THE COMMON CATECHISM

THE
COMMON CATECHISM

A BOOK OF CHRISTIAN FAITH

A CROSSROAD BOOK
THE SEABURY PRESS • NEW YORK

1975

The Seabury Press
815 Second Avenue
New York, N.Y. 10017

English edition © Search Press Limited 1975

German edition *Neues Glaubensbuch*
© Verlag Herder Freiburg im Breisgau 1973

Editiones Herder

Library of Congress Catalog Card Number: 75-1070
ISBN: 0-8164-0283-3

Printed in the United States of America

Edited by Johannes Feiner and Lukas Vischer

with the cooperation of:
Josef Blank (Catholic); Bernhard Casper (Catholic);
Wilhelm Dantine (Protestant); André Dumas (Protestant);
Johannes Feiner (Catholic); Paulus Engelhardt (Catholic);
Heinrich Fries (Catholic); Hans Geisser (Protestant);
Alois Grillmeier (Catholic); Johannes Gründel (Catholic);
Ferdinand Hahn (Protestant); Paul Handschin (Protestant);
Peter Hünermann (Catholic); Walter Kasper (Catholic);
Karl Kertelge (Catholic); Ulrich Kühn (Protestant); René
Laurentin (Catholic); Karl Lehmann (Catholic); Joachim
Lell (Protestant); Peter Lengsfeld (Catholic); Jan
Lochman (Protestant); Ulrich Luz (Protestant); Heinrich
Ott (Protestant); Wolfhart Pannenberg (Protestant); Otto
Hermann Pesch (Catholic); Rudolf Pesch (Catholic);
Trutz Rendtorff (Protestant); Gerhard Sauter (Protestant);
Josef Schreiner (Catholic); Raphael Schulte (Catholic);
Christian Schütz (Catholic); Wolfgang Trilling (Catholic);
Ervin Vályi Nagy (Protestant); Lukas Vischer (Protestant);
Claus Westermann (Protestant); Ulrich Wilckens
(Protestant).

Executive Editors, German edition: Rob van Wezemael,
Otto Hermann Pesch, Ferdinand Hahn
Executive Editor, English edition: John Cumming
Translators: David Bourke, John Cumming, John
Griffiths, Francis McDonagh, John Maxwell, Robert
Nowell, David Smith, Sarah Twohig

Publisher's Preface

This book is the first common catechism or statement of religious belief produced jointly by theologians of the Protestant and Roman Catholic churches since the Reformation of the sixteenth century. It is an important expression of the growing determination of Christians in our time to come together to witness to the truth.

Written by theologians of the major Western Christian tradition, this book provides a coherent and responsible statement of belief not only to Christians, but to a world which, threatened by disaster, may look to Christians for an account of the faith that sustains them.

The many scholars, advisers, and editors who developed this book were not determined to achieve a common statement at any cost, but sought to bear witness to the truth as they had received it in their own traditions. In the long process of writing *The Common Catechism: A Book of Christian Faith* they realized that it was possible to agree on statements covering the major areas of Christian conviction and witness; as a consequence only the last fifth of the book is devoted to matters still in dispute between the churches.

The Common Catechism is ecumenical not only in drawing on the resources of scholars of many nations, but also on all the major Western Christian traditions. The three primary traditions, of course, are the Calvinist, the Lutheran, and the Roman Catholic, each of which has stamped its character on more than a score of major religious denominations, with the dominant emphasis developing along the lines of "Protestant" and "Catholic" or, as with the churches of the Anglican Communion, in a fusion of both. *The Common Catechism* will thus be of universal import to all the Christian churches and will be a source of enlightenment and encouragement to every individual Christian.

Many of the issues that still divide Christians (notably concepts of ministry and sacraments) have also been addressed by official joint Roman Catholic/Protestant commissions in the English-speaking world. Several important statements of this kind are included in the Appendix.

We hope that all readers will find this book a source of light and clarity for themselves, a basis for joint study by clergy and laity of many Christian persuasions, and an effective apologetic tool to help them interpret the Christian faith to the world in which they live.

Introduction

This book provides a joint statement of the Christian faith by Catholic and Protestant theologians.

The community of endeavor among many Protestant and Catholic theologians has become so much a matter of course that it now seems odd that no such book was written years ago. The various branches of the Christian Church are no longer mainly interested in what divides them, but instead in how they are to understand, present and live the Christian faith in the world of today.

Yet some will object that the time is not opportune for a common account of the meaning of the Gospel message, and the arguments against this kind of undertaking are certainly not unfounded: they cannot be shrugged off. The firm trend towards inter-church dialogue began only a few years ago, and in joint discussion during these few years it has not been possible to overcome all the differences that have been recognized as separating the churches for centuries past.

Theologians have been accused of artificially preserving obsolete controversies and of perpetuating the division between the churches by means of new distinctions. It is one thing to compare and contrast, and to reveal things held in common behind diverse pronouncements and traditions. But it is something else again to forge ahead with a joint presentation of the Gospel. That presupposes a far deeper form of community than has come into existence or been apparent to date; it demands a greater degree of maturity. After all, we are still without common ideas and a common language.

Despite and, indeed, partly because of these objections, the publishers, editors and advisers of this work were convinced that the time had come to attempt a common statement of Christian belief. This was clearly an immense task.

It was obvious from the start that the result would not be perfect. But the need was too pressing to be set aside.

In the long run the ecumenical movement cannot be restricted to instances of practical co-operation. The faith and hope which unite us and prompt us to common action must be articulated and expressed appropriately. If this common basis is continually obscured because of persistent unresolved differences, the result might be a stunted form of collaboration which obscures the hope we hold in common.

Moreover, it is increasingly clear that the old notion that doctrine divides whereas practice unites is not necessarily true. In fact the most acute forms of opposition are met with in the very areas where Christians devote themselves to political or social tasks. Only constantly renewed agreement about the meaning of the Gospel can keep the followers of Christ in *one* community despite their conflicts.

It is notorious that the differences between the Catholic and Protestant traditions have not been cancelled. Therefore we sought to express only what was common to them. It soon became obvious that we all accepted the primary importance of setting out the great themes of biblical faith which unite us and which we can proclaim together. That was our first task. We decided that questions which have remained matters of controversy between the churches since the sixteenth century ought not to be shirked but treated in a final section of this book.

The overall plan was born of the conviction that the statements which can be made in common are quantitatively and qualitatively more important than any contradictions. As for the latter, we decided that, after reading the main body of the work, the reader would be able to see how they really looked after all these years of ecumenical dialogue.

What still divides us should not be explained away as inessential. Clearly the last part of this book is also concerned with questions of great importance for the faith and work of the churches and individual Christians, and above all for the structure of the universal Church. Ecumenical discussion of these points must continue. But the body of this book will help to counter the widespread misapprehension that the most important points for initial consideration are the antagonisms between denominations. The possibility of joint pronouncements is in fact much greater than we usually suppose. Even where differences remain unresolved (for example, in regard to the eucharist and the ministry) basic accords are possible. The editors therefore agreed that these questions should not be confined only to the last section of the book, but had to be presented in the earlier sections as well. Ecumenical discussions between Catholic and Protestant theologians have not been fruitless. Several declarations by inter-church commissions which have been issued after exhaustive study in the course of the last few years, show that the denominational front-lines have been pushed back in more than one respect. To the Catholic mind the structure of the Church as given through the offices of the Church is essential. Yet in the last few years Catholics have emphasized more strongly than ever before the fact that those offices, including the Petrine ministry, were established not for their own sake but for the sake of the Church. The various ministries exist in the service of the Church as a whole. They are only understood correctly if seen as structures which contribute to the life and mission of the entire Church. The position of the Church in the contemporary world also makes possible some form of common statement about office. Even though some differences may persist, the eucharist and the Christian ministry are very far from being mere matters of controversy. Hence both topics appear at two points in this book.

The plan of this *Catechism* also takes into account our understanding that not all statements about Christian belief are on the same level. The Vatican II decree on ecumenism rightly speaks of a hierarchy of truths. For Catholics the seven sacraments are major actions of the Church. But Catholics also acknowledge that baptism and the eucharist enjoy primacy as the first two sacraments, and distinguish them from the other sacramental actions. Hence both sacraments appear in the first as well as the final section of this book. There are other, similar instances.

Nevertheless, it is somewhat true that variations in pronouncements betoken central differences; that, for example, divergences in the understanding of ministry derive from differing conceptions of Christ and his work. The objection is valid insofar as the Christian faith cannot be divided quantitatively. It is a whole; if one issue is skirted the whole is vitally maimed. A painting contains some details which are of secondary import. But if they are altered, not only the detail changes but the entire painting must be conceived anew. In the end even secondary questions have to relate to the "hierarchy of truths". They cannot be treated in isolation. But we have to ask how far these points of theological interpretation really divide the churches.

A distinction has to be made not only between primary and secondary truths. We must ask whether a difference involves more than a theological notion. Faith and theology are not the same thing, and it is important not to over-emphasize differences in theological thinking and discourse. Irresolvable differences have often been alleged where in fact only differences of theological interpretation were in question. And these are differences which can and do exist within one and the same church. Nowadays differences of that kind are to be expected within the community of the Church. The Church is "catholic" only by virtue of a genuine pluralism.

How did this book come about? In late 1969 twelve theologians from Germany, France and Switzerland met at the invitation of the publishing house of Herder in order to discuss the project and work out a ground-plan. They soon reached unanimity about an appropriate procedure. It took them a relatively short time to produce a general program which was emended in various ways later. Protestant and Catholic theologians were invited to write a basic text on each of the chapter topics. A Catholic or Protestant theologian prepared the initial manuscript in each case. Then a referee of the other denomination was appointed for each chapter, and gave his view on the standpoint and approach adopted in the text. This method guaranteed common responsibility for each section. To understand the intention behind the book the reader must realize that in this process of reciprocal examination of the various statements which go to make it up, the decisive question was not whether each author could have written every text exactly as it appeared, but whether he could still call himself a Catholic or a Protestant if he accepted this or that text.

Then the individual contributions had to be forged into an organic whole. From the start every author had the carefully established plan in his hands and knew how the work as a whole was supposed to look. The individual sections had to be made consistent and merged into a whole. Fragments of the text had often to be moved from one point to another. Discussions between the editors and sub-editorial staff brought repeated requests to authors for supplementary material, and new authors had to be commissioned for new topics.

The authors have tried to make the material as easy to understand as possible. Specialized theological terms and professional jargon or purely academic analyses of particular points have been avoided. There are no footnotes. The intention is that the reader should not get lost in a mass of details but that he should get things in perspective. The book is intended for all those who are in any way interested in religious questions and present-day theological thinking in the Christian churches. To be sure we could have produced an even simpler and more universally acceptable book. But we were convinced that that was possible only when common theological endeavors were much further advanced.

The first part describes just where.and how the question of God arises for modern man. Only after this is the good news proclaimed by Jesus outlined. Perhaps some theologians would have preferred another structure. Perhaps they would have accepted this one but reached other conclusions in regard to man in the modern world. The editors were aware of these possibilities. The material could have been presented differently. But that very perception implies a major insight. For if the subject-matter could be treated differently, such divergences are not identical with denominational differences properly speaking. It is a question instead of common variations which are peculiar to modern religious thought itself and which cut across the various denominations. They result from the unusually problematic nature of the task which faces all theology in our time—whatever its confessional label.

This book shows that Protestant and Catholic theologians —while remaining loyal to their several traditions—have to set about that task together. Some readers, of course, will be more interested in problems of present relevance than in historical accounts or detailed analyses. To make reading from beginning to end much easier, they can if they wish skip the following sections without losing the essential thread of the work: chapter 2 (the section dealing with the God-question in the past); chapter 8 (the God of the living), apart from the last two sections; and chapter 11 (God's divinity and humanity).

This book is offered to its readers in the hope that it will make even clearer and more vital that community which unites Christians of different churches. The theologians of various denominations who have worked on this book trust that their common witness will arouse each individual Christian to a joint testimony of faith in the Christian life. They certainly do not wish to establish some kind of "third denomination" in an ecumenical no-man's-land between the churches, but to help ensure that Christians co-operate within their own communities in the common growth of the churches towards that unity in variety which is the goal of all ecumenical efforts.

In a sense *The Common Catechism* should be only *an* ecumenical catechism, for as well as being a presentation of the common faith of the Christian churches it is a challenge to reach a more inclusive and more appropriate solution to the task before us: a solution which the publishers, editors and authors recognize as their ultimate goal. Work on this book has strengthened their certainty that ecumenical considerations are not just one aspect of theology but that theology as such has to be ecumenical. Really decisive results in the ecumenical movement are possible only if this truth is taken seriously. If it is, then the Church of the future will look very different from the Church of today.

The Editors

List of Contents

Part One
God

1   God in History

The main purpose of a catechism is to provide an answer: the answer of faith to the questions posed by human life itself and to the question that man himself is. But that answer cannot be given in such a way as to be equally valid at all times and in all places. Man is always changing and asking the same questions in a new and different way. When that happens, the answer of faith must also be expressed in a new way; otherwise it would not be a real answer. But, in its turn, the new answer will not be valid for all time. It must be provisional, because, to be a real answer, it has to focus on man living here and now, in a particular environment. Later, when man has changed once again, a new answer will be required.

This new catechism or summary of belief has not been produced by members of one church or one Christian tradition. It has grown out of a common attempt by Catholic and Protestant Christians to provide the answer of faith to man's questions in the world today. That makes it really "new", since it is the first time that such co-operation has occurred since the sixteenth-century Reformation, and therefore the first time in history. It is above all a risk. Many Christians will say that the time is not ripe for such a venture. Others will welcome it as a promising step forward. That is another reason why the answer provided by this book to man's existential questions can only be provisional. After all, who can possibly be certain of finding the right answer at the first attempt?

The authors of this book had good reasons for embarking on such a risky venture. We were convinced that the questions that were so controversial in the sixteenth century were no longer the main preoccupation of the churches today. They certainly appear again and again in new forms, but usually as aspects of wider questions which are more all-embracing and radical and go much deeper – down to the roots of man's experience. To these contemporary questions, the churches either have an answer which is common to all the Christian traditions, or they have no answer at all. That was the point of departure for the authors of this book. All the leading Christian churches can try to give a common answer to man's questions, for what they have in common is much greater than what separates them. That knowledge has encouraged Catholic and Protestant theologians to offer this new catechism as a guide for people today, both those who have remained faithful members of a church and those who remain at a distance from the churches.

The God question

The essential question to which Christians are bound to give a common answer is the question about God. For a long time now, men have no longer asked explicitly: "Who is God?" or "Is God really there?"; yet all men who think a little about themselves and their existence ask this question secretly. It often appears in a different form or within other questions. Has life any meaning? for example, or Is life absurd? These are ultimately questions about God. What is more, faith can give an answer to questions like this, and everything that faith can say is ultimately directed towards this answer: that God *is*; that man is his concern; and that man can rely on him.

But how, through our questioning, can we arrive at that answer? Where can we look for God? The God question, whether asked explicitly or merely implied, takes as many different forms as the situations in which men live, asking questions about themselves and the world. What form is most suitable for the question? We can hardly ask it in every possible way.

The authors who collaborated to produce this book had to decide between two main ways of asking this question. Should they ask about God with *nature* or with *history* in mind? The title of this section shows that they chose to trace the God question through history. It is quite legitimate to pursue the problem through nature, but the place where western man looks first for an answer to his question about God turns out to be history. What does that really mean?

Nature and the God question

The man who asks about the God of the Old and New Testaments will not try to find him as a God who makes himself known to mankind through some new and transcendent teaching about what holds the world together. On the contrary, he will look for God's revelation of himself in history. We need only look at Scripture to know that any other way of asking about God may be quite legitimate, but it is not the way of asking about the God of the Bible.

It is, however, not simply a question of doing justice to the Bible. We have to find where the God question arises for us. It does so repeatedly whenever we experience how closely we are bound to nature in our inner-most being. We are a part of nature, in so many ways dependent on it and helplessly at its mercy. We are therefore always disposed to see God as the giver of all good things when we receive nature's gifts. We look to God for refuge and salvation when nature strikes us as hostile. We ask what it means when the blind forces of nature pitilessly destroy our lives. We wonder about the significance of sickness, suffering and death, which overtake us as part of nature.

Is the violent and immeasurable cycle of nature merely a blind fate to which we are exposed and to which we have to submit? The answer of faith is that man can trust his life to hostile nature because God is the creator and lord of nature and man can find refuge in him when he is threatened by its forces.

Many people are asking in just this way about God today, as they have done throughout history; they also hear the message of faith and scholarship about belief in God. People on other continents and of other religions are able to ask about God in nature in a much more direct way than those in the West. But even for Westerners, this way of asking is far from meaningless. It seems to become increasingly relevant as the limitations of man's control of the forces of nature by science and technology become more apparent.

All the same, it cannot be denied that western man has achieved a great measure of success in subjugating the forces of nature and thus in changing his relationship with nature. He no longer experiences nature as an abundant yet hostile power, but as something unlimited and creative that he can mould by himself. It no longer reflects God, but himself. News of a natural disaster depriving thousands of his fellow men of their lives and their homes may shake western technological man for a while and make him aware of the limits of his ability, but his reaction is not resignation. On the contrary, he redoubles his efforts to regain control of nature and to prevent such catastrophes from recurring.

History and the God question

Twentieth-century man, so convinced of the ultimate power of science, is constantly shattered by another experience. We are deeply troubled by what men do to their fellows in criminal acts, wars and persecutions and by their failure to live together in peace and justice. We are distressed and mystified above all by the historical aspect of a world in which men harm each other so much by what they do, bring about so many catastrophes, plunge into disaster, and so wretchedly fail to carry out their plans.

That feeling of distress and impotence is increased as our lives become more and more deeply entangled with those of our fellow men throughout the world and the effects of the disasters that we cause can no longer be confined to a small part of the world. We also ask more and more urgently whether our technical control of nature is not changing into a fatal destruction of nature, depriving our fellow men of their means of developing physically and spiritually. This destruction of man's environment confronts us with new tasks, which we still do not take seriously enough; in the meantime one man-made catastrophe is followed by another.

This history of man's control of nature and of his failure to control nature gives rise to countless questions in his mind about the meaning of his existence and ultimately about God. Asking these questions, modern man feels as impotent and helpless as his ancestors did with regard to nature. The power of evil is revealed more clearly here than in any other sphere – in the sphere of sin, as it is called in the language of faith. Is there a God who gives meaning to man in history?

The word "history" is not used here in the sense of a special science or study of past events and their interrelationships. "History" here means the context in which man's life takes place in close unity with all mankind in the past, the present and the future. This history takes place as a series of events in which we either hand on or destroy, preserve or change the tradition inherited from our ancestors.

History is the event in which we act and others act with us, for us or against us. History is the fate on which we are compelled to depend or against which we fight. It is also the space and time in which creative actions occur and every event is totally dependent on all other events. It is the constantly recurring point at which meaning and meaninglessness cross again and again.

In asking about the God of history and looking for his actions in history, we should not think that that is the only possible way of asking about God. There are other ways of asking which are equally necessary. In this book, however, we try to give the answer of faith to the question about God which arises in men's minds from their experience of history. This is because it is directed towards men who are exposed to the experience of history and who can therefore recognize this historical question about God as their own question, even if nature also points the way to God for them.

Again, in asking about God in history, we are not claiming that other ways of asking about God are not legitimate. We do, however, believe that the historical question is the most urgent one for so many people who are conditioned by life in a technical, industrial society. Once again, we must stress that the answers that we try to give to this historical question are provisional and limited. But they must be given. So long as they prove their worth, and testify to a living faith, they will always be answers that help those looking for other ways to God and towards salvation.

We conclude this section with a word of warning against too naïve ideas. The God of Christian faith does not govern nature, nor is he above time and yet in control of human history. He does not preserve the traditional established order, nor does he initiate and guide revolutionary movements to change society. God does not take away from man his responsibility for history. Asking about God in history means being alert to whether man stands alone with this responsibility and his ability to carry it out or whether there is someone who is above the world and yet at the same time in it and who has accepted this responsibility for the benefit of man and the world.

Believing in the God of history means relying on God's presence in the world and on man's ability to give meaning to history because he has received meaning from God. The God we ask about does not deprive man of his responsibility for history, nor dispute his right to it. On the contrary, he gives him courage to act in history because he wants to achieve man's salvation within history. Is that the God proclaimed by the Christian faith? Is faith in that God the real answer to the question about God in history?

Dialogue with other religions

This way of asking about God is, moreover, in no sense new. On the contrary, an understanding of history, of the kind presupposed in this approach and outlined in the preceding section, is an integral part of the western Christian heritage.

The strength of that heritage is revealed in at least one surprising fact. The history of individual societies and civilizations has now become the history of the whole world and only the whole of mankind can now be responsible for this history. Hence there is increasingly close contact between the non-western traditions, which we have arrogantly assumed to be scornful of history, and the non-western religions, which do not presuppose faith in a revelation which took place in history and in a historical mediator, on the one hand, and our western historical tradition on the other.

At the first world conference of religions for peace in Kyoto (on 21 October 1970) the Vietnamese Buddhist monk Thich Nhat Hanh said: "Religion can . . . unite men in their efforts to overcome the really great problems confronting them . . . We shall not be saved by a new system or a new doctrine. We shall be saved by man. How can man find new strength? I believe that this is the task of religions." Asking about the God of history may lead us, as inheritors of the western historical tradition, to a new and very fruitful dialogue with the non-Christian religions.

Marxism – a challenge to Christians

The same question may not be at the mid-point, but it is certainly in the background, of the dialogue between Christians and Marxists. The question of the meaning and the goal of history is, after all, an essential one for Marxists and is, moreover, a question of the meaning of the whole historical process. That entire process must be known if we are to work with a sense of purpose towards the creation of a future society which will enable man to be free. In regard to the question of the meaning of history, Marxists and Christians stand together against any form of positivism which accepts historical facts as valid, but rejects the question of the significance and goal of history as irrelevant and meaningless. In his awareness of this question, the Marxist is at one with the Christian.

On the other hand, the Christian is bound to oppose a

Marxist view that the meaning of history is derived exclusively from man's activity and from the powers of this world. That is an aspect of most forms of Marxism that is unacceptable to Christian faith. The Christian is, moreover, not deceived by the apparently quicker and better results achieved by Marxism in changing the world, in comparison with the mere hopes and aspirations of Christianity. Those who base the meaning of history *exclusively* on what man does embrace the myth of Prometheus and cannot at the same time believe in the God of the Christian faith. Prometheus performed one of the most "progressive" actions of all time for mankind in bringing them fire – but the same action destroyed him.

There is, however, another way in which the Jewish-Christian understanding of history is closely related to Marxist thinking. Both Christians and Marxists think eschatologically: they look forward in hope to a good world in the end. For this element that both have in common, we do not need to turn to Marx's Jewish origins. Both the modern philosophy of history and the optimistic contemporary faith in progress are firmly rooted in Christian tradition. Christians are therefore fully prepared for an encounter with Marxists. In recent years, however, there have been many special inducements, both theological and political or historical, for debate. Protestant theologians above all have been deeply concerned, as the result of intensive research into the Bible, with eschatological realities (the ultimate destiny of the individual and mankind), and in particular with the question of the ultimate form of man's salvation as promised by God.

Immediately after World War I, this question was discussed with great urgency. It can be summarized thus: Does what is new take place (as the "dialectical" theologians maintained) in a call addressed to the individual believer, who then allows himself to be called away from the world and its sinful structures? Or, on the other hand, does this new element occur as a prophetic transcendence of, or passing above and beyond, the socialist movement in the struggle to renew society, as the young Paul Tillich insisted in his religious socialism?

In France, Catholic theologians were able to draw ideolo-

gical strength from a century-old struggle between Catholic
reactionary groups and progressive movements (liberal, social
and finally neo-Marxist groups in the Church). Towards the
end of the 1930s, some of the first representatives of the
so-called "new theology" posed the question of God's incarnation, or "becoming man", not simply in the lives of
individual believers, but in the structures of the world, and
did so within the framework of a very fruitful debate with
Communists.

Inspired by the major thinker, mystic and palaeontologist,
Teilhard de Chardin (1881–1955), French Catholic theologians
insisted that the promises of faith had to act as the impulse for
man's ultimate salvation: to spur Christians on to change
the structures of the world and to make it a better place for
men to live in. This movement culminated in the promulgation
of the Pastoral Constitution, *Gaudium et Spes*, on the Church
and the Modern World, by the second Vatican council and has
been the point of departure for the "political theology" of
recent years.

Man, then, is responsible for the world of the future and,
what is more, that world is one. In it, the other great religions
and Marxism (which might well be called the great counter-
religion of the unified world) together constitute a special challenge to the Christian faith. They compel a man who asks
about God to redefine the place where he should look for an
answer to his question about God. They also compel a man
who already believes in God to ask about God's challenge to
Christians in the history of the other religions and in the
provocation of Marxism.

Abraham

Today, however, the Christian faith is challenged in a special
way and from a quarter that is much closer spiritually to
Christianity. In the many changes that have taken place during this century, three closely related religions have come into
increasing contact with each other, in different ways. These
three communities are similar in that they all share faith in the

one God and they are, moreover, historically dependent on one another. They are Judaism, Christianity and Islam. We shall mention anti-Semitism later, and the part played by Christianity in this phenomenon, but here it is important to note that, since World War II, Protestant theologians have been prompted by an acknowledgment of Christian guilt to think again very deeply about the historical bond between Christians and Jews. The same sense of guilt led the Fathers of the second Vatican council to recall "the spiritual bond linking the people of the New Covenant with Abraham's stock" (Declaration, *Nostra Aetate*, on the relationship of the Church to non-Christian religions). Today, the State of Israel, which evolved largely as the result of Zionism and persecution, is in conflict with the Arab world – a conflict sharpened by the fact that, like the Jews and the Christians, the Arabs regard Jerusalem as their holy city. A solution to this conflict may be possible only on the basis of what all three religious communities have in common. The holy books of all three religions proclaim social justice as the will of God and none of the three religious communities can understand itself fully without considering the other two. Each community of believers can, moreover, understand its own past history and that of the other communities and look forward with confidence to the future only on one condition. That condition is that its members overcome all desire to think of the others as unbelievers, renegades or men whose religious beliefs are outmoded, and learn to accept them as fathers and brothers in faith.

What these three believing communities have in common, the common point of departure for the question about God in history, is their shared memory of the faith of Abraham. This, moreover, brings us to our fundamental theme – what it really means when we say that we believe that God can be experienced in history.

Because of his faith, Abraham is the father of all believers, the father of the believing community. The New Testament writers often claim Abraham as the father of faith in opposition to the Jews (see Mt 8: 11 f; Lk 19: 9; Jn 8: 33–58; Acts 3: 13). In their different ways, Paul, James and the author of the letter to the Hebrews describe him as the model of faith (see Rom 4: 1–24; Gal 3: 6–18; Jas 2: 21–3; Heb 6: 13–15; 11: 8–19). The Quran does the same in numerous passages. We cannot be so closely and directly associated today with the faith of Abraham as the biblical authors for one very simple reason. When the believer in biblical times said "Abraham", he not only meant a historical person living hundreds of years before him. He also meant himself, his own life in the community of believers which derived its faith and its existence from the faith of Abraham. For the Israelites, Abraham was the quintessence of the whole believing people. This has, of course, been called a "mythological" way of thinking, and we can no longer think in that way. We are able to distinguish quite precisely between the Abraham of history and the Abraham of the theology of the biblical authors. But this Abraham theology can help us to understand today what is meant by experiencing God in history. What, then, is this theology of Abraham?

During the early period of the Israelite monarchy, perhaps during the reign of Solomon, the great collector, editor, author and theologian known, because of his use of the divine name Yahweh, as the Yahwist, described Abraham as the primordial figure of faith for Israel. He did this within the framework of the basic idea of the new beginning (Gen 12: 1–4a):

"Now the Lord said to Abram:
'Go from your country and your kindred and your father's
    house
to the land that I will show you.
And I will make of you a great nation,
and I will bless you,
and make your name great,
so that you will be a blessing.
I will bless those who bless you,
and him who curses you I will curse;
and by you all the families of the earth shall bless them-
    selves.'
So Abram went, as the Lord had told him . . ."

In the stories of the fall in paradise, of fratricide and of the flood and the building of the Tower of Babel, the Yahwist has described a history of progressive disaster. In the story of Abraham, on the other hand, he points to the beginning of a history of salvation which was to become world-wide, accepted by "all the families of the earth". The Yahwist was writing with the culminating point of Israel's political power in mind, and he thought of this as the fulfilment of God's promise and as the result of God's activity in history. Yet his text includes a critical question. Israel had been called to be a blessing for all the peoples of the earth. Had she fulfilled this task? There is always a danger for an individual, a people or a nation in possession of power to rest and cling to what has been gained or to increase it. Israel's faith in God's activity in history could, however, only prove its value if the people set out towards a new, unknown future and became a blessing for the whole world.

Abraham's faith

By seeing Abraham in this light, Israel was able to recognize in him another new beginning which formed the basis of her existence as a people: the liberation from slavery in Egypt and setting out in faith under God's guidance (Ex 15: 13; Dt 5: 15; 15: 15). This shows clearly the nature of faith. It is a thankful confession of God's presence and an unconditional trust in him as the one who leads his people to freedom (see Jos 24: 14). We shall have to consider this in greater detail later in this book.

Israel very often failed in this faith, of course, but admitted the failure with an honesty seldom encountered in the history of the world. The prophets of Israel continuously criticized those who looked, not for God's guidance, but for safety in political power and in the legal requirements of cultic practice. In this way, they prepared the people for the eventual collapse of political power and a long period of exile, during which they could once again recover the original faith of Abraham.

At the very time when the great powers in the Near East

could only be enemies or at the most unwelcome partners in a coalition, the prophet Isaiah included both Egypt and Assyria in Israel's blessing (Is 19: 22–5). Again, during the Nazi persecution of the Jews in Germany, the great rabbi Leo Baeck spoke in a similar way of the life of Israel: "Israel's exodus from the 'house of slavery' was a new beginning for the people. But all people were to be given a new beginning. All people were to be born again – all oppressed and enslaved people could hope for their exodus . . . Despite everything that had happened and might happen in the future, this is the conclusion of what is said about the exodus from Egypt." Again, at a time when the Israelites, exiled in Babylon, had to choose between despair and adaptation to their oppressors' way of life, the second Isaiah transformed the familiar idea of God's act of liberation in the past into a new and greater act of liberation on God's part (Is 43: 16–21). Once again, the consequence of this was a call to begin again in faith and trust.

Today, as at the time of Deutero-Isaiah, we all have to choose between flight in the face of despair, impotence and adaptation to the technological treatment of symptoms of a disordered society and faith which, contrary to everything that can be expected, hears God say: "Behold, I am doing a new thing; now it springs forth, do you not perceive it?" (Is 43: 19). Today, "all the families of the earth" and "Israel . . . with Egypt and Assyria" can all be destroyed or blessed together. In this, we are living in the perspective of the Old Testament. The history of Israel, exemplified and summarized in the story of Abraham, the father of faith, is our history. Israel's question about God in history is our question about God.

Called to make a new beginning and set out for unknown territory, we prefer to escape into the safety of the past or seek refuge in an ideologically prepared future. We seldom hear God when we are ready to make a really new beginning, but we can learn from Israel's faith how faith in the God of history can overcome our own historical experience. Faith does not simply add a particular interpretation to historical facts.

Rather, it enables us to act differently. As believers, we know of God's saving acts in the past and, because of this, we choose not to run away from disaster, but to trust in God's salvation. We do not seek to escape from destruction, but to make a new beginning. We do not avoid crisis, but have faith in the future.

Experience of God in history, then, does not mean, in the light of the Old Testament, that we plan to eliminate all risks and to guarantee that everything will be reasonable. Faith in the God of history does not mean that we shall be able to foresee how the whole pattern of events will develop. All that it can do for us is to give us strength to make a new beginning, to set out towards an unknown future, because, through faith, we can remember the past and at the same time be sure of God's presence in judgment and mercy, catastrophe and happiness.

Abraham and Jesus

The Christian sees the connexion between his faith and faith in the God who set Israel free in the person of Jesus of Nazareth as the son of Abraham and the son of David. For the apostle Paul, this connexion was very clear – the universal blessing of the promise made to Abraham was concentrated in his one descendant Jesus Christ (Gal 3: 8, 16). Both Paul and the evangelists – especially Matthew – show how the community of those who believed in Christ entered the life of faith and of the promises made to Israel. Jesus is the Christ, the one God promised to send, God's incarnate action in history. That is why the Christian believes that the history of salvation entered its most decisive phase with the coming of Jesus Christ: "It is the last hour" (1 Jn 2: 18).

This fundamental statement of Christian faith has been interpreted as the closing of God's revelation with the proclamation of the event of Christ in the New Testament. This interpretation is, of course, quite meaningful if "revelation" is regarded above all as the communication of statements or objective knowledge that can be formulated in propositions or as a "content". In that case, Jesus is, as the Christ, the last "content". This content can and must be examined in the light of faith, but nothing can be added to it. Everything has already been said in the Word itself (see Jn 1).

This is, however, only partly in accordance with the message of the New Testament. Two facts are indissolubly linked – the concrete historical form taken by God's ultimate revelation in Jesus Christ and the guidance of the community of believers by the Holy Spirit. It is because of this that we can make a new beginning and set out confidently towards the future. Since the coming of Jesus Christ, human history has been marked by this striking characteristic – the "last hour" is at hand and we are moving towards fulfilment.

The conviction that revelation closed with the New Testament of the Christ event is, however, perhaps too one-sided. What is more, it may be a misconception, containing a possible threat to the essence of Christian faith. This is clear from the fact that believers have again and again been tempted throughout the history of Christianity, and even outside the purely Christian sphere of thought and activity, to break through this closed revelation and look for God's further action in history. The Alexandrian church Fathers, Clement and Origen, for example, strove to achieve a Christian gnosticism which would go beyond simple faith expressed in images and based on the tradition of revelation and arrive at a direct vision of God. In the Middle Ages, Christians were preoccupied with a "third era" which was to come, the "kingdom of the Holy Spirit", a new and definitive period in the history of salvation; and many believed that the herald of this new era was Francis of Assisi.

Again, many attempts were made in the nineteenth and twentieth centuries to break through the closing of revelation. Schelling and the Russian philosophers of religion adopted the threefold division into the kingdom of the Father, the kingdom of the Son and the kingdom of the Spirit. Hegel saw his philosophical system as the fulfilment of Christian history. Marx announced the ultimate, definitive form that human society was to take, and Nietzsche proclaimed the doctrine of the "superman". Finally, to give but two twentieth-century examples, the French religious thinker Teilhard de Chardin outlined the construction of the "noösphere" and the German philosopher Heidegger looked forward to the "arrival of being" as a holy saviour.

Faith as a new beginning

All this points to an essential aspect of faith in the God of history. If Abraham is the father of faith, and faith is therefore always a new beginning made while trusting in God's guidance, then faith cannot be thought of as closed or drawing to a close. In speaking in faith of God acting in history, we do not have in mind a higher form of history on the basis of which our ordinary history can be predicted and regulated for all time. On the contrary, we mean our everyday, concrete human history, which we dare, while trusting in God, to accept as not yet closed. In entering the faith of Abraham and Israel, the Church shows that she is prepared to take a risk with the God who "does a new thing". Jesus was not revealed in the communication of true statements or propositions, but in a making visible and audible of a new and definitive divine act of liberation.

Believing in his resurrection, the Christian knows that God has accepted the world and this discloses a future in which God will always be present in a new way in history. Because God is faithful, this act of revelation is definitive. Because it is an act of love, it applies to all men and to the whole world. God's faithfulness, the definitive character of his revelation is not seen in a series of unchangeable propositions, but as an unlimited opportunity to change the world with courage and trust and to accept the transformations that we have brought about. The universal love of God for man is most clearly seen in man's universal acts of invention and creation.

What kinds of change or invention has faith to deal with today? What kind of new beginning has it to make today and towards what kind of unknown future has it to set out, trusting like Abraham? For what kind of "new thing" that God may do must faith make room today? We have examples in the New Testament of ways in which this kind of new beginning takes place. It is not difficult to see how the New Testament authors expressed their experience of Christ in new ways when new questions were asked, and especially, for instance, when they came to accept that Christ's return would be delayed and their hopes were not to be fulfilled.

On the other hand, however, the questions which are so important to the Christian today were often not envisaged by the biblical authors or the members of the early Church. As we shall see later, the problem of a responsible Christian attitude towards political power did not exist for the Christian minority in the Roman Empire. In the same way, apart from the question of the influence of popular philosophy on the language of Christian theology and on the ethical behaviour of Christians themselves, there was no creative dialogue between the early Church and non-Christian philosophers. Similarly, enormously influential factors which play such a decisive part in modern life – science, technology, the power structure, the struggle for emancipation and so on – were completely unknown during the earliest period of the history of the Church. It is therefore impossible to find a solution to these problems by consulting the Bible and repeating isolated texts. What has been attempted in the fairly recent past, but for the most part the results have been negative.

The Bible can only be used to help us to find a real answer if we examine the central content of the biblical message again and concentrate in our search on its meaning for our own times. In this case, the faith of the Bible has to make a new beginning. The biblical message itself insists, after all, precisely on this. It proclaims above all the risen Christ who is always with us (Mt 28: 20) and who promised that we shall receive the "Spirit of truth" who will guide us into "all the truth" (Jn 16: 13). Because of this central message of the Bible, then, we may be sure that the whole of our history will be ultimately meaningful and that what we do, in faith, in history will not be in vain, however much it may seem to end in nothing. When we speak about God acting in history, then, we mean that a meaning has been given to the history of mankind as a whole and that man may therefore hope to find meaning in history and to make a new beginning and set out in confidence and inventively towards the future. We do not have to do this on the basis of an external law – we may do it on the basis of God's promise.

2   The God question in history

There are two different aspects to this question. The first is that faith as a new beginning is always assuming new forms. In other words, what constitutes faith today does not pre-determine the concrete form that faith will take at a later period in history. The world does not remain unchanged, nor is human life always the same. If faith is indeed a new begin-ning, then it must have a point of departure and a direction, each of which is different according to the historical situation in which man, who is trying to believe, is placed.

The second aspect is that there is at least one element that is common to all the different forms of faith. This common denominator is hope. The believer looks forward to the future and expects with confidence the decisive gift that is coming towards him. Because he does not expect everything to come automatically, however, he does not simply wait passively. He is certain that meaning will be given to his life and for this reason his hope impels him to act. The meaning that he knows he will receive assures him that what he does will not be done in vain and that, even if he is disappointed, he will be sus-tained.

Faith as a new beginning

We have already tried to understand the basic structure of faith on the basis of the faith of Abraham – which of course means on the basis of the faith of Israel. In this chapter, we shall consider how this structure has varied throughout the history of faith. We shall, in other words, try to ascertain how man's faith in God's activity in history has begun again and again in new situations and has taken on constantly new forms. This investigation is very important for four reasons.

The first reason is that the assumption of new forms by faith is by no means a universally accepted idea. The widely accepted teaching of a closed revelation has led to the conviction that, in accordance with God's definitive action in Jesus Christ, all that can take place is a progressively more precise formulation of faith, without any real change in that faith as such. A careful examination of the history of faith, however, gives rise to a different and better result.

The second reason is that it is only by considering the history of faith that we can ever come to know precisely what message Jesus proclaimed concerning God, and what he really brought into the world. We cannot do without a consideration of history, even if our point of departure is the presupposition that history has falsified Jesus' original intentions. We can only really understand a message that is deeply concerned with the history of man by investigating the effect that message has had on history.

The third reason for examining the changes that have taken place in man's faith throughout history is that we can be positively helped towards a better understanding of our own situation (the situation which will provide the starting-point for our own faith and the new form which it must assume) by considering other situations in the past which have given rise to new beginnings in faith.

And there is a fourth reason. An examination of the history of man's faith provides us with models which can show us the way in which faith begins anew and constantly assumes new forms. This does not imply that we are given in advance an answer to the questions that we are asking about faith today, but it does mean that we are given certain indications of the way in which we should look for an answer.

The relationship between faith and life

Certain special difficulties are involved in any examination of the history of faith. The question concerning the changes that have taken place in faith and what man says in faith about God has as a rule been asked exclusively from the point of view of history and it has always been a *theological* rather than an *anthropological* question. In other words, it has been approached from the vantage-point of the historical development of theological concepts and ideas rather than from that of man as an individual and in society.

This, however, was the result of a special situation in which faith was placed, a question which will be discussed later. Generally speaking, the picture that we have been given of the history of faith is relatively abstract, because those who have specialized in this subject have fully recognized that man's speaking about God and the forms in which he has expressed his faith are closely related to the whole of his life. They are not simply connected with what preconditions his way of thinking. In recent years, however, we have become more sensitive to the relationship between man's faith and his life as a whole and have developed a number of scientific methods which enable us to discover this connexion more effectively. We can, after all, only begin to understand the full extent of the history of faith if we include within that history the whole history of man's political, social and cultural life. Quite apart from any theological reasons, many Christian attitudes to life and society can be understood in the light of the conditions of life prevailing at the time as an answer to a concrete situation. Hegel's philosophy, Marxism, sociology and social psychology, to give but a few examples, have presented Christians with a challenge and a task which they have not really fully taken up even now. This chapter is no more than a very modest attempt to draw attention to this problem and to deal with it.

Three basic things are attempted in the sections that follow. In the first place, the factual history of faith as such is outlined by means of carefully selected examples. By this factual history is meant the changes that have taken place in man's speaking about God in faith within the history of the Church as the community of those who believe. Secondly, an attempt is made to show how these changes in fact have taken place as the situation in which Christians live has changed and has challenged their faith and either presented it with a chance to begin anew or else frustrated any new beginning. Finally, some evidence is offered to show that faith has sometimes reacted positively by Christian action in the world and sometimes negatively.

Faith and hope

One of the most astonishing and encouraging facts in the history of faith is that, from the very beginning, faith itself appeared as a public testimony to hope. The so-called *arcanum*, or secret discipline, which prevailed from the third to the fifth Christian centuries and which concealed the Christian message and Christian worship from non-believers was not derived from the Bible, but from ancient non-Christian cultic practices. In the second half of the second century, however, the Church, represented by Irenaeus, Bishop of Lyons, testified, in opposition to the secret traditions of the gnostics, that Christian faith was passed on, not by any form of secret initiation, but by public witness. This is established in principle and in practice in 1 Pet 3: 15 – Christians are regarded as different from their fellow men, and are rejected and viewed with suspicion and curiosity because of the visible hope that lives in them. "Always be prepared," the author of the letter writes, "to make a defence (*apologia*) to anyone who calls you to account (*logos*) for the hope that is in (among?) you." This statement must have been challenging, even paradoxical to men living in the basically Greek civilization of the Roman Empire, since an *apologia* was a public rendering of an account accompanied by valid reasons (*logos*). In the narrower sense, the word *apologia* meant legal defence. To a Greek, or to those influenced by Greek thought, however, hope was above all something that had no reason and was illusory and disappointing.

In Greek mythology, there is the case of Pandora's box. According to stoicism, the dominant philosophy among the intellectuals of the period, hope, like desire, was a "disease of the soul", which man had to try to overcome through an absence of passion (*apatheia*) and by a voluntary conformity with the order of the universe. He must have no more desires and he must confine his expectations to what is possible within his own inner freedom. Paul described the pagans very accurately as men "without hope" (1 Thess 4: 13; see also Eph 2: 12). A group of people – Christians – who proclaimed their hope at the very least must have aroused interest at that period. The reason for this hope, however, was not the unchangeable structure of the world (the *logos*), which was something that the Stoics also looked for, but faith: faith that a saving event had taken place in the world. That event was Christ present as the risen one in the baptized Christian (1 Pet 3: 15, 18, 21).

The "chosen" ones in the "Dispersion" (1 Pet 1: 1) encountered interest in this hope and were warned to be prepared to give an account because they were asked (1 Pet 3: 15). This shows that the need to conform with the order of the world, as preached by the Stoics, did not bring peace to the restless soul of man. Among the perils of the world around him, man looked for security and fulfilment. The mystery religions of the period were especially influential, because they offered man something beyond this life, a remedy of immortality (cf Bultmann on the early Christians).

It was within the context of these questions, which the philosophers of the period were not able to answer, that Christian faith developed an early form of speaking about God in history. This was an authentic beginning, based on a definite situation and resulting from certain habits of thought and a way of life which seemed to be self-evident. It had its origins in the hopes cherished by various groups of Jews existing at the time of Jesus. (We shall discuss this in connexion with Jesus' preaching about the kingdom of God.)

On the one hand, Jesus' words were received with interest and met with success because of the existence of these hopes. On the other hand, however, these very hopes formed an obstacle to his preaching, because, in promising to fulfil the hopes of the Jews of his own time, Jesus also radically changed them. The fundamental hope that Jesus proclaimed and promised to bring to fulfilment – God's activity in the history of man – was closely linked with man's readiness to change the whole course of his life (Mk 1: 15 par) and to look for the "one thing that is needful" (Lk 10: 42), the "kingdom of God and *his* righteousness" (Mt 6: 33; see also Lk 12: 31; Mt 5: 6). Jesus was confronted in his preaching about the kingdom of God with many failures. He preached in the presence of expectations that had become rigid. He met with hostility on the part of the professional representatives of religion and with the tactical and cautious adaptations of other Jews. He encountered the determination of resistance-fighters and a widespread lack of interest among those in whom his word took no root and whose enthusiasm was short-lived (Mk 4: 17 par). His word also fell among those who were preoccupied with riches and the pleasures of the world (Mk 4: 19 par). But to those who believed in him, his resurrection brought clarity – the hope which filled his disciples was the result of God's action through the presence of the risen Christ in them and, through them, in men scattered throughout the whole known world. When the early Christians spoke about God, they meant faith in God's activity through the risen Christ, as a hope resulting in action because it affected man's whole existence.

The light of true knowledge

What very quickly emerged from the claim made by faith in God to give hope to the whole man affecting the whole of his life was a parallel claim to give direction to his thinking. This can, of course, be called a one-sided emphasis, but it was certainly in accordance with a special challenge which confronted the Christian faith of the time. This challenge came on the one hand from the Greek philosophers of the period, especially the Stoics and the neo-Platonists, and, on the other, from those thinkers in the Eastern world and the Hellenized eastern parts of the Roman Empire whose "knowledge" of God and man transcended philosophy – in other words, from the gnostics. On the one hand, then, the philosophers tried to answer man's questions on the basis of intellectual inquiry. On the other, the gnostics looked for a vision of the spirit which went beyond the rational activity of the intellect and presupposed a renunciation of the purely material conditions governing human life.

Speaking about God in such a way that this historical challenge is accepted meant proclaiming God's introduction into the world of the true light which brings to an end all the questions of the philosophers and transcends all *gnosis*. There is every justification in the New Testament for believing that this was done. Paul, for example, announced the claim of faith to "take every thought (!) captive to obey Christ" (2 Cor 10: 5) and to set thought free from the great presumption within which it was enclosed (see 2 Cor 10: 4 ff; 1 Cor 1: 27 ff). The idea of the subjection of thought to and its liberation by Christ as "God's wisdom" was very soon extended to include the growing conviction that all human thought was contained in and transcended by faith in Christ. As such, human thought had to be regarded as a preliminary form of faith (see Acts 17: 22 ff; Phil 4: 8).

It was not simply by chance that the Latin translation of the Bible, Jerome's Vulgate, provided a translation of Jn 1: 9 which arouses interest today and is included in several modern translations: "The true light that enlightens every man who comes into this world" (instead of "was coming into the world"). This light is, according to the Fathers of the Church, the light which shone from the time of Moses until that of Plato. It is the Word, the *logos*, which, according to the Stoics, spread about the world in the form of many *logoi spermatikoi* or "seeded words" and had a deep effect on the world. It is the silver and gold which the Egyptians possessed and which the people of God then claimed as their possession (Ex 12: 36). It is also the "light of the world" (Jn 8: 12; 9: 5; 12: 46), exposing all darkness, evil and deceit (see Jn 1: 5; 3: 19 ff; 9: 39). The so-called Catholic tradition of the inclusion of all human truth in divine revelation and the Protestant tradition of the judgment pronounced on all human thought together preserve both aspects.

Both traditions aim to bear witness to the one light which illuminates the darkness of the world and reveals where there is clarity and where there is darkness. Thus, at the end of the second century, Theophilus of Antioch, one of the Christian authors who have been called "apologists", appealed to the Word that is with the Father and, sent into the world, represents the Father (*To Autolykos*, II, 10: 22), with the aim of drawing attention to the darkness in which the Greek philosophers and poets, who could not think of God as the creator (II, 4 ff), lived and wrote.

In the second half of the second and at the beginning of the third century, Clement of Alexandria also tried to include gnosticism in his Christian teaching about the light which has come into the world. That light, he believed, divided day and night, life and death (*Protrepticus*, 114): "When the light dawns . . . everything is illuminated. It then becomes clear that, of all the Greeks and barbarians who are concerned with the truth, some possess a great deal and others a part, certainly some of the doctrine of truth" (*Stromateis*, I, 57). Clement's theology can certainly be called tolerant, inclusive and transcendent. It contains "the truth mingled with the teachings of the philosophers, or rather it can be found concealed in it and hidden in them . . . which prompts me to say that, to a certain degree, philosophy is also a work of God's providence" (I, 18). "If, according to Plato, it is only possible to learn the truth from the deity or from the descendants of the deity, then we are justly proud to be instructed in the truth by the Son of God . . . We should not, however, reject anything that can help us to find the truth" (VI, 123). The true gnostic, then, is the Christian, because he possesses "concerning good and evil, the whole of creation and indeed everything about which the Lord has spoken . . . the most precise and all-embracing truth, extending from the beginning of the world to its consummation. He has moreover learnt this truth from the truth itself . . . Of all this, he has – even though it may be still concealed from everyone else – received knowledge" (VI, 78).

Redemption as a flight from the world

The "true gnosis" is the fulfilment in anticipation, here on earth, of man's "natural longing" for knowledge and happiness. This stoic conception of "natural longing" was taken over by the neo-Platonists and in this way became very influential in Christian thought during the Middle Ages. It was very much in accordance with the spirit of the age. From the texts quoted, it became clear that knowledge and happiness were identical – the "natural longing" for happiness was seen to be a longing for perfect knowledge. This longing for perfect knowledge or perfect *gnosis* in the light of faith became, for these Christian intellectuals, the goal of Christian hope, their liberation from philosophy. Yet, this intellectual quest for knowledge in fact concealed a far more elemental longing for happiness. The longing for *gnosis*, for an insight into reality which turned men away from the world, was based on a specific situation in which certain men found themselves in social and political life. This is why it was possible for Christian speaking about God as a "true gnosis" to exercise such a powerful influence. Nietzsche expressed the matter thus: "The revolt of the slave in morality begins when resentment itself becomes creative and gives birth to values" (*Genealogy of Morals* I, 10). Although he did not know it, this statement is an accurate description of *gnosis* and its rejection of the world. This negation of the world, experienced as confronting and hostile to the ego, was regarded by Nietzsche as a "creative act". But who could be interested in this rejection of the world? Who could cherish resentment against the world and develop that into a philosophy?

We may in this context quote an expert who has specialized in that period, Hans Jonas. In his opinion, these people were drawn from the same levels of society as the people who belonged to Paul's community at Corinth – "slaves, poor and unimportant people, men with little or no possibility of influencing the world, so that its great events simply passed over their heads". In addition to people at this level, however, there were also, according to Jonas, those who had "once belonged to the ruling class", but who, "since the end of the democracies and patriciates", had been "condemned to a laissez-faire attitude with regard to the dynamism of a world governed by new powers". These men, deprived of political power, regarded the denial of the world that was proposed by the religious teaching of the East as a truth which they could make their own. The world appeared to them as "a mechanism of alien laws . . . as fateful, not as something that could give them a positive task or be the place where they could find freedom".

This, however, has a positive aspect, because man was able to discover himself, through this way of viewing the world, in his own being in confrontation with the world. He could free himself from the conviction that prevailed in Greek philosophy that he was simply a part of the world. Another scholar who has specialized in this period, Rudolf Bultmann, said: "What we have here is above all a discovery of the radical difference between the human ego of all being in the world and the Greek understanding of man, a discovery of man's complete otherness and therefore of his loneliness in the world. The world is not simply something alien to him. It is his prison..." This, then, gives rise to the liberating hope which Christian faith offers to God and which takes on a definite form. Bultmann continues: "This liberation can only come as a redemption which sets man free from his prison by setting him free from himself."

Is this form of faith and hope the whole witness borne by Christianity? Certainly not. Since the time of Paul, the Christian view of man and the world has been both gnostic and anti-gnostic. The Christian message is a message of redemption which at the same time affirms creation. It proclaims redemption *from* the world and it bears witness *in* the world. Christian hope overcomes fear and this is counterbalanced by the joy and gratitude that is experienced in the new Christian being that has already begun. But it was only while they formed a minority without political power that Christians could continue to stress man's redemption from the world and avoid a positive affirmation of the world.

We are fortunate enough to possess a very striking example of this pre-political phase of Christian speaking about God. In AD 178, the cultured pagan Celsus wrote a polemical treatise against Christians entitled *Alethes Logos* ("True Discourse"). Although he himself regarded the state religion of Rome as only one of many possible ways of venerating the supreme deity who was above all religions, he criticized Christians for their uncompromising rejection of emperor worship because, in his opinion, they were thus undermining the foundations of the Roman Empire in an irresponsible way. In 248, the Christian thinker and pacifist Origen concluded a reply to this treatise entitled *Contra Celsum* (*Kata Kelsou*, or "Against Celsus"), in which he criticized the "kings and princes" (VIII, 65), gave a relative value to imperial rule (VIII, 67) and elaborated a picture of what we would now call a political utopia: "If all Romans . . . were to accept the Christian faith, they would, through prayer, be victorious over their enemies or at least have no enemies to fight against . . ." (VIII, 70). Even now, he claimed, Christians support the "rulers" with their prayer. "The more pious a person is, the more he accomplishes with the help that he gives to the rulers – much more than the soldiers going out to battle and destroying as many of the enemy as they are capable of killing . . . With our prayers, we Christians destroy all the demons who provoke warlike undertakings, break oaths and banish peace . . ." (VIII, 73). Rejecting Celsus' well meaning invitation to Christians to accept positions of political leadership, Origen maintained that "the more divine and more necessary service performed for the Church of God" was of greater "benefit to man" (VIII, 75).

Constantine – the turning point

Origen's treatise, of course, reflects a way of thinking characteristic of a minority group. As soon as Christians were drawn into conflict with those in power, however, their speaking about God exclusively as the one who redeemed men from the world was bound to prove inadequate.

It was not long before this happened. From the middle of the third century onwards, Christians found themselves forced to elaborate a kind of "political" theology. The first systematic persecution of Christians took place during the reign of the Emperor Decius (249–51). This came about as the result of a crisis in the Empire. In an attempt to restore unity in the Empire, Decius insisted on unity in the official religion, although that religion was capable of incorporating many different elements. Cyprian, Bishop of Carthage, encouraged Christians to suffer martyrdom in the ultimate struggle against a world that was coming to an end (see his Epistle LVIII of 252). Christians were again cruelly persecuted under Diocletian, who blamed them for the collapse of the Roman Empire, but only six years after the end of his reign, in 311, his successor, Galerius, issued, together with his co-regents, the Edict of Sardica. This edict of toleration declared that Christianity was, with certain reservations, a permitted, legal religion in the Empire (*religio licita*), with the result that it was possible for Christianity to become the state religion of the Empire. Less than two years later, the Edict of Milan did away with the reservations, and Constantine, who proclaimed it, was hailed by Christians of the period as the first Christian emperor.

Christians at once found themselves in a position of political responsibility and very soon they had to bear that responsibility alone. They were confronted by a problem that was unknown in the New Testament: how to use political power in a responsible, Christian way. Hence the Constantinian period is a turning-point; it called for an authentically new beginning, a new form of faith in God in history. Would Christian faith succeed or fail in responding to this new challenge? Would it simply be concerned with the redemption of the individual and leave the world to itself? Or would the assumption of political responsibility by Christians lead to increasing closeness to the world? Would both forms of faith become more closely united and would they lead independent lives?

Even today, the dilemma of the Constantinian turning-point has not yet been fully overcome. Put more precisely, hope of redemption in the "gnostic" sense and Christian political responsibility have not yet become fully united in Christian faith. Even now there is still a danger of Christianity being confined to the individual and of the world being left to its own devices. At best, Christianity provides a kind of emergency arrangement for the world and even approves to some degree of an energetic, violent pursuit of political aims in the world. At worst, Christian faith is transformed into an ideology which supports the political establishment and its violent practices. These attitudes are expressed in different ways of speaking about God. It is valuable to illustrate this phenomenon using examples drawn from history.

Only a century after Origen, who clearly opposed political action on the part of Christians, quite different attitudes can be observed among believers. In an address given to mark the thirtieth anniversary of Constantine's reign, the court theologian Eusebius tried to establish a connexion between faith in God's action in history and his own political experience, seeing the actions of God, the supreme king, in the actions of the Emperor (*Laus Constantini*, 7). Many Christian authors, both in the East and in the West, dealt with the theme of the special divine vocation of the city of Rome and of the Roman Empire, culminating in the supremacy of Christianity. Orosius (born *c.* 375–80), a disciple of the more sceptical Augustine, could not be made less optimistic with regard to Rome and its supreme position, despite its conquest and plundering by Alaric in 410. He was not only a historian, but also a priest who sympathized with the war-weary people's need for security (*Historia adversus Paganos*, III, *praefatio*). For this reason, he provided a suitable theory or, as we would say nowadays, the necessary ideology.

The state of God

Augustine's theology and especially his work *De civitate Dei* (usually known as the "City of God", but better translated as the "State of God") is especially important in any consideration of the connexion between speaking about God and Christian political experience in history. For at least fifteen years, Augustine struggled with the problems which arose for Christians in connexion with the fall of Rome. He did not know whether Rome would ultimately be destroyed or not. If it fell, there was certainly no other order in the world to replace it. Christians could not be blamed for the collapse of the Roman Empire, but the official Christian religion of the Empire did not in any sense remove the constant danger of division which is always inherent in any great empire.

With melancholy irony, Augustine critically assessed the "necessary" just wars which resulted from divisions in the empire (*De civitate Dei*, XIX. 7). The citizen of the State of God is interested in the relative external peace of the worldly state, because this external peace makes it possible for him to go undisturbed on his way towards the real peace that transcends this world and for which his restless heart is always longing.

Augustine's ideas about God's activity in history were, in the period that followed, more influential than any other "political" theology has ever been, but they were, of course, frequently misinterpreted. The main reason for this is that later readers have so often lost sight of the very firm connexion between his theology and the period in which he was living and writing. Augustine developed his ideas basically in order to explain the fall of Rome in the light of God's actions and to forestall any possible criticisms made by non-Christian "political" theologians. He was extremely reticent when dealing with God's activity in connexion with a sequence relating purely to this world of guilt, and the consequences of guilt or good conduct and happiness. His answers are always closely related to the spiritual or intellectual situation in which he was living. We are made aware of that climate of thought by his preoccupation with biblical traditions relating to the end of the world, with the Roman view of the state, and with a neo-Platonic scale of values with regard to the goods that man should strive to achieve.

He made a very clear distinction between his basic models

Augustine used out of context to provide ground for political claim about [...]

of the "State of God" and the "earthly state" on the one hand, and political realities on the other. The State of God was not the Church, nor was the earthly state the Roman Empire. Later, however, a "political" Augustinianism was developed, in which attempts were made to fill in the gaps left by Augustine himself in his original draft version of a political theology. Similar attempts were also made to perfect Augustine's original ideas and to transform them into universally valid guide-lines for political action. These attempts in fact resulted in his theology being torn out of its concrete context of the political situation in which he lived and wrote. The consequence was that, in the period that followed, a form of speaking about God came about which, on the one hand, tried to reply to certain challenging political problems by appealing to Augustine's ideas, but, on the other hand, overlooked what was new in Augustine's situation.

During the very century in which the "State of God" was written, Pope Gelasius I (492–6) introduced the interpretation which was to be accepted almost without question by Christians for hundreds of years – the identification of the State of God with the Church and that of the representative of that State of God with the pope. For this reason, he felt bound to place himself above all earthly rulers, because he had to "give an account to the supreme judge of the kings of this earth". The opposite tendency can be seen at the court of Charlemagne. The Emperor's theological adviser Alcuin clung to the generally accepted identification of the State of God with the Church, whereas Charlemagne himself tended to equate his empire with the State of God.

It was taken almost for granted by the christianized people of central Europe that God's power was represented by political power. They were, moreover, not very interested in the struggle between the various political theologies. What is most prominent in their case is a new form of the individual hope of redemption that we have already encountered in gnosticism. Under the influence of the Irish-Scottish monks who established the Christian Church among them, the Celtic people above all developed a sense of personal guilt in the presence of God and a need for personal redemption. Speaking about God who bestowed forgiveness and grace became, in this environment, a legal system of guilt, penance and expiation by good works. (A very good insight into this system can be gained from an examination of the "penitentials".) The emergence of private confession gave an inner, personal value to this impressive legal system, which has in fact left its stamp on the Catholic understanding of faith until the present day.

The best theological justification of this system was provided by the monk and bishop, Anselm of Canterbury (1033/4–1109), in his presentation of the doctrine that Christ gave representative satisfaction for our sins in his suffering and death. Man's longing for redemption encounters a God who calls for justice, but man is conscious of his failure to meet this demand. God himself therefore, Anselm taught, enables man to avoid demanding too much from himself and allows him to turn to Christ, his representative, who takes his guilt on to himself and redeems him, although he does not release him from the duty of restoring justice.

In this way, there were in the early Middle Ages two manners of speaking about God, both closely connected with the circumstances in which a Christian lived. The relatively few Christians who held power in society spoke about God in the language of the ruling class. The State, Empire or Kingdom of God was there and the question that was debated was whether the political structure of the worldly state or the social structure of the Church was the form in which God's activity in history was made manifest. The many ordinary people without political power, on the other hand, were confronted with the demand, which was often too much for them, to be just and, conscious of their personal guilt, they turned to Christ who atoned for their sins and brought them back to God's grace.

The medieval understanding of the world

As one would imagine, increasing "political" activity on the part of the people as a whole was bound to lead to a new way

of speaking about God in history and a new understanding of
the world in the light of the God of history. This in fact
happened in the great movements which emphasized poverty,
some of which separated themselves from the universal
Church, others remaining in the Church as new orders. In all
these movements, however, the Gospel was understood as a
way of life which could fashion and change the world. This
also happened in the cities among the emerging middle classes.
Finally, it also occurred in the academic movement known as
scholasticism. This trend in the universities was a response to
the intellectual curiosity of the new middle classes, and
resulted in the growth of *sacra doctrina* into the study of
theology as a science (*scientia*). The leading representative of
this intellectual movement as well as of the other two was
Thomas Aquinas (1225–74), whose thought we shall now
briefly examine.

Despite strenuous opposition from his noble family, Thomas
insisted on joining the poor, middle-class order of preachers
founded by Dominic († 1221). His learning was probably less
all-embracing and less directly concerned with the world than
that of his teacher Albert the Great (1200–80) or that of
Albert's Franciscan adversary Roger Bacon (1214–94), but his
thought was above all far more systematic. He was able to
bring together into a unity what apparently could not be
synthesized. These different elements included the new
tradition of Scripture, the recently explored philosophy of
Aristotle and the increasingly influential Islamic and Jewish
philosophy which was at that time entering Europe by way of
Spain. Thomas's attempted synthesis was full of tension, above
all because neither Aristotelianism nor the Islamic philosophy,
which was greatly influenced by Aristotle, accorded any real
place to a personal God who had created the world and yet
transcended it. This philosophical framework of Thomas's
thought was therefore viewed with suspicion, because a purely
worldly conception of man and the world was regarded as
irreconcilable with the Christian faith.

Yet it was precisely the worldly character of this philosophy
which Thomas took so seriously. What is so striking in his

speaking about God – which is his literal interpretation of theo-logy – is that it is predominantly a speaking about man, in so far as man has his existence from God and tends in that existence towards God. Man's being as a tendency towards God is a natural longing (*desiderium naturale*) to behold the very Being in which everything that is has its ground and which is always directly and most intimately present to all beings (*Summa Theologiae*, I, 8, 1–4). God's greatness is shown by his giving to each thing its own being and its own activity. "To reduce the perfection of the creature (in its being and activity)" was, for Thomas, equivalent to "a reduction of the perfection of God's power" (*Summa Contra Gentiles*, III, 69). This provided a new basis for man's freedom: "Just as God does not deprive natural causes of the natural character of their activities, so too does he not deprive intentional causes, by moving them, of the intentional character of their activities. On the contrary, he brings this about in them" (*Summa Theologiae*, I, 83, 1, ad 3).

This is, of course, an open protest against a desecularization of the world, a view which does not acknowledge the autonomous right of things in this world, but regards them only as symbols or references to a world transcending this world. Thomas's view marks the beginning of a process of secularization which has its foundation in the biblical faith in the creation and the incarnation. It is, of course, only a beginning, because the world in the course of becoming secular was seen by Thomas in the context of a great ontological structure in which everything was intimately connected with everything else – the highest with the lowest, God with his creation, the world. This ancient Platonic view of the world was, of course, transformed by Thomas on the basis of biblical impulses and interpreted by him with the help of Aristotelian thought. His theology was therefore a theology of a period of transition. Despite the presence of a great deal of unmanageable material which is not in any way in accordance with a new beginning in theology because it was derived from earlier traditions, Thomas's theology was and is impressively successful.

The dawn of the new era

Those who followed Aquinas were not able to continue in the same direction and develop his theological synthesis with its powerful inner tension any further. The only theologian who bore any affinity to Thomas was Nicholas of Cusa (1401–64), who was, like Thomas himself, stimulated by mystical thought and especially by that of Meister Eckehart (c. 1260–1327). He was more radical than Thomas and attempted to develop the idea that God and the world were identical and at the same time distinct and that man's spirit was both the image of God and what fashioned the world into a unity. These ideas, which seem extremely abstract, are of greater consequence than they at first sight seem to be. It is not simply a contradiction to claim that the world is radically different from God and yet identical with him. It is rather a way of saying that the world is governed by its own inner laws, but is nonetheless kept by God. Again, Cusanus' assertion that man is both God's image and the one who fashions the world means that man's turning towards the world does not in any way encroach on his relationship with God. There is no competition between the "secular" world and God and his claim on man either in thought or in action. The secular world and man acting in that secular world cannot escape from God because they are at the same time also *in* God. As those who have specialized in this question have shown, the philosophical and theological thought of Nicholas of Cusa prepared the way for the natural sciences of the modern era and the completely "godless" methods of research used in them.

Christianity did not, however, accept this challenge and make a new beginning. For centuries, the opinion prevailed in the Church that speaking about God and his activity in the world had to be defended and directed against the claims of natural science. We are now only too aware of the conse-quence of this attitude – the gradual retreat of theology and of the proclamation of the Christian message. Even today we are not entirely consistent in our attitude.

Was it ever necessary? During the post-Reformation period

especially, the blame for this attitude was laid on the continuing tradition of medieval theology in the Church, but in
fact this continuity was illusory. It had been effectively broken
by the teaching of Ignatius Loyola (1491–1556), the founder
of the Society of Jesus and the Father of the Counter-
Reformation. This break gave rise to apparent conflicts with
enormous historical implications. Galileo was forced to recant
despite recognition, for example, by the perspicacious Jesuit
cardinal, Robert Bellarmine, that the conflict was in no sense
objective. The French philosopher, René Descartes, who, as
a result of the condemnation of Galileo, proceeded very
cautiously, was regarded as open to correction. The writings
of Blaise Pascal (1623–62), perhaps the greatest Catholic
thinker of the modern era, were placed on the Roman index
of forbidden books because of his defence of Jansenism (which
was regarded as a heretical movement), especially in his
eighteen "provincial letters". Nietzsche summarized the case
of Pascal with penetrating insight and a mixture of love and
hatred: "There is Pascal! In him, spirit, honesty and enthusiasm are so intimately combined that he is the first of all
Christians. And what a combination this is!"

Pascal's polemics against the Jesuits had an immediate
effect, but his speaking about God, who, he claimed, did not
give himself to man to be experienced directly in nature, but
was to be found in the heart of man prepared to receive him,
was not really heard until the present century. Even today it
is unusual to regard science as a consequence of Christianity
and to think of the latter as responsible for providing the
correctives that can be applied both to science and to faith,
namely the attitude of dogmatic binding force and that of
scepticism.

The Reformation

In referring to the Counter-Reformation and the challenge to
faith made by the natural sciences, we have gone too far
ahead in history. The term Counter-Reformation reminds us
at once of the Reformation itself and this in turn calls Martin

Luther (1483–1546) to mind. It is possible to say of Luther, as in the case of Pascal, that he was one of the greatest of all Christians and that, despite all our reservations, he belongs to all the Christian confessions. What is more, any consideration of Luther, however brief, inevitably brings us back to the point where speaking about God is intimately connected with the Christian's political situation in the world.

Luther based his new way of speaking about God on the evidence of Paul, the Gospel of John and Augustine. He was resolutely opposed to the "modern" tendencies of the theology of the late Middle Ages (the *via moderna*, as it was called in contrast to the earlier *via antiqua*), which had been powerfully influenced by the philosophical and theological thinking of the English Franciscan William of Ockham (*c.* 1285–1347). (Ockham's thought is known not only as Ockhamism, but, because of the importance in his teaching of the theory that a concept is no more than a name [*nomen*], nominalism.)

A man like Luther could only be apprehensive about the Ockhamist view of God, according to which God was almost arbitrarily free and transcendent. He was also fully representative of his generation, and together with his contemporaries experienced and suffered from a profound fear of the strict sovereignty of God and his all-demanding will. His question "how can I obtain a God of grace?" ("Wie kriege ich einen gnädigen Gott?", Weimar edn., vol. 37: 661, 20), for example, is entirely in the tradition of the longing for redemption which characterized the later ancient world and the problem of justice which preoccupied medieval thinkers. In fact, Luther's question represents the ultimate stage in that long tradition, because in it attention is concentrated almost exclusively on the individual as confronted by God.

Luther's question in fact marks a turning-point in the history of faith, from the ancient and medieval form of Christianity to that of the modern era. He found the answer that he was seeking in Paul, the fourth gospel and Augustine. Although it was in some ways a liberating answer, it did not banish fear of God. Indeed, in his polemical treatise *De servo arbitrio* of 1525 ("The Servile Will"), written in reply to

Erasmus' work on free will (*De libero arbitrio*) of the previous year, Luther discussed at a more profound level than in any of his earlier writings the problem of man's involvement in evil and his inability to escape from God.

He learned from Scripture, however, that the "hidden" God had become reconciled with men in Christ and had thus become the "revealed" God of love and mercy for them. That same God did not demand justice or righteousness from those who believed, but gave it to them for Christ's sake. It is, of course, true to say that Augustine and the Christians of the Middle Ages knew, from their exegesis of Paul's Epistle to the Romans, that the "righteousness of God" of Rom 1: 16, 17 was not a justice accompanied by punishment, but justice given to man by God in grace. The completely individual and personal appropriation of this biblical idea among the excessive demands made by all that confronted man as "God's law" or as the consequence of that law meant, however, that the earlier truth was transformed into a new way of speaking about God. Luther's friend Melanchthon summarized this new approach in 1530 in Article XX of the Augsburg Confession: "The one who knows that he has a God of grace, knows God and invokes him and is not without God like the pagans . . ." In Christ, God is above all the one who can be known. He imposes no religious imperatives with regard to works, but accepts man without works. This gives man the freedom to turn towards the world in the service of his fellow men. Paul's text "for freedom Christ has set us free" (Gal 5: 1) thus became a key statement in Luther's reformation. In his document on Christian freedom (*Von der Freiheit eines Christenmenschen*, "The Freedom of a Christian Man", 1520), we read, for example: "A Christian is a free lord over all things and is subject to no one. A Christian is a servant at the service of all things and subject to everyone." The first sentence describes Luther's view of faith, the second his view of love.

The value of individual freedom and responsibility and of direct contact between God and the individual believer is greatly increased in Luther's teaching. The way had, of course, been prepared for this new teaching in the late Middle Ages by mystical theology and religiosity and by the humanism of the period. What is more, Luther's concentration on the individual Christian face to face with God was not an "individualism" in which only the individual had any right. This is quite clear from Luther's teaching about the community. Luther did not regard the Church as a scale of perfection, a structure of rights and duties and a hierarchy into which man was inserted in his correct place. For him, it was a community of equals, the people of God sharing in the universal priesthood of all believers (1 Pet 2: 9 ff), in the early Christian sense. The believer was set free in this community to serve both the community itself *and* the world, because both were, in Luther's opinion, sanctified by faith.

The Church's task was, for Luther, above all the proclamation of the Gospel and the administration of the sacraments on the one hand and, on the other, the activation of the community so that it served the brethren in society, without "ecclesiasticizing" the world, or making it the Church. As such, the world was, according to Luther, the great sphere in which faith was experienced. Faith became a reality and God was encountered not primarily in the Church, but in man's "secular calling", in the world, which was experienced by the believer above all as God's creation and as the place where his kingdom was found. The world for Luther was God's "kingdom on the left hand" where God ruled no less completely than he did in his "kingdom on the right hand", in the work of redemption, the proclamation of which was the Church's task. In a word, the "profane" sphere was the place of sanctification given to the Christian.

It is clear from the matter-of-fact way in which we accept these ideas nowadays that Luther's teaching looked far ahead into the future. At first, however, and during the period that followed the Lutheran Reformation, only fragments of this new vision of the Christian community and the world were effectively realized. It is, of course, possible that the reason for this is to be found in Luther himself. The levelling-down of the hierarchical structures in the Lutheran movement and later in the Lutheran church went side by side with a process which gave increasing importance to political power even in the life of the Church. It is often said – correctly – that it was only the result of unfortunate circumstances that led Lutheranism to dependence on the state. The shock that Luther experienced in connexion with the peasants' revolts on the one hand, and the material interest that the princes took in church property on the other, are relevant in this case. But perhaps the whole development had other, inner reasons.

Faith and activity in the world

Luther was confronted with the problem that had always been present since the time of Constantine – the relationship between the "worldly sword" and the Gospel. In his treatise on secular authority (*Von weltlicher Obrigkeit*, 1522–3), he made a distinction, almost completely in accordance with the Augustinian tradition, between the kingdom of God and the kingdom of the world.

Whereas Christians were, in Luther's view, set free to a new righteousness before God, the "unrighteous" were unable to do anything that was just and "therefore they were in need of justice which would teach, compel and impel them to do good". Luther did not hesitate to criticize the princes fearlessly, but he recognized that they were of necessity "God's gaolers and executioners" and that "his divine anger had need of them to punish evildoers and to preserve external peace". During the Peasants' War, the peasants' leaders appealed to the gospel message of freedom in order to justify their own quest for justice and freedom, but Luther was unable to recognize any connexion between their case and his new ideas about the Gospel and the world and refused to acknowledge their right to political revolt. As one well-known authority on Luther has commented: "The Gospel and especially its presentation of the love of Christ and the commandment to serve others and its teaching about the community led him to be seriously critical of society. This social criticism took the form, however, of stressing the duties and responsibilities of the rulers as norms for their service of the people. He did not believe that, in the light of the Gospel, the oppressed and the persecuted had any rights on which they could insist."

In this way, Luther himself prevented the new way of speaking about God, as the one who set man free to fashion the world in love and justice, from having any real effect on the structures of society and political life. The period that followed can therefore rightly be described as one in which faith withdrew from the world. The idea of the universal priesthood of all believers could develop no further and the Church soon became once again an institution in which the most important part was played by "pure doctrine". God was encountered, not in the expression of faith in the community and its individual members, but only in the Church and especially near the pulpit. The movement known as pietism which began in the seventeenth century was above all an attempt to base man's encounter with God on the experience of brotherhood. Despite its positive achievements, however, it was unable to overcome the less valuable spirit of religious individualism which began to emerge at about the same time.

It is undeniable that, from the eighteenth century onwards, the triumphant progress of the Enlightenment gave a powerful impulse to the growth of individualism in religion. The Enlightenment was, however, able to advance so rapidly because the fundamental movement initiated by the Reformation had lost its first force and had been slowed down almost to a halt. It was therefore possible for the sanctification of the world in the sense in which this was understood by the Protestant reformers to be transformed by the thinkers of the Enlightenment into a process in which the world was set free from the claims of the Gospel. It was similarly possible for God's "kingdom on the left hand" to be changed into an autonomous sphere which could only externally be regarded as God's kingdom, so long as religious terms continued to be used, but which was in reality the realm in which man was the autocratic ruler.

What arose, then, in the eighteenth century (in continental Europe, at least) were absolute states ruled by princes claiming absolute supremacy over their subjects. This total claim was not, however, made public as such, because it was decorated and to some extent disguised by a religious ideology that princes were specially favoured by God. It was only very slowly and painfully that the spiritual life of the Church was able to secure a certain freedom.

The fiction that Europe was as a whole a "Christian body" (*corpus christianum*) was, of course, preserved for a long time for political reasons because it was valuable as a means of maintaining the stability of the established structures of government. Even after the French Revolution, this fiction was made the focal point in the attempted political and religious restoration that took place in the nineteenth century. Yet this restoration also succeeded in banishing faith, in the sense of man's relationship and encounter with God, to the purely personal, inner life of the individual believer.

Increasing rigidity or a new beginning?

Did everything new that began with the Reformation, everything that pointed towards the future, come to an end soon afterwards? This did not happen, because, although Christianity entered a narrow defile in the centuries that followed, this pass was illuminated by two very different lights, each pointing to a new departure.

The first was the discovery of "religion" as an autonomous "province in the human mind", as the German philosopher Friedrich Schleiermacher (1768–1834) expressed it. This return to religion as a "feeling of unconditional dependence" – to quote Schleiermacher again – had the overall effect of reinforcing the movement towards a faith that was above all inward and removed from the world. (That was, of course, quite contrary to the original intention of the man who had discovered this aspect of Christian faith.) On the other hand, however, this view of faith acquired a function that could not have been discovered by the Enlightenment, a status which was, in the long run, of great benefit to the social dimension of faith. At the same time, it encouraged the spread of atheism and thus encouraged believers to reflect deeply about their own faith, eventually with very positive results.

The second factor which urged Christians to explore their faith more fully – sometimes along strange, devious and even dangerous paths – was the increasing emphasis placed on history, above all by Hegel (1770–1831). The effects of this movement can still be discerned in contemporary Protestant and Catholic theology, and the whole question is so important that we shall have to return to it.

This process of purification which had been initiated by these two movements, however, at first took place underground. In the foreground, a battle raged between a reinforced conservative confessional Christianity and a much more open liberalism in the Church and its theology. Piety was relegated by confessional Lutheranism to the immediately religious sphere and every attempt was made to identify the institutional Church with an autonomous Christian community in order to protect Christianity from being overwhelmed by a universal pluralism. This inevitably resulted in a retreat into the ghetto. The Church also lost contact with great and important sections of the population in the industrial society that was rapidly emerging at the time. In a valiant attempt to further the new beginning made by the Reformation, on the other hand, liberal Christians fought strenuously to sanctify the world in the light of a renewed faith and morality. In doing this, however, they associated themselves too closely with the prevailing philosophical tendencies of the period (the Enlightenment, rationalism and philosophical idealism) and in this way to the movement of individualistic academic middle-class thought that these philosophies produced.

The political challenge

At the beginning of the twentieth century, Protestants found themselves confronted with a number of inescapable and fundamental challenges, some coming from outside and others arising from the depths of the history of reformed Christianity itself. These challenges have to some extent changed during the course of this century, but they have not yet been fully overcome, nor have they in any sense ceased to exist.

The first serious challenge to Protestant Christianity in Germany proved of world-wide significance in its eventual implications for the life and nature of a Christian church. It occurred at the end of World War I. The defeat of Germany resulted in the end of the historical supremacy of the sovereign princes of the German Empire over the Evangelical Churches in their *Länder*. These churches remained for a short time in a state of confusion, but very soon gained control of the new situation by pursuing the task of evolving a "free Church in a free state". The results of this policy are at last becoming visible today. In 1933, with the Nazi takeover, the new relationship between the Church and the state was subjected to a serious test and it was the Swiss theologian Karl Barth, who came from a family with a long political tradition as Protestants and as citizens, who was one of the first to urge resistance. The Lutherans who rallied round him formed the so-called Evangelical "Confessing" Church. Before this, the Protestant theology which had stressed the importance and the meaning of the Gospel for the shaping of the world had been regarded with suspicion as a special branch of liberal theology (represented, for example, by Ernst Troeltsch). After 1933, however, the old idea of the "Christian state" had to be finally abandoned and the Church had to recognize that it formed a minority in society. Protestants did not, however, sink into a mood of resignation. On the contrary, they began to reflect once more about the meaning of the Christian mission. They did this, moreover, under the influence of the theological teaching of Karl Barth.

Nowadays, no member of the Lutheran church would venture to suggest that the question of the relationship between the Gospel and politics or between man's speaking about God and the conditions governing his life in the world was one with which theology was not concerned. Protestants have completely accepted the principle that the Christian is above all responsible for the world. Theologians like Dietrich Bonhoeffer, who was condemned to death by the Nazis in

1945, and Friedrich Gogarten († 1967), both of whom stressed the responsibility of the Christian living in the light of the Gospel in a religionless world, have become symbols of this attitude and have an influence which extends far beyond the immediate circle of their theological adherents. We may go as far as to say that it is here that the initial impulse of the Reformation with regard to faith and the world has broken through. It is as though we are experiencing a reaction in this whole process in the deep interest shown by historians in this "left wing" of the Reformation, as represented by such early political Protestants as Thomas Münzer († 1525). A question that is being asked again and again, for example, is whether what was said here was not a word spoken by the God who sets man free, a word which was quickly silenced, with the result that it could for a long time only be spoken *against* the churches.

From as early as the twelfth century and increasingly from the sixteenth century onwards, the right to resist the power of the state has been debated in the Catholic church, although in recent centuries this has developed into a teaching that has lent itself to the maintenance of the existing power structures. The Catholic church has often been criticized for being a "pillar of the establishment" and this reproach is not very wide of the mark. It was not until the end of the nineteenth century that any sense of responsibility for society was aroused on a large scale among Catholic Christians with the publication of a series of papal encyclicals on social themes, beginning with Leo XIII's *Rerum novarum* in 1891.

These initiatives, however, had to take place, according to the teaching of the Church, "on the basis of the natural law" and had to be intelligible and convincing quite apart from faith in the Gospel of Christ. Social criticism based on the Gospel and the power of the Gospel itself to change society were questions which were not raised by Catholic Christians until the present century, when they were asked insistently in France in the 1930s.

Following the example of the fundamental theologian Johann Baptist Metz (a Catholic), both Protestant and Catholic theologians now consciously call this manner of asking questions about faith and society "political theology". The political theologians regard their work as a necessary corrective to a theology which is only concerned with the individual's longing for salvation, as though this desire for salvation, its realization and criticism of the absence of salvation were not at the same time conditioned by the structures of society and man's life together with his fellow men. Furthermore, Old Testament studies carried out in recent years have played a considerable part in making Christians aware of the idea of a God who is concerned with social and political freedom.

It is also most important to mention the enormous influence that the ecumenical breakthrough has exercised on both Christian confessions in the question of faith and social and political life. The ecumenical movement began among Protestants who were deeply conscious of the Christian's social task in the world. The increasingly close contacts between the World Council of Churches and the Roman Catholic church are strongly marked by a sense of the Church's mission in the world, which both confessions have come to understand in a new light. It is therefore not simply by chance that the report of the Conference on Church and Society held by the World Council of Churches in Geneva, 1966, bears a remarkably close resemblance to the Pastoral Constitution, *Gaudium et spes*, on the Church in the modern world, issued by the second Vatican council in 1965. This close parallel is above all evident in the mutual emphasis placed on the bold new beginning that faith must make in order to encounter God's will in history. Equally striking is the insistence of both documents on the need to base all attempts to define the Christian's task in society not on a Catholic conception of the natural law on the one hand or on a Lutheran theology of "order" on the other, but rather on a patient listening to the Gospel. It is in the Gospel that Christians of both confessions can experience a renewed encounter both with each other and with God's claim in history.

The critical study of history

What is the present position? With the help of a number of
examples taken from history, we have shown how Christians
have struggled with the question about God and how they
have tried to answer that question correctly. We have also
learnt how man's speaking about God has always been conditioned by the circumstances of his social and political life.
We have acknowledged the need to question the human,
intellectual, social and political presuppositions governing
every way of speaking about God. We have tried to understand the traditional ways of speaking about God both in
order to gain a deeper insight into their lasting significance
and in order to apply them to our present situation. At the
same time, we have also attempted to verify the extent to
which man's speaking about God in history has been exposed
by these social and political factors to the danger of becoming
an ideological falsification, to the point where it has merely
justified the established power structures in society. This
danger has led many Christians today to subject the traditional ways of speaking about God to a "criticism of ideology".
It has, of course, to be admitted that this criticism is often one-
sided, malicious and even hostile to the Christian faith, but it
does not have to be so. There is a historical criticism of the
Christian tradition which is able to lead us to a deeper understanding of the real nature of man's faith in God.

We shall have to bear in mind all these historical experiences when we come to consider the present situation of
Christianity. Above all, we shall have to reflect how the God
question can be asked today and in the light of what conditions governing life. It is only in this context that we shall be
able to hear the answer provided by the Christian message
and discover the way in which faith must begin again today
and the direction that it ought to follow if it is to be a true
faith in God's dealings with man in history. One very important element in the contemporary question about God is the
fact that many people today regard that question as meaning-

less. We have therefore to look at the whole area in which
questions are asked about God in the modern era.

3   Atheism

No one is compelled to believe in God. It is even possible
consciously to refuse to believe in him. We have the example
of Abraham, called to leave his homeland in obedience to
God's promise (Gen 12), thus becoming the father of faith.
He did this in perfect freedom, hearing God's call and responding to it in faith. It is, however, always possible, because of
this very freedom, for man to reject God's call to faith. He can
also question it – even if he does not in any way doubt that
God exists.

Man's denial of God

Man certainly denies God in the Bible and continued to do so
in the early history of the Christian Church, but he neither
denied God's existence nor doubted the meaning of the question about God as such. When he "denied" God – when, for
example, "the fool says in his heart, 'there is no God'" (Ps
14: 1) – this meant that he was not following God's claims in
his life. God is never called into question in principle or in
theory in the Bible, which in almost every case simply
describes man's questioning God by failing to trust his promise
and, for example, preferring to "speed on horses" and "ride
upon swift steeds" (Is 30: 16). In other words, man places
more confidence in himself or his own weapons than in
Yahweh's power and commandments. He scorns God in practice, turns away from his promise and his teaching and trusts
himself (Jer 17: 5). In turning away from the living God,
biblical man almost always turns towards gods. These gods
are, of course, the forces, such as fertility, political power or
possessions, which man desires for himself, which he fears or
which he wants to depend on. Confronted with the living God

and the power of his word, these gods are merely "idols"
(Ps 96: 5). The stupidity and foolishness of man's turning away
from God and towards idols are revealed in the fact that he
achieves something for a time by serving them, but in the end
nothing (Jer 10: 3).

What can be heard in the history of the people of Israel as
the claim made by the living God becomes concentrated in
Jesus Christ, in whom God's invitation to believe and to follow
him becomes the highest demand of all made on man's freedom. The possibility and indeed the proximity of the absence
or rejection of faith are therefore presented all the more
clearly in the New Testament, which shows us how those who
hear the word of God in Jesus' word have to overcome a whole
series of questionings of this remarkable claim. This process
begins with the "doubts" and the "little faith" of the disciples
(Lk 24: 38; Mt 8: 26), passes through the stage of misunderstanding, in which human ideas are more prominent than the
word of God itself (Mk 8: 33) and eventually reaches the point
where the disciples confess: "Lord, to whom shall we go? You
have the words of eternal life" (Jn 6: 68). On the other hand,
any falling away from this extreme claim on the part of the
Christian who had begun to believe in the risen Christ was
regarded in the primitive Church as the greatest sin of all,
because it was above all a scorning of God (Jn 16: 9).

Philosophical atheism

Questioning God in this way is rather different from fundamentally contesting the reality of God. This type of denial of
God in principle and in theory does not play a decisive part in
the faith of the Old Testament or of the early Church or even
in any of the great world religions. At the most, it appears
only on the periphery of faith.

It is, however, to be found in philosophy even as early as
pre-Christian Greek thought. Protagoras, for example, declared
in the fifth century BC that "man is the measure of all things"
and the Epicurean philosopher Lucretius maintained "that
nature, free of arrogant despots, can achieve everything itself,

spontaneously, of its own accord and without gods" (*De rerum natura*, II, 1093). These are both examples of a fundamental denial of the existence of God. In the first case, God is denied for the sake of man, who regards himself as the ultimate meaning of the world. In the second case, God is denied in favour of nature, to which everything can be traced back. To be precise, we ought at least to say that God is not denied by these Greek philosophers in the sense of the God of the Bible. What they deny are in fact the gods as principalities and powers, as lords of the world who govern the fate of men. What is more, they deny the existence of these gods in order to stress the autonomy of man and of nature.

What we are bound to recognize, however, is that this denial of God which first came about in the Greek understanding of God gave rise to a problem in the subsequent history of the West which was to concern Christianity more and more with the passage of time. If we are to understand this problem, we must bear in mind that the great philosophical systems and especially those which came from Greece were assimilated by Christianity. These systems did not shrink from asking questions about God. On the contrary, because they tried to express everything, they also aimed to express God by an effort of the mind, extending human thought to the uttermost limit. This extreme mental effort resulted in the use of such formulae as the "unmoved mover" (Aristotle), the "simply good" (Plato) and "being itself" to express the mystery of God.

Great thinkers have, of course, always known that God cannot be defined by means of formulas of this kind, which can properly only be used to name things. It is only possible to point in this way to the mystery of God which is still present for human thought at the end of all thought. Since this inward gesture of final release is inherent in all philosophy, however, it was possible for Christian thinkers, who had experienced the reality of the living God, to make use of these formulas in the early and medieval periods of Christianity. They made it clear that there was a fundamental link between the reality of God which called for faith in man and the reality of the world which was examined by philosophers. The reality of

God could never, however, be fully grasped by man examining the world philosophically.

On the other hand, however, this way of thinking and speaking about God brought with it certain dangers and these became more and more apparent with the passage of time. It began to look as though philosophers could really grasp hold of God, assimilate and develop him like any other object of human thought. From that moment onwards, the reality of God had to be questioned radically. This was all the more necessary, because man was at the same time beginning to realize that he no longer needed God as a presupposition in order to understand individual data and situations in the world.

Scientific atheism

A new way of denying God began to develop with the emergence of the natural sciences in the modern era. We are, however, only now beginning to realize that it would never have been possible for scientific and technical thought to have developed at all without the Christian faith, which set the world free from belief in many gods and thus enabled man to devote himself unconditionally to scientific research. In fact, Christians were called "atheists" (*atheoi*) in the Roman state because they did not believe in the gods who were supposed to rule the universe.

It was basically Christianity, then, that enabled man to become scientific man and study the chain of causes and effects within the world itself. But it is quite possible for scientific man to do this without concerning himself at all with God. This principle was stated explicitly at the beginning of the modern era, for example, by the Dutch lawyer and scholar Hugo Grotius, who maintained that nature formed the objective link between men and between things even if it was assumed that God did not exist. The English empiricist Francis Bacon thought that it was dangerous for theology to be introduced into matters which concerned the natural sciences, because the result was always a lack of clarity. The

French scientist Laplace is well known for his statement that he had no need of the "God hypothesis" for his scientific investigations. The medieval understanding of the world, which bore the marked imprint of ancient philosophy, can be called an "ontotheological" understanding of the world: in other words, one in which the reality of all things is always and at once connected with the reality of God's being. As opposed to this view of the world, there is what may be called the methodological scientific atheism which has been gaining ground rapidly throughout the modern era. This is fundamentally a scientific investigation of reality using a method which *a priori* excludes the God question. In this scientific approach, man concentrates wholly on the relationships between individual finite data and phenomena.

This scientific atheism does not necessarily imply any real denial of God. All that it does state is that God is not an object of those sciences that employ this method. If the question about God is approached, a method which is different from the one used by scientists to investigate the relationships between natural phenomena has to be employed. Methodological atheism is quite consistent in excluding the question not only about God, but also about man's existence to a very great extent from the area investigated by scientists. This is, of course, the position occupied by positivism. The practical consequence of this development is a purely functional technical society that is free of all meaning because it never raises the question of its meaning.

So long as it remains purely methodological, there can be no real objection to this kind of methodological limitation of the natural sciences. But the reality of God is certainly not simply methodically disregarded in modern thought. On the contrary, it is explicitly questioned. There are three basic reasons for this.

The first is this. Scientific interest in reality can be and usually is confined to its composition of finite material parts and to its functioning according to certain calculable inner laws. In that case, the early formulas applied to God – "very being", "infinite good", "absolute truth" and so on – either

weaknesses of Deism

become meaningless or else are understood in a purely scientific sense, with the result that God is seen as a thing. In one popular version of the philosophy of the Enlightenment, for example, God was defined simply as the "necessary thing", rather like the computer that controls the whole machinery of the world. During the Enlightenment, it was quite possible to conclude that God was a "computer", because everything seemed to take place in a strictly ordered fashion in the world as it did in a machine and it was equally right to deny this idea of God in the period that followed. A "necessary thing" of this kind cannot, after all, be found or verified anywhere. If it could be found and verified, it could not be invoked with the name "God", because this thing, which is only the last link in a finite chain of causes and effects, requires a justification of its being. We have to apply Kant's question to it – "But why am I?"

There is also a second reason for denying a supreme cause presented in this way. It is clear from history that this "necessary thing" – assuming that it exists – has behaved very indifferently with regard to evil in the world. It is not simply by chance that the problem of theodicy has become so urgent and painful in the modern age: that is, how God, if he is God, can permit catastrophes, injustice and crime in the world. In the context of man's understanding of God as a "necessary thing", it is obvious enough why the question of theodicy has become so significant in the modern era and why it has even been identified with the question about God itself. After all, when God himself is regarded as guaranteeing the correct functioning of the world, then his existence will inevitably be called into question if the order of the world does not function. The question of evil, its origin and its meaning, has never been easy to answer in the light of faith. It is made even more difficult by the modern idea of God.

There is also a third reason why this idea of God which fades out both the unimaginable mystery and the freedom of God also results in a fundamental denial of God. If this "necessary thing", the God who controls the machine of the world, really existed, man would have no freedom No autonomous being who, in freedom of will, was responsible for shaping the world, could really exist alongside the absolute lord of the world. This idea is, however, unacceptable to man who has reached maturity. Because of his maturity, he is bound to protest against a supreme cause – this "spider of purpose and morality hiding behind the great web of causality" as Nietzsche called it. It was above all Jean-Paul Sartre who expressed this protest so powerfully in this century. It is, moreover, a consistent protest, so long as God is thought of in this way. If "God" existed, Sartre said, then that would mean: "I must regard the fact that I am an 'object' to God as more real than the fact that I am an autonomous and free being. I exist alienated from myself and I allow myself to be instructed about what I ought to be by my 'outside'" (*L'Être et le néant*, "Being and Nothingness", Paris, 1943).

Humanistic atheism

It is clear, then, that the existence of God has been called into question in recent years above all because man does not want to be kept in a state of dependence and immaturity by a "supreme cause". Modern atheism therefore appears in the guise of humanism. There can be no doubt that this protest against the existence of God has been nourished by the Church's insistence – in the name of God – on authoritarian doctrines which have been in contradiction to man's inquiring spirit. The case of Galileo in the seventeenth century is a clear example of this. It should not be forgotten in this context, however, that not only the Roman Inquisition, but Luther declared that the Copernican system had to be rejected on the basis of faith.

As a direct result of this connexion between God, represented as the supreme cause, and the claim of the Church, there evolved in eighteenth-century France the argument that God was used by the Church as "clerical deception", in an attempt to cling on to power. This thesis was further developed in the nineteenth and twentieth centuries by such critics of religion as Ludwig Feuerbach, Karl Marx and Sigmund

Freud, who claimed that man's ideas of God were no more than mere self-projections. According to these critics, man as it were concentrated all his anxieties and desires into a quintessence which he regarded as a reality existing outside himself and called "God". He made himself dependent, however, on that God, with the consequence that the ideology of the religions which arose from this quintessential idea was dominated by the notion of supremacy and power. God and religion were used to keep man in a state of subjection. Marx spoke in this context of religion as the "opium of the people", which Lenin expanded into "religion is opium for the people". Freud understood religion as a "collective compulsive neurosis", in other words, as something that was necessary in order to preserve certain stabilizing psychic relationships which also led to a loss of freedom.

The sum total of these explanations of the religious phenomenon is that God is now "dead". The emancipation of man and his increasing control of nature have resulted in God, who was regarded for so long throughout the history of the West either explicitly or implicitly as the one who guided the world, becoming meaningless to technical man. Modern man can live without God as a working hypothesis. For him, God is no longer one of the indispensable objective phenomena with which he associates.

We are, however, bound to ask whether the question about God has in fact been finally settled by the general iconoclasm that has taken place in recent centuries. Many sociologists and philosophers (such as Theodor Adorno and Max Horkheimer) have insisted or now affirm that man has given up asking about meaning on his way towards a scientific understanding of the world. There is no doubt that this thesis seems to be borne out by observation and everyday experience. In modern, technocratic society, man is apparently no longer concerned with meaning and is content simply to make everything function properly. In not asking about meaning, he no longer responds to an unconditional claim and thus excludes the question about God from his life. We must, however, inevitably ask whether he can really continue in this way. There are signs that man's inability to go beyond a preoccupation with the mere technical functioning of things and ask questions about the meaning of his existence is the cause of his greatest suffering today.

If this is really the case, then we have once again to ask what "God" and the "word of God" – terms that have so often been misused – in fact mean. Man's present suffering may, after all, be caused above all by the fact that these terms no longer mean anything to him. It is also possible, however, that asking this question may reveal that many aspects of the contemporary questioning of God are, as far as their inner meaning is concerned, simply a form of the "prayer of the unbeliever" to the living God who has become in the course of history an unknown God, but who is in reality the God to whom the Bible bears witness.

We have, however, once again anticipated what will be discussed later and in so doing have perhaps been unjust to sincere atheists. In any case, we are ready now to consider where and how the question about God is asked today.

4   The God question today

The authors of this book accept the validity of the basic presupposition that history is above all the place where modern man must ask the question about the meaning of his existence and where he must hope to experience God if this hope exists at all for him. The examples that we have so far considered, however, as to how man has asked this question and how he has experienced God in the history of Christianity give the impression of belonging to the past and seem alien. Whenever we have looked at well-known examples in the sphere of the modern natural sciences or of contemporary society and politics, the churches have been in a state of perplexity or resistance.

The basic forms assumed by this questioning of God are, however, familiar to us. God does not arise in the questions posed by scientists or in scientific knowledge and cannot occur there. Concepts which were in the past used in connexion with the philosophical question about God – "being itself", "infinite good" and "absolute truth" – have become empty and meaningless. Attempts to create a view of the world in which the catastrophes of nature, the cruelty of the animal world and the existence of evil in human society are minimized as inevitable but meaningful shadows in a world that is otherwise full of light strike us as dishonest. If we doubt our own freedom, we are bound to reject an absolute God who is in competition with that freedom. If we take these attitudes, which are both intellectual and emotional, seriously, we can no longer be entirely impartial in our search for a "place" where we can ask the question about God and possibly receive an answer. We shall perhaps be partial, prejudiced, sensitive to intellectual dishonesty and allergic to all false notes.

The question of meaning

If we ask about God and at the same time ask where we should ask the question about God, we have to ask it subject to one condition, namely that we may expect *meaning* from the one whom we call "God". We hope to be given a meaning for our existence in this world and thus a meaning for this world, which in its present state does not look for meaning. The God question can only be a real question which concerns us deeply if it is linked to the question about meaning and if it takes us further on our way towards an answer. Are we justified in imposing this condition?

To answer this question, we have to know what meaning is. "Meaning" is not a datum that can be verified, nor is it available like a drug producing a pleasant state of mind. We can only describe what meaning is in so far as it is an object and the possible answer to a certain kind of question, which for this reason we call the question about meaning. What, then, is this question about meaning, as distinct from other questions? In order to answer this question, we must begin with what may be called a "theory of asking".

What, then, is "asking"? The question of "asking" would seem to be superfluous – we all know what asking means because we do it every day. Yet this everyday event is really a strange procedure and it is worth while examining its conditions. We know our way about in life, otherwise we would not have a point of departure from which we would be able to ask. At the same time, there is much that we do not know, otherwise there would not be anything to ask. We know that we do not know much, otherwise nothing would urge us to ask. We can even plan in advance certain directions which our reflective thought should follow into what is not known, otherwise we could ask no questions which are aimed at a goal and which can therefore be answered. In this way, we can achieve an initial result. It is this. When we ask, we reach out from what is known to what is unknown, about which we already know as unknown.

This description of the process of asking is so wide that it includes the question about meaning, of which we have at first only a very vague foreknowledge. There does not, however, appear to be any clear distinction in it between what is already known and what is not yet known. There is also no direction with an aim in view into what is not known in asking. The most important distinction, however, is this – both the everyday questions and the scientific questions that are asked cannot be settled, in principle at least, by an answer. What is not known is, at least in principle, transferred to the sphere of what is known. It would, however, seem as though there is no end to the question about meaning. The inconclusiveness of this question about meaning, however, might be a sign that it is meaningless to ask it. (But what does "meaningless" mean, then?) The methodical prohibition to ask such questions, which certain views about the nature of knowledge dispense with, then seems completely redeeming. We therefore achieve a second result – we want to lift the meaning of the word "meaning" out of the question about meaning, yet we do not know whether the question about meaning is a possible question at all.

The suspicion of meaninglessness

In reality, we tend to ask such questions as: "What in fact is the purpose of it all?" – that is, the daily rat-race, for example, ending with a coronary thrombosis or a pension – "Why do we go on working ourselves to death?" – "For the children?" – "What has she got to look forward to in the years to come?" and so on.

All these and similar questions are quite unscientific, and no scientific ideal can prevent us from asking them. From our examples, we can single out a few typical words which show the totally unscientific nature of the questions that we habitually ask – "in fact", "purpose", "we" and "it all". These words display none of the precision that is to be expected in scientific language. Another characteristic of this type of question is the frequent use of pronouns such as "we", "you", "they" and "it all". Surely "it all" used in a statement or question can never have a precise significance? And "we" or "you" occur as the subject of a question to which no sensible predicate can be added. What "in fact" (!) is meant is "I", but it would perhaps be too dangerous to suggest: "Everything that *I* do might be meaningless or without purpose", because the suspicion "it might be meaningless" threatens my life. For this reason, we banish this suspicion by asking questions in which "I" is replaced by "we", "you" or "they" and "everything that *I* do" is replaced by "it all". Our third result, then, can now be formulated, at least as a rather tentative conjecture: The "suspicion of meaninglessness" seems (today at least) to be the simplest and most obvious form of the question about meaning, but generally speaking we more or less successfully avoid asking it.

If this conjecture contains an element that makes us instinctively avoid placing the "suspicion of meaninglessness" and "I" together in one question, we can go further into this conjecture by asking not "how can we . . .", but rather "how can *I* ask about myself?". But "I ask about myself" is a very imperfect description of the whole process. To be more precise, I must say: "*I* question *myself* about *myself*."

In this question, what is apparently the best-known element of all becomes the unknown element – the "I" occurs three times, firstly as the questioner, secondly as the one questioned and thirdly as the one about whom the question is asked. There can be no doubt that it is the same "I" used three times – the unknown I. Do questions with this structure exist in everyday language? One example comes to mind at once – when I feel suddenly low or in a bad mood, I ask *myself*: "What is in fact wrong *with me*?" If I go more deeply into this question, and do not at once blame another person or a thing for causing my bad mood, I often come to the conclusion that I am annoyed because I have made myself look ridiculous in front of another person, for whom I wanted to play a certain rôle, and in front of myself, when I wanted to see myself playing a certain rôle. I am also annoyed for an even more serious reason – because I am afraid that I was not equal to the rôle that I wanted so much to play. Sociologists assure us that rôle playing is absolutely necessary. This is, however, of little interest to me if I am trying to assert myself in this rôle, through another person, through others or through myself, and am failing to do so.

More questions can be asked, but rarely in the direction which has so far been followed, because it is so dangerous. Continuing in this direction, however, the questions would be: "Why do I always want to play a rôle? Do I need to assert myself through rôle play? Am I not self-sufficient? What in fact is my way of behaving?" In these questions, "I" is always at the very heart of the discussion and is questioned directly. The question "What is in fact wrong with me?" has become "What is the matter with me?" or simply "What am I?" or even more simply "Who am I?"

Even in this pure form of the question about myself, the "I" still escapes me. The ever-circling and penetrating question about myself becomes a disturbing hunt which yields no quarry. It encounters – nothing. And it encounters – death. This experience of nothing was called *ennui* by Pascal, a word usually translated by "boredom". But it is not the boredom that we very busy people believe we do not experience. In reality, we often experience it very acutely, but we have no time for it, because, in Pascal's opinion, we are always trying to run away from it and from the presence of death. Whenever we experience it, we prefer to call it "weariness" or "desolation" (cf Pascal). Pascal, himself a scientist and mathematician, knew that this weariness could not be healed by science. Kierkegaard (1813–55) called it "sickness unto death".

The experiences that we have tried to define in this section are experiences of meaninglessness. The real place where meaninglessness shows its deadly face is not the world where we work and which claims us totally, nor is it the sphere where our expectations of life are finally disappointed. It is the I which asks about itself. We can therefore conclude that, if there is meaning at all, it must be found where we experience its absence. In other words, if there is meaning, then the I which asks about itself is also the place where it is to be found.

I and You

Although not even the least hopeful of our contemporaries believe that it is, the situation would be quite desperate if the question about the enclosed "I" were the ultimate question. The situation is basically changed as soon as another person asks about me and asks not simply about my appearance, my health, my promotion prospects, my achievements or my financial assets, but about *me*.

This asking about another person is known as love. This love is not directed towards an abstract personal core or nucleus, as is sometimes mistakenly said, but towards a concrete person who plays his rôles, has his special qualities, arouses hopes and causes disappointments. We only love a person himself and not simply his qualities if we are ready to stand by him when his appearance, health, success or social status are in danger or are no more. A mother who repudiates her son when he is in trouble has never really loved *him*. A man who wants to divorce his wife because he cannot show her off any more in society has similarly not loved *her*, but only his own appearance in society.

In what way does love succeed in changing the desperate situation of the enclosed I? What we have here is, after all, not an I and a You which are separate and which subsequently enter into a relationship with each other. The person who knows that he is accepted by another person in love experiences the strange and compelling conviction that he receives himself as "I" from the one who loves him, on condition that he also gives himself back to the person who loves him, in other words, provided that he also accepts the other in love. Love and being accepted in love are never experienced once and for all time. Love is a way undertaken together and lasting the whole of a lifetime without coming to an end, unless, of course, an attempt is made to possess the other or to finish with each other. This almost always means the end of love.

But what has all this to do with the question about meaning? The I which asks about itself experiences itself as meaningless if it does not experience itself as received by a Thou, in other words, as a loved and accepted I. Meaning is therefore intimately connected with loving and being loved. Meaning, then, is experienced when I and You literally find fulfilment through mutually giving themselves to and receiving themselves from each other. Three aspects of meaning can be recognized both when this fulfilment succeeds and when it fails.

1. Meaning is not to be found in a single individual action existing in isolation, especially if advantage or success is sought. It is related above all to a life event and to individual action only within this wider context.

2. Meaning is absent if one person seeks another exclusively or even predominantly for his own use or advantage (for example, in casual relationships), in order to possess him (in the "haven" of marriage), or to increase his own status (making a good match). To express this positively, meaning can only be experienced when "I" am there for "You". It is not present when "I" have "You" in order to reach certain objectives.

3. Meaning is both received and actively given at the same time and in unity. We can approach this relationship of simultaneous giving and receiving in this way. Our experience of being accepted, especially in childhood, enables our capacity to accept and to say yes to the other to develop. This experience can only become a fulfilment of life and thus an experience of meaning when it is put into practice in a yes of acceptance said to the You, in "being there for Thee". In other words, the reception of meaning is the condition of all giving and establishment of meaning. It is only in the giving and establishment of meaning that we can experience that meaning is given.

Man's preliminary idea of God

We may now be a little nearer to knowing something about the place where we should ask the question about God. We began by saying that the question about God had to be asked in connexion with the question about meaning. We have in the meantime tried to throw a little light on that question about meaning and on meaning itself. We now have to do the same with the concept of God if we are to obtain an answer to our question about him. We cannot, however, simply clarify what and who God is – this is precisely why we have to ask about him. All that we can do is to proceed from a "pre-understanding" of God – from what we generally understand by "God" without being too precise. We can then combine this with our question about meaning and see where it will lead us. Our preliminary idea may then be confirmed, changed or completely destroyed.

Whether we like it or not, our pre-understanding of God is profoundly marked by the Western Christian tradition. All human understanding is marked by tradition or traditions. Periods of change, on the other hand, are characterized by a loss or a questioning of tradition, which is no longer automatically accepted. It is often possible to observe, in discussing the question about God, how powerfully we all bear the impression of the Western Christian tradition of faith in God.

There is, for example, widespread agreement concerning the irrelevance of asking about the existence of a "supreme being". In any such discussion, some people would say that it is possible or even probable that a supreme being exists, whereas others would say that it is unnecessary to accept such a being and therefore he probably does not exist. If, on the other hand, the question were asked differently – for example, "Is there a personal God?" – more or less everyone would at least agree that this is the proper question to ask. A very common answer to the further question, "What do we mean by a personal God?", is "A being we can talk to" and we refer at once to prayer. Much less common is the addition, "a being who talks to us", although that is no less important.

These ideas are, of course, fragmentary, but what is clear is that, in this question about God, we are not concerned with what Pascal called the "God of the philosophers", in other words, a supreme cause, being or good. What we have here is the God of the Bible, who addresses man and invites man to address him. If we approach the question from this pre-understanding of God, we are bound to say that the place where we may ask about God must be where there is speaking, addressing and answering. There is, moreover, a singular connexion between this and the results of our investigation into the question about meaning. Accepting and being accepted – love, in other words – take place, after all, in the process of address and answer. This, of course, includes the silent address and the wordless answer of the gesture, the sign and the action. On the other hand, when there is no acceptance or love, there is also no address and answer. The question about meaning, then, asked as a question about God, ought to be expressed in the following way. Is there, in and beyond all human address and answer, both of which give or establish meaning, an address to the whole of man's life and a possibility that man will give a lifelong answer? Will this address and this answer continue even if human meaning cannot be established? Finally, is the God of the Bible possibly the God of this address and this answer?

This might seem to be a suitable point to interrupt our

inquiry and discuss the question about the God of the Bible. There are, however, good reasons for postponing this discussion. These reasons are above all to do with personal love as the place where the question about meaning is asked. One very important objection, however, can be raised against the way in which we have set out and elaborated the question about meaning and have extended it to include the question about God. It is this. If the question about meaning and about God is asked from the vantage-point of the possibility of love between two persons, there is always a risk that this question will become a purely private and personal affair. To consider the question about God simply and solely in the context of a personal I-You relationship, as it has been and still is by philosophers of the school of personalism, is, it is claimed, a one-sided approach which reduces the real dimensions both of the question about meaning and of that about God.

This objection is one that we must take very seriously, above all because it may help us to reveal a further dimension of the question about meaning and about God. To do this, however, we must digress a little.

The authority crisis

We are becoming increasingly aware of the phenomenon that people who have been deprived of love as children are later in life incapable of loving or at least severely hindered in their capacity to love. It would moreover seem that, even in countries in which marriage and family life are valued very highly, there is a growing number of people who have not experienced acceptance by and turning towards another person in childhood or whose experience of this is very inadequate. A brutalizing environment without love is often the cause of this, but it also happens that parents who apparently give their children a great deal of love and allow them unlimited opportunities as consumers may in fact be denying them the possibility of being accepted by and turning towards another.

We cannot clearly go into all the possible explanations for

this here, but must simplify radically and say that the source of all man's experience of "I" in turning towards a "You" is the environment that he knows as a child, and especially as a very young child, and this source is constantly in danger. So often the upbringing of the child is either authoritarian – his thoughts and behaviour are strictly regulated and discussion and disagreement are not tolerated – or permissive – he is given everything that he wants. In both cases, however, the child's upbringing is the result of authority on the part of the parents who, whether they are severe or indulgent, imagine that they are already in possession of the only valid norms, and are completely indifferent to all new discoveries. This rigidity, which is apparent even in parental indulgence, shows that the attitudes of an earlier society, with its much greater self-assurance with regard to its values and norms, still persist in the present society. What is more, the same rigidity can also be traced to the fact that marriage and family life have become much more of a purely private matter in modern industrial society.

The extremely complicated structure and development of contemporary society has led to a sense of impotence in the individual rather than the discovery of the meaning of life or of himself. This is undoubtedly why he looks for and hopes to find himself in the private sphere of marriage and the family. This is, however, not so simple as it seems, because married couples no longer come from a familiar world which they share with others. On the contrary, they have first to build up this world together. This is often too severe a demand and, since man cannot live without a stable and easily surveyed world, he will inevitably seek refuge in more or less clearly arranged and established rôles. This in turn will have its effect on the quality and content of the way in which he brings up his children.

What is the effect of this on the question about meaning and the question about God? The child brought up in this way will not experience his parents' turning towards him in love as a liberation of his "I" which gives meaning to his life. He will rather experience it as an encounter, as repression or as a protection from without and probably as a mixture of all three. This fundamental experience of authority will inevitably be transferred to every encounter with other authorities. But, in our tradition, that of the Bible, the content of the word "God" is closely associated with the content of the word "authority". It is hardly surprising that God is experienced as an authority in much the same way as other authorities in our lives. He is either a strong or a weak authority, but he is not an authority that can be questioned.

Questioning traditional authority critically, however, is something that everyone has to do as he grows up and begins to find himself. It is therefore hardly surprising that the gradual process of dissociation from authority should include a dissociation from the authority of God. We can therefore formulate another result, which is this time negative and intermediate. The family ought to be the place where love and therefore meaning are experienced in early childhood and where meaning can be sought as the child grows up to young manhood or womanhood. It should therefore be the place where the question about God is asked. The very opposite is, however, true. The family, which is marked off from industrial society with its inherent threat to destroy meaning, and is therefore a purely private sphere of meaning, would seem to have in fact become a place where meaning is not experienced and where the question about God is not asked.

This negative and intermediate result is reinforced as soon as we recall that, in the biblical and Christian tradition, the authority of God is linked with the name of Father. What was at an earlier period a very meaningful element in man's image of God, however, has now become extremely questionable. The image and the rôle of the father have become very ambiguous in contemporary society. Man's place of work, where he engages in activity that he (generally speaking) dislikes, and his home, where he expects to find love and acceptance, have in the great majority of cases become separated. Many men need to compensate in the home and family for the meaninglessness of what they experience at their place of work. A father cannot transfer to his children a positive relationship with the larger society in which he lives and works and of which his family forms part, simply because he has no such relationship with society as a whole. As a father, then, his share in the upbringing of the children is often limited to sanctioning the mother's intentions: those which have been fulfilled, but most especially those which she has not been able to carry out. He frequently does this in a very special way and his reasons for behaving like this are often incomprehensible to his children. The father, in other words, is often an incalculable figure – what Alexander Mitscherlich has called the "father as bogeyman". God is certainly very often called Father under precisely these conditions and the image of an incalculable and repressive is inevitably impressed on the child's mind. This image of God is not in any sense a help, support or orientation for the young person growing up. On the contrary, it simply reinforces in the young person's mind that people and things are unreliable, alien and threatening.

It hardly needs to be said that we are not accusing anyone or complaining about the existence of "relationships" in the manner of the contemporary scientific critics of society. All that we have aimed to do here is to provide a number of reasons why the changes that have taken place in man's question about meaning and his question about God that is so closely associated with it have to a great extent been conditioned by the society in which we are living. These changes are not primarily the result of moral failures on the part of parents or educators. The contemporary phenomenon of the loss of the father especially cannot be reversed and the father cannot be restored to his former position of honour merely by an appeal to morality. As Mitscherlich has pointed out, we are, at least provisionally, "on the way towards a fatherless society".

In search of new forms of society

It is, of course, possible to go no further than a mere consideration of the situation as it stands. To do so would mean that the question about meaning and the related question about God would literally have no place at all in the reality of life today. Is it possible to avoid this conclusion? It cannot be avoided by the evolution of a new theory alone. The theory must be accompanied by action.

We should above all not regard the situation as we have outlined it above as something that cannot be changed or influenced. We ought rather to accept it as a challenge and try to regain the place where the questions about meaning and about God can be asked again by refashioning human life and society.

There are three possible ways of approaching the analysis that we have made of the situation. In the first place, we can criticize it and our reasons for doing this may be good or they may be apparent, in which case the objective situation will not be accepted. In the second case, we can accept the relationships as they are with resignation, and try to make the best of them. In the third place, we can try to change the conditions which have led to this situation and this seems to be the most suitable solution of all. We should not, however, believe too readily that it is not possible to do this. We should therefore like to suggest certain spheres where changes should and indeed could be made if some answer is to be found to the question about meaning. The main purpose of these suggestions is not to lead to the evolution of a new socio-political programme to change society, but simply to throw some light on that society by means of a few examples.

Firstly, then, we should try to evolve a new form of up-bringing in which parent and child would be partners and the words "authoritarian" and "anti-authoritarian" would no longer apply. A new way has to be found of expressing authority and of making it credible. It is especially important for the young person to grow up accepting responsibility together with others in working together with them in shared tasks and commitments. He must also at an early age develop an understanding not only of "I-You" relationships, but of "we" relationships. This is seldom possible to any extent in the small modern family, the primary function of which often seems to be to protect its members against the anonymity and the immeasurable size of society as a whole. The situation in which the small family finds itself has therefore to be changed.

It would not be possible to revive the earlier type of "extended" family, but there are ways of including the contemporary small family in new, extended social relationships, in which new forms of partnership and even of neighbourliness can develop under the present conditions of living and working. In any case it is certain that the family will only have something to offer in contrast with the challenge made by the "youth sub-culture" if the whole complex of tasks is solved. These sub-cultures are, after all, trying to replace the outmoded pattern of the family with the idea of a "group of equals" and to experience meaning in new forms of partnership. The fact that these new forms often contain irreconcilable oppositions and that these bold attempts often fail does not necessarily mean that we have nothing to learn from them.

A second suggestion is the improvement of the situation of the family by means of the practical implementation of modern town planning. In theory, there has for a long time been widespread recognition of the need to plan towns so that the human environment favours the development of extended social relationships, but in practice this has only been achieved rather rarely. It will only be possible to bring about a new relationship between the family and the world of work which is orientated towards man himself if the physical space in which man lives and works is disposed in such a way that the essential focal points are constantly borne in mind and industry and the services are both decentralized and made to overlap. These changes will not take place of their own accord. They must be initiated by politically conscious citizens by means of "pressure from below". This political awareness also confronts parents and educators with new tasks and responsibilities in connexion with the upbringing of children and adult education. All this must above all take place at the same time, or the circle of conditions for contemporary life in the family and in society will soon become a vicious circle of despair.

It should be possible, on the basis of these and other similar examples, to become aware of the conditions and the relationships which can lead to change, a change which will mean that life in the family and in society as a whole may once more become the place where the questions about meaning and about God can be asked. Man's experience of responsible "we" relationships in the family, the basis of all experience of meaning, can only grow if this experience at the same time grows in other areas of society as a whole, especially in the form of partnership and co-responsibility with others in those questions that concern everyone.

What we have described here is often given the easily misunderstood name of "democratization". This is not the place to discuss whether this word is being used rightly or wrongly here – we are referring to the process in society which allows such forms of responsible "we" relationships to arise. The condition for this is that, both in the smaller and more easily surveyed circles such as the family, but also in the much larger structures of society, there is not simply efficient technical functioning, but an increasing ability on the part of all members of society to perceive what is apparently too immeasurable and impenetrable in society and thus to accept greater co-responsibility and take part in joint decision making.

The threat from world politics

The constant danger of withdrawing from this task in a mood of resignation and of increasing the existing tendency towards purely technical functioning and thus of becoming more and more remote from the question about meaning is especially great in the face of the threat from world politics, which are generally accepted to be of decisive importance for the future of mankind. The whole world is at present faced with two overriding challenges. Firstly, there is the possibility of collective suicide within the space of minutes by the use of nuclear weapons. Secondly, there is the process of rapidly spreading hunger in the Third World encouraged by the economic policy of the industrial nations. In the face of both of these factors, man has developed certain defence-mechanisms.

It is useful to enumerate some of these mechanisms which enable us to "live with the bomb", but it is above all essential to understand that they are no more than defence-mechanisms. We tend to forget the threat or else we try to present the mechanisms to ourselves as reasonable, by arguing that the system of nuclear deterrents has saved us from a third world war. We do not treat seriously enough the carefully calculated forecasts that continued nuclear armament will lead to disaster. We also forget our fears of a menacing apocalyptic situation almost as soon as they arise. We are warned against utopias, but the only argument used against them is "that is how people are". Any attempt to explore ways of establishing peace is rejected by a process of defaming those who take part in this quest and calling them Communist fellow-travellers.

We have evolved a similar set of mechanisms to help us to continue as prosperous members of a consumer society despite the existence of world hunger. We have grown a spiritual carapace to protect ourselves against the pictures and descriptions of distress in the Third World which otherwise would make excessive demands on our ability to feel sympathy. We arm ourselves against the unreasonable demand of admitting that we too are guilty of causing world hunger. (At the same time, however, it has to be recognized that those people who make others feel uncomfortable by using this demand against them often seem to be convinced that they do not themselves share in this guilt.)

We also use a "reasonable" argument in this case, claiming that we can only become capable of helping the under-developed countries if we increase our own level of production and consumption. We point to the differences in time in the development of various countries and conclude from this that we must, for the time being (but how long will the time last?), expect the rich to become richer and the poor poorer. We use clever arguments to show how incapable people in the under-developed countries are of employing the help that we give them with such difficulty properly and efficiently. This justifies our saying that the guilty party is not the murderer, but the victim.

If these defence-mechanisms prove to be insufficient, we have two mutually complementary ways of exonerating ourselves from all guilt. Either we justify our apathy by a process of delegation of responsibility, saying, for example, "we can do nothing about it – that can only be done by the people 'up there'". Or else we try to avoid the fatigue of detailed work by demonstrating and thus quietening our bad consciences. (That does not mean that demonstrations are not meaningful and even necessary – they certainly are, when they take place within a widely embracing "strategic" plan of action.)

The death of God

We have probably said a great deal in this context that is one-sided and unjust, but it may help us to understand more clearly the connexion between these defence-mechanisms, which operate to some extent in all of us, and the questions about meaning and about God. These mechanisms are, after all, fundamentally attempts to exclude the suspicion of meaninglessness coming from a new direction. We should also remember that this suspicion of meaninglessness arises especially in connexion with the direct question about the "I". The answer that we gave to this question was that meaning is to be found in mutual acceptance of "I" and "You". The conditions of this acceptance, however, have run into serious danger because of the rapid changes that are taking place in the modern world. In the past, we tended to seek refuge from "I" in "we", "you" or "they" or even in simple egoism. Nowadays, however, we fly from the dangers of society into the private sphere of "I-You" relationships or into the security of a "group of equals". Both are a flight from the excessive demands made on us by the impenetrable nature and the insurmountable problems of society as a whole.

This flight, however, also ends in an excessive demand,

because neither a purely private, isolated I-You relationship nor a closed group of equals are able to fulfil man's expectation of meaning, unless they are included within a greater whole which makes it possible for the small group to maintain itself. A beginning has already been made to solve this problem, but, in the situation in which the world finds itself now, flight of this kind can only end by confirming our suspicion of meaninglessness. In this case, however, we may presume that flight is only a symptom of what Nietzsche called the "imminence of the most sinister of all guests", in other words, of nihilism.

Nietzsche has coined many unforgettable terms expressing in one way or another the sinister character of nihilism, but the one that has gained currency in recent years is the "death of God". In so far as it is used not merely as a catchword, but is employed significantly, it has acquired various meanings. Our present discussion does not require us to go into these different meanings here. Accepting the risk of oversimplification, we will confine ourselves simply to what Nietzsche himself meant by the death of God.

History – by which Nietzsche meant the whole history of the world – has no meaning. The authority from whom meaning has been expected for millennia, God, has been killed by us. We have drawn the conclusion of history by turning man's will to truth against truth itself. Nietzsche's view of this was that history has shown that truth, which is unchangeable, stabilizes power and that man's will to truth derives from his will to power and is part of it. On the other hand, however, all truth was thought of as established in a higher truth which was at the same time the foundation of all meaning which limited power. Man's will to power has therefore to turn his will to truth against itself, if he does not reject the stabilizing function of truth and at the same time does not accept limitation by the truth.

What happens, on the other hand, if we draw this conclusion from history? The first is a radical criticism, which is synonymous with science. This science knows nothing of a basis or an aim of the whole. It is ready to expel all the worlds that exist behind the world. "In what direction are we moving? Away from all suns? Are we not constantly falling? Backwards, sideways, forwards, on all sides? Are we not wandering through an endless nothing?" (*The Happy Science*). Only the man who, like Nietzsche himself, suffers from this nothingness is able to turn "passive" nihilism into "active" nihilism. The man of "higher history" who is to come has to give a meaning to the meaningless world. But, before this can be done, all ways by which we can seek flight, not only those of apathy, but also those of activity, have to be closed by radical criticism. Among other things, Nietzsche mentioned "history with an immanent spirit, which contains its own goal and to which one can give oneself" (*The Will to Power*). Nietzsche was clearly thinking here of Hegel's theory of (the) spirit, which expresses itself constantly in history. Nietzsche, who scorned socialism, never mentioned Marx and believed that Hegel, with his faith in history, placed responsibility on the spirit. Socialism, in his opinion, put responsibility on the rulers and overlooked the fact that our "age of actors" provided neither solid material nor builders for the creation of a "free society". According to Nietzsche, both the passive fatalists and the active dreamers wanted "to avoid the will, the longing for an aim, the risk of giving themselves an aim" (*The Will to Power*). The decisive aspect, then, is to establish aims and therefore meaning without an authority which will guarantee meaning and which is responsible only to itself. Is this possible?

Nihilism?

Both Nietzsche's opponents and those who have followed him have tried again and again to escape from his nihilistic conclusion. It is even possible to detect this same attempt within the philosophical movement known as existentialism, which is to a great extent composed of variations on the theme first evolved by Nietzsche. Jean-Paul Sartre, for example, experienced in practice during World War II what it means to live as a man who acts responsibly – as a member of the French

Resistance. During this period, he did not persist in regarding the whole as meaningless and, responsible to himself alone in the sense in which this was understood by Nietzsche, in establishing aims and therefore meaning. It is, of course, true that he was not conscious of any meaning in history outside or above history itself, but he expected – and here he was following Kant's thought (a "city of ends" – or purposes) in that history was concerned with the way in which revolution was a condition for the coming of that city. "If the revolutionary wants to act, he cannot regard historical events as the result of fortuitous elements that are not subject to laws" (*Materialism and Revolution*).

The same conviction, that we cannot dispense with faith in and foreknowledge of a meaning in history as a whole, has led to many dialogues between Christians and Marxists. In this dialogue, it has only been possible to speak about the meaning of history if history is seen to be moving towards a goal or aim. This, at least, was the view of many theoreticians who have been involved in dialogue with socialists, since the days of Swiss and German "religious socialism" before and after World War I (Paul Tillich was one of the most prominent members of this movement), since the time of the dialogue of the "policy of the outstretched hand" in France in the 1930s (Maurice Thorez, general secretary of the French Communist Party, played an important part in this), and again since the Christian-Marxist conversations of the Paulus-Gesellschaft in Germany (1964–7).

Christians have at certain times shared an intense experience of "history" with Marxists. This happened especially, for example, in the case of the early "religious socialists" in their critical allegiance to social democracy, in the French Resistance and in the new beginning during and after the Vatican Council (1962–5) in the Catholic church (and not only in the Catholic church). At such times, the meaning of history seemed to have become clearly visible. History seemed, despite all setbacks, to have been moving towards fulfilment, and part of this experience was a consciousness of a way pointing in a new direction, a new beginning.

78

GOD

Doubts could not, however, be silenced for ever. At one time, all Christian-Marxist dialogue was encumbered on both sides with the mortgage of a past (and a present), with the result that inhuman actions were performed and inhuman structures erected in order to save man. On the other hand, the many disappointments experienced in recent years – 21 August 1968 is a notable date – have made us less optimistic and more sober.

Hegel seems finally to be dead, and we are no longer able to cling to the idea that the course of history follows an inner law or plan designed by a transcendent power which we can continue to regard as a theoretical truth and as the basis for all that we do. Nietzsche, it would seem, has been proved right and with him all those who have not diluted his conclusion, namely to ask not about the meaning of history, but only about the meaning that has to be established by me here and now. Heidegger, who is wrongly regarded as superseded, has emphasized that time and history are modes in which man anticipates himself, in other words, in which he projects his life into the future. This anticipation of himself occurs in the life of the individual and it also happens in the whole of historical periods. There is, however, no transcendent guideline in history permitting us to speak of history moving meaningfully towards its goal.

Another existentialist has expressed this idea in a more concrete form. This is Albert Camus, one of the most honest humanists since the "death of God". All that we have to do, Camus believed, was to express the absurdity of life, like Sisyphus in the underworld, rolling the stone again and again up the hill without any prospect of success in the end. This was for Camus everything and it was a great deal – this and standing up here and now for those without freedom and rights, making "a human affair of fate", an affair "that has to be regulated among men" (*The Myth of Sisyphus*).

Camus had this to say to Christians: "I share your dread of evil, but I do not share your hope and will never cease to fight against this world, in which children suffer and die ... What the world expects from Christians . . . is that they set themselves free from abstraction and look at the bloodstained face that is the face of history in our own times . . . Christianity is pessimistic with regard to man, but optimistic with regard to the fate of mankind. Well, as for me, I am pessimistic with regard to the fate of mankind, but optimistic with regard to man . . . Perhaps we cannot prevent children being tortured in this world, but we can reduce the number of tortured children. And if you Christians do not help us, who is to help us? I know . . . and know it often with an aching heart, that Christians will decide to do this only so that millions of voices – and I mean millions – all over the world will join in the cry of the handful of individuals who have no faith and no law, but who are standing up everywhere and without flinching for children and for people . . ." This he said in 1948 in an address to the Dominicans in Paris.

The question about meaning on the way

How far have we got in our search for the place where the questions about meaning and about God can be asked? Our historical situation in the contemporary world of technique and industry has made it extremely difficult for us to find meaning and God in the experience of mutual acceptance of I and You. All attempts to fathom the meaning of history as a whole, including the part played in it by technology and industry, and all attempts to make it a guide-line for our own action here and now seem to be rather overstrained. The sinister guest of nihilism is no longer imminent – he is here, living among us.

The only possibility, then, that remains open to us in our present circumstances is to be ready to stand up for other people when an unconditional demand is made on us. We should, as Camus says, be ready to stand up for tortured children. To look for a "higher knowledge" or for "the whole" would seem to be quite useless. The question about meaning does not become significant until we begin to create meaning as far as we are able to do so – meaning in the sense of "small" meaning, since the "greater" meaning of the whole is concealed.

It should also be noted that Camus did not ask the question about meaning in the address quoted above. All that he did was to express a demand which is still valid. To run away from unconditional demands of this kind is to evade the question about meaning.

Those who make demands like this recognize that the question about meaning as a whole can, at least occasionally, be left open. In acting for men in the world, in showing love and in fighting for justice, meaning is experienced even though it may not be possible to formulate it.

If we trust this experience, the rather surprising consequence will be that the answer to the question about meaning will come not through reflection, but through action. We cannot answer the question about meaning just theoretically. But in making unconditional demands we experience that our action can be meaningful, even if it may be clear afterwards that it was not. The meaning is here once again the "small" meaning – the "greater" meaning of the whole cannot be seen. No breath of the "world spirit" blows in our direction and no programme is produced, providing a solution to all the problems of the present and the future. But, in establishing meaning in the "small" sphere, we experience how the greater meaning of the whole is a continuation of that small meaning. We are certainly moving along the right way if we expect to recognize that small meaning.

What is more, the meaning that we experience by establishing it isn't necessarily so very "small". Without being able to see the greater meaning of the whole, however, we can still do "great" things on a world-wide scale and know how necessary they are. This "small" meaning, after all, always forms part of the greater fabric of relationships, which we must keep in sight if we want to establish the "small" meaning successfully. Since we do not know the relationships that prevail within the "greater" meaning as a whole, we have at least to try to outline a plan of those relationships. This attempted plan will inevitably be provisional and open to constant correction, but it will enable us to act coherently. This type of plan is sometimes called a "real utopia" – "real" because it has an effect on real actions and "utopian" because it does not claim to know the relationships existing between the whole. (This does not, however, mean that this utopia is a pure illusion.)

Let us briefly consider this question in connexion with our two examples, the existence of a system of nuclear deterrents and the increasing distress in the Third World. Both the bomb and world hunger compel us to look for new ways of resolving these and other conflicts and of regulating the economy of the world. The "meaning of history" cannot really help us in this search. If, however, we are to solve world conflicts in the concrete and to formulate a programme of help for the underdeveloped countries, we must try to imagine how a world existing in peace and prosperity ought to look. Thus our activity will begin and end concretely and individually, but it is always guided by a greater plan and directed towards a greater goal. On the one hand, this plan has to be corrected again and again in the light of our experience gained in concrete action. On the other hand, it will not restrict our vision to such an extent that we only see what is close at hand. Such a plan should, on the contrary, keep us looking constantly in the direction of the concealed meaning of the whole.

We can now, on the basis of this presupposition, attempt to formulate the question about meaning in the way in which it presents itself to countless people in modern technical and industrial society. This is also the way in which the same question is understood by the authors of this book. The question about meaning, we may say, is no longer a question about the meaning of history. It is rather a question about tasks, possibilities and perspectives of historical action both on the smallest scale and on the greatest scale. The answers to this question will make themselves known to us at the proper time on the way of this historical activity.

The question about God on the way

Is this way of historical action also a place where the question about God can be asked? In the first place, it is not, because, as a question about historical action, the question about meaning is asked in a completely "atheistic" way. Man's experience of meaning in historical action does not have in any way to refer to God. Believers and atheists can therefore work together without restraint for their fellow-men. There is no danger at all that the dividing line between them will be obscured, because in this case there is no dividing line to be obscured. This is why Albert Camus, for example, was able to invite Christians to take part in unrestricted dialogue on the way of historical action.

Yet the way of historical action is also the place where the God question can be asked. We no longer formulate our question about God as "Who gives meaning to our activity for the sake of our fellow men?" The question does not have to be formulated – the answer is found in our experience of action. We are not compelled, but we may, however, be inclined to ask: "What is the explanation for our being irresistibly drawn into the tension that exists between meaning and meaninglessness whenever we try to bring about a situation of love and justice in history?" Another question that we may ask is: "How can we go on thinking of this attempt to show love and justice as meaningful, especially when it fails so many times and when the success that is achieved is no more than a drop of water in the ocean, just a few children saved from torture?"

The biblical answer to this question is that this attempt is meaningful because behind it is a God who is himself love and justice and who has addressed us in love and justice, a God who reveals himself meaningfully whenever we act in love and justice. We shall return to this later, but in the meantime we are bound to ask whether we can come a little closer to the biblical message by reflection, if this question is posed philosophically.

Is there, for the philosophical question, an alternative to Camus which does not content itself with the "small" meaning as Camus did, yet at the same time does not risk a bad awakening. We do not have to look far for this alternative – it is to be found in the teaching of a twentieth-century Christian thinker who was constantly preoccupied with the question of historical action, Pierre Teilhard de Chardin (1881–1955). It is possible to regard Teilhard de Chardin as the anti-pole to Camus. A consideration of his thought will bring this first part of our work to an appropriate conclusion, because it will enable us to measure the full extent of the question about meaning as a question about God and to come closer to the place where that question can be asked.

God and evolution

It has often been suggested that Teilhard's "optimism" is of a very questionable nature and that his conviction that evolution was moving towards "omega point" at which the cosmos will have reached its highest complexity and consciousness, a situation which is beyond the imagination of man today, is no longer in touch with reality. Those who reject Teilhard's vision base their argument mainly on the observation that the course of world history would seem to be a way downwards rather than a way towards fulfilment. This, however, betrays a mis-understanding of Teilhard's thought (cf *The Future of Man*). It is certain that mankind and the world are confronted with a new phase in the evolutionary process, but it is also true to say that this will not of necessity take place. The level of com-plexity and consciousness that the cosmos has now reached in its highest result, man, means that man must accept co-responsibility for the continuation of evolution. If he does not, the world will enter a situation of extreme danger. This accounts for the "critical moment" of history, at which man has to decide, through action, about the future of the world and therefore about its meaning.

An action which has to guarantee the future of the world and man's health and survival cannot be performed by a single individual. The research and practical steps involved in the many problems of nutrition, population, eugenics and so on that confront mankind today cannot be undertaken by an individual. An entire organization, based on the human com-munity, is required to carry out this task. The precondition for this communal activity is, however, that men become united in a way that has never yet been known. This union of the community of man characterizes the present phase of evolution, which Teilhard called the "phase of socialization".

How is this socialization possible? It must not result in the individual being made absolute, nor must it extinguish him. As a process of "personalizing socialization", it must aim to perfect him. In that case, it calls for interpersonal forces of attraction – interpersonal forces or, more simply, forces of love. If only one community of man is to guarantee the meaningful existence of mankind and its continued survival, then these forces of love must be world-wide.

God as a person

It is precisely here that the question about God arises for Teilhard. He criticized the Marxist solution, according to which the forces of "harmonization" came from men's relationships with and approaches to each other. In his view, it was only the forces of attraction inherent in a real "super-love", in other words, in a real "super-person", who appears "at the same time at the summit and in the heart of a united world", that could release the forces of love among men and finally destroy egoism.

This sounds like a modern proof of the existence of God, but it is not that. Teilhard called it a hypothesis, a concept which was very familiar to him from his work in the field of natural science. This is also a good definition of his way of asking the question about meaning and affirming meaning. He found this hypothesis of the love attracting everything and appearing at the summit and in the heart of the world, in reflecting on the pre-conditions for action. No one can act responsibly unless he affirms the meaning of that action and no one can act with the socialization which alone gives meaning in mind if he regards it as hopeless because the forces of love are insufficient. On the other hand, however, the hypothesis of super-love is not an answer which finally settles the question about meaning. Certainty is to be found in the very

process of acting and in asking about the preconditions governing that action. The question about this hypothesis therefore
arises afresh every time a responsible action is performed. The
hypothesis, then, can be questioned without restraint whenever the sphere within which the question is asked is extended.

Teilhard's ideas and the perspective within which the question about God is asked according to Teilhard are certainly
directly opposed to those of Camus. Teilhard, like Camus,
drew attention to the importance of the concrete decisions
that have to be made together with other men and to the need
to implement these decisions. Unlike Camus, on the other
hand, Teilhard was deeply concerned to include the whole of
the world and its future in his vision. All the same, he did not,
like Hegel for example, suggest an all-embracing plan for the
world, which would carry itself through to completion. On
the contrary, he affirmed an extremely personal love which
gave direction, meaning and future to historical action.

There is, of course, no doubt that Teilhard's Christian faith
played a leading part in these ideas. But why should faith not
be able to direct philosophical thought in this way along a
certain path? We should similarly be able to consider the
biblical message and ask whether this does not proclaim, in
the light of faith, a God of whom the philosopher can only
speak in the form of a hypothesis. In fact, we shall encounter
many different examples of how the Bible transforms the
hypothesis of the highest personal love again and again into a
concrete invitation to believe in the God who is that love and
who has made that love visible. But, since the hypothesis of
"super-love" is situated on the dividing line between philosophy and faith, it is valuable to consider the consequences
that Teilhard, specifically as a Christian, drew from that love.

The first key-word is "adoration". As early as 1934, before
death through atomic explosion had entered the world, Teilhard wrote: "The perspective of total death – and we ought to
reflect seriously about this word in order to estimate the
destructive power that it has over our souls – would, if we
became fully conscious of it, at once enable the sources of
exertion to be victorious in us . . . The time is approaching

when man will recognize that, with regard to his position in a cosmic evolution which he can discover and criticize, he is situated biologically between adoration and suicide" (*Comment je crois*, "What I believe").

In other words, we can only survive the "critical moment" in which we live and we can only carry out the decision that the whole of mankind has to accomplish if we live in hope for a future which transcends time and come together in an adoration which breaks through all meaninglessness. It is only when all this is combined – vigilance for the "critical moment", decision concerning the fate of mankind on earth, hope of a future transcending time and adoration overcoming the suspicion of meaninglessness – that we shall be able to avoid following the obvious ways leading to flight.

Both flight "upwards" to a God who is outside the world and flight "inwards" into the soul, where the world cannot penetrate, are often thought of as indicative of a deeply "religious" attitude. We are also reluctant, however, to seek flight "forwards" towards the future on this earth, a direction recommended to us again and again by Marxism and other progressive ideologies. All these ways are not closed, but are rather combined into one, which is regarded as the necessary and indeed only possible way. Whenever, on the one hand, we experience longing for what transcends the world, this longing can only be satisfactorily fulfilled if we remain at the same time true to this earth by a forward orientation, by moving towards the terrestrial future. On the other hand, if we devote all our physical and spiritual energies to fashioning the future on this earth, then an orientation towards what transcends our earthly experience may at the same time prevent the way forward from being obstructed by our rigidity, intolerance and mutual disagreements.

The human attitude that brings unity is, as it were, the result of the combination of the lines pointing upwards and forwards. It is characterized by Teilhard as "detachment", which he used in the sense of "giving oneself to something greater than oneself". The closest parallel in German to this French word used in a special way by Teilhard is *Gelassenheit* (detachment, disinterest, composure), a word used by the fourteenth- and fifteenth-century German mystics and given new life by Martin Heidegger in his philosophy. This detachment is not, as in late-medieval mysticism, a characteristic of the individual's attitude towards God's dispensation of providence and his own personal environment. It is rather, in the Teilhardian sense, the way in which man fits himself into history. This history is a process of the whole, which man experiences as a claim that makes him conscious of the need to resist many of the tendencies that are active in him.

History was also not in any sense regarded by Teilhard as fate. He saw it as something that man made together with others. This means that it is neither a question of the individual subject, the isolated "I", fitting himself into history, nor a question of an abstract "mankind" entering history. To achieve detachment, that is, man's entering history, the claim is addressed to a concrete community of men and to concrete groups of people, in other words, to a concrete "we". "We" are detached in so far as we act with all people in mind and so to speak represent "mankind" responsible for its future. The place where this detachment is formed is precisely the place where people give themselves to each other and accept each other in love. Once again, then, we find ourselves in the cycle of "I-You" relationships extended to include the whole of mankind in a "we" relationship.

God in history

Teilhard lived this detachment, because he lived from the experience of meaning and of God. He was a Christian and, although he explicitly formulated and devoted his attention to the question about meaning, he was not personally disturbed by it. That is, of course, a very real possibility for most of us. The question of meaning is not always expressed as a desperate search for a meaningful escape from the experience of absurdity. It may equally well happen that, in asking this question, we are impelled to reach out to a "You" that, as the "I" centre of the world, attracts all love to itself: not only the love that comes about between two people, but also all the different forms of love expressed in the unity existing in human society.

According to Teilhard, then, what men experience as the movement of the world is ultimately the attractive effect which emanates from the love of this "I" centre. In the last words that he wrote (in March 1955), Teilhard stated that this world-movement, that is, the attractive effect of God's love, took place, in his opinion, most intensively in research workers and in manual workers. What Teilhard expected from these workers in the future was ". . . (to the degree that the research and manual workers of today are the avant-garde of the human society of tomorrow) a new and higher form of adoration which will be gradually discovered by Christian thought and prayer for the use of all believers in the future" (*Recherche, travail et adoration*, "Research, work and worship").

It should be clear that one of the consequences of Teilhard's thought is that the apparent conflict between faith and science has been overcome. For more than half a century of his working life as a Christian scientist, Teilhard experienced the conviction that faith and science were in competition with each other only when believers and scientists had a one-sided, incomplete understanding of Christianity and science. They were in harmony when they attained their full stature. A faith defined in a "new formula" as "to heaven through the completion of the earth" provides the Christian scientist with a more impelling reason for his research work than any available to his non-Christian colleague.

No longer is man's scientific research and planned activity condemned in the name of faith or altered by those who do not possess scientific knowledge. There has not been a simple diminution or reconciliation of the earlier conflicts between the Christian and the scientific understanding of the world, between the ethics of humanism and those of Christian teaching and between faith in God's providence and the conviction that man fashions his own future. On the contrary, these conflicts have simply ceased to exist. We may almost go so far as to say that, for the Christian scientist Teilhard de Chardin,

man's autonomy – in the name of which God was once regarded as dead – is the work of the living God.

All that we have been able to do here is to give a brief outline of Teilhard's philosophical and theological ideas. Despite
over-simplification, however, his thought has taken us effectively back from the present situation, as stamped by the
thought of Nietzsche and Camus, to the point of departure
that we chose – for very good reasons – for the underlying
theme of this book. In other words, the place where we should
ask the question about God and where we should experience
his presence is, for man living today in the technical and
industrial society of the West at least, above all history. The
answer to this question about God may be found "on the
way", in the "new beginning".

This new beginning is essential to faith. It often appears, to
those whose experience of the world is like that of Camus, to
be a new departure into an almost desperate defiance of
absurdity. Sometimes, however, it is a departure into the
confident hope that we shall be led and attracted by an all-
embracing love. This is at least how it seems to those whose
experience of the world is, despite all absurdity, similar to that
of Teilhard de Chardin.

Both aspects are proclaimed in Christian faith in Jesus
Christ who made this saving and all-embracing love known –
and, what is more, irrevocably known. This love gives both
man and mankind courage to engage in historical action and
then to entrust the future of man and his world to that love.
This question will be examined more fully in the next part of
this book.

Part Two
God in Jesus Christ

5   Scripture

What is the Christian faith's answer to the God question?
The Christian faith says that Jesus Christ is, in his work and in
his person, the answer to the God question. For this reason,
only faith which is concerned with the person and the work of
Jesus can properly be called "Christian faith". A person could
find Jesus' "teaching" very illuminating, and his "principles"
very edifying, but if at the same time he regarded Jesus himself as unimportant he would not have Christian faith. The
question we have to consider in the second part of this book is,
therefore: "Who is Jesus Christ, and what is his work?"

But we can't ask the question just like that. We must first
think about how we know, or where we can find out, about
the person and the work of Jesus. Perhaps we need only open
the four gospels. But we should be on our guard. The four
gospels of Matthew, Mark, Luke and John are not independent
works, but are part of the collection of books and documents
we call the "New Testament". Everyone accepts that the
other writings of the New Testament, from the Acts of the
Apostles to the Revelation of John, are the expression of faith
in Jesus Christ. They set out to describe his importance for the
salvation of mankind and the world from a great variety of
viewpoints – but they say next to nothing about his life. Should
this not mean that the gospels – since they are part of the
same collection (the New Testament) are also essentially the
expression of belief – a faith?

The New Testament is constantly referring back, in literal quotations and more general remarks, to the collection of books and documents which the Jews of Jesus' time called "the Law and the Prophets" (cf Mt 7: 12; 22: 40; Rom 3: 21) and regarded as "Holy Scripture", based on the authority of God himself.

From the start the Christians also regarded these writings as *their* "Holy Scripture", so much so that when they referred to these books they simply said "Scripture". They thought of these sacred books of Israel as the basis of their own faith in Jesus Christ; or, more precisely, they regarded them as bearing witness to a promise which had been fulfilled in Jesus Christ. Therefore, when the Church quite early on, in the second century, settled the uncertainty about which books should be regarded as the binding expression of its Christian faith, it included "the law and the prophets". Following Paul, it called them the "Old Covenant" or "Old Testament" (2 Cor 3: 14).

The earliest Christian writings, recording the faith in Jesus, became the "New Testament"; the name first appears at the beginning of the third century. The two "testaments" together form the single Christian "Scripture". Since that time the list of the various books and the books themselves have been called the "canon", and the scriptural books are also called "canonical" books. The Greek work *kanon* means "guideline" or "standard", and the canon of the New and Old Testaments is a standard of faith which is binding for all time because it preserves in its original form the first expression of the faith.

If this is so, we must expect the gospels also, as part of Scripture, to be not just historical records but the record of a faith. Therefore we should look more closely at the nature of the gospels before we examine what they tell us about Jesus Christ. At the same time we shall deal with some other questions connected with the nature of holy scripture. This will put us in a better position to determine the meaning and value of the frequent references to the Old and New Testaments in the rest of the book.

The nature of the gospels

The gospels are almost our only source for details about Jesus of Nazareth, his life, preaching and death, and his immediate effect on his contemporaries. The rest of the New Testament, as we have already seen, adds little of importance. The few references to Jesus in Jewish or pagan writers (Flavius Josephus, Tacitus, Suetonius) confirm that he lived, but contain no information of independent value. The four gospels are therefore our only source of information about Jesus. There are other "gospels" which came into being considerably later. These generally draw on the canonical gospels, but have a tendency to "decorate" their material with all sorts of abstruse legends or dubious imitations of Jesus' sayings. It is usually enough to read a few paragraphs to see how different they are in type from the canonical gospels. Even the few texts which are closer to the New Testament gospels – such as the "gospel of Thomas", which is made up almost entirely of sayings put into the mouth of the risen Jesus – offer nothing really comparable. The early Church rightly did not recognize these writings as part of the New Testament, nor have we today any reason to revise that decision as a result of our greater knowledge of this literature. In contrast to the canonical gospels, these others are called "apocryphal": inauthentic, and therefore "hidden" or withdrawn from public use in the Church.

The suggestion made earlier that even the four "genuine" gospels are not just historically accurate documentary accounts is justified by the facts. No one at that time wrote documentary accounts in the modern style, nor did anyone expect or demand what we expect and demand from a "historical" account. When ancient writers described events they always wanted to make the meaning and effects of the events clear in the description. That was the usual style of historical writing. That was why no one found it strange that a "report" about Jesus also set out to demonstrate the importance of his person and his action. The authors of the gospels wanted to proclaim their faith and arouse it in others. They wanted this as Christians who believed in a Jesus who had been raised from the dead and established in glory with God. It is clear that in this situation these two elements coloured the "reports", the intention of preaching and faith in the risen Jesus. In other words, the "reports" of the life of Jesus (cf Lk 1: 1–4; Acts 1: 1–2) are never mere reports. Even if they often read like reports (cf Lk 1: 1–4; 2: 1–2; 3: 1–2, and so on) they are often really sermons. Of course, these "sermons" on the life of Jesus include historical information as well, but the "sermonizing" intention dominates the gospels to such an extent that it is quite difficult to discover what parts of them are historical reports of actual events, or what is genuine quotation from Jesus and what the expression of the living faith of the Church in subjection to the final authority of Jesus.

Again, the gospel-writers do not all combine reporting and preaching in the same way. You can see this immediately if you first read a chapter from the gospel of John and immediately afterwards a chapter of Mark. The writer of the fourth gospel is much more interested in clearly presenting to his readers the message of faith in Jesus, the Christ and son of God (cf Jn 20: 31). He presents it in the form of a "history of Jesus", but this is much further from the historical reality of Jesus' earthly life than the other gospels. In contrast with John, all the others appear very similar. In their basic structure all three follow an identical pattern. To a large extent they can be printed paragraph for paragraph in parallel columns in a "synopsis" for convenient comparison. This gave them the name of "synoptic" gospels, and their authors are called "the synoptics". Even their books, though, are anything but "documentaries". Like John, but in a different way, they wanted to preach faith in Christ.

Historical criticism of the gospels

The fact that the gospels are the expression of the faith in Jesus Christ which the early Church had reached through Jesus' resurrection does not give us any ground for supposing that the disciples deliberately "falsified" the true picture of the history of Jesus. If they introduced the features of the risen Lord into the picture of the earthly Jesus, they did it simply because they were convinced that they now knew better who Jesus was all the time he lived on earth and what his actions on earth had meant. The gospel of John says this plainly (Jn 2: 22; 12: 16; cf 16: 13).

Critical suspicion of "falsification" was, however, what first stimulated critical investigation of the gospels in the eighteenth century. Attempts were made to reconstruct the "historical truth" of Jesus and the early Church in contrast to the gospels. One of the most provocative contributions to this movement was the critical questions and suggestions of Hermann Samuel Reimarus (1694–1778), published by Lessing in 1774–8 under the title *Wolfenbüttel Fragments*. The ideas of these early gospel critics are unreservedly accepted today only by the writers and readers of pseudo-scientific popular literature. They were nevertheless the beginning of the development which has produced our modern understanding of the literary and theological nature of the gospels and the perfected methods of scholarly interpretation which we can no longer do without.

In accordance with the findings of modern scripture scholarship we must imagine the tradition which produced the gospels as coming into being in the following way. The living faith of the Church repeated the words of Jesus in its services, its preaching, its teaching, from one community to another, but also filled these words out and made them clearer. It also reworked sayings with genuinely Christian content and gave them the literary form of a saying of Jesus, "put them into Jesus' mouth". The traditional story of the historical actions of Jesus was also given a form which would reflect the main features of the true, living image of Christ. In all this no one felt himself to be "inventing" anything. The general attitude was that if what was taught in the Church was really the truth of faith, under what other authority ought it to be taught than the authority of Jesus, and through the teaching of the Holy Spirit? The Church therefore put what it had learnt about Jesus through faith into the form of words and actions of Jesus himself. The gospel-writers' methods may be compared with the way in which the great icon-painters painted the biblical Christ. They were painting Jesus, but they gave him the features of the exalted ruler of the universe in whom they believed.

We therefore have stories about Jesus which cannot be regarded simply as events from the life of Jesus, and sayings of Jesus which the historical Jesus never uttered. No biblical scholars of any major Church today question this. The only question is how far should we go in finding such "inauthentic" actions and sayings. "Inauthentic" is not really the right word here. The community and the writers who gave these sayings the literary form of words of Jesus, and "attached" these actions to Jesus, did not act like skilled forgers. They merely took seriously in their writing, openly and directly, the implications of their conviction that *all* authoritative teaching in the Church should be passed on as *the teaching of Jesus.* That was the custom of the period. The Jewish rabbis also often put teaching in the mouths of famous wise men of the past, as a sign that they based their claims solely on their authority.

Therefore it is wrong to regard the whole content of the gospels as "historical fact". Our eagerness to get historical statements which can be clearly proved and which are independent of faith or unbelief is a typically modern achievement. Naturally no one wants to stop people looking for historical facts in the gospels. We must merely be clear that the main intention of the gospel writers was to answer different questions. In these circumstances, if we want to know what can be ascribed with relative certainty to the pre-Easter history of Jesus, and what effect he really had on people, we must examine the gospels in detail, saying by saying and story by story. This is the only way to discover what can count as (in this sense) "historically" true or probably historically true, and what remains uncertain.

It will surprise no one to learn that in this work the judgments of biblical scholars differ sharply. It depends on what one regards as crucial to the formation of the gospels, the creative power of the primitive Christian communities and their faith in the risen Christ or the memory of the earthly life of Jesus and his preaching. Some scholars believe that the way Paul speaks about Christ is both the older and the more strictly accurate tradition. In Paul's writings faith and theological reflection begin with the risen Christ, and this starting-point permeates everything else Paul says. In the view of these scholars, the desire of the gospel writers to make a direct connexion between all the elements of tradition which determine faith and the earthly activity of Jesus is a later theological tendency attempting, after the event, to tie faith securely to "historical proof". Other biblical scholars, on the other hand, are anxious to show that the bulk of the Jesus tradition in the gospels is historically "authentic". They see this primitive or core tradition about Jesus as providing the original basis for the Easter faith and the theology which derived from this. Yet another group of scholars thinks that there were two distinctive formulations of faith in Christ in the primitive Church, one based on the Easter event and the other on the earthly life of Jesus. Only in the course of the later history of the Church, they say, did these two formulations of the faith in Christ gradually combine. The first group of scholars naturally sees a sharp break between the "pre-Easter" and "post-Easter" periods, the second group sees an organic connexion, and the third sees both a break and a connexion. Scholars would hardly hold such different views if the New Testament gospels themselves did not produce these difficulties.

But the situation is not quite as hopeless as this makes it sound. The differences of opinion among scholars have to do more with the *relation* between the primitive Church's faith in Christ and the events of Jesus' life than with the question of the importance of Jesus' earthly life and activity for Christian faith. In any case, intensive examination of the biblical texts – in which the differences between denominations for the most part no longer matter – has produced a considerable unanimity about what Jesus himself taught, did, and tried to do and where the primitive Church developed his ideas in response to legitimate new questions and experience of the faith. In other words, we can now say with reasonable accuracy where

the boundary lies in the gospels between historical information
– which is what interests us – and theological interpretation –
which is what interested the primitive Church.

Our task in this book is not to retrace the steps by which
biblical scholarship reached its modern findings – even though
that would be a fascinating story. We have to trace the path
of the message of God which Jesus brought into the world and
which the Christian faith proclaims in his name. But first we
will look at one or two more preliminary questions which
come up in connexion with Scripture.

Old and New Testaments

Once we recognize that the gospels set out to provide evidence
for Christ from the standpoint of faith, the difference between
them and the other New Testament writings is no longer as
great as at first sight. What the gospels do in the form of a
history of Jesus the other writings do in the form of catechetical instruction, exhortation and encouragement – and sometimes also in the form of exploratory "theology". Sayings of
Jesus and stories about him are replaced by excerpts from
confessions of faith in him. It is therefore no surprise that
these writings also contain many old formulas and even complete primitive Christian hymns, which the writers simply
quote on the assumption that their readers already know
them. We shall have to discuss this in detail.

But what about the Old Testament? In spite of all the
quotations from it in the New Testament, is it not a document
of the Jewish faith? Are there not innumerable passages in the
New Testament which explicitly criticize the Old Testament,
or at least the Law? Are we not to take it seriously when
Jesus rejects what "was said to the men of old" (Mt 5: 21–48)
and argues with the scribes, when Paul battles for a preaching
of the Gospel without subjection to the Law? None of this can
be denied. But nevertheless Jesus, Paul and all the other New
Testament authors accept the Old Testament as a witness to
the action of the same God whom Jesus proclaims. The history
of Israel is the history of God's chosen people and the pre-

history of God's action in Jesus Christ. This is why the New Testament, with all its criticism, can still use the old Testament as equally good evidence for Jesus Christ. As early as the second century the Christian theologian Marcion demanded the dropping of the Old Testament and the retention of only a reduced canon of the New Testament, consisting mainly of Luke's gospel and ten of Paul's letters. His attempt was not the only one, but the Church always unhesitatingly rejected such attacks on the Old Testament.

But there is a great difference between the use of the Old Testament by Jews and by Christians. Christians have read it, and still read it, in conjunction with the New Testament; they treat it, one might say, as a Christian book. This is still true when an interpreter tries to understand it with the help of all the historian's tools, which means as a Jewish book, and in the process comes to exactly the same conclusions as the Jewish exegete. As a Christian, he reads the Old Testament as a book which points beyond itself to Christ, and conversely he expects to be able to reach a correct understanding of God's activity in the Old Covenant only in the light of Christ. This is why the authors of the New Testament do not always quote the Old Testament word for word and do not bother very much about keeping to the "historical" meaning of the documents. Quotations may in some cases even be altered and taken out of their original contexts. The non-specialist can often see this for himself by looking up in the Old Testament the quotations used by New Testament authors. In this way the witnesses to the faith of the primitive Church even used literary form to indicate that everything depends on the revelation of God in Christ and that an Old Testament text can be better understood in relation to this than in its own context.

This Christian treatment of the Old Testament is perhaps most clearly visible in Paul. In his view, any independent attempt to understand the Old Testament is wrong. The Old Testament is the book of the promise, and as such a permanent part of Scriptures as a whole, but the promise has been fulfilled in Christ. Christ reveals the meaning of the Old Testament. This remains true down to the present. The Christian

finds in the Old Testament all the more support for his own
faith, all the more help in understanding and deepening his
faith, the more completely he reads it in the light of the fulfilment to which the New Testament writings bear witness.

Holy Scripture and the word of God

Paul wrote to his community in Thessalonica: "And we also
thank God constantly for this, that when you received the
word of God which you heard from us, you accepted it not as
the word of men but as what it really is, the word of God,
which is at work in you believers" (1 Thess 2: 13).

We must try to realize the enormity of this statement of
Paul's. Paul described his own preaching, which was no doubt
brilliant and fascinating, but all the same ordinary human
language, as God's own word, now acting in those who have
accepted it. This is only one – though one of the clearest – of
the New Testament texts which speak of God's word in the
human words of the preacher. When statements like this are
accepted and acquire authority, and when then, as we saw, .
the writings of the people who made such claims for their own
words become "Holy Writ", the logical conclusion is that
Scripture is not merely human words but the word of God
himself. This is what Christianity believed from the beginning, first about "scripture" – the Old Testament – and then
soon, after the canon was fixed, about the New Testament.

But what meaning are we to give to this belief in God's
word in Scripture? Past centuries could have a more naïve
attitude to this truth. Our ancestors had no qualms about
simply identifying Scripture with the word of God himself.
God might not have written Scripture himself, but he had, as
they thought, "inspired" the minds of the sacred writers with
what they had to write. God was the true author of Scripture,
and the human writer was a secretary who provided the
language and the pen. This conception is very well illustrated
in the many old pictures which show the evangelists or other
authors of Scripture with a dove, the symbol of the Holy
Spirit, perching at their ear.

Today we can no longer take such a simple view. The new understanding of the literary features of the Bible had consequences. In a painful transformation, which at times seemed to cast doubt for whole generations on the credibility and reliability of the Christian message, an understanding gradually grew, over two hundred years, that it was totally wrong to think of the biblical writers as divine secretaries. The Bible is first of all human words. It is evidence of the faith and attitude to faith of particular men at particular times in particular places. To such an extent is it human discourse that historians who have not the slightest interest in the Christian faith can use it as a main source for the cultural and religious history of the Near East in the first millennium before Christ and the first century AD. An observer of modern exegetes at work would not be able to tell from their results whether their biblical studies were carried out by a theologian or a neutral historian. Everything we will have to discuss in chapters 6–10 is based on this now unquestioned assumption that the evidence of the Bible may and must be examined as evidence of the faith of a number of men and a number of generations.

Does this mean that the Bible no longer has anything to do with "the word of God"? Not at all, but it does mean that for the future we can no longer say, "The Bible *is* the word of God." Even saying "The word of God is in the Bible" would be wrong, if it were taken to mean that one set of statements in the Bible were purely human words and the rest God's word. We must say something like: "The Bible *is* not God's word, but *becomes* God's word for anyone who believes in it as God's word."

That sounds dangerous. It could be interpreted as meaning that the word of God was a purely subjective matter. We might feel that whether one accepted the Bible as the word of God was a matter of faith, and that was a matter of individual choice. That would be a complete misunderstanding. The reason why only faith is capable of hearing the word of God in the words of the Bible is that the basis of faith is accepting the invitation of the biblical word to rely on the God who made himself known as a liberator in the history of Israel and in Jesus Christ. In the mouth of Jesus we can find a commentary on the way in which this invitation is made in human language: "He who hears you hears me, and he who rejects you rejects me, and he who rejects me rejects him who sent me" (Lk 10: 16; cf Jn 12: 48 ff). Whoever therefore, on the strength of the word of Scripture, believes in the God proclaimed in Scripture, at the same time accepts Scripture as the word of God inviting him to faith in a human way. If someone does not accept this invitation, and does not believe, the Bible remains for him only the human word which it in fact is. Even if historians or students of comparative religion have to admit that this human word of the Bible possesses a range of striking properties which are to be found nowhere else, that does not mean that, as historians or students of comparative religion, they can isolate the word of God scientifically.

When in Scripture we come across, as we often do, the words, "It is written", invoking the full authority of the word of God, that doesn't mean that the word of God is "there on the page", to show to anyone who can read. The word of God comes to men as an invitation and a demand, and its power can only be felt by those who expose themselves to its demand. It would, however, be just as wrong to say that the word of God "occurs" only where the Bible is listened to as the word of God. The word of God, the invitation to faith, has truly been set down once and for all in scripture – a fact which indicates again that God revealed himself in a specific way, at a particular point in space and time, which is another way of saying "in history". And yet it is true that the word of God written down once and for all in the Bible becomes more than mere human words only when the preaching of the community makes it a living invitation which faith gratefully takes up as an invitation from God. And that does not happen without a subjective act; there is no faith without a "subjective", personal life and its connexion with a community. We do not slide into subjectivism because of the structure of faith itself. That faith which knows and feels itself to be completely a personal act on the part of a human being at the same time knows itself to be not men's "subjective" achievement, but a gift of God.

Faith can demonstrate that even to a neutral reader whose interest in the Bible is purely historical. The evidence of the Bible does not allow him to rest in scholarly neutrality, but touches him, turns into an invitation to him to believe – or a reproach. There is no compulsion about this process. Faith does not "make" the Bible God's word by subjectively appropriating it; it discovers it to be God's word by finding it, unexpectedly, unsuspected, unassertively, speaking to the heart as God's liberating word.

Faith is always dependent on the approach of God's word; it "feeds on it", as Luther says. But this word speaks about the historical action of God in the history of Israel and in the person of Jesus Christ, for which our primary evidence is the documents of the Old and New Testament. If faith can hear its own invitation to believe only in this history, it is for ever dependent on hearing God's word in Scripture. This is the reason why Christian preaching can only take place in connection with Scripture. This is also why the Reformers in particular – though they were not the first! – insisted that the Bible is a full and adequate source of knowledge in all that concerns our salvation, our relation to God, our faith, that it is on its own clear and unequivocal and, when listened to with a willing heart, leads to faith. It is true that Scripture must constantly be interpreted afresh for the present, but this interpretation is subordinate to the word of Scripture, not the other way round. That is why Scripture has the "canonical" status mentioned earlier.

We could say a lot more about the Bible. Indeed, we shall come back later to other problems where there are disagreements between the churches. For the moment, though, what we have looked at so far is enough. There were two main points. First, we had to be clear about the literary form of the biblical writings so that we were not misled by the style of modern history books into a misunderstanding of their intentions. Secondly we wanted right at the beginning to avoid the idea that the Bible advances on us like some sort of monster, insisting that we accept its every word because it is the word of God. Scripture is the word of God, it has authority and can command obedience – but only from its power to win hearts through the liberating invitation to believe in God which it can convey to anyone with ears to hear.

6   The God of Israel

When Jesus walked the roads of the hill country of Palestine, entered a house in a Galilean village, or went through the gate of Jerusalem and up to the courtyard of the temple, he followed in the footsteps of countless generations which before him had walked these roads and visited these places in a land which had already known more than a thousand years of civilization, the narrow inhabited strip between the great kingdoms on the Nile and on the Tigris and Euphrates.

The history of the people of Israel is only a small part of the thousand-year history of this land. A long series of earlier cultures had gone before it, of which only the barest traces have come down to us. But the history of the people of Israel which produced Jesus of Nazareth left a record in the book which was Jesus' Bible and is part of the Christian Bible, the Old Testament. The Old Testament contains the prehistory of the Christian faith and important parts of the testimony for it.

Rescue

That prehistory began when a small group of forced labourers, kept in Egypt as cheap labour for big building firms, learnt to believe in a God who promised them liberation. They escaped from Egypt and placed themselves under the leadership of the God to whom they owed their life and freedom. They remained loyal to him on the journey through the desert to the land which had been promised to them together with the promise of freedom. That shared experience of rescue and liberation and belief in a saving God made them a people, the people of the God whom they had experienced as saviour. That original experience of their faith was the basis of their history.

From that beginning the history of Israel curves in a broad arc to Jesus of Nazareth. The beginning is echoed in the angel's announcement: "To you is born this day a Saviour" (Lk 2: 11), and at the end of his journey his disciples proclaim: "There is salvation in no one else." (Acts 4: 12.) Faith says that this is the same God acting. His action stands at the beginning of the new people of God as at that of the old; it is the foundation of the history of both Israel and the Church.

But the saving of Israel at the beginning of its history is different from the saving of mankind in Jesus Christ which is proclaimed in the New Testament. It was a long way from the saving of Israel in their departure from Egypt to salvation "in the fulness of time". Only when we know this way can we really understand what happened in that final salvation. This is what the New Testament itself says. In the story of the young disciples at Emmaus (Lk 24) the unknown traveller explains the events of Good Friday to the still shaken disciples by showing them the meaning of the whole Old Testament, from the salvation at the beginning to the salvation through the death of the Messiah, in whom fulfilment was to come. That is why the Christian Bible contains both the Old and New Testaments.

What is it like, this path that leads from the beginning of Israel to Jesus of Nazareth? Who is the God in whom Israel learnt to believe and whose definitive approach was finally announced by Jesus?

Israel's cry

Before salvation we hear the *cry of the oppressed*. This cry is an expression of the fact that all man's suffering has to do with God. The history of the people of God began with people who were weak and suffering, and cried to God and were heard. They did not yet really know this God, but they could cry to him. The Old Testament describes a history in which

much changes, even the image of God, the way he is worshipped and the way people talk about him. But one thing
does not change: God is always the God who is interested in
human suffering. He is and remains the one who hears the cry
from the depths. Part of the history of God's people is therefore the history of a cry. We hear the groans of the oppressed
in Egypt. We hear the cry out of all sorts of sufferings of
individuals and of the whole people. We hear the cry for the
fall of Jerusalem and the destruction of the temple, for the
failure of the promises to David. It is preserved in the psalms
and other texts.

The cry of an individual's personal suffering reaches its
climax in the book of Job. In the depths of despair a man
accuses God, but all the time clings to God. This history of the
cry in the Old Testament shows how this experience of God
continued through the history of Israel from the beginning:
Israel experienced God as the one who would always hear a
cry of suffering. We can now see why the evangelists later
summed up the sufferings of Jesus in the words of psalm 22
(cf Mt 27: 35; Lk 23: 34 and Jn 19: 24) and why Jesus' cry
from the cross uses the opening words of this psalm: "My
God, my God, why hast thou forsaken me?" (Mt 27: 46). Here
the history of the cry reaches its climax. The gospel writers
want to stress that Jesus has taken on the cry of his people,
and with it the cry of suffering mankind. He has taken it into
his own suffering and death.

Joy of the liberated

The experience of salvation is expressed in the *joy of the
liberated*. It is no accident that what is probably the oldest
song in the Old Testament is contained in the psalm which
follows the account of the rescue from Egypt in Exodus: "I
will sing to the Lord, for he has triumphed gloriously; the
horse and his rider he has thrown into the sea!" (Ex 15: 1–21).
The relief and joyful praise of the saved are so much a part of
the experience of God's saving intervention that the echo of
God's praise accompanies the cry of suffering right through

the Old Testament. "Praise" here means joy expressed in words. This praise which reports the acts of God, which cannot help telling what the liberated have experienced, is the ultimate source of the tradition which starts Israel's history with the rescue from Egypt. The short summaries of God's great deeds in the beginning, which have been called Israel's "historical creed" (cf Dt 26: 5–10), are fundamentally praise; their literary form is that of narrative praise of God. The reverse is also true: Israel's historical tradition has its roots in praise of the mighty acts of God.

From this beginning the praise of God goes right through the history of Israel as constant evidence of the liberating, saving, redeeming action of God. A remarkable illustration of this is provided by a comparison of the song which celebrates the original liberation at the "sea of reeds" (Ex 15: 21) with the songs of praise scattered through the message of the prophet whose work is contained in the second part of the book of Isaiah (Is 40–56). He is not Isaiah, and because he is unknown he is called simply "Deutero-Isaiah", "Second Isaiah". Second Isaiah is merely announcing the liberation of the people from exile in Egypt, but in full assurance of God's act of liberation he includes in his message the rejoicing which will greet this act (eg Is 42: 10–13). Like the cry, the praise is also concerned not only with God's great deeds for his whole people. God's saving action also affects the life of the individual, and each individual can experience his cry turning into rejoicing. The psalms are full of this joy which is expressed in words as praise, and the cry of liberation of the redeemed accompanies the history of the people just as it does the life of the individual members.

This tone of joy bursting spontaneously into words before God is the best expression of the naturalness of the relationship with God which still impresses us today on every page of the Old Testament. The joy is not restricted to the particular experience of a specific rescue, but spreads out to everything a man can rejoice about. Praise of God for an individual saving act swells into praise which celebrates God in all his activity and his whole existence, and grows into powerful hymns to

the creator God which praise God's actions to the furthest
limits.

But praise of God in the Old Testament never gets lost in
generalities. The original experience can always be recognized.
It is expressed in the psalmist's question: "Who is like the
Lord our God, who is seated on high, who looks far down
upon the heavens and the earth?" (Ps 113: 5–6). God is "our
God", the God for men. This basic experience is also in the
New Testament the starting point for the account of Jesus of
Nazareth: God's pity for the suffering of mankind took the
form of the sending of his Son (Jn 3: 16). It is the same experi-
ence which puts the earliest proclamation of God's action in
Christ into the form of simple narrative praise, the delighted
telling of what has happened (Lk 2: 17; Acts 5: 30–2).

The fall of God's people

Praise may stop. The experience of salvation can be forgotten.
Another part of the story of the original rescue tells how
those who had been saved forgot their liberator and made a
God of their own (Ex 32: the golden calf). A third line runs
through the history of the people, the history of their fall. It is
an extremely moving and dramatic story. The Old Testament
has no general concept of sin applicable to all situations.
Transgressions against God's will take place within God's
history with his people, and for that reason what yesterday
was God's will may tomorrow be a transgression. Those who
are firmly established in their righteousness and piety may be
on a path which leads away from God. This is what the
prophets said; this is what Jesus said. It is part of the history
of transgressions that there should be booms and slumps. In
the relationship between God and his people there are good
times, like the early period, and times in which turning away
from God threatens the existence of the people. This was the
situation in the time of the prophets of judgment; they had to
proclaim to their people a destruction which had been decided
upon by their own God. Israel had broken the covenant and
catastrophe was inevitable.

The figure of the mediator

But in this situation something happens which is one of the most characteristic features of the relationship with God in the Old Covenant. The drama began when the answer died away and the people forgot their saviour. God remained loyal to his unfaithful people; he did not forget them. This is expressed in the *figure of the mediator*. In the midst of apostasy from God, and always at the very point when the apostasy had endangered the people's existence, someone appeared to come between them. The mediator in the Old Testament has many forms and many functions, but a central function is to stand between God and the people when a breach threatens. In the early period it was Moses. When the people turned away to the golden calf, Moses interceded with God for the apostates and succeeded in making God relent from his decision to destroy them. From the beginning of the kingdom to the collapse first of the northern kingdom and then of the southern kingdom, the destruction of the temple and the exile in Babylon, the prophets were the mediators. The specific feature of the office of mediator as exercised by the prophets over this whole long section of Israel's history was that no one listened to them. They apparently achieved nothing, founded no prophetic movement which could have given them lasting influence, and acquired no positions of power. Each individual had rather to begin from the start where his predecessor had left off, with nothing else than the word which was given to him.

The history of the mediator now combines with the history of the cry. In the Old Testament there is a characteristic cry of the mediator. It can be heard everywhere where the impotence of his office leads the mediator into suffering. There is the cry of Moses, no longer able to bear the burden of the constantly murmuring and disloyal people. There is the cry of the prophet Elijah when he has to flee before the queen. The climax is the cries of the prophet Jeremiah (Jer 11–20), which give a voice to the crushing despair of God's lonely, ignored and despised messenger, torn between his mission and his human nature.

The suffering servant

A movement can be seen in this history of the cry of the mediator which does not stop within the Old Testament. One sign points beyond the Old Testament. The prophet known as Second Isaiah, who was mentioned earlier, was active during the exile in Babylon. Among the prophecies which derive from him there is a group of sayings or songs which are closely connected with his contemporary preaching of the imminent return of the people, though not merely a part of it. From their main figure, the "servant of God" or "servant of Yahweh", they are called the "servant songs". They are the cry of a prophetic mediator, but one which cannot be tied down to any particular historical figure and points towards the future (Is 42: 1–4; 49: 1–6; 50: 4–9; 52: 13–53). The servant songs clearly start from the mediatorship of the prophet, and in particular from the apparent hopelessness of his task, which was to work in weakness, with no tool but the word, and which therefore inevitably led into suffering when it was rejected. What sets them apart from other statements about the mediatorship of the prophets, however, is that here the suffering of the servant of God leads to death and that this suffering and death of the servant have the meaning and power of *representative* suffering attributed to them. God's acceptance of the suffering and death of the servant is an acceptance which reaches beyond death.

These servant songs are seen by the New Testament faith as the clearest example of the connexion between the Old Testament and the New. This is not just the cry of suffering mankind in general which is taken up into the description of Christ's sufferings (as in the use of Ps 22 in the story of the passion). This is the cry of the dying mediator. Christian faith saw what was only hinted at in the figure of the servant as fulfilled in the story of the suffering, death and resurrection of Christ (cf the quotations from Is 53 in Mt 20: 28; Mk 15: 28 and Lk 23: 33). It follows that if the earliest community understood the sufferings and resurrection of Jesus in these terms they saw in Jesus more than an individual figure taken out of history and in his sufferings more than the sufferings of one man among many. This suffering and God's acceptance of it in the resurrection was in their eyes the culmination of the whole history of the people of God.

Cry, praise, apostasy and new beginning through the office of a mediator form the framework into which everything the Old Testament says about God and the history of men with him is fitted. We must now look at this in detail. What the Old Testament says about the history of God with men, and incidentally about God himself, also falls into three circles.

God and men

The innermost circle of this history is the office of the mediator, from Moses to the suffering servant in Second Isaiah. This office includes suffering. The history of the mediatorship is in turn enclosed in the larger circle of God's communication and action among his people. The outermost, largest circle is made up of God's activity outside the history of his people in the human race and creation. It is often forgotten that the Old Testament does not simply proclaim the history of one people as the history of salvation, but sets this in the larger context of the history of God with humanity and with the whole creation. In this extension of its outlook the Old Testament was Jesus' Bible. It is impossible to understand the innermost circle of this history, the office and suffering of the servant, without seeing it within the two larger circles which are concerned with the path and fate of the people of God and beyond them with the fate of mankind from its beginning to its end and with creation as a whole.

The broader circle of God's communication and actions among his people embraces a history in which an astonishing concentration of important stages in human social organization follow one another: the family (Gen 12: 50), the nomadic group (Exodus, Leviticus, Numbers), the tribes in transition from a nomadic to a settled life (Joshua and Judges), the settled people and the political constitution of the kingdom (Samuel and Kings), and finally the province under foreign rule in which the people can preserve its own life only as a religious community.

The most amazing changes take place in the relationship with God and its expression in the transition from one form of social organization to another. The two most crucial transitions are that from the nomadic group to the settled people with a political constitution and the loss of political independence through the fall of the kingdom and the destruction of the temple. If, in spite of these changes and transitions, we can still speak of a "history" embracing all these stages and a history of God with his people which transcends them all, its foundation lies at the beginning of that history, in the experience of a rescue which was bound up with a promise and which created a mutual relation between God and the people. The mutuality of this relationship with God is expressed in the covenant formula: "You shall be my people, and I shall be your God" (cf Dt 26: 17–18). This relationship with God can face any future and can therefore endure through all the vicissitudes of history.

Historical thought

The overwhelming experience of being saved at the beginning had one more consequence. Since the story of God's mighty deeds was told again and again from the beginning as a motive for praise, a strong habit of historical thinking grew up in his people and made them capable of broad historical views. What we know as the "five books of Moses" or the "Pentateuch" (Genesis, Exodus, Leviticus, Numbers, Deuteronomy) put forward one such view of history. The Pentateuch is not the work of one person, but a compilation from a number of originally independent works whose authors are unknown. The two oldest are those of the "Jahwist" and "Elohist". These are named after the names which each of them most frequently uses for God, "Yahweh" and "Elohim", and were probably combined quite early. Later the "Deuteronomic" and "Priestly" traditions were added. These original works all contain accounts of the early history of Israel. All include legal texts, and these form the bulk of the last two strands. Another sort of historical account is the "Deuteronomic history", which is a product of the same intellectual milieu as Deuteronomy, which was included in the Pentateuch. Yet another attitude to history is represented by the books of the Chronicles, to which the books of Ezra and Nehemiah also belong.

A characteristic feature of these historical books, and of their sources before them, is that they cover amazingly long stretches of time. The Pentateuch deals with the period from the creation to just before the entry into the promised land, including the patriarchs, the escape from Egypt and the journey through the desert. The Deuteronomistic history (Joshua–2 Kings) takes the story from the occupation of the land to the Babylonian exile. The books of Chronicles tell again the story of the first men (though from the beginning to David is all genealogies) and go up to the post-exilic period.

These wide-ranging historical narratives were possible because their authors understood history as an interaction between God and men. It is God's lordship over history that gives them the broad lines which link the periods. One sign that these histories are putting forward a general view of history and not just accounts of individual events is the fact that the core of the Pentateuch is a *confession of praise* (the triumphant account of those who were saved at the sea of reeds in Ex 15), and that of the Deuteronomistic history a *confession of guilt*, the acknowledgment of God's judgment on Israel. In other words, the Pentateuch sees history as Israel's happiness in the presence of its God, the Deuteronomistic history sees it as a judgment which Israel must accept.

This strongly developed historical sense enabled distant and often unintelligible items of history to keep their meaning through the generations in every new period. Israel constantly recalled its history, especially in its religious services, but equally in the families, the meetings of the men, in the villages and at the city gates. This was done not merely for the sake of a past history, but in order through it to understand the present and win power over the future. How often the memory of a past situation determines a decision in the present. The past was never "passed away" in the sense of finished with; it was an inexhaustible source of possibilities for shaping the present and future.

An association of families

The history of the patriarchs with its brightly illustrated stories of Abraham, Isaac, Jacob and Joseph, portrays a time in which the family was the all-important social unit. These stories are a classical expression of the life of the family, with all its particular connexions, conflicts and values. Through the preservation of the traditions of this particular form of social organization the family automatically acquired a permanent meaning, which it did not lose even under the influence of later social systems. The figures of the "fathers" were not models to be imitated, nor were they intended as such. What they did was to transmit an understanding of the fundamental events in the existence of the family, from the birth of the child to the death of the father or mother. In this view a man is not valued for his achievements, not even for his "religious" achievements. He is first of all approved and accepted, like everyone else, in the uniqueness of his existence, which is made up of a birth, life and death all of which belong uniquely to him. When the gospels show Jesus as talking so much about fathers, brothers, children and various aspects of family life, behind all this are the traditions from the time of the fathers. Only with their help can we understand what these sayings and ideas of Jesus meant.

The people in the desert

For the wandering group, which is the form in which we see the people after their escape from Egypt, the determining feature of existence is *following*. Whether someone belongs to the wandering people of God or not now simply depends on whether he stays with them or not. The great temptation is to turn aside from the difficult path into the promised future and try to return to the fleshpots of Egypt. Everything depends on whether you keep your hope in the promise. During the journey through the wilderness Israel had its fundamental experiences as a people, the experience of being saved from its enemies at the sea of reeds and the constant experience of being saved from starvation, thirst, despair and weariness. This time could never be forgotten.

When Israel entered the promised land, it was a strong temptation to adopt the religion of settled life, the religion of the inhabitants of Canaan. Nevertheless they remained true to their faith in the God under whose leadership they had placed themselves in the desert and whose miracles they had experienced. Israel's loyalty to God as saviour right down to the time of fulfilment in Christ meant loyalty to the Saviour-God *in the wilderness*. The time came when Israel lost the land, and had to go once more through the wilderness. During the exile in Babylon the old traditions about the journey through the wilderness came alive again. They became the bearers of a new hope, a new promise. In a similar way, the history of Christianity in its earliest stage began with a wandering group. The determining form of life for the disciples and the first missionaries was also following. Being a member or not depended again here on whether you stayed or not. The first generation of Christians had their fundamental experiences from this life of following. They heard the word of instruction and experienced the miracles of preservation.

In the history of the Old Covenant "following" always had to do with the particular, and was only necessary at certain times and in certain situations. The settled life in the promised land was never called "following". If we give the term "following" a more general meaning and apply it to Christian life in general, are we not obscuring the true meaning of what was described as "following" in both the Old and New Testaments?

Kingship and messianic expectation

There were many changes for Israel in the period of settled life; its relationship with God was also affected. In addition to

God's saving activity his *blessing* now came into prominence. This can be seen particularly in the book of Deuteronomy. The life of the people, and with it the relationship to God, spread out to include political and civil regulations, and intellectual and cultural life, and established a fixed form of worship, to be performed in a particular place at particular times. This fact itself makes it clear that the relationship with God is not tied to any particular form of human society, and for that reason it can be associated with all. What Israel had experienced of its God in the liberation from Egypt and in the way through the desert could now become part of a new way of life. When the threat from the Philistines made monarchy a political necessity for Israel, the king was anointed in the name of God and received a promise that his dynasty would endure.

This promise of descendants, which was announced to King David by the prophet Nathan (2 Sam 7), took on a special importance in the period of settled life. When the Davidic monarchy collapsed Israel faced one of the severest challenges of its history: the promise seemed to have been broken. But against the background of the collapse was now heard the promise of a king for the last age – the Messiah. Or, more precisely, there was a promise that God himself would now look after his people, since the kings had failed (Ezek 34). This – personal or non-personal – messianism is the beginning of the hope on which Jesus draws when he talks about the "kingdom of God". But notice: the line of statements about the mediator, which goes past the prophets to the suffering servant, points directly and without a break to a fulfilment. In contrast the line of messianic promises is broken. The kingdom which is here promised – the kingdom of God or of the Messiah – is to be a kingdom of peace. Power and show are to have no place in it. All this is reflected very clearly in the path of Jesus, and receives its sharpest expression in his death. The scene before Pilate in the fourth gospel shows better than any other that faith saw the two lines of prophecy and messianism once more united in Jesus. Jesus' answer to the question whether he is a king is: "You say that I am a king. For this I was born, and for this I have come into the world, *to bear witness to the truth*" (Jn 18: 37).

Israel's worship

As we might expect, worship in Israel also underwent a rich and varied development. There was no "correct" and immovably valid worship. Just as God travelled with his people through totally different periods of history, so worship can undergo considerable changes. The wandering groups certainly had no system of worship based on a particular place, and even the forms and times could probably vary. It was not until the people settled in the land that a strictly organized system of worship began to take over, with a liturgical place, liturgical times, and a fixed liturgical staff. At first there continued to be a number of places of worship alongside the central sanctuary of the Ark of the Covenant, but finally worship was centralized; this made Jerusalem the only place for solemn worship of Yahweh. During the exile forms of worship began to grow up which, in the absence of sacrifices, were based entirely on readings, sermons and prayer. These no longer took place in the Temple – that lay in ruins in faraway Judah – but in the "synagogue", or "meeting". After the rebuilding of the Temple both forms continued side by side for a time until, after the final destruction of the Temple by the Romans in the year 70, the synagogue form alone survived. But through all periods one thing remains characteristic of Old Testament worship: in a variety of ways, in psalms, creeds, sacrificial formulas and liturgies of celebration, history was recalled, and this made worship sensitive to events of the present and prevented it from suffocating in dead forms. Where this danger existed, worship was attacked: from Amos' blunt accusations (Am 5), through Jeremiah's temple speech (Jer 7) to Jesus' cleansing of the temple (Mk 11: 15–17 and parallels). Worship's firm roots in history and criticism of worship are two aspects of the same fundamental belief: that it is not worship that is holy, but God.

The law

That is equally true of the commandments and the law. Here we must beware of generalizations. The pejorative attitude to the law which we find in Paul (Romans, Galatians) is directed at a meaning which the concept "law" acquired in late Judaism, and it would be wrong to read it into the Old Testament. We must also be careful not to identify "law" and "commandment". The two words describe quite different things, and in origin were not connected. One sign of the difference is that the commandments have retained their positive meaning in Christianity, but the laws contained in the Old Testament have not done so in the same way. The commandment concerns an individual's personal relation to God, in both Old and New Testaments. This can be seen in its linguistic form; the commandments are expressed in the second person. The wandering group experienced the commands of their God as simple necessities of life; they concerned such matters as the direction to take, the time to stop and start the march, and were felt to be part of the leadership of God on which preservation, satisfaction of hunger and thirst and reaching the goal depended. In this context the commandments were experienced as something positive and life-giving.

With the beginning of settled life the law took on chief importance, but it was not fixed from the start in the way that was often assumed in the past. In fact, the existing Old Testament texts show how the various law collections came into existence, grew over the different periods and were transformed. The law is an organic part of Israel's history, and in its various stages of development corresponds to the stages of society in which it originated. Seen in this way, the law is also part of God's guidance and preservation of his people, and it is celebrated as such with gratitude in psalm 119. The misuse of the law as a means of winning one's own salvation is a much later development, and even then the positive understanding of the law as God's guidance to his people on their journey through history continued to exist alongside it.

Wisdom

The Old Testament also includes in the history of God with his people what was at that time generally called "wisdom". The Old Testament includes several books of "wisdom", and wisdom elements occur in many other books. Wisdom in the ancient world had something like the place that science occupies in the modern world. What has it to do with God? The command to subdue the earth (Gen 1: 28) means mastery through work (cultural and technical activity), but also includes mastery through intellectual domination of reality. This is the idea behind wisdom. This "profane" or secular wisdom was given a place in the Bible as a permanent reminder to the people of God that the gift of wisdom comes from God. Both physical and mental activity are part of God's command, and the results of both come from the power of his blessing. Wisdom has an important place in the New Testament in the preaching of Jesus. The parables derive from it, as do many sayings in the words of the Lord. They are an indication that what is unique and extraordinary in the preaching of Jesus is inextricably combined with the very simple and natural.

God the creator

The largest circle in the Old Testament message about God is formed by what is said about God's activity among mankind and creation, apart from the history of his people. The Old Testament begins with the creation, and sees the end as the fulfilment of God's activity in his creation. Only this scope, which embraces the totality of all created things and everything that happens, is adequate to the majesty of the God of which the Bible speaks. In our time, when mankind is being forced to look beyond all barriers and think and plan universally, this universal aspect of the Bible is of the greatest importance. In the Bible the inner line of God's dealings with his people, the history of salvation, is set in the broader context of the account of the beginning and the end.

The history which starts with Abraham in chapter 12 of Genesis follows on from the primeval history (Gen 1–11), which talks about the world and mankind. The transition is in 12: 3: in Abraham all the families of the earth will be blessed. In the apocalypses of both the Old and New Testaments the history of the people of God flows back into the fate of mankind and the fate of the cosmos at the last. In this widest of perspectives the Bible even makes a statement which agrees with the findings of the natural sciences: our planet, the earth, and the human species had a beginning and will have an end. When the Bible talks about God this great totality is always in the background, the totality of mankind and the totality of the cosmos. When it talks about God as the creator and the perfecter who leads his work to its goal ("I am the Alpha and the Omega, the beginning and the end"), it is saying that the totality has a meaning because it has a master.

The statements of the Bible about creation are not intended to commit the reader to a particular view of the origin of the universe and of the human race. Their multiplicity and variety is more a way of expressing the mystery of creation which the human mind can never fully grasp. The talk of the creator and of the creation at the beginning of the Bible and throughout the Bible is intended to point to the ultimate level in which everything that exists is connected with God. Its purpose is to allow the little man – every man – in his place in the immense expanse of space and the immense expanse of time, to be sure of one thing, that he was created unique by God, and that his creator, who is the creator of the universe, gives his life a meaning and is leading it to a goal.

It is in this wide context that we must think of the sending of the Son in time. The whole of mankind and the whole of creation has been affected by the sending of the Son. In the life, suffering and death of this one man God showed that the totality has a meaning, a meaning which everyone can discover from the story of this life. Or, in the words of Jesus, in the life, suffering and death of this one man "God's kingdom" has come closer.

7   The God of Jesus

Jesus of Nazareth proclaimed the imminence of God's kingdom. The evangelist Mark sums up this message of Jesus in
two striking sentences which form a sort of formal proclamation: "The time is fulfilled, and the kingdom of God is at
hand." This forms the basis of the following demand,
"Repent" (Mk 1: 15). Jesus appeared with this "proclamation"
in Galilee after the arrest and execution of John the Baptist
(Mk 1: 14). The identical style of the two sentences (called
"parallelism", and a favourite stylistic form in the literature
of Israel) is meant to indicate that the message has a special
urgency. The time of expectation is over, it says, and God's
kingdom has dawned.

Jesus' sayings and teaching proclaim this message, and the
events of his life, his provocative actions and his death, provide a practical, real-life commentary on it. What does this
message mean, and what is the meaning of the demand for
repentance which Jesus bases on it? What could and should
these two sayings have meant to Jesus' listeners?

The kingdom of God

Most of Jesus' contemporaries hoped for the "kingdom of
God", but they had very different ideas about it. Some
imagined it as an ideal state *in* this world, others as happiness
after it. For some the kingdom of God would transform the
whole universe, while for others it would affect only the
people of Israel. The ideas of ordinary people were of this
second sort. They did not hope for a transformation of the
universe ("cosmic eschatology"), but expected that God would
send the Messiah-King and restore the kingdom of Israel in its
old splendour through him ("national eschatology"). This idea
can be seen, for example, in the spurious ("apocryphal")
Psalms of Solomon (17: 23–51). Many of Jesus' contemporaries

also connected the kingdom of God with the doctrine of the two "ages of the world" ("two aeons") put forward in what is called apocalyptic writing. According to these ideas, "this aeon", the present age of the world, is under the dominion of Satan, the prince of this world. This kingdom of Satan shows itself in injustice, suffering, sickness and sin. The "aeon to come", the coming age of the world, is under the rule of God and will make that rule manifest. It is totally good, and means an increase of life and happiness.

When the people of Jesus' time waited, hoped and longed for this coming age of the world, the kingdom of God, this could influence their attitudes in very different ways. Some became political or religious enthusiasts, others resigned themselves to disappointment, others again kept the hope alive. John the Baptist regarded the approaching kingdom of God primarily as a judgment. He points out the seriousness of the situation. "The time for a decision has come," is the message of his preaching. The Qumran community on the Dead Sea, which was something like a religious order, was waiting for the final battle between the "sons of light" and the "sons of darkness". The Pharisees insisted on punctilious observance of the law, which they believed hastened the coming of God's kingdom. The "zealots" wanted to establish the kingdom of God by force in a guerrilla war against the Roman occupiers. The quiet people in the land hoped for a sudden miracle to reward their prayers and patience. Many had no hope at all. They collaborated with the Romans or lived from day to day. They lived in despair and felt excluded from the number of those with the right to feel that they were God's chosen ones.

Each of these groups was anxious to separate and mark itself off from the others. The exclusive Qumran community withdrew into a monastery in the desert. The Pharisees lived within society, but they kept their distance from the "people of the land", who were ignorant of the law. John the Baptist, too, did not go into the cities, but made penitents come to him in the desert and by the Jordan.

And which group did the wandering preacher Jesus belong

to, who appeared one day in Galilee? To none. He took up
the old and still living hope of the kingdom of God, but gave
it a new meaning. Jesus gave the term "the kingdom of God"
a new meaning by giving the word "God" a new content.
The Romans were still in the country, but Jesus invented no
techniques for driving them out. He produced no signs of any
new paradise on earth. In his proclamation of God's judgment
and the end of the world, unlike John the Baptist's preaching,
the imminence of a universal catastrophe bringing the old
world to an end was not an important part. What was important in it was the announcement that the time of waiting was
over. God's action at the end of time is not just near, said
Jesus, it has already come. God's nearness and saving presence
is taking effect. It can be said that Jesus' preaching gives the
impression of an illusion, but it is impossible to present it as a
national political programme or an apocalyptic threat of
approaching doom.

Jesus also neatly pricked the bubble of exaggerated expectations with his call for people to "repent" – this meant doing
something for themselves and not just waiting for something
to happen automatically. Jesus called for repentance *because*
the kingdom of God was at hand. In other words, because
God has decided to support the world and intends to establish
his own rule once and for all in the world, men must make up
their minds and take appropriate action. Because God's kingdom has come once and for all Satan's kingdom has been
crushed. Because it is directed at the whole world it can
achieve nothing through political or national liberation
struggles. What God's definitive decision for the world is about
is the salvation of men, each man and every human community. Jesus has come to proclaim this decision of God's and
to implement it in word and action. "The kingdom of God is
at hand." In Jesus' mouth this means that God is here for all
who need him. God has begun a movement towards men once
and for all; it cannot be reversed. From his side God has
bridged the gap between God and man. God is meaning and
salvation for all. Men need no longer wait for an "apocalyptic"
catastrophe at the end of time. They have no excuse any more

for resignation. From those who formerly tended to creep away from time or throw themselves blindly into it, for those who were in the past enthusiasts or hopeless pessimists, the time now calls for "repentance", a turning away from all such attitudes and an approach to the presence of God which is advancing on man.

For Jesus, the phrase "kingdom of God" is a little like a signal light. If you try to grasp it conceptually or reduce it to simple terms it becomes very abstract. It has to be talked about in many different ways because the kingdom of God is neither a state of affairs which can be described once and for all nor a general theory, but something that happens, an event. This is why it has as great a variety of forms as those of the situations in which it has so far appeared. For these reasons it is no surprise that Jesus should talk in many different ways about the kingdom of God and even, apparently, contradict himself.

Present and future

A tension between present and future is one of the main features of Jesus' preaching about the kingdom of God. Sometimes he describes it as something of the present, sometimes as something in the future. Sometimes he speaks of it in spatial, sometimes in temporal terms. All this is a result of the nature of the kingdom of God. When God approaches men, this event cannot take the form of a single present situation which, as it were, one could seize with both hands and tie down. The kingdom of God is not simply "present"; it keeps appearing in new forms by making man something new. A man has to be told to let himself go, invited to expose himself, as it were, to the kingdom of God and let himself be remodelled by it. Jesus does not just redefine God, but also redefines man. He tells us that what determines man's nature is that God approaches him in grace and makes him new so that he is freed from his old nature and can make a new start and turn to God.

God's kingdom shows itself among men, and first of all in

Jesus, in a new way of believing, hoping and loving. Jesus himself sets this process off. The kingdom of God is the flame that he lights, the fire he scatters on the earth, the sword he brings, the healing he performs, the expulsion of evil spirits, for which he has the power, the message he preaches, the repentance he stimulates. The fullest appearance of the kingdom of God is in the way Jesus himself lives.

Jesus' acts of power

Jesus himself combined his preaching of the kingdom of God with demonstrations of power. Notably, he cured the sick and drove out evil spirits. This made a great impression on the peasants of Galilee. But Jesus did not allow himself to be labelled or pinned down as a "miracle-worker" (Mk 1: 35–9). Still less did he make use of the effect of his miracles to build up a movement among the admiring crowds and put himself at its head as "Messiah". He himself made the intention behind his demonstrations of power quite clear; they were an extension of his preaching in the form of actions which would reveal the nature of the kingdom of God: "But if it is by the Spirit of God" – Luke says "the finger of God" – "that I cast out demons, then the kingdom of God has come upon you" (Mk 12: 28 = Lk 11: 20). This tells us that the kingdom of God means the release of men from the kingdom of Satan, and its effects of possession, disease and sin. Another important feature of the kingdom of God is revealed at the same time: it does not come only in the "afterlife" and is not just "spiritual"; it is to take up real physical space in this world. Nor is it a "utopia" within the world, something that is always a little bit farther on but never reached; it is present here and now, and its effects can be felt by those who attach themselves to Jesus.

"I saw Satan fall like lightning from heaven," said Jesus: in the face of the kingdom of God the kingdom of Satan is without hope and doomed to decline. God's kingdom is founding a new world in the midst of the old. The sign of this new world is that in the midst of the old world people begin to live in a new way, without fear, full of confidence, comforted, vigorous and healthy – free. Jesus' actions, as it were, push back the barriers which, according to him, Satan had erected around men and open up to them a new sphere of freedom.

Those in this new area of freedom are those who follow Jesus. By following him they become the people of God of the last times. Following Jesus means basing one's life in future on no other protection than the definitive, saving kingdom of God proclaimed by Jesus. This is what the repentance Jesus demands means. That is why the followers of Jesus are what biblical scholars call "the eschatological people of God": the people established and brought together by the coming of God's permanent kingdom. That makes Jesus the witness and inspired founder, the messenger and viceroy of God's rule. His actions create no political messianic party, but set off a process of grouping out of which the people of God of the last times will emerge. For a person who believes, the acts of power which Jesus himself claimed to do in the power of God are unmistakable "signs" of the benefits of membership of this people of God. By relying on Jesus they obtain reconciliation, peace, forgiveness, salvation and freedom, all of which God has destined for those under his rule.

Prophetic provocation

Jesus' miracles in themselves made an impression. But Jesus went further and deliberately provoked people.

He sat at the same table as sinners and ate in their company (Mk 2: 15–17). He broke down the isolation produced by the discrimination against individuals or groups. For example, he flouted the discrimination against tax-collectors which had grown up under the Roman occupation; they fell into the class of the "poor" to whom he had a mission to preach salvation. Jesus' only justification for his actions was God's will to save and his own mission: "I came not to call the righteous, but sinners" (Mk 2: 17). The first community spent a long time thinking about Jesus' provocative association with sinners. One result of their reflections can be seen in the story in Mk 2: 1–12, where Jesus is shown in an argument with the Pharisees, who accuse him of blasphemy against God for claiming the authority to forgive sins.

Again, Jesus provocatively broke the Sabbath laws – at least as the Pharisees interpreted them (Mk 3: 1–6). His healing of the man with the withered hand was a sort of demonstration of God's rule in its immediate concern for human salvation without regard for religious rules. It showed that the will of God was to maintain life and would not tolerate extra laws imposed by the community: "Is it lawful on the sabbath to do good or to do harm, to save life or to kill?" (Mk 3: 4).

Another part of Jesus' provocative prophetic activity was the formation of a group of disciples. It was a remarkable group, which included representatives of every movement in the Palestinian Judaism of his time: publicans, Galileans influenced by Greek ideas and culture, strict Pharisees and Zealots. It was meant as a clear sign for Israel; here was the fragmented house of Israel united in the family created by God for the last times (cf Mk 3: 35). Here were men from all sorts of backgrounds who took the risk of giving up home, family and job at Jesus' word (cf Lk 14: 26; 9: 57 f, 59 f, 61 f; Mk 10: 28 ff). They put their trust in Jesus' explanation of what God wanted, as the whole of Israel should have done. What was provocative about Jesus' action here was, precisely, his combination of all these people in the group of his disciples. Among his followers were people who, according to the dominant views of society, didn't belong together, people "one" didn't associate with. They were people whom it was preferable to divide into cliques and keep apart rather than see together. There were even women among his followers (Lk 8: 1–3; 10: 38–42). Jesus used the most scandalous language in his appeals, a rejection of law, morality and religion: "Leave the dead to bury their own dead" (Mt 8: 22; Lk 9: 60).

What was the purpose of all this provocation? It reached its climax in the incident in the precincts of the Jerusalem Temple which we know by the name of the "cleansing of the Temple" and was probably the direct cause of Jesus' arrest and execution. This deliberate act of provocation in the Jewish capital, in Israel's central sanctuary, is like a banner headline proclaiming the meaning of all Jesus' provocative activity. If our interpretation of the tradition contained in Mk 11: 15–17 and parallel passages is correct, Jesus proclaimed in the Temple, to the crowds of pilgrims who had come to Jerusalem for the Passover, the approach of the kingdom of God. He demanded that the "court of the Gentiles" in the Temple should be made a place of prayer for *all* nations, since the time had now come for the fulfilment of the prophets' promise that in the end the peoples of the whole world would come to Jerusalem to worship God. This prophetic promise about the Gentiles assumes, however, that God's people Israel would first be gathered together, as was prophesied for the last times. This brings us to the clear central intention of Jesus. He quotes the prophetic saying, "My house shall be called a house of prayer for all the nations" (Mk 11: 17 = Is 56: 7). Isaiah in fact calls this saying "a saying of the Lord God who gathers the outcasts of Israel" (Is 56: 8). This gives us a new way of describing Jesus' "programme" and "demand", the gathering together of Israel in expectation of the universal rule of God. The rest of Jesus' prophetic provocative actions fit this description.

The gathering of Israel

That was his purpose. His preaching of the kingdom of God, his powerful actions in the towns and villages of Galilee and on the Lake of Genesareth, all his prophetic and provocative actions up to and including the cleansing of the Jerusalem Temple, had the aim of gathering together the people of Israel. Jesus did not create a movement of repentance like his predecessor John the Baptist. He was not interested in insisting on strict observance of the law like the Pharisees. He did not set up any special community, separate and demanding priestly purity, like the Qumran community. Jesus was not interested in a part of Israel, a remnant, even the holy remnant described by the prophets, but in the whole of Israel. His movement was aimed at gathering people in, at bringing God's salvation to all. This is the reason for Jesus' provocative interest

THE GOD OF JESUS 129

in those who were rejected and banned to the fringes of Jewish society, the sick, sinners, publicans, the despised "people of the land".

In the eyes of religious people Jesus went too far. His intimacy with publicans and sinners marked him out as a friend of those who were regarded as enemies of Yahweh (Mt 11: 18 and parallels). Jesus defended himself by referring to the true will of God. God was more interested in sinners than in the righteous because as the shepherd of Israel he wanted to gather together the whole flock and must therefore take special care of the lost and scattered sheep (Lk 15: 1–7 and parallels). God had sent Jesus to the lost sheep of the house of Israel (Mt 15: 24; cf 10: 6). Jesus explained his mission and the purpose of his actions in words and expressions taken from the Old Testament promises (cf Ezek 34: 15 f). God himself was to gather together his people Israel in the last times, and Jesus claimed that his movement to gather people together was the fulfilment of that promise.

For this work Jesus needed his disciples. They were a sign and instrument of the gathering together of Israel. Jesus needed them to make God's saving will visible and to reach all Israel. He called men to follow him in order that they might make his actions known and carry them on. In his commissioning addresses to the missionaries (Mk 6: 7–13 and parallels; Lk 10: 3–12) he sharply emphasized the urgency of their mission.

On another occasion he compared the gathering in of Israel with a ripe harvest, the gathering of which cannot be put off: "The harvest is plentiful, but the labourers are few; pray therefore the Lord of the harvest to send out labourers into the harvest" (Lk 10: 2 and parallels). Anyone who does not listen to the message of the coming of God's kingdom, which is proclaimed by the disciples with the same authority as Jesus, puts himself on the same level as the heathen to whom Jesus is not sent. The disciples were told to demonstrate this by shaking the dust off their feet (Mt 10: 5; Lk 10: 8–11). Another saying of Jesus, recalling old images of the gathering together of Israel, makes quite clear the claim he makes with his drive to gather: "He who is not with me is against me, and he who does not gather with me scatters" (Mt 12: 30).

Jesus gave an even clearer illustration of the meaning and implications of his actions by forming a special group of twelve. This action was a parable; it was another way of saying that Jesus' claim was directed at all Israel. The twelve were the representatives of the twelve tribes of Israel, which were to be gathered together in the last times: "Truly, I say to you, in the new world, when the Son of man shall sit on his glorious throne, you who have followed me will also sit on twelve thrones, judging the twelve tribes of Israel" (Mt 19: 28; cf Lk 22: 30). Jesus wanted to gather people together for their salvation, for that of Israel and that of the nations. Jesus referred to this again in his complaint against Jerusalem: "O Jerusalem, Jerusalem, killing the prophets and stoning those who are sent to you! How often would I have gathered your children together as a hen gathers her brood under her wings, and you would not!" (Mt 23: 37 = Lk 13: 34).

Jesus' gathering movement had no immediate, striking success. When in the end he expressed his efforts in the provocative incident in the Jerusalem Temple, the result was his arrest and execution. For Jesus' disciples his death was the occasion of a new gathering through the experience of his resurrection. Jn 11: 51–2 says Jesus was to die "for the nation, and not for the (Jewish) nation only, but to gather into one the children of God who are scattered abroad (among the Gentiles)". After Easter the Church came to see itself as a new group brought together by God. The group of disciples, and especially the twelve, were the foundation of the Church. Jesus himself did not directly have the later Church in mind, but the gathering together of Israel at the end of time. Nevertheless the Church is the product of his gathering movement.

In this way Jesus' activity increasingly became a single coherent commentary on his original proclamation of the coming of God's kingdom. His powerful actions announced it, his provocative behaviour was an advertisement for it and his gathering movement started it. For us it is also the basis of our understanding of the nature and themes of his detailed preaching.

The parables

Jesus' intention in the parables is to make clear in word pictures that the kingdom of God has at last begun to make a permanent place for itself in the middle of the existing world. A beginning has been made which cannot be stopped, a goal set up which cannot be allowed to drop out of sight (cf the parables of the seed in Mk 4). The kingdom of God comes and grows "of itself" (Mk 4: 28), untouched by human hand, through God's free activity.

The style of the parables is intended to win the agreement and confidence of the listeners for this kingdom of God. The parables offer a picture both of how the kingdom moves towards men, without forcing them, and how men turn to meet it – or fail to respond. This reveals who God is and the attitude he takes towards the world. God is the Lord who holds the destiny of the whole earth in his faithful hand and leads it to a good end. He is the father of his lost sons. It is possible and right to ask him for help as a father. He has pity on a younger son who made his decision to leave his father in complete freedom and then turned homewards in pain, confusion and despair. But he also wants to bring the older son home. For his sake he leaves the banquet just as before, against all custom, he ran to meet his younger son. He wants to be a father to both without taking their freedom away from them and without abandoning them to their freedom (Lk 15: 11–32). Man, this parable is saying, is the son who is not limited in his freedom by God but, on the contrary, encouraged to make use of it; God's kingdom does not force itself on people. It is an invitation, a gift, which only has to be accepted. Even in the face of death or in total alienation, man can obtain life if he is prepared to go home to his Father's house, accept gifts from his Father, and serve his brothers.

To judge from the parables, Jesus himself is the ideal of "the son". He lives in such a way that his freedom gives others the courage to be free, his faith makes faith possible, his love arouses love. Jesus never directly talks about himself in the parables, but he defends his behaviour as the only one which corresponds to what God really is and to the nature of his kingdom, unconditional love, total faith and unshakeable hope.

Jesus and the law

Jesus' contemporaries believed that God had left an unalterable record of his will in the "law". In this picture, the law was given by God to the chosen people on Sinai, and was now preserved in the tradition of the "elders" and in the interpretation of the contemporary scribes.

Jesus did not see the law as the immovable will of a distant God which demanded meticulous observance on the part of men. He interpreted the law in its original intention, as an expression of God's loving guidance of his people and individual men. He scrambled, as it were, the dead letters, and set the spirit of the law free. By doing this he did not proclaim any sort of human autonomy in relation to the divine law. In Jesus' view the fundamental mistake of his critics was to have made themselves masters of the law by exaggerated subjection to the surface text. They made it detrimental to human life and so distorted its meaning. Jesus' proclamation of the liberation of men from the power of the law attacks such improper submission. This freedom, however, is freedom to love, and this is exactly what the law calls upon men to do.

Anxious liberalism is not the proper attitude to the law. The only standard by which the law can be judged is the kingdom of God: in other words, his loving determination to save man. Jesus claims to know this loving and saving will of God, and he takes for granted that his hearers also have this knowledge. In this he implies that he and all those who listen to him are already living in the "new covenant" described in Jer 31: 31–3: "Behold, the days are coming, says the LORD, when I will make a new covenant with the house of Israel and the house of Judah, not like the covenant which I made with their fathers when I took them by the hand to bring them out of the land of Egypt, my covenant which they broke, though I was their husband, says the LORD. But this is the covenant which I will make with the house of Israel after those days, says the LORD: I will put my law within them, and I will write it upon their hearts."

By interpreting the law as a challenge to men to love freely, Jesus abolished it as a law. God's kingdom is at hand, and this means that the will of God does not just meet men when they come into contact with the written law, even if the guardians of the law have tried to bring the whole of life within its scope. No, the will of God meets men directly, in their lives and in their hearts. This means that there is no "freedom", in the sense that anything not mentioned in the law is "free". God claims a man's whole heart, but because this claim is love it leaves a man at once totally tied and totally free. If this is so, the law in the Jewish sense has served its purpose, and Paul was right when he later proclaimed that Jesus was "the end of the law" (Rom 10: 4).

Jesus' ethics

None of this means that Jesus talked about the will of God only in generalities, without saying anything specific. Quite the opposite: Jesus interpreted the will of God in the form of quite specific advice. This advice was not, however, a rigid and oppressive code, and it is quite wrong to make it one. In any case, Jesus' advice is not just specific, but for those who open their hearts to it perfectly clear and immediately intelligible: "And do not swear by your head, for you cannot make one hair white or black" (Mt 5: 36). "Why do you see the speck that is in your brother's eye, but do not notice the log that is in your own?" (Mt 7: 3).

In these and similar pieces of advice Jesus did not play on a distinction between "intention" and "action", or contrast "situation" and "norm". Terms such as "attitude ethics" or "situation ethics" make Jesus' advice more manageable, but they also take away its sting. People constantly try in this way to provide themselves with standards which can be conveniently applied to human actions, to judge an attitude or assess a situation. But the will of God, which Jesus claimed to know, is in his view not measurable but unlimited: "You must be perfect, as your heavenly Father is perfect" (Mt 5: 48). Jesus did not ask for good deeds, but good people.

Jesus' ethics is the ethics of the kingdom of God. His demands correspond to the final coming of God. They are concerned, fundamentally, with God's rights, not with details of human customs and morals. Hence why Jesus' advice pays remarkably little attention to the actual situation, the conditions in which we live. It is, in the literal sense, "unworldly". This is because the kingdom of God, of which they are the practical consequences, does not reinforce the conditions of life in this world, but questions them, upsets them. The basis and the summit of Jesus' demands are found together in his promise, "Blessed are you poor, for yours is the kingdom of God" (Lk 6: 20). What Jesus' ethics – if we still want to call it that – means and demands is shown most clearly by the story of the rich young man (Mk 10: 17–27). Jesus asks of men nothing that they do not already have. They do not have to acquire anything else, neither new virtues nor anything else, but have to give something up, the feeling of security based on the goods of this world. This is what gives Jesus' interpretation of the will of God its character of an exposure. It can give people a fright: "Then who can be saved?" The only thing that can remove this fear is the thought of the omnipotence of God, whose kingdom it is that makes such demands. By bringing the kingdom of God and inaugurating it in his actions, Jesus himself removes this fear. He does this by interpreting God's will not just in demands, but also by his own actions, by his life and his death. This is why no Christian who adopts the ethic of the kingdom of God can do without Jesus. The way in which men lose their fear of God's will is compassionate action, stemming from a faith which has experienced God's compassion.

We can now see the way in which the disciples of Jesus are enabled, and required, to love their neighbour. The com-

mandment to love God and one's neighbour no longer directs
men to perform particular human virtues, nor to fulfil particular precepts of the law; it simply directs our attention to the
needs of our neighbour. The needs of our neighbour are not
something which can be captured once and for all in the
provisions of a law code; it is not something which can be
calculated or included in a balance sheet. It cannot be made
part of an ethical theory. It is simply the reality untouched by
salvation which surrounds us. To love God, the Lord, means
to love him as a merciful father. I can only do this by
acknowledging the merciful rule he has established to relieve
human distress and by accepting an obligation to all those
who need my love. Jesus did not simply identify love of God
and love of neighbour. He did not regard love of God as in
any way merging into love of neighbour, nor did he make love
of our neighbour into an "instrument" of our love of God. He
preached a God who himself became the neighbour of sinful
man, suffering under the power of death, and came to him.
That is why those who want to love this God will find him
only where he has chosen to go, among sinners, among their
enemies, in the suffering of men and their need of love (Mk
12: 38–44 and parallels; Mt 25: 31–46).

Love of God and love of neighbour as interpreted by Jesus
are therefore not "religious acts", if that means actions which
can be separated from the rest of life. The Samaritan did not
have one eye on God when he helped the injured traveller,
but in the act of helping him he did love God, by loving his
neighbour unconditionally, as God loves him. The indissoluble
unity between love of God and love of neighbour as revealed
in the person of Jesus is not based on any identity between
God and neighbour. Jesus did not abolish the distinction
between men and God. The basis of the indissoluble unity
between love of God and love of neighbour is based on the
fact that there is only one love, God's love. Loving one's
neighbour means passing on this love. This one love of God is
revealed in Jesus.

God's representative

This seems a good point at which to ask what Jesus thought
of himself, what claims he made. The question must be
answered first of all from his words and his intentions. Combining the two, we can say that the most original and most
characteristic feature of Jesus' behaviour is the fact that, contrary to all the usual expectations, he preached the coming of
the kingdom of God as the irrevocable love of God directed,
without distinction, at all men. Everything Jesus said and did

was permeated by this message that God's infinite love was
now starting to take effect without restriction, and that it was
therefore time for the men around him to trust in the power
and faithfulness of this love and pass it on in love for their
fellow men. It was because of this that Jesus called the poor
blessed, preached God's salvation to sinners and called on
them to repent. As a sign of this he cured the sick and the
possessed and collected disciples from among social outcasts
and celebrated the dawning of the time of salvation with
them. In contrast, he called on the "righteous" to accept this
decision of God's. He shrank from no act of provocation to
make the righteous admit that the sinners whom God had
accepted were their brothers, and the brothers of all who were
truly righteous.

In all this Jesus' attitude was so clear, he was so confident
of having God's justice and truth on his side, so spontaneously
impetuous in both kindness and anger, so simple, powerful
and insistent in his words, that the impression was inevitably
given that his message must be completely God's message, and
vice versa. Jesus had a unique connexion with God, and God
was behind him and his actions in a unique way. For Jesus,
men's decision for or against him was equivalent to their turning to God or rejection of God. His disciples were God's
chosen, his messengers God's messengers. "I and the Father
are one": this apparently simple but so profound formula in
which the author of the fourth gospel expresses Jesus' relation
to God in fact sums up the unprecedented claims which is
clearly visible in all the activity of the historical Jesus. Jesus

regarded himself as God's representative and behaved as such to an extent and with an assurance which no scribe or prophet, no one else and no one before him in Israel (cf Mk 1: 21 f; 11: 31 f) had approached. This brings us to another saying in the gospel of John: "He who has seen me has seen the Father" (Jn 14: 9).

This totally uninsistent, but unmistakable and all-pervading, identification by Jesus of his mission with God is ·the real secret of his effect. The tradition has captured the impression made by this identification in its picture of the constant presence of an amazed, hero-worshipping crowd around Jesus, commenting on his teaching, questions and miracles like the chorus in a Greek tragedy (cf Mk 1: 27; 2: 12; 7: 37). Those outside his circle became obsessed with the question of who had given him this "authority" (Mk 11: 27–33); his opponents, the Pharisees and scribes, called him a Satan-worshipper (Mk 3: 22).

Did Jesus himself say anything which would support the conclusion which we have drawn from his behaviour? There are two questions here.

The first is about the way in which Jesus spoke about God in relation to himself. The one and only God and Father, the God of Abraham, Isaac and Jacob, is "his" Father, and this is true in such a deep sense that Jesus made a distinction (or it was attributed to him) between "my Father" and "your Father". This distinction is quite consistent; Jesus never "makes a mistake". "Pray like this: Our Father . . ." Jesus however prays, "My Father . . ." (cf Mt 6: 9; Lk 11: 2; Mk 13: 32 = Mt 24: 36; Mt 11: 27 = Lk 10: 22; Mt 16: 17; Lk 22: 29). The use of "Abba" to address God seems to have been introduced by Jesus (Mk 14: 36; Mt 6: 9; 11: 25–6; Lk 23: 34–46; Mt 26: 42 combined with 26: 39) and was never forgotten. The Aramaic word accompanied the Christian faith into the Greek-speaking communities (cf Gal 4: 6; Rom 8: 15; Mk 14: 36), and became a particular stimulus for reflection on and investigation of the mystery of Jesus.

The second question concerns the description or "title" Jesus adopted. It seems that Jesus said nothing of his own accord about who he was. The subject of his preaching was not his own person, but the kingdom of God. He did not talk about his authority but exercised it.

Jesus' claim

The tradition knows of only a few occasions on which Jesus formally talked about himself. According to Mk 8: 27 ff Jesus once asked his disciples who they thought he was. Peter replied: "You are the Christ (that is the Messiah)." Mark reports Jesus' reaction as forbidding curtly Peter to say anything more about him. He is also described as replying to the acknowledgment of his messiahship by warning his disciples of his approaching passion. Peter then reproached him sharply, insisting that the Messiah should never let anything like that happen to him, and that Jesus, as the Messiah, ought not to fall into the hands of his enemies. Jesus then turned on him a second time, with the words, "Get behind me, Satan! For you are not on the side of God, but of men." However the historicity of this exchange may be judged, the scene shows one thing quite clearly: Jesus did not want to be the "Messiah" in the sense the word was commonly understood by his fellow countrymen. "Jesus of Nazareth, king of the Jews" was not his own description but the charge on which his opponents handed him over to the Roman governor to be crucified (Mk 15: 2 ff).

This charge may have been made against a background of messianic enthusiasm in relation to Jesus among the Galilean pilgrims (Mk 11: 9 f). It is perfectly reasonable to ask whether this enthusiasm did not receive some encouragement from Jesus' own behaviour – possibly, as suggested above, from the "cleansing of the Temple" – but the tradition allows no firm conclusion. That Jesus was the Messiah was always the judgment of others, never Jesus' own assertion. The only exception, Jesus' answer to the high priest's question, "Are you the Christ?" (Mk 14: 61 ff) is probably a product of post-Easter faith. The majority of biblical scholars believe, for solid reasons, that Jesus did not claim to be the expected Messiah, and indeed that in his own view of himself he deliberately distanced himself from this Jewish expectation and tried to evade the title "Messiah" when others applied it to him. Only after Jesus' death was the title "Messiah" no longer liable to mistaken political interpretations, and in its Greek translation "Christ" it became a sort of surname for Jesus.

The position is similar with other titles deriving from Jewish tradition. Jesus himself never described himself as either "son of David" or "son of God". Both titles included overtones from the political expectations of a Messiah (cf Mt 16: 16; Mk 14: 61; Lk 1: 32). And Jesus did not regard himself as one of the prophets whose return the Jews expected in the last times.

The only title which occurs frequently in the sayings of Jesus is the title "son of man". This unusual title probably goes back in the first place to the vision in chapter 7 of the book of Daniel, the so-called Apocalypse of Daniel (Dan 7: 13 f), and occurs in some later apocalyptic writings as the name of a heavenly ruler who will appear at the end of time and judge all mankind. This is exactly the way Jesus at first talks about the "son of man". For example, he promises those who acknowledge him in the present that the son of man will acknowledge them in the coming final judgment. He warns those who now deny him that the son of man will deny them at the judgment (Lk 12: 8–9). To judge by these remarks, Jesus is so sure that he is carrying out God's work among men that he confidently expects the heavenly son of man to determine his decision as judge according to men's attitude to Jesus.

This saying probably does go back to Jesus himself. It occurs in another form, in which the son of man of the last times is identified with Jesus: "Everyone who acknowledges me before men, I also will acknowledge before my Father who is in heaven" (Mt 10: 32). A comparison shows clearly that in this case the post-Easter faith in the risen and exalted Jesus has altered the original wording. Similar treatment of a related saying can be seen in the case of the last beatitude (Lk 6: 22; cf Mt 5: 11). There are many other sayings in which Jesus speaks of himself as the son of man: as son of man he has power to forgive sins (Mk 2: 10, 28) and to suspend the sabbath commandment (Mk 2: 28). It is the son of man who will carry out the last judgment (Mk 13: 26; 14: 62). On the other hand, the rootlessness of Jesus is also a characteristic of the son of man (Mt 8: 20), and this contradiction intensifies as the passion approaches: the son of man will be given up into the hands of men (Mk 8: 31; 9: 31; 10: 33 f; 14: 41). In all these cases it is assumed that even in his earthly actions Jesus is already the son of man, the heavenly representative of God who has come down on earth to men (Lk 7: 34; 19: 10).

These texts are a good example of the way in which Christians after Easter described the earthly life and activity of Jesus in the light of their faith. Jesus himself claimed with total assurance that the final decision about men's relation to God and God's salvation in men was already being made here and now in relation to him. As a result of its experience of the resurrection of the crucified Jesus, the Church regarded the truth of this claim as proved. The son of man of the prophecies was now no longer unknown and anonymous; he was Jesus, the risen one, who now, as the son of man, inaugurated the last judgment from heaven. And not only that, but the mystery of the person of Jesus and his mission, until now hidden in Jesus' claim, was now revealed. All the time on earth, Jesus had been the son of man, the representative of God, whose words were God's words and whose actions were God's actions.

Jesus, God's love made visible

We have seen that these texts give us a clear example of the transition from the (pre-Easter) words and actions of Jesus to post-Easter "christology". This brings us to the heart of one of biblical scholarship's most difficult problems, that of the "Jesus of history" and the "Christ of faith", and we shall return to it. For the present it is clear that, as used by Jesus, the title "son of man" merely sums up what is revealed of his claims by his own words and actions. Jesus is convinced that God is totally behind him and that his work in preaching the kingdom of God as the decisive question for men is identical with God's work. God's kingdom means God's irrevocable decision to save the world. If we translate the language of the first three gospels into that of the fourth, we can say that Jesus is convinced that his work is identical with God's work when he proclaims love as the nature of God and lets himself be controlled by that love even to death. In Jesus God was revealed as love.

Two things follow from this. Firstly: it is only possible to talk credibly about the God Jesus preached when the power which supported Jesus' life also dominates the life of the person who talks about God. This power is unshakeable love which believes in God as love. It follows from this that we cannot tell that it is the God of Jesus that is being talked about from any theory, or from the use of any particular theological language, but only from actions which correspond to this.

Secondly: this characteristic of Jesus, that his life was totally dominated by an unshakeable love, and thus by God, is expressed by the unique way that God is known as "his Father" and Jesus as "the Son". That is to say that this description does not imply a connexion between God and Jesus similar to a natural relationship, but a relationship adopted in freedom. This explains why other men may also be called "sons of God". In their case too it means freely letting God be their father, which in turn means letting their lives be dominated by love. Jesus' "precedence" over other men is unique because no one else let his life be dominated by God as he did. Yet Jesus precedes men in the direction they all have to take in coming into contact with God. For that reason he is the model of human life in God's presence as much as he is the self-revelation of God. The later history of faithful reflection on this mystery said a lot that allowed a deeper understanding of God's relation to Jesus and Jesus' relation to God. The limit which cannot be passed without betraying the New Testament is always the point at which the divine sonship of Jesus is no longer explained as something which is expressed as a life totally dominated by love.

Let us sum up what the story of Jesus tells us about God.

Our starting-point is the fact that Jesus gave the word "God" a new content. God was revealed as the God of Israel who established his kingdom of the end of time in a surprising way, the God who made a move towards men and bridged the gap between heaven and earth from his side. He was the God who had shown himself to be the God of sinners and of the godless and thereby shown himself to be the loving father of all men. By revealing in his words and actions who God is, Jesus himself appeared as in a unique way on God's side. We could say that he himself is the representative of God without qualification, the point at which God made himself known in a way that can never be surpassed. That is what the evangelist John meant when he made Jesus say: "He who has seen me has seen the Father" (Jn 14: 9). And, conversely, Jesus himself starts from the fact that God as the Father was completely on his side, every time he himself acted in the name of God, as a preacher, a banisher of demons, a healer of the sick, an interpreter of the law, the inspired leader of a group of disciples, a prophetic troublemaker, as the shepherd who gathered Israel together and, finally, on the cross.

When God as love completely took over Jesus' life, he also took over his death. If God was completely behind Jesus, then his death too must reveal the coming of the kingdom of God. But if God joined himself to Jesus' life even to death, then death cannot have the last word. This is why we have to say that if Jesus had not risen from the dead the world would have passed away.

8   The God of the living

Try, if you can, to forget the last words of section 7. It is true that the Christian faith stands and falls with the recognition of Jesus of Nazareth as the representative of God, as the "Christ" and "Messiah" whom God sent and confirmed after death. The trouble is that these phrases run off our tongues faster than they ought. The space of centuries has dimmed the scandal in which the Gospel of Jesus Christ long ago made its triumphant progress through the ancient world.

I. THE SCANDAL OF THE CROSS

The scandal consisted in the fact that the man from Nazareth whom the Christians proclaimed as the divinely appointed bringer of salvation had been crucified, executed, thrown out by society. And because the Jewish society of that time thought it saw eye to eye with its God, this man who had been crucified inevitably appeared as a man who had been condemned by God, finished completely. As a former enemy of the crucified hero and persecutor of Christians, the apostle Paul felt this aspect of the Christian Gospel keenly. The famous words of the first epistle to the Corinthians show this clearly: For the word of the cross is folly to those who are perishing, but to us who are being saved it is the power of God . . . For Jews demand signs and Greeks seek wisdom, but we preach Christ crucified, a stumbling block to Jews and folly to Gentiles, but to those who are called, both Jews and Greeks, Christ the power of God and the wisdom of God. For the foolishness of God is wiser than men, and the weakness of God is stronger than men (1 Cor 1: 18, 22–5).

The cross and God

Those words show that the message about the crucified Christ was in sharp contradiction to an expectation of salvation and an associated image of God which, though not simply identifiable with the view of the Old Testament, had become established in the minds of many Jews at the time of Jesus. This was the God who was to reveal his power in signs and wonders, as he had done long ago in the escape from Egypt, when he destroyed his enemies, who were also the enemies of Israel, with one blow, in fact with a single mighty word. He would send his "anointed" ("Messiah") as the saviour of Israel, at the head of an army to fight the enemies of God. Jesus' end on the cross, the contemporary equivalent of the scaffold or the death chamber, did not fit this image at all.

And the Christian Gospel was equally alien to Greek philosophy's ideal of wisdom. Jesus did not correspond to the image of the self-controlled, Stoic sage, living above events in peaceful retirement and pursuit of knowledge, withdrawn from the world and immersed in his studies, nor did news of him attract those who were looking for the higher wisdom. Was the wisdom which was to save and liberate the human race to come from a failure, a man who was not even a Roman citizen and was politically suspect? The claim was beyond all logic and of little interest to a philosophical mind.

In their accounts of Jesus' sufferings, the gospels did not try to reduce the ambiguity connected with belief in Jesus. The story of the soldiers who dressed Jesus in a crown of thorns and a purple cloak and mocked him as "king of the Jews" (cf Mk 15: 16–19 and parallels), or the contemptuous cries under the cross (Mk 15: 29–32) are vivid enough. Whether these accounts describe what actually happened or whether they are more interpretation than reporting, they nevertheless show that the primitive Christian community was aware of the difficulties its claims on behalf of a crucified leader could create for outsiders. "He saved others; he cannot save himself. Let the Christ, the King of Israel, come down now from the cross, that we may see and believe" (Mk 15: 32). It would be wrong to try and minimize these unattractive externals of the Christian message. Jesus of Nazareth, the messenger of God, the mighty prophet, did not just die like any man; he died the miserable death of a criminal. God did not work a miracle to save him from this end.

When, in spite of this, the disciples of Jesus continued to proclaim him, when they even dared to present this crucified man first to the Jewish and then to the international public as the divinely sent saviour, Messiah, son of God and Lord, and in the process developed an amazing sense of their mission, this was not the result of any resentment. No, they had become convinced that God was behind this criminal, that he had declared his support for this "failure" and taken him into his presence.

Cross and resurrection

For the faith of the first Christians there was a firm connexion between the cross and the resurrection of Jesus Christ. This essential connexion is not so obvious for us, and it is useful for us not to repress the problems and questions which arise for us here or try to quieten them with superficial arguments.

The first act of the drama presents no difficulty. Jesus of Nazareth, who preached a startling message about the imminent end of the world and the approaching overthrow of all existing structures (admittedly by God, and not through a violent revolution), seemed so dangerous to those in power that they got rid of him. This puts Jesus in the class of those who in the course of history have had great ambitions which they were unable to realize.

The New Testament doesn't make things so easy for us, however. What it does is to give Jesus' death a complex theological interpretation. These theological interpretations, as we find them in the New Testament and soon in Christian dogmatics, cause difficulties. What does "died for our sins" or "representative expiation" mean? What does it mean to say that the deciding factor in the suffering and death of Jesus was not human responsibility or irresponsibility, but the working out of a mysterious divine plan? And to say that Jesus went to his death willingly, out of obedience to God, his father – who ever chose to die? What are we to make of the assertion that in all this a high-level drama of redemption took place, a battle between God and the demonic powers hostile to him, between God and the devil? These types of conceptual framework, as we might call them today, have become largely foreign to us. We must try to look at the old question of the meaning of Jesus' death in a completely new way, and we shall try to do this, at least in outline, in the following sections.

What does "resurrection" mean?

Even greater difficulties are involved in the second act of the Christian drama of salvation, the claim that Jesus rose from the dead. Thirty years ago Rudolf Bultmann wrote his famous essay, "The New Testament and Mythology. The Problem of the Demythologization of the New Testament Preaching" (1941) (see H. W. Barth (ed.), *Kerygma and Myth* [London, 1953], pp. 1–44). The discussion about the resurrection of Jesus provoked by this essay definitely made a great contribution to clarity about what the message of the resurrection in the New Testament could be saying and does say, and what it does not say. There has not been for centuries such intense discussion of the Christian message of Easter and its meaning as there is today. One result of the discussion, however, has been to emphasize more sharply the difficulties involved in this message, at least for us. One thing above all has become clear. Even if we can solve the problems of the correct interpretation of the texts, to which we shall have to come, we can still not think it is enough just to repeat this message in the biblical words. Accurate understanding of the original meaning of the biblical texts is essential for coming to grips with its message, but it is only a first step.

The second step, a much more difficult one, is to interpret the message as handed down by tradition, and this is a task which cannot be avoided by anyone who wants to have a mature understanding of his faith and make it the basis for a responsible life. There are quite general reasons for this need of interpretation, and they apply to other statements in the biblical message, but in the question of Jesus' resurrection all their weight is concentrated. Modern linguistics and philosophy of language (hermeneutics) have shown in detail that all human statements are dependent on the social and cultural conditions of their time. If this "socio-cultural context" changes in the course of history, the way men look at the world and at themselves also changes. Language necessarily changes too. New words and concepts grow up, and old words acquire new meanings unnoticed. The old words in their old and original meaning no longer say anything; we read them, usually automatically and without noticing, in a new meaning which corresponds to our new understanding of ourselves and of the world. Groups which are strongly attached to traditions and inherited formulas, such as churches and their members, are usually not aware of this inevitable process, and it sometimes becomes a source of conflicts, real or imagined. However, in the question of Jesus' resurrection – if it has now become a question – it is impossible to make progress without taking account of this process of language change.

Something similar is involved in Rudolf Bultmann's provocative reference to "demythologization". The New Testament gospel of salvation based on the cross and resurrection of Jesus was formulated in an environment in which people commonly used apocalyptic and eschatological language and ideas. "The raising of Jesus from the dead" is a term formulated in the language of Jewish apocalyptic, and in this context we know what it means. But while we can understand these ways of thinking by the use of historical understanding, we ourselves no longer use "apocalyptic" language and ideas. If we continue in spite of this to talk about the "resurrection" of Jesus, we become involved in a tension which it would be wrong to avoid.

Rather than avoid it, we must try to see the heart of the problem clearly. In this process our understanding, because it is human understanding, must proceed by approximation; it never reaches its goal once and for all, but always needs correction and revision, because it always grasps only individual aspects and never the whole. One reason for this is that our "socio-cultural context" will also change. In talking about the central elements of the Christian faith we must bear in mind that the language in which we talk about them is human language. We cannot aspire to any sort of "absolute language". This does not mean that we should not express definite opinions on the issues without hesitation, but it does mean that we must be equally honest about the difficulties.

The passion narratives

The sufferings and death of Jesus are described in detail in the passion narratives of the four gospels (Mt 26–7; Mk 14–15; Lk 22–3; Jn 18–19). In the story of the passion all the gospels show a high degree of agreement, much more than in the rest of the traditional material, though even here there are differences, mainly between Mark and Matthew on the one side and Luke and John on the other. The differences are the result partly of special traditions, and partly of the theological and literary intentions of the writers.

The large degree of agreement in this particular section of the Jesus tradition of the gospels seems to justify the assumption that the early Church produced a coherent narrative of the suffering and death of Jesus at a fairly early stage, and that this narrative was widely known. Naturally enough, the primitive Church had a great interest in the details of Jesus' arrest, trial and execution on the cross. There are references to them – the earliest – in Paul. In 1 Cor 11: 23–5 the tradition of the Lord's Supper is introduced by a brief mention of the arrest and execution of Jesus: "The Lord Jesus on the night when he was betrayed. . . ." The Greek word translated "betrayed", *paradidonai*, which can also mean "hand over" or "deliver up", is a constant feature of the theology of the passion: eg, Mk 1: 14; 3: 19; 9: 31; 10: 33; 14: 10, 11, 18, 21, 41, 42, 44; 15: 1, 10, 15 and parallels. Many indications also support the hypothesis that the passion tradition always ended with a short mention of the raising of Jesus, in a similar form to that at the end of the gospel of Mark (Mk 16: 1–8). In that case, the mention has already been expanded by Mark.

In its literary form, the account of the passion is marked by a relatively tight structure in the narrative. The various sections are much more tightly linked than in the other parts of the gospels, where the individual items are only loosely fitted into a framework. This feature also supports the hypothesis of the early composition of the passion narrative. We may also assume with confidence that the account keeps fairly close to the actual course of events. It is true that in the history of critical exegesis almost all the details of the passion story, as of the rest of the gospels, have at one time or another been challenged, and the difficulties in the way of an accurate reconstruction of the course of events have to be admitted. There are questions to which there are no satisfactory answers, such as: how did the disciples know how Jesus prayed in the garden of Gethsemani if they were asleep and Jesus was some distance away? or, where did they get their information about the hearing before the Sanhedrin, the supreme Jewish authority? Critical investigation has, however, led to the important realization that questions such as these miss the point of the biblical passion story. The story of the passion of Jesus in the gospels is not a normal account of a trial or a hearing in the same way as the records of the trial of Joan of Arc. What we have in the Gospel are "stylized" accounts, and the "stylizing" follows a particular principle. The evangelists want to show the last journey of Jesus of Nazareth, the Messiah, as that of the Son of God, to the last obedient in everything to the will of his heavenly Father, "obedient unto death, even death on a cross", in the words of the famous hymn quoted by Paul in the epistle to the Philippians (Phil 2: 8).

In Erich Auerbach's words, "That the King of Kings was treated as a low criminal, that he was mocked, spat upon, whipped and nailed to the cross – the story no sooner comes to dominate the consciousness . . . than it completely destroys the aesthetics of the separation of styles; it engenders a new elevated style, which does not scorn everyday life and which is ready to absorb the sensorily realistic, even the ugly, the undignified, the physically base" (*Mimesis* [Princeton, 1966], p. 72). It is an impression which every careful reader of the passion narratives must feel. The evangelists describe events which, from a realistic point of view, can only be seen as brutal, inhuman and unjust, in a restrained, even a quietly triumphant, tone – a combination which perhaps no one has reproduced as well as J. S. Bach in his passion music. The evangelists achieve it mainly by drawing on Old Testament models of the just man who suffers. Particularly important are psalms 22 and 69 and the song of the suffering servant in Is 53. The account of the sufferings of Jeremiah is also relevant. In this language the brutal details do not disappear, but they are removed from the sphere of meaningless cruelty and taken up into that of a mysterious divine action which takes place before the reader's eyes in unique objectivity and dignity.

One reason for the effect of distance is that, at least in the oldest written tradition of the passion, that of Mark, direct references to the saving nature of Jesus' death are kept to a minimum. It is only mentioned at the beginning, in the account of the eucharist (Mk 14: 22–5). The reader or listener is meant to concentrate on what is happening to Jesus. Some exegetes concluded from this that the oldest tradition regarded Jesus "merely" as a suffering saint and did not attribute any particular saving efficacy to his death, in the sense of a representative expiation for our sins, and they were able to cite the style of the narrative in their support. In most of these interpretations, however, the account of the eucharist was ignored, and it is this in the Marcan tradition which expresses the saving efficacy of Jesus' death. A more important defect of such interpretations, however, is that they fail to notice the intense participation and involvement which the deliberately restrained narrative tone conveys. By simply recording in sequence and presenting what happened to Jesus, by describing the conflicts between Jesus and the Jewish and Roman authorities, and between Jesus and his disciples, they force their readers to take an attitude to the accounts and to the death of Jesus. This is the source of their deep effect down to our own day.

"Kerygmatic formulas"

Alongside the passion narratives the New Testament contains a number of "kerygmatic" (ie, preaching) formulas which refer to death of Jesus, usually in connexion with his resurrection. In 1 Cor 15: 3–5 there is an old formula ("what I also received"): "Christ died for our sins in accordance with the scriptures . . . he was buried," and in Rom 3: 25 another existing formula taken over by Paul, in which Jesus' death is seen as an "expiation" established by God through which believers receive forgiveness of sins and salvation (or, as Paul says, "righteousness"). Again in Rom 4: 25 we find "who was put to death (literally, "given up") for our trespasses and raised for our justification". This is another old formula, and here Jesus' death is connected with the forgiveness of sins and his resurrection with justification. Paul did not just take over these formulas in his own theology; he developed their meaning and reworked them. Their echoes constantly recur in his writings.

At the same time Paul also places the death of Jesus in the line of the persecutions of the prophets, as in 1 Thess 1: 15, which refers to the Jews "who killed both the Lord Jesus and the prophets". This view of Jesus' death as the murder of a prophet also occurs in the Q tradition (Mt 23: 37–9; Lk 13: 34–5). The parable of the "wicked vine-dressers" (Mk 12: 1–12; cf Mt 21: 33–46; Lk 20: 9–19) is also part of this line of interpretation, which sees the rejection of Jesus in terms of the rejection by Israel of the great prophets of the past. These are probably the oldest attempts to understand the rejection and execution of Jesus.

The prophecies of the passion

These short "kerygmatic formulas" have a gospel parallel in the "prophecies" or announcements of the passion. These briefly summarize the accounts of the passion: "And he began to teach them that the Son of man must suffer many things, and be rejected by the elders and the chief priests and the scribes, and be killed, and after three days rise again. And he said this plainly." (Mk 8: 31–2; Mt 16: 21; Lk 9: 22 = Mk 9: 31; Mt 17: 22–3; Lk 9: 43b–45 = Mk 10: 32–4; Mt 20: 17–19; Lk 18: 31–4.) These sayings about the suffering, dying and rising son of man are not, as was previously thought, accurate predictions by Jesus of his passion, but "kerygmatic formulas" similar to that in 1 Cor 15: 3–5.

The title "the son of man" used in these formulas in the place of the "Christ" ("Messiah") of 1 Cor 15: 3 shows that these formulas originated in the primitive Christian community of Palestine. In this community Jesus was regarded as the bringer of salvation who was to come in the last times, whose sufferings, death and resurrection had already brought about the transition from the old to the new age of the world, to the new "aeon". The phrase "the Son of man must suffer" shows that this community understood Jesus' death as an event in a divine "plan". The "must" here means this divine predetermination, not blind fate. This sort of way of imagining "God's plan of salvation" as one whose stages were fixed from all eternity and had merely to be fulfilled in the course of history is part of Jewish apocalyptic, and the same is true of the idea of the "son of man". As we saw, the Christian community at an early stage identified Jesus with the "son of man", or, in other words, it had come to regard the death and resurrection of Jesus as the saving event promised for the last times.

A striking feature of the "prophecies of the passion" is that they gradually fill out the details. From the first announcement of suffering to the story of the passion a sort of intensification can be traced. Luke, for example, introduces the third announcement of the passion at Lk 18: 31 to emphasize the importance of "Jesus' journey to Jerusalem", which forms the framework for the second half of his gospel. Other "kerygmatic formulas" used in this context are the corresponding sections Jn 3: 11–21 and Jn 12: 20–36. We see from this that the gospels use different ways of talking about the passion and resurrection of Jesus side by side. The message of the death of Jesus and his resurrection from the dead is given a number of different literary forms, and these are connected with different ways of interpreting that death and resurrection.

The son of man formulas, which appear three times in Mark – and Matthew and Luke took them over in this form from Mark – have in addition an important function in the structure of Mark's gospel. The first announcement of the passion follows immediately on Peter's acknowledgment of Jesus as Messiah (Mk 8: 27–30; Mt 16: 13–20; Lk 9: 12–21). This is the evangelist's way of emphasizing that the path of Jesus the Messiah is so determined that it leads to the cross. This means that Jesus' messianic secret can only be correctly understood in the light of the cross and of Easter. Anyone who fails to realize this is in danger of falling into a serious misunderstanding of Jesus, as the case of Peter shows dramatically (Mk 8: 32–3). One more point is important to Mark (cf Mk 8: 34–8). This is that by steadfastly following the way of the cross Jesus also indicates the way to be followed by disciples who want to follow him. His way becomes a pattern of life for believers. Only a person who takes up his cross and denies himself, that is, rejects a life based on egotism, can be a follower of Jesus. Only those who risk their lives can win them. Only those who are not ashamed of the crucified Jesus in this world will be accepted by God at the last judgment as he accepted Jesus.

The cross and its interpretation

It is possible – and indeed necessary – to examine and describe the way the New Testament talks about the death of Jesus in much more detail than we have space for here. But even from the material we have already looked at we can establish three points.

1. The question of the death of Jesus forces us to deal directly with the person of Jesus. The final journey of this man itself demands increased interest. There is now no "mission" of Jesus independent of Jesus himself which could divert our attention. The "mission of Jesus" was decided on the way to Calvary. There, and nowhere else, is where it must be examined. This also implies that in the New Testament view the cross of Jesus was not an external, accidental matter. The New Testament witnesses see the cross as firmly connected with the mission and work of Jesus.

2. There is no interpretation of this "path of Jesus" which does not bring out its relevance to salvation. This is the common denominator of all interpretations of the cross in the New Testament. However, the precise ways in which this relevance to salvation is interpreted can be very different. Paul's teaching about the "justification of the sinner by faith alone" is one very important interpretation of the meaning of Jesus' death for salvation, but it is not the only or the only valid interpretation in the New Testament. There are other approaches alongside it of equal validity.

3. None of the New Testament witnesses imagines that

human salvation is automatically assured by faith in the death of Jesus. Faith is not a kind of magic. As much as anything the cross of Jesus is a pattern of life for believers, an example which summons them to imitate it. Following the crucified Lord means living without fear of risks or conflicts whose fatal character is plain. It means relying on the goal which is final freedom, perfect peace, true humanity, all-embracing love and complete joy. In this the New Testament witness on the imitation of the cross coincides with the preaching of Jesus himself.

The New Testament witness to the death of Jesus is theology, even the gospel accounts of the passion. Nevertheless it also contains historical information, and it is this that we will now consider.

The day Jesus died

The fact that Jesus of Nazareth was executed on the cross is one of the most securely established historical facts in the story of Jesus. The exact date of his death, however, can only be established approximately. The gospels all agree that Jesus died on a Friday in the Jewish Passover week, but there is a discrepancy which will probably never be cleared up between the synoptic tradition and John. According to the synoptics, the Friday on which Jesus died was the fifteenth day of the month Nisan (roughly equivalent to our April): that is, the day of Passover itself. Correspondingly the farewell meal Jesus ate with his disciples and in the course of which he instituted the Lord's supper was, according to the synoptics, a Passover meal, as Mk 14: 12–17 assumes. On the other hand, John makes the Friday of Jesus' death 14 Nisan, the day before the Passover itself (cf Jn 19: 28). This was the day the Passover lambs were killed in the Temple, and the Passover meal took place that evening. Consequently, according to John, the Last Supper was not a Passover meal, but a farewell meal with the disciples. John also has no account of the institution of the Lord's Supper, but tells the story of the washing of the feet (Jn 13). Moreover, on John's reckoning, Jesus would have died at the same time that the lambs were killed in the Temple. This follows from the connexion John makes between the death of Jesus and the regulations about the Passover lambs (Jn 19: 31-7). It is the clear intention of the fourth gospel to present Jesus as the true Passover lamb.

The day of Jesus' death is thus established as a Friday, but the date given in the tradition varies. The suggestion that the Johannine description is governed by theological arguments takes us no further because this applies equally to the synoptics. Against the argument that John was trying to present Jesus as the true Passover lamb can be brought the corresponding argument that the synoptics were interested in the Passover meal and wanted to set the Christian Lord's supper against it as the new meal of the Christian community. It is one argument against another.

A further observation is this. It is extremely improbable that the Jewish Sanhedrin would have heard a case involving the death penalty on the most solemn feast of the year. There were explicit rules against this. For this reason a considerable body of exegetes, including a scholar as critical as the pupil of Bultmann, Herbert Braun, favour the Johannine date, 14 Nisan. We also incline to this opinion. This cannot be an absolutely established finding, however, but only a hypothesis of reasonable probability. On the basis of this hypothesis astronomical calculations give the date of Jesus' death as 7 April in the year 30.

The execution of Jesus

Crucifixion was a Roman form of execution. It may go back to the Persians, and became widespread in Hellenistic and Roman times. The Romans used it chiefly for slaves and rebels, whereas a Roman citizen could not be crucified, but was beheaded. As well as being cruel, this form of execution was also particularly undignified. The Jewish historian Flavius Josephus reports a number of instances of mass crucifixion in connexion with Jewish revolts against Rome (*Antiquities* XVII, 295; XX, 129). This gives grounds for the conclusion, which is also confirmed by the gospels, that Jesus was condemned to death by a Roman court, in this case by the procurator (governor) Pontius Pilate (26–36 BC), and executed as a rebel against the authority of Rome. His rebellion consisted in claiming to be the Messiah ("the king of the Jews").

How did Jesus come to be executed? He was crucified as a rebel, but had he really committed an offence against the authority of the Roman Empire? The claim that Jesus was a political troublemaker, even the leader of a group something like the Jewish Zealots, has been frequently maintained. Even on a sympathetic view, however, it cannot be substantiated, even if one takes into account the demonstrative character of Jesus' entry into Jerusalem (Mk 11: 1–10 and parallels; Jn 12: 12–19) and the cleansing of the Temple (Mk 11: 15–19 and parallels; Jn 2: 13–17).

Nevertheless it can be said that the political, social and religious situation in Judaism at that time destroyed Jesus. There is a very important parallel to the fate of Jesus in that of John the Baptist. The evangelists of the primitive Church recognized this very early, and made explicit references to it. The Greek text of Mark 1: 14, "after John was arrested", uses the same word for "arrested" as Rom 4: 25 uses of Jesus' death (*paradidonai*), in a clear attempt to draw attention to the parallel between the fate of the two men. There are also detailed references to the arrest and execution of the Baptist (cf Mt 11: 2 = Lk 7: 18 f/Q; Mk 6: 17–29 = Mt 14: 3–12). We also hear of the belief that John the Baptist rose from the dead (Mk 6: 14–16; Mt 14: 1–2; Lk 9: 7–9), though only as a private superstition of Herod Antipas.

In this context a report in Josephus is also very illuminating. Josephus says that Herod Antipas – the sovereign of both Jesus and John as ruler of Galilee – had John the Baptist imprisoned because he was afraid that his eloquence would lead to an uprising. According to Josephus (*Antiquities* XVII, 118–19), John was, for political reasons, first brought to the fortress of Machaerus, where he was imprisoned and later executed. The movement around John was regarded by the king as a political danger, or at least potentially dangerous, although it had nothing in common with a political movement. At the time in Palestine fear of mass revolts and demonstrations was a widespread and quite plausible reason for taking action against anyone who might be suspected of any such intention, quite irrespective of whether the movement concerned was purely religious or religio-political.

The fate of John the Baptist throws some light on the fate of Jesus. There can be no doubt that Jesus, who after all had let himself be baptized by John, was very well informed about all that happened to him. Jesus needed no supernatural knowledge, but only a clear eye for realities, to work out what, at worst, might be in store for him. If his preaching resulted in anything which had even a remote resemblance to a mass movement or a demonstration, he had to regard a violent death as a possibility. The Roman authorities generally found Jewish affairs difficult to understand, and they certainly could not be relied on to make subtle distinctions between a peaceful religious movement and a violent political revolt. In their view either was a disturbance of the peace, all the more since there was no guarantee that the one might not suddenly turn into the other. The fourth evangelist is almost certainly right in his assessment of the situation when he makes the high priest Caiaphas say, at the decisive meeting of the Sanhedrin: "You know nothing at all; you do not understand that it is expedient for you that one man should die for the people, and that the whole nation should not perish," and reports the fear of armed intervention by the Romans (Jn 11: 47–50). The political situation was such that Jesus appeared as a security risk in the eyes of both the leading Jewish circles and the Roman governor.

An additional factor was that Jesus had challenged the established religious order. The leading group in contemporary Judaism did not welcome the deep disturbance Jesus' attitude must have created in the minds of traditional religious people. Jesus did not directly attack the existing order – he was in no sense an iconoclast – but his radicalism inevitably made the religious feel insecure. If we are honest, we cannot claim that our attitude to a figure like Jesus would be any better than that of the Jewish society of that time. In a sense, the conflict was inevitable. Looked at in this way, Jesus' violent death on the cross merely expresses the inner logic of his message and his attitude. Jesus appeared in the name of God as a champion of radical salvation, radical love and radical humanity in a world which constantly contradicted them. It is the fate of the "absolutely good" person, the man who loves utterly, that, even if he does not condemn others, he exposes the less good and less generous, but deeply religious, by his very existence, the fact of his being as he is and not different, and uncovers false positions and the real conflicts and alienations. In all his teachings and all his actions he constitutes a continual scandal, which either provokes a spontaneous answer of trust and love or attracts deadly aggression. Before the "scandal of the cross" comes the "scandal of Jesus of Nazareth".

The representative

Jesus' rôle as representative is referred to when John describes him as a victim of the groundless hatred of the world (Jn 15: 24–5). Since for Jesus of Nazareth teaching and action, "theory and practice", formed a unity based in his deepest convictions, his death cannot be regarded as inscrutable fate. Jesus died, not although he was a good man, but because he was a good man. Jesus chose and accepted his death, in the sense of an ulti- mate spiritual, existential freedom, because he recognized in it the will of God his Father. "Obedience to God" and his own self-respect, loyalty to himself and the mission he had accepted, were for him identical.

But did Jesus himself regard his death as "a representative expiation for many" in the sense of Is 53? First we must clarify the terms involved. What could "representative expiation" have meant for Jesus, and what can it mean for us? The con- cept of "representation" has something to say to us today. It indicates that a person in a particular position or in a particu- lar situation may act for the benefit of other men and in their place. Jesus did not merely die "for his cause" or "for his convictions" in the usual sense. This "cause" was the liberating, saving kingdom of God expressed as the power of love. Nowhere else can men's true salvation be found, only where the man who is imprisoned in himself, cut off in egoism, the "sinner", comes under the power of love and thereby becomes himself, free, truly human. In this sense Jesus' death was definitely "a representative death for the many" through Jesus' championship to the end of this liberating love of God for men. The evangelist John, here as so often, found the right words: "having loved his own who were in the world, he loved them to the end" (or, "to the uttermost", Jn 13: 1). And again, "Greater love has no man than this, that a man lay down his life for his friends" (Jn 15: 13). If we understand the "representative" quality of love as meaning being totally at the service of others, we find that the death of Jesus has a meaning for us even today – or perhaps more particularly today, in the age of world-wide solidarity. By his death Jesus made the love of God visible once and for all (cf 1 Jn 4: 7–21). Men's salvation consists in a constant effort to meet this love and to let themselves be taken over by it.

But, to repeat our original question, is it possible that Jesus could have seen himself in this way? Even if we leave on one side the evidence which reflects the primitive community's reflection on the death of Jesus (eg, Mk 10: 45 or Jn 13), there are grounds for accepting that the historical Jesus did hold such a view. We can say at least that later interpretations did not misunderstand Jesus. The explanatory words at the Last Supper, "Take; this is my body. . . . This is my blood of the covenant, which is poured out for many," in conjunction with the promise, "Truly, I say to you, I shall not drink again of the fruit of the vine until that day when I drink it new in the kingdom of God" (cf Mk 14: 22–5; Mt 26: 26–9; Lk 22: 15–20; 1 Cor 11: 23–5) may very well go back to Jesus. The problems involved in the history of the Lord's Supper tradition in the New Testament are so complex that we cannot discuss them here, but it may be noted at least that in all cases this tradition is referred to Jesus, even in Paul (1 Cor 11: 23–5). How far each detail goes back literally to Jesus is another question. In each case, however, the interpretative words clearly express Jesus'

own intention. In connexion with a meal, an interpretation of
Jesus' death is given which is at the same time an interpretation of all that Jesus was, did and hoped for. The words "body"
and "blood" do not refer separately to the elements of bread
and wine, but signify a whole, the whole person, who can no
more be divided into "body" and "blood" than into "body"
and "soul". We can now sum up the meaning of the Last
Supper. This meal indicates symbolically that Jesus' death
creates a new and permanent association between Jesus and
his friends, and at the same time establishes the "new covenant" for all. The centre is Jesus himself, given up to death,
but the disciples are also drawn into the fate of Jesus; they
have *koinonia*, "communion" with his work and fate. In the
light of these considerations it appears quite probable that
Jesus himself laid the basis for such an understanding of his
death, which was then developed by the primitive community.

Betrayal and trial

A final historical point. It looks as though Jesus was in fact
betrayed by a disciple, by Judas Iscariot. There has always
been speculation about the motives which led Judas to this
action. The "dark traitor", whom Dante put with Brutus, the
murderer of Caesar, in the lowest circle of hell, has always
exercised a sinister fascination. Judas' development into a
diabolical figure begins even in the New Testament (cf Mk
14: 10–11 and Mt 26: 14–16; 27: 3–10). Disappointment that
Jesus did not correspond with cherished messianic expectations may have played a part. Jesus' arrest must have been
organized by the dominant groups among the chief priests in
conjunction with the Sanhedrin, and carried out by officials
under the authority of the latter, a commando made up of a
not unusually large number of Temple police (cf Mk 14: 43–52
and parallels).

There was probably no formal trial before the Sanhedrin,
but a hearing to decide the charge on which Jesus should be
handed over to the Roman procurator, who at the time was
the only competent authority for capital charges (cf Mk 14:

53–65 and parallels; Jn 18: 13–24, 31–2). The Johannine account is likely to be closer to the actual events here than that of the synoptics, who have built up Jesus' "trial before the Supreme Council" into a great christological confession scene.

In order to bring Jesus before the Roman procurator, a charge was needed which would mean something to a political administrator. This was found under the label "king of the Jews". With this, Jesus was handed over to the procurator as a would-be political Messiah. It would be wrong to regard this as sheer deception or trickery on the part of the Jewish authorities. We have seen from Josephus' account that at this period very different people could make claims to be the Messiah, and in conjunction with very different practices. These included people who worked for a violent revolution, like the "robber" Barabbas who is mentioned as a rival to Jesus (Mk 15: 6–14 and parallels; Jn 18: 39–40), and harmless dreamers who drew the crowds with their talk of the miracles of the coming time of salvation. The Sanhedrin probably included Jesus in this second group. However this may be, the term "king of the Jews" is the important part of the charge in the trial before Pilate in all the accounts of the passion (cf Mk 15: 2, 9, 12, 18, 26, 32; Mt 27: 11, 29, 37, 42; Lk 23: 2, 3, 37, 38; Jn 18: 33, 37, 39; 19: 3, 12, 14, 15, 19, 21), so that there can be little room for doubt about its historicity. Jesus himself had never made such a claim, but it was not difficult, as we have seen, to see him in this rôle. The plan worked. The charge was pressed, although Pilate apparently was not prepared to accept the charge without more circumstantial evidence of revolutionary activity. Possibly pressure was put on the procurator by public opinion. The result was that Jesus was crucified by a combination of political and religious authorities as a rebel, "king of the Jews". This historical fact is one of the main factors which made Jesus of Nazareth a "Messiah". Since, as we have seen, this death cannot be regarded as mere chance, the gospel of Jesus appears from this moment in the shadow – or, better, in the light – of the cross. This more than anything else sets it apart from all those theories which go under the label "utopia" or "ideology". This fact anchors the Christian faith and the Christian hope firmly in the reality of life and its conflicts. No one who does not accept this can penetrate to the reality of Jesus' God.

II. JESUS' RESURRECTION

The death and burial of Jesus are not the last mention of the Jesus tradition in the New Testament. Rather, we hear how the disciples experienced the person of Jesus in a quite new form of life. All the gospels end with a testimony in greater or lesser detail to God's raising of the crucified Jesus from the dead. The message of the resurrection from the dead, the "faith of Easter", was clearly from the beginning part of the gospel openly proclaimed by the primitive community: Jesus of Nazareth, who was crucified, "was raised on the third day in accordance with the scriptures" (1 Cor 15: 4).

Easter Faith

The proclamation of Jesus' resurrection is not an additional, and essentially superfluous, appendage to the story of Jesus in the gospels. It is more an expression of how the primitive community, and with them the writers of the gospels, saw their relation to Jesus of Nazareth "after Easter". For them the person and work of Jesus were in no way finished by the cross; they had brought into being a new movement or development. This led to the formation of a community of salvation, the "Church", characterized by faith in Jesus as the Messiah. It led to the formulation and proclamation of a gospel in which the crucified Messiah Jesus was preached as the "Son of God" who had been raised from the dead, as "Lord" and "redeemer", as the saving act of God. It led to the mission to the nations, to liberation from the Jewish religion of law. In short, it began everything which later led to Christianity's becoming a "world religion", a faith directed to all nations.

According to the evidence of the New Testament documents, the initial event which started off all these others, above all the formation of the community and the public preaching of Jesus as the Messiah, is very closely connected with what is described by the phrase "the resurrection of Jesus". However one may interpret the Easter faith of the primitive Church, it is impossible to avoid the problem of this "initial event", as it may be called for the moment. This problem is the fact that after Good Friday there was a new start for the disciples of Jesus, a new start which requires a satisfactory explanation. There is another difficulty. Even with a relatively superficial understanding of the religious, political and social situation of the time, it is clear that the death of Jesus on the cross ought to have been an almost insuperable obstacle to any attempt at remaining faithful to the "cause of Jesus" or basing any new hopes on its power for the future. In historical terms, the chance of the continuance of the Jesus movement after the Master's death in this way was very small. The cross had been not just a private disaster, but a public and religious one as well. It was certainly impossible to pick up from where Jesus had left off.

Another point connects with this. It would perhaps not be implausible that the disciples, under the impact of the "personality of Jesus" and the liberating power of his influence, should have continued to be loyal to the message of their Master. This could have given them the courage after a little while to carry on the "work of Jesus" in their groups. But it is much more difficult to give a satisfactory explanation along these lines for the fact that Jesus of Nazareth himself, who had been crucified, now became the central content of the gospel which began to be preached. The New Testament does not say that Jesus' message was right in spite of Good Friday, but that *Good Friday itself has become the main theme of faith, through its connexion with the claim that Jesus was raised from the dead by God.*

Thirdly, on the basis of the faith of Easter, the post-Easter Jesus-community understood its relation to its master, not simply as a connexion with a founder in the past, in something like the way that Marxists of various tendencies today claim descent from their founder and teacher Karl Marx. Jesus was regarded, especially in worship, as being active in the present, in the guidance he gave through his Spirit to the communities of his disciples. It is important for us to take account in advance of these clear emphases in the New Testament writings before we approach the texts with our own questions.

Critical exegesis

But these questions must have a hearing. Since the European enlightenment of the seventeenth and eighteenth centuries the Christian belief in the resurrection of Jesus has been a permanent problem. It is noteworthy that modern exegesis has also become increasingly critical in its treatment of these problems. The problems were first clearly exposed since exegetical inquiry made the distinction between the "historical Jesus" and the "Christ of faith" or, more accurately, since the publication by Lessing in 1774 of the work by the Hamburg scholar Hermann Samuel Reimarus, *Wolfenbüttel Fragments*. Two of the "fragments" in particular are relevant to our subject, "The Story of the Resurrection" and "The Aims of Jesus and his Disciples". The first of these detected and laid bare the contradictions between the gospel accounts of Easter with a clear sightedness which immediately ended any thought of harmonization in serious theological study. "How can we ask the whole world, the whole human race in all times and all places, to base its religion, faith and hope of happiness on four such discordant witnesses?" asked Reimarus.

This "fragment" had introduced the question of the nature and meaning of the New Testament evidence for Easter. We have already looked at the question introduced by the second fragment. This concerns the fact that as soon as one takes the risk of looking critically at the gospels the key position in the gospels of the Easter faith becomes evident. The gospels are not simple historical accounts of the life of Jesus, but a description "in the light of faith" or, more exactly, from the retrospective standpoint of the Easter faith. For Mark's gospel this was established by William Wrede finally in his masterly study *Das Messiasgeheimnis in den Evangelien* (1901) so convincingly that there is no longer any disagreement about it in modern exegesis. It is now accepted that *the gospels contain the Jesus tradition in close connexion with the post-Easter witness to Christ given by the believing community of disciples*. This conclusion means, however, that the Easter faith of the first community is inextricably involved with the general outlook of the gospels. It cannot be considered in isolation. This produces a remarkable contradiction. On the one hand, the central position of the Easter faith for the first Christians is now clear, while on the other this makes it exceptionally difficult to use what they say about Easter as a means of getting at that faith.

The biggest difficulties centre upon the question of how the Easter faith came into being. In the course of historical and critical exegesis there have been many attempts to solve the problem by explaining in terms of the practical and psychological needs of the disciples, inability to accept the disaster of Good Friday, the continuing influence of the personality of Jesus, and so on. Today these explanations are expanded with linguistic and philosophical considerations relating to the concept of "resurrection" in the disciples' culture. In both cases the aim is to explain the origin of the Easter faith without assuming "supernatural intervention". What makes complete nonsense of all these attempts at explanation is that they get nowhere near what the gospels so insistently maintained. The texts say more than these explanations can admit. On the other hand, the belief in the resurrection of Jesus as a supernatural event has a characteristic weakness of its own. It can claim the support of the texts in their literal sense, and this is its strength. It largely fails, however, to answer the questions of the historians, and has to put up with the great difficulty of being very hard to give a meaning to in terms of a modern understanding of life and the world.

Emotional religious appeals for blind faith in "historical fact" and accusations of lack of faith on the part of those who feel unable to do this do nothing to get round this difficulty. It is for this reason important to see clearly the blind alleys in which both sides end up. And having seen this, what do we do? If we are not prepared to give up our attempt to understand, our first step must be to examine the content and literary form of the biblical evidence for Easter. A careful analysis of the accounts of Easter, of the history of their tradition, of the precise meaning of their statements and of their literary form is the best way of getting at the primitive Church's Easter faith. Even this preliminary examination should remove a number of wrong views and mistaken questions.

Our next step will be an attempt to get to grips with the statements of the New Testament with as little prejudice as possible. In doing this we must remember that the New Testament evidence itself presents the "risen one" as a reality about which we can talk, but which not even faith can check. One of the most important points to notice when reading the gospel accounts of Easter is that Jesus is no longer available in the same way as before his death. The risen Jesus cannot be tied down, either with historical arguments or with dogmatic theses, because his reality is no longer part of our history. This means that when dealing with the resurrection we must bear the limitations of human language particularly in mind. On this subject above all we can only speak in "images", and this means that our statements can only be approximate and never absolute. The New Testament evidence for Easter is like a set of linguistic models for the Easter faith which were invented by the primitive Church and remain pointers and norms for our own faith. But they are not themselves the reality, only pointers to it, and for that reason we must always examine their meaning afresh in relation to our own needs. This process of looking for and finding the truth of faith contained in these models is a task which never ends.

In considering the New Testament evidence for Easter modern exegesis generally starts from the premise that the epistles of Paul were written before the gospels and contain the earliest written form of the traditions of the primitive Church. On this view the credal formula in 1 Cor 15: 3–5 is the oldest evidence for Easter, and probably originated in the earliest period of the first Jerusalem community (cf 1 Cor 15:

1–2, 6–11). In their present form, the accounts of Easter in the gospels are later.

The profession of faith in 1 Cor 15

This formal summary of the faith, which consists of two (or four) parts, with its core in verses 3b–5, mentions in parallel Christ's death "for our sins in accordance with the scriptures" and his burial, then his being raised "on the third day in accordance with the scriptures" and the appearance of the risen Jesus to Cephas (Peter) and the twelve. There are two pairs of statements: the death and burial go together, and the mention of the resurrection goes with that of the appearance to Peter and the disciples. We cannot say for certain what knowledge the unknown author of this summary had of details described more fully in the gospels (the burial of Jesus, the women's visit to the tomb on the "third day", the first day of the week, the discovery of the empty tomb, and so on).

The bare, formal character of the summary has often been noticed. It gives no more than a minimum of information and merely enumerates the various events without giving details. "He was raised on the third day in accordance with the scriptures": this clearly marks off the raising of Jesus as *a new element* alongside his death and burial. The expression "he was raised" is meant to indicate a new act of God in Jesus after his death, though no description of this act is given. "On the third day" specifies a date, but there is no agreement on the date meant.

It could be the discovery of the empty tomb by the women or it could be the date of the first appearance to Peter. It could also be the period assumed in the apocalyptic writings between the final catastrophe and the dawning of final salvation. If this is the reference, the date is a way of describing the cross and resurrection of Jesus as events of the last times. A reference to Hos 6: 2, however, seems hardly likely, because this text does not appear at all in the earliest Christian proofs from Scripture. Interpreting the date in terms of apocalyptic ideas is attractive, but it may be doubted whether it is possible to bring the summary in 1 Cor 15 into a smooth harmony with the gospel accounts of Easter. There are certainly many points of contact, as in the tradition of a first appearance to Peter and an appearance to the "twelve", but not complete agreement. The primitive Church had no objection to such discrepancies and contradictions because they did not affect the core of the Easter faith.

The proof of the resurrection of Jesus is contained in the resurrection appearances. The Greek word ōphthē, "he appeared", "he made himself visible", is used in almost a technical sense. It is significant that the risen Christ is mentioned as the "subject" of the appearance. He is mentioned first, and the other people mentioned occur as the "object" (the dative in the Greek) of the action. This is the same expression as is used in the Old Testament for appearances of God, "theophanies" (cf Gen 12: 7; 17: 1; 18: 1; 26: 2; 35: 1, 9; 48: 3; Ex 3: 2, 16; 4: 1, 5; 6: 3). Some of the accounts of theophanies in the book of Genesis, such as that of God's appearance to Abraham (Gen 18), are in fact the closest parallels in form to the accounts of the Easter appearances. The credal formula in 1 Cor 15 clearly describes the appearance of the risen Christ on the model of the theophany. The typical features of a theophany are present. A man cannot make such an appearance occur by force; it happens to him. Concealment and appearance are side by side: a reality which is absolutely concealed from men and inaccessible to them makes itself accessible to them, "reveals" itself. The risen Christ reveals himself in this sort of freedom and immunity from constraint; he "makes himself visible".

We shall be careful not to describe the "seeing" involved in these appearances in any psychological detail. The summary in 1 Corinthians says nothing about this secret. Only the content of the appearances is mentioned: it is the Jesus who was crucified who appears to the disciples as one who has been raised from the dead.

Next we are given the names of the disciples to whom an appearance occurred. The order is temporal: first Cephas

(Peter), then the "twelve" (1 Cor 15: 5). The objection that there could only have been eleven since Judas was no longer alive is of course correct, and it was taken into account in the Easter accounts of the gospels. In fact, however, this old formula is referring to the fixed group of disciples formed by Jesus himself before his death. Paul goes on to mention an appearance to "more than five hundred brethren at one time", then one to James, the "brother of the Lord", and one to all the apostles. At the end he adds Christ's appearance to himself on the road to Damascus as a final appearance out of time but equal in status to the previous ones (15: 6–8). Nothing is said about where or when the appearances took place. The only thing that matters is that they took place, and Paul uses the witnesses of the resurrection as a guarantee of the truth of his preaching: "Whether then it was I or they, so we preach and so you believed" (1 Cor 15: 11). This is no irrefutable "proof" of the resurrection of Jesus as a "fact", since as a "proof" it must depend on the evidence of the witnesses. To believe in the resurrection of Jesus means to take the amazing risk of regarding Jesus Christ as a present reality. This is why it has always been emphasized that the object of the Easter faith is not the "fact of the resurrection", but the risen Christ himself and his demands in the present.

Mark's account of Easter

This is the oldest account of Easter in the gospels, and forms the conclusion of Mark's gospel in its original form. Our uneasiness about the present ending stems from a comparison with the other gospels. To all appearances Matthew and Luke knew no other, longer text of Mark, since their accounts of Easter agree only in so far as both agree with the original form of Mark, and both correct this. Apart from this, these two other gospels go their own ways and each introduces particular traditions which strongly reflect the theological interests of its author. This implies that Matthew and Luke have no common material out of which a "longer" ending of Mark could be reconstructed. This is a very strong argument for regarding Mk 16: 1–8 as the original ending of the gospel and 16: 9–20 as a later addition.

It is probably a more adequate interpretation of Mark's text to regard the section 16: 1–8, not primarily as "the story of the empty tomb", but, in the light of its central theme, as Mark's Easter gospel. The real core of the passage is the message the angel announces to the women: "Do not be amazed; you seek Jesus of Nazareth, who was crucified. He has risen, he is not here; see the place where they laid him" (16: 6). The clear intention of the passage is to use the messenger angel as a means of giving the women – and through them the reader – the news of the raising of the crucified Jesus of Nazareth, and to present it as "divine news", and not human invention.

If we look at the passage, at the purely literary level, in the light of this message which is at its heart, we see the "empty tomb" in its proper place. It is no more than an illustration of the message of Easter announced by the angel, and has no independent meaning. It is certainly not a proof of anything. On the other hand, if we try to understand Mark's story starting from the "empty tomb" we are involved in enormous difficulties. The very attempt to "anoint" the body two days after burial involves all sorts of problems. And had the women forgotten, when they set out for the tomb, that there was a stone there which would have to be removed? Why didn't they take someone with them? Finally, the stone, the heaviness of which is emphasized, was already removed – by the angel of course, or, in other words, miraculously. When one goes carefully over the individual details of the story the difficulties in the way of accepting it as a simple "historical account" only increase.

If, on the other hand, we take the whole as a presentation of the message of Easter in the form of a story, it acquires a convincing meaning, and the individual details become intelligible. Mark's gospel then ends with the Easter message handed down by the primitive Church: the crucified Jesus is risen. From this follows 16: 7: "But go, tell his disciples and Peter that he is going before you to Galilee; there you will see him, as he told you." This is a reference to the appearances of the risen Christ to Peter and the disciples, which are also placed in Galilee, a reference back to Mk 14: 28: "But after I am raised up, I will go before you to Galilee." Mark evidently knew the tradition that the Easter appearances had taken place in Galilee, and probably added 16: 7 for that reason.

Mark's Easter gospel adds nothing really new to the credal summary in 1 Cor 15: 3–5 apart from the placing of the Easter appearances in Galilee. Whether an independent tradition of the empty tomb and the women at the tomb existed alongside this common account is another matter. On the whole it seems probable, although in our present version of Mark this tradition has already been set in a larger framework. The whole of Mark's narrative is built around the Easter message, and all the individual elements are subordinated to this. Mark makes no attempt to describe the process of Jesus' resurrection, and this concentration on the message gives Mark's account particular force, as can be seen from a comparison with the alterations made by Mathew and Luke.

Matthew's account of Easter

The story of Easter in Matthew takes Mark's account further. It adds new traditions and transforms the old ones. The Marcan account is taken over as the basis in Mt 28: 1–8. To this is added the story of the guards at the tomb (Mt 27: 62–6; 28: 11–15) and the appearance of Jesus to the women (28: 9–10). There is then a description of how the disciples carry out the command of the angel and of Jesus himself (28: 10): they go to Galilee and are there granted another appearance (28: 16–20). This Easter appearance, which also forms the impressive conclusion of Matthew's gospel, is in its present form the composition of the evangelist Matthew, who uses this section to indicate once more the main purpose of his gospel.

The story of the guards at the tomb is quite clearly secondary, and has an apologetic purpose. It is meant to rebut the accusation of (presumably Jewish) opponents that the disciples had stolen the body of Jesus and spread a false report of his resurrection. This was countered with the claim that the chief priests and elders had themselves made up the story of the deception and bribed the guards to spread it (28: 11–15). The guards are also made witnesses to the descent of the angel who rolled away the stone to the accompaniment of a violent earthquake (28: 2–4). Since the guards were lying on the ground "like dead men", however, they did not receive the message of Easter. The earthquake, like the earthquake at the crucifixion of Jesus (Mt 27: 51–3), is probably meant to stress that the event belongs to the last times.

It is clear throughout the passage that Matthew has altered Mark's original text to remove its difficulties. This is why we are told how the stone was rolled away. The women receive the command to proclaim the Easter message, "He has risen from the dead" (28: 7), to the disciples. In contrast to Mark's account, in which the women leave the tomb in great fear and say nothing (Mk 16: 8), in Matthew they are filled with fear and joy (Mt 28: 8). The meeting of the women with the risen Christ (28: 9–10) becomes a typically Matthean adoration scene, and Jesus also repeats the command to the disciples to go to Galilee.

To remove difficulties is not, however, the only motive for Matthew's "improvements". As has already been said, Matthew interprets the Easter event in conjunction with his gospel as a whole, and the whole weight of the passage falls in this direction. When Jesus appears the disciples veer between worship and doubt (28: 17). The risen Christ is depicted as the exalted son of man, to whom all power in heaven and on earth is given (28: 18; cf Dan 7: 14). It is in this rôle that Jesus addresses the disciples to give them their mission and instructions. The instructions consist in the "missionary command" to make disciples of Jesus among all nations, to baptize them "in the name of the Father and of the Son and of the Holy Spirit", and to instruct them in everything Jesus commanded and taught. As is well known, the text presupposes the practice of the primitive Church with regard to baptism and the mission to the Gentiles. What had been common practice for some time, the making and baptizing of new disciples, is presented by Matthew as the command and the action of the risen Christ. The words "teaching them to observe all that I have commanded you" (28: 20a) should be taken as a specific reference to the great speeches in Matthew's gospel in which the will of Jesus is clearly expressed. The whole stands, finally, under the sign of the great promise of the risen Jesus' help: "Lo, I am with you always, to the close of the age" (28: 20b).

What does Easter mean to Matthew? The exaltation of Jesus to be the heavenly son of man to whom God has given authority over the whole universe, and his permanent presence with his disciples. This presence is demonstrated in the making of new disciples and their instruction in the teaching and practice of Jesus. The ending of Matthew shows how the evangelist wanted us to see his whole purpose in writing his gospel, as the fulfilment of the last command of the risen Christ.

Luke's account of Easter

Luke also takes Mark's account for granted in telling his own story of Easter (Lk 24: 1–11). He makes changes in the Marcan account to fit it into his own theology and expands it by adding material of his own. This includes the story of the disciples at Emmaus (24: 13–35), an appearance of the risen Christ to the eleven disciples in Jerusalem (24: 36–43), a sort of farewell speech to the disciples (24: 44–9) and finally a short account of Jesus' ascension (24: 50–3), identical in part with the beginning of the Acts of the Apostles (Acts 1: 1–11). The reports of appearances presumably come from special traditions, which occasionally show points of contact with the Easter tradition in John. The author of Luke has, however, so skilfully developed these special traditions that the whole section Lk 24: 13–53 must be described as the working out of Luke's own theology of Easter.

Luke has partly smoothed out Mark's account and partly altered it in extremely interesting ways. For example, there are two angels in the tomb (Lk 24: 4; cf Jn 20: 12) who address the women in the significant words, "Why do you seek the living among the dead? He is not here but has risen" (24: 5–6a). This sounds like a title for the whole of the Lucan Easter gospel.

Luke has omitted the command to the disciples to go to Galilee. The key word "Galilee" does however occur – which is a significant indication of the content of Luke's source. The reason for the change is Luke's wish to concentrate all the Easter appearances in Jerusalem and its neighbourhood. For his own purposes no reference to Galilee was necessary, but in 24: 6–7 there is a reference to the prophecies of the passion and resurrection made in Galilee, which have now been fulfilled.

In Luke's version the women do not see the risen Christ, but go to the disciples to tell them of their discovery. They are met with disbelief, and their story is dismissed as "an idle tale". Lk 24: 12, which is a close echo of the Johannine tradition (Jn 20: 3–10), was probably inserted in the text during its subsequent transmission.

What is perhaps the most attractive of the Easter stories, that of the two disciples on the road to Emmaus (Lk 24: 13–35) who are overtaken by a Jesus in the form of a stranger, gives us Luke's view of the disaster of Good Friday and of its transformation by the event of Easter. The stranger revives all the apparently dead hopes which had been placed in Jesus, the "prophet mighty in deed and word", first of all by a new interpretation of Scripture: " 'Was it not necessary that the Christ should suffer these things and enter into his glory?' And beginning with Moses and all the prophets, he interpreted to them in all the scriptures the things concerning himself" (24: 26–7). The story ends with a recognition scene at the "breaking of bread" (24: 30–1), after which the risen Christ immediately vanishes. The language describing the meal scene is such that the reader is forced to think of the primitive Christian Lord's supper. Luke is saying that the community meets the risen Christ in the new interpretation of Scripture and the celebration of the Lord's Supper. In 24: 34 Luke then adds the first appearance to Peter.

The appearance to the twelve (24: 36–43) shows a tendency to "reification" which can be found elsewhere in Luke (for example in the descent of the Spirit at Jesus' baptism, Lk 3: 22). The intention is that the heavy emphasis on the material quality of the risen figure should remove all room for doubt about his reality. The risen Christ is not a ghost, but has flesh and bones which can be seen and touched. To eliminate any remaining doubts, Jesus asks the disciples to give him a piece of roast fish, which he eats in their presence. The scene is not particularly convincing for modern readers, but people in the ancient world reacted differently, we must assume, or there would have been no point in Luke's adding the detail. It is also, of course, a basic human need to assure oneself of reality by sight and touch.

The farewell address (24: 44–9) repeats the themes which Luke regards as important: the fulfilment of the scriptures and their new interpretation in the light of the risen Christ, the command to preach: repentance and the forgiveness of sins are to be preached in Jesus' name to all nations. Finally there is a reminder of what is so important for Luke: "You are witnesses of all these things" (24: 48).

The gospel ends with the short account of the ascension (24: 50–3). For Luke as for Matthew, the Easter event is closely connected with the command to the disciples to be witnesses to Jesus and to bring salvation to the nations. Luke, however, shows more interest in the daily life of the Church, and he combines the topic of mission with catechetical exhortation. The community can experience the presence of the risen Christ, he says, by interpreting the scriptures with reference to Christ and in the Lord's Supper: in other words, in worship.

John's account of Easter

In comparison with the synoptic accounts, the Easter story in John is much more difficult to interpret. This may be due to the longer period of transmission involved, since the gospel of John was completed much later than the others. This gospel also has its own ways of interpreting the event of Easter. There are points of contact with Luke, notably the concentration of the Easter appearances in Jerusalem (Jn 20), though alongside this the "appendix" (Jn 21) reintroduces the traditions of the Easter appearances in Galilee. The editors who added the "appendix" made no attempt to harmonize the traditions, but simply spoke of a third appearance to the disciples (Jn 21: 14).

We will begin with a general summary. In the first section, 20: 1–18, two strands of narrative are intertwined, the discovery of the empty tomb, in this account by Mary Magdalen alone, and the related meeting between the risen Christ and Mary (20: 1, 11–18), and the race between the two disciples, Peter and "the other disciple, the one whom Jesus loved", to the empty tomb (20: 3–10). 20: 2 links the two stories. Next comes the appearance of Jesus to the disciples assembled in the room (20: 19–23) and its continuation in the story of "doubting Thomas" (20: 24–9). Jn 20: 30–1 is the original ending of the fourth gospel. The appendix falls into three sections. Jn 21: 1–14 describes an appearance to the disciples by the Sea of Tiberias, 21: 15–19 reports a special command of the risen Christ to Peter, and 21: 20–4 deals again with the relations between Peter and "the disciple whom Jesus loved". 21: 25 is the final ending, modelled on 20: 30.

In the first section (20: 1, 2, 3–10, 11–18) the oldest element of tradition seems to be the discovery of the empty tomb by Mary Magdalen, possibly already combined with an appearance of the risen Christ to Mary. In addition the Johannine tradition also clearly knew of the appearance to Peter. John retold and developed both traditions to fit his own theology. The theme of the "rivalry" between Peter and "the other disciple" comes in here. Since this theme recurs in the appendix (21: 20–4), we must assume that it relates to something which was very important to the evangelist's circle. The most likely explanation is perhaps that the sources, author(s), editors and readers of the fourth gospel regarded their particular witness, the authority behind the Johannine tradition (cf esp. Jn 21: 24), as a preferable alternative to Peter and the tradition deriving from him. The Johannine circle was unable to deny the first appearance to Peter and his position in the primitive Church, but it remained convinced that the unnamed "other disciple" was the better witness and authority, who had understood Jesus better than all the others.

In the first section Mary Magdalen goes to the tomb early on the morning of the first day of the week and finds it empty. She rushes to tell Peter and "the other disciple". The two disciples then race each other to the tomb. The beloved disciple is faster than Peter, but nevertheless lets him go in first. Peter leads the way into the tomb and sees the cloths lying there. The second disciple then goes in, and "saw and believed". It is striking that Peter's reaction is not described either positively or negatively, but it is stressed that the other disciple believed at once (20: 3–8). We have no indication that Peter also believed until 20: 9, which says that as yet "they did not know the Scripture, that he must rise from the dead". The meaning of the scene is clear; it is impossible to challenge Peter's precedence, and there is no attempt to do so, but it remains true that the "other disciple" came to the true faith at the beginning, even without the Easter appearance. The description of the meeting between Jesus and Mary Magdalen (20: 11–18) may have the subsidiary purpose of attacking the story that the gardener responsible for the ground in which the tomb stood had taken away the body of Jesus. If this is true, the evangelist has dealt with it with great skill by turning it into a case of mistaken identity (20: 15).

The story treats the meeting and the scene between Jesus and Mary at the recognition as the high point. Jesus addresses Mary by name and she replies with emotion, "Rabboni!", "Master!" The famous *Noli me tangere*, "Do not hold me," may be directed against the tendency to "reification" which we noticed in Luke. It emphasizes that the risen Christ can no longer be held in the world of material things. He has another "place", the Father, the realm of God, to which he will "ascend" (20: 17). In this account "Easter" and "ascension" coincide. The Easter story also illustrates the idea, which also comes up several times in the Johannine "farewell discourses", that Jesus' departure is no final parting, but will make it possible for him to be with his friends in a new way. From this point onwards Jesus is not "possessed" by physical contact, but only through faith, which is the basis of the new permanent relation to Jesus.

The objection, at first sight justified, that in the story of Thomas (20: 24–9) there takes place precisely what was forbidden to Mary, ie, someone touches Jesus, is not in fact valid. Thomas does not touch Jesus, but makes his confession "My Lord and my God," at the suggestion alone (20: 28). The important command is not that Thomas should touch Jesus, but "do not be faithless, but believing" (20: 27). According to this story, the risen Christ had no need to fear a physical demonstration, but "Blessed are those who have not seen and yet believe" (20: 29). The story is clearly directed at all believers after the first generation.

The resurrection appearance to the disciples (20: 19–23) paradoxically introduces a supernatural being which comes through locked doors but is yet sufficiently "material" to be capable of definite identification. The author's theological and literary technique here moves with extreme delicacy and sureness along the edge of the unimaginable and inexpressible. He succeeds amazingly in overcoming the problem of talking about something incomprehensible in such a way as to make it vividly intelligible and not just vague. The most important element in this is the recognition that the risen Christ is the crucified Jesus whose side was pierced (19: 34; 20: 27). Any question about the resurrection of Jesus must lead to a discussion of the new permanent relation to the historical, crucified Jesus. The risen Christ makes both the identity and the relation possible. He also grants peace in the form of an all-embracing Easter "salvation" in the way that only he can (cf Jn 14: 27). A part of this salvation is an enormous joy, and the change from fear to joy is an important part of the story (20: 19–20).

The risen Jesus also bestows the "Spirit" on the disciples and gives them power to forgive sins (20: 22–3). The author is not thinking here of an authority exclusive to the holders of particular "offices"; the gift of the Spirit and the power to forgive sins are, like peace and joy, gifts bestowed by the risen Christ on all believers. The Easter peace of Jesus is such that it forms the basis for new relationships among men in which the "Spirit of Jesus" can work. The "forgiveness of sins" means that peace takes effect among men as the salvation won by Easter.

The story of the appearance in Jn 20: 19–23 sums up the whole meaning of Jesus as the revealer of God and bringer of his salvation to men. The risen Christ remains present through the Spirit which he imparts to his disciples, and this Spirit both creates the inner connexion between the believers and the historical Jesus and gives the disciples the power to act independently in the name of Jesus.

As has already been mentioned, the "appendix" in Jn 21 reports an appearance of Jesus in Galilee, by the Sea of Tiberias (21: 1–14). Peter plays an important part in this story (cf Lk 5: 1–11), as also in the following one, in which he is entrusted with the task of feeding Jesus' "sheep" (21: 15–19). This is another clear indication that the tradition of the resurrection appearances in Galilee is older and more historically reliable than the tradition of the appearances in Jerusalem. In this version the first appearance of Jesus, to Peter, also took place in Galilee. This appearance to Peter first must have been the basis for the precedence Peter acquired in the primitive Church. The Johannine tradition expresses this in the appendix in its own way, again with the use of the "rivalry" theme (21: 20–4).

Belief in resurrection in Israel

We have seen that the New Testament evidence for Easter includes very different ways of talking about the resurrection of Jesus. These correspond to different purposes, as the authors fit the gospel of Easter into their own theology. This is one reason why the accounts cannot be "harmonized" and combined into a single account without doing violence to them. And yet they all testify quite clearly to one and the same event, that Jesus did not remain in death, but through God's action lives a perfected life with God, a hope for all those who still live their lives in this age of the world under the shadow of death. It is as impossible to argue this core of the Easter message away as it is to ignore the discrepancies between the different accounts.

Is this Easter gospel totally unique, or had the ground been prepared for it by the beliefs of Jesus' countrymen? It is often pointed out that belief in a resurrection of the dead at the end of the ages came into Judaism relatively late. The first sure evidence for it in scripture is Dan 12: 1–3, which many scholars think was written around 150 BC. In old Israel the belief in a resurrection was unknown. When it grew up, it was adopted at first only by groups which were open to apocalyptic ideas. In the original form there was no thought of the resurrection of an individual man, but of a general raising of the dead, or at least of all the just. The resurrection of the dead in this view is the threshold to the "new aeon" and is followed immediately by the last judgment or the beginning of the time of salvation.

This meant that it was difficult for the Jews to accept the resurrection of an individual if the general raising of the dead did not take place at the same time. Nevertheless, because what was in question was the raising of the dead, the saving of the whole person, the idea of a resurrection is closer to the idea of man held by biblical Judaism than the belief in a survival of the "soul" as envisaged in doctrines of immortality in Greek philosophy.

Naturally, Judaism always regarded the resurrection of the dead as a miraculous event dependent on a direct intervention of God. Where the dead come to life God's power is at work. It is completely inconceivable that a person could rise from the dead through his own power. "Thou art mighty for ever, O Lord: sustaining the living in loving-kindness, resurrecting the dead in abundant mercies. . . . Blessed be Thou, O Lord, who revivest the dead." So says second of the Jewish *Eighteen Benedictions*, a prayer which sums up the essentials of Israel's faith and was recited by pious Jews three times a day.

Although belief in resurrection was a relatively late development in Israel's faith, it was not purely accidental that it grew up in Israel. In fact, it has roots which go deep into the thinking of the Old Testament. We saw earlier that the primitive Christian message of the cross and resurrection of Jesus stands at the end of a long line of Old Testament texts which describe how the just man was humiliated and made to suffer, but how Yahweh intervened and saved him. More recent study has established that these "laments" and "songs of praise" are in fact always constructed according to the same pattern and constitute a distinct literary form (cf Ps 22: 69; 1 Kgs 20: 1–7; Is 38: 9–20; Jn 2: 2–11). The worshipper realizes that illness or persecution by enemies or other forces have brought him close to death. When Yahweh saves him in this situation, it is like a gift of new life.

"Bringing the dead back to life" is even more prominent in the message of a number of prophets, as a way of announcing to the people of Israel the salvation God has in store for his people. The most famous text is Ezekiel's vision of the dry bones (Ezek 37: 1–14). Similarly, the fifth "servant song", the most important of all, describes how the servant of God is humiliated to death and the grave, but God transformed his fate, rescues and exalts him (Is 52: 13–53, 12). We have already seen how important this song was to the primitive Church's efforts to understand the sufferings, death and resurrection of Jesus.

There has perhaps not always been sufficient attention to the extent to which these texts prepare for the Christian message of the resurrection of Jesus. The important point is what they say about God. In the faith of Israel it was a truism that God could rescue his faithful servant from any danger, and in fact did it when necessary. Belief in the resurrection of the dead, when it began, was only drawing the ultimate conclusion from this belief. That ideas about how the resurrection might take place differ widely is hardly surprising, and the different ways of presenting the event of Easter in the gospels are only the echo of that diversity. The different views of the risen state and that of the risen person leave us a great deal of scope.

There are, however, two New Testament texts which show
that the earliest community – and perhaps even Jesus himself
– insisted on the need for a critical distance from all conceptions as regards the essential. The first text is the account of
Jesus' argument with the Sadducees about the resurrection of
the dead (Mk 12: 18–27; Mt 22: 23–33; Lk 20: 27–40). The
other is the fifteenth chapter of 1 Corinthians, the beginning
of which we have already discussed. Both texts describe the
resurrection of the dead as a demonstration of divine power
which cannot be described in detail. The state "after" the
resurrection is simply incomparable with the way we live at
present. What does this imply for belief in the resurrection?
The only thing faith can hold on to, and what it is invited to
hold on to, is God himself. God is not the God of the dead,
but of the living. To believe in the resurrection means to trust
in the victory of the saving power of the living God even in
the face of the inevitability of death.

The God of the living

We have now assembled the most important findings of
biblical scholarship in an effort to understand what belief in
the resurrection of Jesus means and what it does not mean.

Firstly, the only mode in which we can know about the
resurrection or talk about it is faith. Reason alone will constantly come up against various ideas deriving from faith and
will always be able to argue that this message is too much for
it. It is a service to faith to admit this rather than trying to
minimize the difficulties.

Does that mean that we have to believe in the resurrection
of Jesus because it is absurd? No, what makes it an object of
faith is that in it we have to do with God. This is the real heart
of the belief in the resurrection. The believer is confident that
God has a say in death, has something to say on which the
believer can rely in meeting his death and which means that
he need not despair at the deaths of others. This alone shows
us that faith in the resurrection is not a sort of appendage to
faith in God which could equally well not be there, but an

essential part if faith is really faith in God. "You know neither the scriptures nor the power of God" (Mk 12: 24) was Jesus' answer to the doubts of the Sadducees on the same subject.

We can now take the next step, which distinguishes Christians from the believers of Israel. What does it mean when Christians acknowledge Jesus as the one who has been raised from the dead? In the first place simply that the rule that death is no obstacle for the living God applies to Jesus too. "Thou wilt not abandon my soul to Hades, nor let thy Holy One see corruption," in the words of psalm 16 as quoted by Peter in his address on the day of Pentecost (Acts 2: 27). But this is not all.

By acknowledging Jesus in this way, God also acknowledged his position in relation to God and men, as the fully accredited ambassador of God's kingdom, his representative. Anyone who acknowledges the resurrection of Jesus in faith therefore also acknowledges the beginning of God's rule in the person of Jesus, who was crucified. Anyone who does not accept it, who says firmly that Jesus remained in death, can no longer take up the claim that was connected once and for all with Jesus' history in the world, the claim that he was the representative of the living God.

Here again we see that the message of Jesus' resurrection is not an addition which we have to "grin and bear" in order to be good Christians. There is only one choice. Either we make Jesus a teacher of purely human wisdom or in acknowledging the raising of Jesus from the dead we believe in the "God of the living" whose representative he claimed to be. If the resurrection of Jesus is too much to believe, so also is the whole idea of faith in the living God. If that opens up a great possibility for men, the message of Easter does not reduce it, but makes it even stronger.

The resurrection of Jesus means, therefore, that God identified himself with Jesus and his "cause" in a way appropriate to the "God of the living". This immediately makes it clear what meaning this identification has for us. The resurrection of Jesus is not a sort of personal reward for his loyalty to his mission. By supporting Jesus' "cause", God supported what

Jesus said about God's being on the side of men. In other words, just as God acknowledged Jesus, so will he acknowledge every man. It follows from this that in the resurrection of Jesus God has revealed himself as love, and shown that love is the fundamental force which supports the whole world. It is simply this which is being said in a language which has become foreign to us when Paul develops his message of the "justification of sinners by faith alone" in relation to the cross and resurrection of Jesus: "who was put to death for our trespasses and raised for our justification"; "for our sake he made him to be sin who knew no sin, so that in him we might become the righteousness of God" (Rom 4: 25; 2 Cor 5: 21). The point each time is the same. Jesus proclaimed that God had decided to support men unconditionally, had accepted them unconditionally. When he came into the world with this message, Jesus was clearly condemned, and failed, but in raising him from the dead God acknowledged him and irrevocably confirmed that he had accepted men in unconditional love. In this way profession of faith in the resurrection sums up the faith as a whole.

The fact that by raising Jesus from the dead God made himself known as irrevocable love of men also shows that this love, because it is God's love, is directed at life. In other words, belief in Jesus' resurrection is at the same time hope in our own resurrection to a life which can no longer be threatened by any form of death. In acknowledging the raising of Jesus, faith is not acknowledging an inexplicable exception to the normal course of events, but something that gives firm hope that not death, but life, has the last word. In a very important sense, therefore, Jesus' resurrection is our resurrection. We may still want to know other things, such as the difference between the resurrection of Jesus and the general resurrection, the nature and length of the "time" between death and resurrection, and so on, but the main thing is that in the raising of Jesus our life has been guaranteed as "eternal", death-resistant. Does anything else really matter?

More of our questions have dealt with the message which Jesus' resurrection proclaims about our life than about Jesus himself. Does this mean that Jesus' own eternal life, his own resurrection, has become unimportant? Does it not matter much how we imagine his resurrection? The answer to such questions is no longer a problem. We can no more imagine the state in which Jesus now exists with God than we can imagine our own eternal life. We must not forget that the New Testament never "describes" Jesus' resurrection; that is left for the speculations of the later authors of inauthentic (apocryphal) gospels (eg, the "gospel of Peter"). And where the mode of life of the risen Christ is described one thing is always made clear: Jesus did not just "come back to life" as we know life – not even in Luke's "materialistic" account. Our contact with Jesus' life is connected with the gift of the Spirit, which transformed the disciples and made them witnesses to Jesus. What the disciples bear witness to, and what they put into practice, is the love which Jesus revealed as God's nature by his life and death.

When we believe in the resurrection of Jesus, we believe in him who is "the first fruits of those who have fallen asleep", the first practical demonstration, as it were, of God's attitude to men. The message of the resurrection is the climax and confirmation of all that Jesus proclaimed, and in himself revealed, about the nature of God. The whole of the faith stands or falls by it: "If Christ has not been raised, your faith is futile and you are still in your sins" (1 Cor 15: 17; cf 1 Cor 15: 12–19).

9   God in Jesus Christ

Jesus is the source of our faith in God and our love for our fellow men. His word, his life, his death and his resurrection open the way for us to the God from whom the world and mankind may expect meaning, redemption and a happy future. Anyone who believes in Jesus must accept this claim, or else he does not believe in Jesus.

I. JESUS – PROCLAIMED AS THE CHRIST

We have already had to remember that all our knowledge of this claim comes in documents written completely under the influence of faith in the risen Christ. We must now look more closely at the particular features of the New Testament evidence for Christ which follow from this fact.

We can bring all these features under one head: there is a difference between Jesus' own claim and his proclamation in the Church, between our historical information about Jesus and New Testament "christology". Biblical scholars have described this by talking about the distinction between the "historical Jesus" and the "kerygmatic Christ", between Jesus as he was in his earthly life and Jesus as he is preached as the Christ. ("Kerygmatic" comes from the Greek word *kērygma*, meaning "proclamation" or "preaching".)

When we say distinction we mean distinction – and not contradiction. The fact that such a distinction could arise is not surprising, but rather to be expected. As soon as people accepted Jesus' claim and finally believed in him as the Messiah raised from the dead by God, they would begin to think about him. At the centre of this process would be the question, "Who is Jesus really, and what does his work for us mean?" The enormous claims faith makes for Jesus make it impossible to suppress this question, and it even came up among Jesus' first hearers: "What sort of man is this?" (Mt 8: 27; cf Mk 1: 27; Lk 4: 36, and so on), so how could it not be asked by those who acknowledged him as Lord in the presence of the Father? The question, however, was not answered either by a simple repetition of what Jesus had said, or indeed by any single answer. Jesus had not said that much about himself. His effort had been rather to make men think through his behaviour. Any conclusions which might have been drawn from that were now completely dominated by the experience of his resurrection, which changed everything.

One fundamental reason for the absence of a single answer to the question, "Who is Jesus?" is that the first Christians, still overwhelmed by events which made language totally inadequate, were incapable of immediately producing precise, finished formulas. Also, and much more important, everyone was thinking in his own terms, with his own preconceptions and his own questions in his heart, and every preacher proclaimed Christ to the questions and preconceptions of his listeners. And in both preachers and hearers these preconceptions were rooted in social, cultural and intellectual frameworks which influenced their ideas and language – and which often resulted in discrepancies or even contradictions. For this reason we must accept that not only later theology, but the theologians of the earliest period of the Church had different aims and interests in constructing their formulas, according to their audience. Paul, for example, talks in one way to Jews and Jewish Christians and in another to Gentiles and Gentile Christians. In this way the confession of faith in one and the same Jesus developed – even in the New Testament – into a number of "christologies". In the following sections we shall study this more closely.

Gospels and epistles

If we read one of the four gospels (perhaps Mark) and immediately afterwards one of Paul's epistles (for example 1 Corinthians), we notice an important difference. In his letters Paul talks about the Christ who was crucified and raised from the dead, whom God has exalted at his right hand and given a share in his power over the universe. He talks about the Lord of the Church, which is his "body", the future judge, to whom all men must answer. He does not talk about Jesus, the man from Nazareth, his preaching and teaching, his disputes with his opponents and his wonders. Naturally Paul regards it as important that Jesus lived as a man, but what is important to him is not the details of Jesus' life, but its end in suffering and death. Paul's thought as mentioned previously, is completely centred on the man who was crucified and raised from the dead by God. This risen Jesus now reigns as "Lord" in the presence of God in heaven, and will soon appear, at the end of the age, to save believers. The other New Testament epistles, in so far as they cover the same ground as Paul's, talk about Jesus in the same way. They are concerned with Jesus' history at the end of his earthly life and after. On the other hand, the authors of the gospels quite deliberately tell the story of Jesus' life and no more. There are considerable differences in detail between their accounts, but in one respect they agree: they deal in the first place with the earthly life of Jesus. The authors of the gospels believe that anyone who wants to understand who Jesus is must look at the story of his life. We could put it like this: *The gospels answer the question, "Who is Jesus?" by pointing to the earthly Jesus, while the epistles point to the Jesus who was crucified and rose from the dead.*

How is this difference to be explained? It is tempting to suggest that the gospels reflect an earlier stage of the tradition of the faith than the epistles. Early Christianity first clung to the memory of Jesus and the story of his life. Only later did Christians begin to think about the special meaning of the end of his life, and therefore only later did they ask about the meaning of his death on the cross and his resurrection and go beyond the limits of his life on earth.

In fact, the opposite is what happened. Our four gospels all come from a later period than the epistles. The earliest epistles, those of Paul, were written between 49 and 55, whereas the oldest gospel, Mark, came into being in about the year 70. Matthew and Luke come from a later period – we know this because it can be shown that their authors knew Mark's gospel – and the fourth gospel comes from a later period still.

But that is not all. It is not just the history of their composition which tells us that our four gospels originated in a later period of the primitive Church. We can tell this also from their content. The picture the evangelists give us of Jesus is not, as we have already discovered, just the "recollections of eyewitnesses". The evangelists' experience of the faith of the communities in which they lived also comes into the picture. The evangelists portray the earthly Jesus as their faith in the risen Christ saw him – or, in biblical scholars' jargon, they portray the "pre-Easter" Jesus in the light of the "post-Easter" faith. Mark's book opens with the solemn title, "The beginning of the gospel of Jesus Christ, the son of God," and John ends his gospel with the emphatic statement that his book is written "that you may believe that Jesus is the Christ, the Son of God" (20: 31).

Both writers tell their story to preach and to arouse living faith. The Jesus they describe is not just a historical figure, but the exalted Lord and Son of God believed in by the Church in which the authors of the gospels lived and worked. Mark tries to show that even during his earthly life Jesus was already the true Son of God, but nobody recognized this, not even his closest disciples. According to Mark, this realization came only with the resurrection (cf Mk 9: 9). If we follow the fourth gospel, faith in all ages means essentially recognizing in the earthly man Jesus the Son of God who came from heaven and returned to heaven (Jn 16: 28), knowledge which Jesus did not disclose to his disciples until he said goodbye to them and which after Easter is given to the Church by the Holy Spirit (Jn 16: 14). The whole story of Jesus' life as told in the gospels is bathed in the glow of the Church's Easter confession, in the light of the faith in his resurrection.

The gospels and the life of the community

The points we have noticed so far do not on their own tell us anything either for or against an early or late date of composition. They only do this when combined with another point. This is that the authors of the gospels did not get their material from some sort of community records in Galilee or Jerusalem in which the reminiscences of eyewitnesses had been preserved. They found their material already worked up in the religious life of the primitive Christian communities and in their fixed forms of that life. There was something like an annual service to celebrate the two fundamental saving events, the crucifixion and resurrection of Jesus. One of the main features of this service was probably a reading of the story of Jesus' passion. Readings of this sort also formed the background of every celebration of the eucharist, since the account of the institution of the eucharist read at these was originally part of the passion story. Some sort of context such as this seems to be implied in the institution account we find in Paul: "The Lord Jesus on the night when he was betrayed took bread, . . ." (1 Cor 11: 23). The evangelists also took other material from the Church's doctrinal teaching, which soon acquired fixed forms. At the end of Matthew's gospel the risen Christ gives his disciples the command to preach to the nations: "Go therefore and make disciples of all nations, baptizing them in the name of the Father and of the Son and of the Holy Spirit, teaching them to observe all that I have commanded you" (Mt 28: 19–20). This text shows that the communities already possessed some sort of fixed form of words which was used in missionary sermons. This included the baptismal profession of faith and an account of the sayings and instructions of Jesus in a fixed order. The evangelists seem to have made quite frequent use of these collections of the most important doctrinal traditions, especially Matthew, who also was able to use similar work by his predecessors. The way this was done can be seen from a careful reading of the following texts: Mt 5–7 or Lk 6: 20–49 (the "sermon on the mount" and the corresponding "sermon on the plain"), Mk 10 and Lk 10 (instructions about missionary work); Mt 11 and Lk 7: 18 ff (on John the Baptist), Mk 4, Mt 13 and Lk 8 (the collections of parables), Mt 23 and Lk 11: 37–12, 1 (the warning against the scribes and Pharisees), Mk 13, Mt 24–5 and Lk 17: 20 ff; 21: 1 ff (the exhortations in view of the imminent end of the world). Other sources of the evangelists' material are the beginnings of "canon law" in the primitive Church (cf Mt 18: 15–20), the work of the first "Church schools" (cf the material used in Mk 10 and 12), devotional writing (eg, Lk 1–2) and the liturgy (cf hymns such as Lk 1: 46ff, 68 ff, 2: 29 ff).

All these expressions of the life of the primitive Church had helped to shape the image of Christ in many ways for a long time before the evangelists began to write. Naturally, when sources and traditions about Jesus were collected they were shaped by the faith of the Church which collected them. This shape then became part of the gospels which had used the collections. This is why scholars often talk of the kerygmatic character of the gospels, their original character as an aid to preaching. This has a precedent in the historical narratives of the Old Testament, which similarly set out not just to record but to preach and arouse faith. There was, indeed, in Israel no better way of arousing faith than telling the story of God's actions in his chosen people and among the nations, the story of God's actions in earthly history. In the same way the gospel accounts of the history of Jesus are not simply pursuing a biographical interest. It would be incorrect to place them under the heading "Lives of Jesus". Their purpose is rather to tell the story of Jesus as the man in whom God did his saving work among men: "This is my beloved Son; listen to him" (Mk 9: 7). This is why many stories of what Jesus did have a sort of transparency. We see an event in the life of Jesus, but at the same time we see through it the life of the Church. The story of the multiplication of the loaves in the wilderness uses in one place almost the exact words of institution used at the Last Supper (cf Mk 6: 41; 14: 22). The description of the rescue in the storm on the lake, especially in Matthew's version, becomes, almost without our noticing, a parable of the precarious position of the Church, and its saving by Christ, its guardian and Lord (cf Mt 8: 23–7; 1 Pet 3: 20–1).

Paul and Mark on Jesus

We shall take a sort of close-up view of the characteristic difference between the picture of Jesus in the epistles and that of the gospels. This will show that both take the risen Jesus as their starting point, but nevertheless talk about him in very different ways.

The Epistle to the Romans begins with a two-part statement about Christ which almost all scholars believe Paul did not himself compose for his epistle but took over complete from the liturgical tradition of the Church. It is probably a creed used in services: "Jesus Christ who was descended from David according to the flesh and designated Son of God in power according to the Spirit of holiness by his resurrection from the dead" (Rom 1: 3–4).

Two stages in the history of Jesus are here contrasted. Each describes a different position occupied by Jesus, with its own importance. By his human birth ("according to the flesh"), he was of the line of David, a member of the family from which, according to the Old Testament promise, the Messiah should come at the end of the ages (cf 2 Sam 7: 12–16; Is 11: 1–10). But by raising him from the dead and exalting him, God has placed him in a position of heavenly power as "Son of God", the position in which he now reigns by the power of the Holy Spirit. Jesus' earthly and heavenly positions are related as divine and human in general. As "Son of God" in heaven, he possesses the divine power of the Spirit; as "Son of David" on earth his attributes were merely the powerlessness, weakness and poverty of all "flesh". Paul underlines this emphasis in another part of the opening of the epistle: he was not called to be an apostle of the "Son of David", but of the "Son of God in power", the risen and exalted Lord. God's infinite power in Christ is thus behind him and his missionary work throughout the world (Rom 1: 5). For this reason also, his whole theological interest is in the exalted Son of God, and not in the Son of David.

The story of Jesus' baptism in Mark's gospel is quite different. As Jesus comes up out of the Jordan, he sees the heavens opened and the Spirit of God descending on him in the form of a dove, and hears a voice from heaven: "Thou art my beloved Son; with thee I am well pleased" (Mk 1: 11). As in Paul's creed, so here it is God himself who *proclaims* Jesus his Son. In both cases the word "Son" is used not in the sense of descent, but in something like a sociological or political sense. The point is not Jesus' lineage, but his legal position. As "Son of God", his position is like that of the viceroy of an ancient king, who had to be honoured by all subjects like the king himself.

The Pauline creed celebrates the risen and exalted Jesus in his position of heavenly power as the "Son of God". The baptism story in Mark, on the other hand, proclaims the earthly Jesus at the beginning of his work on earth as "Son of God". The creed quoted by Paul divorces the earthly stage and the "Son of David" from the heavenly, post-Easter stage of "Son of God", but Mark's gospel concentrates the dignity of the "Son of God" completely into the earthly, pre-Easter history of Jesus. The evangelist rules out any misunderstanding by repeating the proclamation of Jesus as Son of God solemnly in the centre of his gospel (Mk 9: 7), and the description of Jesus' earthly life ends with the centurion's admission, "Truly, this man was the Son of God" (Mk 15: 39). For Mark too, Jesus is the Son of David, but this is not the important thing. What is important is that he is God's Son and as such David's *Lord* (Mk 12: 35–7).

In Mark, and especially in Matthew, the title "Son of David" itself has an implication of divinity. Jesus is often appealed to by the sick as "Son of David", and the miraculous healings which he then performs are a demonstration of his divine power (cf Mk 10: 46–52). This tendency is common to all the evangelists; for them all the glory, power and saving virtue of God are concentrated in the life and work of the earthly Jesus. This also explains why we find in the gospels traces of what may be very old titles of Christ which later fell into the background but were never forgotten. Such titles as "the prophet" or "the Holy One of God" (Jn 1: 25; 6: 14; Lk 7: 39; 24: 19; Mk 1: 24; Jn 6: 69) are evidence of the effect of his preaching and the power of his actions, and they fell in with the purposes of the evangelists, who could fit them into their picture of the earthly Jesus.

Paul, on the other hand, can say flatly: "From now on . . . we regard no one from a human point of view; even though we once regarded Christ from a human point of view, we regard him thus no longer" (2 Cor 5: 16). "From a human point of view" translates "according to the flesh", which means that Christ "from a human point of view" is the "Son of David" who, according to the creed in Romans, was born "according to the flesh". Christianity, however, and the world after Easter, and the Church which is spreading among all the nations of the world, deal with the heavenly "Son of God in power according to the Spirit". Paul would never have thought of writing a gospel like Mark's. For him the gospel was the message of the man who was crucified and rose from the dead, a message which demonstrated its power in the worldwide mission to the nations (Rom 1: 16–17).

Preaching, not biography

Both the New Testament epistles and the gospels preach the resurrection of the crucified Jesus of Nazareth as God's salvation for the world. Neither set of writers is interested in a "biography" of Jesus. But in that case, why do the gospels put so much stress on the story of Jesus' life, even in a highly stylized form, while the epistles do not? The answer must be that the two sets of writers in some way have a different "assessment" of the same events, the crucifixion and resurrection of Jesus. Let us look at this more closely.

Jesus' tragic death seemed also to have killed all the hopes of his disciples. Their crucified master had been in his own person the guarantee of the truth of his preaching (cf Lk 12: 8 f). His death had made everything uncertain (Lk 24: 21). The most the disciples could hope for was that in the approaching final judgment God himself would vindicate Jesus and confirm his promise of God's presence among men. But until then Jesus' death had destroyed the unquestioning security they had enjoyed in his presence. By their decision to become his disciples they had not just "left everything" (Mk 1: 18, 20; 10: 28; Lk 14: 26 f). By believing in his message about the kingdom of God they had also left the firm ground of the traditional Jewish faith, with its ties to the Law and the Temple. Like their master, they had become heretics in their Jewish world (Mt 10: 17 f). The darkness of abandonment by God, which Jesus experienced on the cross (Mt 15: 34), had also descended on them. Coming to know him as the risen Lord was also the raising up of their own hopes. In "seeing" Jesus, who had been crucified, established in his risen glory with God in heaven, they knew that God himself had finally confirmed the truth of Jesus' claims in the time before Easter. This meant that God had also confirmed Jesus' promise that his followers would be the people of God of the last times.

Confirmed as messiah

Two sets of conclusions could be drawn from this experience. One set would emphasize that the experience of Easter had confirmed the earthly Jesus, and concentrate all its reflection on his activity in the time before Easter as a means to understanding the period after Easter and the future fulfilment. The other view regarded Jesus' resurrection as a "heavenly legal act" which established the risen Christ in divine power and honour. This view would logically require all further reflection to be centred on the heavenly position and function of Jesus in the present and the future.

The first line of thought is embodied in the picture of Christ or "christology" developed by the very first Christian community in Palestine. Just as the witnesses of the resurrection had seen Jesus in heaven, so now these first Christians built up a picture of the earthly Jesus. He had been all along the representative of God who had come down to earth, the Messiah. He had had meals with publicans and sinners and in their company celebrated the salvation of God made available to repentant sinners (Mt 11: 24). This was a vindication of the wisdom of God (Mt 11: 25).

This single basic idea could be developed in different ways. One of these comes through the complex of Old Testament references in the passion narrative as a unique view of Christ: Jesus is the just man who suffers and is saved by an act of God's power.

Another form of christology in the primitive community developed within the tradition of the sayings and speeches of Jesus. Jesus appears in this as the authoritative teacher, the only one who exists – or can exist – in the Church of God, unlike the religion of the synagogue (Mt 23: 8). What he says is divine truth because all things have been delivered to him by the Father so that no one can know the Son except the Father and no one can know the Father except the Son and anyone to whom the Son chooses to reveal him (Mt 11: 27). This unique position of Jesus as the teacher comes out especially in his brilliant victories in doctrinal discussions and disputes with the guardians of the Jewish doctrinal tradition (Mk 2: 1–3, 6). It is presented as a manifesto in the antitheses of the sermon on the mount (Mt 5: 21–48), in which Jesus counters what "was said to the men of old" with his own authoritative and confident word, "But I say to you". The picture of Jesus the teacher thus also contains an important image of Christ. This image dominates a considerable part of the material of the first three gospels, and was later given a further development by Matthew, who sees Jesus as the messianic teacher of the last times, replacing Moses and the scribes.

As a general description of the christology of the primitive community we may say that it developed in the tradition of the pre-Easter Jesus and added to this tradition touches indicating God's confirmation of Jesus by his action in raising him from the dead.

The picture of Christ was drawn differently in the missionary communities outside Palestine. Here the proclamation of the crucified Jesus became the core of the tradition, and theology was mainly a reflection in the meaning of the death and resurrection of Jesus. This can be seen from the titles applied to Christ. One of the most characteristic differences between the epistles and the gospels is the frequency of these titles in the epistles and their rarity in the gospels. First, there is "Christ". This is rare in the gospels and, where it does occur, occurs in passages deriving from a later stage in the tradition. In Paul, however, it is frequent, and indeed central. "Christ" is the Greek translation of the Jewish term "Messiah", and in Paul it refers mainly to the crucified Jesus. Paul says that in his preaching he "decided to know nothing . . . except Jesus Christ and him crucified" (1 Cor 2: 2; cf Gal 3: 1).

This narrowing-down of the title "Christ" to refer to the crucified Jesus is an indication of the deep change suffered by the Jewish term "Messiah" in its christianization. In Israel the Messiah was often imagined as a mighty and victorious military leader who would free the people from foreign domination and make Palestine the centre of the world and the centre of salvation. For the Christians in Paul's communities, in contrast, Christ was the man who, according to God's will, "died for our sins" (1 Cor 15: 3) and who "redeemed us from the curse of the law, having become a curse for us" (Gal 3: 13). In his death "God shows his love for us" (Rom 5: 8). No less for the Christians than for Israel is Christ the one who appears and acts with the full authority and power of God, but this does not mean victory in war, but victory through the love which made him sacrifice himself (Gal 2: 20; 2 Cor 5: 14). He showed his strength in being "crucified in weakness but living by the power of God" (cf 2 Cor 13: 4), and in the way that "though he was rich, yet for your sake he became poor, so that by his poverty you might become rich" (2 Cor 8: 9). The aspect of God which is revealed and set in action by the Messiah of the Christians is his grace, his righteousness which addresses itself to the unrighteous and justifies them (Rom 3: 24–6). Grace does not destroy the godless, but reconciles them with itself: "God was in Christ reconciling the world to himself" (2 Cor 5: 18). The statements about Christ make the closest possible connexion between the death of Jesus and God's love.

Christians proclaim the victory of this love by pointing to the resurrection of Christ. This is the act of power in the man crucified (Gal 1: 1) by which God made Christ's will to give himself up out of love for the salvation of all into an instrument for the salvation of many (Rom 4: 24–5; 2 Cor 5: 14). By raising Christ from the dead God at the same time destined for life all for whom Christ died and saved them from futility (1 Cor 15: 12–20).

Just as Adam, the first sinner, united all men in participation in a fate marked out for death and destruction, so Christ, the first of the righteous, united all the sons of Adam in participation in a fate predestined for those who belong to Christ, which allows them to look forward to salvation and life (1 Cor 15: 21 ff; Rom 5: 12–21). Anyone who believes in the risen Christ and is united with him by baptism no longer belongs to sin and death, but to righteousness and life (Rom 6). All those who are united with Christ in this way together form the "body of Christ", in which individuals are no longer competitors but each finds his place and function in love and service of the others (1 Cor 12: 12–27).

In the Church, the body of Christ, the saved community to be established by God in the last times appears in advance. This community is founded on love and consists in love (1 Cor 13), which means that it is to such an extent dominated by the will of God that in it, as will one day be true of the whole universe, God is "all in all" (1 Cor 15: 28, AV). Because Christians can see the love of God when they look upon the crucified and risen Christ, and because they have experienced the power of this love in their hearts through the Spirit (Rom 5: 5), their confidence in it is unlimited and stretches out, pure, undivided and unshaken, to where the future merges with eternity. "Neither death, nor life, nor angels, nor principalities, nor things present nor things to come, nor powers, nor height nor depth nor anything else in all creation, will be able to separate us from the love of God in Christ Jesus our Lord" (Rom 8: 38–9).

Paul made the new Christian title of Messiah the central concept of Christian theology by deriving its meaning from what God had done in the cross and resurrection of Jesus. He did not apply an existing title to Christ, but applied God's actions in Jesus to the title of Messiah in order to make it a title he could use. This is why all his other statements about Christ and Christians have such consistency and coherence. He produced a solid structure of ideas and images whose power has influenced the understanding of the faith and the actions of Christians in all periods of the Church's history down to our own day.

The Lord

Alongside the title "Christ", Paul uses two further titles, each of which brings out an important aspect of his picture of Christ and is also itself transformed in the process. These are "the Lord" and "Son of God".

The title "Lord" conveys two associated meanings, the unique authority of Jesus and the particularly close relationship to him enjoyed by those who recognize the "Lord" and his authority in faith. "Lord" is a title used frequently by the disciples for their master in the gospels of Matthew and Luke, interchangeably with "master" and "teacher" (Mt 7: 21; 25: 1 f, 19 ff). The Aramaic form of this title was retained in the eucharistic liturgy of the Pauline communities as an invocation of the last times, "Maranatha", "Our Lord, come!" (1 Cor 16: 22; cf Rev 22: 20). With this prayer the community gathered for the meal begged for the coming of the imminent end at which the exalted "Lord" had promised to come down from heaven and gather his own to himself (1 Thess 4: 15–17). "Lord" is therefore, in Paul's language, the personal title used to Christ in prayer (eg, 2 Cor 12: 8 ff), but it has further implications. In the baptismal ceremony the candidate replies to the proclamation of the raising of the crucified Jesus with the affirmation "Jesus is Lord" (Rom 10: 9 ff) thereby accepting Christ as the Lord of the Church whom alone he will serve in the future (Col 3: 24). In his exalted position Christ is also "Lord" of all powers in heaven and on earth, which must join in the Church's confession (Phil 2: 9–11). As in the gospels, Jesus the "Lord" is also for Paul the authority which demands the obedience of the community and each individual (Rom 12: 11; 14: 8; 1 Cor 6: 13; 7: 32, 34; Phil 2: 12).

In this connexion another point should be noted. The Greek word translated "Lord" (*kyrios*) was the invariable translation of the name of God, Yahweh, in the Greek version of the Old Testament which was the Bible of the early, Greek-speaking Church. *Kyrios* was also, in the pagan world, a title of the Roman emperor, to whom divine honours were paid. This gave the primitive Christian assertion that Jesus was the *kyrios* a political significance which began to become important as early as the end of the first century. Since Jesus, whom the Christians acknowledged as Lord, belonged with God the Lord – the "one Lord, Jesus Christ" alongside the "one God, the Father" (1 Cor 8: 6) – there could be no question for Christians of any other Lord, either another divinity or even a secular ruler (1 Cor 8: 5 f; Acts 4: 12).

The Son of God

The third title is "Son of God". We have already talked about its original meaning (Rom 1: 4; Mk 1: 11). The "Son" is God's plenipotentiary. He belongs to God and represents him to God's people and to the world. He is subject to God alone, and no one else (1 Cor 15: 28; Heb 1: 1–14; 3: 6).

The primitive Church developed this idea of Jesus as "Son of God" in two directions. In one it was applied to Jesus' activity on earth. Jesus came from God. He is the only one who knows God and wishes to give his disciples a share in that knowledge by revealing it to them (Mt 11: 27). In John's gospel especially, this idea dominates all that the evangelist says about the mission of Jesus. He came into the world from the Father to make him known to believers (Jn 1: 18; 14: 61; 17: 3), to reveal the love of God and his wish to give men life and salvation (Jn 3: 15; 5: 19 ff; 17: 2). All the Father's authority is given to the Son (Jn 5: 27; 17: 2) and, conversely, the Son does nothing but the will of the Father (Jn 4: 34; 5: 19 ff, 30; 6: 37–39). Father and Son are thus fundamentally one (Jn 10: 30; 14: 9 ff; 17: 21). This is also the meaning of the elaborate hymn with which the author of John's gospel begins his book. Jesus is the "word" which was with God in the beginning and ever since the beginning of all things has been the mediator through whom God dealt with the world – and has now become incarnate in Jesus (Jn 1: 1–18; cf Heb 1: 1–4; Col 1: 15–20).

At the same time we hear of the sending of the Son in connexion with the crucifixion: "God did not spare his own Son but gave him up for us all" (Rom 8: 32; cf 5: 8–10; Gal 2: 20). Paul sees the incarnation of the Son wholly from this point of view. God sent his Son as a man among men because this complete solidarity with sinners was necessary for God's love to be able to redeem them from sin in Christ (Gal 4: 4 ff; Rom 8: 3). The Son became poor to make us rich (2 Cor 8: 9; Phil 2: 6–8). The purpose of the sending of the Son is that believers shall have fellowship with him in the future fulfilment (1 Cor 1: 19) and also be taken up in the present into the legal status of sons of God (Rom 8: 14–17, 29; Gal 4: 4–7). The idea behind all these statements is that in Jesus' actions God's own action is at work, in Jesus' death God's love, in Jesus' resurrection God's power. In other words, calling Jesus "Son of God" is a direct expression of the mystery which was implicitly active and only indirectly recognizable in Jesus' own life. This is why the later Church rightly placed this title at the centre of the doctrine of Christ: "I believe in one Lord, Jesus Christ, the only-begotten Son of God, . . . God from God, Light from Light, true God from true God." The same can be said in the words of the epistle to the Colossians: "In him the whole fulness of deity dwells bodily" (Col 2: 9). Acknowledging Jesus as the Son of God divides those who belong to God from those who do not: "No one who denies the Son has the Father. He who confesses the Son has the Father also" (1 Jn 2: 23).

Resurrection and mission

It may be that our efforts to compare the various New Testament images of Christ gives the impression of an artificial theory rather than of a really illuminating explanation of the facts and the texts. And yet this "theory" receives important confirmation from the way in which the New Testament writers understand and interpret the appearances of the risen Christ. Here again the same difference can be seen between the "christology" of the epistles and that of the gospels.

Paul understood the appearance of Christ to him outside Damascus as a "revelation", as his commissioning by the exalted Lord to be the apostle of the nations (Gal 1: 15–16). This is also the way in which he had understood the previous appearances of the risen Lord to Peter and the twelve, to over five hundred brethren and to James and "all the apostles" (1 Cor 15: 5–11). He saw the meaning of the appearances as being nothing other than to inaugurate preaching and missionary work. Jesus appeared to these witnesses in the heavenly power conferred on him as "Son" by God in virtue of his resurrection. The old creed in Romans says this (Rom 1: 4). The oldest liturgy of the primitive Church accordingly celebrated Christ as a heavenly ruler (cf Phil 2: 6–11; Col 1: 15–

20). It expected his imminent return as the redeemer from heaven (1 Cor 15: 23–8; 1 Thess 1: 9–10). What we, as we follow the Church's year, are used to regarding as two successive events in saving history, the resurrection of Jesus and his exaltation in heaven, coincide in the thought of the primitive Church. This can be seen particularly well in the hymn in Phil 2: 5–11. We expect a reference to Jesus' resurrection, but the hymn talks instead of his exaltation (2: 9).

The appearances of the risen Christ are described differently in the gospels of Luke and John. The gospel writers, just as much as Paul, regard it as important that Jesus appointed his disciples to be his witnesses and to preach (Lk 24: 44–9; Jn 20: 21) and gave them authority to grant or refuse forgiveness of sins (Jn 20: 22–3). For the gospel writers, however, it is the appearance itself that is first in importance. They describe, as an important event, how the risen Christ proved to his doubting disciples that he was really himself, Jesus. The most important message of faith is this, that the risen Christ is, beyond all doubt, Jesus. This is why the evangelists, with different emphases in the details, describe the appearances of the risen Christ as the climax of the history of Jesus. In their view Jesus himself determines the picture which the Church is to have of him in faith throughout the ages. However dazzling the glory of the risen Lord may be (cf Mk 9: 2 ff), however infinite his divine power as Lord of Lords (Mt 28: 18), however high he is exalted as the Son of God, he nevertheless keeps for all time the human face of Jesus of Nazareth. The confession of faith, "My Lord and my God!", with which the convinced Thomas replies to the risen Christ, applies to Jesus, who was crucified, and whose pierced hands and feet he was invited to touch. Once this is beyond all doubt for the readers of John's gospel, it is also clear to them, that is, to the post-Easter Church, that they do not need to make direct bodily experience of the identity of the risen Christ a prior condition of faith, and indeed that they should not want to: "Blessed are those who have not seen and yet believe" (Jn 20: 29).

This brings us to what is far and away the most important concern of the gospels. Strongly though the Easter faith of the

Church has helped to shape the material, no less strongly does the whole theological interest of the gospels concentrate on the picture of the pre-Easter Jesus. The premiss of this approach is that the Spirit given to the Church to "guide you into all truth" (Jn 16: 13) is to "bring to . . . remembrance" all that Jesus said to his disciples (Jn 14: 26). The missionaries who are to go out to "all nations" are to teach them all that Jesus commanded his disciples (Mt 28: 20). The appearance of Jesus as Son of God in the splendour of his heavenly glory is meant to convince the disciples that ever after they must listen to the preaching and teaching of the earthly Jesus (Mk 9: 7). The main burden of the apostles' missionary preaching is the story of Jesus (Acts 10: 34–43).

II. CHRIST THE SALVATION OF THE WORLD

The post-Easter communities – the witnesses of the raising of Jesus from the dead and the many in all sorts of places who soon became believers through their testimony – made the commitment to the kingdom of God which Jesus had demanded as a commitment to Jesus. Even during Jesus' earthly work the decision for or against the kingdom of God had involved a decision for or against him, but now the two elements came together completely. The kingdom, the presence and the love of God – in other words, salvation – was now present for ever in the crucified and risen Jesus. To discuss what this means must be our next task. For the moment we must realize that this fact is the reason why the versions of the faith produced by the primitive Church, for all their adaptation to different audiences, all concentrate on the single task of presenting Jesus as the bringer of salvation sent by God. As the distance from the earthly life of Jesus grows, faith and theological reflection become concerned more and more with Jesus' rôle in salvation. This process began with the experience of Jesus' resurrection and continued, in constantly new and changing presentations for constantly new and changing audiences, for years, indeed, decades, before the production of the writings we know as the "New Testament". There are traces of the process in the New Testament, however, and from them we can work out many of the details.

Antiquarians, editors and theologians

We have seen that the writers of the New Testament were not biographers of Jesus – not even the gospel writers, and certainly not the others. But neither were they only antiquarians, tracking down the oldest reports and traditions – though they sometimes set out to do that as well (see Lk 1: 1–4). Nor were they merely editors, cleverly arranging and working up their source material. They were all these things, and at the same time original and imaginative theologians. Each of them had his own theological position, and each had his own "christology". We should be doing them an injustice if we simply used their writings as material from which to reconstruct the events of the first twenty or thirty years after Jesus' death. We would deprive ourselves of all the wealth of the many-sided preaching of Christ in the primitive Church if we refused to take just a quick look at the differences between the christologies of the various New Testament writers, at least the most important of them. We will start with the gospels, since they are most familiar to us, look briefly at some other New Testament writings, and end with Paul, with whom we started this chapter. Our consideration of Paul will connect with what we have to say in the third part of the book.

Q and the logia: Jesus the Son of Man

We know that the evangelists drew on several sources, though we don't know much about what they were like. Generally we cannot even be sure whether they were written accounts or oral traditions. In one case, however, New Testament exegesis has had a success comparable with the discovery by Old Testament scholars of the sources of the Pentateuch. In a fascinating process of investigation New Testament scholars discovered a book which we no longer possess in its original, separate form but which both Matthew and Luke worked into their gospels. The main contents of this work can be reconstructed by comparing the tradition common to Matthew and Luke and taking away what both have in common with Mark's gospel, which was also one of their sources. This operation reveals the outline of a book which must have included mainly speeches and sayings of Jesus. It is often called the "logia" source ("logia" is a technical term for "sayings"), or simply "Q", from the German word *Quelle*, "source".

As well as being the basis of probable theories about the mutual relations and dependencies in the literary form of the first three gospels – details of which can be found in any introduction to the New Testament – "Q" also introduces us to one of the oldest christologies, which was already less prominent when Paul wrote and had fallen completely into the background by the time of the evangelists. This is why we devote a separate section to "Q" here. This christology interprets Christ as the Son of man. We have already seen how far this title goes back to Jesus. It is uncertain whether Jesus identified himself with the Son of man, but the post-Easter community did so completely, as can be seen particularly well in "Q". In many of the "Son of man" sayings which the gospels take over from "Q", the title has already become a formula which can be quite easily replaced by "I" (that is, Jesus; cf Mt 10: 32 f and Lk 12: 8 f).

How can the title "Son of man" be the basis of a distinct christology? We know that the title is connected with Dan 7: 13 ff, and this indicates that the tradition which produced "Q" proclaimed the imminent coming of a heavenly Son of man as the fulfilment of Jewish expectations for the last times. But, they said, this Son of man is Jesus. The one who "is to come" (cf Mt 3: 11; 11: 3) has now come. The attitude people adopt to the earthly Jesus and his preaching will determine the decision of the Son of man when he comes for the last judgment. In other words, the emphasis of this christology is on the rôle of Christ at the end of time. The community which held this view of Jesus also regarded itself as the people of the last times, and the post-Easter period in which it lived as a time of waiting leading rapidly to the return of Christ. This explains

why the title "Son of man" never became part of a formal
primitive creed. The creeds centre on Jesus' death and resurrection. As time went on and the Church grew, the death and
resurrection of Jesus rather than the return of Christ came to
seem the crucial saving events. The evangelists took over
the "Son of man" texts from "Q", but by this time they no
longer had the power to form the basis of a distinctive
christology and were worked into the new christologies of the
evangelists.

Mark: Jesus the hidden Son of God

Mark makes Jesus' secret an explicit topic when Jesus himself
asks, "Who do men say that I am?" In the gospel this question
is directly contrasted with that to the disciples, "But who do
you say that I am?" Peter's answer is short and sharp, "You
are the Christ" (Mk 8: 27–9). The meaning, however, is not
quite so clear. When Mark wrote this passage his thoughts
were on the way this "Christ", Jesus, ended – on the cross.
This was Mark's main problem in his attempt to describe
Christ, and he devoted the whole of his gospel to solving it.
How he did it can be seen in the continuation of the text just
quoted. Peter's declaration is followed by the announcement
by Jesus of the passion, and by his sharp rebuke to Peter when
he tries to divert him from the path of suffering (8: 31–3).
Jesus' status as "Christ", Mark is saying, can only be understood when we realize and accept that he must follow the path
pre-ordained by God, which leads into suffering. This is his
mission as "Son of man" (8: 31; 9: 31; 10: 33 ff; 14: 21), and by
doing this he is already passing judgment on the world (14:
62).

This context gives the threefold proclamation of Jesus as
Son of God, which has already been mentioned, its particular
undertone in Mark's gospel. Scripture here reveals to believers
what otherwise remained hidden under Jesus' provocative
actions as a man among men until the day of his death. It is
not surprising that his divine dignity should not be recognized.
According to Mark, even his acts of power do not break the

concealment which surrounds his dignity. He helps and heals, but this doesn't make his suffering unnecessary; in fact, these same acts of power may in some cases lead their beneficiaries to follow his path of suffering, as is shown in the case of the cured blind man (10: 52). And at the end it is the crucified Jesus in his final self-surrender whom the pagan centurion acknowledges as the Son of God.

Mark's approach here to an understanding of Christ's status as Son of God is not his alone; it can be found again and again in the New Testament in various forms, and occurs in Paul. These writers must have felt that there was no better way of distinguishing acknowledgment of Jesus' divine status from the gods who became men in the pagan myths or from the divine honours paid to certain men. It meant that there was no longer any danger when, for example, it was said of Apollonius of Tyana that he aroused great wonder by his miracles. There was no rivalry, because Jesus' acts of power were not a demonstration of his personal divine power, but signs of God's love for men, which was fully revealed in Jesus' sacrifice of his life.

Matthew: Jesus, God's true messiah

The evangelist Matthew writes in the first place for the Jews, for those familiar with the Old Testament. For this reason he portrays Jesus as the Messiah promised by God; in his view, his readers can recognize this from the scriptures if they read them properly. It is no accident that when the news of Jesus' birth comes the high priests and scribes quote a prophetic text (Mic 5: 2, 4; see Mt 2: 4 ff). They, however, cannot connect it with Jesus, and this is what the evangelist does with complete consistency. He places the story of Jesus and the Old Testament texts side by side and understands the one as the fulfilment of the other. He applies to Jesus the saying of the prophet Hosea about Israel: "Out of Egypt have I called my son" (Mt 2: 15 = Hos 11: 1). Such "fulfilment claims" – often introduced by the words "this was to fulfil" – are a frequent feature of Matthew's gospel. We must not take them in the sense of a *proof* from Scripture – that would be introducing a modern idea into the Gospel. What the evangelist is trying to do is to understand Jesus as the Messiah in the light of the Old Testament; in other words, in the sayings of the prophets he is looking for testimony to Jesus from God himself. If Israel asks – or, as in the story of the wise men from the East, if Israel is asked – about its Messiah, the evangelist is saying that it must look to God for the answer: Jesus is the one true Messiah, whom Israel must acknowledge. He is the Messiah of God, and as such also the Messiah of Israel.

In line with this Matthew makes Jesus declare that he has been sent first "to the lost sheep of the house of Israel" (15: 24). But at the end of his journey on earth it becomes clear that it is the Israel of God which he has come to gather and lead, the Israel which allows itself to be led by him in the way of *God's* law, the superior righteousness (5: 20) which God wants. In Jesus' actions, culminating in his death on the cross, God's saving will is fulfilled, and he is therefore, even beyond death, as the Messiah of God, the teacher whom his people must follow. Again, it is no accident that it is Matthew who makes the picture of Jesus as the authoritative teacher such an important feature of his gospel.

Luke: Jesus the messiah of the poor

The author of the third gospel also sees Jesus as the Messiah sent to Israel, but, differing slightly from Matthew, he makes Jesus reveal himself to Israel as the Messiah of the poor. Luke's intention can be seen clearly from Jesus' sermon in Nazareth (4: 14–30), which acts as a title for the whole Gospel. Jesus quotes Is 61: 1 ff as a prophetic confirmation of his messianic status. The Isaiah text refers, however, to a message for the "poor", the "blind" and the "oppressed", and Israel cannot understand it. But only those who realize that they are poor, blind, oppressed and need healing can accept Jesus as their saviour. It is as "saviour" that Jesus is revealed to the poor and despised shepherds in the nativity story (2: 11). It is as saviour that he performs his mission to "the lost" (19: 10; cf the parables in ch. 15). Jesus' sermon in Nazareth makes clear that Israel has missed its opportunity of turning to its saviour. Its place will be taken by the Gentiles, when they learn to see themselves as "poor" and "lost".

What Luke only hints at in his gospel he makes explicit in its sequel, the Acts of the Apostles. Here again the gospel is offered first to Israel, but it is the Gentiles who gratefully accept it. Paul's missionary sermon in Pisidian Antioch reveals the author's intention clearly. Out of David's posterity "God has brought to Israel a saviour, Jesus, as he promised" (Acts 13: 23; cf 5: 31). In the preaching of the Church Jesus is revealed as the saviour, since "forgiveness of sins" comes through him and no one else (13: 38). At first the Jews show interest in this message, but their "jealousy" of the Gentiles represses it. At this, Paul and Barnabas, basing themselves on Is 49: 6, turn to the Gentiles, who "were glad and glorified the word of God" (13: 45–8). In this way, the turning to the Gentiles brings out the full meaning of Jesus' rôle as Messiah of the poor and, in this sense, as the salvation of the world.

John: Jesus the word of the Father

No less then his predecessors, the author of the fourth gospel is familiar with the traditional titles of Jesus. He uses them freely, but as a way of setting out his own christology. In this Jesus is the "Son of man", but John deliberately brings the associated rôle of judge at the last judgment forward into the present. It is now that the judgment, the decision on life or death, is being made, according to whether the word of Jesus is or is not heard and accepted in faith (Jn 5: 25–30). Jesus is the "Son of God". Right at the beginning the Baptist testifies to this (1: 34), and it is the disciples' task to bear witness in the same way "that Jesus is the Christ, the Son of God" (20: 31), who promises life to those who believe. In John, though, the title is not connected so closely as by the earlier writers with Jesus' resurrection. The earthly Jesus was – from the first – the Son of God; this sums up his creed. Appropriately, the fourth gospel makes the Jews' gravest charge against Jesus that "he has made himself the Son of God" (19: 7). John introduces new titles for Jesus into his gospel alongside the old ones. Jesus is "the Word" (the Logos, 1: 1, 14), the "only Son" or "only begotten" (1: 14, 18) and the "Lamb of God" (1: 29, 36). The evangelist also regards Jesus' many descriptions of himself beginning "I am" as an expression of his unique position: "I am the bread of life" (6: 35), "I am the light of the world" (8: 12), and many more.

The mystery of the person of Jesus is described in the fourth gospel in a great variety of ways. The evangelist obviously feels that this is the only way he can adequately express Jesus' being and the salvation he brings. *Jesus is what he brings.* That is why he is the Word made flesh, not only in the union of his divinity and his humanity, but above all in sharing the life of men: "and dwelt amongst us" (1: 14). In this human existence he reveals God, the Father, and thereby shows himself to be the life-giving "word" of God. In this period men hear the word of Jesus, and by believing in him who sent Jesus, win eternal life (5: 24). Everything depends on believing in the word of Jesus and keeping it (5: 38; 8: 31, 51 f, 55; 14: 24; 17: 6, 14, 17). The constant reference to "the Father who sent me" sums up the christology of John's gospel. John, as it were, shifts back sayings of the older gospels about Jesus' "coming", for example, Mk 2: 17: "I came not to call the righteous, but sinners." His aim is to reveal the basis of Jesus' messianic activity. What Jesus does is completely determined by his relation to his Father, and so in his actions he becomes the image of the Father.

It is only through the idea of the sending of the Son by the Father that we can see all that John means by describing Jesus as the "Son of God", or simply "the Son" (3: 17, 35 ff; 5: 19–26, and passim). Since the activity of Jesus is concerned with God, and nothing but God, John describes his life as a coming from God and going to God. Because the origin and end of Jesus' life on earth are directly connected with God, Jesus himself becomes in his actions the expression of the love of God and so, for men, the way to the Father. Where Jesus is going the disciples are to follow (14: 3; 17: 24). The "exaltation" and "glorification" of Jesus already throw their light on this way and on its end.

The Johannine epistles – "Jesus has come in the flesh"

We cannot examine the christology of all the other New Testament writings before coming back to Paul. We shall, however, look at one or two more which are of particular interest.

It is not clear whether the Johannine letters were written by the author of the fourth gospel, but they certainly come from the same intellectual environment and their thought is a sort of testing out of John's theology.

All three epistles of John, but especially the first, set out to defend and safeguard the faith in Christ against false teachers. "This is the antichrist, he who denies the Father and the Son" (1 Jn 2: 22): the closeness to the christology of the fourth gospel is obvious from such a sentence. The way to keep off the "antichrists" is to hold fast to the traditional faith in Christ. The "antichrists" have both an inadequate creed and an inadequate practice of love. Who they were can be seen from 1 Jn 4: 2 (cf 2 Jn 7): only the person who "confesses that Jesus Christ has come in the flesh" is "of God". The false teachers being attacked are evidently adherents of the "Knowledge" (gnosis), which regarded the historical, earthly Jesus and his redemptive life and death (cf 1 Jn 5: 6) as unimportant. As a result, they did not understand that Jesus' sacrifice of his life was a binding example for Christians in their lives (1 Jn 3: 16). It is therefore not accidental that the first letter of John stresses so much that true faith in Christ is shown not just by adhering to correct doctrinal statements, but also by perseverance in brotherly love. In the tradition of the faith in Christ this is a new note – and yet it is ultimately the single central message of the life and preaching of Jesus himself.

The Epistle to the Hebrews: Jesus the great high priest

The unknown author of the epistle to the Hebrews is writing to check the drift from the faith which is threatening the

Church in his period, the end of the first century. To do this he adopts a new interpretation of the faith in Christ handed down by tradition. Jesus Christ is the Son of God; this is the basis for everything else. Right at the beginning of the epistle Jesus is introduced as the "Son" through whom God has spoken "in these last days" – that is, finally and definitively – and whom he seated at his right hand at the end of his earthly work (1: 2 ff; cf 8: 1; 10: 12; 12: 2). The epistle shares the primitive Christian expectation of the return of Christ. And yet the old phrases and ideas appear in a new light. Even when the imminent "Day" and the "little time" are mentioned (10: 25, 37), what is important is not the immediacy itself, but the "confidence to enter the sanctuary" (10: 19) and the knowledge that the "unseen" world of heavenly things is near.

What is this "unseen" world of heavenly things? The idea of two worlds which derived from Plato's philosophy may have had an influence, but the real contrast is not with the visible material world in general, but with the world of Old Testament worship. It is from this worship that the writer takes the images with which he describes the realities of the heavenly world, while at the same time showing how it transcends the Old Testament system and makes it no more than a shadow of the heavenly one.

It is this approach which makes it possible for the author of Hebrews – who may have been writing for Hellenistically educated ex-Jews from the diaspora – to connect the title "Son of God" completely with the cross and resurrection and at the same time link it to the heart of Jewish religion, the Temple worship. He presents Jesus as the "great high priest", the "high priest of the good things to come" (4: 14; 9: 11). He exercises his office at the right hand of God and permanently intercedes for us, since heavenly intercession for his followers is the main task of this high priest (7: 25). Through his sacrifice of himself on the cross he has entered once for all into the heavenly sanctuary. His death was a sacrifice which superseded all earthly sacrifices and priesthoods. Through his entry into the heavenly sanctuary he has opened to us the world of invisible things, the world of God's salvation. He is our "sure and steadfast anchor of the soul", fixed firmly in the world of God, "behind the curtain" (6: 19). He has gone before us as "the pioneer and perfecter of our faith" (12: 2; cf 2: 10). The patience with which he endured his sufferings (cf 5: 7–10) has made him a bridge between this temporary and transitory world and the heavenly and permanent world, and has given us a "new and living way" to God (10: 20).

In this we can recognize once more the idea of following Jesus, though it has been modified here by the use of ideas from the Old Testament and Greek culture. Jesus' mediatorship makes it possible to enter the presence of God, and believers may draw near "with confidence" (4: 16; 10: 22), but at the same time there is a break, because the heavenly order is so far above the earthly one. The author of the epistle knows that this can tempt Christians to resignation, and it is those so tempted whom he tries to help with his constant appeal for "confidence". The epistle to the Hebrews could be called a "pastoral adaptation" of christology, christology turned into exhortation.

The Revelation to John: Jesus God's champion

The last book of the New Testament talks about a coming of God and of "his Christ" (Rev 11: 15) which "must soon take place" (1: 1; 22: 6, 12). Apocalyptic and symbolic imagery gives "the revelation of Jesus Christ, which God gave him to show to his servants" (1: 1), a character of its own. The mysterious hints and concealed references to the situation of the Christian community in a world hostile to God can fascinate the reader to such an extent that he can see in them only his own religious and personal problems and perhaps miss the core of the book's message. We may be warned by the history of the interpretation of this book and the interest it has held in all ages for popular preachers and the leaders of sects.

In the midst of all the goings-on in the foreground and background, the author's interest is fixed on God and his Christ. God's rule over the world has been established and is consolidating itself in the face of all opposition from the world.

Jesus Christ has come in the last times to inaugurate and maintain it, and it is in this rôle that he shares in God's rule: "The kingdom of the world has become the kingdom of our Lord and of his Christ, and he shall reign for ever and ever" (11: 15; cf 12: 10). The victorious rule of God will soon be made manifest on the earth. The discrepancy between the harshness of this language and the message of the love of God preached by Jesus is only apparent. This rule means final liberation from the satanic forces which still control the world for a little longer. Their power on earth has already been broken by the work of Jesus, and Christians have only to endure the last desperate struggle of Antichrist. After that they will share in God's liberating victory.

The style of Revelation is strongly "theocratic". Its subject is the rule of the eternal God, and it asserts his absolute majesty against all attacks by the anti-God. The author sees Jesus less in his relation to God than in his saving rôle for the Church and the world. He is "the faithful witness, the first-born of the dead, and the ruler of kings on earth". He showed his loyalty to God and his love for us to the death, by freeing us "from our sins by his blood" (1: 5). Terms from the ritual of expiation and kingly titles therefore both apply to him. He is "the Lamb that was slain" (13: 8; cf 5: 6), "the Lion of the tribe of Judah, the Root of David" (5: 5). The idea of the "Son of man" who comes as judge also recurs (1: 12–16; 14: 14).

All these phrases are, however, used with reference to Jesus' rôle at the end of time. It is as though when the author thinks about Jesus' preaching of the kingdom of God, about his earthly work and especially about his acceptance of death, he sees them together with their fulfilment. His message is that this fulfilment can be kept alive and made a reality by patient and yet active endurance of the persecution which his readers have to suffer.

Paul: Jesus the new Adam

Now from the end of the first century we come back to Paul. His christology is the only one which is available to us directly, without having to be reconstructed. We have it in his own letters. Paul's sermons in Acts, like Peter's, show traces of the theological work of the author, Luke, but in the epistles Paul speaks directly.

We saw before that Paul's concentration on the cross and resurrection of Jesus gave the title Christ and all the other traditional titles and descriptions of Jesus a new content. We must now come back to this, but from a point of view without which Paul's christology would be a mere torso. This aspect has so far only been hinted at. It is the connexion with sin. Today the word "sin" is almost meaningless. Later we shall have to consider why and to what extent it is a word the Christian faith cannot do without. Here we will look at its meaning as used by Paul in connexion with his christology. No one, in fact, has emphasized as much as Paul the place of sin in the Christian faith.

The all-important meaning of Jesus Christ's action only becomes clear to Paul against the background of the history of men without salvation. Believers are linked with Christ for ever, and so removed from this absence of salvation. The history of the absence of salvation is the history of human sin. Since Adam, the first man, sin has "ruled over" mankind. Rom 1: 18–3: 20 gives many depressing illustrations of how sin exercised this rule over Jews and Gentiles alike. It pressed mankind into a sort of slave colony, with Adam as representative for all. Not that individuals can shake their blame off on to Adam. Adam was guilty, but every man since Adam constantly reimplicates himself in the fate which began with Adam.

Only God can release men from this imprisonment in guilt. When he does it it is a gift of new life, but also, and first, a condemnation of sin. But this judgment, which reveals the righteousness of God, ends in acquittal for those who turn to God in faith (Rom 3: 21–6). This acquittal is eschatological: that is, it anticipates the final judgment at the end of time. The believer has his life here and now through and with Christ.

From this starting-point Paul develops a unique view of

Christ as the new Adam. On the one hand is the old Adam with his disobedience, who dragged all mankind into his sin. On the other is the new Adam with his obedience, which benefits all who believe in him. This contrast dominates the fifth chapter of the epistle to the Romans, and fascinates Paul so much that in his eagerness he leaves sentences unfinished and keeps on starting again. "Therefore as sin came into the world through one man," begins 5: 12 – but the parallel does not come until after an excursus (see esp. 5: 13–14), in 5: 18: "then as one man's trespass led to condemnation for all men, so one man's act of righteousness leads to acquittal and life for all men". Jesus is revealed as the new Adam by his act of obedience, in his carrying out of God's will to death, or, in other terms, by his assertion of God's rights over his creation.

In this interpretation of Christ's saving act the last times and the present coincide. Jesus is not the "new" Adam in the sense of a new start guaranteed by God so that the history of the first Adam could now repeat itself with a better prospect. No, he is the man of the last times, the ultimate in man, man as he has never existed before, not just the opposite of the first man but immeasurably superior. As such, Jesus is the head of the new mankind, head of the new believing people of God called by God and redeemed by Christ. He is deliberately not called "father of his people". God is to be the Father, and re-birth by faith and baptism is to be clearly distinguished from natural birth.

The idea of the "new Adam" rightly reminds us of the first chapters of the Old Testament. But Paul, as 1 Cor 15: 22, 45–9 shows even more clearly than Rom 5, is also making use of the idea of "corporate personality". This is an idea used frequently in ancient religions to express the connexion existing between the fates of all men. It can be found in the gnostic myth of the first man: in this redeemer and redeemed form a unity of destiny, which is worked out in the "self-redemption" of the individual soul. Paul's use of this myth or an earlier form of it shows, however, how freely he treats it. He does not sacrifice the gospel to the myth, but the myth to the gospel. The myth will do to describe all men's need of redemption, but the process of redemption does not take place through assimilation to an idea or a higher knowledge, but through Jesus' unique historical act of obedience on the cross. Life and hope for resurrection at the end of time depend entirely on the fact that God raised the crucified Jesus from the dead and made him "the first fruits of those who have fallen asleep" (1 Cor 15: 20).

Only now can we see how other statements of Paul's, which might otherwise look like scattered borrowings from tradition, fit into a system. We have already seen how the cross and resurrection give a new content to the title "Christ". The same applies to another title taken over by Paul from the primitive Church, "Son of God". In Rom 1: 3 ff Paul takes up and stresses Jesus' status as Son of God by virtue of his resurrection from the dead, but he makes the title refer specifically to Jesus' action in freeing men enslaved by sin and death (Rom 8: 2 ff), which enables them to become "sons of God" by imitating him (Gal 4: 4 ff). The meaning of "Son of God" is made clear by the saving purpose and action of God. The same ideas appear again in Rom 8: 29: believers are called by God "to be conformed to the image of his Son, in order that he might be the first-born among many brethren". Gal 1: 18 calls him "the first-born from the dead", and he is also "the first-born of all creation" and "the head of the body, the Church" (Col 1: 15, 18a). These statements interpret each other and agree in the fundamental idea that through his obedience and the sacrifice of his life Jesus is the new Adam, the true man.

The texts which mention the "pre-existence" of Jesus are particularly difficult for modern readers to understand, and must be explained in a similar way. First, the texts just mentioned, Rom 8: 2 ff and Gal 4: 4 ff, show that heavenly existence with God was regarded as the basis of Jesus' sending, as showing that God himself was acting to save men. Two other texts which have already been mentioned in different contexts are of particular importance here, the hymns in Phil 2: 6–11 and Col 1: 15–20. Both, and especially the second, mention a godlike pre-existence of Jesus before his earthly existence. Here again mythological ideas of the period have helped to shape the texts. Paul, however, or the author of the hymns Paul is quoting, has broken into the myth at a crucial point. The hymns do not describe some cosmic process unfolding according to an eternal law, but the obedience of Jesus, who made peace and reconciliation "by the blood of his cross". The reference to pre-historical existence is not intended to start speculation, but as a way of expressing Jesus' universal rôle in the first creation and the new creation. The salvation planned by God and brought about by Christ has, it is saying, left traces in creation since the beginning and will embrace the whole reality of the world. Later this reference to pre-existence on its own, without reference to the context, was to be the starting point for far-reaching christological reflection.

Justification by faith

For Paul it follows from the unique rôle of Jesus' death and resurrection in salvation that the salvation of men must depend on faith in Christ and not on any sort of works of law, if these are understood as necessary to salvation. In the sight of God "a man is not justified by works of the law, but through faith in Jesus Christ" (Gal 2: 16). A little later Paul solemnly gives the reason: "if justification were through the law, then Christ died to no purpose" (Gal 2: 21). This "doctrine of justification" is another "applied christology", in this form associated with the name of Paul. The events of the sixteenth-century Reformation have ensured it for ever a prominent place in the history of Christianity.

Why was this "application" of christology developed? First, to provide a clear explanation of how what took place in Christ took place "for us" and benefits us. The process can be seen – once more – in the beginning of Romans. Paul begins in 1: 3 ff by describing the content of the gospel in traditional credal formulas. Then he interprets these formulations in 1: 16 ff with a summary of the doctrine of justification, which goes on from there to be the subject of the whole letter. In addition, this "application" of christology had a historical origin. Paul was drawn into disputes in which doubts were cast on the sufficiency of Christ's work to bring salvation. Paul's opponents spread doctrines in Paul's own communities which led to a dangerous "and": salvation through Christ *and* through works of the law, which still remained binding on Christians. Apart from the need to take account of the consciences of the weaker brethren – of which Paul showed himself fully aware (1 Cor 8; Rom 14) – there could be no compromise on this. To impose additional conditions for salvation would be a betrayal of what God has done freely and unconditionally. If God has forgiven sins in Christ, then they are forgiven and man is a new creation, and has no need to remake himself by his own works. The slogan "faith alone", on which the Reformers laid so much stress, was also Paul's, and it also agrees with the message of Jesus. Paul's preaching of "justification by faith alone" must count as a binding interpretation of the gospel. This is why, in 1 Cor 1: 18 ff, Paul talks about the justification of man by grace alone without using words and ideas from the Jewish tradition – a clear indication that what is important is not to set out a doctrine of justification in particular words and ideas, but to continually reformulate the basic meaning in one's own words. Justification is a new relation to God in which man is placed without any merit of his own and in which sin is no obstacle to God's love, but is forgiven. This is exactly what Jesus preached under the name "kingdom of God", what he went to his death for – and what God identified himself with by raising him from the dead. One sometimes comes across the view that Paul, and not Jesus, was the founder of the Christian religion and was as such a long way from Jesus' intentions. Anyone who believes that has understood neither Paul's teaching nor what Jesus preached.

God in Jesus Christ

We have now seen something of the way in which the authors of the New Testament worked and produced their various pictures of Christ. We may now want to ask which of them was right.

It is a natural question, and yet our first step must be to

realize that it doesn't mean very much. It makes no sense to
ask which of the New Testament "christologies" is right. It is
certainly possible to ask which form of the preaching of Christ
is most closely connected with the original preaching of Jesus
and which, on the other hand, is newer and more independent.
We have seen what can be said about Jesus' claims, and we
have also given an example of the way in which the attitude
of the evangelists working in the light of their faith influenced
their presentation of the words and actions of Jesus. But even
if in these matters we reached irrefutable results, they might
be of interest to the historian, but they would not necessarily
be helpful, and certainly not crucial, to faith. The point is not
which are the more or less well founded, more or less "true"
and therefore more or less important interpretations. We do
not even need to bother much about whether and how far they
complement each other and combine to produce a single creed.
That only took place to a certain extent, and indeed was only
possible to a limited degree in view of the diversity of situations in which the various interpretations were developed. In
its own terms, each of the New Testament christologies expressed the whole of the Christian faith, with particular
reference to a quite specific audience which had its own questions and its own presuppositions, both of which were different
from those of other audiences. Each of the New Testament
christologies is a breakthrough by faith into a new and different situation (intellectual, religious, cultural, even political)
which forced faith in God's presence in the risen Jesus to keep
on giving a new "account of the hope" that is in Christians
(1 Pet 3: 15). No historical comparison with the words of Jesus
is available to check these accounts; we cannot even show
that they express the same ideas in a different language. All
we can rely on is faith that the Spirit of God guided these
breakthroughs and prompted their authors (Jn 16: 23), and that
the exalted Christ was with them (Mt 28: 20). The answer to
our original question, "Who was right?", might run something
like this: The different pictures of Christ in the New Testament are an expression for different groups of people (but in
every case believers) of the truth about the person and work

of Jesus, and this means that they work out the implications of belief in the presence of God in the risen Jesus Christ.

10   God, Son, Spirit

The last chapter has shown that the New Testament's answer to the question "Who is Jesus?" is that he is the man in whom God himself and his love have come unbelievably close to men. It is for this reason that we can only realize the full meaning of the person of Jesus when we consider the special, unique relation between him and God which made him the mediator of God's presence to men. All the titles the New Testament gives the exalted and even the earthly Jesus are expressions of this twofold relation, to God and to men.

If it were left to us, we might stop there. Or perhaps we might consider the further history of the message of Jesus, and in particular the question how we can continue to accept the testimony of the apostles, but express it in such a way that we can understand it and judge its importance today. But if we are prepared to hear the whole of the New Testament message we cannot stop without considering another element, one we hear about both from the mouth of Jesus and in the New Testament writers. This is the "Spirit", the "Pneuma".

Having talked about God and Jesus Christ, why does the New Testament feel obliged to bring in the Spirit, the Spirit of God and the Spirit of Jesus? A short and slightly over-simplified answer would be: because its task is not just to proclaim that God has drawn near to men in Jesus Christ, but also to answer the question how he is near us. God is with us in Jesus Christ not just when we remember him, as we keep alive the memory of important men in the past. He is with us in such a complete way that the word "memory", and indeed any distinction between past and present, totally fails to do justice to it. This is what the New Testament is saying in its testimony to the Spirit. That is why it attributes every aspect of man's new life in God's presence to the reality of the Spirit, through whom God is near us in Christ.

"God's tempest"

Neither Jesus himself nor the primitive Church could have taken the Spirit of God so much for granted if they had not been made familiar with the idea by the Old Testament. The Old Testament shows us how the use of the term "spirit" grew up, and enables us to understand New Testament references to the "Pneuma" in their correct sense.

Before anything else we must free ourselves from any associations the word "spirit" may have for us. "Spirit" in the Old Testament is nothing like an intellectual or mental power, and certainly not a higher principle controlling human nature. At the beginning it is only with great caution that we can even talk about the spirit as a living force. The spirit is a force which goes out from God, but it is not clear at first what the effect of this force is. Gen 1: 2 contains the famous statement, "The Spirit of God moved over the face of the waters." A marginal note in the RSV warns us that the word translated "spirit" could also mean "wind", and some scholars have suggested that the meaning is "a stormy wind raged over the waters". This is no divine spirit moving over the primeval waters in creative power; the light, heaven, earth and all that is in them were created by God's word. The picture is more likely to be of a raging storm sweeping across the waters of chaos, keeping it in its flux of *tohuwabohu* and preventing the emergence of any shape. Only one thing is certain. This storm is not a primeval element out of God's control or distinct from him. God's own *ruach* is raging over the waters of chaos. Hardly surprising, after this, that the "spirit" should be a feature of God's judgment. The *ruach* can be a punishing, annihilating force. It is like "an overflowing stream" (Is 30: 27; cf 4: 4). Even the famous promise of the outpouring of the spirit "on all flesh" in Joel 2: 28–9, which we normally take in a quite different sense from its use in Acts 2, is a symbol of the advancing judgment. As the end of the passage says, only those who call upon the name of the Lord will be saved. We would be on the wrong track if we tried to read into these texts the associations of a centuries-old tradition of Christian instruction.

The Old Testament does of course also say in many places that the Spirit takes over men to give them salvation and life. Even then, however, it is still not something which is "given" to men. The Spirit always overpowers a man "from outside", and simply takes him over for a short time. It "comes upon" him, and then leaves him again. Putting it in technical language, we would have to say that the Old Testament has a "dynamistic" view of the Spirit. In modern terms, the Spirit is not just a "psychic", but a thoroughly "physical" force. It can take hold of whole groups of men and send them into a state of ecstasy, as in the case of Saul among the prophets (1 Sam 10: 9–12). And not only men are subject to it; the Spirit of God can also shape nature and history (see the famous passage Ps 104: 24–30). In this context we are also told that all earthly life depends on whether God gives it its "breath".

Particularly important for the future is the contrast the Old Testament makes between "spirit" and "flesh". This has nothing to do with the distinction between "body" and "soul" with which we are familiar. "Flesh" means all that is earthly and transitory, "spirit" what is divine. All created things are "flesh"; "spirit" is the power of God, whether creating life or annihilating it in judgment. This is the contrast being made in a text like Is 31: 3: "their horses are flesh and not spirit" (cf Zech 4: 6). The promises of salvation in Ezek 11: 19 and 36: 26 announce that God will give men a new heart and a new spirit; in other words, God's power will take hold of them. Since Is 11 and 61 messianic expectations also invariably included the belief that the Spirit of God would rest on the king of the last times.

The Judaism of the period just before Christ kept this view of the Spirit, but with an important pessimistic nuance: the Spirit of God was now "extinguished". There was a very strong feeling that the action of the Spirit, which had been so powerful in the time of the prophets, had since declined. The promise in Joel 2 became in this mood a comforting hope for the last times – and it was good psychology for Peter's speech on the day of Pentecost to take this as its starting point.

John the Baptist, who was a link between the tradition of Old Testament Judaism and that of Christianity, also shared this hope, but he preached that God's action in the Spirit which was to mark the last times was already at hand. In preparation he called for repentance, and baptized all who were willing: "I baptize you with water, but he ... will baptize you with fire" (Mt 3: 11; Lk 3: 16; Mk 1: 8).

The Spirit and the kingdom of God

The mention of "fire" shows that John is thinking of God's judgment when he talks of the Spirit. Baptism is a seal or mark (cf Ezek 9: 4) which, given genuine willingness to repent, ensures that one will be able to stand before God on the last day. John is the herald of the imminent judgment. It is not mere chance that the gospel tradition reports that after his imprisonment he sent messengers to Jesus to ask, "Are you the one who is to come, or shall we look for another?" (Mt 11: 2 ff; Lk 7: 18 ff).

Jesus' message also announces the beginning of God's final actions. Jesus' work is dominated by the last day; the time for decision has come. "I tell you, every one who acknowledges me before men, the Son of man will also acknowledge before the angels of God; but he who denies me before men will be denied before the angels of God" (Lk 12: 8–9). Nevertheless the action of God, beginning in Jesus, which inaugurates the last times is grace, not judgment. What difference does this make to Jesus' references to the Spirit?

We can answer this question by looking at a saying of Jesus which is preserved in instructive parallel versions. In Lk 11: 20 Jesus says, "if it is by the finger of God that I cast out demons, then the kingdom of God has come upon you". The "finger of God", like the Old Testament expression, "the hand of God", indicates a direct intervention of God on earth. The same saying is preserved in Matthew in a slightly different form: "If it is by the Spirit of God that I cast out demons, then the kingdom of God has come upon you" (Mt 12: 28). The kingdom of God, the kingdom of grace, is the work of the Spirit, and the Spirit acts through Jesus.

In particular, there is a series of stories which emphasize that Jesus is the bearer of the Spirit and acts in the power of the Spirit. Typical of these is the story of Jesus' baptism, in which the Spirit comes down on him in the form of a dove and takes possession of him (Mk 1: 9 ff and parallels). In the same category is Jesus' first sermon in Nazareth, in which he takes Is 61: 1 ff as his text: "The Spirit of the Lord God is upon me, because the Lord has anointed me to bring good tidings to the afflicted." Jesus' exposition begins, "Today this scripture has been fulfilled in your hearing" (Lk 4: 16–21). The time in which the Spirit was "extinguished" is over. The Spirit is at work once more, in Jesus, and this time he will finish his work.

But in spite of this it is surprising how little on the whole the gospels mention the Spirit. One text even claims, "as yet the Spirit had not been given, because Jesus was not yet glorified" (Jn 7: 39). The Spirit is in Jesus, of course, in his words and his actions, but not yet in his followers. The outpouring of the Spirit "on all flesh" is a mark of the time after Easter, not the pre-Easter period. This helps us to understand one of the strangest sayings in the gospels: "Every one who speaks a word against the Son of man will be forgiven; but he who blasphemes against the Holy Spirit will not be forgiven." (Lk 12: 10; cf Mt 12: 32.) The saying comes from a prophet of the post-Easter community. Starting from the saying of Jesus quoted in Lk 12: 8 ff, he contrasts the time of the Son of man acting with authority on earth with the time of the Spirit after Pentecost. There is hope for forgiveness of sins committed in the pre-Easter period, but anyone who resists the revelation and the action of the Spirit after Easter can hope for no forgiveness. The action of the Spirit decides salvation and damnation, since the offer of salvation made in the new era of the Spirit is final, and must be accepted or rejected once and for all.

Pentecost

This hard saying may remind us of other hard sayings uttered by Christians about the impossibility of a second repentance. They show, nevertheless, that the Church continued to insist that before Easter the Spirit was in Jesus, but now it is present to all; all can feel its power. The turning-point is the resurrection of Jesus. According to Jn 20: 22 ff, the gift of the Spirit was directly connected with the appearance of the risen Christ. The more common version is that the Spirit was "poured out" on Pentecost day, the Jewish Feast of Weeks, fifty days after Easter. No great problem is created by the two dates. It is safe to assume that the disciples' experience of the Spirit went back to the earliest part of the post-Easter period. It is possible that this was followed by a big missionary campaign at Pentecost which was regarded as proof of the action of the Spirit, and so linked the "outpouring of the Spirit" for ever in Christian memory with the Pentecost.

More important than the question of the date is the way in which Luke, the author of Acts, interpreted the presence of the Spirit in his description of Pentecost. A sudden noise came from heaven, like the sound of a storm wind, and filled the whole house. There then appeared what looked like tongues of fire; the disciples were all filled with the Spirit, and a miracle of tongues took place (Acts 2: 1–4, 5–13). It is impossible not to think of Gen 1: 2, and of the many biblical texts which describe God's *ruach* as bringing about judgment and salvation. And what about the preaching of John? In his sermon Peter picks on one of these texts, Joel 2: 28–32, and applies it to what is happening before his hearers' eyes.

What was happening? The kingdom of God, begun in Jesus' work and confirmed by his resurrection, was now winning power over the hearts of men. This is why Peter interpreted these events as the fulfilment of the old prophecy, even though his whole sermon was about the crucified and risen Jesus whom God had made Messiah (Acts 2: 29–36). What was now happening was the beginning of God's eschatological activity on an even greater scale, the "greater works" that Jesus had promised that his disciples would be able to do (cf Jn 14: 21). And on the other hand this was nothing but the extension of what was already a finished achievement in Jesus Christ. It was a new experience, but not the experience of something new added to the presence of God in Christ.

Baptism

After his sermon on Pentecost day Peter was asked, "What shall we do?" He replied, "Repent, and be baptized every one of you in the name of Jesus Christ for the forgiveness of your sins; and you shall receive the gift of the Holy Spirit." (Acts 2: 37–8.) What happened to Jesus when he was baptized by John has now become a pattern for every believer. From this point on baptism and receiving the Spirit go together.

Like discipleship in the past, baptism is a sign of willingness to belong to Jesus Christ without reserve. When Jesus' name is pronounced over the candidate for baptism the new Christian becomes his property. At the same time he receives an irrevocable promise of salvation and life. From now on, as the book of Revelation describes it, he wears the mark of his Lord on his forehead (Rev 7: 3; 9: 4; 14: 1). Something like this also happened in John's baptism, but the difference between that and Christian baptism is that everyone who submits to this receives forgiveness of sins in the present, and may live in confidence that he is permanently marked out for salvation and that no power in the world can ever take it away from him.

Since this is so, the receiving of the Spirit must go with baptism. Anyone who is among the saved must be able to feel the power of the new world. In other words, he is filled with the Spirit of God; he becomes a "new creation" and is "born again" (Tit 3: 4–7; Jn 3: 3–12; 2 Cor 5: 17).

This is another place where we must take care not to read our catechism knowledge into the biblical texts. Baptism and the gift of the Spirit do not invariably coincide. The Acts of the Apostles which we have been following so far also tell us of the mission to Samaria (8: 4–17), the conversion of the

centurion Cornelius at Caesarea (Acts 10) and Paul's meeting
with the converted disciples of John (Acts 19: 1–7) – all cases
in which the Spirit was given without baptism or before
baptism. Someone who is baptized in the name of Jesus may
be sure that he is living, as it were, within the Spirit's force-
field, but baptism does not canalize the action of the Spirit.
Both the Old Testament and the New bear witness that the
Spirit blows where it will (Jn 3: 8). It takes hold of whole communities and individual members, whether baptized or not,
and manifests itself in speaking with tongues, prophecy or
eloquence under interrogation (cf 1 Cor 14; Mk 13: 11; Acts
4: 31). It is necessary for Christianity to remember from time
to time that the Spirit is not under its control.

This is not contradicted by the primitive Church's habit of
speaking, as it soon began to do, of the "gift" of the Spirit (cf
Lk 11: 13, and so on). What is implied by this is that the normal, long-term environment of the Christian is the sphere of
action of Spirit, the presence of Christ. But the gift of the
Spirit remains God's gift; only he can give it and make it
fruitful.

The spirit of freedom

Our examination of "Pentecost" has made us concentrate on
the old traditions of the Acts of the Apostles which were put
together by Luke about fifty years after Jesus' death. The first
person to try and think systematically about the nature and
action of the Spirit was Paul. "Any one who does not have the
Spirit of Christ does not belong to him" (Rom 8: 9b). This
means that since the resurrection of Christ the Spirit is the
distinctive sign that a person belongs to Christ and shares in
salvation. Baptism introduces believers, not into a state, but
into a continuing process. They have freedom and a future:
"where the Spirit of the Lord is, there is freedom" (2 Cor 3:
17b), and this Spirit is the guarantee of future glory (2 Cor 5:
5). The Spirit points a man forwards, but not towards a distant
other world, but to perseverance in Christian life in this world
until the fulfilment comes. A person who lets himself be filled

with the Spirit can resist the "flesh" and its temptations to sin (Rom 8: 5–9). He has no need to do "the works of the flesh", and can bring forth "the fruits of the Spirit" in love (Gal 5: 13–18; 19–24). Among these fruits of the Spirit are the "charisms" or "spiritual gifts" which the Spirit sends and which Paul regards as so important to the life of the community (1 Cor 12).

If Christian existence, life in salvation, is only possible through the action of the Spirit, what is the relation between this action of the Spirit and the action of the risen and exalted Christ? The oldest Christian tradition referred almost exclusively to "the Spirit of God", as Paul does too in many cases. But Paul also talks about "the Spirit of Christ" and "the Spirit of his Son". This means that it is none other than the exalted Lord who is present and acts in the Spirit. We might say that the Spirit is a divine force which Christ uses to make his action felt. It is along these lines that we can interpret the mysterious and much-quoted passage, 2 Cor 3: 17a: "The Lord is the Spirit."

God, Son, Spirit

This statement already shows a slight tendency to talk of the Spirit as a person, though the next step was not taken until decades after, by the evangelist John. It has not yet been made in the saying, "God is spirit" (Jn 4: 24). In this, as in Paul (2 Cor 3: 17a), the point is that God is present and active in the Spirit and that therefore the only proper way to pray to him is "in spirit and truth".

In the so-called "farewell discourses" of Jesus, however, in Jn 14–16, we begin to find language in which the Spirit is something like Jesus' representative on earth after Easter. The Spirit is the counsellor and "helper" (this is what the Greek word *paracletos* means; the translation "comforter" is misleading). He makes himself responsible for believers; he "teaches" them and "guides" them "into all the truth". But at the same time he passes judgment on the unbelieving world (Jn 14: 16; 16: 8 ff; 13). It is not now God that acts through the Spirit, but the Spirit himself who acts and is described as a person in his own right – even though it remains true that Christ acts through him and is one with him (cf Jn 14: 18 ff). This "personalization" of the Spirit was to grow in importance in later theology.

One reason for this importance was the fact that from quite early on Father, Son and Spirit were named together in fixed phrases (eg, 2 Cor 13: 13; Mt 28: 19). To agree with the New Testament, descriptions of God's saving act among men must connect it with each of these three names. This is not to say that Father, Son and Spirit have the same "rôle" in the work of salvation; the names cannot be switched around at will. The Father is the source of salvation and the supernatural origin of all grace. He creates, he chooses, he calls. The whole movement that leads men to salvation goes out from him and leads back to him.

The Father himself does not enter history. He does this in his Son, who took the form of a servant and was born of a woman (Phil 2: 7; Gal 4: 4). The whole burden, as it were, of God's saving action among us rests on this Son of God in his human existence. It was his task to proclaim our salvation and bring it about in his work, suffering and death and in his resurrection. All God's "historical" and "this-worldly" saving activity comes from God, but centres in his incarnate Son. "All this is from God, who through Christ reconciled us to himself . . . that is, God was in Christ reconciling the world to himself" (2 Cor 5: 18–19).

The Spirit is the gift of salvation itself, given to us by God in virtue of the sacrifice of his Son and our faith in him. This gift is not a thing, but God's personal presence with us. Even the gift of faith in this presence is the action of the Spirit (cf Rom 5: 1–11). One way of putting it is like this: Christ, the Son of God made man, is "God with us"; the Holy Spirit, sent by the Father and the risen Lord, is "God in us".

God the Holy Spirit

Who, then, is the "Spirit"? As we have seen, some texts

describe a power going out from God, others clearly a person. We need not worry that the New Testament gives us no clearer description. After the New Testament period it still took centuries to reach greater clarity, and in fact in the immediate post-New Testament period not much time was spent on the question. What is important is to avoid falling into oversimplification, and to keep all three strands of statements about the Spirit in mind at the same time. Each of the three acts as a corrective to the others. Talking about the personal reality of the Spirit, we must not deny that he is at the same time the gift of salvation itself. Talking about the Spirit as the gift of salvation, we must be careful to remember that this gift is not a thing, but a personal reality. Our description of the distinction between the person of the Spirit and the persons of the Father and Son must also make it clear that he is nothing other than the reality of the presence of the Father and the Son in men and in the world. Our description of the presence of the Father and the Son among men must make it clear that this presence is not the product of an intellectual effort on the part of men, such as memory, but a reality which transcends all the experiences of reality this world knows.

Ultimately none of this is matter for theoretical speculation. In the New Testament these relations were not expressed in the form of a theory, but in the community's professions of faith, praise and worship. The classical expression of the New Testament community's view of itself, under the action of the Spirit was given by Bishop Cyprian of Carthage in the middle of the third century. He described it as "a people made one with the unity of the Father, the Son and the Holy Spirit" (*The Lord's Prayer*, 23). The second Vatican council quotes this text in its dogmatic constitution on the Church (section 4, end).

Does the Spirit make our picture of God "complicated"? This feeling is tempting particularly to people who are attached to a more or less clear and straightforward philosophical picture, which is of course upset by the statements of the New Testament. The Christians of the New Testament did not feel the sayings about the Father, Son and Spirit as a disturbance, but rather as an indication of the infinite richness of their picture of God. Later periods, however, quite often felt "disturbed", as we shall see. It is a demonstration of the Church's reverence for the inexpressible mystery of God that in this later period it constantly let itself be corrected by these New Testament texts, which are certainly sometimes puzzling, whenever there was a danger of failing to face up to the Christian picture of God and its claims, and it was tempting to look for a "simpler", more "coherent", philosophical solution. We can only talk correctly and adequately about God and man's relation to him when, like Paul, we look at it and describe it, as it were, on a number of levels. We can say that the believer is "in Christ". We can say he is "in the Spirit". This is the same as saying "God is all in all" (1 Cor 15: 28).

The implications of these statements were to provide the following period with the subjects of famous controversies.

11   God's divinity and humanity

The conclusion which the New Testament writers drew from the Easter event runs as follows: The nearness of God, which believers experience in Jesus Christ, transcends all previous experience men have had of God. Another way of putting it is to say that by his latest revelation in his Son God has transcended all his previous revelations (cf Heb 1: 1). By his Spirit God has made men brothers of his Son and gathered them into the community of his children. This overwhelming experience of faith drove the disciples of Jesus to proclaim the news of God's revelation in him and offer all men the salvation which is made available in Jesus.

The first opponents

What for believers was a mystery was for non-believers either nonsense or a scandal (cf 1 Cor 1: 23–4). That God had come near to men as "Father", that Jesus was the "Christ", the bringer of salvation, the "Lord", the "Son of God", this message was a vigorous challenge to the Jews, the Greeks, and also to the Roman State. The Jews, whose political and social structures were based on their religious traditions, put up bitter opposition. The reaction of elevated Greek spirituality and the religious establishment of the Roman Empire, whose ruler could claim divine veneration, was critical and sceptical. This criticism was the background against which the picture of Christ in the New Testament was formed, and such disputes continued after the end of the New Testament period.

In the face of these enormously superior opponents the Christians faced a task of defending and clarifying their faith which made demands on them incomparable with any made of Christianity in later centuries. Only now, when the old Christian traditions are losing their formative power, are we again in a comparable situation. It was natural that the confrontation with Judaism and Greek culture should constitute a particular pressure for deeper consideration of the divine mystery of Jesus and of the mystery of God in general. The directions this reflection took and its results determined the development of the Christian faith. The original stimuluses, internal and external, which led to the formation of the ancient Church's images of God and Christ belonged, of course, to that period, and for that reason some people feel that the questions and controversies of the ancient Church should be left to be buried by the dust of history. Yet it is useful to think about the process by which this image of God and Christ developed. There are quite general reasons for this, which we mentioned at the beginning of Chapter 2 in our discussion of historical change in language about God. What is said here should be taken in conjunction with that. Another reason is that this study will reveal the common basis of Christian faith which unites the separated Churches – whose separation is, after all, based on arguments about God and Christ. There are thus three aspects to our inquiry. We shall look at the formation of the image of God and Christ in the Church's confrontation with Judaism and paganism. We shall examine the importance of this development for the later history of the

Christian faith. Last, but by no means least, we shall see what help this knowledge can give us in understanding the Christian faith in our age which in so many ways thinks so differently.

The foundation and the most important item of the Christian missionary preaching and doctrinal instruction was the primitive Christian belief in the one God and Father who has revealed himself in the Son and is for ever close to men and the world through the Spirit. Only those who accepted this message could be members of the Church. It was not, however, in doctrine that this faith and this image of God received its most important expression, but in the liturgical life of the Church. We find it in the liturgical creeds and especially in the rites of the sacraments. One piece of evidence out of many is the words of Irenaeus in his *Proof of the Apostolic Preaching*: "Faith urges us to remember that we received baptism for the remission of sins in the name of God the *Father*, and in the name of Jesus Christ, the *Son of God*, who took a body, died and rose from the dead, and in the *holy Spirit of God*, and that this baptism is the sign of eternal life and rebirth in God."

The first generations after the time of the apostles – in the period we call that of the Apostolic Fathers – received the faith in God's saving work and its form from the living tradition and writings of the apostles and their pupils. Joining in their profession of faith in the "Son of God" naturally faces us with a difficult problem. How can God remain one God if he has a Son? The related question, how the Spirit too can be God and a "person" without affecting the unity of God, is not such a big problem. Once we can show how the one God could have a Son and yet remain the one God, we also know in principle how to find the answer to the second question. Now, however, we find something rather strange. The New Testament, and the writings produced soon after the New Testament period, seem to show very little anxiety that the profession of faith in the one God might become obscured. The revelation of the one God in Jesus Christ and the Holy Spirit was certainly experienced by the Christians as the revelation of an indescribable mystery, but it was a mystery of the fulness of the life and love of God. It led, not to sceptical questions, but to worship. It was only when the objections of Jews and pagans had to be answered that the questions were revealed. The image of God and Christ now became a problem which it took the Church a hard struggle to solve. The theological controversy we are going to look at here stretched over several centuries. Not every issue of the controversy has importance for us today, but the controversy as a whole is none the less a model for the task of Christian thought in all ages. It reminds us of the twofold task of being attentive to the questions and attitudes of the men of our own time and at the same time being critical of them.

Controversy with the Jews

We have already mentioned that the first attack on the image of God put forward by Christian faith came from Judaism. Far from regarding the proclamation of Jesus Christ, the Messiah and incarnate Son of God, as an enrichment of their own image of God and a new dimension of their faith in him, the Jews took this message as a direct attack on their belief in God. The Jewish belief in one God, their "monotheism", as it existed at the time of Jesus, does not need to be describe in detail. It was by this time firmly established (cf 2 Macc 1: 2; Judith 12: 22 ff; Josephus, *Antiquities* VI, 27: 112). There was no path from this monotheism to the Christian belief in God. God's unity was regarded as a sealed-off existence which made any emergence such as the Christians maintained impossible. In spite of some apparent similarities, the Jewish philosopher Philo (*c.* 13 BC – AD 45–50) was no closer to the Christians. Philo accepted the Jewish belief in the one God (*de opificio mundi*, 61. 171; *Legum allegoriae*, II, 11, 1 ff), but at the same time held the doctrine of a sort of intermediate being between God and the world which he called the Logos, in apparent similarity with the evangelist John. On the one hand his view derives from the speculations of Jewish wisdom literature, in which "wisdom", the first of God's works, was his helper in the creation (cf Prov 8: 22–31). On the other hand Philo's doctrine is connected with Platonic ideas, according to which the visible world is the counterpart of an invisible spiritual world which controls it. In contrast to the prologue of John's gospel, Philo's Logos neither reveals God nor is it a bringer of salvation, and the idea of incarnation is completely foreign to his thinking. There is no short cut from here to the faith of the Christians, and indeed later developments were to show that Philo's ideas instead led the Christian profession of faith into crisis (cf *de specialibus legibus*, I, 81; *de opificio mundi*, 25).

Around the middle of the second century the Christian theologian Justin wrote a book entitled *Dialogue*. It was a fictitious dialogue between a Christian (the author) and a Jew called Trypho. In the book Trypho repeats the Jewish objections against the Christians. They betray the prophets' faith in one God, he says, because they honour Jesus as God and worship him. They hold a faith in two gods; they are "ditheists" (cf *Dialogue with Trypho*, 11, esp., 64 ff). Jews simply cannot understand how alongside the one exalted God who revealed himself in the Old Testament there can exist an earthly, human form of God. That God should become man is for them inconceivable, impossible (*Trypho*, 68: 1). If such a claim is made, it must be referring to another, a second God – and that is the end of Israel's monotheistic creed.

Controversy with the pagans

From the pagans too came fierce criticism. In his work *Against Celsus*, the Christian theologian Origen records an objection which makes very clear the problem created for Christians among pagans by their belief in the incarnation of God in Jesus: "If [the Christians] served none but the one God, their doctrine might be immune to any attacks. But they give totally excessive honour to this man who appeared so recently and still believe that they commit no wrong against God even when they worship his servant." Origen's answer is: "If Celsus had really understood the words, 'I and the Father are one' (Jn 10: 30) . . . he would not be so foolish as to claim that we worship some other being alongside the God who rules all things. Jesus said, 'The Father is in me, and I am in the

Father.'" (*Against Celsus*, VII, 12). Celsus also describes with stinging irony the scandal felt by pagans at the Christian belief in an "incarnation of God" (cf *Against Celsus*, VI, 72–81). It must be admitted that the Christians' pagan opponents had a keen instinct for the problems created by the Christian belief in Jesus as the Son of God, and by the message of the incarnation and crucifixion of this Son of God, for belief in one God and for the very idea of God. This can be seen again in the objections against the Christians made around the middle of the fourth century by the Emperor Julian. Julian was first a Christian and later gave up the Christian faith, and he is for this reason usually known as Julian the Apostate. The Christians had to listen to these objections and answer them.

First attempts at clarification

The Christian answer began with an insistence on the full paradox and tension contained in the statement in the prologue of the fourth gospel, "The *word* was made *flesh*" (Jn 1: 14). This statement was indeed uniquely fitted to express the distinctiveness of the Christian faith both from Judaism and from paganism. Against the Jews it maintained that God's unity and uniqueness was not "closed" and unchangeable in such a way as to make an incarnation and revelation in the form of a human person inconceivable. Against the pagans the statement maintained that God's transcendence was not such that it excluded his entry into human nature and history. This makes it clear how this sentence from the Johannine prologue became both the starting point and the target of all the ancient Church's theological efforts to understand the mystery of Christ.

But in the face of the attacks of non-Christians it could not be enough just to insist on the paradox of the creed. The Christians were not just faced with the more or less primitive attacks of a few pagan polemicists who couldn't really understand what the Christian faith was saying. The Christian faith began to spread in a flourishing period of Greek philosophy. One Greek philosophical school in particular, which traced its origin back to Plato, the Athenian philosopher of the fourth century BC, had a carefully worked out doctrine of God and the world. This stressed the unity of God and his superiority to the world (transcendence) in a way which could not help impressing both Jews and Christians. The result was that Christian thinkers began to believe that this philosophical doctrine provided a tool which would help them to understand their credal confession of the "Son" and the "Logos" in philosophical terms. This led very soon to the first appearance of what would today be called "systematic theology". It was derived on the one hand from the statements of the Old and New Testaments and on the other attempted to make itself compatible with Greek philosophy. By bringing the two together it attempted both to maintain the Christian faith in one God and to make its message about the Son (and Spirit) of God plausible.

An undertaking of this sort was not without its dangers, and the risk was soon felt. To what extent would the enlisting of philosophy lead to concessions to philosophical reasoning at the expense of faith? A tendency in this direction can indeed be seen in several attempts to describe more precisely the relation between the incarnate Logos and the Father. One of these attempts was the doctrine that the Son was subordinate in essence to the Father. This doctrine, which is called "subordinationism", has support from some New Testament texts and can be found in a number of early Christian theologians, including Justin, who has been mentioned earlier, Hippolytus, Tertullian and Origen. The basic idea is that there is a single divine "monarchy", exercised by the Father. The Son and Spirit are subordinated to this "monarchy" in such a way that only the Father possesses the Godhead in the full sense. The Son and the Spirit are only "God" in a weaker sense and in subordination to the Father. In the original Greek terminology of the theory only the Father is *autotheos* ("God in his own right"); the Son and the Spirit are *theos*. The intention of the doctrine is clear. It is an attempt on the one hand to acknowledge the right of Father, Logos and Spirit to the same name, "God", while at the same time meeting the requirements of philosophical reason and of a number of scriptural passages in which the incomparable uniqueness of God the Father is presented as all-important. Even today scholars are not agreed about how far this "subordinationism" in its original form implicitly (and in all good faith) sacrificed the Christian creed and how far it remained faithful to it.

This question is not so difficult to answer for two other attempts which, in contrast to subordinationism, no longer maintained both the unity and distinction between the Father, the Logos and the Spirit. In these there was no longer any effort to distinguish between the divinity of the Father and the Son; in contrast to subordinationism this approach stressed that in Christ man meets God himself. There were many different forms. One theory denies a real difference between Father, Son and Spirit. "Father", "Son" and "Spirit" are not in reality distinguished in God. Christ was only an "adopted man", according to this theory, which is therefore called adoptionism. According to others, whom their opponents sarcastically called "patripassionists", God is only "Father", and it was as Father that he became man and suffered. Such theories can be found in theologians of the second century, such as Noetus of Smyrna, and in the Praxeas against whom Tertullian wrote a book about the year 200. Another theory was that "Father", "Son" and "Spirit" were only different manifestations of the same divine nature. This postulated either different manifestations of God in the course of salvation history or even different forms of the divine nature within the one God himself. This theory is called "Sabellianism" after the theologian Sabellius, its first and most important proponent. Since it regards Father, Son and Spirit as three modes of manifestation of the divine nature, it is also called modalism.

Biblical faith or Greek philosophy?

Around the turn of the third century subordinationism took a sharper form. The author of this was the priest Arius (Areios). Arius was a member of the school of Origen, but where Origen had always submitted his theories to criticism from the original Christian message of redemption, Arius brought the Christian Trinity, "Father", "Logos" and "Spirit" into parallel with another trinity, with which he was familiar from Greek philosophy, "The One" (*hen*), "reason" (*nous* or *logos*) and "Spirit" (*pneuma*). Arius described "The One" as "first God, existing in himself, simple and totally coincident with himself". He is completely transcendent, and in him there is no distinction and no division. Alongside him, "reason" is "second God". This "second God" is midway between the "One" and "matter" (Greek *hylē*), the principle of multiplicity and division. In this schema where is the crucial line called for by Judaeo-Christian faith between God and creation to be drawn? There is only one place, between the "One" and "reason" (*logos*).

We have little direct evidence for Arius' teaching, but as far as we can judge it seems that he did indeed place the "Son" or "Logos" with created things rather than with God. This created Logos was the first of all created things, but he was and remained only a creature. By subtle argument Arius could claim, when discussing Jn 1: 1, that the Son was "god" (*theos*), but not "God" (*ho theos*) like the Father, but for him the Son was at most some sort of created intermediate being such as Platonic doctrines described as carrying out the creation of the world. "When God wished to create the nature which has come into being, and saw that it could not bear the strong hand of the Father and the creation which went out from him, he first made and created another on his own and called him Son and Logos, so that when he had become an intermediary the universe might come into being through him." So runs a fragment preserved under the names of Arius and Asterius. In defending this theory Arius was enormously helped by a scriptural text which spoke of the rôle of "wisdom" in God's act of creation: "The Lord created me at the beginning of his work" (Prov 8: 22). Arius' great opponent, Athanasius, Bishop of Alexandria, has preserved a sentence from Arius' *Thalia* which runs: "Wisdom came into existence as wisdom through the will of the wise God" (Athanasius, *de synodis* 15: 3). It has sometimes been thought that the basic mistake of Arianism was a new polytheism, but this is quite wrong. Where Arius was wrong, and – as we must also say – un-Christian was in uncritically accepting the doctrines of Platonic philosophy and putting an emphasis on the transcendence and uniqueness of God which left no room for the Christian witness to a real incarnation of God. This was the most frequent objection to Arius by his critics: he had, they said, relegated the Son into the realm of creatures.

If we want to use a label like "the Hellenization of the Christian faith", we can see from this dispute where it really applies. It does not apply to the bishops of the council of Nicaea (325) who rejected Arius' teaching. The fathers of the council used a term which fits very well into Greek philosophy, *homoousios*, identical in substance, consubstantial. But far from implying acceptance of Greek philosophy, their use of this term was a direct attack on it. They used it to stress the very point which no Greek philosopher would ever have conceived of, the true divinity of the Son and his begetting – not creation – by the Father. The council of Nicaea chose the *difficilior lectio* of the Christian message. It resisted the temptation to adopt Arius' theory, although it was philosophically more plausible. By doing this it made a sharp distinction between the Greek view of God and the world and the Christian one.

The first council of Constantinople (381) continued and completed this work by similarly defining the divinity of the Holy Spirit and giving it a place in the creed. Christian thought no longer moved along the line: One-reason-spirit. Father, Son and Spirit are now, in simultaneous unity and distinction the one true God, and this triune God is the transcendental origin of the world: the Father brings it into being through the Word in the Spirit. If we understand this correctly, the work of the theologians of the fourth century and the definitions of the two councils of Nicaea and Constantinople, far from constituting the Hellenization of the Christian image of God, are in fact its de-Hellenization. It was not Christian doctrine, but the thinkers who may – with a few

reservations – be called "Christian Platonists", who surrendered to Greek philosophy.

These clarifications were of course by no means the end of
Christian reflection on God, Jesus Christ and the world. Quite
the opposite – we get the impression that the real problems
were only now emerging. Why? Both "God" and "Christ"
were topics which were sooner or later bound to raise new
problems. For the present let us keep to the question of the
image of God.

The problem only became really acute now that there was
no possibility of evading it in terms like "subordination" or
"modes". The one God is Father, Son and Spirit, and this in
true diversity and inseparable unity simultaneously. Unity
versus trinity. What could it mean? By the middle of the third
century and in fully developed form from the fourth, new
questions began to be asked. Should not something like two
"levels" be distinguished in God, the level at which the unity
of God existed and the level of his diversity? Briefly, the
search for such a distinction led to the formulation that God
was three in his "persons" – or, in the Greek technical term,
his "hypostases" – but one in his nature or "physis". Three
hypostases or persons, one nature or essence. *Hypostasis* and
physis were more Greek terms. Would they not do more to
obscure than illuminate the New Testament witness to God?

God three in one

It must be admitted that the attempt at clarification soon led
to a theological venture which may seem to us now to have
been irreverent curiosity. A detailed doctrine of the threefold
internal structure of God, the Trinity, was worked out. The
danger in this is obvious. Whereas in the primitive Christian
witness the threeness of God the Father, who comes to us in
the Son and the Spirit and takes us into his fellowship, is
totally concerned with us, so that we can really only talk about
this threeness in God in connexion with his saving work in
men, this now seems to be completely forgotten. No one now
seems interested in anything but the hidden processes which

take place in God. There are technical terms in theology to
describe these two attitudes. We say that interest shifted from
the "economic" Trinity (from "economy" in the sense of the
system of salvation), about which we learn in the course of
God's revelation in saving history, in the Old Testament, in
the history of Jesus and in the action of the Holy Spirit, to the
"immanent" Trinity, the Trinity as it exists in the inner life of
God. This is another favourite target for accusations about
the Hellenization of the Christian image of God, and in the
case of the Trinity there is often added the charge that this
doctrine means that the God of the Christian faith is being
put out of men's reach. The Trinity seems to float high above
us, above our lives and our fallenness. At no point does it
seem to have anything to do with our salvation.

It is true that the doctrine used Greek terms, but at that
time what other language or culture could have been used to
deal with these problems? And the problems were genuine,
not academic speculation. Can we claim to have got to a position where we can improve on these old solutions, and perhaps criticize them, or at any rate answer the problems in a
way which is helpful to the people of our time?

What is certainly true, and what we must never forget,
whatever reservations we may have, is that the theological
discussions on the doctrine of the Trinity and on "christology"
reached or developed an understanding which none of us today
could do without, the idea of "person" and all that goes with
it. We have already seen how a very clear appreciation of the
uniqueness of man as compared with the cosmos and the sub-
human objects in the world was reached in connexion with
the doctrine of redemption developed by Christian gnosticism.
The discussions on the image of God now put this awareness
into precise formulas. It is true that the final formulation of
the distinction between person and nature, *hypostasis* and
physis, was not reached in the fourth and fifth centuries, but
the intellectual process which led to a deeper and deeper
understanding of what it means to be a person has already
begun, and by the sixth and seventh centuries it had produced
permanent results. The most famous names in this connexion

are those of Gregory of Nyssa in the fourth century and in the sixth and seventh the Greek theologians Leontios of Byzantium and Maximus Confessor and the Latin theologian Boethius.

What was the effect of these discussions on the image of God? The divine nature, which is spiritual and possesses infinite life, exists in itself in a threefold identity which is described in the words Father, Son and Spirit. The reason why the single nature of God should have this triple identity is the infinite fulness of God's life. The single living spiritual nature is the source of the threefold distinction in the selfhood. In the single divine essence God possesses himself in three ways, and each of these three ways is related to the others. Even at the time all this sounded very abstract, but the Fathers and theologians were not interested in abstract "concepts", but in understanding the mystery of our redemption and defending it against misunderstandings. The impulse which drove them to these explorations was anything but a mania for speculation. The reason for their unwavering emphasis on the divinity of the Son and the Holy Spirit was their knowledge that if the Son and the Spirit are not really God we have no share in God's permanence and immortality. Behind their efforts was the verse from 2 Peter which speaks of Christ's "precious and very great promises, that through these you may escape from the corruption which is in the world because of passion, and become partakers of the divine nature" (2 Pet 1: 4). By their reflections on the Trinity within God the Fathers did not want to divert us from concern with the salvation which this triune God gave us, but to guard against a development in which God's salvation would turn out not to be God's because it was no longer God who had brought it about. In the thought of these Fathers God is absolutely one, and yet in himself complex. He absolutely transcends the world, and yet he is interested in the world. He is more than interested, he is present in the world, because in his Son he became man and gave his Spirit to men.

God made man

We have just touched on the second great problem for which Christianity had to find a solution in the face of the attacks of non-Christian philosophy, the real incarnation of God. The problem was to take this message seriously while at the same time ensuring that it was not confused with the myths about gods and children of gods who came down to earth and appeared amongst men. To say of a historical man, such as Jesus of Nazareth was, "This is God", called for an unambiguous justification. The ridicule of people like Celsus and Julian the Apostate was very salutary stimulus for Christians on this point.

In order to understand how this unambiguous justification was developed we must look back once more to the beginnings of christology in the second century. The testimony to Jesus in the writings of the early Christian theologians keeps very close to the words of Scripture. This was not just because scripture was the only source for the authority of their witness, but also because they thought that this was quite adequate. We see again that the sentence "The word became flesh", from the prologue of John's gospel, took precedence over all other biblical statements about the mystery of Christ. It is almost true to say that the first steps towards a "christology" were slight additions to this sentence from the fourth gospel, to make it clearer or to sharpen the paradox. The "word-flesh" antithesis was expanded with terms like "fully", "truly" or "really". At first there was no attempt to give a more detailed philosophical or theological explanation. A good illustration of this primitive antithetical form of the witness to Christ comes from Bishop Ignatius of Antioch's letter to the Ephesians: "There is one doctor, flesh and spirit, begotten and unbegotten, in man God, in death true life, both of Mary and of God, first suffering and then invulnerable, Jesus Christ our Lord" (Ignatius, Eph 7: 2). And in an Easter sermon around the end of the second century, Melito, Bishop of Sardes, said of Christ, "Buried as a man, he rose from the dead as God, really (*physei*) God and man." This simple juxtaposition of true divinity and true humanity was quite adequate to express the idea which in technical theological language is called *communicatio idiomatum*, by which, with reference to Christ, human characteristics can be attributed to God and divine characteristics to the man Jesus. Ignatius of Antioch, for example, talks about "the blood of God", "the sufferings of my God", and so on. If we keep in mind the bracket that holds the antitheses together – Ignatius' "one doctor" – we see the simple point they are intended to make. They all refer to the one Jesus Christ, and this continues to be true even of the final christological formulations of the councils.

There is a simple historical reason for the apparent paradox of choosing Jn 1: 14 as the basis for a christology and then adding such simple, not to say simple-minded, interpretations. The Johannine text was itself the echo of an early controversy over the interpretation of the divinity of the man Jesus Christ. There were Christians who, under the influence of their belief in the divinity of Jesus, etherealized his humanity. They claimed that the humanity of Jesus was mere appearance (and were therefore called Docetists, from the Greek word *dokein*, "to seem"). According to this view Christ was "not really" man. Soon, in the various varieties of Christian and non-Christian gnosticism, this early Christian docetism turned into a massive intellectual attack on the New Testament assertions of the incarnation of God. But there was more to it than a belief that Christ had only the appearance of a body. The Knowledge (which is what the Greek *gnōsis* means) regarded everything bodily and earthly as inferior to the purely spiritual and otherworldly. Christological docetism was only a striking illustration of the hostility to the world inherent in this religious attitude. How was it to be resisted? The problem was all the greater since in the second century the Church's preachers on the whole had little theological training. Indeed, it would be unreasonable to have expected them to meet an intellectual critique of the Christian message which raised problems which were not settled for centuries.

We can now understand the attachment to the text from the Johannine prologue. The author might have been expected to say, "The word became man," but in fact the "exaggerated" formulation, "The Word became *flesh*," was now welcome. It put the reality of God's incarnation in its sharpest form, and was therefore the most powerful weapon against all rarefying tendencies. The bluntness of the Johannine antithesis and its expansions was for this very reason the mainstay of preaching and its main link with the biblical testimony. And many times during the long series of crises which led up to the later councils, when all sides were exhausted and confused by argument, it was proposed that there should be a return to the simple antithetical statements of the primitive Church which kept so closely to Jn 1: 14.

Hippolytus gives an example of how these antitheses were used to defend the biblical statements about Christ against temptations to dilute them. In his attack on Noetos of Smyrna Hippolytus says that Noetos taught that the scriptural statements about the Father, the Son and the Spirit referred only to a single person, so that it could not be said that the Son of the Father took the form of a slave. This was of course a direct contradiction of the Christian message. The case was to be decided by the simple church leaders of Smyrna. Their decision was a repetition of the sort of antitheses we have seen, and on the basis of this statement, which did not clarify the theological issue in the slightest, they had no hesitation in excommunicating Noetos. Part of their statement ran: "We also acknowledge only one God, but as we understand it. We also hold Christ to be the Son of God, but as we understand it. He suffered as he suffered, died as he died; he rose on the third day and ascended into heaven, sits at the right hand of the Father and will come to judge the living and the dead. In this we say what we have learnt." And Hippolytus adds: "Thereupon they condemned him and put him out of the Church, because his self-importance was so great that he had begun to form a sect" (Hippolytus, *Antinoetos* 1).

From the middle of the second century, however, reflection on the mystery of Christ went on peacefully. In particular the African theologian Tertullian, by a happy inspiration, anticipated the later formulation that in Christ two natures were united in the person of the Logos: "We see a double status, not mixed but joined, in one person, the God and man Jesus. . . . The characteristics of each substance were so fully preserved that the spirit (ie, the divinity) in him did its work, the demonstrations of power, works and signs, and the flesh (ie, the human nature) underwent its sufferings, hungry before the devil, thirsty before the Samaritan woman, weeping for Lazarus, afraid to the point of death and finally dying" (*Adversus Praxean*, 27). With the advantage of hindsight one is tempted to say that Tertullian could have saved later theology, and in particular the Greek theologians, much labour. But because he later joined the rigorist sect of the Montanists and was therefore regarded by the Church as a heretic, his theology was for a long time ignored.

Tertullian's formula is none the less the beginning of a long wrangle over the meaning of the unity of divinity and humanity in Christ. Describing it schematically, one can say that in the course of the struggle two factions formed, one concerned primarily to safeguard the unity within Christ, the other emphasizing the distinction between the divinity and the humanity. To follow the turns of the argument in all its details would fill more than one fat book, and would probably make it impossible for readers apart from a few specialists to see that the discussion is about a fundamental problem which is still important today, and more than ever today. To make this clear we shall limit ourselves to a description of the "inner structure" of the discussion, illustrated with some typical details.

Difficulties

What makes this discussion confusing is that the very formula which was the great strength of the ancient Church's preaching, "The Word became flesh," also contained the seed of the crisis. It was certainly a powerful refutation of the Docetists to say, "The Word became flesh," but outside the controversy the question suggested itself, "Only flesh?" Or flesh with a human soul?" If the second, there was then the question of what was meant by "flesh with a human soul".

At this point we begin to see the influence of a particular philosophical doctrine of man which soon became the standard basis for the interpretation of the formula from the Johannine prologue. In a crude and oversimplified form, the basic idea of this view is the following. There is only one Logos, and this Logos is the life-principle of all life in the world. It is spread about the world in a great number of parts or shares. The human soul is one such share in the Logos, a *logos spermatikos*. But what happens if, as the Gospel says, the Logos itself enters flesh? The logical conclusion is that there is no longer any need for a *logos spermatikos*. The one Logos itself fills the place which would normally be occupied by the human soul. On this theory, this is what happened in Christ, the divine Logos made flesh. In this incarnate divine Word the Word is the real inner man, which for that reason transcends all other human existence just as the Logos itself transcends the many *logoi spermatikoi*. At first sight it was the most plausible interpretation of the text of the fourth gospel.

The dubiousness of this view was not noticed for over two centuries, even though conclusions were drawn from it which today seem very dangerous indeed. If the Logos itself is the "inner man" in Jesus, it must exercise total control over the flesh. But the more the Logos is regarded as exercising complete control in the man, the more any opposition from the flesh becomes impossible. This led to the conclusion that in Jesus, the incarnate Logos, all bodily urges were inactive. Clement of Alexandria maintained that Christ possessed complete freedom from all passions (this was known technically as *apatheia*), and even had no digestion. All supporters of this view invariably run into serious difficulties when they have to explain the fact and the manner of Christ's sufferings. The evidence of Scripture leaves no room for doubt, but on the philosophical and theological premises it is inadmissible.

This view of the mystery of Christ is called, for easily understandable reasons, "Word-flesh christology". We find it as early as the third century at the trial of Bishop Paul of Samosata, and it reaches the height of its influence in the fourth century. It cannot be denied that it had two considerable advantages. First, it safeguarded and gave impressive philosophical support to a basic element of the biblical evidence, namely that God really came down into human nature and into history. It is sometimes also called "descent christology". The other advantage was that the "Word-flesh" model was an emphatic statement of the unity of the God-man Jesus Christ, and removed any need for complicated distinctions of what attribute in Christ belonged to which element. To describe this unity a term was already available, "nature" (*physis*). Logos and flesh were described as joined in Christ in a natural unity, just as normally body and soul form a single man. At the beginning of this century the Protestant historian Adolf von Harnack suggested that this view of Christ aroused the religious enthusiasm of the Greeks.

The crisis of "Word-flesh" christology began with the controversies over the teachings of the Arians. It was at first hidden, and appeared not as a crisis in the theory of Christ but as a crisis in the theory of God. This was because both Arius and his opponents shared the same basic view of Christ.

For Arius, however, this view led to the conclusion that the Logos could not be God, but must be a creature. One of the Arians' famous leading questions to the market women of Alexandria was, "If the Logos is God, how could he become man?" This reveals the difficulty. If the Logos really entered into the flesh in the place of a human soul, he cannot be God, because such a connexion with the flesh is excluded by the transcendence of God. But since everyone, including Arius, was agreed that incarnation meant precisely the existential union of Logos and flesh, it must follow that the Logos is not God, but a creature.

As we have already seen, the Church's reaction was at first directed against Arius' conclusion, not against his premiss. Against Arius, the Church maintained the divinity of the Logos, but the dubiousness of the christological premise was still hardly noticed. The principal opponents of the Arians, the theologians of Alexandria, led by Athanasius and his friend Apollinaris of Laodicea, shared their christological assumptions. This gives us some idea of the outrage against contemporary philosophical assumptions perpetrated by the fathers of Nicaea with their teaching of the substantial identity of the Logos and the Father. It took almost fifty years after the council of Nicaea, until the synod of Alexandria in 362, for it to begin to be suspected that the root of the problems raised by Arianism lay not in its theory of God, but in the basic assumptions of its view of man, and, therefore, of the incarnation of the Logos. It began to be asked whether the assumption of a true human soul in Christ, distinct from the Logos, would not do justice both to the full humanity of Jesus and to the transcendence of God, who could not combine with anything created.

From this point the question whether Jesus had a human soul dominates the discussion. From this point also the paths of Apollinarius and the Great Church begin to part. Apollinarius' christology is dominated by the formula "one incarnate *hypostasis* or *physis* of the Logos". For him unity was only conceivable as unity between two elements of a single nature. If Christ had a true human soul, he argued, the Logos would no longer be united with the flesh in a unity and we would have to speak of two hypostases in Christ. For Apollinarius, therefore, his opponents were already condemned by their assumption of a human soul in Christ. Now, however, a new division opened up between supporters and opponents of "Apollinarianism", in addition to the existing split with the Arians. The pressure of this new division forced a gradual retreat, even in Alexandria, from the "Word-flesh christology".

The new controversy was started almost by accident. Julian the Apostate came to Antioch and ridiculed the doctrine of the divinity of Christ and the Christians' worship of "the Galilean". The Christian answer was a cautious loosening of the unity of Logos and flesh in Christ: the worship, it was said, was not directed to the man in Christ, but to the Logos. At the council of Constantinople in 381 Apollinarius' opponents secured the condemnation of his view. From 381 the reaction against Apollinarianism was open, and its leadership was taken over by Antioch, while the theologians of Alexandria searched for compromise solutions which would enable them to retain

the advantages of "Word-flesh christology" while abandoning
the drawbacks.

The dogma of Chalcedon

The reaction against the Apollinarians now armed itself with
unanswerable theological arguments. The crucial point was
made by Theodore of Mopsuestia, the most important theologian between the councils of Constantinople and Ephesus
(431). His argument was that if the infinite Godhead had
replaced the human soul in Christ, Christ's body could never
have suffered any lack, since divine control knows no restrictions. There is therefore a choice between complete control
by the divine principle in Jesus or the assumption of a human
soul capable of suffering. The New Testament evidence leaves
no room for doubt, and this argument therefore led to the
formation of another characteristic christological position,
"Word-man christology". The basic idea in this is not that
God came down into the flesh, but that a complete man,
possessed of a body and soul like all of us, was assumed by
God. The advantage of this starting-point is clear. There is no
longer any difficulty in explaining the scriptural statements
that Jesus suffered or that he experienced emotions like any
other man, was sad, wept, was happy, in short, that he was
totally unlike the Stoic ideal of the man without passions. In
addition, Christ's sufferings can now be described, not just as
the fate of his flesh, but as a fully human act of obedience, a
moral act. There can be no doubt that this approach gives a
more adequate account of the scriptural teaching about our
redemption through Christ's obedience than "Word-flesh"
christology.

On the other hand this view makes it difficult to explain the
unity in Christ. It is an attractive assumption that the man
Jesus submitted in obedience to the eternal Son of God and
became united with him by this means. It is attractive to suppose that the divine Son took up residence in the man Jesus.
These ideas, expressed around 430 by extreme supporters of
Nestorius, the patriarch of Constantinople (not so much by

Nestorius himself), not only avoid the mistakes of "Word-flesh" christology, but also abandon its advantages. Compromise suggestions, such as had been advanced first by Gregory of Nyssa, that a distinction should be made between two natures (*physeis*) and a single divine person (*hypostasis*) in Christ, were still premature. Any mention of "two natures" in Christ was inevitably interpreted as acceptance of a division. In this situation, the opponents of Nestorius, led by Cyril, the patriarch of Alexandria, were able to get the council of Ephesus in 431 to accept the statement that the unity in Christ was a unity of nature, in the sense that there was only one divine-human nature in Christ. In the heat of the controversy, as happened on a number of occasions, Cyril even relied on a forgery which he had not himself examined. Bigots in his entourage had managed to persuade him that Apollinarius' phrase, "a single incarnate *hypostasis* or *physis* of the Logos" came from Roman bishops such as Julius and Felix. Cyril therefore thought that in his fight against Nestorius he was in agreement with the western Church. The result was that Nestorius was condemned in 431 and, as was then normal, shortly afterwards exiled by the emperor.

Cyril, however, did not want to lose sight of the advantages for the understanding of the redemption and of the biblical statements about Jesus contained in the assertion of the existence of a human soul in Christ. Only two years after the council of Ephesus, in 433, he accepted a statement agreed with his opponents which allowed mention of "two natures" in Christ provided there was no attempt to divide the unity of Christ in a Nestorian sense. With this the so-called doctrine of two natures, which later became the official teaching of the Church, was in essence accepted, although the remaining imprecisions of language made further work necessary and the political effects of the disputes saw to it that unrest continued. Finally the emperor took it upon himself to intervene. He summoned the leading bishops of the empire to a council at Chalcedon in 451, and insisted through his commissioners that they work out a formula which would finally re-establish peace. After some opposition the bishops accepted the emperor's instruction and finally drew up the document which, with the creeds of Nicaea and Constantinople, has become the definitive statement of the Churches' faith in Christ, at least in all the major denominations of the western Church and in large parts of the East. Since, unlike the creeds of Nicaea and Constantinople, the creed of Chalcedon is not familiar from the liturgy, we reproduce the full text: "Therefore, following the holy fathers, we all unanimously teach that our Lord Jesus Christ is to be confessed as one and the same Son, the same perfect in Godhead and the same perfect in manhood, truly God and truly man, the same of a rational soul and body, consubstantial with the Father in Godhead, and the same consubstantial with us in manhood, like us in all things except sin; begotten from the Father before the ages as regards his Godhead, and in the last days the same, for us and for our salvation, begotten from Mary, the virgin and *Theotokos*, as regards his manhood; one and the same Christ, Son, Lord, only-begotten, to be acknowledged in two natures without confusion, without change, without division, without separation, the difference of the natures being in no way removed because of the union, but the property of each nature being rather preserved and coalescing in one person and one *hypostasis* – not separated or divided into two persons, but one and the same Son, only-begotten, God, Word, the Lord Jesus Christ, as the prophets of old and Jesus Christ himself have taught us about him and the creed of the fathers has handed down to us."

The most important part of this document is without doubt the phrase "in two natures ... one person (*prosopon*) and one *hypostasis*". This is a final confirmation of the distinction between *physis* and *hypostasis*, nature and person. The expression "one nature" which, though so open to misunderstanding, had still been so important to Cyril, is now finally abandoned. This is the achievement of the council, especially as regards the subsequent development of Christian theology. The clarification is, however, more a clarification of a particular use of particular words than a clarification of the subject. Although the preceding discussions may have produced a clearer idea of the word "nature", there was still widespread uncertainty about the meaning of "hypostasis" and "person", which had previously been used as more or less equivalents of "nature". Much still remained to be done. We will mention here only one name which is of particular importance in this connexion, that of the seventh-century theologian Maximus "Confessor". His work will take us into a final consideration of the importance of Chalcedon's christological statement.

Maximus had a keen awareness of the criteria for true individuality. For him unity was not complete until the two things to be united retained their natural properties while being bound together: "It is clear that a unity of things exists in so far as the physical distinction between them is preserved" (*Opuscula theologica polemica* 8; PG 91, 97A). The more the divinity and humanity in the one Christ remain what they are, the more impressive the mystery of God's incarnation becomes. According to Maximus only the fact that the humanity of Jesus became the existence of the Logos in the world brought that humanity to its full *human* perfection. A humanity exercised by the divine person is "perfect humanity" in the natural sense, perfect in its activity and its freedom. At the same time the humanity of Christ is totally possessed by the divinity through the creative power of God, who controls all being. In this Maximus was returning to an idea expressed at an early stage of the development of the doctrine of Christ. Tertullian had said, "God can change himself into anything and still remain the same" (*De carne Christi* 3.5). If we ignore the word "change" (though it can be given a correct interpretation), this says the essential: through his control over all being, God can give "himself", that is, his Son, an existence in our world and so be in our midst while remaining transcendent.

That was the contribution of Maximus "Confessor". How far does his interpretation of the mystery of Christ unlock the meaning of the creed of Chalcedon? We will take one more look at it.

Old formulas and new doubts

With the doctrine of Chalcedon Christianity seems to have finally settled its belief in Christ, to have found the answer to the question about Christ. And it is true that the creed of Chalcedon, with the creeds of Nicaea and Constantinople, has enjoyed unchallenged acceptance throughout Christendom for over 1500 years. But the creed itself seems to be no more than a summary of what the New Testament says and implies about Christ.

How far does this answer of the Church's really take us? For all the creed's clarity, Christians in every century have had trouble in understanding what the Church was saying – as can be seen from the tortuous labours of theology after 451. How can a man be God? Such a claim could be made in antiquity, because then it was not unusual for stories to be told about gods in human form, and this helped the Christian message and eventually the Church's teaching about Christ. But can a claim like this be repeated today. Has the idea of a "Godman" any place in the way we experience and understand our reality today?

This is not just an intellectual doubt, but a question asked by faith itself. Faith has not only to identify itself with the tradition of the Church; it must also identify itself with the experience of believers, or it remains remote and powerless. Quite a few Christians today would feel relieved if it turned out, and was admitted by the Church, that Jesus was in fact only a man who had said important things about God and men and was a valuable model. Jesus the wise prophet seems much closer to many people today than the "Godman" of dogma. But there is another side. If Jesus in fact was no more than a man, no more than one of the great teachers produced by history, why should we bother about him in particular, and urge others to do the same? If Jesus was only one of us, he was also only one of us in relation to God. In our questions and thinking about God and our relation to God we could take our lead from any other teacher. It is only if Jesus is connected to God in a special way that we cannot do without him.

The Church's ancient dogma may not have been such a bad idea after all. The man Jesus, a man like us, who lived in a quite specific time and culture, must as such be totally involved with God: only this can explain why no one who wants to find out about God can do without him. Somehow the whole Christian faith stands or falls by acceptance of Jesus as true God-and-man. We must resist the temptation to separate his divinity from his humanity or to depreciate one in favour of the other. This, however, brings us dangerously close to mythological or semi-mythological ideas. To see how we can avoid these let us look once more at the text of Chalcedon.

What Chalcedon says

There is a striking phrase right at the beginning of the creed: "following the holy fathers". These "fathers" are the bishops of the council of Nicaea. In other words, in Chalcedon in 451 the feeling was that all that needed to be said about the questions under discussion had already been said at Nicaea in 325. The task at Chalcedon – unnecessary, as the bishops thought, but the imperial commissioners insisted – was to provide additional clarification. Historically, the bishops were certainly wrong. If Nicaea had in fact said all that was necessary, of course the controversies would never have arisen and could have been avoided by a reference to Nicaea. When nevertheless the fathers of Chalcedon believed themselves to be merely repeating in a clearer form what had been said at Nicaea, it follows that here again they dared not make any more "precise" statements about the mystery of Christ than were contained in the old creeds. This is the first indication that we must not import too much philosophy (let alone mythology) into the words and ideas used at Chalcedon to describe the mystery of Christ.

This is confirmed when we glance at the language which Chalcedon in fact chose. At the beginning and again at the end comes the phrase familiar from the second century, "one and the same . . . Jesus Christ", and everything in between gives no explanation, but refers to Christ in antitheses, in paradoxes, in paired terms each of which seems to exclude the other – just as had been done in the second century. The only reason why this was done – and the reason, too, for the meeting in Chalcedon – was that the discussion was in full swing. These terms had played an important part in it and were for that reason unavoidable. This is also the reason for various additions, especially the remark that Christ's humanity included both a body and a soul. Also typical of the ancient Church are phrases like "truly God and truly man", "perfect in Godhead and perfect in manhood". These observations allow a very important conclusion, namely, that the council of Chalcedon canonized no metaphysical "theory of Christ". Still less did it leave any room for mythological ideas. The whole "formalistic" style of the fathers' definitions, far from making the mystery manageable, emphasizes its difficulty. The council doesn't give us an answer to the question, "Who is Jesus Christ?" It gives us instructions about how to think and talk. Whether we go further into metaphysical questions or not, we are required to resist over-simplifications and always to describe the man Jesus in such a way that God is clearly visible in his humanity, and always to describe the eternal Son of God in such a way that he has the features of the man Jesus of Nazareth.

This is once more confirmed when we reach the real heart of the Chalcedon definition. In Nicaea, it can be said, the main issue was to maintain that Jesus Christ, the incarnate Logos, was "consubstantial with the Father". Warned by the agonizing discussions of the intervening decades, the fathers of Chalcedon add a counterweight, "consubstantial with us". This is the climax of all Chalcedon's paradoxical definitions: Jesus Christ is consubstantial with the Father and consubstantial with us.

We have now said enough to enable us once more to refute the charge of "Hellenizing the Christian gospel". The Church became "a Greek to the Greeks" (cf 1 Cor 9: 20–2) – as was no more than its duty – but at the same time it made every effort to prevent an indissoluble union between Greek words and the Christian message. This makes it not only fair, but also important, to emphasize the positive meaning these particular Greek words and ideas had for the future, and still have. First, the council's distinction between person and nature led in the following centuries to an increasingly precise philosophical and theological understanding of personality. If it is true that the christology of the primitive Church contained elements of mythology or Greek philosophy, in this continuing development they gradually fell away. With Maximus Confessor's reference to the creative power of God the Father as the source of the eternal Son's existence in human history all suspicions that the Church's doctrine of the divine incarnation is a new form of mythology are finally removed. No mythical figure here comes down from a higher storey of creation to a lower one, but God's creative power calls into being a human existence for the Son within creation. The discovery and gradual refinement of the idea of person as opposed to nature moved the interpretation of the person of Christ further and further away from the influence of Greek philosophy. The "natural symbiosis" of divine and human, a typical feature of Arian and Apollinarian christology in particular, but also to be felt as a tendency in "orthodox" christology, was now eliminated. Chalcedon had broken the tyranny of the word *physis* in christology.

The prototype of man

The substitution of a unity of person for a unity of nature in Christ removes not only a christological misinterpretation, but also an unsatisfactory view of the relation between God and the world. The doctrine that divinity and humanity in Christ are united in the person of the Logos contains a new view of the relation between God and the world. The "natural" and earthly is now not absorbed into the divinity, but preserved and perfected by the fact of God's making it his own mode of existence.

This immediately implies a new view of man. Human nature is not destroyed or altered by God's entry into the "flesh", but perfected. It is perfected in its own autonomy. The second

Vatican Council draws directly on the interpretation of the incarnation proclaimed at Chalcedon in the idea of the "autonomy" of the Christian which it expounds in the pastoral constitution *Gaudium et Spes* (41–2): "Whoever follows after Christ, the perfect man, becomes himself more of a man. . . . All this corresponds with the basic law of the Christian dispensation. For though the same God is Saviour and Creator, Lord of human history as well as of salvation history and so the 'saving God' can, as it were, push the 'creator God' into the background, in the divine arrangement itself the rightful autonomy of the creature, and particularly of man, is not withdrawn. Rather it is re-established in its own dignity and strengthened in it."

This autonomy implies humanity perfected, and perfected through the closest possible connexion with God, such as exists in Christ, the highest instance of human nature and union with God. In this way the creed of Chalcedon points forward.

If we look back for a moment at what was said in Chapter 7 (especially towards the end) about the mystery of the person of Christ, there is one last point to consider. We began by seeing what we could find out about God from the man Jesus, his preaching, his life, his death and resurrection, and also found out something about Jesus in the course of our inquiry. The inquiry which ends in the Church's creed moves in the opposite direction. We ask about Jesus on the basis of what we know of God. The answer of the creed is that he is the eternal Son of God whom God sent into the world for our salvation. These are two quite different ways of trying to find out about Jesus. But there is no contradiction between them – quite the opposite: each requires the other and we always pay a high price if we adopt one at the expense of the other.

Theological work which took the creed of Chalcedon as its basis has quite often in the past – contrary to the intentions of the council itself – neglected the connexion with the historical Jesus of Nazareth, and as a result has found itself accused of talking about a mythological figure. The keen modern interest in the man from Nazareth, his life, his preaching and his end, is for this reason good, and the Church's faith can only be strengthened by such firm ties in history. But if our interest goes no further than the man from Nazareth, Jesus in the end inevitably becomes a wise man, a social revolutionary or whatever, and there is no longer any reason why the salvation of the world and true faith in God should depend on him in particular. If the Church's creed, through the power of its 1500-year-old tradition, achieved no more than preventing us from settling the question "Who is Jesus?" with a pat answer, if it was no more than a permanent reminder that in this particular man from Nazareth something happened in our history which bursts through all comparisons and therefore always leaves new questions to be asked, then the old and often strange sounding creed would still be of importance for us. But in fact its importance goes further.

Even if we avoid exaggerations and simplifications, the creed can still remind us of something which we can easily forget in our modern style of asking about God in Jesus Christ. That is the fact that God has given us salvation *in abundance.* Look back at the first part of this book, in particular at the end of chapter 4. Left to ourselves, wouldn't we have been quite happy with an argument which showed convincingly that God takes an interest in the world, holds its fate and the fate of mankind in his hands and accompanies them along the path (and the wrong turnings) of history with his love? No human expectation and no human longing could ever have stumbled on the truth, that "God so loved the world that he gave his only Son," (Jn 3: 16), that "the Word became flesh and dwelt among us" (Jn 1: 14). God does not just redeem us; he is not just, as Teilhard de Chardin said, the magnet for all human love "at the summit and at the heart of the world". In Christ he is in our world, to live for and with us perfect human existence in the sight of God.

12   God's love made visible

The closing remarks of the last chapter once again lead us on to a new topic. When we mentioned that the old creed is a warning to us against simplifications, this presupposed that when we talk about Jesus Christ today we have to do more than just repeat the old definitions. For believers Jesus Christ is not just a figure from the past, but the living and present Lord. This means that the way in which faith in Jesus Christ is expressed also cannot be fixed once and for all, but must live and constantly grow. To acknowledge Christ in faith means more than repeating a dogmatic definition correctly. It is only faith when the confession of faith in Jesus Christ is alive and relevant to the changing situations of men in history.

We saw that the struggle for such a relevant confession of faith in Jesus Christ began in the New Testament itself, and the last chapter should have given us some idea of how fiercely the struggle continued into the early Church. The statements of the creeds and definitions about Jesus Christ as true God and true man in a single person, which still unite the major Christian churches today, are in no way obsolete. The following points cannot and are not intended to replace them, but start from them. They were established at the time in a critical and open encounter with the world of Greek culture and philosophy. We are now faced with the task of finding a way of enabling men of our times to realize the truth expressed in the old articles of faith. The struggles to find the right mode of expression that took place then shows us today how we can and should try to understand and express the mystery of the individuality of Jesus Christ and the meaning of his cause. Belief in Jesus today as well has to undertake an examination of, and confrontation with, the cultural tendencies of our time, just as the old Church and its theologians did. We have to do so even though we know from the start that we shall never be able to seize all the aspects and all the richness of the mystery of Jesus in any one single attempt at understanding it.

We must ask quite emphatically – in Dietrich Bonhoeffer's words – "Who is Jesus Christ for us *today*?" Or, to put it a different way, how can we today come to see that Jesus Christ, in his person and his work, is our salvation as the Christians of the first centuries tried to understand and express it in the world of their experience?

The creed and secularization

In trying to answer this question, we must first look at the reasons why so many of our contemporaries find the creeds of the fourth and fifth centuries at first sight utterly remote and strange. Where does this strangeness come from?

The secularization of the world since the scientific and industrial revolutions has changed the situation of believers in many ways. Apparently or in fact, the religious questions about salvation, redemption and God no longer exist for many people. As a result of this, the traditional phrases of Christian preaching and the Christian creed, which were meant to answer these questions, seem to them no more than empty husks or the remains of a pre-scientific mythology. The classical teaching of the incarnation of the Son of God in Jesus Christ suffered as a result in two ways. Either it was not understood at all, and ignored as a curiosity of religious history, or it was misunderstood as a myth in which God clothed himself in the humanity of Jesus like a disguise and appeared on earth like the old gods in human shape. Many ideas and phrases from popular piety gave strong support to this misunderstanding.

In this sense, a "demythologization" of our ideas and language about Jesus Christ is an urgent necessity – and not just in connexion with the resurrection. But this sort of demythologization is only legitimate when it does not openly or implicitly assert that there is no longer any point in faith, but instead "reinterprets" for the outlook and consciousness of modern men in such a way that it presents them with a challenge which is also modern. The old message must become a new invitation to faith in God and must be understood as an invitation.

The Gospel of Jesus Christ can only be such a challenge if it has something to say. Some modern attempts to "reinterpret" the Christian faith produce a pale interpretation by which no one could ever live or die. In these Jesus Christ becomes just a symbol of all men's universal human experiences, the model of a free and realized human life or an image of the grandeur and the tragedy of man. Of course, the intention behind such attempts is to help modern man when he tries to find out about Jesus Christ, but such a purely "secular" description of Christ performs only one half of the task which the Fathers of Nicaea, Constantinople and Chalcedon set themselves. It shares the preoccupations of contemporary thinking, but does nothing to question its assumptions, although this is as necessary today as ever. If we start from this sort of "secularized" view of man, we must logically end up by making man, or society or mankind as a whole, the highest good. But such an idolization of man by himself only replaces the old myth by a new one, and one which is more dangerous because it can so easily turn, as we have seen, into totalitarian ideologies and systems.

But if man accepts his finitude, his limits, and realizes that the power of evil and injustice in the world make it impossible for him by his own power either to fulfil himself or to establish a perfectly just and happy order of society, he must accept the possibility of a salvation which he cannot make or plan for himself. Only in this way can he banish the fear that a demythologized, secularized view of the world will turn into a new myth. Only in this way can he prevent the demythologized "Son of God" and "Godman" from becoming the symbol of a new myth of man – which will be essentially the old myth of Prometheus.

If we now on our side reformulate our question about Jesus Christ and think again about how we should talk about him, we cannot help seeing that our answer to mankind's endless longing for sensual fulfilment and perfect justice cannot be an eternal vision enthroned beyond the terrors of history. The only answer which will do is the message about the God who united himself with men, himself became a man and entered into the hazard and history of our humanity, even to the ultimate experience of isolation and abandonment in an unjust and violent death.

The classical doctrine of the incarnation of God and its formularies did not forget this; far from it, this was just what they were trying to say. The problem was that with their resources they were unable to say it clearly. In spite of all its critical aspects, the old doctrine remained imprisoned in the Greek philosophical concept of a God who was absolutely unchangeable and could not suffer. This made it very difficult indeed to understand how God could *become* man (and so in some way change), suffer and die on a cross. Our modern approach can therefore help us to reach a fuller understanding of the original meaning of the message of Jesus Christ and to get through to the biblical message about the God who is with men and acts in support of the oppressed, the poor and the powerless. There is another side to the much-discussed "crisis of traditional christology". Our modern approach and attitudes are another chance, a new possibility of reaching a more authentic and fuller understanding of what "traditional christology" was trying to say.

The starting-point: the resurrection of Jesus

How can we today understand who Jesus Christ is and what he means for us? Like Christians in all times, in our search for an answer we must first turn to the evidence of the gospels. We have seen, however, that the gospels do not just tell us who Jesus was during his earthly life, and what he said and did; they are also testimony to his identity in the Christian communities of the time. In other words, they are testimony not only to the earthly Jesus, but to the Christ who rose from the dead and is present now. To bear witness to the earthly Jesus alone would make no sense for faith, because from a purely human point of view his message and his claim were disproved on the cross. His death is not only a sign that no human life can reach fulfilment in this world. It was the killing of an innocent man who had relied on God as no one else had ever done and had championed men in the name of God. At first sight the cross of Jesus opens up an abyss of meaninglessness and destruction.

There is only one alternative, despair or hope against hope. The cross points back to Jesus' message and claim. If he, who claimed to be God's representative, died on the cross, it would seem that God either did not confirm his claim or did not have the power to do it. If this is so, all the hopes which were based on God as a result of Jesus end in despair. But anyone who hopes against hope (Rom 4: 18), and in spite of this end accepts Jesus and his claim that through him God identified himself with men even to the point of sharing their failures, can only do so reasonably if he is sure that God maintained and confirmed his loyalty to Jesus and his work, and through him to all men, even in Jesus' death. We have seen that the claim that Jesus rose from the dead has precisely the function of inviting us to believe this. Both then and now, only one thing gives any point to our bothering about Jesus and believing in him, his message, his claim and his mission, and that is belief in his resurrection. The start and the heart of faith in Christ in all ages has been the belief that the man who was once crucified is alive now.

God's kingdom in love

Only because faith knows who Jesus Christ is today can it finally know who he was in the past. Finally, because knowledge of Christ always begins with our hearing who Jesus Christ was in the past. By confirming Jesus as his representative even in his death, by raising him from the dead and identifying himself with him, God has irrevocably declared that Jesus was, from the beginning, the man through whom God's kingdom came into the world. This kingdom of God is simply the occurrence of God's limitless love for all men. Jesus sums up the nature of this rule of God in love by calling God

"Father". The title expresses both God's absolute sovereignty over men and his nearness to men and men's closeness to God. Both, God's power over life and death and his sovereignty over men, have been finally confirmed by Jesus' resurrection.

We can now see that the claim that Jesus rose from the dead is not a supplementary article of faith, additional to Jesus' message and work during his life. The statement of his resurrection is what brings this message and work into operation. It makes the kingdom of God in love present in human history in a new and permanent way. If we ask how it is present, Scripture's answer is the Holy Spirit. It is the Spirit who makes the person and work of Jesus, God's kingdom in love permanently present in history.

We can now sum up the essence of the Christian message as follows. Faith in Jesus Christ reveals the identity of God and his importance to men in a way which is revolutionary in comparison to all other ideas. It reveals him as the one who is free in his love and loves in his freedom. For love he sacrificed himself to associate with men – with men who rebel against him. In spite of this he remains absolutely sovereign, and never surrenders or loses his identity. It is in the madness and weakness of his solidarity with men that he reveals the freedom and glory of his love. Only this freedom of God in love can bridge the gap which runs through our world. Only this love based on freedom can reconcile contradictions without neutralizing them, and maintain tensions without reducing them. Only this can hold down hope against hope, and prevent it from floating off into the absurd.

It would clearly be the wrong approach to try to prove the reality of God's love in Jesus Christ. A message which by its nature is addressed to the unforced acceptance of faith cannot be "proved". This does not mean, of course, that we cannot ask questions about the truth of the New Testament's claims. Their truth is not something which can be "proved" by external arguments, but proves itself by confirming our experience of being human and enabling us to understand and accept the greatness and the wretchedness of man. In our human lives we usually veer hesitantly and uncertainly between greatness and wretchedness, hope and despair. We usually purchase firmness and certainty at the cost of one-sidedness. What makes the message of God's love in the life, cross and resurrection of Jesus Christ so convincing in itself is that it rules out one-sidedness. Jesus Christ says something to us about both the greatness and the wretchedness of man. By recognizing our wretchedness in Christ we are preserved from arrogance, and by recognizing our greatness in him we are saved from despair.

By showing us the freedom of God's love, Jesus Christ shows us the true humanity of human nature and enables us to live it. To do this, Jesus' claim must have immediate credibility, and what gives it that is its power to account for all the elements of our life, its questions and mysteries, its happiness and its sorrow. The author of the fourth gospel gave this power classical expression when he made Peter say, in the name of the Twelve, "Lord, to whom shall we go? You have the words of eternal life" (Jn 6: 68).

"Son of God"

Starting, as we have done, from the cross and resurrection as the centre of the Christian faith enables us to understand in a new and deeper way what it means when the New Testament itself, followed by the creeds of the early Church, calls Jesus "Son of God" and "true God and true man in a single person". We need not be troubled by the fact that the christology of the early Church is more interested in the incarnation than in the cross and resurrection. Jesus' obedience even to the cross shows us the attitude which dominated his whole earthly life. He surrendered himself completely to the control of God's love and thereby became – in another phrase of Dietrich Bonhoeffer's – "the man for others". In giving himself to God for men, Jesus wanted to be nothing in himself or for himself, but everything in God and for God, and everything for men.

This twofold gift of himself to God and men consumed his life to its end. Through it his human sacrifice and human obedience became nothing less than God's visible love for men, the instrument God used to make his love present in the world. We can therefore say that by letting himself be totally taken over by God's love and opening himself completely to it, Jesus becomes in his own person the form in which the kingdom of God's love exists for us. This is what is meant by the Christian creed's description of Jesus as the "eternal Son of God", and not anything similar to the myths of ancient religions. It says that in his human openness to God and men he is the personified love of God. His words, actions, sufferings and signs are the words, actions, sufferings and signs of God's love in him.

Scripture talks more about the function of Christ, the later tradition of the creeds more about his nature. But "functional christology" and "nature christology", as they are often called today, are not opposites. They represent different stages, and different legitimate approaches, within Christian thought. The statements about the function of Christ always include statements about the nature and person of Christ, whether or not these are made an explicit part of the theory. The confession that Jesus is the Son of God and that in him God himself approaches us says something about both the function and the nature of Christ.

We can now also understand quite easily what the other old definitions mean when they refer to Jesus as "true God and true man in one person". The freedom of God in his love, with which we come into contact in Jesus Christ, and the freedom of the man Jesus in his gift of himself do not exist side by side in isolation, and still less does either restrict the other. The divine element in Jesus does not reduce his human awareness or his human freedom. Nor does his human autonomy threaten his union with God. The situation is the opposite: the unity of God and man in Jesus is complete because God and man remain God and man without restriction. It is because Jesus let himself be taken over by God in complete human openness and surrender that God and his love became a person in Jesus. The statement "Jesus is true God and true man in one person," is therefore a commentary on the statement "Jesus is the Son of God." It stresses a perfect unity which at the same time includes the sharpest possible distinction between divinity and humanity. This means that when we say "Jesus is the Son of God" or "Jesus is God made man", this is not the same as saying "Peter is a man." In a confession of faith in Jesus Christ the "is" has a quite unique meaning, different in kind from the meaning of other "is" statements. It is therefore a mistake when many critics of the faith describe the statement, "Jesus is the Son of God," as mythology. They are rejecting something the Church has never taught. This means also that it is perfectly possible for them in fact to have true faith in Christ in the New Testament sense even though they reject a correct definition as a result of a misunderstanding.

It must be admitted that misunderstandings are only too easy, and we may not always have escaped them in our attempt at a new interpretation. Our language uses general ideas and models and for that reason cannot do justice to the unique importance of Jesus Christ. Only faith lived by the individual and the community can produce clarity and confidence here, and draw the line between faith and mythology. This is why the important thing is not the correct formula correctly interpreted, as something independent, but talking about Christ in such a way that we say what the formula sums up in technical language, that in him God's love became a part of our world and gave us the right to hope against hope.

The salvation of all men

The reinterpretation of the old doctrine of the "two natures" in the "one (divine) person" of Jesus Christ which has been outlined here should have made it finally clear that faith in Jesus Christ involves more than just "believing in" abstract formulas. If Jesus Christ in his person is the entry of God's love into the world and as such the basis of hope for all men, everything said about the person of Christ must also say something about his meaning for us – and only if it does so is it a "correct" and "accurate" statement about Christ. But the opposite is also true. It is impossible to describe the importance of Christ for the salvation of individuals, mankind and society without at the same time offering as an explanation of why, and on what grounds, one believes that Jesus Christ in particular has this importance for salvation, a particular account of the person of Christ. Anyone who wants to think and speak correctly and accurately about Christ must always be on their guard against two temptations, to abstract doctrine and speculation and to purely "practical", "pragmatic" Christianity.

This brings us to another question which we have not yet considered: how can the particular historical figure of Jesus and his particular fate be the source of salvation for all men? In the past a number of images were used to explain this which go back to the New Testament. One such image comes from law, and describes Jesus, by his death on the cross out of love and obedience, as "meriting" the grace and love of God for us, making "satisfaction" to God's righteousness for our guilt. Another image comes from worship, more strictly, from the sacrificial system. This presents Jesus' death on the cross as a sacrifice of reconciliation, though even in the New Testament this was not understood as meaning that Jesus reconciled God in the sense of making him relent from his anger and return to his love of men. Such legal and liturgical ideas have a basic validity because in this area we can never do without images. In using these images, however, even tradition had to take precautions against the danger of thinking of God too much in human terms, in the bad sense. It is of course impossible to sway God like a temperamental ruler, or to negotiate with him in terms of a mutually advantageous bargain.

The best way to bring out the meaning of these images is perhaps like this. We saw that Jesus allowed himself to be taken over completely by the love of God, and gave himself completely to God and men, even to the extent of sacrificing his life. This was something new in history, something that had never happened before: at a point in history the vicious circle of evil was broken and the love of God appeared in its pure form in the person and life of a man, unobstructed by any human failing. It was impossible for it not to have an effect on other men, the fellows of this one man before, with and after him. All men are joined in fate, for good or bad, salvation or destruction. No man lives for himself alone. The situations of other men affect me, not just externally, but in my own being. We can illustrate this by thinking about ourselves. There are various factors which condition my life, even direct it. I had these parents, have this job, have these and these neighbours, speak this language, feel attracted by this sort of people and repelled by these. My life is also determined by the fact that I grew up and my ideas were formed in such and such a country in the twentieth century with its experiences, that I live under such and such a political system, with a government which follows such and such policies in association with such and such other governments in the world. And so on. If I imagined for a moment that any of this were different, I would have to admit that then I too would no longer be what I in fact am.

One of the basic features of the situation in which all men in practice live is that their lives are marked by violence, hate, lies and guilt, by many sorts of far-reaching pressure. Simple experience, which no theory is strong enough to refute, tells us that we can never finally free ourselves from this through our own efforts. If in this situation Jesus Christ breaks through the vicious circle of evil in his person and his actions and sufferings, the fundamental conditions affecting the lives of all men are in that moment altered – this is the result of the interrelatedness of men. A new possibility of making sense and making a success of human life has been created, a possibility which no one could have expected. It doesn't affect men automatically; it is a possibility, and it is up to each person to decide whether to let it take him over or to leave it alone sceptically. The decision to let oneself be taken over by this possibility is what we call faith, faith in God based on Jesus Christ. A person who takes the risk of believing in this way breaks through the vicious circle of evil with Christ and like Christ, and enters the solidarity of a new human race. He is no longer without an alternative in the world of violence and lies. He finds he is free and recognizes Christ as the source of this freedom (cf Gal 5: 1, 13). In the language of tradition, he is "redeemed".

We shall talk in detail later about what this means in practice. For the present we have seen enough to say that what took place in Jesus Christ did indeed have importance for all mankind; the only ones who cannot see this are those who do not take up the freedom offered in Christ but remain in unbelief. This freedom, which is what tradition calls "grace", "redemption" and "salvation" is not a "thing" distinct from Jesus himself which can be separated from him. He himself is this freedom for men, and it is given to men in their meeting with him in faith. Anyone who refuses this meeting in faith does not see this offered alternative of freedom, but only the continuing pressures of ordinary life; he remains stuck in these and in the experience of constantly failing attempts to win freedom for himself.

But what is the position of those who do not take hold of the redeeming freedom made available in Christ because they do not know him? What is the position of those who do not know him because he has never been preached to them? We shall have to look at this question later on its own, and from the point of view of its practical consequences. Here we can, and must, look at the principles involved.

Scripture tells us (1 Tim 2: 4) that God in his love desires the salvation of all men. In addition, what we have said about the solidarity of all men excludes the assumption that some men should have the chance of reaching freedom and salvation and other men should not – except by a deliberate rejection of the chance. All this makes it impossible to believe that men may be without salvation and have no possibility of obtaining the freedom and redemption given to Christians through faith simply because through no fault of their own they have not heard the message of Christ. Because his love is universal, God has built the whole of creation round Christ (cf Col 1: 16 ff). This means that the fact of Jesus Christ has left traces, pointers, hints, all over human history. Wherever a person tries to imitate what had its purest expression in Jesus, the selfless love which reaches out to one's fellow men, there he meets Christ (cf Mt 25: 31–46). Wherever a person tries to accept the darkness of his existence and his future in hope and obedience, it is a reflection of what was achieved once and for all in Jesus Christ. Such a person, though he may not know it, is being guided by the model of the new man which was revealed in the Christ of history. In acting as he does such a person shares in the freedom, love and hope which have come into the world through Christ. In this way even a person who has never heard of Christ can nevertheless meet him unconsciously and anonymously and obtain the salvation he brought.

"And he will come again"

God's rule of love, which came into the world with Jesus Christ and gave us the freedom to love, fulfils the hopes of the Old Testament and also the hopes of all mankind for salvation, redemption and reconciliation. But the salvation and freedom brought by God's kingdom are overshadowed by the cross. Reconciliation takes place in the midst of a world which is still unreconciled as a whole. Therefore when we say that the hopes of mankind have been fulfilled it does not mean that hope is no longer needed. It means that hope now has a ground and strength.

Jesus Christ is the fulfilment and perfection of all human history. But another way of saying this is that he is its real beginning, and all the future belongs to him. Nothing can downgrade this beginning or improve on it. When faith expresses this in the New Testament by saying that Christ will return at the end of time to judge the world, we would be wrong to take this as a myth, as meaning that Christ will somehow re-enter our space and time. This belief in the coming of Christ means that the future of every single man and of all history is part of God's kingdom of love, which is among us through Jesus. "At the end", therefore, God will be "all in all" (1 Cor 15: 28). But what is this end? When is it? This is a question which we shall ask again at the end of this book. It is not one that science can answer, nor one that provides food for curiosity. Our only source of information about this "end" is hope, which deals with things not seen (cf Heb 11: 1), and hope does not provide a theory for the course and end of history.

But hope does provide a course of action. A person who believes that God's love does not pass away, but lasts, also has a right to hope that human love will last and that what is done in love will last (cf 1 Cor 13: 8). When the hope which is based on Jesus Christ urges us to build our lives completely on God's rule of love, that is no empty promise, but an encouragement to work for a love which is no longer bound to fail. In this love it is a Christian's task to be a figure of hope for others just as Jesus Christ, the love of God become a person, became the messenger, token and source of hope for us. That is what makes the Christian the "new man".

Part Three
The new man

13   The "new creation"

The first and second parts of this book have considered the
question of God and presented the answer that the Christian
proclamation of faith claims to give to this question. The next
two will try to show how this answer is translated into terms
of the many different aspects and factors of human life, and
what can and does happen to people's lives as a result.

"Proving" the faith?

We have deliberately talked about *how* this answer is translated into terms of human life. The question *whether* the
Christian proclamation of faith is any kind of suitable answer
to the question about God is one that we do not even begin to
ask. This is not through oversight but because it is not a relevant question. We must resist the temptation to "prove" the
faith, even indirectly, or at the least to demonstrate that it is
reasonable and in fact self-evident to give the Christian message the assent of faith. If it could really be conclusively shown
that it is reasonable and self-evident to believe, then who
could escape the charge of being unreasonable or even wilfully
bloody-minded? But everything we have had to say about the
Christian message up to now makes it clear that it is directed
towards nothing other than the *freedom* of the human heart.
And everything we have said about the question to which the
Christian message is intended to provide the answer makes it

clear that a real answer is not one that says: "You *must* believe, accept the message, belong to the Church . . ." but instead one that says: "You *can* believe in God." A faith that people were forced or obliged to accept, even only on intellectual grounds, let alone by means of physical force, would be neither the faith preached by the proclamation of the Christian Gospel nor an answer to the questions that inevitably arise from human life.

If anyone should raise the question of "proving" the faith what we have to do is simply to present in the clearest possible terms what this faith says and means and then to bring this into contact with the fundamental questions of human life that were our starting point. What happens next is totally outside the control of any third party. It is fundamentally and exclusively something that happens between a free man and God, and either there takes place in this freedom the believer's encounter with God or this does not occur. And even whether this has really happened or not is not something that anyone can judge from outside, since the acceptance or rejection of a certain set of propositions, the use or non-use of a certain set of terms is as little decisive as is the phrase "I love you" for establishing whether this is genuinely love.

There is, however, something else we can do. We can try to describe what happens in the case of someone who believes. Indeed, this is something that belongs to the actual message of faith. Faith changes a man's relationship to himself and to his life, his relationship to his fellow men – and his fellow men both in the smaller world of family and immediate neighbours and in the larger world of the whole of mankind – and finally his relationship to the universe, of which the earth on which he lives forms only a part.

If we begin with the first aspect of the change faith effects in someone, that is in his relationship to himself, that is not without reason. When we developed the question of meaning as the question of God, there too we began with man's search for his own identity – and expanded the question later to include questions about human society and finally the evolution of the universe. It seems obvious to adopt the same procedure in the present case. Admittedly it is correct that, if we believe the Bible, God's revelation of himself was always directed primarily to the community, to his people, and it gathered people together to form his people – and it was only through the mediation of the community that it reached the individual human being and directed itself to him. Nor is it in any way admissible to make the individual the centre of the world to such an extent that even problems of a universal scale – and that means problems that affect the life and death of the whole of mankind – would have to take second place to the claims of the individual, of any single human being. But that does not alter the fact that, leaving the social and universal aspects on one side, the question about belief in God starts today, and perhaps particularly today, with the individual's question about himself. Even if belief in God itself expands this question to broader dimensions, and perhaps from a certain point of view discloses its pettiness and egotism, it is nevertheless relevant to begin describing the effects of belief at this point and simply to allow it to reach the point where it becomes necessary later to broaden our perspective.

In the preceding paragraphs we have in fact already raised the matter that we now have to expound in greater detail – whenever in fact we were forced to "interpret" the Bible's statements so as to elucidate the language of the past that has now become strange and alien in such a way that it fitted in with our actual present-day life. At least one tendency became clear in this, in that faith was expected to bring about a change in man. In this way what follows puts together a number of details that have already been mentioned. On the other hand we must now try to describe in concrete terms, less closely tied to the interpretation of biblical texts and more closely linked with our present-day life, what happens in the life of a man if he believes the biblical message – the biblical message translated into the terms of our life.

Salvation

The Bible itself is aware of a concept that comprises the effects of faith in man's life, the concept of "salvation". In Hebrew, the language of the Old Testament, we find corresponding to this concept the word *shalom*, which we usually translate as "peace"; in Greek, the language of the New Testament, we find the word *soteria*, which is also translated as "deliverance". When this word or the corresponding verb occurs in the New Testament, it denotes the totality of what Jesus Christ has brought into the world for man's sake through his life, death and resurrection (cf eg, Acts 4: 12; Rom 1: 16, 5: 9 ff; 1 Cor 3: 15, 5: 5, 2: 5 and 8; 1 Tim 1: 4, 2: 4 and 15). Corresponding to this Jesus is the "Saviour" (Phil 3: 20), the mediator of salvation (cf Acts 4: 12; Jn 14: 6, 15: 5; Heb 9: 15, 12: 24). It is "in Christ", "through our lord Jesus Christ" that we have salvation (cf Rom 5: 1 ff, 11; 2 Cor 5: 18 ff).

Words like "salvation" and "saviour" have, however, become somewhat devalued over the centuries and must in all cases be used with care. But the word "salvation" is a fundamental term in the biblical language of the Christian faith. If we are not able to say we have a share in salvation we must stop talking about our faith. Hence the usefulness and necessity of a brief consideration of what this word means.

Salvation carries with it the idea of wholeness, perfection, the absence of decay and division. A world that has been "saved" is a world in which human life is no longer threatened, no longer illegitimately cut short or confined – though the question of what conditions such a world would have to fulfil is always open to dispute. If then Paul says: "It (the Gospel) is the power of God for salvation to every one who has faith" (Rom 1: 16), what he means is in general terms something like this: faith in the Gospel makes man whole, its power breaks the power of everything that can threaten man, it gives life that no death can overcome. In fact this, as the second part of this book has shown on practically every page, is the exacting message of Christian belief.

The opposite of salvation

Because the human mind has a tendency to think in terms of

pairs of opposites, the very word "salvation" itself begins to arouse awareness of the profound and characteristic tension that inescapably runs through the Christian message and forms an essential part of its contents. We use such sayings as: "Nothing in this world is perfect." Anything we describe as perfect is in fact only approximately perfect, and there is nothing so whole and entire as to lack all flaw. This applies to physical objects just as much as to man's life and work and to the structures of human society. Anyone who introduces the fundamental Christian concept of salvation into this context is immediately faced with a new and important question – whether Christian faith has in fact healed and made whole the flaws and divisions in the world and in human life. Has salvation, in fact, driven out its opposite? Has Christian faith, has the God who proclaimed this faith brought about more salvation in the world than men could themselves bring about if they were only to make sufficient effort?

We have to answer: No! Certainly the Church and Christians throughout the centuries have done much that was "saving". And yet the world does not give the impression that today it is saved and made whole to a greater extent than in the time of Jesus. And even we ourselves, if we believe, can on careful consideration feel ourselves to be only half way to salvation: salvation is the object of our hope more than it is something that we already enjoy. Salvation is not in any way something that we can already have had our fill of, whether it is a question of our own salvation or that of the world.

But this depressing conclusion does not discredit the Christian message and Christian faith. At no time has there been the suggestion that if only a man believes he can expect for himself here and now an existence that has already been redeemed and made whole and live in a world that has already been redeemed and made whole. On the contrary, from the start there runs through the message of faith the tension between the blatantly unredeemed present situation and a future salvation that is expected, hoped for, and longed for. The believers of the Old Testament always knew God as the one who was to come, who would come forth to save, but on whose coming one could rely and depend precisely because in the past he had been present to save and was present here and now. Throughout Jesus' proclamation of the imminent reign of God there is to be found from the start, as we have seen, and often in a very confusing form for those who interpret the texts, the tension between, or one could say the simultaneous presence of, present and future. God's reign has come upon us, it is there, Jesus is the representative of the imminent God – and at the same time God's reign is not there yet, it is only dawning, and now is the hour to decide for it. Finally the death of the herald of the kingdom of God on the cross could only have destroyed every illusion that God's reign would put the world right at a stroke. The "salvation" that is given to men by the presence of God does not for a moment exclude the failure of him who was the representative, the messenger, the witness of this God-with-us, his "Son".

The message of Jesus' resurrection does not remove this failure of the cross but instead confirms and strengthens it. He who is risen is Jesus, the crucified, and it was in the light of their experience of the risen Jesus that the disciples realized from the start that this death on the cross "had" to be. This person who has been crucified now lives with God, and he does so as "the first fruits of those who have fallen asleep" (1 Cor 15: 20). That is to say, his life does not undo either his or our death, but instead "merely" gives the hope that death and failure in this world do not have the last word and the final victory. And still within the period covered by the New Testament, in the further development of the infant Church, we observe how the final misunderstanding was destroyed. Whereas the first Christians reckoned on merely a short span of time between the first beginnings of the reign of God in Jesus Christ and the ultimate achievement of salvation through his return (cf eg, Rom 13: 11), whereas Paul advises his congregation at Corinth no longer to be preoccupied with things that are wholly connected with the old world that is passing away and are therefore now of no importance, and this because of the shortness of the time (cf 1 Cor 7), the later New Testament writers, especially Luke in his Gospel and in the Acts of the

Apostles, soon realized that Christ's return had been "postponed", that the Church had a longer period of time before it between Jesus' death on the cross and resurrection and the end of the world. But coming to terms with this "postponement" did not involve any crisis, because from the start Christians knew that the tension between present and future is of the essence of the salvation that has been opened up to men through Jesus. The development of the image of Christ in the New Testament and in the early Church, considered in this way, takes into progressively more serious account the tension between present and future. The image of God's accredited representative of the reign of God, preaching the time of decision, failing, crucified, broadens out into the image of Christ who in his life, death and resurrection becomes the "fulness" and "centre" of the ages and opens up to all men the way to God (cf Mk 1: 15; Gal 4: 4; Rom 8: 1 ff).

Christian faith has never talked of any salvation other than that whose manifestation and consummation are still awaited, which remains a continual object of hope, and which nevertheless is already present, is spreading unceasingly, and thus forms the basis of our hope. Even today that is what the word "salvation" calls to mind – precisely because of the unavoidable contradiction between its meaning and the reality. In this connexion present-day Catholic theology tries to understand the meaning and essential significance of religious orders and the religious life. A life lived according to the so-called "evangelical counsels" of poverty, celibacy and obedience is a demanding one and distances the religious to some extent from certain aspects of life in our world, thus indicating that Christianity awaits the returning Lord who reveals and fulfils salvation.

The Spirit

But at the same time the use of the word "salvation" shows up its weaknesses. It could lead us astray into answering the resulting question of where this salvation is to be found with a slick reference to hope and the future. We could be tempted to find comfort in the following consideration, that faith does not in any way commit us as it were to demonstrate salvation here and now. What we have to demonstrate is our hope in salvation, our certainty with regard to the future that allows us to endure all immediate experience of the lack of salvation. We could tend to see the misgivings of unbelief with regard to the Christian message of salvation precisely as a necessary indication of this very message of salvation.

On the other hand the Christian really ought to be glad if the doubter relentlessly persists in asking where salvation is to be found. If faith speaks of the tension between the present and the future, it ought not to do so in such a way that the present is for all practical purposes not taken seriously and is excluded. This not only opens up a credibility gap – after all, one is on the other hand laying stress on the tension between present and future that is involved in salvation – but it is also a considerable playing down of what the biblical message says on the *presence* of salvation "here and now".

What does it say? At this point we must once again mention a reality that has already been the subject of explicit treatment: the Spirit. We have already pictured to ourselves why the New Testament regarded itself as obliged to bear witness to the Spirit: in order to exclude the possibility of Jesus Christ being only one among many great men in human history who continue to have an effect on people's lives because people remember them and allow their actions to be guided by their example. But at that stage we were interested in the consequences for the image of God in Christian faith that flowed from the biblical witness to the Spirit. Now we must take another look at this evidence of the Spirit from the point of view of seeing what it has to say about the person who believes.

Remembrance

First of all, the "remembrance" or "commemoration" of Jesus Christ which according to the witness of the New Testament is provided by the working of the Holy Spirit is not in any way a mere "calling to mind". Remembrance can give life not only a direction but a new direction. It can help us to recognize the particular historical situation we are living in, the influences that mould us, and from this definite hopes and expectations for the future are aroused, the desire for change is stimulated, and the power to come to terms with the present gains strength. Nor is remembrance something that concerns only the individual. A community can preserve a particular remembrance, can be formed around a definite remembrance and the power it has. This kind of remembrance is in the most general terms called "tradition".

We do not of course need to have recourse to special "supernatural" influences to remind ourselves that even the remembrance of Jesus Christ can develop this kind of power and can arouse this kind of expectation: that is to say, confidence in the presence of God that Jesus proclaimed; hope in a world that has been made whole, a world in which the barriers between men have fallen just as they fell in the circle of those around Jesus; expectation of a clear decision of those who through faith belong to God, even if they have been expelled from society, and those whose lack of faith comes to light even though they see themselves quite differently.

The history of the Church and even of the world as a whole in the period since Jesus Christ shows that remembrance of Jesus has been able to develop this kind of power even when faith in Jesus' presence through the Spirit has not been sought or has long since been given up. Roughly at the time of the Enlightenment two hundred years ago, when people began on a large scale to reject the Christian message in the form in which it had been transmitted to them, a form involving Church membership and confessional allegiance, a time when all that people wanted to retain of Christianity was what went with the religion of reason they were striving after, a time when in keeping with all this all that people wanted to see in Jesus was a highly gifted teacher of human wisdom and human morality, then precisely at this time this kind of "remembrance" of Jesus succeeded finally in carrying through what belief in Jesus in its ecclesiastical form had only insufficiently been able to achieve: the abolition of slavery. The doctrine of human rights which is accepted at least in principle throughout the world and which as such is without a doubt not the achievement of the Church is nevertheless inconceivable without the Christian understanding of man and thus without the "remembrance" of Jesus. And, despite all the practical political problems that remain unsolved, there is broad agreement that Christians because of what they believe can and must support the efforts of the peoples of the Third World to achieve self-determination, freedom and a way of life in keeping with human dignity.

These are only a few examples of the way in which remembrance of Jesus develops its power to shape the future and to give hope even outside what one generally calls Christian belief. But why does the New Testament nevertheless rightly insist that remembrance itself is not enough, that we must rather talk of the Spirit if we want to describe how the salvation promised for the future is already present?

Spirit and faith

The first reason is that there is a difference between recognizing Jesus, in whatever way we like, and believing in him. Someone who believes in Jesus regards him as more than one of the great men in the history of mankind who to the best of their ability have made a lastingly valid contribution to the world. To believe in Jesus means to recognize and grasp hold of the appearance and the irrevocable presence of the love of God in him, in his person, in his life, in his death, in his resurrection. But of this belief Paul says: "No one can say 'Jesus is Lord' except by the Holy Spirit" (1 Cor 12: 3). To talk of Jesus, to recognize him, to grasp something of his contribution to the history of mankind is something man can do with his own mental and spiritual resources. The New Testament says that to believe in Jesus does not belong to the unaided resources of the human mind and spirit. It is only the Spirit of God and Jesus that gives that. Faith is a gift, is grace.

But this very faith tells man – and this is the second reason

– that Jesus does not just go on having an effect but is present. He is the one who lives, he is with his own until the end of the world (Mt 28: 20). And this once again takes place through the Spirit which is with the Church and leads it into all truth (Jn 14: 16, 16: 13).

This then is the first and immediate reason why the New Testament must speak of the Spirit and cannot be content with the concept of remembrance. It is not thanks to himself alone that man can believe in the living Jesus who is present to him and to all who believe. But should this mean that Christ's presence in the Spirit is something that happens above and beyond the rest of our spiritual and mental life, outside the area where remembrance develops its power? That would be a misunderstanding. Indeed, we are explicitly told that the Spirit will "bring to the remembrance" of those who believe all that Jesus has done and said and what he means (Jn 14: 26). In actual fact the working of the Spirit takes on the form of our normal spiritual and mental life, becomes as it were incarnate in it. For this reason, that which the faith of Christians attributes to the power of the Holy Spirit always appears to those who do not believe as mere remembrance of Jesus with no power beyond that of remembrance. It would be completely false to adopt the idea that first of all Christians had at their disposal all the usual possibilities provided by memory and then thought that thanks to their belief in the Holy Spirit they were able to have recourse to yet an additional source of knowledge that was not available to others. For the Catholic teaching that those entrusted with the Church's teaching office enjoy the especial assistance of the Holy Spirit in their proclamation of the Church's doctrine must not be interpreted in this way – even if one must admit that on both sides of the confessional boundary this is not infrequently stated to be the Catholic view.

The remembrance of Christ that is characteristic of faith is certainly also knowledge of a special kind (cf 2 Cor 5: 16) but it develops its power in all the forms that are normal for ordinary kinds of remembrance: critical reflection on the original message, study of Scripture and the many different ways in which it has been interpreted throughout the history of the Church, the question of the contemporary meaning and significance of the gospel message, discussion and not infrequently dispute about all the intellectual and practical questions thrown up by this message, and concern for the continual reform of the Church to correspond with Jesus' demands, in the spirit of Jesus, and so on. In all this the Christian believes in the presence of the Lord, in the working of the Spirit who keeps the community of believers in communion with Christ throughout all these conflicts and often throughout failure and defeat and incomprehensible situations.

This conviction is moreover something we find most clearly expressed as early as the time of the primitive Church. Thus the same Paul who at the conclusion of his letter to the Galatians speaks of the "fruit of the Spirit" and explicitly includes peace and love in this (Gal 5: 22–4) had earlier fought so hard for his understanding of the gospel in opposition to other views, both in his own mission territories and in the Church of Jerusalem, as to bring the Church to the brink of splitting into separate denominations (Gal 1–2). Clearly he did not feel that the Spirit's gifts of love and peace were inconsistent with serious disagreement. Similarly we read in the Acts of the Apostles that at the meeting generally referred to as the Council of Jerusalem, at which it was a question of the Church remaining united or becoming split, there at first broke out no small dissension among the brethren. Nevertheless it does not seem at all out of place for the concluding decree to begin with the words: "It has seemed good to the Holy Spirit and to us . . ." (Acts 15: 1–29).

The presence of Christ

But is there not all the same something in the outward form of remembrance which the Christian can refer to when he insists on the distinction between the working of the Spirit and mere remembrance on its own? Certainly one's immediate general response would be to say that the working of the Spirit comes to light the more the dominant tone in the discussion and also any dispute comes from a desire to follow Jesus himself and his message of imminent salvation. This indication of the Spirit at work is that much more credible the more the Church's search for truth is marked by love, by desire for peace, by selfless commitment to this task. Of course the qualifications that have just been made apply: brotherly love and peace do not mean the absence of conflict and a smooth artificial agreement. But if discussion within Christendom of questions of faith, the structures of church life, internal church reform, and the Church's influence on society at large is marked by ambition, obstinacy, greed for material gain, desire for personal domination, and a yen for individual convenience, then it will be difficult to make out that thanks to the working of the Spirit this internal church dispute has nevertheless a good effect and is distinct from a free-for-all struggle for political or economic power.

But we can still point to two special aspects. A unique phenomenon characteristic of the history of the Christian Church, and one that must strike even an impartial historian, is that Christians have never thought they could finish with Jesus Christ once and for all. In the case of other great historical personalities it is possible after some time more or less to settle the issue in agreement. Of course books appear from time to time which suddenly overturn what had been taken as the firmly established verdict on some great man of the past. But for the most part one can say that when all the available documentation has been examined and when all the historical data about some major figure in the history of mankind have been reviewed the possibility does fundamentally exist of saying after a certain time that his contribution to the history of mankind is such and such. With Jesus Christ the situation is surprisingly different. Those who believe in him have at every moment to reckon with the prospect, which not infrequently they are forced to face up to, of starting all over again from scratch in their judgment of Jesus Christ, in their expectations of him, in the direction they give their lives in imitation of him. This is something that applies to the relationship between the different epochs in the history of the Christian church

290 THE NEW MAN

(compare in this context the examples cited in chapter 2), and not infrequently does it apply too in the life of small groups within the Church or even of individual Christians – such as in the case of a religious order trying to reform itself, a national church adopting a new policy, a Christian suddenly being "converted" after years of unquestioning conformity, or a theologian perhaps making an entirely new start after several years of theological work. It is precisely this that faith must attribute to the Spirit. The believer will never be able to say, however many years of intensive study he may have devoted to the question, that everything is clear to him with regard to Jesus Christ. In the most variegated way faith must be ready to allow itself continually to be surprised afresh by the reality of Jesus and the claims this makes and to make a new departure. Otherwise it is not faith.

It is precisely here that yet a further distinction from ordinary kinds of remembrance appears. The great men in the history of the world remain in the past, however great the power that their remembrance may be able to develop. But the remembrance of Jesus means in the literal sense a remembrance of the future. We remember the Christ who is present as the person whose revelation is yet to reach us. Once again this characteristic is something that the New Testament attributes to the Spirit (cf Acts 1: 6–11).

Hence it is like the keystone in the New Testament witness to the working of the Spirit when the sacrament that has long been called the sacrament of faith also imparts the Spirit (Jn 3: 5). For baptism makes a man a member of the community of those who count on Jesus coming again and recall and commemorate this in every celebration of the Eucharist (1 Cor 11: 26).

The new creation

Have we now come closer to our goal of describing how salvation is already present and what it does to people? In itself the key-word "Spirit" has not yet let us escape from the realm of the abstract. A further description of what is meant by this did indeed lead us into areas of everyday down-to-earth – and often unpleasant – experience. All the same, where it was down-to-earth it was more a dispute over the presence of salvation than about salvation itself. Salvation itself, as communion with God in Jesus Christ, still remained obscure and abstract even when considered in the light of the Spirit. Now, however, it is not only said of the Spirit that it leads us into the truth, a process often involving considerable tension, but that it simply is, quite all-embracingly, the gift of salvation: the spirit of adoption as sons through which we can address God as father (Gal 4: 6), the spirit of love that God has poured into our hearts in order to make peace with us and to give us access to his presence (Rom 5: 1–5), the conclusive pledge and first fruit of the perfect redemption for which we hope (Rom 8: 23, 2 Cor 1: 22). Can we explain this in a little greater detail?

Paul's remarks about the fruits of the Spirit (Gal 5: 22–4) or the continual association of the Spirit and brotherly love in Jn 14–16, to quote only these two texts, are already using a very down-to-earth language, as can hardly be disputed. This will be dealt with in detail later when we consider the basic patterns of Christian behaviour. But the New Testament itself provides a key-word that as it were sums up and includes all that Paul and John are enumerating and that at the same time characteristically maintains the tension between present and future. "If anyone is in Christ," writes Paul, "he is a new creation; the old has passed away, behold, the new has come" (2 Cor 5: 17; cf Gal 6: 15). And it is as if John in his own way were providing a commentary on this passage of Paul's when he makes Jesus say to Nicodemus that man must be born anew (Jn 3: 5). That faith trusts God to make things new against all expectation has from the start been apparent to us as an essential characteristic of faith. When Paul and John wrote about the new creation, were they recalling the words of the prophet: "Remember not the former things, not consider the things of old. Behold, I am doing a new thing; now it springs forth, do you not perceive it?" (Is 43: 18–19)? But what is meant by the term a "new creation"?

The desire to become new, and even the phenomenon of

someone radically changing himself and becoming new, are in themselves familiar to us. Even all the small changes of rôle that we make daily in the various situations of our life and the demands of our job are already this kind of becoming new, even if only on a small scale. Often enough this kind of change of rôle can in fact involve someone becoming radically new – that is, if it also involves giving his life a totally new direction. For we do not just play rôles but are the rôles we play. How often too are we not moved or even saddened by the unreal desire to start anew all over again, to do things all over again and better, to be faced once again by some fundamental decision? And it is not infrequently that simple but profound disillusion with ourselves leads to the wish to be someone else, to make something quite different of ourselves.

All this is in no way alien to what is meant in the Bible by the term "new creation". But it is at one and the same time too little and too much. Too little, because it does not reach the genuine profundity of the biblical concept; too much because what the Bible means is much simpler and plainer than our complicated desires for newness. In biblical language it could be expressed by saying that a believer becomes a new creation through being able to exist before God, having peace with God again, being reconciled with God. It is not by chance that Paul goes on immediately after the text quoted just above to say that through Christ we are reconciled to God (2 Cor 5: 18). This kind of language presupposes that we have already before this been aware of the reality of God and of our fallen state in his sight. It is only on this condition that the word of reconciliation can move us in such a way that we feel as if created anew. To translate this biblical evidence into the world of our experience we would perhaps express ourselves in the following way: we are a new creation through being able to stand before God. In other words, through faith we become aware of the reality of God and build confidence from the certainty of his presence.

To say this is to say also that the "new creation" is not something we possess, something the possession of which we can produce tangible evidence for. If we look around us, there is nothing at all tangible that has been created anew. What is new is our confidence that rests on faith in God's presence, a faith that first of all has to withstand the entire onslaught of the world's appearance to the contrary. Faith comprehends the presence of God, but it is a hidden presence. Present and future are both to be found in this hiddenness, since what is hidden is present while at the same time allowing the expectation of a future public demonstration of its existence.

If therefore we now want to describe what the presence of salvation, the gift of the Spirit and the faith that the Spirit creates make of a man, then we must ask what the effect on a man is of this totally un-self-evident, totally quixotic confidence in God's hidden presence in this world.

Freedom

The first key-word, and once again one that is all-embracing, must be freedom. No other word serves us better to express what it is all about. True, it is correct that freedom has not always been the concept that sums up what Christian faith makes of a man. Even in the New Testament the "freedom of a Christian man" (Luther) is the explicit theme of only one piece, the letter to the Galatians. The other New Testament writings mention it only in other contexts – admittedly very emphatically and in a variety of ways. Starting with the oldest texts of the New Testament one could construct a history of the concepts that have summed up the Christian faith: the reign or kingdom of God, light, life, the true philosophy, redemption, justice, order, piety (*pietas, devotio*), justification of the sinner, the accord of faith and reason. These are all concepts which expressed and comprised the summing up of a whole basic understanding of Christian existence.

If today we regard freedom above all as this kind of inclusive concept, then this is more than merely the addition of yet another term to the list of such earlier concepts. All the earlier terms used in this way to sum up what Christian faith is all about could only be used for this purpose because they indicated a liberating effect that resulted from Christian faith, admittedly at times an effect that operated in one particular direction. For the chosen people of the Old Covenant, with centuries of oppression and being reduced to political insignificance, it was a liberating proclamation for them to hear, even given the misunderstandings that occurred, that God had not in any way abandoned his people but was with them and was entering into his kingdom. For the sceptical and world-weary intellectuals of the end of the ancient world it was a liberating proclamation to hear that the divine logos, the fulness of all intelligence and all reason, had appeared on earth and that, as Clement of Alexandria said, it was no longer necessary to labour away in the Greek schools of philosophy in order to gain a little wisdom. In the political insecurity of the time of the early Germanic kingdoms it was a liberating message if one could say that Christian faith brought with it a justice that everyone could depend on. In this way we could progress (cf also the examples in chapter 2).

Similarly today freedom ought to be a concept that sums up what Christian faith is all about – because it expresses the way in which the Christian message answers the question that is raised about God today. We have earlier explained that the question about God today arises from a variety of different forms of oppression and threat and, resulting from this, from various forms of suspicion that everything has become absurd and lost its meaning. It is only if Christian faith has something to say that brings freedom, whatever form this proclamation may take, that it provides an answer to this question. To put it the other way round: the statement that God is a God of "order" may in itself be as correct as possible. But to put this idea today at the centre of the proclamation of the Christian message means to threaten as profoundly as possible its liberating power and thus its evangelical character, its sense of being the "good news". This is because in the conditions of the complicated and stiflingly over-organized world we live in the word "order" degenerates through "law and order" to suggest an additional element of oppression – the precise opposite of what the Christian message is meant to, and must, be.

Freedom from care

Now of course it is a question of describing this freedom in a little greater detail. Not every personal, social or political freedom that we think worth fighting for is thereby connected with the "freedom of a Christian man". And moreover a freedom that is understood as giving rein to arbitrary licence is a perversion of Christian freedom. On the other hand we need not fear that we are on the wrong lines in making an essential connexion between the freedom of the children of God and efforts for social and political liberation. To put it another way, it is not every political trend, conditioned as it is by the particular situation, that is justified by the biblical message. Often enough faith will seem decidedly cumbersome and unwieldy in comparison with political programmes and expectations. Nevertheless the longing to do away with the structures of social and political oppression, the demand to tear down the barriers between people that create the lack and opposite of freedom – these are something that Christian faith can only describe as legitimate and right.

But these are examples of the working of Christian freedom in practice, not in essence. The believer has a more profound freedom than social and political liberation is able to give. It is first of all freedom from the pressure of being obliged oneself to ensure the meaning of one's personal life. Not that the believer is relieved of the duty of establishing meaning at every level that has already been mentioned. Not that the meaning of one's personal life and of the life of the whole of mankind does not also depend on whether meaning has been successfully established in this way. But there is a difference between taking up the duty of establishing meaning in this way from an awareness that it is the only chance of bringing a little meaning into a meaningless world, a little hope into a hopeless humanity, and taking up this task because I already know that this meaning has already been established and that my efforts merely allow it to become tangible and concrete. To put it in biblical terms, the fundamental freedom of the Christian consists in the fact that he must not be anxious about himself (cf Mt 6: 25 ff; Lk 12: 22 ff). Certainly he must exercise forethought and prudence, for others and also for himself, but he is freed from any radical anxiety about himself, over whether it is not finally all the same whether he has lived or not. Faith tells him that he as himself is called by his name with eternal love. We can use another word to express what is meant, a word we have already used: composure. The composed person is not reserved, he does not build up around himself a defensive bastion against life, he does not keep the world and other people at arm's length. He trusts himself to events, throws himself into the whirl of the tasks set by history, because through his faith he knows he can do this, he must not be afraid of losing himself, since God is everywhere close to him, in the magnificent and just as much in the sinister moments of the world and of history.

Freedom from the pressure to look for meaning, freedom from anxiety about oneself, composure: all this necessarily includes freedom with regard to the whole area of what is usually called purely human rules and regulations. We do not want to, nor must we, play down the fact that what is meant here includes internal church structures, regulations, and laws, and indeed simply social values that are conditioned by social surroundings. To insist on this is neither self-evident nor unimportant. There have been moments in the history of the Church when the power of the Gospel seemed threatened with suffocation, not with regard to the great questions of the world but with regard to an impenetrable and agonizing system of church regulations, customs and sanctions which may have all once upon a time had a good reason for their existence but which finally hardly fell behind the Jewish law and its interpretation by the scribes in their continually increasing number and complexity. It was against this kind of danger that Paul wrote his letter to the Galatians. It was in this kind of situation that Luther wrote his prophetic work *Of the freedom of a Christian man*. And in this kind of situation the believer has the right and duty of continually recalling explicitly how sharply and critically Jesus himself expressed himself against "the tradition of men" when it reaches the point of making God's commandments void for the sake of "traditions" (Mk 7: 1–23).

That Christian freedom is fundamentally concerned with ecclesiastical regulations too is logically compelling once the Christian's basic freedom from anxiety about himself has been grasped. Once it is established that God through my faith sets me free from anxiety about myself, then no human regulation can arouse fresh anxiety about myself in me. But if it comes to the point that human regulations arouse serious anxiety in me about myself – that is to say, anxiety about the meaning of my life, anxiety about salvation – then the basic freedom from anxiety about myself has been removed and Christian faith and freedom can no longer be identical.

Freedom to love

This of course does not in any way mean that church regulations and laws are nothing but purely arbitrary and meaningless constructions that have nothing to do with the believer. We have only to pay attention to the fact that they are and remain nothing other than a help towards and an indication of the right use of freedom, that they do not shut off the area of freedom that God has opened up. Given this, there are good reasons for church regulations and even church laws. One can even say that there must be rules and regulations for the sake of freedom. This is because every exercise of personal freedom naturally restricts the freedom of other people. An arrangement must be found so that the unavoidable restrictions on the exercise of freedom are somehow shared out equally and so that the end result is not the right of the strongest. This simple consideration is the basic reason for positive law in every society and thus too in the Church. Church regulations have to exist in order to regulate the ordered life of the society – and therefore they both are capable of and need revision as soon as the society's conditions of life have changed to the extent that revision is necessary. Keeping to regulations of this kind – we are not discussing here the problems of the most suitable way of working them out – is therefore basically nothing other than an expression of respect for the freedom of fellow-believers and thus finally an expression of love. This love can and should go even so far as to follow rules that are really out of date or superfluous rather than to disturb the conscience, and perhaps even the faith, of a fellow Christian who does not see things so clearly. This is the view not of some prelate devoted to the niceties of legal order but of the very apostle who has proclaimed the freedom of a Christian man as no other New Testament author has done – Paul (Rom 14: 1–23; 1 Cor 8: 1–3).

We have thus already mentioned the third key-word by which Christian freedom can be recognized: love. Ever since Paul warned his Galatians against abusing the freedom they had been given in Christ for concessions to the "flesh" (Gal 5: 13), no one can suppose that Christian faith means freedom from ethical duties. Quite the contrary. Because the Christian is fundamentally free from radical anxiety about himself and from the domination of the purely human, he can all the more unreservedly surrender himself in love for his fellow-men and in working for justice in human society. This can be put the other way round. Where he does not do this unreservedly, this can only mean that he is still occupied with anxieties about himself that prevent him from committing himself totally to love and justice. Naturally the saying that the devil is to be found in the small print applies here too. Often it can and will be very difficult to decide what corresponds to love and justice. This will be gone into in detail later on. But if there is something distinctively Christian in the area of ethical behaviour then it is to be found here in the indissoluble link between radical freedom and unreserved love. And if non-Christians too think and act in this way this is no reason for Christians to be disturbed. God does not belong to a Church. The churches are his instrument with which he approaches the whole of mankind. If somewhere in the world confidence, freedom, and commitment for love as they are preached by Christian faith are to be met with outside the Church, the Church should not try to bring this under its control as rapidly as possible but should rejoice that God's work is being done here even without its help.

Forgiveness

And there is a fourth key-word we must mention to characterize Christian freedom: forgiveness. To forgive someone does not mean to regard what he has done as something that has never happened, not to want to acknowledge it or simply to forget it. In certain circumstances forgiveness can mean precisely not forgetting. Forgiveness means refusing to allow someone else's past to be a reason for not accepting him. Forgiveness does not mean approving some past offence but rather approving and accepting some person together with his past offence. Forgiveness in this sense is a fundamental term of Christian faith – first of all indeed in relation to God. Whether we cherish old ideas of sin as an offence against God or prefer quite "modern" ideas of sin as man's self-alienation, faith in God's saving presence always includes the confidence that God has accepted us and all men as we are – that is, with our past offences, with what contradicts him. This indeed is his forgiveness, that our weakness and also our only too real guilt do not prevent him from accepting us. In this sense God's forgiveness is an indispensable component of his liberating presence and our trust in his forgiveness an indispensable component of our freedom.

Forgiveness among men means nothing other than that we should behave towards our fellow men in precisely the same way as God behaves towards us – and for our part liberate them just as God has liberated us. Forgiveness is thus not simply one particular requirement of the Christian ethos among many: it is a fundamental requirement of faith itself. How unthinkable any view to the contrary would be is made clear by Jesus in the parable of the unforgiving servant (Mt 18: 23–35).

There are two New Testament texts which seem to bring together in concentrated form the entire connexion we have been presenting between freedom, love and forgiveness. One is Jesus' enigmatical saying: "Whoever would save his life will lose it; and whoever loses his life for my sake, he will save it" (Lk 9: 24). Anyone who wishes to provide his own guarantee of the meaning of his life in all circumstances will find that this is impossible. But anyone who starts from the premiss that he does not need to cling on to his life but can risk it in any way because this is something that is taken care of without any contribution on his part will discover that this is the only life worthy of the name.

The other text is the magnificent series of ideas developed in chapters 2 and 3 of the letter to the Colossians – but read in their context. Here the apostle is answering his opponents, who were smothering Christians with minute regulations and thus making them anxious about their salvation. The Christian is dead to such regulations, that is to say, he is free. But what is involved is nothing less than the reality of the resurrection. The Christian is free from the pressure of regulations of this kind precisely because he is risen with Christ. The consequence of this is not arbitrary irresponsibility but the love which is developed in fundamental Christian attitudes and patterns of behaviour and which ultimately cannot exclude those who are beset by anxiety and lack of freedom.

Faith and hope

It is not pitching it too high if one holds the view that what is distinctively Christian emerges most clearly in the believer's attitude and relationship towards the future. To put it another way, it is in this attitude and relationship towards the future that the "new creation" which takes shape in Christian freedom shows its face most unequivocally.

The fundamental term that Christian tradition has from the start used to express this is hope. Both hope and its characteristic nature have already been discussed. We obscure this characteristic nature if we succumb to one particular temptation, that of equating faith quite simply with hope. Admittedly, some scriptural texts, some statements in the theological tradition could give rise to this. Are not faith and hope equated when Abraham's faith is summed up by the fact that he hoped against hope? (Rom 4: 18.) Did not Luther anticipate entirely modern considerations with his view that God is hidden behind the contradiction of everything that reason and faith itself are forced to think of him and that faith therefore consists in hoping in a – desperate, defiant – "nevertheless" that God breaks through this contradiction? Such a view of things we cannot simply term wrong. And from this point of view we can understand how many Christians and theologians find themselves in such sympathy with trends of thought which do not admittedly arise from the foundation of Christian belief but which in a quite similar manner are penetrated by hope, give rise to hopes and thus come to terms with the hopeless present. It is not by accident that Christians discover a mental and spiritual affinity with someone like Albert Camus or with utopian visions of the social and political future which have as little justification in the concrete present as the Christian message of salvation but which promise to further matters through the impulse of hope.

Nothing of this is lacking in Christian faith. But what distinguishes it from the existential "nevertheless" and from utopian visions of the political and social future is that in all seriousness it bases this hope on the presence of what it hopes for. This is expressed by the New Testament in a whole series of characteristic passages. Thus Paul adopts the pregnant formulation: "In this hope we were saved" (Rom 8: 24). Hence faith does not simply project itself into an absolute future because the Spirit, the "earnest" of the future we are promised, is already in us (Rom 8: 23). And it is precisely this that is solemnly summed up in that passage in the letter to the Hebrews that in Christian theology has often provided the starting-point for studying the indissoluble connexion between faith and hope and at the same time the distinction between them: "Faith is the assurance of things hoped for, the conviction of things not seen" (Heb 11: 1).

Thus Christian hope introduces into the life of the believer that characteristic paradox that allows and obliges him to project himself entirely into the future and at the same time, in resignation and patience, to trust himself to the present, including all its unpleasant aspects (cf Rom 8: 25). One is tempted to say that it is this urging on to confidence in the present, understood by faith as radically accepted by God, that marks the distinction between Christians on the one hand and on the other genuine existentialists, Marxists, and political revolutionaries – even though the question still remains whether a Christian is a Christian through and through, an existentialist through and through, or a Marxist one completely purged of all Christian influence. This fundamental paradox that runs through the Christian life is summed up in that enigmatic idea of Paul which in its immediate sense is connected with the second coming of Christ that he expected as close at hand: have as though you had nothing (cf 1 Cor 7: 29–31).

Suffering

The Christian attitude and relationship towards the future becomes particularly tangible with regard to suffering and death. The kind of suffering we have in mind here is not that for which we ourselves are responsible or which in some way or another is the outcome of human failing. There is only one attitude a Christian can adopt with regard to this kind of suffering, and that is to work away with every possible means to overcome it and to eradicate its causes. But side by side with this kind of suffering for which human beings are responsible there is another kind of suffering that is beyond human understanding and beyond human redress – the kind that ranges from natural catastrophes that cannot be prevented to incurable diseases. What is the meaning of faith in the presence and future of salvation for the Christian's attitude and relationship towards this kind of suffering?

First of all, a Christian will renounce every attempt to provide some kind of ultimate explanation of this kind of suffering or to show it to be meaningful or logical. Of course he can put theories forward, work out considerations about the origin and perhaps even the future usefulness of suffering. This is something Christians have been doing right up to the present. Anyone who finds this kind of exercise useful can of course do so today, only he must refuse to impose theories of this kind, however "religious" they may be, on other people and on his fellow Christians in the name of faith. But in general the desire for this kind of explanation seems simply to be on the wane today, when we are more aware of the whole extent of suffering in the world for which no one can be held responsible and for which no explanation is possible. It is not by accident that today we should be so thankful for the presence among the holy books of the Church of such pessimistic works as the book of Job or Qoheleth (Ecclesiastes), books which mercilessly lay bare the unsatisfactory nature of all explanations for the suffering in this world.

Secondly, a Christian will, obviously, sympathize – suffer with those who are suffering. He will be at one with those who suffer, and he will not simply let this solidarity remain a question of feeling sympathetic but will use all the means at his disposal to transform this feeling into actions to help those who are suffering and to alleviate their sufferings. One of the finest characteristics of our age is that this kind of practical assistance is no longer confined to the circle of our immediate neighbourhood but rather that we have developed the imagination and the technical organization to provide assistance anywhere on the globe where human beings through no fault of their own are facing suffering and the threat of death. Sharing in this kind of assistance – which can well include a continuous critical appraisal of its effectiveness – is something which must be self-evident for a Christian today.

For the rest a Christian will let suffering remain an unsolved question. Nor will this be a matter of smiling at it or retaining one's composure but accepting it in its full horror. And it is precisely at this point that it starts asking too much of his faith. For this faith should and must retain its confidence in God's presence in the face of suffering. His faith tells him that suffering does not abolish the presence of God. It merely makes it clear that God's love is something we cannot fathom and that it has standards other than those that we are used to. His hope tells him that God will ultimately let the meaning even of this be seen – though at the moment a Christian has and can have no kind of idea what sort of meaning this will be.

And finally a Christian will remember the cross of Jesus – not in order to provide himself with consolation but in order to understand that if the God in whom the Christian believes could let even his own son, and with him the whole business of his lordship in the world, come to failure on the cross, if this failure did not involve any contradiction of his essential nature, then there is quite simply no suffering in the world that could provide a basis for objecting to belief in God's presence.

Death

A Christian must similarly refuse to try to know too much in too great detail with regard to death. Here too in the past, from the time of the Bible on, people wanted to know and thought they knew so much in so much detail that today we can only shake our heads over it all. This is because precisely here, at the darkest moment of human life, Christians were understandably especially liable to link their faith in eternal life with ideas about the whole scheme of things that came from other sources. In this way the Christian tradition about death and about life after death is like a tree that bears so many blossoms and so much foliage that one can hardly discern its trunk. Yet blossoms fade and foliage withers when the weather alters with the changing seasons.

But an attentive reading of the biblical texts would have warned against indulging in too much speculation. However powerful the imagery of many biblical statements about death – and above all about the future of the world – and however difficult it may be to bring these various images into agreement with one another, the decisive biblical statements about death leave more questions open than they answer. First of all, Scripture seems less interested in the fate of the individual at death than in the future of the entire world. We shall return to this later. But on the other hand the New Testament leaves no doubt but that every individual has an eternal future to look forward to (cf Lk 16: 22–8, 23: 43). But this future does not involve anything new but merely makes plain what is already present and what faith already discerns in the signs that are now evident (Mk 4: 11 and parallel passages, 4: 30 ff and parallel passages; Mt 11: 25, 24: 27 ff; Mk 13: 24 ff, 14: 62 and parallel passages). There is only one distinction between present and future. In the present the reign of God that is already dawning means nothing but mercy and the offer of salvation for everyone, including those who are despised and lost (the "poor" and sinners: cf Lk 4: 18; Mt 5: 3 ff; Mk 2: 17 and parallel passages; Lk 15). The future, on the contrary, brings with it God's reign or kingdom in the double form of salvation for those who have accepted his mercy and judgment for those who have rejected it (Mt 13: 24–30, 24: 40 ff, 25: 31–46).

If we want to know more exactly what form salvation and judgment take there are in fact some texts which seem to provide a clear answer – but eventually in each individual case do not turn out to provide what had been expected (cf Mt 5: 3–13, 8: 12, 18: 34 f, 19: 28, 25: 31; Mk 9: 47 ff, 10: 29 f and parallel passages). On the contrary, we are explicitly told that conditions at the coming end of the world are completely different from what we now know, so that we cannot form any kind of idea of them (cf Mk 12: 24 ff and parallel passages, 14: 25 and parallel passages; 1 Cor 15: 35–53, and so on. Wherever clear language is used, the formulation that we shall be "with the Lord" (2 Cor 5: 8; Phil 1: 23; 1 Thess 4: 17) seems to say as much as needs be said. And there is one other thing we learn. That is that for those who are "with the Lord" it will be eternal joy, as is shown above all by Jesus' parables of the wedding-feast and the great supper (Mt 22: 1–14; Lk 14: 16–24; cf also Mt 5: 3–12; Mk 10: 29 ff; Mt 19: 28).

How then will the Christian encounter death? Inasmuch as dying and death are the natural course of things, they are part of suffering in the world, and the Christian will encounter them in the way we have described above. Inasmuch as dying and death are more than the rest of suffering, that is, inasmuch as they mark the end of everything with nothing to be discerned beyond them, the Christian will call to mind his faith in the resurrection of Jesus, the first-born of those that sleep. All that this faith says is that in Jesus God has anticipated what is intended for all men. That means that we know no more than formerly – since we cannot form any kind of idea of Jesus' resurrection and of his new life. But we know that God is the God of the living (Mk 12: 27), and this means that death sets no barrier to God's power and that therefore it is not the final word on man's life.

The Christian does not need to know or to believe anything more about death. Everything rather depends on making death the last act of faith in the God who raised Jesus from the dead. It is easy to understand that this act must take place before we find ourselves on our deathbed.

It is similarly easy to understand that this final act of faith is nothing other than faith pure and simple, admittedly achieved in view of the approach of death. And it is yet again easy to understand that we do not know when we shall have to make this final act. There is therefore a definite sense in which the Christian's entire life must be a life of faith looking forward to death or, as people liked to put it formerly, a preparation for death. According to each individual's personal temperament, age and experience, this life looking forward to death can take on a very different style: from profound seriousness that is continually aware that all things pass away, through an obvious composure that as it were forgets death and does not regard it as so important, to an explicit anticipation and even longing for death. When the French writer Charles Péguy was asked on his deathbed how he felt, he gave a classic Christian answer: "I am very curious."

Creation and new creation

We must conclude the considerations of this chapter by taking up once again the key-term "new creation". It has wider dimensions still. Up to now we have described how from the old Adam of sin, egoism and despair a new man is made who risks the freedom of the children of God. But in talking of the "new creation" Paul has indeed recalled the beginning of all things. He is of the opinion that what faith does to a man is so powerful that it can only be compared, and is in fact similar to, the origin of all things in God. What kind of sense can we make of this?

"Creation" as a statement of belief about the entire universe will be considered later. Here we are asking what it means for man. Even if we had no biblical statements at all about the creation of man in the image and likeness of God, what we have expounded so far would have to force us to the conclusion that the God who in his saving presence reveals himself to us as love itself cannot be anything other than love where our salvation is not at issue. From this it follows that the fact that there is a human misery from which we must be redeemed by God cannot be traced back to the God who saves us. It is man who is fundamentally responsible for this – however many distinctions and limitations we may have to make in working this out in detail. Hence our faith in God's saving action in Christ makes us recognize the lack of salvation in the world as sin and the consequence of sin. At the same time it forces us to recognize that God himself made the world good – and that man too was made good.

It is in the light of this consideration that we must read the statements of Scripture about God the creator, especially as the creator of man (Gen 1–2). We cannot naïvely read these statements as the first instalment of a history of the universe. Nor can we even read them as the first utterance of faith about God. That was only possible as long as God himself was not a question but self-evident certainty. In the context of what we have said earlier about the "death of God" we can only regain the ability to use the language of faith in God the creator by means of faith in God the redeemer.

This however makes talk of God the creator nothing less than an addendum to faith's message of salvation. It is rather that it places this message in its true context. The reign of God, God's presence, God's work of redemption in Jesus Christ is not a repair-job somewhere on the margin of cosmic history, nor is it some distinction, however splendid, conferred on man to raise him up over against the context of the whole. Rather is it the redemption of man, now beginning and once completed, the accomplishment of God's will throughout the entire universe even against the rebellion of his free creation. And the greatest proof of the power of this will is that God does not accomplish this by breaking or forcing man's will but by winning him through the gentle attraction of his grace, in other words through the invitation to believe in his love and to live from it.

Hence since the apostle spoke of the new creation the question has been raised throughout the history of theology, which is the greater, the creation of all things at the beginning or the redemption of man. Thomas Aquinas' answer was the redemption of man, since the gift of grace, even for only one single man, is greater than the creation from nothing of all things, which cannot receive grace (STh I–II 113: 9). Martin Luther declared that the justification of the sinner showed in the highest degree that God is God, since more than anywhere else it here becomes evident that the creator God is essentially nothing other than the outpouring of love. And according to Teilhard de Chardin, Christ the redeemer is the goal and final point of the evolution of the universe, of that evolution which is brought into and held in being by nothing other than a personal "super-love" at the summit of all things. The presence of salvation in Christ and hope in the world to come allow us to understand man and the world as God's creation. But it is precisely here that it becomes clear what man's redemption and perfection, what the meaning of history really is.

14   The old Adam

Here it would be as well to talk about sin. If we have acquired some grasp of what is meant by the new man, by the "new creation", and by the goodness of God's original creation, then we can and must understand that the apparently alien term sin is in fact a fundamental term in the language of Christian faith. One cannot talk about the new man and at the same time not want to accept the fact that there was – and is – an old Adam which the new man formerly was. Faith in the gift of salvation at once discloses the true face of the opposite of salvation, the condition from which God has already redeemed us through his forgiveness but which nevertheless remains with us right up to the end of time. This condition is called sin. We have already had to discuss it several times beforehand, but what we are trying to do now is to bring together what would otherwise remain a series of scattered references.

But why at this point? Would it not be better within the framework of ethical questions? The reason is that sin is something more than sinful behaviour. Sin is a situation in which man finds himself, as will be shown in what follows. Sinful behaviour makes this condition of sin apparent and has the effect of continually establishing it afresh. To look at the question from a different angle, this condition of sin and every individual evil action that takes place stand under God's gift of forgiveness – if man only accepts it. So it makes sense to discuss sin – and the ethical questions that arise – at the point where we are discussing the salvation that God gives. The believer looks back at the old Adam of sin. If he sins, it is a backsliding into a past that is over and done with. When on the contrary the question is what kind of behaviour is demanded by faith, there should be less readiness to raise the alarm of the danger of sin, as if man's salvation were once more at stake all over again, but rather an attempt to show what the believer has been set free by God for: for love.

This way of introducing the discussion of the subject of sin has moreover an excellent basis in the New Testament. When in the first part of his letter to the Romans Paul paints all men's entanglement in sin so blackly, this is not because he was by nature a pessimist. Rather it is that he is looking as if in fascination at what he knows he has broken free from. When in the seventh chapter of the same letter he uses the first person to picture the way in which the sinner is fragmented, then this is a looking back at his own lost existence before he arrived at faith. When he gives a very concrete list of the "works of the flesh" (Gal 5: 19–21), then this is within the context of the Spirit that gives strength not to succumb to these again. When he emphasizes the inevitability of sin for all Adam's descendants (Rom 5: 12 ff), then this is only to show how God's grace in Christ is still more powerful. This way of discussing sin clearly does the utmost to take God's saving act seriously. And Paul himself is the chief witness for how little this view does to play down the damaging nature of sin. We shall therefore now try to be faithful to this witness.

Sin as an individual act

Evil is one of the fundamental problems of mankind and despite all attempts to explain it it will always remain a mystery. In the world we encounter not only natural suffering and calamity which we can do nothing about but we also encounter evil in the strict sense: consciously willed behaviour by an individual person for which he is personally responsible. Even in our own case we are continually discovering that we are capable of being evil, or at the least fail to live up to the ideas and expectations of our fellow men. If this failure in faith is understood as rebellion against God, then it is called sin.

Awareness and feelings of guilt are among the basic experiences of men and women. They cannot simply be explained away as the result of a repressive upbringing or the suppression of the instincts. Sin is similarly one of the believer's basic experiences. One must not try to turn it into merely a survival of pagan awe of the numinous.

By sin, therefore, we first of all understand the action of a person who abuses the freedom that has been given him in full awareness and with full responsibility. Sin can therefore only be committed by someone who is mature and responsible. Sin in fact has the same primary meaning as wrongdoing: an evil action. All that the word sin indicates is that it is directed against God, while wrongdoing implies that it arises from personal decision. Hence it is not so much the individual external action in itself that is decisive for the degree of evil involved but rather the extent to which it is a matter of personal decision. Sin is properly to be found in the heart of man.

Sin and the condition of being a sinner

The deepest root of the individual sinful action, the essential sin, is unbelief. Sin is an abuse of that freedom that is laid hold of by faith. It abuses freedom before God to glorify itself and abuses freedom for love for arbitrary egotism. This abuse is brought about only by unbelief that will not accept that God alone gives freedom. Hence John and Paul often speak simply of sin in the singular. It is the origin of individual sins.

The individual sinful action thus has its roots in a false relationship of man to God. In the sight of God man is a sinner. It is precisely this false or distorted relationship to God that is at the root of sin. Faith cannot agree to any understanding of wrongdoing and sin that neglects God. And the other way round, when human society, justice and peace in the world are threatened, faith traces this back first of all to this damaged relationship to God. Of course this does not enlighten the non-believer. Sin after all is not just wrongdoing and failure with regard to one's fellow men, and certainly not just an external offence against a commandment, but a turning away from God, a lack of thanksgiving and faith. The reason for this turning away is to be found in man himself – so truly is he free. Hence he should not be too quick to shift the responsibility for the evil he does on to fate or destiny – nor even on to original sin.

Turning away from sin – just like deciding for God – involves a lifelong effort. Hence the call to conversion is something that is always applicable – at every moment. Even though he has been "justified" man continually stands in need of forgiveness by God. Every individual sinful action is a part of the history of our life. It was this that the Reformers had in mind when they spoke of man's total corruption. It is not merely individual actions but an entire life that is continually marked by sin that stands in need of God's forgiveness. But the facts of the case go even deeper.

Man – sinner from youth onwards

Knowledge of good and evil points to a flaw lying deep in man, a flaw that is continually expressed as conflict. This fundamental awareness of man's evil and sinfulness is expressed in the opening pages of the Bible in the story of the fall of man. Sin, as disobedience, selfishness and rebellion against God, is as it were pictured as man's first action. This story of the fall portrays for us man as he is and always will be: someone who again and again succumbs to the temptation to sin and decides against God. Susceptibility to evil clearly belongs to the nature of man as we know him. "The imagination of man's heart is evil from his youth" (Gen 8: 21).

There is one other thing the story tells us. Man has no excuse for sin – neither supernatural powers nor human weakness. Both aspects – the reality of sin and man's responsibility for it – are to be found in the doctrine of original sin, a doctrine that it is very easy both to misunderstand and to misapply.

The consequences of sin

It would be reading too much into the story of the fall of man if one wanted to describe illness, suffering and death or even the drudgery of human work and the pains of giving birth as direct consequences of sin. They are part of human life in this world as it is known to us. What reason there is for them is hidden from us. It is something different that faith sees as a consequence of human selfishness and human sin: man's alienation and isolation, the breaking down of his relationship not only to God but also to his fellow men. Sin is revealed plainly as man's separation and isolation from his fellow men and from God. Sin gives rise to death. Hence Paul describes Adam – man in general – as the originator of death for all men (1 Cor 15: 21 ff).

Death, however, is more than physical death. In Paul it

describes the entire hopelessness of man's condition, born as he is into a community of sinners and himself becoming a sinner. With sin man serves death, not life. Wherever someone demands his rights autocratically and without regard for others, is concerned only for his own affairs, wherever he enriches himself at the cost of others, controls and exploits his fellow man, wherever he cheats others who are of good faith, exploits others' need and dependency, wherever as an individual and as a member of society he egoistically rejects what is demanded by the future, wherever in marriage he goes his own way and neglects his partner for someone else's sake, wherever the promise of loyalty is broken, wherever too parents will not let their children be free to lead their own lives but are selfishly concerned for proofs of their affection – in all these cases man does not place himself at the service of life and its development but instead destroys life and thereby serves death. Evil and sin bring about suffering, bring life to naught, give rise to death.

Sin and wrongdoing as evil circumstances

This kind of annihilation and death as a consequence of sin and of man's nature as a sinner extend throughout all spheres of life in this world and reach their most fearsome aspect in the breakdown of peace, in war, and in mass murder. Hence we must also talk of sin and wrongdoing in a sense beyond the purely personal. We encounter evil in the established structures of this world and of human relations. Inasmuch as till the end of time this world is exposed to the power of evil and to human evil actions and remains characterized by them, one can talk of a dialectic of evil in the world. We encounter evil both as the action of the individual who is personally guilty and can be made to answer for his actions and in a way whereby men come together and are drawn together in entanglements and conflicts, in co-operation in injustice, persecution, war and killing. No kind of clear distinction is at all possible here between personal guilt, shared guilt, and joint responsibility for causing it all. Alongside and behind every individual wrongful act there is somewhere to be found as equally responsible the surrounding world with its lack of understanding and its fateful power of disaster.

Hence it is not going far enough merely to look for evil in individual persons and at the same time to overlook the fact that it can become institutionalized in so many established forms and patterns of society and of a particular economic system in which the rich continually get richer while the poor just get poorer. A realization of the repressive structures of a particular form of society or of an evil system is the foundation on which all this rests. But when repressive and unjust conditions are maintained unaltered, when they are not unmasked but instead whitewashed, then in this lack of vision sin becomes once more apparent. The same applies in reverse to those who suppress or deny all personal awareness of guilt and place the entire burden of wrongdoing on to social conditions alone, in the opinion that the alteration of social conditions would in itself rid the world of evil. This view forms the starting-point for various vulgarized forms of Marxist socialism. To do this is to gloss over the dialectic of evil in the world just as much as in a purely individualistic understanding of wrongdoing that tries to get rid of evil in the world merely through the good will of the individual.

Original sin

This extension of sin from the actions of an individual to the structures of society and the entire circumstances of the world has long been the subject of the doctrine of original sin. Since this doctrine has recently come in for heavy criticism and discussion, especially within the Catholic church, we must briefly examine it more closely.

Original sin has in the past frequently been thought of in terms of biological inheritance. But this connotation of inheritance is not entirely accidental. Briefly, what the doctrine is saying is that the first man Adam through his disobedience of God's commands lost the holiness and perfect justice before

God in which he was created and thereby fell into the servitude of evil and the power of death. In this Adam did not merely injure himself but all his descendants. They are all therefore through their descent from the first man sinners from birth, and it is only God who can rescue them from this sinfulness through the redemption he has given in Christ.

Theologians, especially those following in the tradition of Augustine, have of course tried to explain in greater detail these basic statements of the doctrine of original sin. Two aspects have always aroused their especial interest: the way in which Adam's sin is transmitted to his descendants, and the consequences of this sin for the life of the individual human being. It has, for example, been said that original sin is none other than sexual desire, with the result that every individual act of procreation, necessarily involving sexual desire, makes the person who is born as a consequence a sinner. Another opinion was that sexual desire in itself may not have been sinful but that thanks to Adam's turning away from God it, like all bodily and instinctive drives, had now become selfish and could now beget nothing other than a body selfishly dependent on its sensual drives and instincts. This, however, as it were infected the soul which God had created innocent and infused into the body and dragged the soul down with it into the selfishness of the body and thus into turning away from God. In this way every man and woman became a sinner through the very fact of human reproduction. Sinfulness thus becomes in fact a kind of inheritance that is passed on from generation to generation.

As far as the consequences of original sin are concerned, there has for example been endless discussion of the extent to which original sin turns man's freedom for good into a compulsion towards what is sinful and the extent to which his freedom is maintained. Or illness and physical death were understood as immediate consequences and effects of original sin, since a body that is no longer subordinate to God through the Spirit but is instead self-seeking has been abandoned to destruction.

Disputes over original sin

All this, and yet more still, need not occupy us any longer here. However, at the fifth session of the Council of Trent the Catholic church did raise the doctrine of original sin to the status of a dogma. But, as can be seen from glancing at the decree on original sin, all that this did was to confirm the basic statement involved in the doctrine without any commitment to more detailed theories. However, the doctrine of original sin has become a firmly established element in Christian doctrine as a whole and in the way it is proclaimed, not only in the Catholic church but in all the major churches, to such an extent that one can say it has gained great popularity, with the result that the contemporary discussion arouses considerable disquiet.

There are essentially three reasons for this popularity. First, the doctrine of original sin provides a very good foundation for presenting the history of mankind's salvation (and mankind's lack of salvation) in preaching and in instruction. God created man good and perfect, but man withdrew his obedience from God and thus plunged the whole of mankind into damnation until Christ, God become man, rescued mankind from this condition. Secondly, the doctrine of original sin helps one to provide an apparently very satisfactory answer to one of man's fundamental questions, the question of the origin of evil in the world. One can go further. When evil in the world becomes of such an extent that people can hardly trust other people as we know them any more, the doctrine of original sin and of the consequent sinful condition of everything offers a welcome explanation and in fact an excuse. Thirdly, the Church has for centuries baptized infants. What reason and meaning is one to find for this if these infants are not sinners and thus do not need baptism? But how can they be sinners when they are not yet themselves capable of sinning? The only explanation seems once again to be that these children are in fact sinners thanks to original sin, even if they personally have not committed themselves to any sin.

Why is this doctrine the subject of discussion today? To

begin with, the question has for some considerable time arisen, thanks to the progress of research into the history of mankind, whether the whole of mankind is in fact descended from one original pair of human beings or whether we are not rather descended from several such pairs that bred independently of each other. All presently available indications favour the latter view. But the switch from the theory of monogenism to that of polygenism obviously removes one of the bases for the doctrine of original sin as it has traditionally been understood and expounded. This logically presupposes that the history of the human race began with only one pair of human beings – quite apart from the fact that research into human origins does not allow us in any way to have quite such a wonderful and immaculate view of the first human beings before the fall as was often described by catechetical instruction on original sin.

Coupled with this progress in scientific research are the new findings of biblical scholarship. We have already pointed out that chapter 3 of Genesis does not only talk about original sin in the sense of the Church's later doctrine, it does not even talk of one single original historical pair of human beings at the start of human history but instead simply of man. What it is saying applies to all men and to every individual man. Admittedly sin and its consequences are represented as an all-embracing condition. But what the biblical writer meant was not that one man originally brought about this condition for all men but that every man, without being able to excuse himself, causes this condition of sin and brings it on himself and his fellow men.

Similar considerations apply to the other biblical passage to which the doctrine of original sin has always appealed, the apostle Paul's statements on Adam's sin in chapter 5 of his letter to the Romans. Paul too certainly talks of men's sins as a condition that has affected everyone descended from Adam. But it is not a question of an inherited sin but about the sinful actions of men which they, following Adam, have themselves committed. The only honest and decent course is to admit that, inasmuch as it rests on these passages, the traditional doctrine of original sin depends on a misunderstanding.

Christian faith without original sin?

Does this mean that the doctrine of original sin is something obsolete, a curiosity from the past history of the Church and of theology? Is the most that can be said that it has a certain meaning for the Catholic church inasmuch as it provides a test case for the attitude of Catholics to what has been solemnly proclaimed as a dogma? Far from it. It is not too much to say that today we are in a better position than we were to understand what original sin is all about, thanks to the new insights and findings provided by the criticism and the discussion. The following points must be maintained:

1. The purpose of the doctrine of original sin is not and has never been to provide us with information about the origins of the human race that cannot be provided by science. The doctrine of original sin provides just as little solution to the question of the origins of the human race as the account of creation in Gen 1 and 2 does to scientific questions. We must say goodbye to this kind of idea, even though it means that much in our proclamation of the Gospel is no longer as simple as it was.

2. Nor does the doctrine of original sin give us a convenient answer to the question of who or what is to blame for evil in the world. Anyone who wants to use the doctrine of original sin to provide a greater or lesser excuse for his own sin is forced to say precisely the opposite by the biblical passages, that in fact no man can shove the responsibility for sin on to others, whether other men or supernatural powers. It is an abuse of the doctrine of original sin to use it to exonerate one's own denial and to whitewash evil in the world. But that is what the doctrine of original sin emphasizes in its traditional form by misunderstanding the biblical texts. But in order to do this it has retained the challenging statement of the biblical texts in the form of a powerful paradox that claims what no one can really understand – that the sin of Adam (conceived of as a historical person) is really and truly the sin of all men.

3. One must also say goodbye to the idea that it is only the doctrine of original sin that provides a satisfactory reason for

the practice of infant baptism. Infants were being baptized in the Church at a time when the doctrine of original sin was as yet unknown in the form in which it is being discussed today. Augustine was the first to link infant baptism with original sin, and indeed regarded the custom of infant baptism as an argument for original sin. Today we cannot any longer think along these lines. There are good reasons to justify the practice of infant baptism, but original sin is not one of them. It is only when one has provided a solid foundation for infant baptism by examining other aspects of Christian doctrine that it makes sense to ask what the relation of infant baptism is to what the doctrine of original sin is all about.

4. But what is the doctrine of original sin all about, and what does it still have to tell us? To answer this question there is once again no better help than to look at the relevant biblical texts and make a close examination of the Church's doctrine. There are no important biblical passages and no decisive church statements that talk about original sin for its own sake. It is something that is only mentioned in the context of the promise and the working out of salvation in Jesus Christ. The biblical story of the fall concludes with the passage that people like to call the *Protoevangelium*, or primitive gospel: "The Lord God said to the serpent, 'I will put enmity between you and the woman, and between your seed and her seed; he shall bruise your head, and you shall bruise his heel'" (Gen 3: 14–15). In chapter 5 of the letter to the Romans, Paul mentions Adam's sin simply in order to show that God's grace in Jesus Christ is that much greater. And the Council of Trent only discussed original sin in order to lay the necessary foundations for the next subject on their agenda (at the sixth session), the sinner's justification by God and his grace. The core of the doctrine of original sin, whatever form it may be given, is that Christ is the redeemer of all men because all men without exception stand in need of God's redemption.

Therefore the doctrine of original sin takes the demand of the message of faith to its logical conclusion. If for the self-sufficient person it is already sufficient encouragement for him to thank not himself but God, then it is a real challenge to tell him that he has committed himself to denial and refusal and goes on doing so without being able to escape from this situation by his own ability – and that every optimistic over-assessment of his own powers and capabilities is out of place in view of the condition of sin which is both imposed on him from outside and which he consciously assents to. This theory or that of the origin and extent of evil in the world is possible, and scientific theories of evolution may today contribute new perspectives which play an important part in the contemporary discussion of the doctrine of original sin. But, quite apart from these theories, Christian faith is not possible without the fundamental statement of the doctrine of original sin, since faith cannot refuse to say that man needs God as the source of his being and redemption.

Sin and redemption

In this way the doctrine of original sin summarizes something that applies to every individual sin in the light of Christian faith – that the Christian can never mention sin and wrongdoing without at the same time mentioning the forgiveness that has been promised to men in Christ. Even in the desperate situation of sin men are given the promise of being saved by God – and that is what the opening pages of the Bible reveal. God has mercy on man, and for this reason justification, redemption and salvation cannot come about through man's unaided power or through the merits of his good works. So while on the one hand sin reveals man's powerlessness, on the other God reveals the greatness of his grace. In Christ human sin and wrongdoing become a "happy fault" (felix culpa). Augustine even speaks of "Adam's truly necessary sin that brought forth so great a redeemer" – a phrase that has been introduced into the liturgy of the Easter vigil.

"Mortal" and "venial" sins

Even someone who has accepted God's mercy in faith must be afraid of falling again into actual individual sins and of remain-

THE OLD ADAM
321

ing a sinner. Falling back into the past that is over and done
with remains an unfortunate possibility. Sin holds its sway
over man right up to death. God needs to forgive us not once
and for all but every day. What can be said about this persist-
ence of sin?

In this context Catholic doctrine makes a distinction between "mortal" and "venial" sin. What is meant is that in the
life of the believer there are sins that do not completely
destroy his status as a child of God, though they disturb it:
sins of omission, everyday faults, minor offences against love
– of God and of one's fellow men. At the same time there are
sins which, if committed with the necessary awareness,
decision and responsibility, separate one from God and destroy
everything that a man becomes through faith. The Bible talks
of sins that exclude one from the kingdom of God (cf Gal
5: 19–21; Eph 5: 5; 1 Cor 6: 9 f; Col 3: 5–8).

In theory this distinction between mortal and venial sin may
be unequivocal. In practice things are somewhat different.
Often one simply cannot say whether and to what extent some
attitude that seems insignificant, some so-called venial sin may
not hide a fundamental rejection of God and a deep-rooted
egoism that amounts to a total turning away from God, except
that the person concerned does not admit this turning away to
himself. Hence the Christian will take seriously weaknesses
that at first appear insignificant and everyday faults and ask
himself whether he has not remained a sinner in a much more
radical sense, someone who in the depths of his heart will have
nothing to do with God. Does that mean we must be frightened
and ask ourselves to what extent we have remained sinners
while all the time our heart impels us to actions that are not
the fruit of God's Spirit? The Christian does not obtain a clear
conscience with regard to sin as long as he weighs up the
degree to which it is "mortal" but as long as he takes God's
forgiveness at its face value – and passes it on to his fellow
men.

The distinction between moral and venial sin does not thus
help us much further forward. Salvation, the grace that God
gives, are not something we possess. Man must continually

accept them afresh, decide for God, break away from egoism into the freedom of the children of God. There is no better way of achieving this than of remaining aware how deep are the roots in the human heart that have been struck by the tendency to oppose God. But if the distinction between mortal and venial sin encourages one to be complacent about sin, then this distinction should decidedly be dropped so as not to minimize the abyss in man's heart.

15   The community of the faithful

One can be a Christian and a believer only in community with others. That has always been the case. A person may reach his personal decision about faith in one of many different ways. But once that decision has been made, it can only be realized together with others. Even a person born into the community of the faithful, and who grows up in it as the basis of his family life and education, must later on decide for himself whether he believes, and hence whether he wants to join in the community and the communal life in faith.

We usually refer to the community of those who believe in Christ as the "community" or the "church". These words are associated with a variety of widely differing concepts and interpretations which fortunately derive from the same root.

"Church" is a word borrowed from the Greek. *Kyriake* mean "those belonging to the Lord" or "the community of the Lord". Since the Reformation, however, the term has been used primarily to designate its visible structure and universal form. Since Luther, Evangelical Christians have stressed the inner reality of the community of the faithful and its practical embodiment in the local community, or parish. The original notion is that designated by one Greek word in the New Testament: *ekklesia*, which stands for the local community as well as the community of all the local churches, which together form the Church as a whole. Community and church are interchangeable. The local community is a church, and the universal Church is a community.

To start with, there are four main questions. Firstly, we shall examine the origin or roots of the community or Church, by which we mean the "historical Jesus", his mission, and the "apostles" he gathered round him.

Secondly, we shall try to understand the beginnings of community formation after Easter, by examining the foundation period of the Church, including the communities of Gentile Christians in the areas where Paul conducted his missions.

Thirdly, we shall outline some important characteristics of the communities and their organization in the post-apostolic period: ie, after the time of the apostles' personal activity, but still within the period that produced the writings of the New Testament.

Fourthly, we shall consider the relationship of "ministry" and "community" which may help us to come to terms with the problems of our own day.

I. THE ORIGIN OF THE COMMUNITY

What is the historic origin of the community? How and why did men begin to gather together in Christian communities?

Easter

Many people think that the origin of the community is in the extraordinary events after Jesus' death through which he showed that he was living. The "appearances" – no matter how they are interpreted – resulted in the "cause of Jesus" not being given up for lost. Indeed they acted as a challenge to carry it on. "Jesus' cause" served to unite the disciples and created a feeling of community among all who supported it.

But talk of "Jesus' cause continuing" does not really convey the full significance of "the resurrection of Christ". Even if we were to accept this definition, it does not account for the origin of the Church. Just what is this "cause of Jesus"? What exactly is the "Jesus thing"? We can only understand it if we take into account the things Jesus did before his death. Even though the Church was only founded after Easter, that was in no sense an absolute beginning. What Christ wanted, what he lived and died for, must by then have been well enough known to provide a starting point.

If "Jesus' cause" is a kind of programme, a philosophy of life, a new religion, a message, and hence a "cause", then the common knowledge of what he wanted and what had to be carried out need only have led to the formation of a kind of "action group" or association with a common programme. But, as far as we can tell, the community saw itself in different terms right from the start: as a community founded by and in Jesus Christ, through whom it derives its permanence. Or, to put it differently, it saw itself as a community instituted by God through the deeds of Jesus of Nazareth – through his message, his death and resurrection, and through the communication of his Spirit after Easter. The risen Christ appeared to those individuals who had had a closer contact with him than the mass of the people. On the whole, the Easter experience happened to people who knew Jesus personally and already had an attachment to him. They had to be able to "recognize him anew", as in the gospel accounts. The appearances undoubtedly came as a surprise to *all*, since no one did or could count on them. And yet these experiences alone cannot explain why people devoted themselves so whole-heartedly and with such conviction to "Jesus' cause". Yet that is just what did happen. So we must conclude that devotion to his message, his aims, his deeds and his "cause" is indissolubly bound up with attachment to his "historical person". The events that followed Easter are not enough to explain the origin of the Christian community.

Before Easter

We must probe further and look for the origin of the Church in the events preceding Easter. First we must make one point clear. We are not concerned with the often-repeated question as to whether Christ wanted a community or not, or whether he envisaged or expected one in the future. Any such questions are fundamentally dubious because they aim at knowing what we can never know, namely Christ's own thoughts and intentions: his innermost thought-processes. In that case a wide variety of divergent suggestions is to be expected. For our present purposes, we must stick to what is definitely discernible in tradition.

We remember that Jesus came with the news of the coming of "God's kingdom". Jesus does not proclaim this kingdom as a doctrine *about* God, the end of the world, or the future of human society. Instead, the kingdom of God is announced as an *event* or happening that is beginning there and then. The coming of Christ is also the coming of the kingdom of God. It determines everything Jesus says, does and suffers. For mankind this means that the irrevocable moment has arrived, the moment for a final, categorical decision. Everything is at stake: life or death, salvation or destruction.

Jesus does not remain alone. Because the preaching of the kingdom of God is so urgent, it has to be done as quickly as possible. For this task, helpers and co-workers are needed. All four gospels contain reliable reports that even in the early stages Jesus gathered "disciples" round him (cf Mk 1: 16–20). There were already many examples of this custom. Wandering preachers and the Greek schools of philosophy used to collect pupils and move round from town to town. The scribes (rabbis) taught their pupils how to interpret the law (the "Torah") by means of years of study and training. Revolutionaries like Judas of Galilee (cf Acts 5: 37) mobilized "combat groups" in order to topple the Roman regime and to pave the way forcibly for the "kingdom of God". John the Baptist sparked off a powerful popular movement, and gathered flocks of men around him for support. Jesus was close to him and was caught up in his movement. Some of John's "disciples" then became followers of Jesus. Jesus shared this one factor with all such preachers: he gathered people round him. And this is where the origin of the community seems to lie.

Disciples

We must look closer. The group that gathered round Jesus is in some respects different from all other examples. Here it is not a question of an individual coming to him and asking to be included in the circle. On the contrary, Jesus calls *him*. The would-be rabbi, on the other hand, came to the master in order to learn the "Torah". Jesus simply called "those whom he desired" so that they should "be with him" (Mk 3: 13 f).

The student rabbi was trained for years so that later he, too, could be a "master and teacher". By contrast, Jesus founds no school, and demands no studying, memorizing or organized teaching. The basic pledge is made directly in relation to his *person*; his disciples participate in his life and fate. They have no home or permanent dwelling, but wander round the countryside with him (cf Lk 9: 57 f).

What is the significance of this pledge to his person and his life? Are we to understand it as a kind of "princely court" such as great men like to gather round themselves? Or as a kind of servitude like that practised by the rabbis, whose pupils also had to wait on their teachers? Jesus' followers were certainly involved with his work and "mission". But in what sense? Did Jesus want to form an élite group, distinct from the masses, with special privileges, but subject to higher demands? Or was it to form the core of a new "community" within the old "community of Israel" – and simultaneously a protest against the prevailing constitution, as was the case with the community at Qumran? The text in Mark to which we have already referred gives no specific answer to these questions. For Jesus' aim in calling the disciples was not merely that they "be with him" but, as the text continues, "to be sent out to preach and to have authority to cast out demons" (Mk 3: 14). They were to take part in his *work* – in the task of proclaiming the kingdom of God. Like Jesus, they were to make this reign or kingdom of God visible through their actions.

Did the "disciples" really do this? It is historically certain that Jesus sent these men out on at least one occasion. His talks to them before sending them out to preach in Mk 3: 13 ff;

6: 6–13 (=Lk 9: 1–6); Lk 10: 1–10 according to the logia source, and Mt 9: 35–40, 42 in a combined form also reflect the later mission of the Church. The discrepancies between the different texts reflect the different missionary situations involved. But they all share the same historical basis to which the following factors definitely belong: the mere fact that he sent the men out, the command to preach the kingdom of God (cf Lk 10: 9), the authority to drive out demons, the command of the kiss of peace, the spartan outfit ("no purse, no bag, no sandals", "nor a staff": Lk 10: 4; Mt 10: 10), and probably the command to go out in pairs. The disciples were sent out to villages and towns all over Israel, although Jesus' actual sphere of influence was confined to Galilee and his own district. They were pressed for time, speed was imperative ("salute no one on the road": Lk 10: 4). People spoke of a kind of "major invasion" of Israel. Everyone should come into contact at least once with the power of the word and the demand of the hour. The gospels also describe how the apostles returned and told Jesus of their experiences (Mk 6: 30; Lk 10: 17 ff). On the whole, though, this campaign seems to have been a failure in the same way that Jesus' own appeal to all Israel finally died away.

The "messengers'" preparations for their task are remarkable indeed. They are to take only the base necessities. They may not even wear sandals, nor take a bag for provisions, nor a staff. What is the significance of these radical stipulations? Surely they are not intended to symbolize an ideal of frugality or unpretentiousness, as with the Cynics in Greece. Nor are they intended as a ascetic means of illustrating the seriousness of conversion, as with John the Baptist. The reason is to be found in the basic premiss of the whole "cause": the supremacy of the kingdom of God over all other things. The messenger is so absorbed in this that he has no time left for any practical consideration or provision (cf Lk 10: 4–12).

Followers of Jesus

The same maxim seems to apply not only to those directly

commissioned by Jesus, but to all vocations. Those who are
called are so absorbed by the new claims made on them that
all other considerations seem unimportant. Whoever joins
Jesus must leave his job and home, and even give up close ties
to his family. The four fishermen of Lake Genezareth (Mk 1:
16–20) and the tax collector Levi (Mk 2: 14) were torn away
from their jobs. "And immediately they left their nets and
followed him" (Mk 1: 18). Whoever wants to follow Jesus
must leave house and home. Jesus puts it as if in a commandment: "He who loves father or mother more than me (and that
means here the kingdom of God that I bring with me) is not
worthy of me" (Mt 10: 37; Lk 14: 26). Nowhere is this more
unequivocally expressed than in the request of a man who
wanted to follow Jesus: "Lord, let me first go and bury my
father. But Jesus said to him, Follow me, and leave the dead
to bury their own dead" (Mt 8: 21 ff). His reply showed an
unforgivable disregard for the law (the fourth commandment),
tradition and the duty of reverence to the dead. For many
Jews the fourth commandment was the most important of all.
Throughout antiquity, the burial of the dead was the natural
duty of the relatives or son, and under rabbinical law it was
also regarded as a special labour of love. But even this counts
for nothing against the supreme demands of the hour. Once
the first move has been made, once the hand has been put to
the plough, there can be no turning back. This unconditional
detachment Jesus demands is only comprehensible if it really
is the last moment – the last chance. There are no contemporary parallels to such behaviour and demands.

To be able to devote oneself wholly to the communal cause
requires total freedom from all property and possessions.
Jesus' disciples live communally, not out of one purse, but
from what people give them. On one occasion there is mention
of some women among his followers who served him by providing for his disciples out of their own money (Lk 8: 1–3). To
a man who wanted to be accepted as a disciple, Christ said:
"Go, sell what you have, and give to the poor, and you will
have treasure in heaven; and come follow me." (Mk 10: 21.)
It can be summed up as *following*. Jesus himself says so when

summoning the disciples: "Follow me!" This involves an obligation to him, and simultaneously a detachment from all other spheres of life. One determines the other.

After Easter, "following Jesus" was occasionally interpreted in a purely spiritual way, in the sense of shaping one's life in imitation of him. Basically though, "following" means to be bound unconditionally to Jesus and his work.

Rules for the apostolate

Was there an organized circle of disciples with established rules and customs? Certainly, such things as communal meals seem to indicate that there was, though we have no means of proving it. Jesus did not have the time systematically to build up a new community. The urgency of his task and the short time allowed him did not permit it. But in the last analysis the external institutional form is less important than the *inner* "rules" the former is intended to embody. These "rules" are determined wholly by Jesus' personality and actions. One rule is given particular emphasis: that there be no leaders and no servants among them. He himself is "among you as one who serves" (Lk 22: 27). There is no distinction between lesser and greater; and no ranks or titles or special claims: "If any one would be first, he must be last of all and servant of all" (Mk 9: 35). Those who belong to him and "follow" him must also be living examples of what the lordship of God means: that there is only one Lord, but that all are brothers and that, as Jesus himself showed, true greatness manifests itself only through service. This was later applied to the "ministry" of the Church, as we can see from the passage in Luke: ". . . rather let the greatest among you become as the youngest and the *leader* as one who serves" (Lk 22: 26).

The twelve

One more question about the institutional character of the circle of disciples concerns the "Twelve", as the group (except at Mt 10: 2) is described throughout the gospels. Within the mass of disciples there is a small group of twelve men. The names sometimes vary in the different accounts, but the number is always the same (cf Mk 3: 16–19; Lk 6: 14–16; Mt 10: 2–4; Acts 1: 13).

The establishment of this circle is presumably to be attributed to Christ himself, despite certain assertions to the contrary. The oldest known account, in 1 Cor 15: 5, includes the Twelve among the witnesses of the appearances of the risen Christ, thus presupposing their existence at that time as an established group. It is hardly conceivable that a group of twelve men should have formed of its own accord *after* Easter (with Judas as a member) without any previous indication.

This is quite clear if we realize the significance of the number twelve, and that the group of men numbered twelve. Twelve symbolized the twelve tribes of Israel, represented by their twelve "Fathers". In establishing this circle of twelve men, Jesus must have intended to convey that his mission embraced the whole of Israel. God's demands on this nation were thus made visible. The validity of this interpretation is proved primarily by the fact that the mass of the people – mostly simple and uneducated – had to understand the symbolic character of this circle if it was to fulfil its purpose. The circle of the Twelve was a sign to Israel – a sign that it should repent and be converted. The chance of salvation was to be given to the whole nation and to every individual in it.

This symbol of the Twelve is characterized by the same earnestness and inability to compromise as everything else Jesus said or did. Unfortunately some people think that the Christian faith is concerned solely with the conversion of the individual, with his personal faith and reconciliation with God. This is not wrong, but it is not everything, and in the sense of the New Testament not the primary factor. God's will and Jesus' mission are directed towards the whole human race. Israel therefore stands for the whole of mankind, and is itself represented by the circle of the Twelve, who in turn symbolize God's love for mankind and his desire to grant it salvation and perfection.

The fisherman Simon, son of John, is the first name mentioned in all four gospels. He is also called "the rock" (Aramaic: *kepha*; Greek: *petra*, "petros" being the masculine form) and is described as the spokesman of the group. The word "rock" is scarcely applicable to his character, which is depicted on the contrary as easily excitable, indecisive, and not wholly reliable. It must therefore refer to his specific function or position within the group. Hence the risen Jesus appeared to him first (cf Lk 24, 34; 1 Cor 15: 4), and during the period immediately following the ascension he was the leader of the community in Jerusalem.

But even in the period before Easter we can see the first signs of a tension that has remained with the Church up to the present day. Namely, the tension between the mass of the disciples and the group of Twelve, between the common calling and the symbolic institution, and even between the Twelve and their leader, Peter. These various tensions cannot be simply put aside. But they pose no threat to the unity of the disciples and the Church if they are understood in their original relationship to the kingdom of God, of which they are to a certain extent the symbolic representation. These tensions will not be overcome or settled in the future, but remain related to the fulfilment of the kingdom of God that still lies ahead of us. They are the symbolic beginning of the fulfilment of the kingdom, and as such at all times point beyond themselves.

II. AFTER EASTER

At first Jesus' mission was wrecked by his death. It split up the group of Twelve and the wider circle of his disciples. The encounters with the living Jesus brought them together again, convinced that his work had not been in vain after all. On the contrary, God himself had intervened with all his power and raised Jesus from the dead, thereby initiating the new creation. All of a sudden this became absolutely clear, and necessarily made the disciples aware that "Jesus' cause" was by no means lost. Just the opposite, through Jesus' resurrection it became truly legitimate and had to be brought to the people. Hence in all accounts of Jesus' resurrection and appearances to the apostles there is the underlying thought of the *mission*. These mysterious yet overwhelming encounters with the risen Jesus must have been intended to have this effect and must have made a deep impression on the apostles (cf a clear example in the case of Paul in Gal 1: 15 ff).

Later on the missionary task was expressed in different words. For instance: ". . . and that repentance and forgiveness of sins should be preached in his name to all nations, beginning from Jerusalem . . ." (Lk 24: 47). The most powerful articulation of this thought comes at the end of Matthew's gospel, where the permanent task of the Church is given the classic formulation: "All authority in heaven and on earth has been given to me. Go therefore and make disciples of all nations, baptizing them in the name of the Father and of the Son and of the Holy Spirit, teaching them to observe all that I have commanded you; and lo, I am with you always, to the close of the age" (Mt 28: 18–20).

What did this mean for the progress of history? In the first instance, the demand imposed on Israel was understood in a new light. There was a revival of conviction that the lordship of God was coming, which then developed into belief in the one through whom God had acted so wonderfully. For the community in the early period after Easter, assembly and mission were one and the same thing. The assembly did not take place for its own sake, in order to form a separate community within the politico-religious union of Judaism. Rather, it was formed in order to pass on the message to all Israel. Jesus' disciples became his "missionaries". "For we cannot but speak of what we have seen and heard" (Acts 4: 20). The group of Twelve also reassembled in Jerusalem and remained there as the symbolic embodiment of Jesus' demand to the whole nation. The field of missionary activity expanded rapidly and soon spread "to the end of the earth" (Acts 1: 8).

Community as assembly

With the resurrection of Jesus the way was open to the world of God. This was the experience of the Easter appearances, which could not but be interpreted in this way in Israel at that time. Those who experienced them necessarily saw themselves as the eschatological people of God. This can be seen in the words used by the early communities in Palestine to describe their members: words such as "saint", "called" and "chosen", all of which suggest a distinctly fervent outlook.

The word "community" (of God) (=the Greek *ekklesia theou* and the Hebrew *kehal Jahwe*) was probably introduced by the Jewish-Christian communities in the Greek-speaking world. The word *ekklesia*, "community" (of God or Jesus Christ), dominated the whole mission, even in the Graeco-Roman areas. The assembly led to the first forms of community. The profession of faith in Jesus as the *messiah* or *kyrios* ("Lord") had to be put into words (cf 1 Cor 16: 22: *maranatha*= "Our Lord come!"; 1 Cor 15: 3–5; Lk 24: 34). The community in Jerusalem took part in the official temple services, but at the same time developed a certain life of its own. In terms of religion, laws and way of life it still regarded itself as an inherent part of Israel, though independent assemblies undoubtedly took place very early on – to "break bread", to pray, to exchange ideas and to help one another.

The profession of faith in the "messiah" also requires entry into the community – in other words an outward act of decision. This profession of faith unites and divides simultaneously. Entry into the community is symbolized by the act of "baptism". The historical origin of Christian baptism is unknown, but the immediate source is certainly the baptism by immersion instituted by John the Baptist. The *meaning* of the act, however, is absolutely clear. Through his profession of faith in Jesus the messiah, the candidate for baptism enters into the newly-declared people of God, and hence into the community of the faithful. Through this act he is able to participate in the reality and intensity of this new world.

The first Christians described this as the "Spirit of God". For it was God who had created the faith, given them the language to proclaim it, granted them perseverance when in need, or persecuted or in prison, and aroused in them an overwhelming joy and the hope that from then on everything would be all right. On account of these experiences the community saw itself as the work of the Spirit of God. This conception of the community was also fundamental to the missionary communities outside Palestine, as can be seen above all from Paul's letters. Superficially, it may seem as if the community originated "from below" – as an assembly of people united by a common conviction. The community, however, saw itself right from the start as originating "from above", through God's calling and the working of his Spirit. This is a fundamental truth that must hold good in the Church at all times, regardless of any temporary differences in the form of community life.

Formation of the community through the missions

At a certain point in time which we can no longer trace, a missionary movement spread outwards from Jerusalem. It is possible that other Christian groups were formed after Easter in Galilee, Christ's native region, and that they conducted their own missionary campaigns, but we cannot be sure about this.

The first step mentioned in Acts is a mission conducted in Samaria (Acts 8: 5–25). The second, more important, step was Peter's admission of the first Gentiles to the community, also described in detail in Acts (Acts 10: 1–11, 18).

The mission in Palestine presumably lasted longer. The missionaries apparently had a hard struggle, yet the final result was disappointing. Like Jesus himself, they failed because of a "lack of faith". Traces of violent hostilities and persecutions during this period are to be found in particular in the texts of the "logia source". Nevertheless, some communities were founded in Palestine (cf Gal 1: 22), and persevered stubbornly until the catastrophe of AD 70, when they began to decline in importance. They ceased to exist entirely from about AD 135 onwards. The Jews, under the leadership of the Pharisaical rabbis, only made the final break with Christianity towards the end of the first century – by excommunicating all Christians.

The community in Jerusalem contained a number of different

"factions". One of these, the so-called "Hellenists" – presumably Christians from the Jewish diaspora – appears in chapters six and seven of Acts. This group consisted of seven inspired men working as missionaries, who seem to have adopted a more critical attitude to the Jewish law and temple rites. Stephen, the most outspoken among them, was finally stoned by the Jews, as a result of which the first wave of persecutions broke out. The members of the Jerusalem community scattered in all directions (Acts 8: 1). But instead of having a dampening effect, these persecutions became the starting point for a new mission. The faith spread to Phoenicia, Cyprus and Syria. Antioch, the capital of Syria, was to play a very important rôle in the campaign. The community there became very significant in the development of the early Christian communities in that it was the first community established in a "Gentile" area, and consisted of a mixture of Jewish and non-Jewish converts. It even superseded Jerusalem in its missionary zeal, sending out many missionaries, mostly to the southern part of Asia Minor. It "discovered" Paul and drew him into the missionary operation. Paul undertook his first long journey that we know of, together with Barnabus, as a delegate from Antioch (Acts 11: 25 ff, 13: 1–3).

Paul's community

In the period between about AD 45 and 65, Paul played the most important rôle in the missions. Born and brought up in Tarsus in Cicilia, he was educated at the temple school in Jerusalem. In religious terms he was committed to the doctrines of the Pharisees, and during the 30s he was a violent enemy of Christianity, until overwhelmed and totally converted by a heavenly encounter with Christ. From that time on, his entire life and work was dominated by this experience. In his Letter to the Galatians he gives just a brief account of his life up to the year 50 (Gal 1–2). After the journey with Barnabas he decided to work independently, and set off alone on his first long journey through the centre of Asia Minor as far as the west coast, and from there to Europe. On the way he stopped off at Philippi, Thessaloniki, Berola, Athens and Corinth. His second journey, from 52–5, took him mainly to Ephesus, where he spent at least two to two and a half years, building it up into the centre of his new missionary area in Asia Minor. After that he returned to Jerusalem to hand over a collection of money to the non-Jewish Christian community there. This journey ended with his arrest, followed by two years' imprisonment in Caesarea and transportation to Rome, where he died a martyr's death.

Admittedly, there had been a few Gentile communities before, but it was Paul who first fought for and enforced the rights of the Gentile communities which had not made the detour by way of Judaism: that is, circumcision. He also broke through the boundaries of Palestine, Syria and Asia Minor, and brought the message of the Messiah to Europe. It was above all thanks to his efforts that the decisive barrier between the Jews and Gentiles (the law of Moses) was finally dropped. For, after the crucifixion, death and resurrection of Jesus, it had ceased to have any significance as a path to salvation. With penetrating insight, Paul recognized that the law and the "cross of Christ" – as he put it – were mutually exclusive. Either one or the other is the true path to salvation, but not both. What God had accomplished through Jesus Christ was radically new. The whole situation of the world was new. The individual who accepted this situation with faith (Paul calls this being "in Christ") was himself "a new creation" (2 Cor 5: 17). For the new people gathered together by God there can be no different conditions of entry – Jews and Gentiles are treated as equals. The call to the faith is also the call to freedom; in other words to free access to God and to the freedom of mutual love (cf Gal 5: 1–13 ff).

Paul's letters give us considerable insight into the life of the Pauline communities, their difficulties and problems, but also their great vigour. They give us the most colourful and concrete picture we possess of any early Christian community. Of all the problems that emerge we must examine one closely: the relationship between the community and Paul's apostolate; that is, the "ministry" as such.

Paul considered himself equal to all; in his faith, in his un-deserved vocation, and in his hopes for perfection. Together with all other believers he belonged to the "body of Christ". By this he meant the direct sense of belonging to the risen and ever-present Lord, and sharing in the salvation he had brought. But at the same time he meant the community of the faithful, both in terms of the multiplicity of its members and of their mutual support and solidarity (cf Rom 12: 4–8; 1 Cor 12; Col 1: 18, 24). For this reason Paul often speaks in the first person plural. .

But Paul also stood over and above the communities, as an apostle. The term "apostle" had existed before his time and had roughly the same meaning as "missionary" (envoy, mes-senger), but he gave it a far deeper significance. Indeed, he emphasized the authority of the apostles to an almost extreme degree, though he was probably driven to this stand by the numerous false charges, hostilities, persecutions and cam-paigns directed against his work. He saw this authority first and foremost as the power to preach the word of Jesus. "Woe to me if I do not preach the gospel!" (1 Cor 9: 16). Hence a missionary canon was also included. The apostles had to bring the good tidings to all who had not yet heard them. To the Jews he had to become "as a Jew", so that he "might win those under the law", and though himself "under the law of Christ", to those outside the law" he "became as one outside the law" in order to win over the Gentiles (1 Cor 9: 20 ff).

The power and authority to spread the word included the power to found and lead communities. Paul himself had strict control over the direction of his communities, and for this reason they were probably relatively slow in developing their own constitution. He dominated everything, and demanded unlimited authority as an apostle of Jesus. He did not, how-ever, want to "lord it over your faith" (2 Cor 1: 24), and sub-mitted himself to the community of "those who were apostles before" him, out of concern for the overall unity of the com-munities (cf Gal 1: 17; 1 Cor 15: 11).

Service in the Pauline communities

Only in the community at Philippi do we hear of "deacons" and "bishops" (Phil 1: 1). In Greek these terms originally referred to separate activities. *Diakonos* usually referred to the table-servant, though it was also applied to menial workers and slaves. *Episkopos* generally referred to minor employees, such as overseers in the building trade or in the government service, and was rarely associated with religious rites. In Philippi the deacons and bishops seem to have joined together in a kind of college, in which differences of rank were apparently irrelevant.

In his first letter to the Thessalonians (5: 14), Paul mentions certain members of the community who "are over you in the Lord". The Greek word for "to stand over" can also mean "to labour at", and presumably both meanings are intended when Paul admonishes the faithful to respect such people. He certainly did not use the word "to be over" in the sense of an official position. In the lists of different gifts and services given in 1 Cor 12: 4–11, 28–31 and Rom 12: 6–8, mention is made of some which clearly refer to a kind of leadership (for example, "prophets" and "apostles"), though they are followed by extremely modest services, such as "he who gives aid" and "he who does acts of mercy". The sole forms of "ministry" to be found in the Pauline community are his own apostolate, and the "hierarchy" of apostles, prophets and teachers which was valid for the whole Church (1 Cor 12: 28). Paul describes all such activities and vocations as "gifts of mercy" or "spiritual gifts". The great variety of these gifts is the expression of the eschatological or prospective community and of the general manifestation of the Spirit. Through these gifts the community was edified, kept vital, qualified to bear testimony, and stirred to worship and praise, as well as prepared for service. The community in Corinth, in particular, was "not lacking in any spiritual gift" (1 Cor 1: 7). There was such a chaotic abundance of gifts that Paul wisely intervened to establish order (1 Cor 12–14).

In doing so he raised two points which are still of fundamental importance. Firstly, that the various gifts and tasks are
not given to the individual for his own personal edification or
satisfaction, but for the good of *all*. Each must see what he
personally can do for *others* and the cause as a whole with the
gifts with which he has been endowed. And secondly, all activities and tasks related to the community and its testimony
are to be considered as gifts of the Spirit. In other words,
stress should be laid not only on the striking, spectacular and
inspiring gifts such as prophetic speech, enraptured speaking
in tongues, miracles, healing, or special strength of faith.
Equal store should be set by the more humble gifts such as
works of mercy, care for the lonely, encouragement and comforting words, practical and often dirty work, help for the
poor and sick, and even financial administration.

Paul introduced certain lasting attitudes into the community. Each person has some contribution to make, according to his ability and gifts. The variety of gifts should not
lead to confusion, but should contribute to the organization of
the whole. No one should want to be the master of his
brothers. All who profess the same faith and are endowed with
the same Spirit are of the same rank – there is no distinction,
for instance, between "priests" and "laymen". Among Jesus'
disciples there are no priests, and in the Jerusalem community
former priests were simply counted among the general body
of the faithful (Acts 6: 7). Jesus is the only priest in the New
Testament. During the founding period of the Church the
only "ministry" was that of the apostles, which was a unique
institution that could never be repeated. Even the "prophets"
were soon regarded as an institution confined to the early
Church (cf Eph 2: 20). In this respect, too, Jesus' community
or Church is a "new" foundation.

We cannot assert that the original and sole legitimate constitution of the Church was a "charismatic" one in the sense
of 1 Cor 12 and Rom 12. Nor can we assert that the priestly
constitution that emanated from Palestine and Syria is the
only possible constitution for the community. The two forms
should not be played off against each other, because they

belong to different historical situations, while expressing
different trends which can easily be linked.

In the later texts of the New Testament we read that the
Church was built on the foundation of the apostles (and prophets). While Revelation mentions only the apostles (Rev 21:
14; however cf 18: 20), Paul's letter to the Ephesians refers to
both apostles and prophets (Eph 2: 20; 3: 5). The truly fundamental significance of the early Christian prophets was only
understood later, when they were placed on a par with the
apostles. Even in Paul's writings their decisive importance for
community life emerges, though the apostles always maintain the first place. The apostles were, after all, the founding
ministry of the Church.

The ministry

But what happened when the apostles had died and could no
longer carry on their task of guiding and leading the community? Who led the communities then? Here, too, we find
the answer in the New Testament.

It would be an oversimplification and not in accordance
with the historical facts to state that the office of the apostles
passed to anyone other than their immediate successors – as
was claimed by the First Letter of Clement in about AD 100
(42–4). Similarly, we cannot simply say that several different
forms of constitution existed simultaneously and that one of
these was finally "victorious". Unfortunately, we cannot trace
the full historical development of the ministry. Our overall
picture is far from complete, and is full of transitions, intermediary steps, exceptions, local differences, tensions and
rivalries, as well as the concurrent existence and fusion of
what were originally separate community forms and services.

No matter how complicated the various aspect of this
development, we can nevertheless state with certainty that
in the post-apostolic period there were community leaders

(Acts, Jas, Rev, 1 Pet, Heb, and the pastoral letters). There are various descriptions for them. The Letter to the Hebrews speaks of "leaders" (Heb 13: 7, 17, 24), the Letter to the Ephesians of "pastors" (Eph 4: 11); while most of the other texts of the later period speak of "presbyters" or "bishops" (Acts 14: 23; 20: 17; Jas 5: 14; 1 Pet 5: 5; 2 and 3 Jn; 1 Tim 5: 1; Tit 1: 5: – to quote just a few examples).

The word "presbyter" is by far the most frequently used. It has a long history going back to the Old Testament and the Jewish tradition. It was probably first adopted by the Christian ministry in Jerusalem and Palestine, from where it spread via Syria and Asia Minor to Europe (cf the First Letter of Clement to the Corinthians and Romans).

Almost everywhere in the New Testament the presbyters are united in a college, from which we can deduce that they conceived of their ministry as a communal one. The historic prototype is found in the constitution of the Jewish synagogue communities. Each local Jewish community had a committee of presbyters (a "presbyterium"), normally consisting of seven members. The Jewish communities in the diaspora also had such synagogue committees. The clearest picture of the first Christian community in Jerusalem is obtained from Acts (21: 17–26), where mention is made of a college of presbyters headed by James. This concept of the priesthood was linked with the title and function of the Greek *episkopos* or bishop. Acts 20: 17, 28 shows just *how* the two were linked. Similarly, in the pastoral letters the two titles appear together, though there they are linked in a different way, thus indicating the irregular structure of the ministry. The superiority of bishops over presbyters is not definitively stated anywhere in the New Testament. Both belong to an administrative group in which the two forms are merged.

Hence the post-apostolic Church possessed a circle of leaders, most of whom were called "presbyters". The college of presbyters governed the local communities. This was the presbyters' most important function, to which many other activities were linked. To a certain extent, though, other offices were considered independently, such as the "evangelists" and "teachers" mentioned in Eph 4: 11. The presbyters themselves also took over a certain amount of proclaiming and teaching (cf the pastoral letters). The task of preserving the true apostolic tradition and protecting it from abuse is frequently emphasized (cf Acts 20: 28; the pastoral letters).

Offices of the ministry

Right from the early stages there were signs that a special "class" would develop within the community (cf 1 Pet 5: 5; Heb 13: 7, 17, 24; 1 Thess 5: 12). Those in office were exhorted to carry out their tasks in the spirit of Jesus, in other words to serve and not to rule (Lk 22: 26). They should be on their guard against the desire for gain or power, and should not regard their ministry as a burden (cf 1 Pet 5: 1–4). Those holding an office should take Jesus as their model and thus become models for their communities. Even at this stage there are indications of the problems that were to increase with time (cf 3 Jn 9: ff). The first letter of Peter stresses that the aim of this ministry of leadership is not to draw the gifts and deeds of others to itself, but to make them effective for the good of all: "As each has received a gift, employ it for one another, as good stewards of God's varied grace" (1 Pet 4: 10).

The office of prophet continued to play a rôle for some time to come, and only faded out when it came into disrepute in the middle of the second century. Teachers are named as an independent class in the writings of Clement of Alexandria in about AD 200. The letters of Ignatius of Antioch describe the development of the "monarchical episcopacy" in Antioch, in which the bishop is the representative of God, while the presbyters under him are the representatives of the apostles.

The "hierarchical" order of bishop, presbyter and deacon first developed in Antioch, though that remained for a long time the sole instance of this practice. Even in Rome in the middle of the second century there was only a college of presbyters, to which the bishops and deacons likewise belonged – as can be seen in the anonymous text *The Shepherd of Hermas*. The office of presbyter and bishop began to assume ever greater importance in view of the urgent necessity to quell various "false doctrines" and to defend apostolic teaching. At the same time, prophets and teachers declined in importance. The so-called "Doctrine of the twelve apostles" (the Didache) is characteristic of the transitionary period at the turn of the second century: "Elect bishops and deacons worthy of the Lord, meek men free from greed, sincere and experienced. For they celebrate the divine service of the prophets and teachers for you. Hence you should not look down on them, for they should be held in honour among you together with the prophets and teachers" (Did 15: 1 ff).

So we cannot simply say that there were various different forms of constitution and ministerial structure existing along-side each other in the New Testament, from which we today can choose at will or try to combine. The early period of the Church was dominated by the ministry of the apostles, while the post-apostolic period was characterized by the ministry of the presbyters; that is, the college of presbyters.

IV. COMMUNITY AND MINISTRY

The community

1. Those who have found their way to faith are called on to help each other and to gather together in a community. This is a necessary consequence of the acceptance of faith. It is not a result of mutual agreement or the desire of the individual, as is the case with a club or party assembled out of mutual interest. When a person accepts the faith he does so, according to the New Testament, "from above", through God's will. No one makes this decision as a result of insight or personal desire, but because he is moved to it by God: "For it has been granted to you that for the sake of Christ you should ... believe in him" (Phil 1: 29). This corresponds to what we have already said about Jesus' calling of the apostles. Alongside the terms "brother" and "brotherhood", the most frequently used name for Christians, especially in the gospels, is "disciple". With the circle of disciples round Jesus in mind,

the communities regarded themselves as disciples of the "glorified" Christ (Mt 28: 19) and accepted the same instructions for life that Jesus had given his disciples. Like them, the communities also saw themselves as having a "mission". They wanted to bear testimony to what had been given to them and what they had experienced.

God's demand on mankind, his call to faith, is spread by his envoys or messengers, who preach the word. The message comes down to mankind from above and challenges them to submit freely to the word. This cannot happen any other way, for the message does not derive from human knowledge or experience, but is the expression of what *God* has done. Faith, as Paul often says, is simultaneously the "obedience of faith": it does not come through reflection or study, but through hearing it. Faith is brought to the people by authorized messengers. "For every one who calls upon the name of the Lord will be saved. But how are men to call upon him in whom they have not believed? And how are they to believe in him of whom they have never heard? And how are they to hear without a preacher And how can men preach unless they are sent? . . . So faith comes from what is heard, and what is heard comes by the preaching of Christ" (Rom 10: 13–15, 17).

For that reason the community regards itself as called upon and founded by God. It is the gathering of all who have heard and obeyed the word. The mere existence of the community is a symbol of the final salvation brought about by God through Jesus Christ.

To interpret its *essence* in "democratic" terms would therefore be to overlook its uniqueness totally – even though "democratic" forms certainly belong to its concrete structure and are appropriate to the realization of its mission. There have always been such forms. Today they must be rediscovered and developed in a way appropriate to the age. Essentially, however, the community is not a democracy according to our understanding of the word. For it is not dependent on the will of the people – on the "sovereignty" of the people. Rather it is the listening, obedient community of those called upon and sent by God.

Ministry and community

2. This enables us to understand the proximity of "ministry" and "community". However, the first thing to note is that the New Testament offers no comprehensive definition or term for what we call the "ministry", any more than it does in the case of "sacrament". The nearest thing we come to "ministry" is the frequently used term *diakonia*, or service, which takes up and continues Jesus' own commands to his apostles and disciples. Even Paul, despite the authority he claimed for himself, understood his task as a form of service (cf 2 Cor 5: 18). The word "ministry" is therefore an abstract expression intended to cover the diverse structures and offices that appear in the New Testament. What unites these offices and functions?

All are called to the faith together. In faith all are equal. But as well as this co-existence in faith, in the common calling and hopes, there are also a few men entrusted with a special mission which is not given to all. The many different tasks within the community are not distributed in a "democratic" way. This could certainly be the superficial impression of procedures such as the "'choice" of the seven men (Acts 6: 5), the sending out of Barnabas and Paul (Acts 13: 1–4), and the calling to duty by the laying on of hands of the college of presbyters (1 Tim 4: 14). However, these special tasks are generally recognized as coming "from above" and are carried out in the "Spirit of God". The Acts of the Apostles, in particular, are so emphatic that the real guidance of the Church comes from God that the human activity involved is often completely overlooked. Paul describes these special tasks as "gifts" *to* and *for* the community ("gifts of mercy", "spiritual gifts", "charisma"). So while the members of the community are all united by their common calling, some of them are entrusted with certain special tasks. Both "ways" originate in God and in his Spirit and are the expression of the "eschatological existence" of the community. All these special tasks can be described as "ministries", though perhaps the word "services" is more apt, as it conveys most clearly the spirit in which they were understood and carried out.

This simultaneous co-existence and differentiation can be discerned in *all* instances of special services or offices mentioned in the New Testament. The same applies to the apostles, prophets and teachers (cf 1 Cor 12: 28) as does to the presbyters, deacons and bishops, to the men and women particularly involved in missionary work, and to those given a specific apostolic mandate, such as Titus and Timothy (cf Paul's letters to them).

In none of these cases is it of fundamental importance whether they are specially commissioned by one of the apostles; whether they feel themselves personally called by the power of the Holy Spirit, like the first Christian prophets; or whether they are commissioned or at least authorized by the communities. The moment they carry out one of these special tasks, they automatically face the community in the above-mentioned sense. As Paul points out, the community recognizes that they are empowered by the Spirit of God and acknowledges this "gift" in its midst. The community thus submits itself to the power of the Holy Spirit through which it is endowed and expands.

This applies even in the special case of Paul. He testifies that he was called directly by God, and that he did not receive his gospel through man, but through a revelation of Jesus Christ (Gal 1: 11, 15). He did, however, seek contact with the original apostles so that they might confirm his authority to preach the Gospel to the Gentiles: "And when they perceived the grace that had been given to me, James and Cephas and John ... gave to me and Barnabas the right hand of fellowship" (Gal 2: 9). The essence of every ecclesiastical office lies in this simultaneous co-existence and differentiation.

This tension is in a way an expression of the Church's "imperfection", for it is not the "lordship of God" pure and simple, but merely paves the way for it. The Church does not possess the divine truth once and for all, but must continually be retold it. Nor does it consist of a free inter-play of offices and manifestations of life. On the contrary, it stands in need of an inspired structure and guidance.

When we speak of *the* "ministry" in the Church today, we

generally mean the special service of leading a community or a larger area. This service is of particular importance because it embraces the whole community with all its different tasks and offices. If we try to justify this "superintendent" service by saying that it is responsible for the smooth co-operation of the other services, we by extension see it as differing from them.

Basically, there should be just the *one* ministry that can be adapted to the various needs of the Church, according to whether it is a town or country parish, or a special area such as a student community, or a larger territory. In other words, priest, bishop and pope (or the corresponding offices based on territorial divisions in other churches) should share one and the same ministry. This one special service, or ministry, can also be justified in terms of the command to preach the word, which includes the service of leadership, or rather, of which the service of leadership is one form of expression. This is particularly fitting, since the "ministry" of the Church consists essentially in the ministry of the word and the preaching of the Gospel, and requires utter conviction on the part of anyone who wishes to practise it. But in both cases (based on the "classification of services or on the command to preach the Gospel) the assumption is that within all the different offices there is one basic ministry to which they are all related. Whether this ministry, as in the western Church, ought always to be associated with a celibate life is (again) under discussion. What is in question is not the meaning of staying unmarried "for the sake of the kingdom of God". As a genuine gift of grace and as a freely chosen way of life it will always be meaningful. But to discuss the ramifications of this particular question would be to step outside the framework of this book.

16   Life before God

The believer sees himself as a divine creation, liberated by his trust in God, moved by God's Spirit, and enjoined to love. He shares this as a matter of course with all who are united with him in the community of the faithful, or, more clearly, with all who through their belief in Jesus see themselves as God's people. All this characterizes the life of the Christian and affects his behaviour accordingly. For he must devote himself to *God* and to his *fellow men* (cf Jesus' dual command to love in Mk 12: 28-34; Mt 22: 35–40; Lk 10: 25–8). And he must serve God and his fellow men in the dual dimension that is the essential feature of the Christian way of life: as an individual solely responsible for his own life and decisions, and as a member of a community – the Church – without which individual Christian life is not possible.

The consequences of this relationship to *others* necessarily manifest themselves in the ethical sphere. In the personal ethical attitude between individuals, in the socio-ethical attitude between one community and the other, as well as that between the individual and the community. We shall come back to these questions later. At this point we have to consider the attitude of the individual and the community to *God*. This means that we must discuss prayer, worship and the sacraments.

I. CRITICAL QUESTIONS

Any inquiry into prayer and worship must start with the fact that they are no longer self-evident. And by that we mean not only for non-Christians, but precisely for Christians themselves – even for those who regard themselves as convinced members of their Church. We shall start by examining a few of the key phrases of this fairly recent calling-in-question of prayer and worship.

Too demanding?

The most obvious reason for prayer being called in question lies in the immeasurable practical difficulties that have ensued from life in the modern industrialized world, destroying the old habits of private and family prayer. People nowadays work round the clock. It is virtually impossible to organize a timetable which all the members of the family can share. The morning is usually the most tense time of the day, and the evening the most "profane" and distracting. And up-to-date forms of genuine leisure still have to be discovered and developed. Under such conditions the good old customs of personal or communal prayer each morning and evening, or even family bible-reading sessions or communal church-going can scarcely survive. We must be thankful if even grace before meals – in so far as the family still eats together at all – does not die out too.

But in addition to the problems caused by the pace and rhythm of modern life, we must also take into account the effects of the environment. Key phrases such as the over-abundance of stimuli, continuous distractions, lack of concentration, stress and "managerial stress" are truisms for the critical observer of modern life. Prayer clearly demands a certain amount of time and concentration, and hence it is dying out. We must be thankful if just an occasional hint of the old practices remains.

But Christians cannot live in a continual conflict between the acknowledged tasks of the Christian way of life, and the chronic impossibility of ever fulfilling them. The question inevitably arises as to whether this conflict can possibly be the will of God. Since it is obviously not against the will of God that we should meet the demands of everyday life, it is difficult not to wonder if we are not mistaken about prayer; whether the private and communal forms of prayer are not forms of life belonging to the past that have no relevance to the modern world.

Prayer as escapism?

This brings us to the fundamental problem concerning prayer. The gulf between prayer and the world, between the specific activity of prayer and what we do the rest of the time, has never made itself so keenly felt as today. But should faith drive us into a kind of schizophrenia? If faith is a way of understanding the world and our own existence, and of fulfilling our

life in this world, how could it ever come to terms with the gap
between prayer and secular life?

In an earlier age, one could have answered that it was
precisely through prayer that the Christian could gain and
maintain the necessary distance from the world, and if need be
protest on God's behalf against the world and its demands.
The gulf between prayer and worldly existence is inevitable,
because the world, being practically orientated, is the exact
opposite to God. But a Christian today can no longer think
along these lines. On the contrary, he considers any such conception to be a misunderstanding of the Christian interpretation of the world, and is proud to have rediscovered the truly
Christian approach. God and world are not of themselves
rivals, so long as the world and its demands do not set themselves up in opposition to God. It is God's will that man should
rule the world, that he should make it into God's garden
through his own efforts, and that he should serve his fellow
men with all his strength.

The recent "secularization" of all spheres of life started out
as a distinctly anti-Christian, anti-religious enterprise. Today,
however, theologians are trying to see it as the final consequence of the Christian faith. For it was the Christian faith
which cleansed the world so thoroughly of false gods, that
Christians in the old days were branded as "atheists". And it
was this same Christian faith that made the world into a really
"secular world", and made men free to develop its scientific
and technical resources. But surely this brought with it the
death sentence for prayer? Should the Christian withdraw
from the world and approach it only from a distance – and still
hope to fulfil God's will?

In the chapter on prayer in his book *Honest to God*, Bishop
Robinson pinpointed what hundreds of thousands of Christians
of all denominations had long felt but dared not admit:
whether a Christian may "disengage" himself from the world
in order to pray.

Robinson's conclusion is clear: prayer in the traditional sense
is dead. If it is to be meaningful at all, it must be understood
in a totally different way. For instance, as a means of reflecting

on one's tasks as a believer in this world, or as a brotherly talk with those in need of loving help. In other words, commitment or "engagement" rather than "disengagement". Robinson does, however, acknowledge that people need a genuine pause for breath, that they need to withdraw from the pressures of everyday life now and then in order to gather their thoughts and strength. If we wish, we may call this "meditation". But this sort of meditation does not have the same characteristics as prayer. It does not speak directly to God, nor does it unload on him any problems we might have. Meditation in this sense is not intended as a means of withdrawal from the world, but as a source of further strength to carry out our tasks in the world.

For many people this raises another objection, namely that prayer not only presupposes a false, un-Christian understanding of the world, but that it also weakens or detracts from a person's service in the world. It sucks off energy which we need for this task. For the person who prays needs energy to concentrate properly. And in order to distance himself from the demands of his work, he must first find the necessary time. Prayer also reduces our will to solve our own problems because it inevitably tempts us to let God solve them for us (hence the word "petition"), instead of tackling them ourselves. Prayer then becomes a "substitute activity"; and that, psychiatrists tell us, is a very destructive tendency.

A false image of God?

This brings us to the strongest modern objection to prayer: that prayer implies an image of God which the Christian faith cannot justify. Traditionally, prayer means a personal I-You conversation with God. That forces me to think of God in human terms. That is not all. Since I expect something from God through prayer, I have to imagine God as a sovereign with special powers whom I hope to persuade to help me.

Surely prayer confirms that ineffectual picture of a "loving God" which one can no longer preach to children, let alone to adult Christians? Surely this kind of prayer constitutes the gravest possible danger to belief in God, since those who practise it might one day suddenly discover that there is no such thing as this "loving God", but that he is a totally enigmatic being whom we cannot grasp with human standards? In short, does not God's transcendence, his absolute "otherness" forbid us to think of him as a person and to address him in the direct I-You form? Surely the Christian image of God forbids prayer?

On balance, the current debate about prayer can be reduced to the basic formula: meditation but not prayer is permissible. However meditation in the sense of exercises in concentration and of gathering enough strength to cope with the stress of everyday life is by no means a privilege of the Christian faith. Indeed, one can learn it far better from the Indian masters of meditation. Hence Christians today can be seen rejecting outright the traditional form of prayer – or interpreting it in a quite different light. They show intense interest in yoga techniques, transcendental and zen meditation and so on – and enthusiastically recommend them to others.

In view of all these widespread and serious objections, is there still any point in talking about the meaning and necessity of prayer and worship in the *traditional* sense, even if the traditional forms have been modified?

II. PRAYER

Inevitable though these considerations may seem, so too is the argument in favour of prayer as it appears in the Bible. For Jesus and for the authors of both the Old and New Testaments, prayer is such a foregone conclusion that they never discuss its meaning or justification at all. While referring to it as something to be taken for granted, they issue repeated warnings not to neglect it.

We have already seen just how vital prayer, in a great variety of forms, was to the people of Israel. So we propose to quote just a few of the instances in the New Testament where prayer is mentioned – "proof" is scarcely necessary.

The tradition of prayer

The Gospels are full of accounts of Jesus himself praying (for instance, Mk 1: 35; 6: 46; 14: 26 par; Mt 11: 25 ff; Lk 6: 12; 22: 23; 23: 34, 46). And in the seventeenth chapter of his gospel, John depicts Jesus as summarizing his entire mission and works in a long prayer.

Jesus not only prayed himself. He also continually exhorted his disciples to pray (for example, Mk 9: 29; Mt 9: 38; Lk 11: 5–13; 17: 18; 18: 1–8). And he taught them how not to pray and how to pray correctly (Mt 6: 5–13; Lk 11: 1–4).

The early Church clearly followed Jesus' commands (Acts 1: 24 ff; 4: 23–30; 12: 5) and handed them down as precisely as possible (Eph 5: 19 ff; Phil 1: 3; 4: 5; Col 1: 11 ff; 3: 16; Heb 13: 15).

In the tradition of the Church we find the same attitude to prayer as a matter of course. Much thought was devoted to the meaning and significance of prayer, but it is indicative that none of the churches ever had to protest against arguments disputing the meaning of prayer. In the seventeenth century the Catholic church had to contend with "Quietists" who disputed the necessity of prayer. They claimed that the person who attains to Christian perfection need not and should not petition God for anything further, on the grounds that this would amount to a revolt against God's absolute will.

Whoever wishes to contest the meaning and justification of prayer must bear in mind this unequivocal attitude on the part of all Christians and believers since time immemorial. So either we have to assume that despite its ancient tradition, prayer was merely a particular form of expression of man's relationship with God that was valid for a specific period in history. Or else we are forced to suspect that there must be some logical error in the critical objections to it. If we adopt the first of these two alternatives, it would be more honest to make a complete break with prayer and not to try and give the word a new meaning which would have no connexion with what was formerly understood by "prayer". The question is whether we shouldn't at least give the second alternative a try.

If, as we suggested, we set about finding any possible logical error in the arguments, we are automatically presupposing that the problem of the meaning and justification of prayer cannot be solved simply by reference to tradition and the Scriptures. These can and must force us to question the validity of our criticism, but they themselves do not indicate just where the error lies. In other words, blind obedience to the exhortations found in the Scriptures and tradition cannot in themselves bring us any further in our critical reflections.

We have to investigate the intrinsic reason for the necessity of prayer, and this we cannot find in Scripture because the problems that beset us today were unknown in biblical times. We can no more hope to find a solution to current problems merely by quoting certain passages from the Bible than we can hope to justify prayer by saying that the Bible says that we should do so. How then, can we prove that prayer is an inherent part of the Christian way of life?

Perhaps we can look at it this way. Prayer is an essential part of Christian life in faith because faith itself can be realized only through language; therefore it shares the same basic form as prayer. You can no more believe without prayer than you can swim without water. We shall elucidate this statement in three steps.

Man and language

1. For various reasons we are now more aware than ever before that human existence is totally dependent on the medium of language. We have come a long way from the view that language is merely an indifferent instrument used to describe realities and convey information. For each piece of information is far more than it might appear to be at face value. Each piece of information changes the situation and relationship between human beings. No age has ever understood better than ours the power that can be wielded through the control and manipulation of information. One need think only of the happiness or misery that can be started by a specific piece of news. And we all know what a beneficial effect the smooth exchange of

scientific information has on human relations and co-operation. This can even be said of the so-called "inhuman" technical language of the various specialized branches of knowledge which are so full of abbreviations as to be totally incomprehensible to the layman.

If this is the case when words are used as a means of conveying information, then it must apply all the more so in cases where words function to either help or hinder communication. When a judge pronounces a verdict, when a politician wants to establish contact with his audience by means of a speech, when lovers express their love for each other, or when a bridal couple give their pledge in front of a registrar or priest – in all these cases it is not simply a matter of giving and receiving information. As a result of the words spoken something happens between the participants, and a situation is either created or changed. Similarly, the unspoken word, in the form of a sign or gesture, can create or change a situation. In this sense silence can be equally eloquent and change or influence a situation for better or worse.

Hence man's whole conscious life, from the everyday trivialities to the most vital decisions, takes place within the medium of words. We also know more than previous generations about the significance of whether a person's mother-tongue is of Asiatic, African or European origin. And even within these categories we know that a person's character and outlook on life vary according to whether his mother-tongue is English, French, German or Italian. One symptom of this situation is that even among the related European languages – as compared for instance with the Asiatic languages – there are innumerable words which are virtually untranslatable into any other language because they more or less embody the wholly untranslatable individuality of the people of a specific linguistic area.

So the first step towards finding a justification for prayer is contained in the simple question: can the realization of life in faith conceivably be excluded from the general rule that human existence can be achieved only through the medium of language? If we were to answer this question in the affirmative, then faith – itself an all-embracing way of existence and of understanding human life – is presumably outside and above the normal structures of human existence. Though not impossible in theory, this is highly unlikely in practice.

Faith and language

2. So far we have discussed language from the point of view of the human situation, though the points made are also applicable to Christian belief.

Earlier in this book we have often used the word "message". We have also spoken of the "witness" of the gospels and the Christian tradition, as well as the Christian "preaching of the word" and of "sermons". These are all key-phrases connected with language and words. Whoever questions the possibility, meaning or content of the faith cannot avoid getting involved with words. For the believer the words contained in the "message" have a special significance; he accepts them and says Yes to them. Faith is essentially the *answer* to the message conveyed through the written word of the Scriptures and the spoken word of the priest or teacher who interprets them and makes them relevant to the present. Hence faith is inherently language- and word-bound.

The word of God

3. As yet we have not touched on the decisive point about prayer. Faith would still be linguistic if it consisted merely of acquiring greater insight and expressing it in the form of propositions. Such propositions – of which there are many examples in Christian faith – would be written in the third person. For instance the sentence: man is a creation of God. Or: God loved mankind and saved them from damnation. But one of the age-old charactertistics of prayer is that it uses the *first* not the third person. Instead of "he", prayer uses "you". "I", and "we". Can this also be attributed to the phenomenon of faith as the answer to the message?

If so, then we logically have to see the *message* proclaimed in the scriptures in terms of an *address* or invocation, in fact as the *word of God himself*. Only then can faith move beyond the message and its content. Only if it is conceived of as the answer to the message can it be forced to turn directly to God in the I-You form. Only then could one say, indeed one has to say, that *faith itself is prayer, the basic form of all prayer*.

One of the fundamental assumptions of the Christian faith is that it is based on the "word of God", and that it sees its sole justification in the fact that it complies with and answers the word of God. Faith listens to God's appeal to mankind and conveys mankind's answer to God. Luther could not have attacked the old Church more sharply than by accusing it of having neglected this verbal character of the faith as the mediator between one person and another for the sake of purely theoretical "doctrines". Luther did not contest the "doctrine" that is undoubtedly contained in Scripture. His chief concern was that the scriptures should be understood as God's encouragement and promise to mankind – in the form of human words.

Faith and prayer

We have already seen that the Bible and hence also the Christian prophecy are simultaneously the word of man and the word of God, and have discussed how this is to be understood. Luther had by no means discovered something new – he merely brought an old treasure out into the open and made Christians aware of it again. Christianity has not forgotten this refound truth to the present day.

This brings us to the goal of our reflections. If we read the Bible and the prophecies connected with it as an invitation to us personally, rather than as an account of the faith of others who lived long before us, then the answer of faith is no longer merely the endorsement of a doctrine, but of a person. The basic linguistic expression of the faith no longer runs: "I believe in it", but "I believe in you". And this is the basic form of prayer – the original prayer, so to speak.

If these observations on the necessary interdependence of

faith and prayer are at all valid, several other quite problematical points should also become clearer.

In the first place, the relative importance of the vital concept "the word of God" would be established. "The word of God" defines a reality that can only be discovered and meaningfully expressed by means of prayer. We can talk in neutral terms about the "content of the Christian faith", or "the message of the Bible", or "Jesus' cause", or the "Christian image of God". But we should not refer to the "word of God" in the same way, as if it were to be found somewhere in a tangible form, rather as the "message of the Bible", is contained within Bible.

Even within the faith we cannot really speak of the word of God as long as we continue to use the third person, which after all is the form of a *declaration* of faith. By the "word of God" we mean that singular feature of the Bible by which it evades all scientific probing and offers the reader a personal invitation to faith. This invitation can only be responded to in terms of an *answer*; in other words in the I-You form of faith which is prayer. Prayer is where the word of God is continually being extended and embraced. The same applies when the word of God is rejected – except that it results in the denial of prayer.

This explains what is meant by that easily misunderstood formulation: God is a person. That this does not mean that we should think of God according to human standards (and be furious if he does not live up to those expectations) scarcely needs to be demonstrated. But with all this lofty speculation about God's "otherness", we should not forget that the ease with which the Bible conceives of God according to human models nevertheless presents a challenge for us. As we have already seen, the Christian faith has always protested fairly promptly whenever attempts have been made to raise God, because of his transcendence, out of the world of reality altogether, to the total neglect of his real "humanity". Some of the traditional images of God, for example that of the "Father" or the authoritarian "Almighty", have become dubious, but this only means that *these* human models for God have become questionable. It does not mean that it is basically wrong or against the faith to think of God in "human" terms. If the image of God as "Father" is no longer helpful, would it not be possible to think of him as a friend and partner?

What does this concept of "God as a person" really mean? Quite simply, that he speaks, talks to us, and wants us to talk to him. Since, as we have seen, the word of God is only heard through prayer, "God as a person" is clearly not something that can be analysed and depicted. No matter how many "transcendental experiences" we may achieve, "God as a person" as taught by the Christian faith can only be approached through the dialogue offered by prayer and through our reply to the invitation to faith. It is precisely here that the traditional concept of prayer as a "conversation" becomes problematical. If we understand it to mean that the person who prays may expect a verifiable answer from *God*, then it is misleading and immediately conjures up the ready-made image of "God as a person" that we have already rejected. *If* prayer is a "conversation", it is so only in the sense that man *replies* to the word spoken by God and only heard and grasped through the faith.

From this we can deduce one fundamental principle applicable to all other practical problems connected with prayer. If prayer is conceived of as the "verbal faith" whose basic form is "I believe in you", then every prayer – regardless of the words or form it chooses – must continually repeat this phrase in endless variations, or else it is nothing more than the "empty phrases" of the Gentiles which Jesus criticized so sharply (Mt 6: 7 ff). Equally, the question of the frequency of prayer depends on how often a person needs to exercise his faith and his existence in the faith by means of repeating this phrase or one of its many variations. It would be almost superfluous to remark that this question can be answered in a great many different ways depending on the period in time, the specific person involved, and even on his particular stage of life. On the other hand this does not mean that people should pray "according to their mood". Faith demands to be practised as an inherent part of one's *everyday life*. If prayer is to assist in this process – which it certainly can – then part of the "necessity" of prayer is that it should be practised regularly.

By this we do not mean that it should become an idle routine. On the contrary, it should become a truly human, freely asserted form of "exercise".

It is obviously not appropriate to describe faith as a "duty" or "'obligation" *ensuing from* faith. This would be tantamount to saying that a swimmer is obliged to use water. In reality it is more applicable to say that prayer is the *characteristic form* of the living faith. The meaning and necessity of prayer can only be denied if it is considered unnecessary to practise the faith openly. By which we mean not merely to speak about it openly, but to practise it openly as well.

In summing up we can say that the necessity of prayer can only be disputed if we reject the "word of God". But the necessity of prayer which we feel should not be disputed is not the inevitable result of a demand or duty. It is inevitable simply because it is the natural correlation to faith. One cannot say that because someone believes he should draw the consequences and pray. The only plausible formulation is to say that someone prays because he believes explicitly.

Explicit faith

But is this necessity to practise faith explicitly so obvious as we might think? Is faith something that must be stated explicitly, rather than a way of coming to terms with life?

This brings us to the core of all modern criticisms of prayer. Previously the tendency was to see prayer as the sole sphere in which man enters into a direct relationship with God. Work was seen as a service to the world and hence a distraction from God. The ideal was to save as much time as possible in which to be "free for God", to quote Thomas Aquinas' famous formulation (STh II – II 24, 8; II – II 194, 1–3). Service in the world and to one's fellow men has to be justified in the face of this ideal. The entire philosophy of monasticism rests on this fundamental idea with its concepts of withdrawal from the world and the "heavenly life" on earth.

John Robinson and his school rightly insist that life and service in the world should not have to be justified before faith, but *are* the true way of faith. Withdrawal from the world, relaxation and "disengagement" are necessary for prayer. But just as we cannot judge a person's abilities by what he does on holiday, so we cannot judge his strength of faith by his prayer, but only by the practical evidence of his everyday life. The decisive objection to Robinson's argument is how he deduces that this means the end of prayer in the traditional sense. Prayer is the time when we pause for thought and distance ourselves from the daily task of living in order to be with God. And just as a working man has a right to build up new energy, faith cannot be held suspect if it reserves the right to pray.

This introduces the idea of prayer as something "continual" and "inexplicit". By this we mean that a Christian to a certain extent sees his entire work – from the trivialities of everyday life to the highest intellectual achievements – as an indirect form of prayer without words. The reason for this is simple. If a person accepts his life and work in faith, then everything he does and experiences will be pervaded by faith. If he were to express what his life and all its details really meant, he would have to say that everything was a gift from God – or attributable to him. Expressed in words, this would bring us back to the basic form of all prayer and faith: "I believe in you".

Ever since the days of the New Testament this idea of prayer has been precious to the entire body of the faithful. It has been instrumental to all Christians and teachers (of prayer), even in practical suggestions such as a "daily dedication" or "morning offering": "And whatever you do, in word or deed, do everything in the name of the Lord Jesus, giving thanks to God the Father through him" (Col 3: 17; cf also Eph 5: 20). Explicit prayer only expresses what is accomplished through the life in faith. And only if life is accepted, mastered and accomplished in genuine faith does explicit prayer express the truth. Otherwise it is a lie.

This leads us on naturally to the extension of prayer in its communal form, which is worship.

III. WORSHIP

If we want to compare prayer and worship without going into too much detail, we have to say that worship is the prayer of the community, the communal prayer. But it is still prayer, because it requires the readiness to hear, answer, receive and participate in what God imparts to us.

The particular problem

As in our discussion of personal prayer, we must start by establishing a few basic points. There can be no doubt from the scriptures, and in particular the New Testament, that communal prayer or worship is both a self-evident part of community life and something to which the faithful are continually exhorted. Nowhere is there a hint of the modern questioning of prayer. Some of the biblical exhortations to prayer which we have already mentioned refer to communal prayer in community worship. They are not so exclusively concerned with personal prayer in a "quiet corner" as a superficial reading of the passages might suggest. But we cannot solve our problems concerning either personal or community prayer solely by reference to the evidence of the Bible. In any case we are free to choose our own particular form of personal prayer. The difficulty with community prayer or worship as we know it is that it uses forms and texts which we ourselves might not have chosen. And we cannot change this form one day to the next. Indeed, we have no right to think of making our own idea into the sole valid norm. As with personal prayer, we shall have to go back to the essence if we wish to convince ourselves of the meaning and necessity of worship.

In order to do this we must go back to what we have already said about the relationship of faith and Church. If faith in the sense of the biblical message – regardless in what form – cannot exist without reference to the community of the faithful, then prayer must also extend beyond the sphere of the individual. It is, after all, the verbal expression of the faith itself. So the basic form of prayer: "I believe in you" is now extended to: "We believe in you".

The specific necessity

The specific meaning and indeed necessity of this extension from "I" to "we" is best understood in the light of what we have already said about prayer as a means of gathering strength for faith. Communal prayer is a way of reflecting on faith in community with one's fellow believers. The Church is united by its common belief in God's presence in this world in the person of Jesus Christ. Every day each individual member of the community of the faithful must accept, master and sometimes even endure his existence. In today's inevitable and necessary "diffusion" (*diaspora*) the Church cannot possibly see itself as the community of the faithful in the original sense of the word. It can only hope to achieve this by gathering together away from the contrary demands of reality – not in order to escape from this reality, but in order to gather renewed strength to combat it.

By worship we mean that the faithful gather together to reflect on what unites them as a Church. *Duty* cannot be the primary consideration here any more than it is in the case of personal prayer. The most important factor in worship is the actual gathering together in an assembly of all who believe in God's presence. In this assembly they are freed from the continual pressures to defend the faith. There are none of the communication problems they have to contend with at work with those who do not believe. Just as a family celebration or a party with friends can give us strength in our daily lives, the communal prayer in worship gives us strength to go on living in "diffusion".

From this we can deduce some clear rules for the structure of worship, which if neglected can destroy its essence and true "gathering function". The dominant factor in worship is not the working character, but the festive atmosphere. There should be relaxation rather than tension, peace and quiet rather than agitation and activity. There should be no planning, just a purpose-less "gathering together". And it should not be regarded as a duty, but as a gift of faith. Contrary to many critical reservations worship is *rightly* directed inwards, towards the Church itself, and not outwards, towards the tasks of this world. Church and world were, it is true, separated – indeed treated as opposites – for far too long. And there is certainly some justification in the current efforts to re-establish the connexion between community worship and the everyday lives and activities of Christians. Nevertheless, worship should not be turned into an organized meeting any more than a family celebration should be turned into a working conference.

Worship and preaching

Community worship differs from personal prayer in that it is definitely directed towards the outside world. It is public and visible. Everyone, even non-believers, may participate. In this way the personal reflection of the community of the faithful assumes the character of a public confession of faith. It becomes a public invitation to faith. It is thus a way of preaching the Gospel.

Interestingly, this is not due so much to the fact that the scriptures are read out and preached upon. What is far more important is that people pray together in public. Everyone who sees and hears knows what it means and can deduce from it what Christians believe in. We encounter a structure similar to the one we found in personal prayer. Namely, that the Church and its individual members express verbally in worship what they otherwise realize through their deeds. As in the case of personal prayer, the two are interdependent.

This "preaching" element of worship also explains why it has to forgo a certain element of individuality. In other words, why established structures, and in certain contexts fixed formulas, are both desirable and necessary. For only by using well-tried texts and structures does it become clear that what is at issue in worship is the testimony of the *whole Church*, and not the more or less incidental form of expression of any one group of

Christians. However, the structures of Church worship are by no means unchangeable. The Church is, after all, the community of all the faithful. If their understanding of their faith changes in any way, then the forms and texts of community worship must be altered accordingly – by all *together*.

Fixed texts and forms have a definite significance for community worship as a "gathering" and celebration. For no gathering, least of all this one, can cope with a constant stream of new ideas absorbing all its attention. A certain regularity of form guarantees the truly liberating function of community worship. It lets the faithful know what is coming, or at any rate gives an approximate indication of the changes that are to be expected, and contributes to what worship is and should be; namely the communal pause to gather new strength to counteract the strain which is imposed on the faith every day.

With these reflections on the nature of worship as a vehicle for preaching the Gospel, we have reached an excellent point at which to say something about those particularly sacred forms of worship that we call the sacraments.

IV. THE SACRAMENTS

The sacraments are the one area over which confusion reigns in all churches. Where the sacraments are concerned, the emancipating message of the gospels often seems to have been forgotten. Instead, the different churches are dominated by varying degrees of excited exhortation, moral pressure, obligation and sometimes even force and sanctions against any objectors.

In the Catholic church in particular, a Christian is judged to be a "practising" Christian chiefly on the basis of how regularly he receives the sacraments. Whether he devotes his entire life to the care of the poor and suppressed is in a sense irrelevant. If he never or only occasionally comes to the sacraments, he cannot count on the approval of his fellow Christians or priests. However, it must be said that preachers seldom succeed in making the sacraments seem "attractive". In order to achieve

a fairly regular reception of the sacraments they only too
often have to support their recommendation with a moral
appeal to Church discipline.

Baptism and the eucharist

We must be fully aware of this unhappy state of affairs when
we consider the sacraments within the general context of community worship.

To begin with, they are drawn into the perspective, already
discussed, of the peaceful celebration and the communal
gathering of strength in the faith. Equally consciously, we rele-
gate the traditional view – held by nearly all churches with the
notable exception of the Orthodox churches – of the sacraments
as "means of grace" or "means of salvation" firmly to second
place. But before going into the reasons for this we must first
deal with the *general* concept of a "sacrament". There is a
strong suspicion that precisely this general concept is to blame
for the popular notion of the sacraments as "means of grace".
If this is so, then it would also be responsible for most of the
confusion to which we referred.

For this reason we shall start by discussing the sacraments
one by one. At this point we shall confine ourselves to those
sacraments which are accepted without dispute by all the
churches, even if they are interpreted in different ways. These
sacraments are baptism and the eucharist. Any necessary comments on the other sacraments, for instance the different value
laid on them in the Catholic church and the churches of the
Reformation, will be dealt with at the end of this chapter.

Baptism and the eucharist have been celebrated in the
Church from the earliest days. These two rites are so old that
even the earliest texts of the New Testament do not mention
explicitly when they were introduced into the Church. They
are simply taken for granted as a self-evident custom which
needed no further justification.

So what the New Testament does is present a more profound
interpretation of what must have been common knowledge at
the time. Baptism is discussed along these lines in chapter six

of the Letter to the Romans (probably written in about AD 56) and in the Letter to the Galatians (3: 27; probably written in 52 or 53), whereas the eucharist is dealt with in 1 Cor 10: 15–17 (probably written in 54). But when it comes to the institution of these two rites by Jesus, even the oldest accounts (1 Cor 11: 23–6, written in 54, mentions a far older text) are not to be understood as verbatim reports of the act of institution. On the contrary, they refute the formula used in the liturgy. In this context we can quote passages such as Mt 28: 19 with reference to baptism, and Mk 14: 22–4; Mt 26: 26–8; Lk 22: 19–20; and 1 Cor 11: 23–5 with reference to the eucharist (cf also Mk 6: 41; 8: 6 par). Mention has already been made of the difficulties this presents in any attempt to ascertain the date and precise form of the Last Supper.

Baptism originally took the form of the total immersion of the baptismal candidate in water. The words and formulas probably differed greatly at first. Mt 28: 19 indicates a form very similar to that still used today – "in the name of the Father and of the Son and of the Holy Spirit". Other texts, especially in the Acts of the Apostles, seem to indicate a baptism "in the name of Jesus Christ" (cf Acts 2: 38; 8: 16; 10: 48; Rom 6: 3; Gal 3: 27).

Baptism symbolizes two things: unconditional allegiance to Jesus on the part of the baptismal candidate, and Jesus' inviolable love for him in return. In this way baptism symbolizes admission into the Church as the "body" of Christ (Acts 2: 41; 7: 12 ff; 1 Cor 12: 13; Eph 4: 4 ff). It bestows on those who are baptized a share in the Spirit which forms the Church and gives it its unity (Mk 1: 8 par; Jn 2: 5; Lk 24: 49; Acts 1: 5; 2: 38; 1 Cor 12: 13; Eph 4: 4 ff; Tit 3: 5).

To judge from the information given in these texts, baptism was a unique event through which a person was received into the Church for ever. The eucharist, on the other hand, was repeated at regular intervals (1 Cor 11: 17–20; Acts 2: 42, 46), probably weekly (Acts 20: 27). Bread was broken and distributed, after which a communal chalice was handed round to drink from. The accompanying words were apparently more uniform right from the beginning than those used in baptism, as can be seen from a comparison of the four separate accounts of the Last Supper in the gospels. Nevertheless, even here there are some significant differences which throw some light on its antecedents.

In all four accounts the words of institution spoken by Jesus connect the eucharist with his death for mankind as well as the new covenant instituted by it between God and man. Only Luke and Paul mention Jesus' *submission* when *blessing the bread* and identify the *chalice*, ie the *shedding of his blood*, with the new covenant. The accounts given by Mark and Matthew, though similar, omit this mention of Jesus' submission to the will of God. Nor do they identify the chalice with the institution of the new covenant, but link the wine directly with the blood of the covenant.

Hence Luke and Paul give greater prominence to Christ's *action* in dying for mankind, while Mark and Matthew lay more emphasis on Christ's *offering*. The formulation in Luke and Paul is probably based on the idea of the suffering Lord who died for our sins found in Is 53, together with the motif of the "new covenant" from Jer 31. Mark and Matthew, on the other hand, combine the idea of the death of reparation from Is 53 with the concept of the blood of the covenant in Ex 24. In addition, as can be seen from 1 Cor 5: 7, they also saw a connexion with the slaughter of the pascal lamb. There are reasons to believe that the formulation used by Paul and Luke is older than that in Matthew and Mark – although the difference in date between the four accounts cannot amount to more than a few years. Mark and Matthew concentrate more on the "factual" offering, and probably contribute the first step towards the subsequent doctrine of the "real presence of Christ" in the eucharist under the appearance of bread and wine.

We also find this interpretation in a fairly advanced form in John (6: 53–6), although biblical scholars are not all agreed whether this passage actually refers to the eucharist.

All four evangelists are in complete agreement over the significance of the Lord's Supper. The eucharist unites Christians with the death of Christ and makes them members of the new covenant until the coming of the Lord (1 Cor 10: 16; 11: 26; Jn 6: 54; and the actual accounts of the Last Supper).

Instituted by Jesus?

What is special about these liturgical celebrations or "church services"? The answer is simple. These celebrations of baptism and the eucharist share the unparalleled distinction of being instituted and ordained by Jesus himself. This answer is right, provided we do not oversimplify it.

None of the New Testament texts which attribute the sacraments of baptism and the eucharist to Jesus himself is in fact a straightforward account of an act of institution performed by Jesus during his life on this earth. What these texts actually reflect is the practice and faithful interpretation of these actions by the early Church. The authors do ascribe baptism and the eucharist to Jesus personally – but not in an *historical* sense, as we might somewhat hastily conclude. One thing is certain, that they see the foundation of baptism and the eucharist in Jesus' *work*, death and resurrection. If we are looking for an historical act of institution, we have to try to reconstruct it from the texts.

However, this is not quite so hopeless as one might think. A historian can state with a clear conscience that the practice of baptism and the eucharist was introduced into the Church as a matter of course immediately after the death of Christ. Despite the parallels that exist in both the Jewish and Greek traditions at the time of Christ, both baptism and the eucharist have some features that do not derive from any other similar institution.

As in other similar cases, we are faced with two alternatives. Either the early practice of the Church constituted the first distortion or at least deviation from Christ's intentions, or else we are forced to conclude that this practice goes back to some declaration of intent in Christ's part, even if we cannot reconstruct it in detail. The latter solution seems the more likely of the two, as even a historian would agree. Otherwise we should have to credit the first Christians, and in particular the simple fishermen of Lake Genezareth, with a virtually superhuman originality and inventiveness.

So if we say that Jesus Christ instituted the sacraments of baptism and the eucharist, we are in fact saying that ever since the Church began it has celebrated the sacraments of baptism and the eucharist, and regarded the obligation to do so as being founded in the death and resurrection of Jesus Christ. This does as little to answer *our* question as the reference to the relevant passages in the New Testament does towards establishing the meaning and purpose of prayer. Once again we must examine the *intrinsic* reason for these actions.

Special significance

To begin with, everything we have said about the significance of community prayer in worship applies equally to the sacraments. What distinguishes baptism and the eucharist from the "ordinary" forms of worship can be summarized in the following four characteristics:

1. Ordinary forms of worship are concerned with words (prayer, reading, sermon, singing, and so on), and perhaps also with gestures such as sitting, standing, kneeling, the kiss of peace, and so on. Baptism and the eucharist in addition involve material elements – water, bread, wine. They are the "visible word" or *verbum visibile,* as Augustine and many others after him so aptly put it.

2. The communal reflection on the faith, which constitutes the essence of every form of worship, is extended in the case of baptism and the eucharist to embrace every aspect of faith. One could say that baptism and the eucharist are the most "complete" forms of worship. Through baptism man is included in the work of salvation and enters into a community of fate determined by Christ's cross, death and resurrection. Man is not merely changed by this process, he is "born anew".

The eucharist likewise embraces the whole faith and the whole of human life. This is most apparent in the structure of the liturgy of the eucharist in the Catholic mass. In *this* respect the eucharistic prayer stands apart from the controversies over the "real presence of Christ" and the "sacrificial character" of the eucharist which the Christian churches have so far failed to resolve.

The liturgy of the eucharist begins by exhorting us to give thanks to the God who loves the world and mankind. In the prayer of thanksgiving we remind ourselves that God has manifested himself throughout the history of mankind. According to the season, mention is made of God's various acts of salvation in history. God finally manifested himself in the person of Jesus Christ, who shared our human existence right up to his death on the cross. That is why the community gathers together to worship – reminding itself of what Jesus did for mankind by this divine act of salvation, repeating in his name what he has done for them and reminding itself of the consequences this deed has for their lives.

And then the community dares to say to God what no man could think out for himself: *Our Father.* The eucharistic prayer commemorates the Lord's Supper and contains the entire message of the faith. And when the community concludes their worship with an "Amen", they have given testimony to their entire faith.

3. As we can see, baptism and the eucharist are not only the most "complete" forms of liturgical worship. They constitute the real essence of the faith. Other forms of worship can and should deal with any of the various aspects of the faith, but baptism and the eucharist are what makes Christians into Christians.

4. Baptism and the eucharist unite the community of the faithful not just in spatial terms, throughout the world, but in temporal terms, throughout history. We today are baptized and celebrate the eucharist in the same way as the first Christians in Jerusalem or Galilee. For this all-important reason the Church should and must hold on to at least the basic structure of the traditional rites of baptism and the eucharist.

Admittedly, at the time of their institution these rites were easily understood by all, and not in the least outstanding. They fitted into the cultural setting in which they were celebrated.

To us, however, two thousand years later, and in a different cultural environment, they are somewhat foreign. We need a commentary in order to understand them properly, and that reduces their emotive power. Rites which have to be elucidated and explained are rather like a bunch of flowers which would have to be analysed before one could realize that it was meant to express a birthday greeting.

Nevertheless, it is a good thing that the Church sticks to the old rites. For they represent the Church's identity throughout the centuries. They also serve to remind us that God revealed himself to us in *history* – not through any abstract theories or doctrines. Whoever does not want to keep up the old rites should not, to be logical, accept that God manifested himself to us through a member of the Jewish nation who lived at the time of the Emperor Augustus and the Roman governor Pontius Pilate in the area that now comprises the modern states of Israel, Syria, Jordan and the Lebanon, came from a poor background, spent a few years as a wandering preacher, and was finally executed by the Romans as a result of religious misunderstandings and false political charges.

"Sacraments"

A comparison of baptism and the eucharist shows that despite many differences they also have a number of features in common. Both are celebrated and performed within the community as the "visible word". Both go back to Jesus himself, at any rate in the sense that they were instituted according to Jesus' will, through his cross and resurrection. And lastly, both happen *within* the *community* to *individual* members of the faithful. These common features have for centuries been expressed by the overall term "sacrament".

Now this concept is unknown in the New Testament. In fact in the sense that we understand it, it was unknown before the Middle Ages. To be more precise, they did in fact know and use the word *sacramentum*, but it embraced far more than what we understand by the "sacraments".

In its original meaning the word *sacramentum* designated

the military oath of enlistment, or the sum of money put up as bail in a court case. In the Latin Vulgate it was used as a translation for the Greek word *mysterion,* and thus came to mean a "mystery" (the most famous instance being Eph 5: 32). There is clearly a wide spectrum of further meanings between the original "oath of enlistment" or "bail" and the subsequent "mystery". Hence the word *sacramentum* is used to describe such differing concepts as the faith, the truths of the faith, the Trinity, the work of salvation, and the symbolic Old Testament prototypes, to name but a few. A decisive step forward was taken at the turn of the third century by the African Father of the Church, Tertullian, when he used the word *sacramentum,* in the sense of an oath of enlistment, with reference to baptism. According to him, a candidate for baptism promises to dedicate himself to the service of Christ just as a soldier pledges himself to the service of his emperor.

Augustine introduced the interpretation of the word "sacrament" as we know it today. According to him a sacrament is always present when an outward sign accompanied by the uttering of certain words symbolizes the invisible mystery of God and his salvation of mankind.

Augustine had by no means definitively solved the matter, as can be seen from the fact that for a long time afterwards there was still no specific *number* of sacraments. In the eleventh century, for example, Petrus Damiani, a monk and later cardinal, counted twelve sacraments: baptism, confirmation, the annointing of the sick, bishops and kings, the consecration of churches, confession, the consecration of canons, monks, hermits and nuns, and marriage. Curiously, the eucharist is missing. The washing of the feet of Maundy Thursday was likewise often regarded as a sacrament. The seven sacraments currently recognized by the Catholic church only came into force in the twelfth century – and in the sixteenth century they were to be the subject of a further dispute.

In view of its history the concept "sacrament" is hardly the most suitable material for a successful theological debate. It is a helpful abbreviation for a number of special liturgical rites, the precise number of which is in a sense irrelevant. A closer understanding of what the concept really means can only be obtained by examining the sacraments individually. But this is nothing new. For example Thomas Aquinas, whose treatise on the individual sacraments in his *Summa Theologiae* presupposes a general treatise on the essence of a sacrament, nevertheless illustrated this general *essence* of the sacrament by reference to the specific example of baptism (STh III, 60–5). On no account should the general concept "sacrament" lead us to forget the unmistakable individual significance of each separate sacrament.

The essence of the sacraments is far more important than the question of how many of them there are. The classic Catholic definition of the sacraments is as follows: the sacraments are the symbolic actions of the Church instituted by Jesus Christ through which those who receive them become sharers in the fruits of Christ's crucifixion and resurrection. According to the classic Evangelical, and in particular Lutheran, definition, the sacraments are the combination of a divine promise with an outward sign (element), instituted by Jesus Christ. It is not difficult to see the obvious difference between these two interpretations. The Catholic interpretation emphasizes the *Church's action*, and does not explicitly mention the divine promise. The danger here is that the sacraments then tend to be abused or wrongly regarded as some kind of semi-magical ritual. The Protestant interpretation emphasizes the *word* and omits any specific reference to the liturgical action. In this case there is a danger of the sacraments eventually being understood as purely individual acts, which would result in them no longer playing a central rôle in the life of the Church. Instead they would be relegated to the use of those individuals who think they need them.

The dangers of one-sidedness have fortunately long been recognized by both sides. They have both successfully endeavoured to counteract the inherent danger of their particular interpretation of the sacraments, without giving up the more valuable aspects of their own tradition. For this reason we can already attempt a definition of the essence of the sacraments that is acceptable to all Christians, regardless of the current differences in emphasis and practices.

The sacraments as a form of worship

Any such definition of the essence of the sacraments necessarily leads us to conclude that they are to be understood as a form of *worship*. For they comply in the fullest sense with the meaning and essence of community worship outlined above, though of course they differ from the "ordinary" forms of worship as far as the special features just mentioned are concerned. The concept of worship embraces both the Catholic emphasis on community action and the Protestant stress on the preaching of the word.

Perhaps we could suggest the following formulation. The sacraments are special forms of worship instituted by Jesus Christ through his death and resurrection, by means of which the word of the Gospel is proclaimed to the faithful, both as individuals and as a community, in the form of an explicit action and certain significant words. The sacraments are thus the focal point of all life and activity within the Church. They are important not because they convey anything further or different what the Christian receives as a matter of course in the Church, but precisely *because* they are the focal point of all activity in the Church.

From this we can see that it would be inappropriate to compare the influence of the sacraments with the effect of faith and the acceptance of God's message. At various points throughout the history of the Church, the pious faithful were in danger of regarding the sacraments as an *alternative* to faith in God's revelation. In other words they were regarded as a means of obtaining salvation "on the cheap". For the sacraments do, to quote the old formula, "by their nature" seem to bring about salvation, and thus spare us the effort of faith and the personal involvement it requires. What this formula in fact means is that the sacraments are the guarantee that God keeps his promises to mankind, that his message is not just so many empty words. It does not mean that Christians are dispensed from the need to believe. Rather it is intended to protect them from any unworthy priest administering the sacraments. Because the sacraments are "by their nature" means to salvation they cannot be endangered by any unworthy person who administers them. But then, how could a Christian receive a symbol that by its nature appeals to his deepest faith, except in and through faith?

This clarifies one other point too. People can no more be forced to receive the sacraments than they can be forced to believe. The Church must continually offer the sacraments to the people. It must invite them to receive the sacraments, make them as attractive as possible, and try to make the old symbols as clear as possible by means of carefully chosen words and liturgical structures. What then happens depends entirely on the faith of each and every individual. As with faith, the practice of the sacraments may differ greatly from one stage of life to the next. So any attempt to enforce a specific rule by any means other than exhortation and invitation would turn the focal point of the Church's life into a form of organized hypocrisy.

Confession

We shall conclude these reflections with a few comments on the other sacraments. Of them all, confession is the one that is most frequently the subject of dispute between the various denominations.

Its foundations in the New Testament cannot be contested (Mt 18: 18; Jn 20: 22 ff; Jas 5: 16; 1 Jn 1: 9). Nevertheless the practice of regular confession – the "first" confession being that in baptism – was apparently not nearly so widespread as baptism and the eucharist in the early days of the Church (Heb 10: 26–31; 1 Jn 5: 16; Rev 2: 5, 16; 3: 3, 19 ff). But from the second century onwards the Church evidently developed liturgical forms of confession which were structurally very similar to baptism and the eucharist. In those days no one doubted that confession ensured that the penitent would be reconciled with God.

The various forms of confession practised today by the various churches differ greatly from that practised by the early Church. But even where confession is not recognized as a sacrament (as in, say, the German Evangelical church), no one doubts that through confession Christians are granted the forgiveness of their sins and reconciliation with God. Confession hence belongs in one form or another to the liturgical life of the Church. Together with baptism and the eucharist it occupies a special position alongside the "ordinary" forms of worship. The fact that the Evangelical church does not place confession on a level with baptism and the eucharist, ie that it does not regard it as a sacrament, has other reasons. But it would be wrong to say that one church has confession and the other none.

Infant baptism

The children of Christian parents have been baptized as infants for centuries, though the biblical scholars are still disputing whether this practice is in fact indicated in the New Testament. There is certainly no explicit statement on the subject. And it is disputed whether some of the accounts of neophytes being baptized with their "whole household" (Acts 16: 15; 1 Cor 1: 16) include the baptism of infants.

Because of this uncertain information in the New Testament, and the deeper insight gained into the relationship between faith and the sacraments, and last not least because we are no longer constrained by any extreme interpretation of "original sin" – the baptism of infants and children has been a much disputed topic in the churches.

1 There is no compulsory reason for Christian parents to have their children baptized as infants, particularly when the parents themselves are no longer close to the Church or the Christian faith. To insist upon it would lead to the misunderstanding that baptism bestows something on the person being baptized regardless of his own personal involvement. This would inevitably reduce the sacrament to a kind of magical

formula, which can never have been the original intention of infant baptism.

2. It is *most appropriate* for Christian parents to have their children baptized as infants. For this demonstrates that neither the parents nor the Church think that proven faith or morality are *prerequisites* for God's mercy. In other words, the practice of infant baptism is the Church's overt acknowledgment that God's mercy is the determining factor in everything. Hence the Church can permit infant baptism. However this fact does not constitute a forceful argument because in the case of adult converts (for instance in the missions) the situation is clearly different. Faith itself must ensure that no one regards it as a prerequisite for God's mercy.

3. Infant baptism is only justifiable when there is the opportunity for a *Christian education*: in other words, the child can grow up in the kind of surroundings in which it can encounter the invitation to faith in an appropriate manner. In the case of infant baptism the strict obligations imposed on the catechumens in the early Church are replaced by the duty of giving the child a Christian education. The child baptized and brought up in a Christian family has the distinct advantage of being introduced to the faith right from the beginning. This is the unearned grace that comes through infant baptism. Nevertheless, the child must still answer this invitation in the freedom of its own conscience, just like any unbaptized child.

4. Within a Christian family the invitation to faith can obviously come without infant baptism. If Christian parents are of the opinion that they should allow their children to decide freely whether they wish to believe and be baptized, there can be no fundamental objections. The question of infant baptism can only seriously be regarded as a test case for an argument for or against the faith and the Church by someone who has a false idea of the essence of the faith and the sacraments.

17   Christians and non-Christians

A Christian believes in Jesus Christ as God's definitive and insurpassable action in the world, and is required to invite all men to share this faith. What does this imply about the attitude of believers in Jesus Christ to the history, culture and religion of non-Christian peoples?

We have noted this question as a special challenge to the Christian faith today. Its importance comes home to a Christian when he spends some time in a non-Christian country. Indians, Chinese, Japanese and others tend to ask a Christian missionary or tourist: "Is the entire culture which our country evolved before the Christian missionaries came to preach their faith worthless?"

The question is justified. In the past Christians concluded from their belief in the redemption of the whole world and all men by Christ that any other religion had to clear out with all its trappings immediately Christian preaching appeared. Even today in conversations with non-Christians a Christian can often feel the unhappy results of a Christian claim to absoluteness understood and maintained in this way. Many non-Christians have the impression that Christians consider themselves the only people in the world who have no need to search for the truth, for they already possess it. In the eyes of many non-Christians this makes Christians seem arrogant and intolerant people with whom it is impossible to communicate and who are best avoided.

On the other hand, many European Christians have begun to suspect any form of Christian mission. Why shouldn't other peoples be allowed to live in a world which is their own and reflects their particular history? And if religion is part of their world, why shouldn't they be allowed to keep their traditional religion? Who can prove, many Christians ask, that the Christian religion is so much better and truer than other religions, or even than no religion at all? Sometimes people don't ask such basic questions, but try to measure the value of a religion more or less by the contribution it makes to the development of a country. They say things like: "It's all right to have Christian missions in India to get rid of sacred cows, but in Japan there's no point. The Japanese have created a rational modern civilization without Christianity." But this sort of attitude is just as dangerous as the old Christian claim to superiority, for the crucial question about the truth of a religion disappears and is replaced by another, very western "value" as the absolute standard of measurement: namely technological development.

I CHRIST AND ISRAEL

In the discussion of the relationship of Christians to non-Christians the people of the Old Covenant, the people of Israel, is a particularly sensitive and painful topic. This is because any attempt to discuss it inevitably brings in the heavy load of guilt which stands between Christians and Jews. This is not the guilt so often attributed by Christians to Jews of having had Jesus crucified; only a few years ago this charge was officially withdrawn by the Catholic church (Second Vatican Council, *Declaration on the Relationship of the Church to non-Christian Religions*, 4). The guilt in question here is Christian guilt. In order to understand how this guilt came into existence, it is useful to remember the earliest history of the Christian faith.

The old people of God and the new

The first Christians did not think of themselves as a new community, a "church", but as part of the whole people of God which was Israel, to whom Jesus had come as Messiah. They prayed in the Temple (Acts 2: 46) and made no attempt to separate themselves from Israel, because they regarded Jesus as the fulfilment of the promises given by God to his people Israel. This situation did not last. Soon the Christians became more and more a community in their own right, a church alongside Israel. They began to think of themselves as the new people of God which had replaced the old Israel. There were a number of reasons for this. The preaching of the Christian faith was on the whole unsuccessful among the Jews, whereas the preaching of the Gospel unrestricted by the law had great success among the pagans. As a result, the Christian Church grew mainly in non-Jewish areas: in Syria, Asia Minor and Egypt. Jerusalem was destroyed in AD 70 and the Jewish Christian communities were driven out to the fringes of the Arabian desert. From the beginning of the second century Jerusalem was a Gentile (or Gentile Christian) city.

This disaster of the Jewish people encouraged the Christians in the belief that the Jews were no longer God's holy people, but had been judged and rejected by God: "The kingdom of God will be taken away from you and given to a nation producing the fruits of it" (Mt 21: 43).

It was also a great advantage in dealings with the Roman authorities to place great stress on the responsibility of the Jews for the death of Jesus. In this account Jesus was not a revolutionary executed by the Romans, and the destruction of Jerusalem in AD 70 became God's punishment of his murderers. None of our four gospels is completely free from a tendency to present things thus. Luke and Acts portray the Jews as perpetual troublemakers, slandering the loyal and peaceful Christians (Lk 23: 13–15; Acts 7: 54 ff; 12: 1 ff; 13: 45; 14: 15; 17: 5 ff; 13; 18: 12 ff; 21: 27 ff), and in the gospel of John we find the hard saying, which is even put into the mouth of Jesus: not Abraham, but the devil, is your father (8: 39–44). The Old Testament was now more and more interpreted as a Christian book; that it was the holy book of Israel was forgotten or denied. Very early on the so-called Epistle of Barnabas – written by an unknown writer of the early second century and attributed to Barnabas – could even state that the Jews had been idol-worshippers from the time of Moses. They had never accepted the covenant granted them by God (4: 7–8). According to this writer, the Old Testament was never meant literally, and the Church is therefore right to interpret it allegorically: that is, to understand it as metaphorically referring to itself (cf 10: 2). Anyone who thinks in this way will naturally no longer ask what the fate of the people of Israel means, or what God's purpose for this people is. Israel is already judged. The case of this people is closed; they are the victims of God's wrath, and as such rightly the object of Christian contempt. Today we no longer think in that way, but it is good for us to know that the majority of the Christian churches did conceive things thus – and for centuries. It is also important to realize that one of the roots of anti-Semitism goes back to the New Testament.

In the course of two thousand years the guilt of Christians in regard to the Jews has become enormous, but it should not make us forget *why* the New Testament talks of a guilt of the Jews. Israel did not see, did not recognize, the salvation God wanted to give it in Jesus Christ. As so often in the history of the Old Covenant, Israel kept its heart hardened against the friendship and mercy of its God. A Christian of the first period who saw himself separated from Israel for his faith in Jesus Christ could hardly see things in any other way. But Israel's guilt in this matter is a guilt before God, not a sin against its fellow men. Israel has to bear it and answer for it before him who has nonetheless remained its God and still guides his people.

Therefore, in spite of the New Testament, there is no excuse for Christian anti-Semitism. Anything the Jews did to the earliest Christian communities in their initial persecution is quite insignificant compared with what the Jews have had to suffer in later periods from Christians. It is not at all surprising that the behaviour of Christians was not designed to lead the Jews, apart from a few exceptions, along the path of faith in Christ. Christianity has not done its duty to Israel, nor has it yet clearly seen and acknowledged its failure and its mistakes. It took the events, persecutions, torture, humiliation and mass-extermination of Jews in Germany and German-occupied Europe in the 1930s and 1940s slowly to open many people's eyes and reveal the appalling arrogance of Christian anti-Semitism. We can do no more than mention the fact that to the Christian guilt about the Jews there has today been added guilt about the Arabs. We are not paying for our guilt today;

the horrors which the Jews suffered in Europe are projected on to others. Conversations with Israelis often reveal that they can see Arab policy towards the state of Israel in terms of what happened under Hitler, and so perhaps misunderstood it. When, as Christians, we are prompted by our faith to reflect on God's dealings with Israel, we must start with a confession of guilt. We must think about a guilt for which we have not even as yet really asked forgiveness. So far Christians seem to have been satisfied with generously overlooking the splinter in their brother's eye.

Paul on Israel

All this means that when we try to understand the meaning of Israel's fate in accordance with the biblical mesage, we should not start with texts which may encourage misinterpretations, or which themselves betray hostility towards the Jews. We must keep to texts which try to understand God's intentions for his people in the light of faith. From this point of view the most important text in the New Testament is Romans 9–11. Here we see Paul examining the question of Israel with exemplary clarity, and moreover with painful involvement.

Paul suffers because the majority of Israel have rejected the faith (Rom 9: 1–3). But he suffers not so much because he is also a Jew, but mainly because Israel is the people to which God gave his word and his promises. His basic question is: "Has not God's word been contradicted by the facts? Has the word of God failed?" (Rom 9: 6).

The problem of Israel involves nothing less than the truth and faithlessness of God. This means that for Paul two answers to his question are ruled out in advance. The first is the view that the choice of Israel has been cancelled or in some way transferred to the Church – a view later maintained by most Christian theologians. Paul takes God's word seriously, the word he spoke to Israel in history; he cannot simply abandon it. Paul knows that God has revealed his name in history (cf Rom 9: 14–17). Without this revelation of God in history no one could talk about God. The other view which is ruled out for

Paul is the claim that the unfaithful Israel, which misuses God's law in an attempt to appear righteous, is accepted by God in its own righteousness. If this were so, there would be two ways to salvation: the way of grace opened by Christ and the way of one's own achievement, which was chosen by Israel. Right from the start Paul cannot argue in one line. He has to find the answer between two impossible views. Or, as we would put it today, he has to argue dialectically.

In the ninth chapter of the Epistle to the Romans Paul stresses God's absolute sovereignty. God is God, and man can as little argue with him as the pot with the potter who made it (Rom 9: 20). God graciously admits some people to eternal glory and condemns others to eternal destruction, and no man has the right to challenge him (Rom 9: 21 ff). Whether it is comfortable or not, the idea of a "double predestination" is here clearly stated. For Paul, however, this idea is not a general statement about the world, but a idea which, as it were, goes to the limits of conceptual possibility. Such "limiting concepts" are necessary to show man his place. What Romans 9 is really out to stress is that *there is no human right to grace*. Grace to which one had a right would not be grace. This is why grace is not under our control. So, in the case of Israel, God chose Abraham, but that did not automatically give his sons the right to be sons of God. By his free choice God chose only Isaac and not Abraham's other sons (Rom 9: 6 ff). Similarly, the Church cannot ultimately dispense the grace of God. It is not in his place. In his interpretation of Romans (one Epistle to the Romans, first edition 1921), Karl Barth logically replaced "Israel" in his commentary with "the Church" – which gives the text remarkable force.

In Rom 9: 30–10, 21 Paul develops another idea: In Christ God drew near to men (10: 8). There is no other nearness of God. If Israel wishes to persist in following the law and be close to God by *this* means, it will live in isolation from the real closeness of God, it will incur guilt against God's love. The righteousness Israel fights for is *its own* righteousness (Rom 10: 3), whatever its merits. Israel heard the message and did not believe (10: 14 ff). It is impossible and wrong to reduce this guilt. As far as men can judge, it means final separation from God.

Two further ideas are connected with this. God did not bestow his grace on the whole of Israel, but of his free choice only on a part, a "remnant". In so doing he acted in the same way as in the Old Covenant, in free grace and without being tied. Every charge against him is illusory. The second idea is that in a marvellous way God has made something great out of Israel's failure. He has made it possible for the Gentiles like a wild shoot to be grafted on to the tree of the people of God in place of the unfaithful Israel (Rom 11: 11–24). Not that this gives the Gentiles any sort of right to God's grace (Rom 11: 20–1).

Three things are now clear. First, it is quite impossible for man to argue with God about the fate of his people. Second, to all human thinking Israel long ago passed judgment on itself by its guilt. Third, God has more than kept his word. Only now does Paul proclaim the "mystery" that the whole of Israel will be saved even through its "hardening" (11: 25–6). In this it is clear that the saving of Israel is really grace, the free act of God which he owes to no one. Israel has no right to salvation. It takes place in spite of Israel's disobedience and by means of it (11: 32). God has kept his word; his choice and his promise stand. But none of this can be calculated in advance. It is a pure, incalculable and uncontrollable miracle. Not without reason Paul ends his expositions with a great hymn of praise (Rom 11: 33–6).

Christians and Jews

In considering the relationship between Christians and Jews we can learn important lessons from this text of Paul's.

1. Questions about "God's plan" for Jews or non-Christians are often prompted by mere curiosity. Answers to such questions merely satisfy curiosity. It is unfortunately true that answers of this sort can be dressed up in biblical quotations and prove acceptable in "the best" Christian circles. In contrast, it is notable how clearly in Rom 9–11 Paul accustoms

his readers never to lose sight for an instant of the difference between God and man. Questions prompted by mere curiosity are the ones he does *not* answer. Even Rom 9–11 leaves many questions open: the time of the final salvation of Israel, whether all Jews will be saved, what will happen to the Jews (and pagans) who died before Christ, whether God's grace will lead finally to a general redemption (*apokatastasis pantōn*, or salvation and restoration of all – maintained in Christian tradition mainly by Origen). Even Paul's faith has to say in many different ways: "I don't know." This is not resignation or despair, but simply leaving to God what is for God alone to decide.

2. Paul's discussion of the fate of Israel is strictly *theological*. His thought was inspired neither by curiosity nor by sympathy with the unfaithful Israel, but by a concern for the right way to talk about God. God must remain God, that is, remain true to his word. Paul realized that only if it was clear that God remained true, and more than true to himself and his historical word under all circumstances would questions like the one about the meaning of Israel's fate no longer be a problem, even if there is not a solution to all the details and perhaps no "solution" at all. Perhaps it would be wrong for such problems to be given "solutions". Perhaps things are like this so that human beings are constantly forced back against the difference between God and man, which always remains to some extent obscure. This obscurity is no longer oppressive, however, once it is clear that God's word cannot fail. To show this is Paul's aim in Rom 9–11.

3. This section of Romans shows clearly how important, but also how dangerous, are theological inquiries into "salvation history". The point of such inquiries is to stress that God spoke his word in history. It is only because he has constantly confronted men with his historical word that we can talk about him. But the danger is also clear. We may be tempted to try to discover God's "plan" in history. God's purposes are not visible in history. Even the light of revelation does not make it easier to interpret history. Paul knows that the history of mankind as a whole can be interpreted only as a history of the absence of

salvation, of sin, the history of Adam (Rom 5: 12 ff). God's word always remains strangely "open" in history. Hence anyone who confidently offers a "theology of salvation history", always runs the risk of writing his theology from God's point of view. This is not inevitable, but it is a risk. Paul sees it clearly, and reminds men of their limitations. Although he never ceases to insist that God's word never acts anywhere other than in history, he rejects any attempt to explain history in simple terms.

4. The section gives us a model for the use of the Old Testament in the Christian Church. On the one hand Christianity will never be able to stop using the Old Testament. It is only from the Old Testament that the Christian community can learn the word of the God who has remained true to himself and whose faithfulness is the source of salvation for Israel as it is for all men. On the other hand the Christian Church will never be able to forget that primarily the Old Testament contains the word of God which was spoken to Israel. It cannot forget this because it takes history seriously as the sphere in which God's revelation operates. But if it does this, the sort of thing which happened very early in the Christian Church is ruled out: that is, treating the Old Testament as unqualified testimony for the Christian faith. Paul does not claim that the whole of the Old Testament speaks the language of his faith. But any simple choice between the Christian and Jewish interpretations of the Old Testament is also ruled out. The Old Testament speaks to both: to Christians and to Jews. Neither Christians nor Jews enjoy the grace of God as a possession, but both need constantly to hear anew about the wonder of grace. This gives both a common duty, to listen to the word of the Old Testament as it speaks to each.

II CHRIST AND THE GENTILES

The New Testament writers show a reluctance to speculate. That could be the reason why we have hardly any texts dealing with the relationship of the faith to non-Christian religions or considering the fate of non-Christians. Only a few texts tell

us anything, and then only in passing. One is Col 1: 15–20.
It is an old hymn in praise of Christ, quoted by the author of
Colossians. It begins:

> He is the image of the invisible God,
> the first-born of all creation;
> for in him all things were created,
> in heaven and on earth,
> visible and invisible . . .
> all things were created through him and for him.
> He is before all things, and in him all things hold together.
> He is the head of the body.

The community which sang this hymn celebrated Christ as the
foundation and principle of all creation. In doing so it took
over ideas from Stoic and Hellenistic Jewish philosophy. The
hymn also makes use of countless traditional ideas. More importantly, we must be careful in trying to turn the worshipful
prayer of this community into factual assertions. For all these
reasons the usefulness of the text for our problem is limited.

Christ and non-Christians

But we can learn something from it. The hymn contains three
central statements about the relation of Christians to non-
Christians.

1. The community knows that Christ is the only "image" of
God. Only through Christ is the unknown God made visible
and knowable.

2. In celebrating Christ as the one who was before all things,
through whom and for whom all things are and in whom
everything holds together, it is saying that beside Christ there
is no power that can stand. Implicit in this hymn is the belief
that all the authorities and powers (the gods of the non-
Christians included) have been vanquished. These powers are
fictions, and have always been so.

3. In this hymn the community proclaims it complete openness to the world. The world is Christ's world. It is creation.
The community can therefore live in the world without fear

because it knows the Christ has been from the beginning the Lord of the world, its "first principle".

It is also valuable to see clearly what we *cannot* find in this text. It offers no basis for any "natural" theology. It does not talk about two different forms of existence of Christ, one hidden and secretly governing the world and one made manifest by the resurrection. It is the hymn of a community which has experienced the reality of Easter and knows that the power of the risen Christ is an unlimited power which gives way to no worldly power and embraces the whole creation. Even the first couplet of the hymn is an expression of faith in the *risen* Christ, and the natural implication of the whole hymn is the preaching of the power of the risen Christ, *mission* (Col 1: 22 ff). It is not the assertion of an unconscious unity existing from the beginning of the world in which all men somehow participate, "Christ in you" (Col 1: 27) is not a Christ dwelling from the creation in men's hearts, but the Christ preached by Christians to non-Christians.

In other words, Col 1: 15 ff is the foundation of the mission. The last thing the text offers us is materials for a pseudo-universal religious philosophy which would make the Christian mission superfluous. That may be in various ways uncomfortable, but if so it is all the more important to be quite clear about it. It is precisely where we find the New Testament's statements hard to understand that we cannot find solutions by avoiding uncomfortable statements. It is only after we have seen that in the view of the author of Colossians the hymn we have quoted implies mission, that we can ask what is involved in preaching to the Gentiles.

Here again the Epistle to the Colossians gives us clear advice. Preaching to the Gentiles does not mean showing the inferiority or viciousness of non-Christian religions. Nor does it mean – at least in the first place – calling on them to change their traditions and customs. Mission means constant repetition of the news that Christ has reconciled the world with God, and that God has now drawn near to the world, the Gentile world. Mission means telling people that God has always loved the world and, through Christ, has always been its Lord. This love of God applies without discrimination. In Paul's language, the love of God is shown in the preaching of justification by faith alone, without works. That means that God in Christ loves the Jews as Jews, the Greeks as Greeks: everyone as the people they are. All are equally near to God. In Christ there is neither Jew nor Greek, slave nor free man, male nor female (Gal 3: 28). This love of God holds whether men accept it or reject it, whether they know about it or not. Its basis is Christ, not human piety, and as the hymn proclaims, Christ has been from the beginning with the creation.

So we see that for the earliest Christians the question of the truth of intrinsic value of non-Christian religions was almost impossible to form. Naturally even when we find mention of it, mainly in Hellenistic Judaism and Stoic philosophy. Even Paul sometimes refers to it. For example, he can take up the Stoic idea that all men can know God, but he does so only to show how far Gentile life has been perverted, and how little of this knowledge of God has been preserved by the Gentiles (Rom 1: 18 ff). Or he can go the other way and give a very favourable account of the Gentiles, and say that they do God's commandments by nature (Rom 2: 14–15), though only to hold them up to the Jews and say: "Don't you think you're better than the Gentiles." Taken *together*, the two passages show how far Paul was from working out a single theory of the problem.

In the rest of the New Testament the most favourable judgment on the Gentiles is in Paul's speech on the Areopagus – which was written not by Paul but by Luke, the author of Acts. Here, in Acts 17: 22 ff, world history is turned into the prehistory of the Christian faith. Man is by nature capable of knowing God, indeed related to God (17: 28). In this speech God *is* and has been for a long time close to men, but they only see this because of the order visible in creation and not because of the love of Christ. In this text the message of Christ comes like an appendage at the end, and one which doesn't seem particularly necessary (17: 30–1). What are we to think of this speech? Is it a "takeover" of the Christian message by Hellenistic "natural theology"? Or has Luke simply tried to be a Greek to the Greeks (1 Cor 9: 19 ff)? Both views are possible.

But the end of the Areopagus speech shows that "natural theology" is at most a peg on which the preacher can hang his message, and in no sense a way to salvation. Only the preaching of the Gospel of Jesus Christ produces belief or unbelief in the hearers.

Christians and non-Christians

What does all this tell us about the relationship between Christians and non-Christians? The result of this survey of the New Testament may be disappointing. We have found that there is no New Testament "doctrine" of non-Christian religions. Attempts have frequently been made in the history of theology to construct such a doctrine. One such is based on the idea of a "primary revelation" of God to mankind. Or attention is transferred to the doctrine of "natural" knowledge of God. Ideas of this kind appear only on the fringes of the New Testament, and even then are not expressed in a single way. Consequently, when we approach the question of non-Christians we must first admit that we know nothing. This is salutary, not only because the realization of human ignorance constantly brings us up against the difference between God and man, but more importantly because through this ignorance a community is established between Christians and non-Christians, a community in a common inquiry, in which neither has an advantage over the other.

When Paul talks about non-Christians, he talks about justification by faith alone, not by works. For him the essence of faith is that it is not a human achievement, an effort of the intellect, but a gift, the chance of real life made available by the experience of God's love. This love of God is directed in the same way to all men. There are no conditions to it; it depends only on God's free choice and not on man and his actions. The beginning and the end of Christian conversation with non-Christians must therefore be the experience of this ultimate community established by the love of God. Christians and non-Christians are loved in the same way by God, each in his own situation. Christians and non-Christians therefore share a reason for gratitude, since both are loved by God. Because of this, this deepest community between Christians and non-Christians must be the main content of Christian preaching to non-Christians.

But the community goes very much further. Christians and non-Christians are human beings, and neither are "possessors". God is not at their command, and neither side has bought rights in God's grace. Paul reminds us: "Do not become proud, but stand in awe. For if God did not spare the natural branches [ie, in the original context, the Jews], neither will he spare you" (Rom 11: 20–1). But the community also consists in common ignorance, as in the case of God's "plan" for the non-Christians. Being a Christian does not mean being on a higher level of knowledge. Theologians themselves from non-Christian countries have constantly emphasized that the important task cannot be to build "bridges" to the non-Christian religions so as to give non-Christians a place in an existing Christian "system". Rather, they say, the important point is that the bridge has *already* been built, by God, or, in the words of Ephesians 2: 14, that the dividing wall has *already* been broken down.

That does not stop us asking questions. Almost thirty years ago Dietrich Bonhoeffer suggested that Paul's slogan, "justification by faith alone", might today mean justification without being religious first. Can this proposal be applied to the relationship between Christians and non-Christians to allow the conclusion that for non-Christians "justification by faith alone" means justification without having to accept the Christian faith? Whatever fascination the idea may have for us, it is misleading. God loves Jews as Jews, Greeks as Greeks, and Indians as Indians. But they are not justified by being Jews, Greeks or Indians – that *would* be the salvation by "natural theology", which the message of Christ rules out. Paul knows nothing of any justifying faith which is not faith in *Christ*. This faith is not, like "religion" in Bonhoeffer's language, initial capital, a precondition, a qualification, but the acceptance of the justification which God gives for Christ's sake without any prior qualification. But this faith includes "conversion", and in that sense Jews do *not* stay just Jews, Greeks just Greeks, and Indians just Indians, when they are justified "by faith alone". Nevertheless Bonhoeffer's idea quite rightly turns our thoughts in a different direction.

Christian mission

Paul and other Christian theologians became Greeks to the Greeks for the sake of the Gospel (cf 1 Cor 9: 19 ff). A close study of the New Testament shows the astonishing degree to which the message of salvation changed its form on its entry into the Greek world, and entered into Greek thought for the sake of the Gospel.

The big question now is: the Christians may have become Greeks to the Greeks, but in their dealings with other men have they largely *remained* Greeks? In the past Christendom enclosed itself within a fortress of dogma, and has still not in any important way been able to free itself from its marriage to Greek philosophy. Perhaps in Europe there is no need to. But is what suits Europeans necessarily right for non-Europeans? Certainly all Christian attempts so far to break out of the Greek mould which has formed the Christian faith have made very little impression. For the most part they have remained on the level of liturgical and stylistic adaptation and have not touched the level of doctrine. There is scarcely a single element of Christian teaching – the dogmas formulated by the Church and even the very idea of dogma – which does not in some way show the influence of Greek ideas. Is this form of the Christian faith so simply identical with the faith itself? For non-Christians confronted with this European Christianity must there not be a possibility of "justification" without the prior condition of the European form of Christianity? Is it not time for the faith to make a fresh start?

It is certainly a fascinating experience to see how the Jews, for example, are today rediscovering Jesus – not the Son of God Jesus Christ, but *their* Jesus, "Brother Jesus". If we are honest, we must admit that this rediscovery is taking place, not thanks to Christian influence, but in spite of it. Dialogue with the Jewish interpretation of Jesus is valuable for Christians, and necessary, because it helps to free our own picture of Jesus from centuries-old premises and unquestioned assumptions. Similar developments are beginning to take place in Hinduism and Buddhism. Here we Christians can do no more than humbly join in the dialogue, and mostly it is we who profit most from this non-Christian discovery of the Christian faith.

But these people mostly remain non-Christians, Jews or Hindus. Can we be satisfied with this? Is not the experience of the love of God established in Christ, which goes out to all men, identical with membership of the community which thanks God for this love, with membership of the Church. Indeed, but when we say this we must bear in mind two points. We must remember how much most non-Christians, now as in the past, see the churches as representatives of the claim for the superiority of European ideas. We must at least be "generous" towards nọn-Christian Indian or Japanese, for whom not only, say, our ideas about sin, our doctrine of Christ, but even the way in which we approach the question of God, are often as strange as they have become obvious to us. We must be at least as "generous" with these fellow men of ours as God, who loves them without conditions.

And the second point. We should not forget the Church in Calcutta with a huge fan on the ceiling; it was operated by hand by Indians to blow cool air on the English who sat below praying to their God. That church is a symbol of times gone by which are nevertheless more relevant than we suspect.

We mustn't forget these two points when we have to formulate a principle – not to be "theoretically correct" and universally valid, but true to and for the present.

There can be no salvation without faith, but perhaps for the moment – and we may hope only temporarily – Christian faith can only exist among non-Christians as "non-church" or non-"Christianity" in the European sense. Even then this formulation is only acceptable when we remember at the same time that where true Christian faith exists, Christianity and the

Church necessarily also exist – though perhaps in a form which is for us at the same time puzzling and liberating.

After all, what are Christianity and the Church based on if not faith? Our principle must be taken first as a confession of our guilt. At the same time, however, it does lead us towards a new understanding, as we can see in a number of ways. We have recognized the questionable nature of the missionary work of earlier ages which was so strongly marked by western culture, but have not yet discovered any really practical model which can be used by Christian missionaries. At best we are in the stage of experiment and the search for new and better ways. Moreover, the so-called "young churches" are still a long way from finding the form which will allow them to "go native" and so accept yet critically reassess their own culture. To a large extent these churches are still foreign bodies in their own environments and are only now beginning to develop their own theology and their own forms of church life and organization. Finally, before we become too worried about the "riskiness" of our formulation, we should re-read Mt 25: 31–46 to see that the boundaries between those who belong to Jesus and those who do not by no means coincide with the "official" boundaries of the Church. The Church too will be judged. And at the judgment of the non-Christians it will be seen that many whom the members of the Church would never have expected will be at Jesus' side.

There is one last lesson to learn from "justification by faith alone", and that is a deep respect for all that is human. This includes respect for religion as an expression of human nature. That respect has its foundation in the fact that God loves men without conditions. Far from being in conflict with a correctly understood claim for the superiority of Christianity, it follows from it. Absolute claims can be made only by God's love, not by its human interpretation or embodiment. And it is the very absoluteness of God's love, directed to all men in all circumstances, which gives rise to this deep respect for what is human, because it is loved by God. This realization should also guide us in our dealings with the representatives of other religions.

Part Four
Faith and world

18   Man in history

The Christian faith says no less than this: through the life, death and resurrection of Jesus of Nazareth, God himself took up and answered once and for all the age-old question as to the meaning of human life. Does this mean that the question is "settled" – contrary to all expectations? The scriptures tell us that we have the treasure of this answer "in earthen vessels" (2 Cor 4: 7). We do not possess any complete, universally applicable picture of man. The faith does not outline any "ideal" picture of human life in which reality is necessarily overshadowed. On the contrary, the faith is a definite way of accepting life with its *unanswered* questions. It also knows the perfection towards which our whole earthly existence is aiming. But this perfection is unattainable. Only God knows this perfection. As yet we have no insight into it.

And yet we read in John: *Ecce homo!* – Behold the man (Jn 19: 5). When faith reflects on its ultimate theme, Christ, it simultaneously introduces a kind of "anthropology", and makes statements about mankind. These statements do not form any definitive system but do open up various "perspectives of human life". We must now try to describe some of these "perspectives" in the light of the whole story of Jesus. We shall discuss three areas of debate which are currently mentioned in dialogue with non-Christians: the history, social nature and "transcendence" of man.

Man in history

Paul summarized the story of Jesus of Nazareth in the following words: "But when the time had fully come, God sent forth
his Son, born of woman, born under the law" (Gal 4: 4). "The
sending forth of the Son of God", "the fulfilment of the times"
– such phrases are reminiscent of the abundant, but to our ears
rather gloomy sources of antique mythology. And yet this
phrase represents a decisive break-through from the mythological way of thinking. For this "Son sent by God" is no demi-
god but the historical person, Jesus of Nazareth.

This is just what Paul emphasizes so concisely – Jesus' full
historical existence as a human being. "Born of woman" – the
fundamental biological criterion of human existence. "Born
under the law" – the concrete position of this humanity in
religious and cultural history. Nature and history in the form
of concrete space and time are not unknown to this "Son of
God". We must not overlook the fact that this story of the Son
of God is a "special", unique and incomparable story in the
eyes of the apostles.

But this does not in the least minimize the significance of the
earthly, worldly history of mankind. On the contrary, God
takes the nature and history of this world so seriously that he
identifies himself with it in the person of Jesus. His "story" and
his "fulfilled time" lead him into the midst of human time, at a
specific moment in the history of the world. Jesus of Nazareth
participated unconditionally in the history of the world until
his death under Pontius Pilate. This should determine once and
for all that mankind should accept the world and history as its
existence. We started out by saying that we *can* look for God
in history, and now we have the answer of the faith, that we
should look for God in history; in the concrete history of God-
made-man in the person of Jesus Christ who lived and suffered
our human existence with us and for us.

In the light of the story of Christ we can see that man is determined as a *historical being.* We can now repeat the precept
with which this book opened. Through the Christian faith,
man's history was revealed to him.

Of course man had always been historically determined. His characteristic feature right from the beginning was that he was not simply a "creature of nature", but a "cultural being" open to change, able to shape his own destiny, and living and suffering in history. Yet in his human experience of history and his reflections about himself – as mirrored in mythology, religion and philosophy, his attitude to history remained generally helpless and negative. The ancient oriental religions, for example, were predominantly "static" and made no allowance whatever for history. Ancient philosophy looked for the universally valid *Logos* – the precise opposite of that inscrutable, "illogical" thing known as history. According to it everything truly human, the real meaning of being human, lies beyond the historical process. This was clearly a dead end from which man's soul, the real core of his existence, had to be liberated.

By contrast with this, the biblical way of thinking seems radically new. One is tempted to say that it was through the Bible that man first became fully aware of himself, his faith, and his thoughts in a historical context. For in the light of the biblical message the history of the world no longer appeared to be godless. We must emphasize that the God of the Bible is the God of history, not only from the time of his "identification" with history in the personal history of Jesus, but already in the Old Testament. The Old Testament is the history book of mankind. In it man experiences himself as a historical being. His all-important past is no longer something shrouded in mythology as in oriental religions. On the contrary, the Bible recounts the history of events that really took place, such as Moses bringing the people of Israel out of the land of Egypt, Jahveh's act of salvation in the history of Israel. Man's present is full of history – for instance the prophets and their involvement in the present. Man's future is not directed towards the beyond, as the ancient philosophers had thought, but towards actual history. This consists of the coming of the Messiah promised by God and awaited with such eagerness and devotion. For when man's salvation (and downfall) is decided *within* rather than beyond his own history, then he is not saved *from* it but *for* it. For biblical man living within this unfathomable history is no blind fate but a meaningful chance, which he is free either to take up and develop in faith, or else to let slip and abuse if he has too little faith.

The biblical faith stemming from these sources acted as an incomparably effective "historical initiative" in European history. We use the phrase "biblical faith" deliberately, and not "Christian religion". Both are inseparable, and yet there is an important distinction between them. For Christianity's purpose was not exclusively that of transmitting the message of the Bible. It was also a sacred institution with a hierarchical structure which by no means acted *solely* as a source of "historical initiative". On the contrary, its slowness and inertia sometimes even paralysed the progress of history. On the other hand, the "historical initiative" of the Bible also made itself felt outside the Church: for instance, in the nonconformist lay movement of the twelfth and thirteenth centuries, or in the Hussite movement of the fifteenth century, or indeed in the conscious decision to break completely with Christianity. Marxism, for example, and its specific kind of "historical initiative", is unthinkable without the impact of the legacy of the biblical prophecies. Wherever this legacy asserted itself inside or outside the Church it led to the dissolution of all myths and "eternal" doctrines, so that the wide scope of history could be reopened to mankind once more.

Man in community

Some of the most important Old Testament texts about mankind taken up by Jesus are those at the beginning of the Book of Genesis. The most powerful statement of all is probably contained in the verse which played such a vital rôle in the history of dogmatic theology and philosophy: 'So God created man in his own image, in the image of God he created him; male and female he created them" (Gen 1: 27).

The closing phrase is "male and female he created them". Man can only achieve true humanity within a fundamental "duality", as male and female – in other words in a community. Sociability, the characteristic feature of the community, is the basic structure of human existence. Where man's social nature or inclination is threatened, human existence itself is in danger.

The Bible, though in other respects a veritable gold-mine of controversial ideas, never relinquished this insight contained within its first pages. In the eyes of the Bible man is never self-sufficient or introspective. He is an "extra-vert" continually on the move from God to man and from man to God. His "core" is a movable centre. By which we do not mean that man has no centre. Biblical man does have a centre, or rather, he himself *is* this centre. He bears his own name – an unmistakable, inviolable ego. He is no anonymous, irresponsible, subservient creature of the herd, but in the fullest sense of the word a "person" and the master of his own destiny. The biblical "I" is not infrequently spoken with great emphasis – as in the psalms. That the concept "person" developed a far greater significance in European thought than it ever did in ancient philosophy (take Augustine for example) is not just by chance due to the influence of Christianity.

And yet this emphatic "I" attributed to man by the Bible is never introspective. In the psalms in particular it is above all the actual self or ego which expresses itself by confessing its sins and giving thanks to God. Wherever this I appears it immediately refers away from itself towards others, towards the You of God and its fellow beings. This self is a totally different one from that found in non-biblical philosophy. It does not find itself by granting unlimited sovereignty to the non-self. The ego finds itself through the support of its non-ego, namely the ego or self of God and its fellow beings. The biblical "master of his destiny" is no superman as conceived by Nietzsche, capable only of dominating over and despising others. Just the opposite, he is the master of his *own* mind and his *own* movements. Once again we encounter one of the questions with which we began this book: the promise of an answer.

The gospels talk about this – and hence the call to follow – using one of the most meaningful words in the New Testament: love. Nowadays this word is somewhat worn and debased. But in the New Testament it has a distinctive ring when applied to the life of Jesus of Nazareth. It is a precise comment on man's social nature.

By social nature, we do not mean just man's erotic nature. All too often the word "love" is interpreted only in this sense. Erotic love is the egoistical search for someone else as a means of satisfying one's own desires and instincts. By extension, even the "platonic" search for intellectual enrichment from someone else is basically a form of erotic love. Erotic love is obviously an important and necessary part of human existence. We *need* other people in an erotic way. The New Testament interpretation of love is not out to brand erotic love as a sin which should be eradicated. The Old Testament Song of Songs warns us against any such fanaticism. But if eros becomes our predominant attitude to our fellow men or even God, then it becomes a perversion of man's social nature.

The way of Jesus was different. His kind of love is *agape,* not *eros.* By this we mean that Jesus is there for *others* and not the other way round. "For the Son of Man also came not to be served but to serve" (Mk 10: 45). This perspective radically changes the rôle that the other person plays in my life. He is not there simply as a possible source of enrichment, ready to be exploited by me. Nor as an awkward rival best got rid of. And how often does the mood of an erotically-determined person sway between these two extremes! In the New Testament sense of love I encounter my fellow man as a genuine opposite, a fellow being in God. He is taken up by Jesus' love. This love does not transfigure him so that I want to be morally indignant with him. Jesus' love does not teach us to divide the world into black and white, heaven and hell. We should not see our fellow men as exclusively good or bad. What it does teach us is that other people are our life. Without them we cannot exist. Hence everyone, even a stranger, is my *neighbour.* His life affects me too.

So far we have discussed the relationship between one individual and another. This is understandable, because this is how love begins, from heart to heart. But it is most important that we understand that this is not the only manifestation of love. Christ's love is more than a simple "affair of the heart". According to the unequivocal evidence of the New Testament this love has a "religious" and even a "cosmic" dimension. It not only functions between individuals; it also penetrates the larger community of the Church and indeed society as a whole. It is love "incarnate". True Christian love cannot avoid becoming incarnate. Nor is it indifferent to social structures; it takes account of social and political life. In this sense the social nature of the faith – if we may be permitted to express it this way – is socially orientated. For it seeks new structures for human love and charity. And precisely in our day, the problems of others are also the moving force of society and its institutions. In the eyes of the Christian faith, man is a social being.

Transcendence

The Bible treats the historical and social aspects of human existence seriously, and avoids the danger of a purely individualistic religious "metaphysic" or "introversion". It also reveals the classic religious theme of man's "transcendence": that is, his relationship to everything that goes beyond himself and his own person. This involves not only his relationship to God, but the basic problem of the image of man.

We have only to glance at the current discussion about the essence and reality of man in order to see that the question of transcendence plays an extremely important rôle. Significant discoveries of modern biology have demonstrated that man is a creature open to development and that he is still developing. He does not adapt instinctively to the natural environment like the animals, but has to discover and create his own world by feeling his way and making experiments. Does this not mean that man is always trying to move beyond himself and his limits – in other words that he is a "transcending" being? This, surely, is what modern philosophy is trying so emphatically to express.

Existential philosophy, for instance, stresses that man is not what he is once and for all, but is continually changing. Marxists also appreciate man's transcendence in a totally new way – precisely through their dialogues with Christians. It would seem that despite the otherwise confusing intellectual situation of the day, all are agreed on the transcendence of man. Man is a being which necessarily has to transcend itself.

But the Christian faith does not content itself with a general discussion on this matter. It also discusses just what this transcendence of man *is*. At this point we have to return to the passage from Genesis quoted above. This time, however, we wish to emphasize its central statement. "So God created man in his own image, in the image of God he created him" (Gen 1: 27). Man becomes man because God made him into his equal, raised him up above the dumb existence of the rest of creation. He made man into his own "confederate", and continues to encounter him as the unmistakable You of his own self, his own I. The conclusion of this thought is that the original and only aim of this self-transcending being, man, can only be this one absolute, transcendent God.

Negative transcendence

Wherever contemporary theology confirms this biblical insight, it proceeds with extreme caution, full of self-criticism, and – as many people think – almost uncertainly. In modern theology – right up to the beginnings of so-called "atheistic theology" – the traditional concept of God is changing. Modern atheist criticism, as represented with particular intensity by the philosophy of Ludwig Feuerbach, has not been overheard.

This criticism includes such questions as to whether "God" is not just a concept through which man depicts his own infinity. But in that case our original sentence would surely run: God created man *to* his own image. The philosophical criticism of traditional metaphysics has also come under fire. For does not the metaphysical concept of God in fact amount to what one could call a "negative" transcendence, in other words a transcendence created for man's own benefit? Does this not do harm to man's historical reality? To sum up both views, does the concept of God not in fact estrange man from his historicity and his social nature on the one hand, and from his human self-transcendence on the other – in fact from all the decisive dimensions of his existence?

The Christian faith has to consider with due gravity all these questions, if it is to be honest with itself. In John Robinson's terminology, we must be "honest to God" in our thinking and living. In Christian theology and piety God has all too often been untenably humanized. And how much oriental mythology and ancient metaphysics have nevertheless found their way into the dogmatic history of the Church. For the theologian of today, in the midst of this whirlpool of criticism and self-criticism, "honest to God" means that he must reflect on the real purpose and aim of the biblical faith. If this is done, many of the criticisms will undoubtedly be stilled.

The problem is man's *real* transcendence. But quite apart from the Christian faith, has the fact of human transcendence been taken seriously enough if the age-old "religious experience" is simply dismissed as an illusion? On the contrary, the existence of religion is a sign that man's "openness" cannot stop at the limits of his consciousness and the finite world. To express it in biblical terms: is the God of the Bible not a fixation of the "free transcendence" on an object? Do not the entire Old and New Testaments instead try to say that God is the free, unattainable Lord, who resists all human attempts at reducing him to an object through religious cults, myths or philosophical concepts?

The God of the Bible is the Lord of history, the coming God, the God who comes towards us, and hence our unattainable deliverer and judge. This refutes the final objection against God, namely that this transcendence could estrange man from his historicity and his social nature. The God of the Bible enters into the midst of history and society in the person of Jesus of Nazareth. By freely entering into this covenant with man, he proves that he does not negate or destroy man's historicity and social nature. On the contrary, he demonstrates that he is man's creator and deliverer, as the historical and social God. In this way the Christian faith still believes it can hold on to God as the true transcendence of man – despite all critical and self-critical doubts. We shall try to elucidate the meaning of this true transcendence in two concluding points.

Liberating transcendence

Human self-transcendence seems to be threatened from two directions. The first temptation is obvious and generally comprehensive: "bad finity". This is an attitude which cannot endure the "emptiness" of unattainable transcendence, and tries to replace it with a substitute as quickly as possible. This superficially quells the discomforting feeling. Where God is silent, the gods and idols speak. Man is sacrificed to the gods of the instincts, superstition, money, race and nationalism. But this kind of "transcendence" is not liberating. It enslaves man, and alienates him from himself. Man's "openness" closes up. We all know only too well how many false cults based on false transcendence twentieth-century man has instigated and suffered to the bitter end.

The God of the prophets and apostles forbids this alienation. When this God comes, man will be freed from all the entanglements of his earthly existence and led into the "openness" of the "absolute future" (Karl Rahner). This is true freedom. Free *from* and *for* the ties and obligations of this world.

The world of the gods and false idols with its false transcendences will be "deprived of its divine attributes" and "demythologized". It will be restored to man in its true, worldly reality. For the man created in God's image, God is the only transcendence which does not alienate. Augustine, one of the chief witnesses of this true transcendence in the history of European thought, expressed it with incomparable perception: "You made us for yourself, and our heart is restless until it rests in you" (Confessions 1: 1).

The transcendence of mercy

Our true transcendence can also be threatened from another side; from the "false finity". By this we mean the interpretation of transcendence according to which it incessantly tries to surpass itself. This leads into a void. Optimistically, this can be described as the evolutionism of the first hour, or the progress into infinity. But it can also – and this is more often the case – be given a pessimistic overtone, by describing it as the pilgrimage from one Nothing (when we did not yet exist) into another (when we shall be no more). Many people today feel that existence in this dark void is the only possible honest approach.

Biblical faith in God as the transcendence of man also applies to this human need. It takes man's needs seriously, even in their sceptical and pessimistic forms. It does not clarify them. It sees man's needs as the "sighs of an oppressed creature", the signs of alienation. And this is a reality which the Bible treats with incomparable seriousness. Our world is an alienated world. Not only on account of the natural finiteness of the world, the lack of development, or fatal misfortune, but because of man's abuse of his freedom; in other words, the betrayal and inertia of the chief representative of creation, God's associate in the covenant, man himself. If we look at the reality of this alienated world, the temptation is to join forces with the sceptics and pessimists, and give up all hope.

There can be only one real reason for a Christian still not having to join in the cries or silence of the pessimists: his belief in the true transcendence of man. We describe this (and in doing so try to indicate the word "God" as well) as the "transcendence of mercy". Both words should be emphasized. *Transcendence*: faith in God means belief in that "opposite" which does not rise on our historical horizon through the powers of given reality. How could alienation ever be overcome under the conditions and with the means of the alienated world? This is not the "opposite" that vanishes into the void of a meaningless process. It is the God who comes into the world in his free initiative and sovereignty. This freedom is expressed in biblical terms with the word "*mercy*".

The God of the Bible is not a nameless abyss. He is no almighty, hidden Absolute. He is the God whom we call Jesus Christ; the God with a human face; the God of man. His mercy is the true transcendence of man. It does not clarify the world

of man just like that, but it does open the world and its alienation to hope. And so it makes sense to act and suffer openly
in all personal and social situations. In other words: to live
humanly.

19   History and cosmos

Christian faith makes man new in that, even as it liberates
him, it binds him to God and unites him in community to his
fellow men. Yet what this newness does to man is simply to
bring him back to the original calling which he had lost. This
too is something we have touched upon. The central point of
this "new creation" is the resurrection of Jesus. In it it is clear
that any man who believes in God has managed to achieve
contact with life itself – that very life which rises triumphant
over every form of death. But is this "all"? Is the creative
power of faith confined to the new union between persons,
between God and man, between Christ and the Church,
between man and man? Does not faith also transform the
relationship between man and cosmos, between person and
world? The world, that is, not of humanity but of things and
living creatures. Does not the resurrection of Jesus transform
the cosmos at this level too in its turn?

This is a question which we cannot evade, if only because
we have already introduced this idea of "world" as a vital
factor at several points in our considerations. Evolution, physical forces and processes, man's mastering of these, and the
possibility of his misusing them; all these constitute a special
factor in the question of God as it affects us *today*. It is the
root cause of the fact that even from the aspect of our relationships with our fellow men and our social life the God question
is becoming so acute. Conversely Scripture insists that man
cannot blame the world or material things when they oppress
him, for only man makes them his enemies. Whereas in the
foregoing chapter we provided a brief résumé of the Christian

faith in its understanding of what man is, we have now to consider how that faith understands the world.

I. THE NEW CREATION OF THE WORLD IN JESUS CHRIST

The New Testament does speak of a new creation of the world through Jesus Christ. Before Christ the world was in bondage to mysterious principalities and powers which held the sphere which exists between God and man under their sway. But by his resurrection Christ has cut his way through the sphere ruled over by these powers and broken their strength. They can no longer set a barrier between God and mankind (cf eg, Rom 8: 38 ff; Col 2: 14 ff; Eph 2: 13 ff).

Principalities and powers

In biblical times statements of this kind were not merely understood, they struck an answering chord of joy in the hearts of their hearers. For they were in harmony with views on the nature of the cosmos which were in any case current coin. For ourselves, such statements strike us as mythological. We no longer see any hosts of rebellious angels or any tyrannical powers oppressing the cosmos and blocking the horizons of our lives. But what, in that case, are such passages saying to us? There is a real temptation here, and one which is sometimes actually succumbed to, to find substitutes for the old mythological ideas drawn from the world of modern civilization. Thus we may find, for instance, economic and technological "pressures", or the drives of the subconscious as described for us in depth psychology, taking the place of the powers and spirits in the air. Certainly it would be a false loyalty to the New Testament for us to feel obliged to commit ourselves to such "translations". It is the *message* of the New Testament that we have to "translate" and not its cosmological ideas. The vital point is that believers must in practice keep a firm grasp on the cosmic dimension of Christ's redemptive work.

The New Testament has something more to tell us than the

sole fact that *man* has received grace through Christ, has been accepted as a child of God and co-heir with Christ, and now no longer lives by that which was, but rather by that which is and is to come (Rom 8: 12–17). Also, and more than this, the whole of creation is waiting with eager longing for its liberation and glorification, and is ardently yearning to experience the fact that it is not nothingness (Rom 8: 18–25). Not only man but the cosmos is caught up by the power of God in its act of new creation. This truth is expressed in the gospels by means of a number of points of detail included in the narratives of the passion and resurrection. During the crucifixion a darkness fell upon the earth from the sixth to the ninth hours: the reversion of the world to chaos (Mk 15: 33 par; cp Gen 1: 2). By contrast the ascension of Jesus into heaven symbolizes the power of the Lord in the new creation (Mk 16: 19; Lk 24: 51; Eph 4: 9 f). On this aspect the Johannine gospel is more guarded, but to compensate for this provides the fullest description of all of the glorified body of Christ, which is both present in this world and yet at the same time not subject to its limitations of space and time. This, once more, has a mythological ring. How, therefore, are we of *today* to understand the process of renewal wrought by Christ in its effects upon the cosmos?

Greek and biblical world-pictures

We should begin by reminding ourselves of the fact that the Bible views the world through different eyes from those of the Greeks in their religion and philosophy. For Greek thought the world considered as cosmos is a divine reality, the origin of all things, mankind and gods alike. Hence the root problem which constantly arises is whether any "divine principle" is to be discovered within this cosmos. The Greek tragic poets raised the question of whether fate does not signify necessity and freedom suffering. The philosophers, seeking to rise above the chiaroscuro of the tragedians, search for the "logos", the spiritual force giving form to things and presiding over the world and mankind. The myths of the cosmogony lead human reason to the idea that an ultimate rational meaning might be found for the whole if that reason could succeed in separating the essential from the inessential, the spiritual and intellectual from the sensible and material. On the basis of both approaches, the understanding of the world of the tragedian and the philosopher alike, man promises himself freedom.

The thought of the authors of Scripture proceeds in the opposite direction. Here it is not the cosmos and the element of the divine in it that occupy the centre of the stage. Here, rather, the centre of the cosmos is man. Man alone, and not the world, is called to be God's image and the partner to his covenant word. Man alone has received God's revelation, and this revelation to man is now the expectation and hope of the world. The world is merely the environment (*Um*welt) of man, his wider environment (Gen 1) and his more immediate one (Gen 2). It stands ready, as it were, for him to receive and is the sphere of his authority. But above all it is the sphere of God's direct and unremitting action. At the same time it is the sphere of encounter and converse inasmuch as it is here that man either praises God or alternatively rebels against him. Hence, whereas with the Greeks it is the dialogue between man and world about God that is crucial, in the Bible the decisive factor becomes the dialogue between God and man about the world.

Yet in Scripture, even though, by comparison with Greek ideas, the world has lost its sovereign position, it is still involved and affected by the central events of the covenant between God and man, by sin, by the incarnation of God, the cross, the resurrection, and the grace and future glory of man. The world is not the agent of the work of salvation, but it is involved in it. It throws back the echo of the words uttered in promise and responded to in faith between God and man. Hence man no longer turns to the world in order to achieve some experience about God from it – in this sense the Bible puts an end to all "natural theology". But at the same time man cannot turn away from the world either, for it is here, and nowhere else, that God makes it possible for him to hear echoed the message of his own liberation. The world is affected by the salvation

wrought in Jesus Christ just as, for example, the wider and
narrower worlds of man described in Gen 1–2 are affected by
the reality of the covenant and by the factor of belief or
unbelief in the relationship between God and man. The world
as the Bible views it is a companion to man, whose life,
together with his, is affected by the adventure that unfolds in
terms of sin and grace.

It is this involvement of the world in man's saving destiny in
God's sight that is being pointed to when the world is called
"creation" in the Bible. In its root meaning what the word
"creation" expresses is not a physical statement, as for instance
that the world was created out of nothing, but rather this significance that the world has of being the stage on which the
history of God with man and of man with God is played out.
This likewise explains why in the Bible the world of God and
man alike can be addressed as a person – as, for instance, when
it is exhorted to praise God (Dan 3!) and thank him, and so not
to have any pretensions to self-glorification – properly speaking exhortations addressed to *man*. Here the world too can,
like man, be called to account for its attitude towards God at
any given time. God does not address the world directly, but
he does guard against any fresh resurgence of the hostile
forces which were thrust back at the creation (Gen 1),
unleashed anew in the Flood (Gen 6), and overthrown by the
resurrection of Jesus until they are finally destroyed at the
Last Day (1 Cor 15: 24–8). The world, like man, is capable of
rebelling against God at any time. Yet even as God watches
over man so he watches over the elements also (Ps 46: 4; 74:
13; 89: 10; 104: 7; Job 3: 8; 7: 12). It is in and through the faith
of man that the world is intended again and again to recognize
its true vocation.

Cosmos and faith

This brief digression into the history of ideas has been necessary in order that we can understand at this point the sense in
which the Christian faith ascribes to the resurrection of Jesus
a significance which bears not only upon man but upon the

world, the cosmos. To entertain the idea that as a result of
Jesus rising from the dead something happened to the world
independently of man – behind his back, so to say – would be
in accordance with the Greek divinization of the world. At no
stage within the biblical conception of the world is anything
of this kind to be expected. In the view of Scripture the world
has meaning only in relation to man. He it is who makes its
vocation clear, recognizes it and calls it by name, and renders
it serviceable to him by his technical skills. If man loses the
meaning of his own existence the world loses its meaning in
turn, and remains isolated and a void. But in believing in Jesus
Christ in all the dimensions of which we have been speaking
up to now man may come to discover and recognize once more
the meaning of his existence, a meaning which is greater than
all failures and disruptions. And if he does this, then the world
too profits by this discovery of meaning. To reiterate: this is
achieved only in and through the activity of man, but this
activity has effects upon the world itself. Faith is once more
in a position to regard the world as a friendly and profitable
companion. It no longer remains alien, incomprehensible, and
hostile to it. Henceforward the believer will have a different
relationship with the world; henceforward it will appear to
him in a different guise. No longer can it be maintained that in
principle man and nature are enemies from birth.

Of course it would be just as untrue to say that they have
been brought into perfect harmony with one another. Nor
does faith assert this. Just as faith itself, with its characteristic
tension between present and future, between the "even now"
and the "not yet", is in a state of chiaroscuro, so too it is with
the world. The world has experienced only the further effects
of the atonement. It, no less than man himself, is ignorant of
what form the further effects of the redemption in all its fulness may take. We are ignorant of how the fulness of our own
redemption will appear, and we are ignorant of how the world
will appear when it has been permeated through and through
with the redemption, when it has been made whole. So far the
world is delivered only from futility; it has not yet been freed
from bondage (Rom 8: 20).

But faith knows that heaven and earth, so far from being the empty stage of an absent God, are actually God's dwelling-place. From this follow two apparently disparate consequences. The first is natural science. The world cannot escape God, and at the same time it must be the world of man. As a result it is laid open unreservedly to the probings of scientific research and to technical exploitation – right up to those limits beyond which it would no longer, in the end, be the world of man at all. The second consequence is the liturgy, which draws the world into the relationship between God and man. In the personifying parlance of the Bible the earth appears as a festal procession of the earthly bride as she prepares to meet her bridegroom. At times the Bible combines nature and cultivation, things and events, the lights of heaven and the treasures of the nations, without drawing any distinction between what has been provided for man from the resources of nature, and what has been made by man himself with his cultivated skills. It is as though the world were an environment in existence before us and surviving after us (cf Rev 21). What is important in this is, once again, not the details but the underlying statement that the whole world resounds with the echo of the redemption. Revelation has its own way of conveying this when it describes the throne of the Lamb that was slain as set at the central point of the cosmic liturgy. The gospels content themselves with minor details on the periphery of the event, while the epistles include those statements about angels and spirits which strike us as so surprising. But Revelation uses this same conception to develop its portrayal of a supreme celebration in which the world derives a blessing from the fact that now God and man confront one another face to face.

The world and ethical conduct

Once more we have fallen deep into the language of imagery, a language which seems to have more to do with poetry than with scientific thought. It seems as though we have absolutely no other way of speaking about the matter. And this is under-

standable provided we bear in mind this point: that we know
only *the fact that* the world too is affected by man's faith in
the redemption without knowing *how*. For the rest, the Bible
itself guards against any excessive speculation in this area –
this same Bible which gives rise to our use of the language of
imagery. To seek to know in the most exact detail – that is the
chief concern of the gnosis and apocalyptic which go before,
and follow after, the Bible. Scripture has one very realistic
way of keeping its optimism in check in the statements it
makes about the world in its redeemed state, namely its
ethical teaching. The response of the believer to his redemption in terms of ethical conduct counteracts of the enslaving
effect of the incomprehensibility of the cosmos (cf Gal 4: 3, 9;
Col 2: 8, 20). To *act* ethically is to deny, at the cosmic level,
the idea that one is at the mercy of a blind fate, just as at the
human level the rule of reason, of law, puts an end to the
quest for signs and wonders. Hence ethical conduct debars
man from the two ways in which he is forever seeking to
evade the full significance of his redeemed state: he can
attempt to make heaven out of the earth for himself by his
shaping and organizing of it – in other words he can set up
his ego at the heart and centre; or he can take the opposite
course by maintaining that nothing can ever really achieve its
full consummation; that history is only the beguiling reitera-
tion of a fate which has already run its course, that freedom is
an illusion of faith and reason alike, that hope is as futile as
astrology. Faith has to take its stand against both these
attitudes: both against the despair arising from a fatalistic
view of cosmic history, and against human presumption. It is
the task of a Christian ethic to come to grips with both of
these outlooks.

At this point a serious objection to Christian faith will be
raised: is it either conceivable or possible to escape from
both these attitudes of fatalism and presumption at the same
time? Christian faith brings God so near to man that we no
longer see how this God can still have anything in common
with what the word as used in the religions of the world
commonly conveys, namely a sovereign law of the cosmic

order. Corresponding to this we have the unique tension involved in the Bible's statements about Christ. He is Jesus of Nazareth and at the same time he is the cosmic Logos through whom the world was made. He is the one whom the disciples encounter anew on the Lake of Tiberias, and he is the apocalyptic sign in heaven. The New Testament *confesses* that both are identical; to understand it is hard. Faced with such alternatives we are inclined to opt for the God of humanity. But even as we do so God seems, as it were, to be robbed of what is implied in the name God in relation to the universe. The opposition to Greek thought is then complete. We no longer look for any revelation of God from contemplating the cosmos. It is only by contemplating humanity that man is to experience who God is, and that is a profoundly biblical idea. Yet the question then arises: Has God any connexion with the non-human element in the universe? Or, to state the same question in the terms of the nineteenth-century critique of religion: Is not the idea of a God who upholds and guides the universe simply a "projection" of our own anxieties and hopes, prompted by the incomprehensibility of the universe itself? At this point credal theology has to venture upon an incursion into contemporary biology and cosmology.

II. BELIEF IN THE CREATION AND NATURAL SCIENCE

The Christian and biblical faith numbers among its most important tenets the avowal that God is the creator, that the world is his creation, and that man is the centre of it. Man is that creature which is *conformed* to its creator in a literal sense inasmuch as he is at once the image of God and the ruler of the world. It is only when it is linked to this faith in the creation that the resurrection of Jesus, the heart and centre of Christian faith in the redemption, achieves its unmistakable significance. As we have already seen, the resurrection is not a piece of wonder-working designed to still man's craving for the miraculous and the supernatural. Nor is it a fantasy which the disciples conjured up to overcome their dejection at the death of their Master. Nor yet is it a myth intended to "solve" the riddle of death – in no sense do we gain any detailed knowledge of an afterlife on the basis of our faith in the risen Lord. The Christian believes in the resurrection of Jesus as inaugurating a new world, and from the midst of this world the Church conducts her mission of preaching and waiting for that world to come to its fulness.

The significance of this is that in the resurrection of Jesus God takes up afresh his initiative as creator. We can understand what the resurrection of Jesus means only if we view it as falling between the creation at the beginning and the new creation at the end. If it is impossible to isolate this belief from the message of the cross, it is no less impossible to separate it from belief in the creation without it falling under the suspicion that it is some odd fantasy of faith that has been conjured up. But the converse is also true. Belief in the rising from the dead of Jesus, whose crucifixion is a fact of human history, definitively frees belief in the creation from the danger of being regarded as a *mere* subjective viewpoint concerning the origins or the future of the universe, and one which is incapable of verification. Each of these events, the resurrection and the creation, supplies the key to the interpretation of the other. When, therefore, we consider more precisely how we of today believe in the creation, we achieve a better understanding of what the resurrection of Jesus means.

Now today this belief in the resurrection to stand in ominous contradiction to that scientific knowledge regarding the evolution of the universe which we have acquired from other sources. Let us describe in brief outline the three main difficulties.

Bible and natural science

From the seventeenth century onwards men have come increasingly to abandon any attempt at reconciling what the Bible has to say about the world with the findings of science about that same world. The world cannot be both a world that is the concluded outcome of the activity of God himself and at the same time an open world in process of expansion within limits which are more or less narrowly defined. In order to bring home to ourselves the extent to which the two viewpoints are opposed, and the impossibility of reconciling them, we need only to read what Bossuet wrote as early as the seventeenth century in his *Discours sur l'histoire universelle* (*Discourse on the History of the Universe*). According to Bossuet the period between the creation of the world and the coming of Christ amounts to 4004 years. The Flood occurred 1656 years after the creation. 1757 years after it the Tower of Babylon was built. 2083 years after it Abraham received his call. 430 years later, and 856 years after the Flood, the Hebrew people came out of Egypt, and in the same year Moses received the tables of the Law. And so on.

In contrast to this "theological geophysics" we have the hypothesis put forward by modern natural science to the effect that the universe originated more than ten milliards of years ago in an initial explosion, and that after a further seven milliards the earth will meet its end in a collision with the sun. The advent of man is placed at the centre of a biological stage of evolution lasting three milliards of years, and this in turn is preceded by a radio-chemical stage lasting one and a half million years.

Set side by side, the figures in these two series speak for themselves. On the one hand we have a writing of history dominated by theological interests and fitted into an appropriate cosmological setting. An avowed faith in the creative word of God to man is naïvely juxtaposed with an account of the world regarded as the more immediate environment of man and things. When we turn to the other version we have the vastness of the figures making up a night of darkness within which man's historical awareness and the degree of understanding which natural science affords constitute only a tiny speck of brightness. If we wish to interpret the creation spoken of in the Bible as a real cosmic event, then we must identify it with an initial explosion of energy devoid of any kind of recognizable connexion with the much later history of mankind. In Scripture the creation is the setting of a deeply loving intercourse between God and man, the setting of a covenant which is renewed in the resurrection of Jesus. But on the view just described it becomes instead something so utterly impersonal that it can be described in terms of an "explosion" and "evolution", something in which, it seems, there can be no place either for a personal God or for a man who has experienced his call.

Nature "unplanned"?

The second blow dealt to the traditional Christian idea of the creation comes from the side of the biologists. They deny that there is any plan implanted, so to say, in the womb of nature, and governing the processes that unfold within the world of living beings. Very recently this position has once more been made challengingly clear by the French Nobel prize winner for biology, Jacques Monod in his work on *Chance and Necessity*. The great opponent of this book is Teilhard de Chardin, who has upheld the theory that it can be established from biological evidence that beings rise progressively from the stage of lifelessness to that of life, and thence to the further stage of intelligence. This theory is rebutted by Monod with all the vehemence of a pamphleteer. Taking pains to make his position clear even to the uninitiated, he draws upon a vast array of learning so as to broaden the findings of contemporary research into the origins of life. According to Monod the universe is devoid of any teleological principle. As he sees it "teleonomy necessarily presupposes invariance". In other words biological mutations which occur initially by chance and then persist take priority over all successful or "so to say wondrous" teleological adaptations which we can establish in nature. The accidental arises unplanned, and then becomes a factor that is passed on of necessity. But here we are not surrounded by any hidden purpose which was already in operation before we arrived on the scene and, as it were, now receives us within the cosmic order. The idea of creation as essentially constituting an environment favourable to, and specially shaped for man to shelter and nourish him – this is a vision which has been made familiar to us by passages such as

Gen 1–2. But it is an idea which science compels us to abandon. Ideas such as selection and mutation are intellectually
speaking far more honest than that of creation.

Obviously man *himself* can supply a goal for his activities,
but – and here Monod reverts to the language of Albert Camus
– in his enjoyment of this power man stands alone in the midst
of the "gentle indifference of things". "The old covenant is
destroyed; man knows at last that he is alone amid the indifference and immensity of the universe from which he has
emerged by chance. It is for him to choose between the kingdom and the shades." The idea of "creation" as a cosmic plan is
dying. But can some form of "creation" still survive in and
through the factor of human decision? No doubt it can, retorts
Monod, but in saying this we must bear in mind that we are
creatures bereft of any surrounding order of creation, and
therefore bereft of any universal creator. The idea of creation
should be replaced by that of the freedom of man in his loneliness, an idea which is more closely in accordance with the
truth.

"Projection"?

The third and most bitter onslaught of contemporary science
upon the Christian idea of creation runs as follows: it is a
"projection" of our psychological experience onto the universe outside ourselves. If, for instance, we believe that our
freedom is exercised only within the framework of a divine
plan embracing the whole of existence (and in fact throughout the entire biblical and Christian tradition this idea is taken
for granted) what we are in truth doing is nothing else than to
transfer our knowledge of the teleological functioning of our
own central nervous system to inanimate nature. Monod's
name for such a projection is "animism". In accordance with
the experience which we make of ourselves, and of the
manner in which we foster and bring to fruition our aims, we
generate within ourselves the image of a God who controls
nature. The evidence for this is so copious that it is felt possible to find support for it even from the Bible itself. Can we

not in fact say that the Israelites transferred their convictions as to the meaning of their national history to a creator God and his creation as a whole? Is it not a fact that in Israel the belief in a creator God emerged only *after* the belief in God as deliverer from Egypt, which belonged to an earlier tradition? And is not this conclusive proof of the rightness of the theory? Once we are able to view the matter in this light we must arrive at a similar conclusion with regard to the idea of the risen Christ as the renewer of the universe. The primitive Christian community has projected its personal experience of the liberating force of the Easter event onto the cosmos, and so has come to regard Jesus as the head of the new creation. On this showing to believe in the creation means to transfer some particular interior experience of renewal and vocation to the external universe. Today science requires us to admit that if we believe in the creation we are exceeding the bounds of any kind of verifiable knowledge of the world, because in doing so we are basing our position on views the origins of which do not go beyond human living and experience. This means that the idea of creation is an unreal one.

But once belief in the creation wavers, *ipso facto* belief in the resurrection does likewise. For unless it is legitimate to take this as connected with belief in the creation it can only be something which in the gospel message it is precisely proclaimed not to be: a piece of wonder-working, a fantasy, a myth. How, therefore, is it possible today to commit oneself to belief in the resurrection in its cosmological dimensions – and that means to belief in the creation?

Jacques Monod's powerful attack upon an interpretation of belief in the creation which makes excessive claims for it is a salutary one. It forces us to inquire afresh into, and to seek a fresh grasp of, the real meaning and the real import of belief in the creation as presented in the Bible. For the Bible is not, in fact, concerned, as Bossuet supposed (and countless teachers of the catechism have still not wholly given the idea up), to hand down a chronological record of the history of the world such as will satisfy human intelligence. Even with belief in the creation it is belief in the word of God that we are concerned with, a word that confronts us with a question and a demand, and includes us in a promise. We have already mentioned the point that in biblical thought man stands at the centre of the creation, because right from the outset the concept of creation is bound up with the idea of the covenant between God and man. The idea of man occupying the central place is based not on a naïve ignorance of the extent of the universe in terms of space and time, even though in fact the biblical authors were ignorant of this. This idea seeks, rather, to emphasize the point that belief in the creation sees man as that creature which is not merely the subject of an anonymous becoming, but has a meaningful history. Those to whom the biblical accounts of the creation were addressed were not modern practitioners of natural science, but the tellers of the cosmogonic myths of Babylon, in which man remains an insignificant element in a cosmic process. Similarly the belief that is avowed in the resurrection is a protest alike against an attitude of gloomy submission to the elements of the world as the arbiters of one's fate and at the same time against the futile speculations of the apocalyptic literature, prompted as they were by idle curiosity. To sum up: creation implies a vocation for man – whatever further may remain to be said about it even in the Bible does not constitute the message of the creation itself but the formulation of that message, which contains elements of the apocalyptic and mythological.

Faith and projection

Admittedly we are still not immune from the charge of indulging in a "projection". For what is the real difference between a statement of faith and the transference of an interior way of seeing things to the world outside? There is, in fact, one important difference: a projection, the psychologists tell us, proceeds outwards from one's own ego, which, terrified by its own loneliness, seeks a means of calming itself. By contrast with this a statement of faith has its basis not in our own personal psychological activities, but in something initiated by another: a word or action which we cannot be forced to accept, yet which we cannot utter or initiate of ourselves. This applies even to faith at the human level and as between men, and *a fortiori* to faith in God. Furthermore, faith in God as creator seeks actually to *counteract* precisely the mythical cosmogonies – in other words the projections. It is in history, in the exodus from Egypt, in the experience of the resurrection of the crucified Lord, rather than directly in any experience of nature, that the community of believers is made aware that it has been delivered from an unspeakable fate by a creator God. History, with man at its centre and at its close, rather than the universe in process of evolution – that is where faith in the creation is located. As Karl Barth has put it, "The covenant is the *goal* of creation, the creation the *way* to the covenant." A small but strongly characteristic detail in the language of the Bible serves to sum up this viewpoint. In Hebrew one and the same word, *toledot*, meaning "generations", is used to designate the descendants of the principal figures in the history of God with man (Adam, Noah, Shem, Terah), and the "ancestry" of heaven and earth (cp Gen 5: 1; 10: 1; 11: 10, 27, together with Gen 2: 1).

A closely parallel state of affairs can be recognized when we turn to the belief that in the resurrection of Jesus Christ the world was created anew. The crucial point here is not the few remarks about the risen body of the glorified Christ, but the question with which the individual is confronted, namely whether he will believe the promises of the Gospel that God is the God of life. The knowledge of the cosmos yielded by the science of our times (it is no accident that such knowledge begins to advance at that point in history at which the self-enclosed Christianity of the Middle Ages begins to disappear) does a positive *service* to faith in that it forces it to conceive of God not as he who produces but as he who speaks, and of Christ not as a demiurge after the Greek pattern but as the Word of God.

Belief in creation and evolution

Yet even now we still have not found answers to the two

questions which cause us most embarrassment: Is it or is it not the case that the course of development of the cosmos is governed by an all-embracing plan? Does belief in the making of the universe mean no more than this: that our faith in the renewal of the heart is transferred to inanimate nature? To put the question another way: How can we of today achieve the transition from the interior world of the human spirit to the physical world outside?

On the basis of the factors just mentioned it is no longer difficult to find the answer. The first question is, as we now no longer need to substantiate, a wrong question to put to faith, a question which belief in the creation is quite incapable of answering and never seeks to answer. To the second question faith's answer is "no!". It is not we who envisage nature as renewed; rather it itself is so. What we mean by this is that it stands under the "secret and hidden" benevolence of God (1 Cor 2: 7). What surrounds man is not "the gentle indifference of things" referred to by the existentialist writer Albert Camus or the biologist Jacques Monod, but the "blessing" which God has poured out upon things. The world is not (any longer) hostile to man, but rather shelters and nourishes him. Hence the unspoiled world of Gen 1–2 finds its counterpart in the portrayals of the appearances of the risen Lord (Lk 24: 30, 42), in the great catch of fish at the Lake of Tiberias (Jn 21: 6), in the joy of the friends at the meals which they shared with the risen Lord (Lk 24: 30, 42), or in the signs of power which accompanied the disciples in their work of preaching (Mk 16: 15–18; Mt 28: 18). The world is an anticipation of God's grace – and this is not something that man himself decides under the impulse of his own yearnings; this is something that his faith actually *discovers*. It discovers it, then, as a knowledge that brings release to man who, in biblical times, was labouring under the dread engendered by the myths of an impersonal cosmogony or of the spirits in the air, and who today is oppressed by the prospect of the loneliness of human existence within the boundless void of the cosmos.

Faith discovers it. This realization, then, that the world shelters and protects man is not a finding that has emerged as the outcome of scientific observation: "By faith we understand that the world was created by the word of God, so that what is seen was made out of things which do not appear" (Heb 11: 3). If, therefore, anyone wishes to adhere to the rules of life of the old democrat, according to which "everything that exists in the universe is the outcome of chance and necessity", faith can hardly gainsay him. Conversely, another may take up the position of Zeno the Stoic of old and say that the world is a finely structured living being, "A city encircled by walls, in which everything functions according to reason, so that the one who moves through all that exists deserves the name of Zeus or Dia, for everything lives through him" (Diogenes, *Laertius* 7, 147). And to such a faith has no help to offer. As between these two positions scientific observation cannot tip the scales to one side any more than to the other. Faith in the creation means recognizing in the (limited) power of disposal which man has over the cosmos, and in the (limited) means of habitation which the world has to offer, a sign of the favour of the covenant God towards his human partner. The hostility between man and nature – in addition to the hostility between man and man which is one of the characteristic signs that the creation has been robbed of its pristine brilliance (Gen 3: 17–19) – seems, in the light of faith in the creation, to be in no sense necessary, and in the light of faith in the resurrection of Jesus to have been brought to an end. In his attitude towards the world the believer takes this as his starting-point.

Now it is possible to say that this too still remains a projection. Nevertheless, apart from the argument already mentioned, that it would be difficult for man to express such a view of the world of his own resources, there is yet another factor which faith can point to in the hope, if not of allaying this suspicion, at least of drawing its sting. It is precisely not a function of belief in the creation to present itself before the world as an assured conclusion. A world that is relentlessly threatened is actually *entrusted* to the believer. It is for *him* to preserve it and to regard this task as an unhoped-for gift. Anyone who considers this as a projection should himself stand trial, for if he attaches such importance to the world as his habitation, then *ultimately speaking* he is finding it no more alien to him than the true believer.

In the light of all this, faith in the creation, fortified as it is by further faith in the resurrection, should no longer ask, "When and how did the world originate under God's hand?" Its question should be, rather, "What service has man as God's creature to perform for the world of created things?"

III. MAN'S DOMINION AND SERVICE

The task which has to be discharged, and which constitutes both dominion and service simultaneously, might be summed up as follows: To make meaningful history out of fate (regarded as a meaningless and irresistible flux of events), trusting in the promise given to us in the resurrection of Jesus. Every word in this description is important.

Fate and history

To make history out of *fate*. The world which surrounds us, the world in its narrower or its broader sense, does in fact constitute fate in the sense attached to the term here. It is true that we no longer believe in spirits in the air, into whose power man is delivered defenceless. But nothing that we know from natural science about the cosmos and its technological exploitation makes us feel that our view of the world as fate is any less valid. The sense which it gives us of being, to a large extent, powerless, is not diminished by our awareness that we ourselves have played a part in the shaping of it. Faith in this context means to resist the experience of being governed by fate, to *decide* one's own life, and to make the surrounding world the material and subject of this decision.

To make *history* out of fate, therefore. What history and historical living signify is a topic which we have already considered at several points and from several different aspects. Here we have to add to what has already been said by showing how the believer draws the cosmos into the history of his

own existence. He includes it as the friendly natural environment which God of his grace has placed under his control –
for it seems unfriendly only if man fails to view it through the
eyes of faith or if he misuses it. To *make* history out of fate.
What this actually means is that faith in creation and a creator
is not an "aspect" from which to view the world, but an act. It
consists in resisting fate as fate by accepting it, especially when
it is a painful fate, and making it into a decision that is lovingly
taken, just as Jesus did when he accepted his fateful course
and made of it an act of obedience to his Father. The repeated
"so it must come to pass" which is the gospels' comment on
the way of Jesus (Mk 8: 16 par; 14: 21 par; 14: 49 par; Lk 2:
34; 24: 26) is their way of keeping firmly before our eyes how
Jesus, by his own obedience, "made" that which God
demanded of him out of fate – for every day of his missionary
work he had to prove this afresh in his dealings with the
world. So too it is with the believer in his life.

To say this is to say at the same time that faith does not
eliminate the factor of the fateful in the cosmos. Faith knows
of a way, offers a possibility, of circumventing fate – for this
present age it still remains true that fate and meaningful
history are intermingled with one another. It is the same when
we are told in traditional terms: "This world remains subject
to the cross – despite the reality of the resurrection." If one
takes a different view, if one refuses to attach due importance
to the fact that the cross and fate are inescapable realities, the
final outcome of this in terms of thought is illusion, and in
terms of our dealings with the world is terror. Since Jesus
exhorted his disciple to take his cross upon himself, there can
be no doubt that illusion and terror are incompatible with
Jesus' way.

And yet so far as faith is concerned, the cross and fate have
only the first word, not the last. For faith makes meaningful
history out of fate *by trusting in the promise given to us in the
resurrection of Jesus*. It is "only" a promise – and not a reality
already present within our grasp. This is why faith in the creation, like faith in the redemption, also takes the form of hope.
But like this latter kind of faith too it does take its rise from

reality which is already present. God's blessing *is* upon the cosmos. The resurrection of Jesus manifests it afresh once more. Hence faith can have trust in the cosmos, just as it can have trust in the world of mankind. It can hope in the revelation that the cosmos is no longer threatening but "familiar", just as it can hope in a world in which the divisions between men have been healed.

We shall attempt to explain this still more clearly and in somewhat closer detail in connexion with two concrete questions of our own day: the question of the "single human race" and the problem of what position a Christian can adopt towards Marxism.

One human race

How far mankind can be said to be one is problematical. Certainly unity can be estalished at the biological level, especially from the uniformity of brain structure. Yet the variations from the intellectual, psychological, and cultural aspects are so wide that they throw all the biological unity into the shade. This fact emerges most clearly when we consider how difficulty it is for people from different countries to overcome differences of national character so as to achieve a fruitful interchange through the medium of language. Formerly it was possible to allow this state of affairs to continue unchanged without raising any problems so long as mankind lived in isolated national and linguistic groups, the boundaries of which were rarely crossed. But, as we have already reminded ourselves at an earlier stage, modern technological developments are such as to confront the *whole* of mankind, regardless of the stage of development that has been achieved, with two alternatives only: either happiness or ruin. When, therefore, faith declares that all men are "children" of their "Father in heaven", and that God calls each individual by name, this statement has definitively passed beyond the stage of a purely theoretical idea. It has acquired a disconcerting relevance.

What should be made of this statement by those who believe in God the creator? We are discovering anew, in terms of a concrete example, everything that we had begun by stating in more general terms. The unity of mankind in virtue of its creation by God is not an established conclusion in the sense, for instance, that science can establish the biological unity of mankind. Still less does it constitute any explanation of this biological unity. This is not a question to which faith has an answer any more than the question of the physical origins of the universe. What faith declares about the unity of mankind represents a suggestion that is *offered* of a *possible* way of becoming united. The whole of mankind, engaged as it is in a quest for meaning, and inquiring into the meaning of human behaviour in history, experiences the fact that it can become one – provided it recognizes that it is the creation of God who loves it and has given it the earth, this speck of dust within the cosmos, as a pleasant garden.

If this unity is to become *real*, then this can only be achieved through action on man's part; the action, namely, of seizing this opportunity, taking it as his starting-point, and shaping his dealings with the world in accordance with it. For in fact the alternative could be for man to blow the world up. In a word: The unity of mankind is a *promise*. In the resurrection of Jesus God has manifested that he is the source of a life that rises victorious over death, and it is here that we have to hearken to this promise, a promise that had been obscured up to that point through the human race being split up into different groups. "For the promise is to you and to your children, and to all that are far off" (Acts 2: 39).

Marxism and Christian faith

Marxism is the most influential theory of history that we know today. The challenge which it represents to the Christian faith lies precisely in that fact. For there is an intrinsic connexion between it and the atheism it professes. It seems almost rash to offer any observations on it within the space of a few words. We shall confine ourselves strictly to the question of the Marxist interpretation of history in its attitude towards Christian belief in the creation.

Ultimately speaking Marxism has the same aims as belief in the creation, namely to equip man to make meaningful history out of fate. In this, it is true, Marxists regard belief in God as a wrong path, because on their theory it detaches man from the inescapable material and social conditions of his life. In Marxist eyes man as Christian faith views him is an abstract idea which has never had any real existence.

Now it cannot be gainsaid that Marxism does come to grips in earnest with the material conditions of human living. Doubts must be raised as to whether the belief in creation and a divine creator which it attacks is in fact the Christian one. The main question to be put to Marxism, however, arises from within the system itself. It regards itself explicitly as a scientific theory concerning the course of *history* as *governed by certain laws*. Marxists are not disturbed by the fact that much that happens in history does not conform to such laws. These are accidental occurrences on the surface of things.

At this point Christian believers will ask: "Is the factor of *fate* not being somewhat underestimated here? Has not Marxism evidence enough of the fact that history does not consist only of developments that take place according to its own laws? That it also includes other and anomalous events which it is not given to man to shape or alter – at any rate not in the concrete particular instance – but which, on the contrary, he has to accept and *so* try to weave into the fabric of history? Are such anomalous events eliminated from history the moment the means of production have been taken over by the state in the sense implied in the Marxist theory of history? To put it in theological terms: Does this Marxist view of man's resurrection still assign any meaning to the cross he has to bear? Is it, then, so realistic as it itself supposes?"

On this question there is one significant test to be applied: the use of propaganda. The theory of history is threatened unless history constantly progresses upwards. Again and again when this is not the case Marxism succumbs to the temptation of putting matters right by propaganda and bad unconvincing apologetics. The question might be posed the other way round. In denying the element of the incomprehensible, the fateful, in history – what the Bible calls the power of sin – is not Marxism, with its rigidly unbreakable laws, transforming history itself into a fate which oppresses man and alienates him from himself by depriving him of his freedom? Does history still continue to be history once it is turned into a rigid process which can never be questioned?

At the same time Marxism has, better than any other interpretation of history, accorded due importance to the transition from fate to meaningful history. Certainly on this point everything is ascribed to the power of man as the creator of meaning, and the Christian, in view of the finitude and the sins of man, will never be able to place such confidence in his powers. Nevertheless Marxism is here posing the same question to which the Christian finds an answer in his belief in the creation and the resurrection. Despite all the controversies about atheism, the image of man, and the communist system of government, Christians should recognize that the Marxists are, as it were, their closest relations so far as understanding of, and responsibility for, the world in faith are concerned. Each could help the other to achieve a greater realism on various points.

What, therefore, is man's contribution to the created order? Under the promise of Jesus' resurrection men must find every day, individually and collectively, the courage to construct anew, out of the fate constituted by the course of nature, the meaningful history of mankind as a single race in the world given to it by God. The unity which mankind could grow towards in this way is not a fact that can be demonstrated, but it can become a reality that can be observed. And it would allow room for all conceivable differences and contrasts between groups. From this let us turn to one final consideration: How are the providence of God and the responsibility of man related one to the other?

The providence of God and the responsibility of man

Faith in divine providence is indissolubly linked with faith in God as creator. But from ancient times onwards it seems no less unavoidably to lead to fiercely controversial problems. What can still survive of the responsibility of man which we have here emphasized so much if we accord all due importance to the idea that God's providence directs what takes place in the world? Evidently the message of the resurrection of Jesus, so far from ridding the world of this problem, renders it still more acute. On the one hand in raising Jesus from the dead, God gives to man, while still living in conflict with the world, such an answer as he had never for one moment foreseen. What, therefore, remains of his responsibility? The second reason is that in the world about us no sign can anywhere be discerned of any change or renewal resulting from this event of Jesus rising from the dead. What, therefore, is left of "providence"?

The only way in which we can find an answer is for us to realize that the problem thus presented is apparent rather than real. It stems from a conception of "providence" as a kind of human activity on a supra-dimensional scale which constitutes, to a greater or lesser extent, a constant rival to the activities of mankind. Even though the believer has to trust that God does have an activity of this kind, he still knows nothing of what it is, any more than his belief in the creation tells him anything about the way in which the world began. What he "knows", rather, is that the world remains under the benevolence of God, and that in virtue of this man can be bold enough to feel at home in the world and to assume responsibility for it. In the light of this the idea of "providence" assumes a quite different meaning. It tells us nothing about God *as director of the world*, but tells us rather about God as *faithful*. Belief in providence is no guarantee against the misfortunes which occur in human life and activities, but constitutes, rather, the pledge that God is faithful to his promises even in the face of rebellion and faithlessness on man's part. Over and above this the idea of "providence" implies that God will direct all to a good end even though his decrees remain totally hidden (Rom 8: 28; 11: 33–6) – in other words that his faithfulness has an indefectible goal in which salvation and consummation lie hidden. Thus the concept of "providence" is closely connected with that of forgiveness, the only difference being that it also points to the cosmic dimension of belief in the redemption.

On this interpretation there cannot be any tension, much less any conflict, between the providence of God and the responsibility of man. If man recognizes his responsibility for the world, both the world of mankind and also – arising from this – the world of nature, then he is fulfilling God's providence which fulfils its own function through this attitude on man's part. For God's providence over the world signifies nothing else than the fact that it is intended to attain its purpose for man through man himself. If he *fails* to recognize his responsibility towards the world then God will not act as a stopgap to make up for his failure. Yet he does maintain his "good will", his promise, his offering of the new creation. No evil in the world, and no guilt on man's part cause him to withdraw them. Faith's answer on the message of God's providence, therefore, consists not in a theory about how God's acts are related to man's freedom, but is embodied rather in Paul's question: "If God is for us who is against us?" (Rom 8: 31).

20   Faith and love I: Basic principles

I. FAITH AS THE BASIS OF CONDUCT

"In order, therefore, for a man to do good works we need nothing more than to say to him: 'Only believe and thus you will do it all of yourself.' You do not need, therefore, to demand prolonged good works from one who believes this. For faith will teach him everything, and then all the things he does are well done, and are nothing else than Christian good works, however small they may be. For faith is so noble that it makes everything which is in man good" (Martin Luther).

This is the context in which we must come at last to saying something of human conduct on the basis of faith – for this is a question which has already been raised repeatedly in connexion with all the topics discussed in this book (above all those treated of in the chapters of parts III and IV), and from many different points of view. In formal terms: We are now inquiring into the question of faith and ethical conduct, or, in the language of the Bible, into faith and love. Luther's challenging words can serve to put us on the right track.

Spontaneity in conduct

A point that is striking in what Luther has to say about ethical conduct is that for him it is not a fulfilling of demands. If the believer does good he does it without obligation or demand, spontaneously and from an inner impulse. This idea seems unrealistic and, moreover, in contradiction to holy Scripture. Why should there be commandments of God, which Jesus too exhorts us to observe, and, indeed, as a necessary condition for salvation (cf Mk 10: 19; Mt 19: 18 ff; Lk 10: 28; 18: 20)? Why does Jesus speak of – not to say threaten us with – the judgment (Mt 25: 31–46)? Why do Paul, and still more James and other New Testament authors, exclude from the kingdom of God those who fail to observe specific ethical modes of conduct (Gal 5: 21; 1 Tim 6: 14; Jas 2: 8–13; 1 Pet 4: 17)?

We could adduce a crude legalistic morality from the New Testament. Yet we must neither isolate the relevant passages from their contexts nor overlook other statements expressing the opposite point of view. The same Jesus who confirms the commandments and speaks of God's judgment finally declares that eternal life is precisely *not* a reward corresponding in value to works that have been performed (Mt 20: 1–16). And in the parable of the unmerciful servant it becomes clear what the true reason is when God condemns an individual: he who fails to understand that he must act towards his fellow men as God acts towards him, namely with compassion and love, will find that God withdraws from him the unmerited gifts which he had bestowed upon him. All that will remain to him is what he himself has "earned", namely nothing. From his place in the debtor's prison he will be able to recognize how far that will carry him (Mt 18: 23–35).

The first reason, therefore, why faith must take immediate effect in action is thanksgiving for the compassion and love of God. If anyone needs a specific commandment in order to recognize that he is obliged to have an attitude of love towards his fellow men, he has not yet realized what has been bestowed upon him in faith. But the intrinsic connexion between faith and love extends still deeper. As we have already seen repeatedly from many different points of view, the heart and centre of Christian faith is this: the world and mankind are upheld by the love of God which makes everything whole and overcomes death. This is the basis on which man can live in this present world and work for it in a spirit of hope and trust.

Now how else is the love of God, considered as the basic force of the world, to be manifested except through human love in all its forms and at all its levels? In other words how else is faith in salvation to be made intelligible except by man acting in a manner corresponding to salvation, namely on the basis of love? The deepest reason for the indissoluble connexion between faith and ethical conduct is that salvation, which faith proclaims as the gift of God, precisely consists in a world and a humanity which is wholly under the dominion of love. All ethical conduct, therefore, is connected with salvation. It is sustained by the idea of eternal life. There would be only one way of escaping this conclusion: if salvation were *only* a benefit to be hoped for in the future, one which was to be imparted to us *after* this present life. But since Jesus has proclaimed the saving and redeeming proximity of God as a *present* reality (albeit a hidden one), any such idea is ruled out. *This present* life holds out the opportunity of salvation. It *is* already the beginning of "eternal" life, as the Christian knows from the resurrection of Jesus. What still remains to be achieved is not salvation itself but its final manifestation and consummation – just as our eternal life too has still to reach its final consummation through death.

While, then, we cannot doubt *the fact that* faith takes effect in love and through love, still difficult problems do arise when we ask *what kind of* ethical conduct it is, in that case, which corresponds to faith. This is a question which we now have to investigate, first in principle and then in terms of certain selected individual examples.

Bible and Christian ethos

If faith is the basis of ethical conduct, then it is to be expected from the outset that Scripture has a special importance for the moral decisions and moral conduct of the Christian. For it is in Scripture that the message of faith is to be heard in its original form. Over and above this, it is here that we are instructed about the basic ethical principles that follow from faith.

Nevertheless it is not enough, when the Christian seeks to know what decisions he ought to take, what actions he ought to perform, for him simply to concentrate his gaze on the Bible. Scripture does not offer us a manual of moral duties for the Christian. All the concrete moral directives, for instance the Ten Commandments, the "Sermon on the Mount", the catalogues of virtues and vices in the epistles of Paul, are, as we know today, to a large extent conditioned by their age and their cultural environments. We must guard against supposing that the ethical directives of the Bible are wholly "original" throughout. Often they have been taken over point for point from collections of laws and precepts belonging to the cultures and religions of surrounding nations. We should not be over hasty, therefore, in elevating the moral directives of the Bible into a timeless "ideal order of Christian living". And this also applies to the directives contained in the New Testament.

The ethics of Jesus is the ethics of the kingdom of God. When, therefore, we search the pages of the New Testament for pointers to ethical conduct on the basis of faith, our constant concern will be to discover this ethic of the kingdom of God and to create from it the motive forces of our conduct. What then emerges as a right course of action in the concrete may wholly coincide with the demands of the ethical systems of other religions or philosophies – we may remind ourselves, for instance, of the Hellenistic list of virtues contained in Phil 4: 8 ff. What distinguishes the Christian system from these others is not the kind of action involved but that with which it is connected. The Christian acts well towards his fellow men because the kingdom of God is present. And this means because God has taken man irrevocably into his love, and because on this account, if the believer were to be unloving in his conduct, he would be casting off once more the very faith which he had previously accepted from his heart. Scripture is the basis of ethical conduct because it keeps the Christian constantly and fundamentally aware of this connexion.

In saying this we have already enunciated the supreme ethical rule of Christian living.

Love of God and love of neighbour

The twofold commandment of love of God and love of neighbour is the supreme ethical directive for the believer. "On these two commandments depend all the law and the prophets" (Mt 22: 40). Once again we must guard against claiming that these two commandments belong exclusively to the Christian faith. Yet is should be noticed that here they are preached as a twofold commandment and made to provide a critique of the piety of the Old Testament which was based on the Law. Precisely in this respect they do seem to be characteristic of Jesus and of the Christian faith. Thus it is possible to conclude that by comparison with the great number of individual laws contained in the Old Covenant, and still more by comparison with the complicated interpretation of these by the scribes of Jesus' own time, the whole system of ethical conduct presented in the New Testament appears to be radically simplified. The Christian "only" needs, so to say, to love God and his neighbour and he has done everything which the Law – the Law of God! – requires of him.

Now this word "love" at first constitutes an empty formula capable of being filled out with content of various kinds. How often this word is actually forced out of its true meaning in order to apply to things and attitudes which have nothing to do with what the New Testament understands by love! Yet the biblical passages – above all, once more, the attitude of Jesus himself – leave no room for doubt as to the nature of love. In the so-called "golden rule" Matthew provides a paraphrase of what really constitutes the essential content of this command-ment of love: "Whatever you wish that men would do to you, do so to them, for this is the Law and the prophets" (Mt 7: 12). Luke expresses himself in still more radical terms and, as it were, looks for the meaning of love hidden in the cross of Jesus himself: "But Jesus said to all, 'If any man would come after me, let him deny himself and take up his cross daily and follow me, for whoever would save his life will lose it, and whoever loses his life for my sake, he will save it'" (Lk 9: 23–4).

It is significant that in these two sayings which the evan-gelists place on the lips of Jesus love is not merely raised to the level of an ethical demand, but at the same time yields a new understanding of human living. What Christ has to say about "losing one's own life" establishes a rule for achieving fulfil-ment in human life which, despite the difference in times, psychology and philosophical anthropology too can only agree with. The individual man precisely does not attain to that unfolding of personality and that fulfilment which he seeks by a self-sufficient concentration on his own happiness. It is only when he breaks out of this prison of his own egotism and opens himself alike to the Thou of his fellow man and to the We of the community that he can find his life's fulfilment. In this kind of love the supreme criterion governing moral decisions is one's fellow man. It is with him in view that we have to weigh up in every situation precisely which values are to take priority. Anyone, for instance, who wants with all his heart to fulfil the obligations of fraternal love, love and loyalty to his married partner, or responsibility for his family, will often have to surrender his own selfish desires. Such a renun-ciation of the immediate fulfilment of one's personal desires and of the satisfying of one's own impulses will only be achieved if one holds firm to the basis for it, the essence of love. It is at once obvious that this renunciation will have to be practised ever afresh.

Conduct arising from love of this kind can no longer be regulated by laws. The standard of what is good is not the law but what is of service to man. "The sabbath is made for man and not man for the sabbath" (Mk 2: 27). In accordance with this we must arrive at the corresponding principle: "Morality is there for man and not man for morality." Every moral action which is not based on that love which proceeds from faith, but rather begins and ends with the law, is in contradiction to the preaching of Christ.

The simplicity of Christian love consists finally in the fact that it is totally disinterested. The Christian must love good men and evil alike, and be ready not only to love his enemy but actually to lay down his life for his neighbour. Jesus himself preaches such love to us by his example, extending this right to his death on the cross. Only by achieving such complete lack of self-interest will human love become that "agape" which is so different from the self-orientated "eros".

This basic ethical demand of love can in principle also be the light of a non-believer's way. But faith makes man particularly open to these insights because it has no means of escaping from them if it is to remain faith at all. But with regard to the principle that it is in selfless love of neighbour that man puts into effect his love of *God* – in other words that love of God and love of neighbour are one – this is something that the Christian learns not from any philosophy but solely from the message of faith.

The "Sermon on the Mount"

When we search the New Testament for guides to ethical conduct we must perforce attribute special importance to one major section of text in particular, the so-called "Sermon on the Mount" (Mt 5–7. The corresponding section in Luke is the so-called "Sermon on the Plain", Lk 6: 20–47). This section of text has the effect of a complete and concise summary of the ethical message of Jesus. What is expressed in the paradoxical formulations of the Sermon on the Mount is the radical and uncompromising character of living by faith in the Christian sense.

We can misinterpret the Sermon on the Mount in two different ways, and thereby evade its demands upon us. First we may regard it as expressing a special code of morality designed for a small circle of disciples. The text itself offers no justification for this. On the contrary what the Sermon on the Mount proclaims is that the righteousness of *all* who wish to live within the kingdom of God must be "greater than that of the scribes and pharisees" (Mt 5: 20). Jesus demands something more of his followers than a mere external fulfilment of the Law. He also requires them to be right in the hidden dispositions of their hearts, and to seek for the kingdom of God before all else. Without compromise or curtailment certain radical demands are laid down which call in question every kind of worldly wisdom in man's estimation of himself. Among these demands are to be numbered the prohibition of anger, the demand that the disciple shall be ready to forgive, the forbidding of divorce, the forbidding of the use of force to defend one's own rights, the requirement of love of neighbour ("golden rule") and love of enemies.

The second way of misinterpreting the Sermon on the Mount is to turn these requirements into readymade laws capable of being applied as they stand in any age. The very reason that in the Sermon on the Mount Jesus is in fact seeking precisely to overcome every kind of legalistic morality is in itself enough to show how absurd this approach is. Moreover, to turn the requirements of Jesus in the Sermon on the Mount into laws in this sense can be done only at the cost of depriving them of their radical force: by trying not to take them literally, and therefore not to accord them their full importance.

What, therefore, does the Sermon on the Mount demand if on the one hand we are to do full justice to its radical character, and on the other must not interpret its requirements as laws capable of immediate application? The directives of the Sermon on the Mount are, as it were, models which show the attitudes to which faith can lead man if it is true faith. In love the believer breaks through the destructively mechanistic outlook of the behaviour pattern which seems so "natural" and "right". We should do nothing to derogate from the uncompromising character of the conduct illustrated in these prototype examples, but prototypes are not intended to be copied. Rather they point to where we can discover the way for ourselves. The Christian is not obliged to follow the clauses of the Sermon on the Mount point for point, nor should he try to do so. Rather he should use his own creativity to discover and to do what constitutes, in *his own* concrete situation, radical Christian conduct of this kind, as shown to us in the Sermon on the Mount in its application to the situation of Jesus' own hearers. This brings us straightaway to a further question.

Intelligence and Christian ethos

Scripture, then, does not provide the Christian with any ethical prescriptions ready to hand and immediately applicable either in the form of laws or in any other way. The question therefore arises of how the Christian is to recognize in the individual concrete instance what decisions and what lines of conduct his faith obliges him to. There is only one answer: he has his intelligence for this task. Guided and led by the orientation which love supplies, and impelled by its driving force – that love which God himself has bestowed in the hearts of man (cf Rom 5: 5) – this reason of his must discover for itself what is required in the individual concrete case. And since love is no prerogative of Christians, the task of using reason to discover this applies to believers and unbelievers alike. The common quest of mankind for the principles of rational ethical conduct has left its mark in the various presentations of a "natural law" of morality. Biblical texts too ascribe to the "Gentile" the power of right moral judgment: "When Gentiles who have not the Law do by nature what the Law requires, they are a law to themselves even though they do not have the Law. They show that what the Law requires is written on their hearts, while their conscience also bears witness and their conflicting thoughts accuse or perhaps excuse them" (Rom 2: 14 ff). Reason's power to make discoveries of this kind can also be applied so as to arrive at rules of morality which are completely its own, though it has educed them from Jewish or Gentile thought. This too is something which can be recognized from the New Testament and the history of the Church.

In its function as providing an ethical standard, intelligence or, as we also say, human "nature" (for it is reason that distinguishes man from animals) is the underlying source of manifold kinds of mistrust. All too many of its moral judgments have already been proved erroneous. Furthermore the Christian is aware of the crippling and blinding influences of sin on human knowledge, and will not be over-trustful of it on this account either. This mistrust is justified. Yet it cannot invalidate the function of reason to discover what is ethically right. Where else except in the reason is ethical duty to be recognized? As sustained by faith, reason can even lay itself bare in its own sinfulness. To put demands upon it does not mean to withdraw from reason, but rather to use reason in maintaining a constant criticism of oneself, measuring oneself by the standard of the love of God as inspired by faith, by the standard of the need of one's fellow men in all its personal and social implications. Hence in arriving at moral judgments reason must, today more than ever, take due cognizance of the findings of the various sciences – those for instance of the study of human behaviour: of sociology, psychology, medicine, and economics.

Even then there are manifold dangers of falling into error. How is man to guard against wrongly estimating which of several values is to take priority over the rest? For instance which comes first: love of one's spouse in marriage and one's family or the generation of new life? And, if we take love as our ethical standard, is it good or bad to practise birth control? Or how is the Christian to guard against arriving at a false decision in cases of conflict? For instance, which comes first, human life as such or the prevention of grave injury? And in the light of this is abortion ethically permissible or not on the basis of the so-called eugenic prognostications? Or how is man to establish the borderline between positive civic justice and an ethical precept? For instance must the state impose and defend certain specific ethical requirements by punitive sanctions? Does love of neighbour take priority over truthfulness, and should we on that account tell untruths in order to protect another from unjust persecution?

Even conscientious men can arrive at wrong decisions in these areas, and the teachings of Jesus, the New Testament, do not provide the kind of help that descends to individual concrete details here. They have nothing whatever to say about the burning ethical questions of our own time. Yet in many ethical questions on which they do in fact provide an answer we of today are no longer in a position to follow them at all. Or should we, for instance, "render to Caesar the things that are Caesar's", namely taxes, without at the same time asking whether they will be used to finance wars or social justice and peace (cp Mk 12: 13–17)? Should we, without further consideration, leave our parents and family in order to become missionaries or helpers in the under-developed countries (cp Mk 1: 16–20; Lk 14: 26 ff)?

If then, despite all dangers of error, the Christian still commits himself to decision and action, then it must be only after subjecting himself to conscientious self-criticism, and in an attitude of readiness to accept fresh self-criticism in the future! And above all in a spirit of trust in God's forgiveness which, despite all denials and errors, has accepted man once and for all.

Faith and world

On the basis of the foregoing considerations we are now in a position to say how faith in general conceives of the world, and what the believer's attitude towards it is. Reason as guided by faith and love is competent to discover what is demanded of the Christian in the concrete instance. This same reason is evidently the power with which man finds his way in the world and shapes it as he desires. If, therefore, faith has no occasion to be in principle mistrustful towards reason, then it has no grounds for suspecting the world as such either. This provides fresh confirmation from a new point of view of a point which we have already drawn attention to at an earlier stage in connexion with faith's understanding of the world. Now that we are considering the question of faith and ethos we have to draw the consequences from it: any kind of disdain for the world is forbidden to a Christian. Just as God himself has definitively accepted the world in Jesus Christ, so too the Christian has to accept the world. Hence it is that Paul can invoke the incarnation of God in Jesus Christ to restate in fresh terms the task laid upon us by God as creator. "All things are yours, whether . . . the world or life or death, or the present or the future, all are yours and you are Christ's and Christ is God's" (1 Cor 3: 22 ff).

Obviously nobody can overlook the fact that the attitude of man towards the world always entails also an element of the "unforced". And a further factor which always enters into man's attitude towards the world is human self-will and sin. Hence Paul and John both warn us against becoming "conformed to the world" (Rom 12: 2; 1 Jn 2: 15–17). They exhort us "to deal with the world as though we had no dealings with it" (1 Cor 7: 31). But in saying this they are thinking not of the world which God has made good, but of that which is the outcome of the sins of fallen humanity. There can be no "conformism" with *this* world for the Christian. The believer cannot unite himself in solidarity with a world which exalts itself and refuses to acknowledge that it owes its existence and all the possibilities that lie open to it not to itself but to God.

Asceticism

In the light of this we can understand why "ascesis" (asceticism) too is to be numbered among the factors belonging to the life of the Christian. In its root meaning this word, derived from the Greek, signifies "exercise", "training". What is meant by it in the context of Christian conduct does in fact appear on the surface from time to time as the outcome of unusually hard and exacting training. A Christian may, for instance, strive by these means to avoid giving in unrestrainedly to his impulses and desires, to achieve interior freedom from the pull of his instincts, to break the dominion of his bad temper or his ill humour, and so on.

But an individual may also use the same "ascetical" practices for different purposes, for instance in pursuit of the ideal of so-called "Stoic calm", "imperturbability", or "impassivity". The Christian attitude to the world, however, has nothing whatever to do with all this. The difference between Christian ascesis and the other form consists solely in the fact that it has its basis in faith. What we have said about faith as the basis for Christian conduct in general (see above p. 433) applies to this also. The external actions that are performed may be as like as two peas in a pod. What makes the difference is their basis and their goal. By his use of ascesis the Christian seeks to root out, as far as possible, the obstacles to love, and thereby the roots of self-idolization. Often, in fact it begins with self-indulgence with regard to spontaneous inclinations and instinctive desires, and ends with self-will becoming a tyrant and refusing to recognize any law except itself. If, therefore, the Christian toils arduously in his ascetical practices to become independent, free, and disciplined with regard to all the more carnal tendencies in his behaviour, whether internal or external, then ultimately speaking what he is doing is simply banishing the idol of his own ego from the throne in order to make room for God, the creator and redeemer, to have sole and all-embracing dominion over his life. Ascesis is not only "a struggling against" but "a striving for" – for the freedom which love requires.

For this reason it is quite unnecessary for ascesis in all cases to impose great strains. On·the contrary a right use of the practice of relaxation is also a function of ascesis, and it should equip the Christian to arrive at a sound judgment as to when good discipline requires him to "let go". Anyone who rejects this or regards it as unnecessary would not merely be contradicting the unequivocal findings of psychology and medicine. Viewing the matter from the opposite aspect, he would also be putting in peril the kingdom of God in man. For the man who is forever tense, forever at full stretch, constantly controlling his every action down to the last detail, is again in acute danger of attempting to build himself up by his own efforts, seeking, as it were, to owe nothing to anyone apart from himself. Or, to put it in biblical terms: "justifying himself". Just as for about the past fifteen years good behaviour for drivers on the roads has become no longer a merely technical question but an ethical one too, so too, in the age of increasing automation and ever shorter hours of work, the right use of free time has become an ethical problem. New tasks for Christian ascesis are coming to light here, and it is only to outward appearance that they seem no longer to have anything in common with the old questions covered by ascesis.

The very last thing that Christian ascesis means, therefore, is flight from the world. On the contrary, it is faith's protest against the enslavement of self-sufficiency. In its ultimate depths, then, it is a protest against the ascetical ideal precisely of that philosophical movement which so deeply impressed the Christians of earlier ages: the philosophy of the Stoics. Without any pretensions to self-sufficiency, or according an absolute value to man and the world, it still remains true that the world has been committed to the Christian as his task. At a later stage we shall have something more to say about certain concrete details in this task of the Christian for the world, these being of special significance precisely for our own times.

II. CHRISTIAN CONDUCT AND LAW

From the outset we have had to draw a clear dividing line between the conduct that stems from faith and that which has its source in law. Conduct proceeding from faith is something more than the fulfilling of commandments or the observing of laws. This is far from being self-evident, for concepts such as "law", "commandment", "prescription" constantly reassert their importance anew in contexts where ethical questions are being discussed. This is all the more true here, seeing that we have just underlined the importance of reason for discovering what actual ethical principles demand.

For and against the law

An ancient definition runs as follows: "Law is an order imposed by reason to serve the common good, promulgated by him who has responsibility for the community as a whole" (Thomas Aquinas, *Summa Theologiae* I-II, 90.4). We should conclude, then, that reason's task of discovering the ethically right course attains to its ultimate goal at that point at which the members, either of the Church considered as the community of believers or else of secular communities, take responsibility for the community. They do this by issuing rules for the behaviour of the individual towards his fellows in the form of directives, the terms and purpose of which are clear, and which are arrived at as the outcome of mature deliberation.

We can even transfer this concept of "law" to God himself. God is Lord over the whole community of mankind. As its creator, upholder, and redeemer, he himself has taken over responsibility for it. If he promulgates to men some measure designed to promote the communal life of mankind in the form of a law or a divine moral directive it becomes completely clear. The degree of importance which the individual attaches to ethical obligations arising from faith should then be measured by the degree of importance he attaches to observing the law of God, And how, in that case, is it possible to dispense with the concept of "law" and similar concepts as a result of reflecting upon what it means to act from motives of faith? It seems that we can do that only if we take back again what we have already recognized, namely the rôle of reason in all this and its significance for Christian action.

To this a further and still more weighty consideration may be added. Certainly the Christian will find it hard to forget Paul's sharp attacks upon the Jewish law and its representatives, the scribes and those sympathizing with them in the Christian communities. Certainly the law does contain commandments and directives for action, and demands that something should be done. But according to Paul the condition of man is such that he himself is in no position whatever to fulfil these demands. The law, therefore, is a *statement*, presented in the guise of a directive, about man's position in God's sight. It brings it home to man that he has all along refused to obey God's commandment. The law drives him still deeper into sin because now he is fully aware that he is transgressing God's commandment, whereas formerly his disobedience was naïve and inculpable. The law beguiles him, impelling him to put forth his utmost efforts, still despite all to achieve righteousness in God's sight through fulfilment of the law; and thereby it drives him into the sin of sins for humanity as such, the temptation to live in God's presence by his own efforts instead of by God's grace – in a word in a state of unbelief. For Paul the law, so far from being a way to salvation, is a force of perdition. In the Epistle to the Galatians Paul actually goes so far as to represent the law as deriving not from God but from "angels". In the passage concerned Paul takes these to be God's adversaries, God, as it were, lets the law run its course in order to render men ripe for the promise in Jesus Christ (Gal 3: 19–29). In the Epistle to the Romans Paul no longer expresses so radical a judgment on the law, but here too the law is a force of perdition (Rom 7).

But when we survey Scripture *as a whole* we find a whole *range* of passages on the law which are quite different in tenor from those of Paul. From this we must conclude that that particular interpretation of the law which Paul is attacking is not that of the Old Testament (nor yet that of all the other authors of the New Testament either), but rather a version of what law means which he himself had encountered directly in the course of his work as apostle and pastor. For a believing Jew a statement such as "the letter (of the law) kills" (2 Cor 3: 6) is an enormity. Israel felt God's law not as an enslavement but as a distinguishing mark showing that she had been singled out and preferred before all other peoples. She felt it not as a power of death but as a source of life. This view of the law, so far removed from that of Paul, achieves its most sublime expression in psalm 119. We find an echo of the joy and thankfulness for the law expressed here in the New Testament itself when Matthew records Jesus' saying: "I have come not to abolish the law and the prophets but to fulfil them" (Mt 5: 17). Jesus Christ is not the end (Rom 10: 4) but the consummator of the law.

Incidentally we of today are, perhaps, once more in a somewhat better position to understand this joy in the law than the men of earlier ages. For in fact we no longer find ourselves oppressed by innumerable prescriptions, each one pettier than the last, and often merely ceremonial in character, on which, so we believe, our salvation depends. Thus for instance Paul had to insist in his preaching to the Christians of Galatia that they were called to freedom (Gal 5: 13). We find ourselves faced with immense ethical problems, to which a solution is hardly yet in sight, and yet on which the survival of humanity depends. In such a situation to receive ethical directives of the highest authority and the utmost reliability would not be an enslavement or an oppression, but in fact a liberation. Even if we are unable to discern any such ethical directives to provide solutions to our problems, still we can understand why men who believe in the same God as Paul, whether Jews or Christians, do not necessarily have to have the same view of the law and its significance as Paul himself.

And finally what even Paul himself has in mind is not that Christians should be exempted from following moral directives and fulfilling moral demands. When he attacks "the law" – whatever he may be understanding by this term – he does so in any case precisely because he wants to show his hearers what the true will of God is. Hence he can also speak of the "law of Christ" (Gal 6: 2; 1 Cor 9: 21), or the "law of the Spirit" (Rom 8: 2), and produce long and extremely detailed exhortations in which he enumerates all the things which this "law of Christ" requires of us.

It seems, therefore, that to speak of a Christian ethic without law is making the wish father to the thought. Hence it is not surprising to find a long tradition of Christian ethics making positive use of the concept of law, setting out the ethical principles following from faith as divine law, and explicating it further in human laws based on divine authority. In the light of this we can understand why obedience to laws that have been justly enacted should be regarded as an ethical and a Christian virtue.

Right up to the high point of the Middle Ages men were conscious of being secure from the danger of falling into the error against which Paul had struggled. No one had any idea of looking for salvation in God's sight first and foremost by observing the law. The fact that God decides to act on behalf of man, saves him and redeems him, accepting him even in his errors and faults, is a pure gift which no one can merit. It is only *subsequently*, and on the basis of what God has already bestowed, that the law comes into play. It expresses in binding and unequivocal formulations the duties which faith lays upon the believer. To discover the law of God in its detailed applications from Scripture, from reflection in a spirit of faith on the content of the Christian message; and to "translate" all this into terms which are intelligible to man and suitable to his situation at any given time: all this is the task of that special branch of theology which is sometimes called "theological ethics" and sometimes "moral theology" according to the differing points of view of its practitioners.

And yet there does arise among Christians and non-Christians alike – not only today but today more than ever – a spirit of resistance and hostility towards any theological ethics with the concept of the law as its focal point. In order to understand this hostility and to decide how far it is justified it will be helpful to begin by briefly pointing out certain relevant factors.

Divine law

At first it was wholly right and reasonable for the moral consequences of the Christian faith to be preached, as we have already mentioned, as the law of God, or alternatively as human law deduced from the law of God. But the further the history of the Church progressed, and the more complicated human living in the Church and in a developing (western) society became, the more difficult it became to manage with only a small collection of laws (for instance the Ten Commandments together with a brief commentary). It was found necessary to produce ever fuller definitions and draw ever finer distinctions in order to define what constituted the law of God and legitimate human law, and to apply them to specific situations and "cases".

By the end of the Middle Ages this way of treating the law of God had led to a form of theological ethics which is justifiably and necessarily characterized as "legalism" in its conception of what constitutes Christian behaviour. On the one hand its practitioners believed that they could arrive at a clear and unequivocal description of the sovereign will of God only in the form of the law. On the other hand not only the simple Christian, but also many theologians and educated Christians, could no longer find their way through all the complicated ramifications of the system which had been devised, and all of which was preached to Christians as the law of God and the legitimate interpretation of it. No other course remained open to them than to fulfil the law unquestioningly, and to forego any inquiry into the intrinsic, objective value of what was required of them. Christian behaviour was now focused no longer on the basic requirement of love, but rather on the requirement of obedience. The more exacting and the more meaningless a given demand appeared, the higher was the value attached to the obeying of it. In this connexion the faith of Abraham was regarded as a supreme example precisely of a blind obedience of this kind. Thus the concept of "law" was, to an increasing extent, externalized. Since it was no longer possible or desirable to inquire into the intrinsic justification of what the law demanded, it became the essence of ethical behaviour to observe the law as such.

Law and Gospel

It was against this "legalistic approach" that the Reformers reacted. With great vehemence Luther reminds Christendom of the fact that Paul actually *draws a distinction* between law and Gospel, between law and promise. Salvation comes only from faith in the Gospel. The law, on the other hand, is the *adversary* of the Gospel. It represents a constant temptation to man not to accept salvation as a gift from God's hand, but to attempt to earn it for himself by his own powers through observance of the law. Luther does not intend, any more than Paul himself, to absolve the Christian from his ethical duties. Already in his *Sermon on Good Works* (1520) he rejects the imputation of his opponents to the effect that he is preaching libertinism and freedom from any moral obligation (Weimar edition, vol 6, 205). But he invokes Paul's authority for the view that the concept of law should precisely be excluded in describing what is essential to Christian behaviour. The law is a negative entity. It is intended to lay excessive demands upon man, to drive him absolutely to despair, to "kill" him in order to bring him to the realization that it is not his own works, but only God's grace, that can save him. For one who has arrived at the faith the law certainly retains its importance, but now no longer as law in the true sense, something that makes demands and threatens its transgressors with penalties. Now it survives merely, so to say, as an aid to the believer in his task of discovering what is ethically right and arriving at a right decision. For ultimately speaking he himself has to discover what God requires of him on the basis of his own faith and in the light of the needs and claims of his fellow men. For the believer as believer there is no longer any law in the strict sense of the term. Law still remains only so as to ensure order and harmony in the life of human communities. For we must reckon with the fact that such communities will include among their members non-believers and wicked men as well. And these latter must be compelled to observe good behaviour by the law.

Calvin's reaction is different. In contrast to Luther he

attaches less value to the *distinction* between law and gospel, and emphasizes rather the *transformation* of the law when, so to say, it becomes filled with the Gospel. The believer regards the law with different eyes, fulfils it spontaneously from love and not from compulsion. The law is thereby actually given a higher value – and at the same time the "legalism" of the late Middle Ages, which had blind obedience as its highest ideal, is radically overthrown.

Law and salvation

As in other spheres, so too here, Catholic theology reacts against the attacks of the Reformers by reinforcing the approach confirmed by tradition. For the development of the sacrament of penance had long since come to have an unfortunate consequence. This was a tendency to reduce ethical questions in practice to what could be treated of in the confessional, a tendency which, while it does not appear in the main stream of theology, certainly does so in the practical instruction given to ordinary Christians. The question which took priority over all others was how precisely a distinction could be drawn between "venial sin" and "mortal sin". The Ten Commandments of God were used as heads under which to summarize Christian moral teaching, and Luther still follows this method in the "Sermon on Good Works" and in his "Greater" and "Lesser" Catechisms. Moreover it had long been the practice to compile exemplary "cases" in the so-called "penitential books" and in manuals for confessors (this method is called for "casuistic" from the Latin "casus" = "case") so as to offer suitable aids to the simple people in deciding what course they ought to follow, and suitable criteria to the confessors in judging of particular cases and giving advice. Hence it is not surprising to find that now the law appears as an unambiguous standard of universal validity for assuring at, or evaluating, moral decisions. Anyone who attacks the law must incur the suspicion of seeking to evade the clear and unequivocal will of God for unworthy motives.

Hence the Fathers of the council of Trent (1545–63) assume

the rôle of passionate advocates in defence of God's moral law and its importance for the life of the Christian. They misinterpret the real purpose of the Reformers' attack, and fail to recognize what it is directed against. Hence they formulate the following declarations, chiefly against Luther: "If anyone says that it is impossible even for a justified man with the help of grace to observe God's commandments, let him be anathema. If anyone says that nothing is prescribed in the Gospel except faith, and that all the rest is inessential, neither commanded nor prohibited but open to choice, or if anyone says that the Ten Commandments do not apply to Christians, let him be anathema. If anyone says that a man who has been justified, or in any way made perfect, is not bound to observe the commandments of God and the Church, but must only believe, as though the Gospel were nothing more than a sheer and absolute promise of eternal life with no condition of fulfilling the commandments attached to it, let him be anathema. If anyone says that Christ Jesus is given to men by God as a Redeemer whom they trust but not a law-giver whom they have to hearken to, let him be anathema" (*Decree on Justification*, canon 18–21).

Now Catholic moral theology sets the concept of law still more in the centre of the stage and an ingenious system of "casuistry" is developed. On close examination this casuistry is seen to spring from a kind of pastoral compassion. Not every confessor, far less the simple people, is capable of understanding the complicated distinctions and lines of demarcation of the theologians. And because of this the intention is to illustrate, by means of clear representative "cases" drawn from everyday life, what God demands, and to make it easier to arrive at a corresponding course of action. At the same time, however, this casuistry intensifies that tendency to "legalism" in determining Christian behaviour of which we have spoken above. For now still more it presupposes that the will of God can be set down in unequivocal prescriptions governing human conduct. Hand in hand with casuistry, therefore, there emerged the so-called "systems of moral theology". These are nothing else than methods of arriving at a right interpretation of the law as applied to ever more complicated cases. Again pastoral considerations prompt a methodological inquiry into "precisely what is still allowed" – and must plead guilty to the charge of laxity. Moral earnestness seeks to prevent "laxism" of this kind, and takes its stand upon the strictest possible interpretation of law. It in turn must plead guilty to the charge of inhuman "rigorism". The basic axiom remains undisputed: moral life consists in fulfilling laws. It is possible to present a purely legalistic approach in terms of the fulfilling of external duties and laws as in itself constituting an attitude of "waiting for heaven".

Salvation without law

Today even Catholic Christians, prompted by a spontaneous instinct more than by any other reasons, reject any such system of ethics based on the concept of law. They do not hesitate to associate such systems with the behaviour and outlook of the Pharisees at the time of Jesus. The hidden purpose of an ethical system of this kind is to have the self-satisfaction of being able to say "I have done my duty". And Catholics too feel this to be downright un-Christian. This feeling of the Christian of today towards those who present a purely legalistic ethical system as Christian ethics is a sound one. In entertaining it the Christian finds himself in the best of company. We are led to the same conclusion by four considerations, for which by now we have already paved the way.

1. First a wholly practical consideration. Every law, every directive leading to action, must be simple. But this is precisely what we cannot say about the concrete situation at any given time in which the individual has to take action. Under certain circumstances the situation may be very complicated. Even if there is such a thing as a "commandment of the hour", still it is in any case never possible to formulate a law expressing this commandment. This is precisely the point which has been demonstrated by the history of casuistry. In the honest effort to do justice to the endless multiplicity of situations, it has finally come to be thoroughly bogged down amid the

countless "cases" to which it has attempted to supply an answer. Anyone who satisfies himself with doing only that which the law commands remains stuck at a pre-Christian stage, because he has failed to take into account the fact that God can speak to him precisely through the unique situation. Anyone, however, who strives to respond to the "commandment of the hour" will find no adequate help from any law. But he is now conscious of the seriousness and the radical nature of the commandment of love, which obliges him to selfless effort on behalf of his fellow men. And through faith he has the strength to fulfill it. He must now discover for himself what this commandment of love requires of him in the concrete individual instance here and now. One law taken in isolation is just as unavailing as a mere glance at the Bible to instruct the Christian in this. A further point that he must constantly take into account is that in the end he will precisely not feel any satisfaction with himself, but will rather be brought to recognize that he has remained a debtor to his fellow men and a debtor to God.

2. With regard to Luther's teaching on "law and Gospel" we are permitted to form our own opinion as to how far we shall regard it as valid. But in any case there is one point which cannot be contested. Luther has loudly summoned Christendom, and European thought in general, to an awareness that the concept of "law" as used by Paul is simply not to be included under the same definition as that which we are accustomed to think of as "law". We have only to read the Epistle to the Romans or the Epistle to the Galatians to recognize this at once. Neither that "law" which, as Paul sees it, is the opposite of living by faith, nor yet the "law of Christ" or the "law of the Spirit", have anything to do with that which the practitioners of theological ethics had in mind when they used the concept of law. Unless, therefore, we are to exclude the Epistles to the Romans and the Galatians (and certain other texts from the gospels as well!) from the New Testament, we can no longer be so undiscriminating in our use of the concept of law. The idea of "law" as it has come to be developed and used in systems of philosophical ethics, or even in

jurisprudence, needs considerable modification before it can be regarded as coinciding with the biblical concept of law. Despite all appearances to the contrary, it is only in a limited sense that what God expects and demands of the Christian in his conduct can be expressed in the form of law. In no case can Christian conduct in all the depths of its meaning be covered by an exteral observance of laws.

3. This point has still greater force when we reach back beyond Paul (and the legalistic preaching of his opponents) to the understanding of law which we find in the Old Testament itself. Israel's joy in the law is based upon the fact that the law was precisely not a "dead" and abstract letter, but was regarded as a personal message of God to his people. It was in the law that God led his people through history. It is not for nothing that Martin Buber, in his now famous translations of Old Testament passages, avoids the word "law", and prefers to translate the Hebrew "Torah" as "directive". Only in this way is it, in fact, actually possible to explain that the law that was in force in Israel underwent changes and nevertheless remained the one law of God. From this point of view also, therefore, we may conclude that any concept of law in terms of philosophical ethics has no place in our considerations of the nature of Christian conduct.

4. Finally the content of that which is presented to us as the "law of God" in Scripture was demonstrably drawn to a large extent from the laws of the surrounding peoples and reflects their ethical outlooks. Furthermore this content was, in part, modified in a significant manner so as to apply to the special circumstances of Israel. This makes it finally impossible for us to imagine that God dictated his requirements for men to this or that biblical author in the form of laws, and that the compilation thus arrived at now constitutes for all ages the binding norm for Christian conduct.

The ethics of responsibility

At this point let us bring all that we have said in connexion with our inquiry into faith and love to its due conclusion. First we must say without reservation that there are binding duties and obligations laid upon men by the will of God, but God has not regulated man's moral conduct by means of laws. This statement can no longer appear shocking. God has not made his relationship with man, or man's with him, depend upon fulfilment of the law as its condition, but rather established this relationship on the basis of an unconditional gift. In other words there is no law in the sphere of man's *relationship with God.*

The same is also true of man's relationship with his *fellow men.* It is not the case that God has intervened directly and in person to promulgate laws to govern this. On the contrary, the claims laid upon the man who has been received by God are those which stem from the unconditional love of God for all men, and he has to apply this standard in regarding his fellow men in order to discover what is truly of service to them, and how he must act towards them in accordance with this. Man learns what God's will is, therefore, by combining his faith in the love of God with a comprehensive view into the real lives of his fellow men at the individual and social levels. Another way of expressing the matter nowadays is to say that man learns to recognize the will of God by hearkening to the *claims of his fellow men* and to the "commandment of the hour" in a spirit of faith as *the claims of God himself.* When, therefore, we speak of this attitude in terms such as "law", "order", "commandment", and "obedience", we are failing to attain to the true and essential element of Christian conduct. We come closer to the reality when we speak of a "call" and a "response" – of "responsibility". If we wish provisionally to reduce it to a single formula we must say that the Christian ethic is not an ethic of the law but an ethic of responsibility. And again, "to take responsibility" is not in itself a prerogative of the Christian. But what is special and peculiar in this Christian ethic of responsibility is that the only true sense in which the believer can respond to *God* is for him to take responsiblity for his *fellow men,* while conversely the individual, by taking responsibility for his *fellow men* is thereby in fact responding to the call of *God.* This connexion between the two follows obviously from the nature of faith. Paul expresses it in an image when he says that the ethical conduct of the Christian is the "fruit of the Spirit" (Gal 5: 22). We do not command a fruit to grow; it grows of itself from the inner power of the tree. And it is of service to man.

God's will – in human law

Now it can be the case that precisely service of our fellow men requires that what needs to be done and what is demanded of us shall be expressed in the form of a clear unequivocal and binding directive – a law. This is the case above all when what is in question is not merely the personal need of an individual, but the requirements of a whole community, and those arising from their community life. This applies to many laws handed down to us in Scripture, and above all to the Ten Commandments. Scripture itself calls laws of this kind "divine law", "the law of God". This does not mean that God himself has issued them in a direct sense – there has always been individuals who formulated such laws, or again who copied them or introduced fresh modifications to them from time to time. They are called "divine law" because they give expression to something which faith has recognized and proclaims in the name of God as the will of God for men in the concrete. Besides, in this connexion Israel knew how to draw a very precise distinction between that which constitutes the will of God for man in a quite fundamental sense – as expressed, for instance, in the Ten Commandments – and applications of law which, while they were indeed proclaimed in the name, and under the authority of God, were capable of being changed as human relationships changed within the national community. Faith in holy Scripture discovers the word of God in the words of man in that it reads and understands these words as an invitation to belief. And in the same way faith discovers the will of God through the medium of laws which have been formulated and set down by men. When the believer reads the law in this spirit, what he finds in it is not an abstract impersonal norm, even though it might appear to be such, but an expression of God's own purposes.

Does this apply to Christians too, despite the fact that action proceeding from faith can never in its essence be dependent upon laws? Yes, this still does apply to the Christian also, in those cases, namely, in which he has to recognize that amid all the freedom which faith bestows upon him he needs the guidance and help of the law in order to act aright. The Christian does also encounter the will of God through the medium of human laws, and when there are sufficient reasons for it he can use such laws to help him in acting as faith tells him to. But there are several reasons of this kind, and they are so cogent that we can absolutely speak of an abiding function and significance of law as helping us to act out of faith. We can say this even though we have rejected every kind of legalism as a guide to Christian conduct. We shall survey the most important of these reasons and thereby try to achieve an understanding of how the believer of today can encounter the will of God and be reached by its claims upon him in human laws.

The function and significance of the law

First. Laws are necessary for technical reasons or reasons of organization. Thus if it were only a question of this individual acting aright towards that one, we could perhaps be satisfied simply with appealing to faith and trusting to the impulses stemming from it. But where men are living together in a wider community, rules with universally binding force are needed in order to ensure peace and security. Such rules, designed to ensure the security of community life, can also take the form of laws. At first sight this still has little to do with ethical behaviour, but all the more to do with intelligent organization. Examples of laws of this kind are, for instance, the traffic regulations, the franchise laws, or the trade regulations. Since these are concerned more with organization than with ethical principles the Christian can and must observe such laws even in those cases in which they have been promulgated by an unjust régime or one which despises ethical principles.

Admittedly it is questionable whether there can ever be laws which are *exclusively* organizational in character, and wholly free from all ethical considerations. For example we are more than ever aware today that the traffic regulations have been designed to serve an obvious ethical purpose, namely the best possible security for human life, and that therefore they must constantly be undergoing improvement. A lawgiver who enacts traffic regulations that are inefficient, or a driver on the roads who breaks the traffic regulations, is more or less directly endangering human life and acting inethically. Thus even in this example we can see something which is still more manifest in a whole range of other laws which go far beyond any rules of organization in their aims. Laws do in fact have a function in determining ethical conduct – even that ethical conduct which consciously seeks its roots in faith. For instance in laws which prohibit the taking of human life, or protect the life of the unborn, or provide security for marriage and the family, what is in question is certain basic human values applicable to the individual and the community, values which, whatever variations of detail there may be, are firmly upheld by all the different cultures and ideologies in common.

Laws and directives of this kind embody not only the pronouncements of the human authorities who have raised these requirements into laws at any given time, but also the experiences and convictions of many cultures and human traditions. Laws precisely of this kind, even in their human formulation and expression, come to be proclaimed in Israel and in the Christian Church as the law of *God*. This is an expression of the conviction that in them man is confronted directly with the will of God, which faith recognizes and acknowledges. Hence we can understand why it should be that a century-old tradition of Christian moral theology speaks of an identity of content between the "natural law" and the "Ten Commandments" of the Old Testament. What this means is that faith is convinced that laws of this kind, which

have an unmistakable ethical content, can on the one hand
(with the help of a little reflection on the nature of man and
the conditions of his community life) be applied to human
living, and on the other be preached in the name of God as
divine law.

Obviously not all human law is concerned with absolutely
primary ethical requirements of this kind. Between laws of the
technical and organizational type and laws which express
direct ethical requirements lies a broad spectrum of greater or
lesser ethical significance. But who, for instance, can dispute
the fact that modern tax laws or laws against land speculation
are, or ought to be, concerned with the same justice between
men as that which was preached of old in Israel and even
among more ancient peoples as a basic requirement laid upon
men by God?

But to reiterate again at this point: Why do there have to
be laws of this kind, seeing that it is not external observance
of them that in itself turns human conduct into ethical conduct proceeding from faith, but solely and exclusively that
will to achieve integrity and love which is born of faith and
which, provided it is genuine, has no need of law? For this
there are two main reasons. The first is simply that there is
never a stage at which faith itself is once and for all mature
and fully developed. On the contrary it grows and ripens, and
also undergoes reverses and fresh beginnings. And because of
this it cannot be expected that faith of this kind, weighed
down as it is by human weakness, will be unimpeded in its
function of determining our ethical behaviour in all circumstances and cases. Egoism and self-interest will draw even the
believer into temptation again and again, and will often gain
the victory over him. And from a different point of view it
is indispensable that community life among men should be
protected at least from the more blatant effects of human
egoism. Laws, together with the punitive sanctions attached
to them against their transgressors, have the function of ensuring at least a minimum of at least external ethical conduct in
order that man may not finally reach the stage of preying upon
his fellow men. Even among believers it is in fact character-

istic human behaviour – or better characteristic human lack of behaviour – to need a certain compulsion in order to do, or to refrain from doing, even relatively light things, and to find it very difficult to do, or refrain from doing them, without such compulsion. Luther calls this function of the law the "first use of the law", in other words its initial function, which the law must exercise even before we come to discussing its significance for salvation. The theologian who asserts this is the very same who, more than any other since Paul, has regarded the law as something to be banished from Christian life.

The second reason: the law enables us to a certain extent to demarcate certain areas of mortal danger within the sphere of ethical conduct. For in fact the process of seeking, inquiring, and deciding does not eliminate the risk of error from the individual even when he is a believer. We must abide by our earlier statement: ethical conduct that proceeds from faith can never be satisfied merely with observing laws and precepts. But laws do impart to ethical conduct a quality which might be described as a negative sureness. This applies chiefly, of course, to the quite basic and primary ethical laws such as, for instance, the prohibition of killing, but it also applies to legal ordinances derived from these, and applying them in concrete detail. They demarcate a boundary such that once it is overstepped there can no longer be any question, whatever the case, of ethical conduct or obedience to God's will. Could we ever be in a position to assert that the believer never has any need of a negative sureness of this kind for his behaviour? In these two functions, the positive and healthful compulsion, and the negative sureness, lies the whole significance of the law as conducive to ethical conduct. Obedience towards the law does not turn human conduct into conduct proceeding from faith. But without observing the law there cannot be any conduct proceeding from faith because even in human law we encounter God's will in manifold ways.

The limits of law

But side by side with this factor of the law's significance a further corollary, following no less directly from these considerations, is that the law has its limitations. Even the best of human lawgivers can never be sure that in the laws he has formulated he has given appropriate expression to the true needs of human life, to the relationships between individuals, and thereby to the will of God itself. Furthermore the world in which men live is changing. Much that was demanded as a matter of justice yesterday can today be injustice, and perhaps gross injustice. In the manner of their formulation, therefore, all laws are subject to the conditions of a particular age and stand in need again and again of reappraisal, improvement, or supplementation. And this becomes increasingly true in proportion as their application is extended so as to cover the individual details of human life. One and the same basic and primary ethical principle can and must assume the most varied formulations and refinements as it is applied in the various situations and epochs of human history. Thus for instance we of today may justifiably ask whether something of the will of God for mankind is not expressed in the "Charter of Human Rights". Do not the human rights presented here constitute interpretations of the Ten Commandments as applicable to our own situation in a manner similar to that in which the law in Israel interpreted the will of God for men as expressed in the Ten Commandments in its application to Israel's own concrete situation? At any rate it would not seem a false position for the Church today, following God's call, to give her support to these human rights and exhort mankind to observe them, seeing that they state the requirements of God's justice in these times just as the laws of Israel stated these requirements in biblical times. At all events it is only when human laws show that regard for the conditions of life of those to whom they refer, only when they are "reasonable" in the broadest sense of the term, that they can also convey an ethical summons to the human personality in its freedom, a summons in and through which faith recognizes the will of God.

Finally all that we are considering here applies also to those laws which cater only for believers and have force only within the community of believers, the Church, since it is only in the light of faith that they can be understood and recognized as meaningful. Such would be, for instance, the laws governing the observance of Sunday as a holy day. It is plain that a Christian living in a society with a whole range of different philosophies and outlooks cannot impose laws of this kind on those of his fellow citizens who are not Christians. At most he can attempt to convince them that such laws have a universal value for human living as such, for example by pointing out the advantages of having one rest day after every six working days. The Christian can justifiably ask his fellow citizens who are non-Christians to have due regard to the religious convictions of Christians, seeing that these too do in fact constitute a group within the society and have the same rights as other groups. It is likewise clear that Christian conduct requires something more than merely the external observance of such laws, and if we fail to recognize this we fall back into all those errors which Jesus condemned so severely in many of his contemporaries. But as in other contexts so too here such laws are capable, within the sphere of their application, of bringing to bear a healthy compulsion which is of assistance in subduing the hidden egoism which persists. And they can also indicate the boundaries which in the long run cannot be overstepped with impunity or without damage to our faith. It is true that considerations of this kind are on no very heroic level. But they are realistic – for in fact the majority of Christians are not heroes.

III. CONSCIENCE

Already at several points we have emphasized the importance of reason in arriving at an ethically right decision. But what gives the voice of reason its force? From ancient times this problem has come to be discussed under the heading of "conscience". It is only through a "voice" of personal conscience that man experiences any sense of obligation, whether it comes to him in the form of a law or not.

The voice of conscience

As used today, the word "conscience" has more than one meaning. Two different approaches can serve to bring this plurality of meaning home to us. On the one hand a saying which tends to be used in connexion with complicated ethical questions is "act according to your conscience!" On the other a point that is especially emphasized is that "conscience must derive its orientation from objective ethical norms". On the first approach conscience itself is the source of the good. It is only acting *against* conscience that is evil. On the second approach conscience is the faculty by which we apply in action certain norms accepted as binding, these being for their part sources of the good.

A perfectly simple explanation of these shifts of meaning is to be found in connexion with those historical points which we have noticed in tracing the development of the concept of law in theological ethics. We may follow the opinion of the medieval theologians to the effect that a divine or human law, or an ethical norm which is either divine or else legitimately enacted by men, constitutes a single unequivocal criterion of the good, admitting of no exceptions. In that case all that we have to do is to judge whether a given concrete situation in which a moral decision has to be taken does or does not fall under this criterion. If it does so fall then it follows that the individual who finds himself in such a situation and is bound by such norms must bring his decision and action into conformity with them. Here the term "conscience" is taken to mean precisely this concrete judgment to which we have referred. On this showing the voice of conscience has, as the upholders of this approach like to put it, the form of a so-called "practical conclusion", one, that is to say, which is orientated towards action and a "practical" outcome. To take one example. It is an ethical norm that an individual must look after his parents when they are in need. These are my parents and they are in need. Therefore I must look after them. Conscience – in other words this practical judgment as to what must be done here and now – has a positive effect. It admonishes and warns the subject prior to his action, and confirms and commends him after it to the extent that that action is in agreement with its own dictates. Where this has not been the case conscience has a negative effect. It accuses and condemns, disturbing the subject and taking the form of a "bad conscience" leading to the "gnawings of conscience".

This concept of conscience is far from being obsolete. In innumerable cases the circumstances are just as described, and they are so in all cases in which a man's ethical obligations are in principle clear. We are aware, however, that sometimes this is not so clear as a guide to action for the Christian as was supposed in the theology of the Middle Ages. And this is because of all those factors which are not covered by laws. Hence it is necessary to broaden the concept of conscience. Conscience does something more than merely apply a norm to a concrete situation. In certain circumstances it must actually play a positive part on its own account in order really to discover what is the good and right course of action here and now. There is a special sense in which the term "conscience" as used today signifies an activity of creating and discovering for oneself. And as used in this sense its range is co-extensive with that of reason itself in its function of discovering new truth. What the two concepts of conscience, the "old" and the "new", have in common is that conscience is always concerned with the concrete decision to be taken here and now. In this respect it is different from the function of reason in general. Where reason searches for the guiding principle that is universally valid, conscience applies the knowledge thus acquired precisely to the particular concrete situation calling for decision and action.

But there are still greater depths to be explored in this question. We experience the fact that our conscience is "stirred" even *before* we bend our efforts to acquiring the knowledge that we need to act upon, and *before* we deliberately take up any given position. Even before the "practical judgment" which we have described, and before the individual decision of conscience itself, it generates, as it were, a spontaneous insight in which it brings to the individual's notice the idea: "This is what you must do" or "This is what you must avoid". Underlying this a still more basic impulse is at work, the impulse, namely, to do good rather than evil, which manifestly belongs to the very nature of man. The medieval theologians were accustomed to call this impulse the "primitive conscience" (*synderesis*). It is only through this primitive conscience that the voice of conscience in the individual concrete instance acquires its impelling, binding, and, in appropriate cases, disturbing force, and becomes something more than merely a neutral judgment of the understanding.

If, then, the voice of conscience is rooted in human nature itself, then finally we must conclude that conscience extends to deeper levels in us than all that activity of the understanding and the will which is designed to lead to action. The voice of conscience is an experience at the heart and centre of the personality, and it summons man to be at one with himself in his concrete decision. The "bad conscience" accuses man of having lost this oneness with himself – *hence* the disquiet. Faith establishes a connexion between this universal human experience of the primitive conscience, together with its effects in the concrete, and the Spirit of God which enters into man, orientates him towards God, and impels him to opt for the good. Where sinful man has the experience that his bad conscience will not relinquish its hold upon him faith can bring him to the judgment that despite his sins man remains so possessed by God that he can understand how far God's will exceeds his own acts. For the believer the disquiet arising from his state of alienation from himself is turned into repentance before God.

The binding force of the voice of conscience

Whether, therefore, the rôle of conscience is confined simply to providing an "application" of an ethical norm, or whether, without the help of any clear norm, it discovers in the concrete what is the good and binding course by examining the situation for itself, one point is clear. The idea of a self-willed conscience or one that recognizes no obligations is wholly ruled out. The conscience is not released from its obligations by the fact that it has a more vital function to perform than merely the applying of a norm. It is no whit less bound by its obligations then than the believer himself is when he no longer has any laws to guide him in arriving at a right course of action. The conscience is always a predisposition to what is good, to hearkening to God's will.

This predisposition can be blunted, and that is blameworthy in God's sight. But a more important factor – and one that applies to reason in general – is that the voice of conscience can err. It can make wrong applications of an ethical principle. In attempting to discover what is good in the here and now it may stray from the right path. Yet so long as the error is not recognized as such, even an erring judgment of conscience remains binding. For it continues to be in principle a call to what is good, a call to responsibility before God. Even in a course of action which is materially wrong by reason of a mistake which conscience has made, the judgment arrived at can be a judgment for God. If, and to the extent that, the voice of conscience is guided by genuine conviction and a sincere quest for the true and the good, it still remains binding. It is the direct and ultimate tribunal by which human action must be judged. God will judge man according to his state of conscience.

The second Vatican council has this to say with regard to conscience: "In the depths of his conscience man detects a law which he does not impose upon himself, but which holds him to obedience. Always summoning him to love good and avoid evil, the voice of conscience can when necessary speak to his heart more specifically: do this, shun that. For man has in his heart a law written by God. To obey it is the very dignity of man; according to it he will be judged.... Conscience is the most secret core and sanctuary of a man. There he is alone with God, whose voice echoes in his depths. In a wonderful manner conscience reveals that law which is fulfilled by love of God and neighbour. In fidelity to conscience, Christians are joined with the rest of men in the search for truth, and for the genuine solution to the numerous problems which arise in the life of individuals and from social relationships. Hence the more that a correct conscience holds sway, the more persons and groups turn aside from blind choice and strive to be guided by objective norms of morality. . . . Conscience frequently errs from invincible ignorance without losing its dignity. The same cannot be said of a man who cares but little for truth and goodness, or of a conscience which by degrees grows practically sightless as a result of habitual sin." (*Pastoral Constitution*, art. 16).

At the same time, however, we should not be too ready to excuse ourselves on the grounds of an inculpable error of conscience or, when we have acted in a way that is materially false and wrong, by saying that it was done "in good conscience". One root cause of possible errors of conscience is described in Scripture as a hardening of the heart. What is meant by this is that hardness of heart towards God which leads to an attitude of unwillingness to subject our personal opinions to critical inquiry, and also to insensitivity or laxity of conscience. Such an attitude can also arise from our own personal faults. To this extent the fact that it is possible for conscience to err manifests one particular aspect of the fact that the world to which its owner belongs is one still dominated by sin and in need of redemption in Christ. It is precisely his awareness of the danger of self-deception, of self-righteousness, and of the innumerable possibilities of error, that will make the individual watchful and critical of his own judgment when he is tempted to regard it as the voice of conscience.

Authority and conscience

At this point the problem of "freedom of conscience" arises. Without freedom there can be no moral conduct, no responsibility. The factor which directly determines moral conduct, however, is the voice of conscience. It is to this that the ultimate moral obligation must be attributed. Hence no one should be obliged, or even forced, to act against the voice of his own conscience once he has clearly recognized it to be such. This freedom of conscience and of honest conviction is numbered among the basic rights of man. Moreover in the sphere of ethical conduct it is the will and mental attitude of man that we are concerned with, and not merely his external actions. And here any kind of compulsion would remain futile and meaningless. In connexion with the problem of religious freedom the second Vatican council defines its position on this point in the following statement: "This Vatican Synod declares that the human person has a right to religious freedom. This freedom means that all men are to be immune from coercion on the part of individuals or of social groups and of any human power, in such wise that in matters religious no one is to be forced to act in a manner contrary to his own beliefs. Nor is anyone to be restrained from acting in accordance with his own beliefs, whether privately or publicly, whether alone or in association with others, within due limits. ... The Synod further declares that the right to religious freedom has its foundation in the very dignity of the human person, as this dignity is known through the revealed Word of God and by reason itself. This right of the human person to religious freedom is to be recognized in the constitutional law whereby society is governed. Thus it is to become a civil right." (Declaration on Religious Freedom, art. 2.)

The constitutional authorities and those representing them are likewise obliged to observe these basic rights. For instance anyone who, on religious or other grounds, is unwilling to take an oath as a form of religious attestation should not be compelled to do so. But when we say that the authorities should respect the freedom of conscience of the individual this does not mean that they should acquiesce in error or capriciousness, but rather that they should recognize man's responsibility for his own actions. After all it would be disastrous if men sought to invoke the principle of freedom of conscience to evade authority's every claim to respect and legitimate obedience.

It is true that this can also lead to conflict. For cases can arise in which the claims of authority, on the one hand, and conscience on the other, are mutually irreconcilable and exclusive.

In such cases we should begin by examining whether and
to what extent that which passes for the voice of our own
conscience may perhaps be emanating from self-sufficiency or
a desire for our own comfort. It is in fact the task of authority
to draw man out of his state of isolation and his limited outlook and direct him towards the wider sphere of relationships
in human life, and especially to take an interest in the needs
of the community as a whole. Moreover until the contrary is
proved we should actually proceed on the assumption that this
is what authority intends.

Precisely for this reason the directives or laws issued by the
authorities for the sake of the community often constitute a
necessary corrective to the promptings of the individual's own
conscience. Only an individualistic outlook and a self-
sufficiency of a very dubious kind could in principle reject
such correctives on the part of authority to the voice of one's
own conscience as invalid, and thereby *de facto* uncritically
equate one's own personal opinion with the voice of conscience. Precisely because the individual has a responsibility
in conscience to do his utmost to arrive at a right decision he
is bound, again in conscience, to inform his conscience
amongst other things by listening to authority. Nevertheless
there are cases in which, even when one has subjected one's
own judgment to "questioning" in this sense, and given
earnest consideration to some difficult problem, the conflict
between conscience and authority still remains unresolved. In
such cases the individual concerned must follow his own inner
convictions, that is the voice of his conscience, in determining
his course of action, and no authority, no superior, no church,
can prevent him from doing so.

Hence it is obvious that in cases of conflict of this kind, in
which human authority demands something of us which is
manifestly contrary to the clear decision of our own conscience, so that to comply would be to disobey this decision of
conscience, then obedience to the voice of conscience takes
priority. For "man must listen to God rather than man" (Acts
4: 19). The conflict of the individual with authority – even
that of the individual Christian with ecclesiastical authority –

is not necessarily or in all cases a bad thing. If a right solution to it is eventually arrived at, it has a positive significance for all those involved. It causes the individual to accept a still deeper degree of that personal responsibility and power of decision which is laid upon him, and thereby brings him to a higher degree of moral maturity and development. But at the same time it also rouses authority from any false inertia or rigidity. This means that the necessity of finding just solutions to such conflicts demands a process of developing maturity throughout the life of society and the Church alike, and also throughout the life of the individual in society and in the Church.

Conscience as redeemed or unredeemed

Theologians of the Reformed churches do not always adopt so positive an attitude as that which we have indicated here towards the value of the voice of conscience. In particular they see a constant danger of human self-will and autonomy. The conscience of the "natural" man who has not yet given his allegiance to Christ in faith bears traces of his unredeemed state. This appears when it becomes the expression of a dangerous autonomy on man's part and tends to close his spirit still more to faith. The voice of conscience is accounted "the most godless self-righteousness" (Dietrich Bonhoeffer), as the attempt of the individual person to justify himself as knowing good and evil in the sight of God, of his fellow men, and of himself. Only the miracle of faith overthrows this autonomy on the part of the natural man, and discovers the law of action in Jesus Christ. The redeemed conscience of the believer consists in a surrender of the state of "being a law to oneself" (autonomy) on the part of man in favour of an attitude of "having one's course determined by another" (heteronomy) – and in fact by the law of Jesus Christ. The conscience set free in Jesus Christ summons me to unity with myself in Jesus Christ. "Jesus Christ has become my conscience. This means that now the only way in which I can find unity with myself is in the surrender of my ego to God and mankind. It is not any law, but the living God and living humanity as I encounter them in Jesus Christ that constitute the origin and the goal of my conscience" (Bonhoeffer).

Is the opposition so radical as it sounds? Protestant theologians who believe so speak of the *source* of the free conscience. All that they say on this point we must say too. But what we are concerned with precisely *here* is the way in which we *hearken to* conscience *in the concrete individual case*. It is no contradiction to say on the one hand that Jesus Christ is the unifying point of my personal existence, and yet at the same time to understand conscience as summoning me from the depths of my being to achieve unity with myself. The believer is aware of no other unity apart from that which is bestowed upon him in his faith in God through Jesus Christ. If the conscience that has been redeemed in faith asks where unity with itself is to be found, then it is asking not for self-righteousness but for that which God himself wills it to achieve.

IV. CONCERNING THE FREEDOM OF A CHRISTIAN MAN

All the lines of argument which we have been following up to this point on the subject of "faith and love" converge in the single supreme idea of the "freedom of the Christian man". This is still true even of those considerations (which may have sounded a little "pessimistic") which we put forward with regard to the significance of the law. For even to allow oneself to be helped to a certain extent against one's own weakness by the law is still a free act of faith.

The actual *phrase* "the freedom of a Christian man" is in fact the title of one of Martin Luther's shorter writings from the year 1520 which has become famous. But the subject matter is one of the key themes of the New Testament (Jn 8: 31 ff; Rom 6: 18; 8: 2; 1 Cor 7: 22; 2: Cor 3: 17; Gal 5: 1 ff; Jas 1: 25; 2: 12; 1 Pet 2: 16). We have already at an earlier stage given some consideration to it. Here we must revert to a special aspect of it in order to inquire what consequences this freedom has for the question of conduct proceeding from faith.

In our earlier arguments we have already defined the place of our present problem within the total discussion in the formula: "Freedom *for* love". A freedom which seeks to do without love ceases to be freedom at all. But how can this be? How can freedom remain *freedom* when love acts as a *binding commitment* upon it? How can this binding effect of love remain a *binding commitment* so long as freedom retains its own nature? At this point a whole series of particular questions arise, which may serve to test whether the arguments which we have put forward so far are valid. For in order to maintain them we must answer these questions successfully.

Freedom of the will

We may begin with the question of whether man is capable of taking any free decisions at all. If this is not the case, then any further considerations concerning freedom and binding commitments would be mere idle speculation. Now the usual explanation that is given runs as follows: It is only possible to speak of responsible and morally accountable actions on man's part, and in accordance with this of personal guilt also, so long as man is capable of free choice and decision. On the other hand human freedom is finite. It remains limited and circumscribed by the fact that the subject in which it inheres, namely man, is made up of body and soul, so that it is exercised only in and through the appropriate organs (the human brain, on which depend the power of the reason to acquire knowledge and of the will to take decisions). And a further factor which circumscribes it is the influence of the environment, the "milieu". In view of these manifold circumscribing factors, is it not more honest to deny that the will has any freedom of decision?

Arguments against the existence of a free will capable of making decisions come initially from the direction of natural science with its analyses in terms of cause and effect. The whole range of human decisions which are regarded as free can be proved in reality to be to a large extent predetermined by character, environment, and upbringing, and by various psychic and physical factors. They constitute in a greater or lesser degree reactions to impulses from the environment. Now it is precisely when we achieve a deeper insight into these manifold preconditioning factors of human behaviour and human life in general that doubts arise with regard to man's freedom of decision. In nature we encounter a strict sequence of cause and effect which we recognize as a law admitting of no exceptions. This is now applied to human nature as well. According to this principle of "natural determinism", therefore, man's behaviour and decision-making is determined by a complex network of physical factors which it is perfectly possible to calculate in advance. "Freedom" – if we still want to use the term – appears from time to time as an insight into the necessity of this process and of the laws which govern it.

According to another theory, this time deriving more from biology than physics, man is so largely programmed from the outset by numerous hereditary factors (genes) that the only scope for further formation that remains is for external guidance to be brought to bear to develop the good traits and repress the bad ones. A related school of thought maintains that man is so largely predetermined by social factors that he is no more than the product of his social relationships. This is precisely a state of affairs which could be exploited by the most varied political systems once they had achieved power, so as to render man amenable to their wishes and aims.

Yet not only philosophers and natural scientists, but theologians have denied that man has any freedom of will. It is true that these latter have had different reasons for doing so. At this point we must refer to the Reformation theologians. In 1521, in the course of his teaching on the predestination of man, Melancthon, the collaborator of Luther, emphasized that God alone is our salvation and that our will contributes nothing to the process. In 1525, in his work, *On the Lack of Freedom of the Will* ("De servo arbitrio") Luther himself took issue with the humanistic teaching on freedom of Erasmus of Rotterdam. This controversy gave rise to numerous misunderstandings. Today it can be accounted as to a large extent settled. Yet it is important to notice two points. First,

Luther and Melancthon never had any idea of denying that man was responsible for his own actions, and second, what Luther meant by the "lack of freedom of the will" can be understood only against the background of his teaching on the "freedom of a Christian man".

One argument against all deterministic denials of freedom is the simple fact of experience that from the most ancient times man has been held accountable for his actions. Man himself resists compulsion or repression. The fact that he is a responsible being faced with the task of taking decisions is constantly being borne in upon him afresh. We too can, as a matter of conscience, decide to resist inclinations, desires, or general trends of the age. We can "swim against the current" and say "no!". And this shows that we do have an awareness of being free.

Still more, precisely in reaction against the deterministic denial of human freedom, others have put forward that theory of man's total freedom from commitment of any kind ("indeterminism") which has come to play so significant a rôle in certain currents of contemporary philosophy (for instance in existentialism). Man, so we are told in this kind of philosophy, is constantly confronted with a choice. And he can and must be completely free and immune to influence in responding to this choice.

Freedom in peril

The truth lies midway between the two extremes. It cannot be denied that human conduct appears in many ways restricted, predetermined, and sometimes seems as though it were following a preordained programme. On the other hand there is undoubtedly a scope for choice. Now the implication of this is that the responsibility which man must take for the use he makes of his power to choose, together with human freedom itself, is not absolute but limited. It is a relative freedom. Freedom implies that man – even in the midst of external influences and internal impulses – is able to act without any *compelling* influence from without, but on the contrary on the basis of his own insights and decision. This does not exclude, but rather presupposes, that he has prior reasons impelling him to action (motives). Otherwise human action would never be set in motion at all. But action which is motivated is not action which is unfree. It is *conditioned* but not *forced*. Freedom consists precisely in the fact of deciding which motives are to determine his action.

Admittedly in all this we have depicted an ideal situation, the wholly good man who can rely on his own insights and motives. Experience shows how far the realities fall short of the ideal. Man's "autonomy", or his freedom in the concrete, is not only circumscribed by all kinds of factors in his environment; above all it is constantly endangered within its most immediate sphere by that egoism and self-will, pride, and quest for mastery and power, which break out again and again. And it is also imperilled by the egoistical exercise of power over others. Freedom is endangered by the fact that it can lead to an absolute enslavement to evil, and in that case survives only as an appearance of freedom. In brief freedom is endangered by sin. This sounds strange. It would be possible to reply: Sin is a *misuse* of freedom, but is it a *danger to* freedom? Is it not precisely part of the essence of freedom that no one can *prevent* man from doing evil when, without any influence being brought to bear, he decides upon it?

The freedom of the children of God

It is true that there is one consideration which can immediately make us cautious. If being able to sin belongs to the essence of freedom, then we cannot call God free. For he cannot sin, since that would mean that he would be acting against his own nature. And we find a further positive pointer even in that law already referred to which lays down that only he who is ready to give up his life will find the fulfilment of it. Hence anyone who seeks to cling on to himself in a spirit of egoism gains nothing but loses all – certainly the opposite of freedom. Can we achieve a still closer insight into this truth?

We can only be free provided that we do not have to be

preoccupied with looking after our own interests. Once we do become preoccupied about ourselves we are unfree, for in that case we *have to* seek for something, do something, make sure of something. We *have to* fulfil some want that we feel. We *have to* build up some security for ourselves. Every day we can feel pressures of this kind. But the person who is most radically unfree is he who feels compelled to devise the meaning of his *entire* existence and to construct it for himself. By contrast he is most radically free who does not have to trouble himself at all about the meaning of his existence because he is so certain of this that it never occurs to him to question it at all. Again the matter can be expressed in these terms: that man is radically free who has all his powers at his disposal for other activities and other *men* because he does not need them for himself – in a word, therefore, the man who is free for love.

Who can be radically free in this sense? There are only two possibilities: either God or a being of such a kind that God himself has taken over the task of caring for him in his personal life. The first possibility provides its own answer. Man is not God but a being which feels its own state of want on every side and ultimately the most radical want of all, the unanswered question of the meaning of its own existence. By contrast the second possibility is one which the Christian with all his heart asserts of himself – to such an extent that he accounts it a fault in himself when his practical conduct makes it seem as though he is not that kind of creature.

What follows from this for the relationship between freedom and sin? It is quite impossible to produce a definition of the essential nature of human freedom without including in it a mention of God. Human freedom is freedom under God as creator and redeemer, and this not because God has after all been unwilling to leave us altogether free, deciding rather to reserve some transcendent sphere of control for himself, but because without God we are burdened with all the crushing task of caring for ourselves, and it is this that robs us of our full freedom.

We are now in a position to understand that if sin means setting oneself up against God, refusing to accept that one is a creature and that one is loved, seeking to live by one's own resources – in brief if sin is self-orientation, then it *must* of necessity destroy freedom because it is cutting man off from the source of all genuine freedom. And even though when he has done this man is still just as able to "choose freely" between this and that, he is not really free for he is acting under a relentless compulsion to pursue his own interests and cares. And conversely anyone who radically binds *himself* to God is binding himself to the source of freedom. To be obedient to God, therefore, is not a moral virtue which I "*have to*" practise, but means recognizing God as the upholder of my freedom. To love my fellow men is not an oppressive "duty" which I have to grit my teeth in order to fulfil so as not to forgo my chance of salvation, but means committing all my powers to his service, powers which I do not need for myself seeing that God himself is looking after me. The more unreservedly I "lose" my life in service and love the more this manifests that freedom and life which I "gain" from God by letting it be bestowed upon me.

This is precisely what is meant by that "glorious liberty of the children of God" of which Paul speaks (Rom 8: 21). Its nature is summed up in that saying which John attributes to Jesus: "My food (ie, my life) is to do the will of him who sent me" (Jn 4: 34). And in one passage which is positively liturgical in solemnity the second Vatican council draws the ethical conclusions of this: "Only in freedom can man direct himself towards goodness. Our contemporaries make much of this freedom and pursue it eagerly . . . For its part, authentic freedom is an exceptional sign of the divine image within man. For God has willed that man be left "in the hand of his own counsel" (Ecclus. 15: 14) so that he can seek his Creator spontaneously, and come freely to attain to blissful perfection through loyalty to him. Hence man's dignity demands that he act according to a knowing and free choice. Such a choice is personally motivated and prompted from within. It does not result from blind internal impulse nor from mere external pressure. . . . Man achieves such dignity when, emancipating himself from all captivity to passion, he pursues his goal in a spontaneous choice of what is good, and procures for himself, through effective and skillful action, apt means to that end. Since man's freedom has been damaged by sin, only by the help of God's grace can he bring such a relationship with God into full flower." (*Pastoral Constitution*, art. 17.)

Is man's course predetermined by forces outside himself?

On the basis of what has been said above we can find an answer to a question which we have already touched upon at an earlier stage. Is God a *rival* to man in his freedom? Does man's binding commitment to God destroy his power of self-determination (autonomy) or does it subject him to determination by forces outside himself (heteronomy)? The atheism of recent times does in fact believe that it is compelled actively to oppose belief in God in order to liberate man from this state of being determined in his course by forces outside himself. But this would only be justified if God were a kind of lawgiver or "inspector general" who imposed arbitrary rules upon men, a God who made men subject to his moods and whims and stunted the development of their personalities. Now those who condemn belief in God in this way do in fact believe that it has this effect, and on the basis of this idea hold that the further idea they conjure up, of religious leaders as a group of men seeking to achieve dominion over their fellows, is not altogether groundless. But all this has little to do with the God of the Bible, who has compassion on men, has accepted them irrevocably in Jesus Christ, and thereby precisely guarantees their freedom. It is only the situation we ourselves create when we regard God and man as opponents confronting one another that can give rise to the idea of any rivalry between them. But this is something which the Christian, no less than the atheist, must resist with all his might.

The grace of God and human freedom

It is only in virtue of a binding commitment to God, therefore, that man is truly free. But he *can* refuse to be bound to God in this sense. Hence we encounter human freedom in two forms: first as an uncommitted freedom, the freedom that leads to decision, and second as a committed freedom, or the freedom of decision. In the uncommitted form of freedom (freedom of choice) no decision has yet been taken. The individual can decide either for or against that which he has recognized as good and true, and ultimately speaking for or against God himself. This is a decision which he can in no sense evade. Even the refusal to take a decision, the state of continuing to live in a state of indecision, would in itself be a decision, namely a negative one: a refusal to decide upon the good. Paul's way of expressing the matter involves the idea of man being a servant. He must enter into service with some master. But he is given the power to choose *whose* servant he will be, the servant of evil and sin or the servant of God and justice: "Do you not know that if you yield yourselves to anyone as obedient slaves you are slaves of the one whom you obey, either of sin which leads to death, or of obedience which leads to righteousness? ... Having been set free from sin, you have become slaves of righteousness.... For just as you once yielded your members to impurity and to greater and greater iniquity, so now yield your members to righteousness for sanctification" (Rom 6: 16–19).

But even when man does commit himself to a decision he does not cease to be free, but rather his freedom acquires a new form: the new freedom of the state of commitment to God which is identical with the "freedom of the children of God". It is precisely *through* obedience to God that it really is freedom, as we have described. Hence we can actually say: freedom and binding commitment go hand in hand. The deeper the commitment to God the greater is the freedom.

This perhaps provides us with a basis from which to unravel a perennial problem of theology, namely the question of *freedom and grace*. There can be no doubt that the Christian is free because he himself has taken the decision to commit himself to God. Or, to put it quite simply, because he believes. But the effect of this *decision* is nothing else than to *accept* something: the gift of a life and a hope which man cannot bestow upon himself. The *decision* is a grateful *response* to an invitation. The connexion between the two is similar to that which exists between freedom and binding commitment. The decision is *at the same time* an act of God and an act of man. If it were not a decision it could not come to be a gift, a grace. If it were not a gift then by his decision man would have committed himself to nothing.

Whereas the Reformation theologians in their teaching turn their attention first and foremost to the free gift and the grace of God's action upon man, Catholic teachers concentrate more strongly upon the free and responsible action of man himself. We should not underestimate the contrast. But we can say that the only way in which the two points of view can become mutually exclusive is for us so to interpret the relationship between God and man that what man does is no longer the action of God and *vice versa*. In reality, however, two interconnected situations are involved here, each of which demands the other as its complement: the free act of man is at the same time a gift of God's grace.

The further question of *how* man's decision to commit his life to God is achieved is in its turn a special question in itself. As a rule it is achieved not in a single isolated act, or so to say at one blow, but in a lifelong process of growth, of "exercise" in the good, and at the same time of failures and fresh beginnings.

21   Faith and love II: Selected questions

In this book we cannot attempt any comprehensive ethical system for believers covering all the problems involved. In view of the immense ethical problems with which we are confronted by the age we live in, anyone attempting such a thing within the space of the few pages at our disposal here would make himself a laughing stock. The six selected questions which follow, therefore, are not intended in any sense as a miniature manual of ethics. Their purpose is, rather, to *illustrate* by means of a few concrete examples how a Christian is to discover ethical standards and arrive at ethical decisions in the light of the foregoing considerations of the principles involved. In the examples chosen we shall be attempting to grapple with contemporary problems. But the selection is not based on any prior judgment as to whether these represent the most urgent ethical problems. A factor which has influenced our selection far more is the question of whether a given problem can so be discussed within the space of a few pages that we do not fall into the error of a crude oversimplification. Anyone, therefore, who, as he may, finds something missing in the pages which follow is invited to test them precisely from this point of view, and to see whether it is in any sense possible to present them wholly adequately within the limits imposed here. Conversely, anyone who has understood the way in which we are attempting to answer ethical questions in what follows will no longer be devoid of assistance in tackling other ethical problems.

I. RELIGIOUS FREEDOM AND TOLERANCE

"We should try to overcome the heretic with writings, and not with fire." So Luther wrote in 1520 (*To the Christian Nobility of the German Nation*, Weimar Edition, VI, 455, 21). At the time this was written it constituted a quite revolutionary idea.

From intolerance to tolerance

The demand that other communities of believers and "confessions" should be tolerated was, in fact, first raised only after these various communities of believers were already in existence within one and the same political federation. Moreover the circumstances in which it was raised were such that any hope of religious and ecclesiastical unity had by then come to be abandoned – in other words it was in the period following the sixteenth century. In the Middle Ages ideas were quite different. The way to faith is indeed a matter of the heart's own free decision. But once anyone has embraced the faith he can no longer abandon it without guilt. If he persists in doing so, then he should be treated like someone who has become deranged or sick and forced to return to that which constitutes his own personal salvation. This explains why the theologians of the Middle Ages showed tolerance – at least in theory – towards Jews and heathens, and did not wish to see any compulsion brought to bear upon them to embrace the faith. Apostates and heretics, on the other hand, were to be "brought back" by means of threats and the application of physical punishments. As late as the later Middle Ages the opinion was still being upheld that the threat of external penalties could effectively bring about inner conversion. In medieval society the "heretic" occupied a precarious position outside the law, or at any rate his rights were diminished. Not infrequently these conditions were also imposed on those who were not heretics at all. If one man wanted to drive another out of society he needed only to brand him as a heretic. It was attitudes of this kind that gave birth to the spirit and practice of the Inquisition, lasting right down to the period of the Counter-Reformation following upon the council of Trent (1545–63).

This also applies to the initial stages of the Reformation movement. As the Reformers saw it, the state was obliged to accord full civic rights only to those Christians who were orthodox believers in their creed, while against the adherents of any other faith it should actually bring means of compulsion to bear in appropriate cases. As time went on, however, such ideas became increasingly a dead letter. The principle expressed in the religious peace of Augsburg in 1555 was "A man must have the religion of the land he lives in" (*Cujus regio ejus religio*). And this marks the beginning of religious tolerance. The maintaining of a single creed is now restricted to the particular land, the particular free city, and it is the ruler or the appropriate authorities who decide which creed the citizens are to follow. But at the same time the empire as a whole "tolerates" a plurality of confessions within the single confederation of states. It is a tolerance born of necessity, a question of putting up with an evil that cannot be avoided.

What this leads to can be foreseen. At first the prince of a given state "tolerates" believers belonging to other confessions besides his own within his territory. In the end the state becomes religiously neutral, "secularist", and guarantees its citizens full freedom of religious practice in accordance with the classic formula of King Frederick II of Prussia (1740–86): "In my state everyone shall be blessed according to his own way." Today we are at last standing at the end of this long process of development.

Tolerance and religious freedom

The necessity of "putting up with" an evil that could not be avoided finally came to be transformed into a demand for *positive* tolerance, an attitude of due regard for the religious convictions of others. Freedom of religion is part of freedom of conscience. Convictions of faith are binding in conscience. Just as a man should not be forced to act against his conscience, so too he should not be prevented from living by, and acting according to his religious beliefs in private and in public. On the same principle each individual is entitled publicly to stand up for these beliefs, and to attempt to win others over to them. He is entitled to conduct a "mission". The demand that they should recognize the principle of religious freedom has not always seemed easy to Christians, especially in those cases in which they represent the majority of the society or population of the particular state concerned. Nevertheless the Catholic church too has, in the course of time, come unambiguously to express her assent to this principle in the *Decree on Religious Freedom* of the second Vatican council. Christian believers are indeed convinced that God has revealed himself in Jesus Christ in a unique manner and one which is binding upon the entire world. But this faith must be accepted in freedom. The opposite course would be in contradiction alike to the nature of faith and to the dignity of the human person. To demand religious freedom, therefore, means something more than merely seeking to "put up with an evil". Freedom of religion, like freedom of conscience, of which it constitutes a part, is a basic right of the human person. The individual may be in error. Others may be quite certain that he is so. Nevertheless the only course which does justice to his dignity as a person is not to prevent him from following the convictions of his own faith. Whenever the churches preach religious freedom as a basic right they are entering upon a new and more mature stage in their history, and leaving the Middle Ages behind them. But when the opinion is put forward that the duty of the churches is merely to act as a guardian to the believer and protect his faith from factors which threaten it, the effect is to arrest the Christian at the childhood stage of his faith. Once the principle of a universal right to religious freedom is established it is not merely the state that gains an increase in internal peace, but the Church too which gains an increase in maturity of faith from this fact.

Truth and tolerance

If the *state and society* guarantee religious freedom this does not mean that *the individual and the Church* are absolved from the responsibility of seeking for the truth. On the contrary, religious freedom is precisely the full freedom to seek for the truth. Some might interpret tolerance as an attitude towards the strivings of the human spirit for truth in which in principle all views are considered equally valid as containing an equal admixture of right and wrong. But to hold this would be to misunderstand the idea of tolerance. Such misunderstanding may be natural. It is born of that despair which arises from the innumerable failures of Christians in their attempt convincingly to establish and to live by the truth. And yet the logical outcome of a "tolerance" of this kind, which accords the same validity to all, would be to require of the Christian that he should cease to be a Christian at all. It is no intolerance on the Christian's part if he rejects such a demand. It is intolerance to demand a "tolerance" of this kind from him. True tolerance seeks to ensure that men shall be free to accept faith and preserve it. But it does not seek to prejudge the issue of what the truth which is believed in should be, or even of whether there is any such truth at all.

True tolerance, then, excludes any attitude of disputatiousness or desire to dominate, or any self-conceit on the part of those who "have" the faith. True tolerance actually makes them ready, conscious as they are of the imperfect nature of their own knowledge (cf 1 Cor 13: 12), to discern the marks of Christ even in other communities of believers, Christian and non-Christian alike, or even among declared critics of the Christian faith. In view of the process by which the world is growing together into "one world", Christians certainly have much still to learn on this point.

Like any basic right, the right of religious freedom too has its boundaries, boundaries that are defined by the freedom of our fellow men. Religious freedom should not endanger peace within the community or between nations, and should not fail to respect the principles of justice and humanity. Anyone who, under the cloak of "religious freedom", still violates these principles must be prevented in accordance with *the very same* principle of "religious freedom" which he is professing. It is easy to recognize all this in general terms. Problems arise when we come to the concrete particular case. Nobody, for instance, finds it difficult to see that human sacrifices can never be permitted in the name of religious freedom. But what is the situation with regard to modern cults of witchcraft and other kinds of superstition? Should society, the state, and the Church "tolerate" these?

II. TRUTH AND TRUTHFULNESS

"You shall not bear false witness against your neighbour." So runs the eighth commandment of the decalogue (Ex 20: 16; Deut 5: 20). "Let what you say be simply Yes or No; anything more than this comes from evil," says Jesus in the Sermon on the Mount (Mt 5: 37). And he uses the words of the prophets to criticize his own critics: "This people honours me with their lips but their heart is far from me" (Mk 7: 6; cp Is 29: 13). Truthfulness before the courts, truthfulness of speech in general, truthfulness in one's deeds – three witnesses from the Bible to God's demand for truthfulness. God does not lead men into deception. Hence among men too truth must prevail. The Church has to preach this requirement of God to all men.

Truthfulness in speech and in action

But not only the Church. The requirement that what we say must be true, and that our actions must be in accordance with the truth because the opposite of this, namely hypocrisy, would simply be a lie without words, is so rudimentary and so evident that no one needs any special revelation to be able to recognize it. Truthfulness of speech and action is the necessary prior condition for trust between man and man, and only when men trust one another can they live together in peace.

Thus the prohibition of speaking untruths is found not only in the Ten Commandments of the Old Testament, but also, for instance, among those five chief commandments which constitute a popular summary of the ethics of Buddhism. In the New Testament the requirement of truthfulness is regarded as obvious from the outset. At no point is it found necessary to set forth the grounds for it. It is simply insisted upon. "Putting away falsehood, let everyone speak the truth with his neighbour, for we are members one of another" (Eph 4: 25). Now if we look for some more profound basis, over and above the requirements of community life among men referred to here, we may notice that the authors of the New Testament seem to discern a deep correspondence between the action of God in Jesus Christ on the one hand, and human truthfulness on the other. For Paul the preaching of the gospel is the "word of truth" (Col 1: 5). According to John, Jesus himself calls himself "the Truth" (Jn 14: 6) and characterizes the devil as the father of lies (8: 44). Anyone, therefore, who lies and lives by lying has for his father not God but the adversary of God. To the extent that we can discover anything about the "character" of Jesus from the gospels, not the least outstanding of the distinguishing traits which men saw in him seems to have been intrepid truthfulness. With him outward presentation and inward attitudes, words and thoughts, actions and "disposition" are one and the same, and continue to be so even at the cost of mortal danger to himself. We may recall the impression of his disputes with the scribes and the authorities of the Jewish faith.

All this is so clear that any elaborate justifications of it could only be boring. Problems first arise when we ask whether and where truthfulness has its limits. Or, to formulate it more precisely, whether life (especially in the complicated social structures of our own age) gives rise to situations in which considerations precisely of love and trust among men make it necessary to separate our outward presentation from our inner attitudes, our words from our thoughts, our actions from our dispositions.

The limits of truthfulness as a duty

To begin with the simplest point: what we say must be true. But we neither can nor should say everything which is true and which we know in all circumstances or at all times. An initial limit to the duty of truthfulness is imposed by the state of receptivity of the person to whom we are speaking. If for one reason or another his receptivity is only a limited one it may be desirable to cloak our words and speak to him indirectly and in images, or at any rate not to tell him everything or to descend to the most precise detail. One simple example is the instruction of children in questions of religion or the origins of life. Everyone regards it as obvious that we have to use images and figurative descriptions here, which are suitable to the child's own powers of understanding. And we may see whether such ways of speaking to them constitute truth or lying by asking ourselves whether the answers we give to them lead to error, so that they will subsequently have to be withdrawn, or whether they are the sort of answers that are open to further expansion or deepening when the children are ready to accept the full truth of the matter. Thus in response to a child's inquiry of where human life comes from we may reply with the fairy tale about the stork. This is a lie. But an alternative reply might be that God forms the child under the heart of the mother. This is a true answer but one that is open to further filling out, even though the further question of whether it is still the most effective answer from the point of view of sex instruction for children still always remains open to dispute.

In the case of a child this is a simple and obvious state of affairs. But in politics there are many occasions on which what is essentially the same state of affairs calls for the highest skill, and necessarily must do so. Since words are deeds (Wittgenstein), in other words since they have effects which may be either welcome or unwelcome to the speaker, and since on this account they must be well weighed, it very often happens in the case of a politician that the words he utters must be both true, and at the same time so open that, according to the effect they produce in any given case, they can be expanded, interpreted, rendered more precise, or, on occasion, even withdrawn, without thereby incurring the accusation of lying.

How often it happens that a politician can only indicate! How often he has to "send up a balloon", and on the other hand how often too his armoury includes the specially sharp-edged weapons of polemics! Then too truthfulness becomes a matter of great skill when it comes to choosing one's words. In many cases the borderline is not very clear between veiling one's words, using subtlety, or a kind of honesty which is calculated rather than spontaneous on the one hand, and actual lying on the other. But the one point which is beyond dispute is that in such cases, and in the sense we have indicated, there are limits to the duty of telling the truth.

The same point can be established by a consideration of what the opposite course leads to. An exaggeratedly literal adherence to the facts *can* actually lead to misrepresentation. If we present facts or statements out of context, then even though our words are true to the realities of the case, still, unless we provide some further comments, they may nevertheless give rise to a false picture of those realities. A quotation from literature, a press notice, an extract from an interview, can lie even though every word is correct. Incidentally one actual example of such lying through "faithfulness to the realities" is pornography. It is, in fact, more a matter for the eighth than the sixth commandment. The details of the human body as represented in pornography are true. But it falsifies the truth about human sexuality because it refuses to concern itself in any way with the connexion between this and the human person as a whole. And incidentally it is this that constitutes the difference between pornography and a representation of the human body (even in photography) which is genuinely artistic.

Words are only truthful, therefore, when they have due regard for the whole context in which they are uttered: the powers of understanding and the probable reactions of the hearers, and the connexions between the matter being spoken of and other matters. We reach the limits of this duty to conform our words to the truth, to be faithful to the real facts, at that point at which to do so would, having due regard to all the circumstances referred to, do harm. For to go beyond these limits would, in the end, lead to a situation in which there was no longer any faithfulness to the real facts at all, and this would contribute not to trust or peace, but to mistrust and disharmony.

Conflicts of duty in relation to the truth

Sometimes we come across the idea that a lie is only a lie and only forbidden in those cases in which it harms our fellow man. Anyone entertaining this idea will certainly agree with the following two quotations: "To tell a lie for charity, to save a man's life, the life of a friend, of a husband . . . hath not only been done at all times, but commended by great and wise and good men. Who would not save his father's life, at the charge of a harmless lie, from persecutors or tyrants?" (Jeremy Taylor, quoted by Newman). And: "What man in his senses would deny, that there are those whom we have the best grounds for considering that we ought to deceive – as boys, madmen, the

sick, the intoxicated, enemies, men in error, thieves? I would
ask, by which of the commandments is a lie forbidden? You
will say, by the ninth. If then my lie does not injure my neighbour, certainly it is not forbidden by this commandment."
(Milton, quoted by Newman.)

A Christian will have his reservations here. So long as we
maintain any connexion between the Gospel as the "word of
truth" on the one hand, and human truthfulness on the other,
we shall be unable to confine our judgment on this kind of lie
merely to the aspect of whether it helps or harms others. At
the same time both passages are justified in pointing out that
conflicts can arise in matters of truthfulness to which no easy
solution can be found, and in which, on the contrary, one duty
conflicts with another. The classic cases are familiar to us. The
duty of being truthful can come into conflict with the duty of
keeping a secret, of protecting the basic personal rights or the
privacy of others, of shielding the innocent from persecution
at the hands of the unjust or of an unjust state acting in contempt of the rights and freedom of action of the individual.
Such a state may, for example, make listening to foreign
broadcasts a crime and attach disproportionately severe penalties to it. It may require us to betray our relatives and friends
or seek to extract damaging information against a third party
from us. Often in such cases mere silence or evasive answers
are too insecure or are quite impossible. The only way of
guaranteeing the necessary protection for the party in danger
is by means of direct falsehoods with the deliberate purpose of
deceiving the inquirer.

In such cases anyone who, while maintaining his basic love
of truth, and with the utmost conscientiousness, uses a false
statement as his tool, could hardly be regarded as breaking
the commandment of truthfulness. By way of justification we
can begin by pointing to the fact that the individual in this
situation has chosen the lesser of two evils, the choice between
which was forced upon him, and that his choice at this
moment was in accordance with the dictates of love, of justice,
and of peace.

Perhaps we may go still further. It may reasonably be asked

whether one who makes unjust inquiries or makes them for unjust purposes has any right to an answer in accordance with the truth. In such cases the false statement amounts to a form of self-defence against the threat which the unjust inquiry represents. The purpose of the false statement is not to deceive or to undermine trust but quite the contrary. This in no sense represents a compromise with the notorious saying, "the end justifies the means". The question is not whether an individual can lie in order to do good, but whether that individual can and must do something good – namely speak the truth – when it will be used to promote evil. The principle which states that our words must be in conformity with our knowledge is no merely formal law without regard to the effects of this, any more than the weighing of benefits to others against probable injuries constitutes the sole grounds for the prohibition of lying.

Truth at the sick-bed

A special case of the conflict between truthfulness and other duties arises when we are dealing with someone who is gravely ill or even destined to die. The question then arises whether, and at what point, we should tell him of the seriousness of his state, or alternatively whether we should withhold and conceal this information. In principle there can be no question here of the right of the sick man to the truth. In accordance with what we have already said it is the ability of the patient himself to receive it that establishes where the limits of truthfulness lie. Sometimes the relatives, hospital staff, and doctors shield a sick man from knowledge of his true condition, or only reveal it to him very gradually, in order to avoid weakening his will to live or to bring him to come to terms with his condition in a human way by carefully calculating how much to tell him of it at any one time. And in all this there is nothing to object to seeing that it is in conformity with a wise and prudent love.

It becomes problematical when even the best will to live can no longer contribute anything to the recovery of health, when death is certain. Should we allow a man, possibly despite his expressly asking for the truth, to die, so to say, unawares? Should we expect so much of him that we make him recognize the truth of his condition only at a stage when he is bereft of outside help? Should we thereby deprive the sick man of the chance of turning his death into a human act, and so simply let him end his life like any non-human creature?

The questions are all the more serious in view of the fact that what is in question here is (so there is reason to suspect) not so much the problems of the sick man himself as the problems of those about him. Are we helpless in the face of death? Do we shrink from letting the sick man have the remainder of his days, letting him accept what is his own and helping him to die? At all events, anyone who upholds the policy of silence towards one who is mortally sick must ask himself in all sincerity whether his true motives are not along these lines. The most recent medical and psychological researches have shown that communication with, and help for, the dying are perfectly possible. The Christian, able as he is to create from Jesus' own rising from the dead a hope that transcends all death, is the very last who should be silent at the sick-bed from motives of a false kind of consideration for the sick person.

III. SEXUALITY AND MARRIAGE

Man and woman

Right from the outset the Christian faith must reject as false any kind of individualistic understanding of man and his relationships with his fellow men. This also applies to the Christian understanding of the relations between man and woman. In the second (earlier) creation narrative, that of the so-called Yahwist (Gen 2: 4 ff), the man, whom God addresses, finds in woman a partner, a human Thou to be his helpmeet in life. For the author of the first (later) creation narrative (Gen 1: 1 ff), man and woman taken together constitute "man" (Gen 1: 27). According to the evidence of the Bible here, which the

Christian faith upholds without reserve, man and woman are permanently orientated to one another, and can fulfil the task for which God has created mankind only by sharing their lives and in partnership with one another. This also applies in a quite uncompromising sense to the single man or the single woman.

It is true that anyone who seeks to hearken to the whole of the witness of the Bible concerning man and woman cannot leave out of consideration the message contained in the ensuing chapters of Genesis. The narrative of the Fall shows how, when man turns away from God, this does not leave the relationship between himself and woman unaffected. On the contrary, the alienation between men, the destruction of the state of partnership, finally degenerating into envy, violence and fratricide – all this stems originally from the damage done to the relationship between man and woman. Both forfeit their paradisal freedom and lack of constraint. They are made to live their lives out in an earth filled with thorns and thistles, each concerned merely with his own troubles. And a further factor which has its source in sin is the man's unwillingness to take responsibility for his own personal guilt, his attempts to shift the blame on to his partner, finally even on to God: "The woman whom thou gavest to be with me, she gave me fruit of the tree and I ate" (Gen 3: 12). As with sin in general, so in a special way here, the alienation between man and woman develops into the crimes of adultery, rape, incest, sodomy, homosexuality and prostitution. "They are an abomination to the Lord" (Dt 22: 21 ff).

As we have already said, we cannot read too much into the narrative of the Fall. It does not suggest that human labour is merely a curse and a consequence of sin any more than it encourages us, for instance, to regard the pangs of motherhood as a decree of divine punishment such that we may not take any measures to mitigate it. Married women who are Christians may try to make the process of giving birth as free of pain as possible by means of pain-killing drugs or anaesthetics. And in doing so they are in no sense offending against their faith. What the biblical author has in view is the trials and sufferings of man and woman in their lives together as he saw it *at the time when he wrote,* and it is this that he has ingenuously associated with the fact of guilt and sin, and God's resistance to sin.

It is true that the basic truth of sin retains its force for Christians in this context too, and to say anything else would be unrealistic, an illusion. Faith's view of the relationship between man and woman must always include both these extremes at the same time. Men and women are the creation of God and good, and it is only in union with one another that they constitute "man" in the full sense. At the same time the power of sin threatens to bring their relationship to a profound crisis even though God has forgiven us for it, and continues to forgive us again and again. For despite this, sin is still a reality in this world and this age, and continues to exercise its power. Faith must pay heed to both factors in inquiring into the ethical consequences for the relationship between man and woman.

The equality of the sexes

On reading the first pages of the Bible we receive the impression that the according of equal rights to man and woman, not only in God's sight but also in the life "society", is much clearer here than in many passages in the New Testament (cp eg, Gen 1: 26–30, 2: 18–25 with 1 Cor 11: 3–9; Eph 5: 22–4; Col 3: 18; 1 Cor 14: 34 ff). Here, too, as so often elsewhere, the social relationships which the biblical author takes for granted have found their way into the written text. It is true that on a really full examination all obscurities disappear. In that same eleventh chapter of 1 Corinthians in which Paul speaks in so "patriarchal" a manner he continues: "Nevertheless in the Lord woman is not different from man nor man from woman. For as woman was made from man, so man is now born of woman. And all things are from God" (1 Cor 11: 11 f). In other passages Paul expresses the matter in still more radical terms, and regards the difference between the sexes as abolished just as much as the differences between nationalities and classes. "There is neither Jew nor Greek, there is neither slave nor free, there is neither male nor female, for you are all one in Christ Jesus (Gal 3: 27 ff). In accordance with this he makes no distinction between the sexes in giving honour to the body, in which sex finds expression. "Your body is a temple of the Holy Spirit within you, which you have from God. You are not your own. You were bought with a price, so glorify God in your body" (1 Cor 6: 19 ff).

In such passages we are simply hearing an echo of what Jesus himself has laid down in word and deed. When he calls all men to the love of God, Jesus sharply calls to account those who would erect barriers of discrimination, whether national, social, or religious, between themselves and the rest of men. He points to the sins from which no one is free, and thereby enters into judgment with those who self-righteously claim to be above their fellows, and accuses them of hypocrisy. It is wholly in harmony with this that he rejects any discrimination against women and rejects the privileges accorded to the husband in the process of divorce as he found it being practised. Since God has bound them both, neither should separate from the other, the husband from the wife any more than the wife from the husband. "What God has joined together let not man put asunder. . . . Whoever divorces his wife and marries another commits adultery against her; and if she divorces her husband and marries another she commits adultery" (Mk 10: 9–12).

Sexuality and love

With regard to the concrete ethical questions of human sexuality with which we are confronted in our modern world, we can learn virtually nothing about these from Sacred Scripture. Here too we find one further indication of the fact that the Bible is not a manual of moral theology. This does not mean, however, that faith has no standards to bring to bear on the sexual life of mankind on the basis of its own message. Like the life of the Christian in general, this particular department of his life is subject to the law of that selfless love which was exemplified in the life of the Lord himself, and which faith gives us the freedom to live in our turn. Sexuality as such, and even in itself, gives man an orientation beyond himself to an encounter with the Thou. Sexuality, however, is not in some sense a mere part of man. On the contrary, sexuality is a specification of the whole man. This fact alone makes it clear that what human sexuality is essentially concerned with is not merely certain physical functions of man, but rather his very status as a person.

Even in itself, and quite without reference to faith, therefore, we are justified in saying that human sexuality is designed to liberate man from a mere self-orientated striving, and to bring him to a deeper self-realization and maturity in his encounter with another. Christian faith does not add anything new to this whatever. All that it does is to impart to the believer the greatest conceivable motivation to find himself in losing himself by committing himself to another. This is the freedom of the children of God, which is a freedom to commit oneself to love. From this, two compelling consequences can be deduced: it is inadequate to say that the sole function of the sexual instinct is to contribute to the maintenance of the species. It is likewise inadequate to exercise the function of human sexuality merely for purposes of physical pleasure. The powers of human sexuality extend beyond their functions, their "purposes", even the supreme purpose of maintaining and propagating human life on the earth. The contrary position could be maintained only if human sexuality were merely one special quality of man, instead of being an integral part of his very being.

Any purely egocentric exercise of sex merely for the fulfilment of lust likewise contradicts that love to which sexuality itself offers an opportunity of fulfilment, and freedom for which is bestowed by faith. Sexual desire as such certainly does not, of itself, constitute egotism. It belongs integrally to the sexual encounter, and the couple involved should lead one another to it and expect it of one another. At the same time, however, there is a kind of sexual activity which reduces the partner to the status of an object for satisfying one's own needs, and reduces the sexual encounter to a means of enjoyment. The effect of this is to impart a shallowness and lack of meaning to human sexuality, and it can ultimately lead to a brutalizing of the sexual act. Faith, therefore, can only emphasize and, from its own point of view, insist upon a truth which medicine, psychology, and philosophy too have recognized: human sexuality needs to be shaped, guided, "humanized" and even "redeemed" by the personality if it is not to remain a purely biological activity and response at a "sub-human" level.

Nowadays the idea of a "separation of sexuality and love" has become a much discussed slogan. So long as this is taken to signify an ethical programme, a Christian can find nothing to agree with in it. Certainly sexuality and love are in no sense identical, as we have just shown. Again it can perfectly well be the case that even though an individual is capable of loving and ready for it, he is sick and deviant in his sexuality. In such a case an "isolated" medical or psychological treatment of his sexual attitudes may, under certain circumstances, become necessary. Nor need one feel constraint or be afraid of coming into conflict with ethical principles if it subsequently turns out, merely in the case of this or that individual, that in practice his way of breaking through the sexual inhibitions occasioned by his upbringing, and thereby of finding his way to sexual maturity and above all to a capacity for real loving, has been through a temporary period of sexual promiscuity. All this is something quite different from laying down as a matter of principle that sexuality and love have nothing to do with one another, and can or should actually be taken as separate and practised in isolation from one another. What is sexuality precisely as *human* sexuality if it remains at most at the level of a party game, and any permeation or shaping of it by personal love is excluded?

For the same reason the Christian will also find it impossible to give adequate expression to his total attitude towards sex in the axiom "Thou shalt never hurt the feelings of the other party". Love, which has the *person* of the other in view, and not merely his body, his charm, or his erotic attractiveness, seeks to do something more than merely to avoid inflicting any harm upon him or hurting his feelings in any way. A lover intends to make his personal happiness dependent on making his partner happy, and obviously *this* also constitutes a motive for never hurting the feelings of his partner.

The chief sign that a sexual relationship really has become an expression of personal love is that the two partners are prepared to take over responsibility for one another and, in appropriate cases, for the new life that they are awaiting. The readiness to do this distinguishes their whole sexual behaviour very clearly from other forms of sexual activity which do not entail any such readiness to take responsibility. They induce a critical attitude towards many questionable examples to which the term "love" is attached, and which are loudly proclaimed to be such nowadays. Again this outlook induces an attitude of uprightness and genuineness in the sexual relationship and prevents either party from imposing upon the other in any way, arousing false expectations, or making questionable protestations. It makes love independent of the fashionable trends or the spirit of the age, because it has grasped the real content of the term "love" at too deep a level for it to need any kind of instruction from such fashionable trends or from the spirit of the age.

Love and marriage

Now that we have come so far it takes only one short step further for us to see that the individual has only genuinely assumed responsibility in the sexual relationship when he or she has taken it for good. Without such a commitment and lasting responsibility the giving of himself becomes all too easily either a lie or a yielding to degradation. Hence when we say that the giving of oneself in sex, if it is to achieve its full significance, involves a commitment to the married state as its prior condition, this is no useless survival from an out-of-date morality, but simply a logical conclusion based upon the nature of the case. This should not be taken to imply that marriage in the human, and also in the Christian, sense invariably and in all cases begins only with the ecclesiastical or civil "legal enactment" of marriage. Even within the Church, to say nothing of secular society, the juridical forms and juridical consequences of the formal and public marriage ceremony have undergone too many changes for us to be able simply to identify the human reality of marriage with this formal marriage ceremony as governed by regulations which may be more or less accidental, and perhaps too more or less reasonable. On the other hand, in virtue of the very faith which he holds, the Christian is least of all in any position to reduce marriage to a purely private affair between two individuals.

The Christian has views of his own, sometimes contrary to the spirit of the age with regard to love and marriage, and he attaches significance to the practice of announcing marriages publicly. And it is precisely for this reason that if there were no public and juridical form of marriage, and no way of publicly recognizing marriage as an institution at the juridical level by society and by the Church, that he would actually have to devise such public and juridical forms.

Besides, the situation which we meet with in this question is similar to that which we have already observed in considering the question of the meaning of law in a Christian's life. Certainly as a Christian sees it, the sole and exclusive ground for marriage is the personal love between man and woman, and his faith tells him that such marriage is not only based on human assent, but is supported by God's love and faithfulness in Jesus Christ. Yet here too it is only in rare cases that married people constitute heroic examples of the mature freedom of a Christian man. The public announcement of the commitment to the married state in the presence of society and of the community of believers actually provides the married people themselves with a certain security, a protection from the fickleness of the emotions. We do not so lightly withdraw a public act of assent as one which has been made only in the presence of two individuals.

An additional point is that the Christian will regard his marriage and the attitude of readiness to found a family as a matter of importance within the community of believers as well. If it is true that the essence of Christian conduct consists in acting towards one's fellow men as God has acted towards us, then marriage constitutes the primary and supremely important instance of this. We might say that the task of a Christian marriage is for the married partners to transform themselves and their families into the incarnate love of God. In this the married partners are doing on a small scale exactly what the Church as a whole is doing on the large and world-wide scale. Both proclaim the fact that God loves the world and has accepted it, and both attempt to make this clear in their deeds and to cause the reality of Redemption to become actual. This is precisely the reason why the Catholic (and likewise the Orthodox) church regards marriage as a "sacrament". The Protestant churches tend to reject this doctrine, but not because they would dispute the points briefly outlined here; rather it is because they have a somewhat different concept of "sacrament", and one which does not apply to marriage.

And what does it mean when men fail to make love and responsibility real in their sexual relationships, but simply yield themselves up to the explosive force of their instincts? We should not shrink from the radical conclusion that such conduct remains beneath the level which man is capable of attaining to, and which he is called to attain to. Nor should we lightly dismiss the danger that such conduct, once it becomes a custom that is taken for granted, prevents man from arriving at personal maturity, firmness of character, and a capacity for love that is genuine and fully human.

There is always something pitiful in an uncommitted sexual relationship, yet we should neither over-dramatize the particular failing nor ever be too ready to take the judgment-seat and condemn those concerned. Precisely in these times the reasons for such conduct can be so manifold that they make it totally impossible – at least for an outsider – to distinguish between what is culpable and inculpable. It may be that hereditary factors are partially responsible, or simply what we are nowadays accustomed to call "damage from the social environment". Or perhaps on both sides there may be a reaction against overwhelming stresses at work. Or it may be that the individuals involved are in despair and looking for escape from a threatened atrophy of their emotional life in the modern technical world. Or alternatively the whole thing is simply a transition stage on the way to maturity, a fumbling attempt on the part of a subject who is not yet sure of his own sexuality. If serious medical and psychological research, as distinct from any cheap magazine stories, regards such explanations as possible in modern times, we in the Church should be open-minded enough to take due cognizance of their findings and not to judge our fellows by the principle that what should not be cannot be. But it would help no one, and only damage the individual himself, if, as the outcome of all this, the Christian were no longer bold enough to say what he has to say with regard to sexuality and love on the basis of his faith in God the creator and redeemer, namely that the only way in which a sexual partnership can attain to the full heights of human behaviour of which it is capable is for it to have marriage as its goal; the will, that is to say, to enter upon an exclusive, lifelong and fully human partnership of love.

Responsible parenthood and birth control

In marriage man and woman are called by God to parenthood and thereby to a sharing in his creative work (Gen 1: 28). As a consequence of this it has long been assumed that the proper and primary goal of marriage is the propagation of the human race, and that any marriage act not undertaken with this end in view is sinful. Neither in the Catholic nor in the Protestant churches is this idea still maintained in the form described. We see marriage primarily as a union between man and woman in virtue of which they become "one flesh" (2: 24), and only as thus united constitute "man" (cp Gen 1: 27). It is not biological propagation as such, but rather that opening of love to new human life which nips in the bud any "egoism as a couple" that constitutes the deepest, innermost meaning of parenthood. No married couple can buy their way out of this love.

But surely there can be serious reasons, under certain concrete circumstances, for restricting the generation of new life, or even avoiding it altogether.

If, therefore, we say nowadays that the decision as to the number of children should be left to the conscience of the parents, this does not mean that they should exclude children for motives of pure egoism or for material considerations (avoiding disturbance in the home, lasting responsibilities, restrictions of living standards, and so forth). In view of the increasing hostility to children in our society, we should actually be insisting on this point almost more, nowadays, than on family planning as a right and a necessity.

But there are genuine grounds of conscience for restricting the number of children, and in some instances even for totally excluding them, which have nothing to do with an egoistical or unchristian refusal to have children. It can be the case that the health of the parents, and especially of the mother, is not equal (any longer) to the task of bringing up children or perhaps even of giving birth to them. The financial and social conditions may be too wretched to admit of any healthy upbringing for children. The cost of providing the necessary living space may be exorbitant. Today we should even go so far as to ask whether certain specific callings practised by the parents may not represent a serious danger to the bringing up of children, for instance if they entail an exceptional amount of travelling, frequent changes of home, or temporary family separations. Responsible parenthood implies that before deciding to have a child the parents will weigh up these factors carefully. Again younger married people can and must take due account of these considerations from the outset, and not wait until they have already had as many children as they can cope with. These are reasons for a responsible planning of the births of children at the personal and family level.

But nowadays we cannot escape from recognizing certain additional reasons at the political level, and in view of the population figures. Nowadays it has come to be recognized as an assured fact that mankind is heading for a catastrophe unless the population explosion can be arrested. Some like to lay the blame for this chiefly at the door of medical progress, the fall in infant mortality, or the increasing expectation of life. But this is hardly a tenable position. At most it has a statistical validity as applied to the world population taken as a whole. In reality the population figures rise most steeply precisely in the poor and, for the most part, under-developed countries. In Europe, on the other hand, it is precisely because of medical progress and a general knowledge of the uses of medicine on the part of the population that the initial increase in births has been slowed down, and in certain areas actually reversed, as for instance in Germany. However, on an overall view we have to reckon with a doubling of the world population within the next twenty-five years. Up to the present no one has been able to say with any precision where these millions of human beings are to live or how they are to be fed. Viewed in this perspective, the population explosion cannot be deprived of its force as an argument for regulating births merely by saying that it does not represent a threat to Western civilization.

We cannot, on the one hand, emphasize responsibility for the single human race and, on the other, seek to limit our considerations of the political and ethnographic aspects of family planning merely to the national level. A further question is whether it is justifiable to deduce from this that the state can prescribe and supervise measures of birth-control as part of its own function. In the political and social conditions of our society we must judge any such procedure as an unjustifiable intrusion on the state's part upon the privacy of its citizens. But in different political and social conditions it can be the case that a state may be directly threatened by the consequences of the population explosion, and have serious grounds for fearing a breakdown in food resources, health, or peace among its citizens, and then it must undertake a civic policy of birth-control as an extreme and temporary measure for as long as the level of education, the economic situation, and medical welfare do not hold out any prospect of the citizens acting independently and for themselves to achieve the necessary limitation of births. That would be in accordance with the so-called "subsidiary principle" according to which the state should only intervene in the lives of its citizens at a certain point, but then is actually obliged to do so – the point, namely at which the citizens themselves or the adult groups and associations among them are incapable of helping themselves in ways that are more effective. Such an intervention on the state's part, however, would be justified only provided that at the same time it were undertaking all possible measures in terms of the economy and the health and education services to render its own intervention superfluous as soon as possible.

Provided the grounds for restricting the number of children are justified and in conformity with love, the various methods of achieving this are in themselves of no particular ethical significance – apart from abortion and those methods which are designed to prevent the implanting of the fertilized ovum. The ethical value of the methods employed depends, rather, to a large extent on the attitude and experiences of the married partners themselves. If one partner finds a particular method distasteful, repellent, or offensive to their human dignity, then that method is immoral in that particular case, even though other married couples may not feel the same about it and for this reason are justified in using the same method for themselves.

In the Catholic church preference is officially given to the "rhythm" method, but circumstances are conceivable – and not *merely* conceivable – in which some method of actually preventing conception cannot be forbidden; in those cases, namely, in which the "rhythm" method is not sure enough, while at the same time it is absolutely imperative to avoid having a child (or any further children). If under such circumstances as these married people conscientiously decide to use some other method, no one should accuse them of "misusing their marriage". They are in no sense acting from mere caprice, but are rather shaping their course on the basis of an intelligent and conscientious evaluation of the benefits between which they have to decide. It is true that the encyclical

Humanae Vitae of Pope Paul VI, which appeared only in 1968, still rejects any such considerations, and lays down as a binding principle for the allowing or forbidding of contraceptive methods that the integrity of the marriage act at the biological and physiological level must be preserved. In spite of this, many Catholic theologians, pastors and married people themselves continue to stand by the chief objection which was put forward even before the encyclical was published, namely that to approach the question in this way is to deny the totally human character of the self-giving of the partners in marriage and to reduce it to a purely biological level. It is the aspect of the marriage act as an expression of love, rather, that in cases of conflict must take priority over the biological functions, and this makes contraceptive methods which derogate from the normal integrity of this act permissible in certain cases. In August, 1968, the Conference of Catholic German Bishops (and it was not alone) in a declaration encouraged those concerned to a conscientious continuation of the discussion in all its aspects, and exhorted them to pay due regard to the factor of the married people's own responsible decision in conscience on this question even when their practice was not in conformity with the encyclical. Other hierarchies throughout the world have made similar statements.

IV. BODY AND LIFE

Life: a high, but not the highest good

There is no civilization which does not attach a high value to human life at the physical level. It is true that the life of the individual is never regarded as a good in itself and in isolation, but always in the relation it bears to the lives of others, to the community, as well. Hence all civilizations (while they may differ in points of detail) recognize certain exceptions to the prohibition of taking human life. These exceptions range from killing in self-defence or killing in a "just war" to the exercise of the death penalty or killing someone who is grievously sick on grounds of compassion and sympathy. But abstracting from this, human life is universally recognized as sacred and is protected both by laws and also by religious convictions or taboos.

For the Christian, God is the ultimate origin of all life, and especially of human life. In the last analysis these are the grounds on which faith judges that human life is sacred and that man has no direct or absolute right of disposal over his own life or over the lives of other men.

At the same time, however, the Christian recognizes, still on the basis of his faith, that physical life is not man's highest good. For the Christian the highest good and the highest goal can only be the progressive unfolding of his relationship with God in faith and love, and his relationship with his fellow men in love and justice. All other values of human life are subordinated to this supreme goal and must contribute to its achievement. They have a "relative" value, and this means that they are related to the higher good which constitutes the absolute meaning of human life as a whole.

From this it follows that even the earthly and physical life of man cannot be his highest good. Situations can arise in which the meaning of human life as a whole can be fulfilled only by man laying down his physical life. Right from its origins Christian believers have regarded the voluntary laying down of physical life for the sake of one's beliefs or for the sake of the Christian creed as a supreme form of human consummation, and have venerated it as martyrdom, as *the* ultimate form of "witness". Yet there are other situations of this kind too which require, or at least justify, the laying down of one's physical life – chiefly those in which it constitutes a direct act of love, being done in order to save either one or several or many of one's fellow men. Thus for instance if a doctor risks his life in the service of the sick, or a railway official endangers his life in order to prevent a collision, or a pilot steers a crashing aeroplane away from houses at the risk of his life, and so on.

Have we any rights of disposal over our own lives?

There is no need to discuss the principles underlying the idea that no man, but God alone, can take it into his hands to decide how long the life of other men is to last. With regard to the situations indicated above, which were formerly regarded as exceptions, there is an increasing conviction nowadays that the death penalty is ethically indefensible. As for the question of whether it is permissible to kill in war, light is thrown on this by what the Christian has to say about war in general. Yet questions still arise even for the modern Christian with regard to certain problems which have emerged as a result of the progress of medical science.

The first problem has been given a distinctive label, "Death on demand". There can be two motives for this: first to cut short the pain of dying; we shall have something more to say about this below; the second motive is to make available at the cost of one's own life some vitally important organ which will save the life of another. The basic principle is clear. Anyone who believes in God as Lord over life and death must exercise control over his own life in such a way that it does not contradict the meaning and goal of that life, namely the consummation of love for God and the service of one's fellow men. Hence we can expose our own lives to danger from motives of love for others. But what we cannot justify is, for instance, for a healthy individual to ask someone else directly to end his own life in order that his heart can be transplanted into the body of another. For the healthy man cannot decide here and now that he has already reached the full realization of the meaning of his own life in love, and that therefore he can bring his own life to an end.

Protecting the life of the unborn child

The question of rightly evaluating conflicting goods has a special importance in the discussion of whether there should be any penal sanctions attached to abortion. What value does the human life of the unborn have compared with the just claims of a wife, a mother, or a family? Should the free assent of the mother to an abortion or the health of a child already born take priority over the right of a living being already conceived but not yet born to be born and to live? We must distinguish two questions here. The first is, should the state relax the statutory penalties hitherto attached to abortion, or should it leave them in force? The second question is, what judgment should a Christian arrive at on the basis of his faith with regard to the question of whether abortion is or is not ethically permissible?

Even if we hold that abortion is ethically unjustifiable we may still have good grounds for supporting a relaxation of the statutory penalties attached to it. The state – and above all the kind of state that is neutral on philosophical or religious questions – is a guardian not of morals but of peace, and it should foster the life of society as a whole so as to make it as fruitful as possible for all groups within it. Since, as experience shows, it cannot in practice eliminate abortions, the question arises of whether it is not the lesser evil to bring them under control as far as possible by legalizing them instead of leaving the women concerned – above all the poor and those who are in needy circumstances through no fault of their own – to the back-street abortionist. It would be well for Christians too to help actively in getting rid of the special social stigma attached to those who have had abortions. There are injustices and crimes which are far more abominable than having been brought by one's state of need to have an abortion. And yet society treats these other crimes more or less as though they were a mere sowing of wild oats.

A quite different question is whether the Christian can in principle regard abortion as permissible. The Christian churches have pronounced themselves unambiguously on this point. The second Vatican council declares: "For God, the Lord of life, has conferred on men the surpassing ministry of safeguarding life – a ministry which must be fulfilled in a manner which is worthy of man. Therefore from the moment of its conception life must be guarded with the greatest care, while abortion and infanticide are unspeakable crimes." (*Pastoral Constitution*, art. 51.)

Apart from those borderline cases in which a choice has to be made between the life of the mother and the life of the child ("medical grounds"), the Christian will find himself unable to agree to a termination of pregnancy in any other circumstances – in other words when it is undertaken on grounds of a state of social need ("social grounds") or when the child is expected to be injured in health ("eugenic grounds"), or when a rape has taken place ("ethical grounds or grounds of rape").

We do not wish to give the impression that we can dismiss the whole serious discussion of this problem in a few brief sentences. But let us concentrate upon only one important aspect. The question would perhaps be easier to solve if we knew exactly when human and personal life begins, whether it begins already at that point at which the ovum is fertilized by the sperm-cell or only when pregnancy begins, in other words once the fertilized ovum has been implanted. Or is it at a point a few days after this, when the individual life has been definitively established, or even a few weeks later with the development of the brain functions? These are points on which the medical specialists are far from agreeing with one another.

Hence all we can do in order to throw light on our ethical duty with regard to the unborn life is simply to take as our starting-point the fact that with fertilization a process is initiated which is highly probable to issue, without any further interventions, in an individual human life. It follows that man cannot have any power of disposal over this process, any more than he can over life itself. To this some like to rejoin that for a very long period in the past the Church was not so "hypersensitive" in her treatment of life that has already been born as she is today in her demands as to how the life of the unborn should be treated. But the logical consequence of this is not that we should permit abortion, but simply that we must examine our consciences with regard to how we have treated of the life of those already born.

Although the medical and biological findings do not provide us with an altogether clear picture as to when human life begins, still a point which *is* clear is that human life is something more than biological life. In rejecting abortion on moral grounds, therefore, we can avoid hypocrisy only when precisely as Christians who uphold this point of view we at the same time do everything to ensure that the human life brought into the world because of this position of ours is capable of being a *human* life in the true sense. In other words we must provide social assistance for children who are injured in health or unwanted. In general it is important to establish an atmosphere in which children are more welcomed than is generally the case in our society. Again we must eliminate any kind of discrimination against children born out of wedlock, whether in society or at work. Finally those who are involved: above all, therefore, the women who have to fear that they may one day be faced with the question of a possible abortion – must be suitably instructed as to the various possible methods of contraception. And what they need here is those methods of controlling conception which are absolutely sure, practicable for everyone, and not harmful to health.

Suicide and euthanasia

A clear distinction must be drawn between the laying down of one's own life on behalf of another and what has traditionally been called suicide. In the philosophy of the Stoa as well as among the Teutons and the Romans suicide was glorified as a courageous use of freedom – indeed as a sign of philosophical self-mastery. The early Church initially wavered as to whether it should be regarded as permissible for virgins to kill themselves in order to avoid being raped. But as early an authority as Augustine arrived at a radical rejection of any kind of suicide on the grounds that it is a form of murder. Since then the ending of one's own life on one's own authority has come unanimously to be condemned in the Church as immoral.

Today too we must abide by this condemnation to the

extent that we can in practice speak at all of a "self-*murder*" which is based on full knowledge and a free decision. Admittedly we of today are in a better position than those of earlier ages to realize how major a part psychological factors can play in a "self-murder" – to the extent, in fact, that we must often be in doubt as to how far responsibility and freedom really have entered into the act and have not rather been substantially diminished. The idea of "self-murder", therefore, is one which we should be cautious in applying because "murder", as distinct from "killing", implies the taking of a human life as the outcome of conscious design and free choice. Hence it is better to speak of "self-killing" ("suicide"). In the majority of cases it is the outcome of a "short circuit" in which the reason is temporarily by-passed, and it often takes place in a phase of deep depression. Not infrequently self-killing is also the individual's ultimate attempt to draw the attention of those about him to himself and his needs, or even to take revenge on his fellow men in that by his death they will be given a bad conscience for their neglect. Who will seek to judge or condemn in such cases?

Nevertheless, while the Christian can indeed bring understanding to bear and refrain from judging in such cases, he cannot recognize that there is any objective justification for suicide. Since it is hope in God's love that brings Christian faith to life, neither weariness of life nor frustration and despair are attitudes which can be reconciled with that faith. The believer never ceases to recognize the meaning of his own life and the lives of others in God, even in those cases in which, by any human standards, this life has become futile and has seemed to lose its meaning.

In its original significance the term "euthanasia" was taken to mean helping someone to die, namely by easing and cutting short the pains which a dying man has to suffer when death is certain. It is not to be condemned on moral grounds when the doctor or relatives of a dying man seek to erase his distress and pain by means of medicaments, and thereby actually make it possible for him to prepare himself while there is still time for a good death.

Today, however, the term "euthanasia" is generally used in a more restricted sense to signify the killing of a patient at his own request, or even the bringing to an end of a life which, so we are told, is "valueless". It is at this point that we overstep the bounds of what faith in God as Lord over life and death can recognize as justifiable. When a sick man asks for his own death at the hands of the doctor and with his assistance, this simply constitutes self-killing in another form. It is indirect suicide. This is something to which the Christian cannot assent.

Nevertheless in practice the question arises in a totally different form in the vast majority of cases. Nowadays modern medicine has opened up vast possibilities to us of prolonging the life of someone who is mortally sick far beyond the point at which any hope can still survive of being able to restore him to health and activity. In this situation the question confronting the doctor, hospital staff, and relatives is not "Should the doctor 'kill' the sick person in order to cut short his pain?", but, even in those cases in which it is possible, from a medical point of view, to apply the kind of treatment which prolongs his life, "Should the doctor do this once his treatment has become meaningless?" In practice this question is immensely complex because the borderline between artificially maintaining life and meaningless treatment is difficult to define. The decision as to whether treatment should be broken off always includes a certain risk of "indirect killing". Even a wrongly estimated dose of a pain-killing medicine can have the effect of an overdose and thereby hasten death. Just as it is impossible in these matters always to avoid mistakes in medical treatment, so too it is quite impossible that there should be one specific moment in any given case at which it becomes altogether clear what the ethical decision should be which has to be taken. It is only by balancing a number of considerations against one another that this decision can be arrived at, and this too must necessarily entail a risk of error. The conscience of the doctor and of all those involved needs, therefore, to be particularly sensitive, and reverence for life must be as deeply rooted as possible. For the rest, the doctor need not be alone in having to take responsibility for the decision. It should be arrived at by consultation between the doctor, the relatives, and, if possible, the sick person himself.

There are two considerations which, taken either singly or together, may make it easier to decide whether to break off the measures designed to prolong life. Once we have reached the point of questioning the value of continuing such treatment we may ask ourselves first whether it can be continued only at the cost of depriving others of certain vital helps to save their lives, and second whether the life of another individual could be saved by giving him one of the organs of the dying man which is still sound.

V. PROTECTION OF THE ENVIRONMENT

"Subdue the earth!" (Gen 1: 28). This call included in the creation narrative has been taken by men of all ages to signify the task of controlling nature by the means at their command, and thereby so altering their environment that it becomes "the friendly garden of God". In recent times, however, we are beginning to ask ourselves, already with some disquiet, whether in our days the message of the creation narrative should not be the precise opposite of this in the task it lays upon us: "Do not subdue the earth beneath you any longer!" In November 1972 Konrad Lorenz, an expert on animal behaviour and theories of instinct, gave a talk on West German television about the limits to growth. For those who worship at the shrine of unrestricted technical and economic development he inscribed the following statement in their album: "What we need is a new ethic to teach men gently that the ideology of growth can no longer continue along the lines they advocate." In fact the technical possibilities of intervening in the natural order have so greatly increased over the years that man is capable, not merely of bringing about the sudden death of all life upon earth by nuclear weapons, but also of bringing about a gradual death by so manipulating nature through his "dominion" of it that it can no longer offer any adequate source of nourishment, any living space, or any possibility of development, which is worthy of human beings. For the forseeable future the situation is already that the continued existence of human life upon earth is still possible only through a responsible direction of man's "dominion over the earth", and it seems far too dangerous to allow it to come to this. Hence there is only one way of counteracting the gradual suicide of mankind: mere "growth ideology" must be discarded. We must be perceptive enough to see that it is immoral. In countries with the living standards of western civilization the renunciation of any further unrestricted growth must come to be recognized and accepted as an ethical commandment.

Yet this is only the first step. The balance of nature is already perilously disturbed. The cyclic process by which the air is renewed and the waters of the earth – including many of the oceans – purify themselves, is already so damaged that it can hardly be repaired as quickly as it needs to be for the sake of mankind without human assistance. All this has been made clear enough in the last few years by the specialists.

Today, therefore, man should in no sense continue to do all that he is capable of. It is a good sign to find that today, in the sphere of western civilization, it is no longer possible for any politician or any major industrialist to be able to dismiss the problem of protecting the environment as of small account. The people have come to be alerted on this point, and a universal awareness of the problem has come to prevail. And yet often this remains at the level of mere lip-service. Cases even occur of the public being deliberately misguided and deceived about measures for protecting the environment which are in reality quite inadequate. It is not possible for us in the present context to develop any kind of political programme for all this. But a few ethical principles can be laid down. In this field Christians should make themselves the champions of a human world without regard to their personal interests, advantages, or disadvantages. All too often they have, in common with many others, shown themselves willing to accept certain ethical judgments only at a point at which the forces of destruction were already making themselves felt.

1. The fatal mechanism which leads from the plundering of nature for purposes of increased production, to fresh methods of plundering, and finally to damaging the natural order, must be broken through. It is true that every economic system is worked out in terms of research, production and marketing. But any such system becomes inhuman and immoral when it is operated at the expense of man himself. Now this in no sense applies merely to the producers. Production can only increase when increasing needs and demands – whether stimulated or spontaneous – offer greater marketing possibilities. Protection of the environment from industrial damage is possible only if all consumers are personally ready to do without any superfluous increase in consumption which does not contribute anything to the human quality of life. It will be evident without any prolonged argument that major tasks arise here for the future education, especially of a young generation which, unlike older ones, has never known from the experience of war how *little* a man needs in order to be genuinely human.

2. Anyone who causes damage to the environment must make a decisive contribution towards eliminating that damage. Again this is not to point an accusing finger at industry alone. The principle we have enunciated does not imply any pre-judgment on the political question of the so-called "law of holding the author responsible". On the contrary we recognize that the tax-payer too is involved in the protection of the environment. And the more reluctant the tax-payer is to forgo the higher consumption which industry and its products make possible, the stronger the ethical grounds are for applying our principle to him too.

3. So rapid has the process been by which the problem of the environment has come to impinge on man's awareness, that as yet the legal provisions for it are in many respects totally inadequate. Here the political task of creating the appropriate juridical basis for such protection becomes an ethical duty for politicians and all other responsible parties. The unanimous findings of the specialists must lead to clear legal provisions for the protection of the environment deter-

mined not by any vested interests but by considerations of the well-being of all. And when these provisions are transgressed it should no longer be regarded as a mere "sowing of wild oats".

4. It should surely be evident too that, as a further factor connected with the protection of the environment, the regulation of births and the containing of the population explosion has become an ethical duty. It is irresponsible to generate more human beings than the earth can sustain while still preserving the environment intact. We have already discussed the consequences of this.

5. From the ethical point of view the need to work out far-seeing plans for the future at the international level seems to be of the utmost urgency. What help is it, for instance, to have laws and penal sanctions for the protection of the environment in one country when their good effects are frustrated by overriding laws in a neighbouring country? Air and water recognize no boundaries. What use is it, for instance, to forbid the sale of specific products on the home market on the grounds that they are harmful to the environment in some way, when they can be sold for export with impunity? This point again is far from being one that is merely of concern to politicians and leaders of industry. Awareness of the necessity for, and ethical consequences of, protection of the environment must increase at the international level. Only so will protection of the environment become a further factor contributing to peace instead of being a fresh source of frustrated resentment and finally of international conflict.

What we are saying here applies primarily to the industrialized countries of western civilization. Having formulated this basic principle of arresting growth, which, as we see it, has become a basic ethical requirement, it would be pharisaical of us to apply it wholesale to the so-called developing countries. For not only are living standards in these far removed from our own, but often they can hardly guarantee a minimum level of subsistence for their populations. We shall have to return to this point in connexion with the final concrete ethical question to which we shall now be turning our attention.

The New Testament

Christians of today have begun to learn to cope with the range of problems entailed in the question of war and peace. Here once more the fresh insights afforded by biblical scholarship have been a potent factor. We have been forced to recognize that war as an instrument of politics can neither be justified nor condemned on the basis of the New Testament alone. Jesus recognizes the power of armed forces and of war as realities of this world (Lk 14: 31 ff; cp Jn 18: 36). He also characterizes war as a punishment imposed by God (Mk 13: 2; Lk 19: 41–4). Above all the so-called "eschatological discourse" (cp ch 20) characterizes war as a plague specially reserved for the final age. For the rest we cannot glean any direct information from the New Testament on the question of war as waged in the past, and still less on the question of whether war in its modern forms can ever be justified. Anyone who seeks to draw his arguments from the Bible can only base his position on the message of the New Testament as a whole.

Now this message speaks of love, righteousness, reconciliation and forgiveness. Even the Old Testament calls God the God of peace: "I think thoughts of peace, not of destruction, says the Lord" (Jer 29: 11). This peace is a gift of God and at the same time a task for man to achieve. And special emphasis is invariably laid on the point that justice will be accorded to the lowly, the poor and the oppressed. The same word "shalom" means "peace" and "well-being" in general. The coming messiah is called "Prince of peace" (Is 9: 5), and his work will be peace. It is like an echo of these voices emanating from the Old Testament when John represents Jesus as saying: "Peace I leave with you; my peace I give to you; not as the world gives do I give to you" (Jn 14: 27). The peace-makers will be called blessed (Mt 5: 9). Again the disciple of Jesus must have love for his enemies (Mt 5: 44; Lk 6: 27; 10: 29–37).

Christians are "called" to peace (Col 3: 15). The peace of Christ which surpasses all understanding must dwell in their hearts (Phil 4: 7). Christ himself in his own person is peace and reconciliation (Eph 2: 14–17; cp 2 Cor 5: 18 ff).

The message of such words does not in any sense bear directly on the ethical questions of war and peace which perplex us today – above all by comparison with those other words which seem to accept war as an unavoidable evil. And yet these words do have a "political" meaning. One point which is regarded as beyond dispute among Christians of today is that such a message radically rules out any *war of aggression* which is undertaken solely for the sake of increasing the power of a people or a régime, or simply to heighten personal or national prestige. Admittedly the point is not yet wholly obvious. Right up to the fearful experiences of the First World War there were nations which, despite a strongly Christian influence, regarded war of aggression as legitimate for the restoration of national honour, to impose specific ideas of national unity on others, or to eliminate economic rivals. But while the magic of war as a "school of virtue" (Machiavelli) is radically a thing of the past so far as we are concerned, the magic of the idea of military service as a "school of the nation" has, by contrast, still not altogether died out.

The "just war" – yesterday and today

It is admittedly questionable whether we would have arrived even at the new exegetical insights, to say nothing of the change in our estimation of war, without the experiences occasioned by the progressive development of modern techniques of war. It is this that in practice gives rise to the question of whether there can ever be such a thing as a "just war" at all under present-day conditions, a war, that is to say, in which the Christian too could take part with a good conscience.

The theory of the "just war" has been carefully and consistently worked out within the Church from that point onwards at which Christians first found themselves in a position of political responsibility. As for Jesus himself, so too for

Christians, wars have constituted a painful but inevitable factor in this world of sin. It has, in fact, consistently been denied that it is permissible to wage a war of aggression. But the question of whether under certain circumstances it could be permissible to wage "just" wars to avert some injustice that has been inflicted is not one which it has been possible simply to dismiss out of hand. Reappraisals have been attempted of a few biblical statements on the subject (admittedly these have to some extent been misinterpreted), above all in the light of philosophical findings concerning the nature of man and of the life of human societies. The conclusion has been that a war is permissible and so "just" provided the following conditions are fulfilled:

1. It must be undertaken and waged exclusively by the leaders of the state and not, for instance, by private individuals.

2. It must constitute a last resort and the only way of protecting the people of the nation concerned from harsh and unjust injuries imposed upon them. A necessary prior condition, therefore, is that all other possible ways of settling the conflict peaceably must have been exhausted. In the conditions of modern warfare the injury to resist which it is justifiable to wage war is in practice reduced to the case of a military invasion. But this means that the only surviving form of a just war is a war of defence in the strict sense.

3. The evil and damage which the war entails must be less than the injustice or alternatively the injury which it is designed to avert.

4. The confrontation in war must be confined to the forces actually engaged in it. Not only the innocent, women, old people and children, but the wounded and prisoners too, must be protected throughout from the warlike activities.

5. The war must have the chance of a victorious outcome within a calculable period. Otherwise that law comes into force which lays down that the injustice should be borne as the lesser evil.

Of all these conditions of a just war the only one which can still be fulfilled under modern conditions is at most the first.

All the others fail to apply in virtue of the fact that it is no longer possible to keep the war within the necessary bounds. It is impossible to weigh the injustice that is suffered against the evil of war, because the direct and indirect effects of modern systems of armament – above all of atomic weapons – can in principle no longer be controlled by the parties waging the war, and hence the civil population cannot be spared from the effects of the warlike activities. Again it is hardly possible nowadays to calculate the chances of victory, and not infrequently under modern conditions war entails a risk that the very things which it is intended to defend will be ruined and brought to nothing.

Under these circumstances war, even the most justified war of defence, has ceased to be a morally permissible means of achieving justifiable demands in international relationships. It is true that in theory this could be made subject to certain provisos. War is not a legitimate means of achieving political ends in those cases in which the waging of it involves the use of modern techniques of armament. But it would be legitimate so long as it could be restricted to the use of weapons which still did not involve any violation of the conditions of a "just war". However any such consideration is utopian. Nowadays nations throughout the world are so politically and economically involved with one another – the very situation for which the slogan about the "one world" has been coined – that any merely local or regional conflict carries with it the danger of a total war such as can never be justified by any theory of the "just war". If, therefore, it is true that justice and peace constitute the social and political form of love, then there can no longer be any question for believers of solving the question of the necessary prior conditions for a just war. The only question for them that still remains can be how absolutely to outlaw war as such. Incidentally the more Christians press for precisely this outlawing of war, and for the development of new forms of solving disputes between nations, the clearer it will become that precisely here a specifically Christian contribution can be made to coping with the problems of present-day international politics. For a glance at the current state of international politics shows that the non-Christian nations, or those who do not to any marked extent bear the imprint of the Christian faith, are still a long way from regarding war as not permissible on ethical grounds.

Peace and order

An unconditional commitment to peace and an unconditional outlawing of war on the part of Christians is not the same as an utopian pacifism. The Christian is not so naïve as to believe that all future wars can be excluded if only we ourselves have this will to achieve peace. As in the past, so too in the future, we have to reckon with unjust attacks as prompted, for instance, by the sheer desire to achieve greater power or greater national honour. Anyone, including Christians, vested with the responsibilities of government, has the task of keeping any injustice which threatens as remote as possible from his own nation by all permissible means. In this connexion there still remains wide scope for estimating which of the various means for averting such injustice will be politically the most effective, even when we have avoided the two extremes: on the one hand that utopian pacifism which is prepared to put up with any kind of injustice, and which, so far from being demanded, is actually rejected by believers, and on the other the modern form of defensive war which is no longer legitimate today. In this sphere the more politically effective a given means of defence is in protecting the rights of a nation, the better it is from the ethical point of view. The scope for choice and evaluation which we find here is one within which not merely our political judgment but our ethical judgment at the same time can operate. Precisely for this reason very varied political convictions can be entertained among Christians without prejudice to their common faith. They can have different ideas as to how best to discourage a possible aggressor from launching his attack. Very recently an explicit pronouncement on this point has been made in the Catholic church by the second Vatican council (*Pastoral Constitution*, art. 74).

A Christian's faith and his commitment to peace, therefore, are faced with a further prior decision as to whether it is better for a given state in the concrete to adopt a neutral policy or to engage in a defensive pact; whether it should have no armed forces at all, or merely symbolic ones, or alternatively whether it should have armed forces sufficiently powerful for its own defence. It has to be decided whether it is not even permissible to build up a system of atomic defences to frighten off a possible opponent and to make him feel that any attack he might be planning would be incalculably risky to himself. One might do this even though one was firmly resolved never to use this system of atomic defences. A further point which, for the same reasons, the believer cannot decide *a priori*, is whether in any given case military service or the avoidance of military service constitutes the decision which he, as a Christian, has to arrive at in conscience if he is not to be false to his own faith.

Admittedly with these last considerations we have reached the extreme limits of what the Christian has to say on the subject of war. For surely, according to all experience and serious estimates of the future, it is just as utopian as any radically pacifist position to suppose that one could have arms, perhaps even very advanced atomic ones, without them ever being used, in other words that one could find any basis for lasting peace between nations in a "balance of fear". As the Christian sees it, therefore, any reliance on an alleged balance between modern systems of armament and equipment for the purpose of warding off the danger of direct attack can be permitted at most only as a temporary expedient, and only provided that the Christian himself for his part is simultaneously doing all in his power to collaborate in developing new ways of resolving conflicts, achieving a supervised programme of disarmament, and creating regulations for peace which would be internationally recognized.

If, therefore, in view of those extremely limited possibilities of waging a just war of defence, a Christian refuses to engage in armed service in case of war on the grounds that in the concrete circumstances he no longer regards it as ethically permissible, he is, to say the least, arriving at a decision of conscience which is in harmony with his faith. This still holds good even though he may not condemn another for engaging in such service on the grounds that he has arrived at a more optimistic appraisal of the possibilities of containing the conflict within local and technical bounds, or alternatively on the grounds that he simply does not feel himself strong enough to persist in an attitude of resistance towards the state once it has made national service compulsory. Since in case of war this can be a Christian's duty under certain circumstances, the authorities should also respect without discrimination the decision in conscience of a young man who, even in time of peace, refuses to serve in the forces on the grounds that he rejects any use of force or threat of force between nations. Any state which takes seriously the basic right of its citizens to freedom of conscience must make legal provision guaranteeing the right of the individual to refuse national service on grounds of conscience. Despite this, however, the maintaining of armed forces for the reasons mentioned is not to be rejected on ethical grounds in all circumstances. And in view of this it does not derogate from the right to refuse service in the forces if the state requires the conscientious objector to give a corresponding amount of service in social or non-military fields. In any case this has the further advantage of showing that his refusal to serve in the forces does in fact proceed from conscientious objections to war, and not from other motives. But it must be the concern and the task of the Christian to see that these considerations are strengthened rather than weakened. Even though the state and society may discriminate against the conscientious objector, Christians should give an unmistakable example of non-discrimination and of what it is to have an informed conscience on the whole range of the problems involved. It is in no sense *ipso facto* certain that a military attacker can be discouraged from his designs solely by the threat of warlike retaliation.

In this connexion a new type of scientific research has come to the fore in recent years, to which the name "research into peace" has been given. It attempts to track down more thoroughly than has been possible hitherto the causes of military confrontations in all their manifold complexities, and to work out proposals for, and methods of, settling even acute conflicts, or at least of showing how they can be endured, without recourse to arms. Again the question of non-violent resistance is studied at length by these researchers, which shows that what they advocate is in no sense simply to tolerate any kind of injustice or any attack. The Christian has no reason to adopt an attitude of mistrust in principle towards the "research into peace", even though in points of detail many proposals may strike him as unrealistic. It is still better to examine even the remotest possibility of maintaining peace than to place a naïve trust in the power of weapons, an attitude which, at basis, has not yet overcome the romantic glorification of war of former ages.

Peace and prosperity

Among the deeper underlying causes of modern wars one in particular is coming increasingly into the foreground nowadays: the contrast in terms of riches and poverty between the modern industrial states and the nations of the so-called "Third World". If war is really to be abolished for the future poverty and hunger must be overcome before all else. Theoretically speaking this has been recognized and acknowledged for a long time. The political economists, above all in the wealthier countries, have to draw the practical consequences of this in view of their policy of investment in the Third World, and the Christians living in these countries have to use all possible means to bring their political influence to bear to this end. Here once more scope for political and ethical evaluation is open to them in the same way as in the question of the best means for averting war, stopping short at using force in retaliation. But in any case the goal to be aimed at is clear. It must be recognized that it is impossible to ensure world peace unless solidarity is achieved between the rich and the poor of this earth. And this means, unless the rich are prepared to forgo any increase in their consumption and to give assistance to the poor in the struggle against economic wretchedness. Only so can it also become clear that the "human rights" which rich and poor states alike have subscribed to, are not in practice to become a mere form of words.

22   Conclusion

This book began with an inquiry into the question of "God in history". In the portrayal of Abraham we introduced what was to be the *leitmotiv* of all the discussions which followed. Faith breaks into the uncertainty of history, involving, as it does, an attitude of trust in God as the Lord of history. The first part of this book ended with the crucial question of how the inquiry into the idea of God and faith in God fitted into the whole spectrum of questions, whether optimistic or pessimistic, hopeful or despairing, into the meaning of history.

The presentation of God's message in the sacred writings of the Old Testament, in the history of Jesus, and in the New Testament's witness of faith, showed us again and again how impossible it is for the believer ever to escape from the history of mankind, and how on the contrary he is made again and again to commit his life to it afresh, often at the cost of pain. His attitude towards the future, towards his own state as involved in history, and, in the broadest sense, towards the world in general, is, therefore, something which sets the Christian apart from his fellow men. For, as he sees it, the entire future is determined by God, and because of this he can still make his way through history in a spirit of sureness and hope, however dark the future may be. In his ethical conduct he does not try to fulfil the abstract norms of a law that ignores the world. His actions proceed, rather, from that freedom to commit himself in love which removes all obstacles and enables him to dedicate himself to the needs of man in his situation in history.

It is both necessary and consistent with its purpose, therefore, that in this book the main section should conclude with the question with which it commenced: the question of history. We would be evading the ultimate test of the validity and soundness of our arguments if at this point, and in the light of the message which we have set forth, we did not once more raise the question which was left open, and necessarily had to be left open, at the end of the first main part: what is the meaning and goal of history? Here, at the end of this book, this question must take the form: what does Christian faith have to say about the meaning, goal and end of history?

Christian faith's answer to this question is in terms of that which is traditionally called the "doctrine of the last things" ("eschatology", from the Greek "eschaton" = the last). According to this teaching the "last things" for the individual man are death, judgment, the vision of God (heaven), or eternal separation from God (hell). The "last things" of the world and of history as a whole are the second coming of Christ ("parousia"), the resurrection of the flesh, the general judgment, and the dominion of God as finally and definitively revealed. In this the whole of creation attains its ultimate goal, and it is this goal that constitutes the meaning of its entire existence and its history. The process is portrayed in terms of a chronological sequence of coming events which at the same time signify a radical end to all history. Scattered details are taken from the Bible purporting to show what *form* events will take at this time, and the whole is joined together into a single continuous and unbroken "system" of eschatology, although it is only at the cost of a certain forcing that some of the scattered details can be brought into harmony with the system as a whole.

Today, however, strong rivals have emerged to this view of history, as developed by believers in the past. Even non-Christian philosophies of life have developed a view of history, a projection of the future in various forms. In contrast to former ages faith no longer enjoys a monopoly in supplying an answer to the question: and what will come at the end? On the contrary, these new answers that are being suggested seem closer to the realities which we know, and are clearly powerful influences in changing social, economic and political

530 FAITH AND WORLD

conditions. And because of this they tend to put faith's answer into the shade. Again developments within Christian theology, itself constitute a further factor. Today we have at last come to recognize how disparate the various statements are which we find in the Bible concerning the "last things". We can precisely *not* fit them together into a single harmonious "system". Apart from this certain philosophical considerations regarding both the nature of man himself and the meaning of history have shaken many of the assumptions which had previously gone unquestioned. The doctrine of the "last things" is falling into serious danger. Christians too are already beginning to withdraw their belief in eternal life and the "resurrection of the flesh".

Is faith, therefore, on the point of striking its colours at the first shot? At all events we do need to reconsider the whole question realistically, and not to shrink from subjecting many long-cherished ideas to a searching examination if this proves to be a right and necessary course. Only then can faith make its own contribution to the current discussion concerning history and the future. For this we must begin by examining the sources of faith and asking ourselves whether in the past our reading and interpretation of these may not perhaps have been mistaken or inadequate.

I. WHAT DOES FAITH SAY ABOUT THE FINAL CONSUMMATION?

As we have already said, when faith speaks of history it has in mind the goal at which it is aimed. This means that it considers it from the point of view not of the past but of the future. Now there are various ways in which we can speak of the future. Which is faith's way of speaking of it?

History and future

Religions do exist – and they existed above all among Israel's neighbouring peoples – whose prime concern is to interpret and explain to the individual inquirer the meaning of the cosmos and the cycle of nature with its eternal alternation of generation and decay. We usually call such religions – not always without a certain arrogance – "non-historical" religions. Whether this judgment is justified or not the faith of Israel at all events is concerned in the highest degree, and almost exclusively, with interpreting history. This concern stems from Israel's own historical experience: the deliverance from bondage in Egypt which welded the people together as a people. In the course of its own history and as a result of its own memories, ever fresh and ever imparting new shapes to it, Israel's vision of the advancing course of history in general, even as seen beyond its own national boundaries, became wider and more penetrating.

We have a characteristic example of this in the Old Testament: the book of Genesis in its present form and as shaped by the redactors. This book is intended to record the origins of the people of Israel, and thereby to interpret its own current life. But it is not until the twelfth chapter that we find the first mention of Israel as embodied in Abraham, the father of the nation. A wider cycle of narratives leads up to, and converges upon the figure of the patriarch: the story of Noah, the founder of the second family of man after the Flood. Noah, however, is the connecting link between this and the first family of man which perished in the Flood, that descended from Adam. The meaning is this: Israel is the people chosen by God for the salvation of all mankind – to be a "blessing" to all nations. But this is no arbitrary act on God's part. It is God's way of making a new beginning with mankind after it has rebelled against him for the second time. The fact that Israel as the people of God continues to exist shows that God is carrying out his original purpose for mankind and for the world.

But can we still say that these ideas are "historical"? Assuredly not in the sense that they constitute a record of "historical facts" after the modern pattern. Neither the creation narrative nor the stories of Noah and the "patriarchs" are intended to supply us with factual "information" as to the origins of the world, mankind, or the people of Israel. But they do tell mankind something about his own existence in time, about his present position in space and time in the light of God's call to him. Adam and Noah are "mankind" as living in the *present*. Abraham, Isaac and Jacob are the people of Israel as it exists at the time of the *author himself*. The book of Genesis regards man not as one particular instance among many equally important ones within an eternal cycle of reality, but as the one to whom a call has been addressed, a call which has its roots in the creative deed of God and is meant to be answered and responded to as *immediately present to the men of all ages.*

Promise

In this sense what the Bible has to say about man does not constitute "factual history" at all. And yet for all this it does at the same time regard him as a being of meaningful history. Now the very fact that we can recognize this leads us to suppose that the Bible's way of speaking about the goal and end of history is exactly the same as its way of speaking about the beginnings of it. It is treating not of the "material facts of history" but rather of its "inner meaning". The statements in the Bible about the end and goal of history, therefore, do not constitute a preview of future events in the history of the world and mankind. If this supposition is correct (and comparisons drawn from the scientific study of religions and philosophical considerations serve to confirm the observations of the exegetes), then we must renounce the idea that "eschatological" statements, statements about the "last things", are telling us something about what will take place in the future.

Even if sometimes we may have the impression that the catastrophes and wars which we experience today are in conformity down to the last detail with what we find written in the Bible about the events of the last days, still we must guard against taking the eschatological statements of Scripture as a libretto for the final act in the drama of the world's tragedy. Just as there are no eye-witnesses to the "first things", so too there are no prognoses for the "last things". Indeed we may even ask whether we should regard statements about the future as on the same level as statements of historical fact is not precisely to contradict the essential meaning of future as such. The statements about the "last things" contained in Scripture are not intended to anticipate what lies before us, but to set in motion human actions orientated towards the future.

We can throw further light on what has been said by noticing carefully the way in which the Bible speaks of the world of man's environment in connexion with the goal and end of the history of the cosmos. There can be no mistaking the fact that the Bible portrays the "end" of the world as in very deed an "end", as a cosmic catastrophe, as the downfall of heaven and earth. Such ideas belong to a well-defined stock of ideas found in the civilizations surrounding Israel, and it comes as no surprise to find the biblical authors too seizing upon these traditional views, which it never occurs to them to question. Finally we cannot expect their ideas to correspond to our Copernican view of the world. Yet it is striking to notice how the thought of the Bible, focused as it is upon man's existence as involved in meaningful history, constantly, and to an increasing extent as it develops, introduces fresh shades of meaning into the ancient stock of ideas used to portray the world. Such shades of meaning come to the fore whenever emphasis is laid on the fact that it is *man* who is called to take responsibility for the shaping of history.

The author of the first chapter of Genesis exercises a sovereign control in manipulating the ancient ideas of mythology, which he takes up and transforms to his own ends. But this chapter reaches its climax in verses 28 ff. Here man is called to be ruler of the earth, and henceforward it is his destiny actually to *make* out of that earth a world that is *his own*. It is not laid down *a priori* what is to be made of the earth. This depends, rather, upon man's own decisions in his human history. And misfortunes and sufferings within history are likewise brought about precisely by man's own actions.

We notice a similar position – to take a further example – with regard to the preaching of the prophets. When they call for "conversion" they are not thereby demanding a return to *earlier* conditions. They are calling for a decision for the *future*, which must be better than the present. But this sense of meaningful history, this orientation towards a future in the thought of the Bible, appears most clearly in the concept of the *promise*, the root form of biblical statements about the future as such. We must examine this somewhat more closely by concentrating upon the three different types of promise which we meet with in the Bible. This will have the incidental effect of showing that the Bible has not one way, but several different ways, of speaking of the future.

The charismatic saying

The simplest and best known form of statement about the future is the *charismatic saying*. It predicts future events in order thereby indirectly to influence the present. For the most part such charismatic sayings apply to the people or its representatives. But the Bible also contains charismatic sayings for individuals (eg, Amos 7: 17; Is 22: 16 ff; 1 Sam 10: 2 ff). No uniform judgment can be arrived at with regard to the source and purpose of such charismatic sayings. In estimating their worth it is prudent to see what kind of fulfilment they achieve. In this one can often recognize whether in an alleged charismatic saying the speaker has merely taken a superstitious refuge in signs and portents which are chosen arbitrarily, or whether he has noticed genuine portents of the future and given his "prognosis" the form of a charismatic saying.

But with such charismatic sayings the most interesting question is not what their source and underlying intention is, but how far they do predict the future at all in such a way as either to leave the individual free to take his own decision, or to withdraw this decision from him. It is no accident, for instance, that the charismatic saying is expressed in the form of an oracle. The oracle is ambiguous. It calls for interpretation and decision, and thereby keeps the future open and undetermined. It is not surprising to find pseudo-prophets too uttering alleged charismatic sayings so that these finally fall into decay through their misuse. This explains why it should be that in Israel charismatic sayings never achieve an over-riding influence or come to dominate the whole attitude of the people towards the future.

In addition we should notice a somewhat different point. The concept of faith found in the Old Testament excludes any smooth and unbroken correspondence between a charismatic saying and its fulfilment. No charismatic saying uttered in the name of God excludes the possibility that its fulfilment will be full of unexpected surprises. Hence Israel's faith consistently extended more to the fulfilment of the saying than to the saying itself. This meant that despite all charismatic sayings the future remained constantly open and indeterminate. More than this, indeed, often it was only in the light of its fulfilment in fact that the true meaning of a charismatic saying came to be recognized, and that thereby a meaning came to be attributed to it which extended beyond the particular set of circumstances at any given time, and beyond its immediate fulfilment. It is in *this* sense that the New Testament asserts that in Jesus Christ and the Christian Church the inspired sayings of the Old Testament are fulfilled. We have already adduced examples of this at several points. We may remind ourselves, for instance, of the prophecies of the Suffering Servant of God or of the Virgin's Son of Is 7: 14.

Prophecy

Another form of biblical saying concerning the future which must be distinguished from the charismatic saying is *prophecy*. Whereas the charismatic saying speaks of the future in order to influence the present, prophecy speaks of the present in order to have an effect upon the future. The prophetic word, then, has the present in view even when its immediate message relates to what is to come. The preaching of the prophets at any given time is focused primarily upon the questions and demands of the hour. It is the immediate moment that provides the prophet's message with its concrete content as he demands of his hearers, "Believe! Hearken! See! Recognize!" or "Repent!" (cp Amos 5: 6; Hos 6: 3; Is 7: 10, 14;

Jer 36: 3). That which Isaiah presented as demanded by God, namely resistance and steadfastness in the face of an invading enemy, was viewed in Jeremiah's message a hundred years later as resistance to God's will.

But in that case what has the prophet's word to do with the future? Prophecy *criticizes* the present and summons it to a decision as to the future. This means that prophecy regards the present not in isolation, but from the viewpoint of the future which is to emerge from it. The future will bring to light what the value of the present is. This is why the prophet presses so strongly for clarification and decision here and now. The word is his weapon. For the word has the power to indicate the portents of the future under which the present stands. In this way his word opens up the future by making decision both possible and inescapable.

Apocalyptic

The best known, but, as has been shown, by no means the only, type of biblical statement about the future, and by no means the most important either, is found in *apocalyptic*. The apocalyptic (its literal meaning is "unveiling", "revealing") saying paints a picture of what is to come. In this respect it performs the same function as the charismatic saying. But one way in which it differs from it is that it speaks not merely of one particular event in the future but rather of the future of the entire universe. And a second point of difference is that apocalyptic does not call upon man to shape the future. The apocalyptic writer gives us, in some degree, a glimpse behind the scenes, and seeks to show us things of the future which, while they are still hidden to us, have already been brought to full reality in God's sight. This action of God in the future is something which man can only wait for. What this future demands of man is not to be shaped or controlled, but to be awaited in a spirit of patience and repentance.

The apocalyptic writer addresses his message to people who are oppressed or persecuted and in need of consolation. The vision of the healed and redeemed world as an already existing reality with God is intended to strengthen their confidence that God's designs will in the end be brought to a triumphant conclusion despite all resistance. We would be misinterpreting the apocalyptic literature, therefore, if we were to allow ourselves to be beguiled by the literal meaning of the term "apocalypse" into supposing that it is intended to unveil future events. Apocalyptic does not itself reveal anything, but proclaims a future revelation. Apocalyptic statements give expression to the fact that God's final revelation of himself is still something constantly to be awaited. It does not provide us with any kind of chart mapping out the course of future events.

The traditional doctrine of the "last things" is to a large extent based on the apocalyptic sayings of the Bible. We can now understand why such sources should be used only with caution. If we are over hasty we can all too easily read wrong interpretations into them and say more than the text allows. Furthermore the New Testament itself has taken up an unambiguous position with regard to apocalyptic. The influence of apocalyptic ideas on the first Christians was, in fact, very strong. We can see this by noticing how many apocalyptic elements have survived in the New Testament. Among them we must in fact include not merely the "Secret Revelation" of John, but also the sayings of Jesus concerning the end of the world and the Great Judgment, the numerous sayings of Paul with regard to the Second Coming of Christ and the way in which we shall be united with him. And yet in that same New Testament we can see how as the early Church developed it adopted a critical attitude towards apocalyptic and finally came to avoid it. For it is not apocalypse but the gospel that has become the characteristic form of Christian literature. The fact that the three first gospels each include a "Little Apocalypse" within their structure (Mk 13; Mt 24; Lk 21) is positively symbolic. The *gospel* envelops and interprets apocalyptic and not *vice versa*. What is true on a small scale of each of the gospels applies to the Apocalypse of John within the structure of the New Testament as a whole. The apocalyptic elements in the New Testament are traces of the strivings which took place in order to achieve a truly Christian under-standing of the future. They have given valuable assistance in understanding the message of Christ by making it clear that the gospel also provides consolation and hope in a present that is devoid of either. But precisely what *form* this consola-tion and this hope take is something that we can learn from no apocalypse but only from the gospel.

And what does the gospel tell us? It focuses the preaching on the "last things" upon the manifestation of Jesus Christ. What has taken place irrevocably in Jesus Christ – it is this, and nothing else, that constitutes the basis for all statements about the future. What Christian faith has to say about history and the future is the outcome of what has been said to us in the gospel. If a point is reached at which an apocalyptic state-ment is intended to be something more than a means of expression for conveying the message of the gospel, then it becomes impossible at that point to justify apocalyptic lan-guage any longer. Faith's message about history and its goal, therefore, is expressed in three ways: in the forms of charis-matic sayings, prophecy and apocalyptic. We neither can nor should seek to bring all of them under a single common denominator. Nevertheless they do have one thing in common. All three kinds of saying about the *future* have a function in and for the *present*. To speak of the future clearly means to speak either with reference to, or against the background of, the present. Statements about the future are a particular kind of statement about the present. This is a point that we must bear in mind as we now turn to the question, "Precisely *what* does faith tell us about history and the future?"

II. WHAT HAS FAITH TO TELL US ABOUT THE FINAL CONSUMMATION?

According to biblical ideas history begins without any pre-liminaries. The first act in the drama of history is the creation, portrayed as God's first deed in history. Even here at the starting-point the single great theme which is to run through history is defined: the theme of *life*. This theme extends over the whole span of Scripture from the first page to the last (cp Gen 1: 21-7; 2: 7; Rev 22: 17-19). History itself is nothing else than the history of life which, in progressively narrowing perspectives, runs right through the biblical account of history. It begins with the widest perspective: the origins and development of the cosmos, and the history of mankind at the universal level (cp Gen 9: 9-16) is drawn into the narrower limits of the history of the people of Israel as we are told, "I have set before you life and death, blessing and curse; therefore choose life" (Dt 30: 19), and then leads into the personal history of the individual as the psalmist prays: "God will ransom my soul from the power of Sheol for he will receive me" (Ps 49: 15). If we seek to know what the meaning of history is as seen through the eyes of sacred Scripture we must notice how life is thought of in its pages.

The history of life

The decisive aspects are already laid down in the creation narrative. God blows the breath of life into man's nostrils (Gen 2: 7). This shows that life is essentially God's *gift*. Henceforward it is in history that God imparts the gift of life anew. This gift is at the same time a gift of *freedom*. God sets man in the garden which he has planted (Gen 2: 8, 15). Life can only be a gift if in his personal history man recognizes, accepts and preserves it as such, if he commits himself to that life in common with his fellows which is offered him by God. Finally God gives man the task of being fruitful, of tilling the garden and having dominion over the earth and the other creatures. Life signifies the *task* of extending the life-giving dominion of God throughout history.

Gift, a gift of freedom, and a task are the roots from which the single and continuous history of life grows, and which supply history with its meaning and its future. But if life is indeed the theme of history in this sense, then the future must necessarily remain open. If it were predetermined, then its outcome could be anticipated, and in that case life would no longer be a gift of freedom and a task, for then there would

no longer be anything to shape and form, only a state of frozen
inertia and an anticipation of death.

This is the basic message of Scripture. What does it have
to tell us in greater detail about history on this basis? History
involves a relationship of tension between two extremes, two
poles which never coincide. At one extreme stands God as the
dispenser, guardian and Lord of life who, in his gift of life,
himself becomes present (cp 1 Sam 17: 26). Opposite to him
stands man, chief among, and representative of, all those upon
whom life has been bestowed. Thus history becomes the stage
on which the interplay between two freedoms is enacted, the
freedom of God in bestowing, and the freedom of man in
receiving and having gifts bestowed upon him.

The relationship is not one between two entities of equal
status, and yet it is God's will that it should be a relationship
between two partners. It is aimed at community of life
between God and man. History can be described either as the
realization of God's dominion or as the perfecting of man and
the cosmos, according to which of the two poles we direct our
attention towards at any given time, and again depending on
this we can give a corresponding interpretation of the meaning of history. And yet these are not alternatives but statements which mutually complement one another. For the more
God is Lord the more man achieves fulness of life.

On such a view of history it is vital to recognize that God
and man appear *both at the same time* as subects, upholders
and enacters of history. In collaboration with, and in subordination to, God, man remains, in the deepest sense, the subject
of history. If we take the Bible at its word, therefore, then
we should not so represent the end of history to ourselves that
it seems that God's action either eliminates or takes over from
the action of man, or that man's action eliminates or takes over
from the action of God. God in his sovereign freedom allows
for the free collaboration of man in history. It is above all to
this indispensable rôle that the prophets draw their hearers'
attention. Salvation or judgment, life or death, lie within the
decision of man. In every moment of history life is subject to
decision. Thus we understand why sometimes in the prophets

all temporal distinctions become blurred. Everything is "near", everything takes place "soon" (cp Lk 18: 7 ff; Rev 1: 1; 22: 6). Hence man can also achieve repentance and conversion at any moment, as soon as an appeal is made to his free decision.

Here, then, we also find an answer to the question of whether history admits of any genuine progress, anything that is really new. Since history is a history of freedom, that which is underivably new is included in it, so that there are some things such that we cannot know what they will be or how they will turn out. Even if we are convinced of the reality of evolution as an irresistible process, this is no sense gives us any greater knowledge of the future. Evolution, taken in itself, is blind to meaning and goal, or at any rate we cannot perceive that it has its eyes open. This means that man, involved as he is in his physical side in this process of evolution, and being a part of it, can and should of his freedom give evolution meaning and fulfilment.

Evolution itself is, as it were, material awaiting his decision. We can and should take up a specific attitude towards it. We can and should turn it into a blessing for mankind. Thus in the history of life we meet the development of the cosmos, the history of mankind as a whole, and the history of the personal life of the individual. And within this all these are inseparably intermingled. Now if we still ask what the faith of the Bible and Christianity teaches about the "last things", what it "knows" and "says" about these as they affect the world and man, then the only answer we can give is that it summons man to awareness that he must be true to his inalienable and creative rôle as a free creature in the here and now.

The God of life

Although man is reminded with urgency and compelling force of his freedom and his task in the history of life, this does not represent a demand that is hopelessly beyond his strength. For God has hazarded a still more far-reaching intervention on the stage of history. This intervention, freely undertaken by God, never ceases to maintain its initiative whatever shoals and hazards it may encounter in history. Nowhere does this become more clear than in the attitude of God towards the unending history of human unfaithfulness in mankind as a whole and in Israel and its representatives in particular. God's surpassing initiative is inexhaustible and never discouraged by any failure on man's part. This divine initiative, bordering on folly, is ready at any time to take up man's cause. This is incomprehensible except on the supposition that God's freedom is nothing else than the very root cause of love and life itself. This is why God does not betray his own gifts. In the experience of God's mighty deed, which both *is* free and sets man free, the avowal of God as the "living one" is brought to maturity in Israel's faith (cp Ex 3: 14; Jos 3: 10; 2 Kgs 19: 4; Ps 42: 3; Jer 2: 13; 10: 10; Dan 6: 21, 27).

Since he is the "living one" in this sense, God is at the same time the God of "faithfulness". God keeps faith with his creation and his creatures in that he bestows life upon them and maintains them in life. This is something that Israel in particular experienced and confessed: "Know, therefore that the Lord your God is God, the faithful God who keeps covenant and steadfast love with those who love him and keep his commandments" (Dt 7: 9). Despite punishment and judgment Israel experiences her God as he whose faithfulness cannot be shaken even by all the acts of faithlessness on the part of the people. Again and again at the conclusion of these acts of faithlessness on the people's part they receive a new promise, new life and new faithfulness from God. The longer the history of life endures the more the promise and the experience of God's faithfulness increases too.

In the last analysis all statements in the Bible about the future owe their origin to belief in this faithfulness. The assent of God to his creation, which is made effective in history, simply does not admit of the idea that life is destined to be brought to an end forever in death. The message of faith concerning the "last things" is therefore incapable in principle of providing any physical science or history of the events of the final age. It speaks not of future happenings, but rather of

God, whose faithfulness gives man confidence as he advances into the future. *Eschatology* is *theology* – and nothing else. Eschatological statements of faith have no other purpose than to strengthen man in the belief that God will continue to give life whatever vicissitudes may befall in the future, and that he is faithful to this promise of life. If we read the "sayings about the future" of the Bible in this sense, then we shall neither expect too much of them nor interpret them wrongly.

Christian faith says that the history of life, as a history of human freedom and divine faithfulness, attains its unique and unsurpassable climax in Jesus Christ. It is not by chance that John records this saying of Jesus: "I came that they may have life and have it abundantly" (Jn 10: 10). Indeed he identifies life with Christ himself. "I am the life" (Jn 11: 25; 14: 6). In Jesus faith sees life itself, because in him the history of life, both past and future, is freed of its obscurity, and in him all the riches of life's experiences and life's blessings are gathered up. In the further course of history it is no longer possible to ignore this fact. Why should this be?

It is at this point that we have to draw the ultimate conclusion from the witness to Jesus' death and rising from the dead. As faith sees it, this rising of the crucified Lord from the dead has imparted a new dimension to everything which has been accounted life hitherto. What life really means is something that we know only in the light of the risen Lord. The conclusions which follow from this for the believer, and the new vision it gives of history and the future to which it is leading, have been formulated by Paul in the following terms: "We are ... always carrying in the body the death of Jesus, so that the life of Jesus may also be manifested in our bodies. For while we live we are always being given up to death for Jesus' sake, so that the life of Jesus may be manifested in our mortal flesh" (2 Cor 4: 10 ff). In Christ that which we understand by life has been transformed and purified. The meaning of the history of life now consists in the fact that this life, which at first is still hidden (Col 3: 3), is extended by the service and life of the Christian community until through Christ God becomes all in all (1 Cor 15: 28). In Christ the faithfulness of God is proclaimed as a faithfulness *in* death and *beyond* death. As God's assent to life has proved itself true in him, so too it continues to do so in all who stand united with Christ in his fate. Hence the believer looks for nothing greater than that he may always be with his Lord (1 Thess 4: 17).

God the faithful

It is quite impossible for us to work out in more detailed terms what this union of life with Christ, and this universal expansion of God's faithfulness, signify in terms of concrete content, and how the entire cosmos too is drawn into the process. To describe this, Paul, like other writers, avails himself of a series of apocalyptic images which we have already spoken of in relation to the problems they entail. However searchingly we inquire into them faith must still be satisfied with the fact that God's faithfulness has proved itself to us in the death of Christ, and that henceforward Christ, as God's faithfulness in person, is now the reality which radically specifies man and the world. This compels us to exercise an ascetic restraint instead of indulging in curious questioning, while on the other hand it helps us to realize more profoundly what faith possesses and hopes for in Christ as the quintessential meaning of history and future.

We must confess, therefore: we do not actually *know* anything about the "last things". We cannot in any sense picture them to ourselves. In place of this, the Christian's adherence to Christ can become deeper, and it enables him to view his own "last things" his death, in a different light. In former ages men described death by saying that it consisted in the separation of the immortal soul from the body. Today the notion of a "purifying" separation of body and soul has become open to question. Present-day philosophical views on the nature of man regard death as the event which withdraws man from the relationships by which he is surrounded. Death is the total absence of contacts outside oneself. To this Christian faith rejoins: the death of Jesus has deprived death of its power as the last word on the life of man. Hence in dying man is offered a share in God's victory over death. The very nature of life itself is such that it summons man to this. For the life of the individual man, so far from being self-enclosed and aimed at nothing beyond itself, only achieves its fulfilment by making its due contribution to the great history of life which makes its mark upon, and in part predetermines, every individual life right from the first. This has still greater force when we view life in the light of God who is the giver of life. On this view eternity acts as a portent governing the past and the future which life includes, showing where they lead. "Resurrection from the dead" means nothing else than that life is offered an eternal future.

This eternal future of life, however, is promised to the *whole* man. This is what it means when Scripture tells us that we are destined to rise from the dead. This statement can be, and has been, misinterpreted in two different ways. We can seek to find here a scriptural basis for the philosophical doctrine of the immortality of the soul. Conversely we may take it to represent the doctrine that the body will be given back or restored. The first interpretation is false, the second superficial. The true meaning of the biblical witness to the resurrection from the dead is that man *as single and undivided*, together with his history, will survive and be preserved for all time. To express it in modern terms, we should formulate the witness of the Bible as follows: it is not body considered as a biological and chemical structure, but the *person* which will rise from the dead.

For the rest, the life of one who has risen from the dead will be subject to different conditions with which we are unfamiliar. If, for instance, we ask whether any material conditions are attached to this other life, or what other kind of relationship it will have to matter, then we have no direct answer to give. At most we can give an indirect answer by pointing to the fact that the combination of spirit and matter which characterizes our real mode of existence is one in which the two overlap with one another. If there is in fact an ultimate underlying unity to the world and history, then they too will survive and be preserved in the life of the resurrection. To say otherwise would be in itself, once more, tacitly to impose illegitimate limitations on the witness of the Bible. But *how* the combination of spirit and matter will be preserved is a point on which faith has to forgo any detailed answer because it has none. Yet this is no loss. The real message of faith is in fact far greater. Given that man has to meet God, this God whom he has to meet is the *loving* and *faithful* God. It is an intrinsic contradiction to suppose that this loving and faithful God will abandon to destruction the man with whom he has entered into relations and dialogue as his partner.

We can misinterpret this hope in an egotistic sense. For the reproaches of those who blame Christians for their lack of selflessness in their hope for eternal life are all too justified. Yet what is involved in this hope is not primarily any longing on man's part. It is concerned with *God* in that faith *must* trust in God that he will save, preserve and "raise" all life. Without this trust faith would be failing to take God seriously as God. On the basis of such considerations we of today have come to avoid using conceptual models to explain the after-life of the dead which are all too conditioned by time, for instance the idea that death comes "first" and "later", at the "end of the world", the resurrection of the flesh and the general judgment.

If the question of "points in time" must be raised, then we must say with modern theologians that the individual resurrection from the dead is achieved in and at the time of death. At this point a Catholic Christian will ask about the significance of the doctrine of a "place of purification" (purgatory). But there is no contradiction. Since man never achieves fulfilment in this life but remains a sinner, only God's mercy can fulfil man in his guilty state. The passage through death to a resurrected life is therefore a refinement or clarification: a painful release from everything opposed to God, a maturing of everything incomplete. The prayers of the Church for the "souls in purgatory" can help in that process as much as prayers and petitions on behalf of other people in suffering. This idea of "purgatory" which is held by some Catholic theologians today and makes possible a new discussion of the subject with Protestant Christians, does not call for a precise chronological image of the kind already referred to and helps contemporary theologians to reach an appropriate understanding of the individual resurrection from the dead. Correspondingly, in conceiving of the resurrection of all men we must say that it is the gathering up of all men in God as the origin of life, a past that is saved in a present that is God's. From 1 Cor 13: 12 we learn that what is involved here is not a dead past but a living and speaking one. For all our ignorance of detail, for all the obscurity of the "last things", the question may be raised: should the believer find it so difficult to accept that in the faithfulness of God as manifested in Christ everything is raised to fresh heights? This faithfulness is too great for man to conceive of it in petty or narrow-minded terms.

The immortality of man and the resurrection of the dead are, furthermore, inconceivable without the co-existence of others who together constitute the communion of the saints. If the *whole* man is to receive life in its final and definitive form, then his co-existence among his fellow men must also be preserved in the future of eternity. The future of the individual and the future of mankind belong together. This is a truth which we already find adumbrated in the witness of the manifestations of the risen Jesus. The resurrection of Jesus from the dead causes the union of the disciples with Christ and among themselves to emerge in a hitherto unprecedented manner. The biblical images of the banquet and the marriage convey the same message. They symbolize the final definitive state of salvation and enable us to recognize that in it those relations with our fellow men which are essential for human existence will be preserved and perfected in the community of the Body of Christ.

End or consummation?

All history begins and ends with faithfulness of God, which is in essence a faithfulness to life itself. Within the broad scope of this idea, which is so basic to the Bible and Christianity, there is room for the entire creation, for all developments

within it whether possible or actual, for every kind of history
and future. If we wish to make this basic perspective of the
Bible our own, then we must say that to the eyes of faith
history and the future remain essentially open and undetermined. History is not the enacting of a drama in accordance
with a divine libretto. Precisely for this reason, however, the
question arises of whether the consummation of history consists of a future that is *absolute* – one in which history as such
will cease – or a future that is *relative* – one in which history
as history will be prolonged. One point is sure. The goal of
history – in biblical terms the "last day" – constitutes not that
in which it is broken off but that in which it is consummated.
In this work of consummation as faith sees it, God and man as
God's free and chosen partner will "share".

The development of the cosmos and of history takes place
through acts of freedom, and this means through the activities
of the spirit. If we take this seriously then world and history of
themselves point to a spiritual factor at their heart and centre.
Faith identifies this with Christ. Hence Teilhard de Chardin
calls him the "omega point" of evolution. What is revealed to
the natural eye as "evolution" is revealed to the eye of faith as
a continuous interplay of divine and human initiatives within
history.

Once more faith must satisfy itself with this. The question
of whether the end to which this interplay between divine
and human freedom culminating in Christ will one day be
brought will be a relative or an absolute end is not one that
will be resolved by *faith*. The *consummation* of the world and
of history do not *ipso facto* mean the same thing as the *end* of
history. It would represent no contradiction to faith if the
consummation of history were to consist in an unending dyna-
mic process.

Thus the believer is confronted with the future and with
history as entities that are essentially open and indeterminate.
Ultimately speaking, he knows nothing of them. But this openness has nothing to do with mere random chance, scepticism,
or fatalism. It is an openness such as love and freedom create.
The believer knows that in his life he is committed to a loving

Thou from whom he can expect all, meaning, future and life. The faithfulness of God in Christ empowers him fearlessly to look into the future and advance into the future. Because God in his faithfulness knows what avails to salvation, the believer can, without disquiet, forgo all detailed knowledge of the future. He can view it in an attitude of total freedom, openness and eagerness. He no longer seeks to know or to receive anything specific from the future, for he looks forward eagerly to *the* supreme future, that which comes from God ever anew. The believer aligns himself, as it were, on the course marked out by God and *wins* the future. For him the future has, in Christ, acquired a name and a programme. This means that the future constitutes a decisive dimension of the Christian faith precisely *because* the Christian does not "know" anything about it. The basic way in which the Christian comes to terms with history and the future is called *hope*. The Christ of faith points the believer outwards and forwards. But hope is only a living force, and will only avoid being a "flight in a forward direction", so long as it does not forget the past of Christ which is gathered up in the Cross. Only so can the Christian continue to play his part as man in history and remain identical with himself.

For the Christian, however, consummation is not merely a subject of hope but precisely on this account a duty and task for the present, requiring him to *act out* his hope. As a factor of history human freedom is an active, creative freedom. Openness to the future, rightly understood and rightly lived, gives human action an unconditional freedom. Making the example of Christ his standard, the Christian accepts the conditions of history and acts according to them. He shapes the future not at his desk or merely in terms of theory and scientific knowledge, but in action. Here once more we find that we have come full circle. Our view of the "last things" leads us to commit ourselves resolutely to action. For only so can we decide once and for all whether it is to be life or death that determines the future (cp Mt 25: 31–46).

Hence a Christian preaching on the "last things" has two focal points: the assertion of God's unshakeable faithfulness to all life, and the summons to action of hope in all spheres of life. Only these two key notions of "eschatology" can do justice to the future. Anyone who considers them, it is true, still knows only very little about the "last things" of man and of the world. But he knows enough to believe hope, love, and to be able to live a life that is full of meaning.

Part Five
Questions in dispute between the churches

23   Preliminary considerations

In this book theologians – or rather Christians – belonging to two major denominations have tried to formulate a joint expression of the message of Christian belief. The fact that this endeavour is possible and indeed necessary gives rise to the question where and why these denominations still differ from each other.

Even though they are in no way exclusively differentiated by setting altar against altar, church against church, doctrine against doctrine, that is at least part of what differentiates them. Their view is that they exist on their own, separate from the others, and that to a great extent they are obliged to develop their activities on their own rather than jointly with the other churches. All the shortcomings, difficulties, rivalries and competition within Christianity have their origin in the fact that up till the present the various denominations are not the outcome and expression of a legitimate and indeed desirable pluriformity within the all-embracing unity of the one Church, but are instead a multiplicity that has not yet found its way to achieving an all-embracing unity.

Christian belief itself says that this state of affairs ought not to last, and must not last: that it should be the object neither of idealistic glorification nor of fatalistic resignation. Faith itself provides the foundation for the obligation to be concerned for the unity of the Church – a unity of which we do not yet have any precise idea but which must in any case become recognizable as a visible unity. Faith itself bids us to do what unites, and to break down whatever prevents or impedes this unity.

It is a cause for thanksgiving that the present situation of the denominations, both in themselves and in their relations with each other, is no longer the same as we have described – as, indeed, we were obliged to describe it on the basis of the facts. The relationship between the churches is no longer something static but is instead moving towards unity – and it is not the least of this book's aims to bear witness to this. The situation is no longer the same as it has been for centuries. The process of strengthening and hardening each church's defences, of emphasizing what is peculiar and individual and thus what is divisive, has been interrupted. What has begun instead is a process of movement, of considering what is held in common and of rejoicing over what is held in common. But this movement has not yet reached its goal. The different denominations still persist in retaining not just their individual peculiarities but also the points at which they are in opposition to each other. In the concluding section of this book we must describe these points of opposition, indicate their mutual origins and background, and try to work out how deep they go and how important they are. At the same time we must recognize that we are working within the perspective of a further objective rapprochement in the future. Admittedly the way to unanimity on certain questions is not yet in sight. But more frequently it is apparent that former points of opposition have already for the most part been overcome and surpassed. Often, indeed, it is difficult to go on talking about "open questions" or "questions in dispute". The disputes that remain often occur already within the joint unity of the confession of faith.

Thus this fifth part is in no way some kind of appendix on a subsidiary subject. What it is concerned with is rather questions and doctrines that have a fundamental effect on the life of the churches and of their members but which cannot in contrast to the subject-matter of preceding sections, be given a common formulation without reservations. Until now we have talked about the common content of opposing viewpoints; now we must talk of opposing viewpoints among those who hold common views. If this is the situation, then our concluding question is all the more urgent: what is the present function and significance of the divided churches?

24 Scripture and tradition

The problem of Scripture and tradition – the question of the relationship between the Bible and non-biblical ecclesiastical tradition and of its actual determinative significance for the Church's doctrine and life – has been an especially heavy burden on the churches for a long time, because meaningful dialogue on the many related questions that are raised seemed no longer at all possible. That the situation is different today we owe on the one hand to the recent findings of biblical scholarship on both sides of the denominational fence, on the other to the results of two important events in the institutional life of the churches: the Faith and Order Conference of the World Council of Churches, and the second Vatican council of the Roman Catholic church.

Scripture and tradition in primitive Christianity

The reason why the dialogue on Scripture and tradition was for a long time unable to make any headway was because – in connexion with the doctrinal decisions of the Council of Trent, which we shall deal with in due course – two opposing viewpoints stood over against each other and no compromise seemed possible between them. The Reformers and the churches of the Reformation took the view that Scripture alone was binding on the Church; the Catholic church, that both

Scripture and the "oral tradition" of the Church that was being guided into all the truth by the Holy Spirit were binding on the Church. First of all we must free ourselves from this kind of antithesis, since it is both historically and factually an oversimplification.

Indeed, in primitive Christianity one cannot set Scripture and tradition in opposition to each other in this way, for the simple reason that the "New Testament" did not yet exist. As far as Jesus and the original Christian community were concerned, "Scripture" was what today we call the "Old Testament", and well into the second century the Old Testament remained "the Church's Bible". The list of books belonging to the Old Testament had in essentials been fixed for some two hundred years, though there had been no fundamental decision on the question within Judaism. It was only at the turn of the first to second century that Jewish scholars completed a definitive delineation of the Old Testament "canon". This was indispensable if Judaism was to be reorganized after the catastrophe of the Jewish War (AD 66–70) and the destruction of Jerusalem.

This had no influence on the Church's attitude to the Old Testament since the Church and Judaism had already begun to go their separate ways. If nevertheless there is essential agreement between the Church and Judaism on the canon of the Old Testament, this has another reason. The fact that the business of collecting the Old Testament writings together had come to an end became for Jesus, for the apostles and for the primitive Church a matter of principle, because God had now acted afresh and definitively in Jesus. The traditions of Israel were not just supplemented or continued in the person and life of Jesus but rather what Jesus was, said and did marked a totally new beginning. In Jesus' preaching, actions, suffering, death and resurrection and in the outpouring of the Spirit the power of God has broken through, salvation is there. Israel's covenant organization as the people of God was necessary for the Old Testament. But now "the law and the prophets" are the book of God's promises and are binding simply as such. The facts of the situation mean that there can no

longer be an independent and autonomous canon of the Old
Testament with its own law. The canon, the guiding line, now
is what God has done and is doing in Christ. The Christian
reads Scripture as a book from which now for the first time
the veil has been lifted (cf 2 Cor 3: 6–18).

What was promised by the Old Testament is proclaimed as
fulfilled here and now by the "good news", the "glad tidings"
of the Gospel (cf Lk 4: 16–21; Mt 11: 5 ff; together with Is
52: 7 and 61: 1). But here the Gospel is as yet not Scripture,
not something written down. What Jesus himself did and the
preaching of the original Christian community constitute "the
Gospel". But this preaching was not confined to expounding
a handful of dry basic formulas, any more than the preaching
of Jesus himself. In connexion with the preaching of the
"Gospel" there arose a tradition that was very much alive and
rich. The sayings of the Lord were passed on, as were Jesus'
parables, formulations of belief, liturgical texts, catechetical
summaries and so on. This tradition is in fact "oral", and until
the 60s no one took the trouble to fix it in writing. The letters
that the Apostle Paul wrote much earlier (between AD 49 and
55) cannot be brought into the argument here since they all
presuppose the existence of the oral preaching of the Gospel
and are concerned simply to clear up particular questions that
had arisen in communities that the apostle was for the time
unable to visit personally.

But this kind of oral tradition was not left without any protection against being falsified. Within the complex multiplicity
of traditions there was a "standard" tradition against which
every other tradition could be judged. This standard – or, to
use the technical term, "normative" – tradition existed from
early on in the form of firmly established formulas which were
not open to misinterpretation but were only capable of being
accepted. I Cor 15: 1–11 is the clearest example of this, but
in no way the only one. But in a Church that was steadily
expanding this protection could not be permanently satisfactory. Thus in the "post-apostolic age" – round about AD 65–
100, in other words after the deaths of Peter, Paul and James
the brother of the Lord – there arose most of the New

Testament writings – written with the precise aim of collecting the traditions inherited from the apostolic age on the basis of this "normative" tradition.

The gospels are particularly indicative of the way in which this aim was carried out. The material available was collected and arranged according to definite themes. The immediate consequences can easily be guessed: the rôle formerly played by the formulas of the normative tradition, that of providing a standard for all other traditions, was now filled by these writings or "scriptures". Nor did things come to a stop with individual writings. The gospels, the letters and the other works were brought together in groups – and soon the question arose as to what ought definitely to belong among these normative writings and what ought not. From the historical point of view we cannot throw light on all the details of the process whereby the Church formulated the view that was to lead to its final answer. But we can discern what in fact was the guiding principle. If the Old Testament is concluded because its promises have been fulfilled, then the collection of apostolic writings is complete because the Church knows that it is bound to the once-and-for-all history of Jesus and of his first messengers. All the available efforts to establish in writing the original tradition of what God was doing in Jesus and all written record of the apostolic preaching were thus brought together to form a new "canon". Already by the middle of the second century there is essential agreement on this canon, even though discussion continued into the fourth century on individual books such as the Letter to the Hebrews or the Revelation of John. But this meant that the "Gospel" in its original form had become "Scripture"; that from the formal point of view it had the same character as the Old Testament. At the beginning of the third century the name "New Testament" began to be used for this Gospel that had become Scripture.

From this historical sketch we can now draw weighty conclusions for the question of "Scripture and tradition". No longer can a completely independent complex entity called "Scripture" be given precedence over and placed in opposition to a "tradition" separated from it – as has often happened on the Protestant side. Tradition and Scripture in the New Testament stand in a mutually shifting relationship – and similar conclusions can be drawn for the Old Testament. But equally unilateral emphasis cannot be put on the deep significance of oral tradition in primitive Christianity, leading on to the view that the establishment of this in writing, in other words the emergence of the New Testament as "Scripture", is only a secondary process of less importance – as there was and is a tendency to do on the Catholic side. One must not let oneself be led astray by the apparently simple and unequivocal concept of "tradition". In the primitive Church there was a wealth of tension between "the" tradition, that was established in fixed formulations and provided the standard, and the traditions that actively expounded and developed it.

After the normative tradition had become "Scripture", this opposition and tension arose afresh between Scripture and traditional interpretation, since, just as formerly with "the" tradition, "Scripture" had to be placed within the context of the present and interpreted – a process that continues today. From one point of view the relationship and the tension between Scripture and traditional interpretation can be tracked back to the New Testament itself. From the other point of view it has never been seriously disputed that there has been and must be one legitimate tradition of interpretation. It is no wonder that this tension continually gives rise to the question where the tradition of interpretation splits off from "the" tradition – in other words, where, in the language of Mk 7: 8, the tradition of interpretation becomes simply a "tradition of men".

It is thus precisely on the basis of the New Testament that the findings of biblical scholarship have led us to a better understanding of the true core of the old dispute over Scripture and tradition. Scripture and tradition are not fundamentally in opposition to one another – but they can quickly become so. Every living interpretation runs the risk of falling victim to the pressures of the age and situation in which it is formulated, inasmuch as ultimately it is drawing on its own resources. For this reason it needs a standard. It is only if interpretation remains continually critical of itself in the light of this standard that Gospel and faith stay protected from falsification even when they are subjected to creative reformulation. In the primitive Church this standard was provided by the fixed formulas of the normative tradition. Today it is provided by the scriptures of the New Testament.

The early Church and the Church of the Middle Ages

The risk of falsification by means of a tradition of interpretation that goes beyond its proper limits is nearly as old as the Christian message itself. The authors of the New Testament writings had already had to fight against "false teachers", and this struggle continued after the emergence of the New Testament. Indeed, the establishment of the "canon" was itself to be a weapon in this struggle: certain writings that had been tolerated up to now were no longer recognized as binding and – to some extent – were dropped from public official church use.

But this was only a partial help. The false teachers themselves claimed support from the New Testament writings. Thus the struggle over the right interpretation of tradition became a struggle over the right interpretation of Scripture. But what arguments was one to appeal to? At once the appeal was made once again to traditions that had stayed alive in the Church – in the individual churches. This explains why the bishops were soon to play a decisive rôle in this dispute. In the early Church it was still easy to trace the line of succession in office back to the apostles – only a few generations separated them from Jesus' own times. Therefore one should have confidence in the bishops' ability to stand immediately and reliably in the right tradition. Hence a special grace or *charisma* was ascribed to them of discovering the truth in disputes over faith and doctrine.

But the older the Church grew the less this simple solution became possible. The binding doctrinal statements of individual bishops were taken over by decisions of synods and councils that had to decide between truth and error when matters of belief were in dispute. What these Church assemblies understood themselves to be doing was to expound and explain Scripture and existing tradition. But on the other hand their decisions now for their part formed a new Church tradition. We are aware of the powerful influence that has been enjoyed right up to the present by the confessional and doctrinal tradition forged by the councils of the early Church. Even during the Reformation this tradition was never called into question. On the contrary, the "consensus of the first five centuries" often provided the starting-point for disputes between the two sides.

But even in the early Church this process of building up tradition had had an increasingly wide effect. Characteristic of this is the famous statement by Vincent of Lérins, who died around 450, in his *Commonitorium*. His test for genuine tradition was "what has been believed everywhere, always, and by all" (2: 5: *quod ubique, quod semper, quod ab omnibus creditum est*). Our faith, he said, must first of all be guarded by the authority of God's law, in other words, Scripture. But the canon of biblical writings, for all that it was complete, needed a definite standard according to which it should be interpreted: as could easily be ascertained, these writings were interpreted in very different senses. Therefore a plain and unequivocal decision was needed. There was progress in doctrine inasmuch as it was made progressively clearer and more explicit. But there was no change of doctrine. It must not be affected in its specific characteristics, there must not be a multiplicity of conflicting views. One's concern and passion should serve not progress and development but the "view that what is characteristic of Christian discretion and consideration is not to transmit to succeeding generations what is one's own, as something new, but to guard what one has received from earlier ones".

But tradition was not understood and continued in the Christian Church in quite the simple and unequivocal sense in which Vincent of Lérins had described it. In the view of the Eastern church a legitimate development of tradition existed only in the case of the seven "ecumenical councils" held between 325 and 787: it was, in other words, a process that came to an end with the eighth century. In contrast, the view was always held in the Latin-speaking church of the West that the process of the formation of tradition was something that continued, since new times brought new challenges that demanded new forms for the response of faith. Thus, for example, there arose the dispute with the Eastern church over the *filoque* clause ("and from the Son"). The Eastern church wanted to keep the text of the confession of faith or creed drawn up at the Council of Nicaea in 325 and expanded at the Council of Constantinople in 381, and in this Nicene creed this phrase does not occur in the confession of faith in the Holy Spirit. After a lengthy dispute the Western church finally in 1014 inserted the statement that the Holy Spirit proceeds from the Father "and from the Son". Up till the present there has as yet been no agreement with the Eastern church on this question.

Further councils held by the Western church, as well as other developments, led during the course of the Middle Ages to a wider formation of new traditions. But the broader this stream of tradition grew, the greater grew the danger of Scripture and tradition becoming significantly separated from each other. What was the use of scientific theology retaining its sober moderation and being able to distinguish between binding traditions recognized by the Church and the many other traditions on which the Church had never come to a decision? It was the latter that defined the Church's daily life, and they permeated it to the point that the best minds in the Church had the impression that gradually what was essential in the Christian message, that gradually *the* tradition was here being overgrown and lost to view.

Scripture in the view of the Reformation

Martin Luther was thus by no means the first member of the Church to go back to Scripture as the only binding standard in the face of this danger. But Luther set about this task with such energy, in connexion with all the other new directions his theology was taking, that his work and his teaching set the whole question of the relationship between Scripture and tradition in motion again. In his disputes over questions of belief he wanted to allow as valid only those arguments that were drawn from Scripture. Decisions of councils had no binding authority as far as he was concerned. Admittedly the expression *sola scriptura* – "Scripture alone" – which was later to become a slogan in religious quarrels, does not actually occur as early as the sixteenth century, even though in fact Luther meant precisely this when he coined phrases like "only Scripture" or "God's word alone", and it was in this sense that the 1577 Formula of Concord used the words "only the prophetic and apostolic writings of the Old and New Testaments".

It would be a complete misrepresentation of what Luther was concerned about if one were to accuse him of having turned the Bible into a "paper Pope". He discerned distinctions within Scripture according to whether the writings concerned "are about Christ's business or not . . . Whatever does not teach Christ, is not apostolic, even if it is Peter or Paul who is teaching. But again whatever preaches Christ can be taken as apostolic, even if it is Judas, Annas, Pilate or Herod at work" (Preface to the Epistle of James, WA 7: 385: 27). What one must then say is that for Luther the word of God is to be found in the sayings of God and of Christ contained in the books of Scripture that have come down to us.

Balancing the distinction made on the one hand between the inherited stability and certainty of Scripture and the word of God that was proclaimed in it, was on the other hand the strong emphasis laid on the authority of God's word. Everything in the Church was subject to the dominion of this word of God. There had never been any foundation for this authority other than the explicit statements of Scripture and the witness of the Holy Spirit in the conscience of the faithful. Nobody thought it was necessary to base this authority on tradition too.

But Luther did not by any means break radically with tradition. He never called into question the early Church's development of doctrine. Traditions in the Church's doctrine and life that were not in contradiction with Scripture he allowed to continue. Other theologians of the Reformation wanted to be much more thorough-going here and were prepared only to allow as valid what was explicitly taught by Scripture. But their view did not prevail. All the Reformers were concerned to fight against was one particular false tradition that obscured the truth of Scripture. If they appealed to the Bible as the unique source of our knowledge of God's revelation and as the ultimate standard for the Church, what they wanted was simply to give fresh validity to nothing other than the "good old tradition". In this sense they were "traditionalists" and thought of themselves as such. And they had no time for those who saw the standard for the Church in the possession of the Spirit by individual believers and in their experience of its effects. Luther called these people "enthusiasts" and "fanatics", and they are still given these labels – even though today serious people ask whether this is not to do them an injustice.

The Council of Trent

In the face of this Protestant challenge the Council of Trent (1545–63) was obliged to state its mind on the question of tradition and to justify the existence and validity of the different traditions in the Roman Catholic church. In doing so tradition was expounded as something existing in its own right alongside Scripture. It was decreed that tradition should be accepted and honoured "with the same love and respect" as Scripture (DS 1501). A tradition that coincided with Scripture was called *traditio inhaesiva* (inherent tradition). If it explained a biblical passage that in itself was obscure, it was called *traditio declarativa* (declarative tradition). If in questions of faith or morals a tradition went beyond Scripture, it was called *traditio constitutiva* (constitutive tradition).

The Catholic church's dogmas of Mary's immaculate conception and assumption are based on this kind of *traditio con-*

stitutiva. In this context the conscious belief of the people of God has become the primary criterion for valid tradition.

But it should be noted that the interpretation of the Tridentine doctrinal decrees on this point has today become a matter of dispute among Catholic church historians. The point is made that the Council's deliberations, as can be seen from the record of its proceedings, put *traditio* (tradition) and *consuetudo* (custom, usage) on the same footing. The Reformers' attack was also directed at the dominion of *consuetudo* in the Church. It was only a later interpretation that thought it had found here the basis for a theory of "two sources" of revelation of equal authority and used this as a foundation for further developments.

The way in which the relationship between Scripture and the representatives of tradition was for a long time seen in the Catholic church can be shown by a quotation from the encyclical *Humani generis* of 12 August 1950. This rejects the view that "the teaching of the Holy Fathers and the sacred magisterium should be weighed as it were in the balance of sacred Scripture as this is expounded by exegetes according to purely human criteria, rather than that this same sacred Scripture should be expounded according to the mind of the Church, which was established by Christ the Lord as the guardian and interpreter of the entire deposit of divinely revealed truth" (DS 3887).

The arguments that lie behind the words of the encyclical are not confined to one denomination or only to the Roman Catholic church. In all churches a fresh consideration of tradition and of its relationship to Scripture has become necessary. The results of this new attempt to think this problem out are to be found on the one hand in the report of Section II of the fourth Faith and Order Conference held in Montreal from 12 to 26 July 1963, and on the other in the second Vatican council's dogmatic constitution on divine revelation, published on 18 November 1965. We shall deal with these two documents in chronological order.

The faith and order conference

It must always be remembered that up for discussion at
Montreal under the heading "Scripture, Tradition and Traditions" was a much broader complex of questions than we
are concerned with in this connexion. It was not just a matter
of problems affecting two major denominations, but a discussion between representatives and observers from the whole of
Christianity throughout the world.

In the discussion fresh consideration was given to an old
distinction, that between "tradition" and "traditions". The
Gospel itself and its being carried on was to be understood as
included within "tradition": the "paradosis of the kerygma,
the contents of which is Christ himself". It is self-explanatory
that with reference to this "tradition" one can say that this
kind of tradition has remained alive since the time of Jesus,
and that against this background Scripture is something that
came as a later supplement because it first emerged afterwards.

In the light of this starting-point the opposition between
"Scripture" and "tradition", as it has been known to us since
the sixteenth century as the subject of the controversy,
appears as a marginal problem. In contrast, the question
seriously to be pursued is how "traditions" within Christianity
are on the one hand differentiated from the one single "tradition" and on the other are yet connected with it. The investigation goes further, into the question how traditions that
embody the true tradition are to be distinguished from those
that represent a purely human tradition.

One criterion for the true tradition was provided by the
New Testament at the moment when it was recognized by the
Church and its canon was established. But hardly had this
standard been discovered and set up than the Church was
faced with the question how these writings of the New Testament canon were to be interpreted correctly. Although it is
unanimously agreed that the correct interpretation of Scripture can only take place successfully under the guidance of
the Holy Spirit, it is clear that the traditions of the different

churches conceal distinct "hermeneutical principles", in other words different criteria according to which Scripture must be interpreted. It was stated in Montreal that every part must be interpreted in the light of the whole of Scripture. What was meant was, in other words, that the key to the understanding of Scripture lies in the incarnation, the atonement, justification, the message of the rule of God or in Jesus' moral teaching. A consequence of these different principles of interpretation is that individual passages of Scripture are given different interpretations while at the same time agreement can be established over long passages taken as a whole.

Considerations of this kind were concluded at Montreal with the question whether the ecumenical situation did not demand searching for the one tradition and seriously examining individual particular traditions. Together with this concluding challenge the representatives of the churches gathered at Montreal let it be known that for them tradition in the sense that they had defined it represented a reality over which no dispute was possible.

The second Vatican council

The text that the second Vatican council worked out on the question with which we are concerned also has behind it a tough theological debate. But, compared with Montreal, Rome offered a better situation, inasmuch as everyone belonged to one and the same church, could take up the formulations of previous councils, and had more time and more consultors at their disposal.

"The tradition" is discussed in chapter 2 of the constitution on divine revelation, a chapter headed: "The transmission of divine revelation." It was noted that the chapter dealing with tradition is embedded in a broader context in which four whole chapters are devoted to Scripture – and it should also not be overlooked that the catchword "tradition" is entirely lacking from the heading to this chapter.

On the basis of the statements of the Council of Trent and the first Vatican council, the second Vatican council defines the relationship of Scripture and tradition. At the first glance it is apparent that it is now the word "tradition" in the singular that comes to the fore – at Trent there was more talk of "traditions" in the plural. That is a clear point of contact with the text of the Montreal Faith and Order Conference. Similar contact occurs between the council's affirmation: "This sacred tradition and sacred Scripture of both the Old and the New Testament are like a mirror in which the pilgrim Church on earth looks at God, ... until she is brought finally to see him as he is, face to face," and the demand made at Montreal to look for "the tradition".

The idea that the apostolic tradition is subject to a certain progress is adhered to. But this progress is defined as a deeper understanding of the faith, not as the creation of new doctrinal statements from the explicit belief of the people of God. Thus the close link between tradition and Scripture can be maintained, since both arise from the same divine source and aim at the same goal. In this way the Fathers of Vatican II avoided setting Scripture and tradition up side by side as two more or less independent sources of our knowledge of the faith. As far as concerns the magisterium, the Church's teaching authority, which has the task of expounding the word of God whether written or handed on (note the clever combination of Scripture and tradition), it is expressly stated that this teaching authority is not placed above the word of God but has the task of serving it. If one asks what the source is from which the teaching authority works, then once again in this context the "one deposit of faith" is named. The Council of Trent's demand that Scripture and tradition should be "accepted and venerated with the same sense of devotion and reverence" is also repeated. We must wait to see how this earlier formulation will be interpreted in its new context and which interpretation will prevail within the Catholic church.

In conclusion, it is probably not going too far to say that even within the Roman Catholic church it is felt to be a lack that the critical ingredient is missing from the chapter on tradition. At least this can be heard clearly today in Catholic theology and in judgments on the church's way of life.

Admittedly, in the Catholic understanding of things Scripture is not the only means whereby what the Bible is concerned with is brought to men. But it is the Bible alone that provides the criterion for judging whether what men have been brought into contact with from other sources is really what the Bible is concerned about. In this sense the Catholic too can say "Scripture alone". The promising element at all events is that the Council has created a new starting-point: tradition as communication in God's activity of giving. This brings to the fore a principle from which the dialogue between the confessions can gain fresh perspectives of hope. Thus on all sides a new starting-point has been created that makes it possible "to fulfil with courage and strength the Church's major task of handing on to men in this new world culture the tradition, the word of grace and hope, as in the past it was preached in Jerusalem, Greece, Rome and Gaul, yes, as far as the uttermost ends of the earth" (Montreal, 1963).

25   Grace and works

What disrupted the unity of the Church in the sixteenth century was not the dispute over Scripture and tradition. Despite the dominating rôle this subject played in the struggle, what really disrupted the unity of the Church was another disputed question which lay at the heart of all the disagreements. The question was the significance for our salvation in on the one hand God's grace and on the other what men did themselves – by works. In technical theological language the dispute was over the "sinner's justification before God". For the fathers of the Reformation this question represented the *articulus stantis et cadentis ecclesiae*, the article of faith by which the Church stood and fell. They repeatedly made their obedience to the Pope dependent on the latter guaranteeing freedom in the Church to the preaching of the Evangelical doctrine of justification. But this did not happen. Instead the Council of Trent during the years 1545–7 formulated the

Catholic counter-position in the decree on justification (Session VI) and established it as a binding dogma. The Lutheran doctrine of justification is to be found in its dogmatically binding form in, especially, the 1530 Augsberg Confession, in the 1531 Apologia for the Confession, in the 1537 Schmalkalden Articles, and in the 1577 Formula of Concord. What is this dispute all about?

Luther's radical insight

It is best to begin by having a brief look at Luther's early life. He entered the religious life, a monastery, in order to find peace with God and with himself. In this he shows himself to us as totally a man of the Middle Ages. Peace, salvation and justice in the sight of God were, as Luther had learned, decisively dependent not only on Christ and on God's grace made present in him, but also just as much on people's efforts to achieve perfection in their lives, and the highest level of the perfect life was that of the cloister, the religious life. "God will not deny grace to him who does what is in him" was a guiding principle of late medieval theology and piety, and someone who happened to be in the "state of grace" needed good works in order to achieve eternal life. It is well known that Luther fell into despair in his efforts to live according to these principles. At the core of his being he discovered ineradicable selfishness; he felt he was "distorted in himself". Since nothing of his own could have value before God, he felt he was rejected by God and deprived of salvation. Nothing was changed by receiving absolution in the sacrament of penance or by regularly taking part in the eucharist. "Fear drove me to despair, since nothing but death remained for me and I must go down to hell," he was to write later in a poem.

It was in these personal religious experiences that the way was prepared for the Reformation. It took place "because Germans have and had the need to be pious" (Clemens Maria Hofbauer, the Austrian Redemptorist saint who died in 1820), and because Luther made his "reformatory discovery" in the New Testament, particularly in Rom 1: 16 ff. God gave grace

and salvation unconditionally; God's grace was intended precisely for the person who is and remains a sinner and who as a
Christian has nothing to show that could really save him. Salvation was to be sought and found in God's grace alone and in
no way in our own works. For this what was needed was faith
alone that accepted God's gift. This kind of grace that is
unconditionally guaranteed to faith is, Luther declared, the
"justice of God" spoken of in the Letter to the Romans.

The Council of Trent on grace and works

This basic insight of Luther's from which the Reformation
sprang found its final form for the time being in the Lutheran
church's confessional writings mentioned above. From the
Catholic side these are opposed by the Council of Trent's
decree on justification. A look at the boundaries that were
finally fixed here shows how they had their roots in Luther's
early experiences.

As before, what is in dispute between the confessions is the
way in which God deals with the sinner and leads him to salvation. The Catholic doctrine formulated by the Council of
Trent at its sixth session says roughly the following. God
desires man's good. He makes him a new man through a
power which comes from Christ and his work of redemption
and which flows into man like a stream. This power is called
"grace". Grace first of all affects the non-Christian through the
proclamation of the word which arouses in him the first stir-
rings of faith, hope and love. Here the Council of Trent corrected the late medieval view by stating that these first
impulses towards good also arose from grace and not from
man's natural capabilities. If someone who was so affected
allowed himself to be baptized, then transforming grace took
complete possession of him and made him into a new man.
This process the Council of Trent called "justification". Thus
the justification of the sinner consisted of "a passing from that
condition in which man is born a son of the first Adam to the
condition of grace and of 'adoption as sons' of God through
the second Adam, our saviour Jesus Christ" (DS 1524). The

person who has been baptized and filled with grace then leads a life full of faith, hope and love. This life will then be reckoned to him as meriting eternal blessedness. If he should fall into serious sins, then the sacrament of penance helps him to regain his state of grace. At the end of the ages the Christian will exhibit his life to the eternal judge as a white garment made resplendent by God's grace and thereupon receive eternal life as his reward.

The dispute over grace and works

The essential features of the objection brought by the Reformation against the Catholic doctrine sketched out above are as follows. It is an illusion to think man even as a Christian could ever attain such a degree of perfection that the inner disposition of his life and his deeds could bring him eternal life as a reward. If there is any such thing as salvation and eternal life, then that is only because God, through a judgment of grace, acquits man for Jesus' sake, man who even as a Christian remains a sinner (*simul iustus et peccator*, at one and the same time both justified and a sinner). This acquittal through grace was called "justification" by the Reformation. To this the Christian is directed every day until the end of his life. "Grace alone" saves men: no human work has any power here. For it is "Christ alone" who has made satisfaction for the salvation of mankind. It is to dishonour him to want to place human merits alongside his merits. God's law serves to keep his lack of ability as clearly as possible before man's eyes. It is only when we come to faith that man has any contribution to make – and this is not really man's own contribution at all but simply the means God has given him so that he may receive God's verdict of grace. This is what was meant when alongside "by grace alone" (*sola gratia*) and "Christ alone" (*solus Christus*) the Reformers made "by faith alone" (*sola fide*) a valid summary of their position against the Catholic view.

There was, certainly, one misunderstanding which the Reformers vigorously rejected. "Our people are falsely accused of forbidding good works," says the Augsburg Confession (xx). Luther himself in 1520 wrote a "Sermon of good works" and in his two 1529 catechisms provided thoroughgoing interpretations of the Ten Commandments. What was decisive for the Reformers was simply this, that doing good should never be regarded as a *condition* for salvation: it was rather a *fruit* of the *unconditional* gift of salvation and an expression of thanksgiving for this. There is no trace of an egotistical concern over working out one's own salvation.

It was because the Reformers saw their threefold "alone" – "Christ alone", "by grace alone", "by faith alone" – threatened in the Catholic system drawn up at Trent that they protested. It was because the Catholic church for its part saw the Reformation giving rise to moral anarchy and thus threatening fundamental statements of Christian belief that it condemned the Reformation. And that led to schism.

Polemical escalation

Four hundred years later, how does this dispute appear today? It would certainly be dangerous if the fact that we are historically distanced from it had the effect of making us less deeply affected and agitated by the concerns of sixteenth-century Christians. But on the other hand this very distancing allows us to recognize in their disputes much that is conditioned by their time and situation. And this recognition enables the attempt to be made to overcome unnecessary disagreements without betraying the truth.

The greater historical distance first of all allows us to realize better than formerly that many theses and statements have been conditioned by the very counter-position they were drawn up to answer and have thus been made more one-sided than they need have been. An understandable example of this one-sidedness is the way in which, in the face of a system of thinking in terms of man's religious and moral contribution to be found in late medieval theology and piety, the Reformation should have brought the unconditional nature of God's salvation, achieved without human works, into the foreground. After Luther's death one of his particularly zealous adherents, Nicolaus of Amsdorf, took this one-sidedness to the extreme position of saying that good works were downright harmful for salvation and eternal bliss. It was no wonder that, faced with this kind of one-sided approach, the Council of Trent should for its part have reacted with defensive polemics and placed the emphasis on good works and their meritorious effect.

A closer examination nevertheless enables us to discover not only in Luther, but in all the other Reformers, an awareness of something like the importance of good works for salvation. The phrase "by faith alone" directed exclusively against all works must for example be read in conjunction with a statement of Luther's in the preface to the Letter to the Romans in his translation of the Bible: "Oh, there is something living, active, powerful about faith that it is impossible for it to do good without doing it unceasingly." Faith, precisely as the means whereby God's grace is received, is itself the doer of good works. On this point recent research has asked whether in Luther himself certain aspects were not still interconnected and became over-distinguished from each other in the later development of his teaching, especially under Melanchthon's influence. Such a distinction would already be problematical if one considers that faith has necessarily got something to do with conversion and repentance. All this is of course first apparent when it is considered from the standpoint provided by the longer perspective of history. Perhaps, in order to represent Luther's view correctly and completely, one would have to say that no one will achieve salvation *without* repentence and without good works, but that on the other hand no one gains salvation *by means of* repentance and good works, since even the most excellent of Christians is in his continuing imperfection and guilt driven back on God's infinite mercy.

If the Fathers of Trent had heard the witness of the Reformation expressed in this way, would they have formulated wherever possible certain problematical statements about the "meritorious effect" of good works differently? For the Council's statement that justification opens up to man the achieving of a new life in faith, hope and love is something that no

Reformer disputed in peaceful debate. And even the difficult assertions about the meritorious effects of good works sound a little differently if one considers that according to the Council of Trent "God's goodness towards all men is so great that he wants his own gifts to be their merits" (DS 1548).

Differences of language

The dispute was further burdened by the fact that at crucial points people were talking different languages. The Catholic side was indebted to the medieval tradition of thought, marked by the conceptual system of Aristotelian philosophy. In contrast the Reformation had broken through the medieval tradition at essential points by going back directly to the biblical mode of thought and speech. Thus for example what the Catholic side understood by "grace" was primarily, as described above, that divine power flowing into man, while the Reformation used this word to mean God's gracious disposition and activity. The two do not have to exclude each other if one starts from the point that God's grace necessarily creates man anew because it brings him into a new personal relationship of love and forgiveness to God and because this love and forgiveness provide the motive power for his life. But the difference of usage left the disputes a legacy of considerable confusion.

The concept of "faith" provides a similar case. According to the medieval tradition of thought, "faith" meant the human understanding saying yes to God and to his revealed truth. In contrast the Reformation understood by "faith" man's total giving of himself in trust to God with *all* the levels of his being, and thus it included in this concept all that according to medieval Catholic usage was expressed by the concepts of "hope" and "love". The result once again was a lot of talking at cross-purposes, and someone contemplating the dispute from the standpoint of the present day reaches the verdict that it was burdened by a wealth of misunderstandings.

But to say all this is not to say that in reality both sides were fundamentally saying the same thing. There remain not just differences of emphasis but also genuine differences of substance – as in the questions of the rôle played by sin in the life of the Christian, the rôle of good works for salvation, and where the decisive emphasis is to be placed in God's action of justification. But it is quite clear that both sides do in fact stand closer to each other than was recognized in the heat of the dispute in the sixteenth century.

Paul or James?

In order to reach a suitable verdict on the range and importance of the differences of doctrine that actually occurred in the sixteenth century it is especially necessary to subject these to the light of the New Testament witness. That is what modern theological scholarship has done, reaching the following conclusions.

First of all, the New Testament itself contains a multiplicity of statements on the relationship between grace, faith and works. Side by side with the fundamentally important view of Paul we must also consider that of James. In contrast to the crucial Pauline statement of Rom 3: 28: "For we hold that a man is justified by faith (alone) apart from works of law" there stands the text of Jas 2: 24: "You see that a man is justified by works and not by faith alone." As far as Luther was concerned this contradiction was one of the reasons for devaluing the Letter of James as a "letter of straw". As far as we are concerned this difference of language should be taken as an indication of how very differently one and the same message can be proclaimed in different situations and in response to different challenges. What Paul had to fight against was a Judaic piety centred on the law and its fulfilment and thus on the purely human contribution. James in contrast was up against an ethical laxity and irresponsibility that claimed support from Paul, even though that was a misunderstanding of Paul.

Besides the Letter of James, it is above all the Gospel according to Matthew and its account and interpretation of Jesus' message that should be named as witness to a tradition of preaching and doctrine specifically distinct from the

Pauline one: "Not every one who says to me, 'Lord, Lord,' shall enter the kingdom of heaven, but he who does the will of my Father who is in heaven," Jesus says in the sermon on the mount (Mt 7: 21). No more than in the beatitudes is the fulfilment of the law turned simply into the condition for salvation in this passage: it is rather an attitude that points far beyond such an outlook, an attitude that indeed aims at being like God (Mt 5: 48). But man's attitude and behaviour are unequivocally presented as decisive for his eternal fate. And moreover even in Paul's own writings statements are to be met like that of 2 Cor 5: 10 which can only with difficulty be brought into agreement with the sentence from Rom 3 quoted above because they too ascribe to what the Christian does a decisive significance for his ultimate salvation. Is it that ultimately the Reformation offered a one-sided interpretation of Paul himself too?

Paul and Luther

Here we need to bring in the second conclusion reached by modern theological scholarship. This is that none of the positions adopted at the time of the Reformation can simply be brought into congruence with any one of the views of the New Testament. Attention has in fact been drawn to considerable differences between Paul and Luther. Luther's thesis that the Christian is at one and the same time a sinner and justified and that he is therefore dependent on God's continual mercy is not to be found in this form in Paul. Rather, according to Rom 8: 1, there is with those who are in Christ Jesus no longer anything that could bring about their condemnation. But does this in itself provide a verdict on Luther? Could not his position have been a relevant translation in terms of the Christian situation of the sixteenth century? Was it not possible fifteen hundred years after Paul to know of the experience of the Christian's existence as a sinner in a quite different perspective from what was possible for Paul?

For the discussion between the denominations yet another example is especially important. If Paul talks of justification, he is not thinking in terms of the pair of alternatives that played such a prominent part in the Reformation, which saw justification either as God's judgment or as an inner transformation. What justification meant for Paul was rather entering into the realm of God's dominion and his justice and thereby changing masters. When God utters the judgment of grace over a man he makes him the servant of his justice. Accepting God's judgment of acquittal in faith means thereby and at the same time taking on the service of justice, a service that is expressed in a new life and in good deeds. God's unconditional gift of grace is as such man's subjection to his authority, for he who has received grace is and continually becomes a different, new man through this gift of grace, since he surrenders himself to God and mankind in love and trust. From this point of view the contrast between Rom 3: 28 and 2 Cor 5: 10 becomes more understandable. And Paul is seen to be a kind of bridge thrown across the trenches between the separated churches of the West.

Grace for the world

If this interpretation is correct, then it cannot today be a matter of us simply subscribing to the Reformation against the Council of Trent or the other way round. Still less can we play the biblical witnesses off against one another. Today rather we are faced with the question how Christians can jointly find new and revelant words for the one message of salvation of Jesus Christ, with its essential and unavoidable tension between grace and works, in the situations of the contemporary world – a task that each has to undertake from the starting-point of the emphasis of his own tradition but at the same time with regard to the other traditions. Characteristic of the situation in which contemporary mankind finds itself is the fact that to a very considerable degree the problems of the individual have become entangled with the problems of the world and of society as a whole. For this reason the proclamation of the Christian message must make it more than ever clear that God's approach to us in Jesus

Christ is not simply grace for the isolated individual but "grace for the world". It is in Christ that God has loved the *world* (Jn 3: 16), it is in Christ that he has chosen a *people* for his own (Tit 2: 14): the individual shares in God's love only as a member of mankind and of the chosen people. What strikes the contemporary observer is that in the dispute over grace and works in the sixteenth century both sides showed remarkable one-sidedness in allowing the individual and his relationship with God to stand at the focus of their interest. Today it is a matter of grasping and of making it possible to grasp that God's judgment of grace saves man from the inescapable involvement in guilt of mankind as a whole. And by doing this God opens his attack on mankind thus involved in guilt, on its urge to be self-sufficient and its self-justification, on all lack of reconciliation, lack of love, and manipulation of man by man. In this case "faith alone" would again be two things at once: being borne up by God's love, which in the midst of all the hopelessness of the world shows itself in the encouragement of forgiveness and in a wealth of goodness that is continually allotted to us – and the service of love towards the world, a service which God uses as the means of his attack on the world of despair and of his mercy towards those whom he loves. The Christian community could be the place where this grace and this faith continually came to a conscious encounter. And this would then be salvation – the salvation that the men of our generation hunger after just as much as the men of four hundred or two thousand years ago. It would be the salvation that God grants here and now and in the midst of the world, but in such a way that at the same time there becomes visible a glimpse of the hope for the promised world that has been granted salvation, the world that will be God's eternal world.

Since the Church split in the sixteenth century there has from time to time appeared in Lutheranism a fatal tendency towards a passive attitude to the world – the consequence of a misunderstanding of "by faith alone". On the Catholic side the contrasting danger has now and then been shown of a harmful tendency to think in terms of the purely human contribution. Today it is no longer unthinkable that a relevant understanding of what living by faith means today can transform the sixteenth century dispute over grace and works into a joint witness in our contemporary world.

26   The sacraments

The churches' teaching on the sacraments does not give rise to quite so much hope as the former disputes over grace and works. Admittedly, it is already possible to go so far as to say that, in the matter of the sacraments, there are no differences of doctrine between the Christian churches that are fundamentally and for ever irreconcilable – as the following considerations will show. But at the same time there are differences, and when we trace these back to their roots we come up against profounder differences and points of opposition between the churches than could be recognized at first – as too will be made clear in what follows. It is only if we can find a road towards unity with regard to these profounder differences that the disputes of yesterday can be transformed into joint witness in the question of the sacraments too.

The starting-point

We must start from a fact that is undisputed and that should not be under-valued: the fact that the major Christian denominations have sacraments. The criteria for recognizing the Church and the basis for its unity are always, in the view of the major churches denominations, purity of doctrine and the correct administration of the sacraments (Augsburg Confession VII). The sacraments moreover belong to the active working out of faith in the "everyday" life of the Church, today perhaps more than ever. At all events people in all the churches are increasingly aware of the significance of the sacraments. If therefore there is a difference of doctrine between the denominations with regard to the sacraments, then it is not the kind of thing that can be reduced to the formula of claiming that sacraments exist here but not there. Nor can the difference be expressed in such terms as on the one hand "grace by means of the sacraments alone" and on the other "grace by means of the Word alone" or however such formulas might still be drawn up. The consequence is that the denominational differences in sacramental doctrine must rather arise from the fact that for example different things are understood and expressed by the term "grace" or "word"; and these above all have their roots in the fundamental doctrinal differences that divide the denominations. If these latter were to be overcome, then the former would be overcome along with them.

But that is not the only source from which different views of the sacraments can arise. Another source is in fact the different development of the life of the Church in the different denominations. The actual life of the Church took on different forms as a result of the fundamental and divisive differences of doctrine. The consequence is very remarkable. Before the Church divided, in other words just before the Reformation, the one undivided Church possessed a large wealth of different forms of liturgy and of church life. After the Church split in two, one denomination placed more emphasis on some forms from this rich legacy and neglected others, while the reverse happened in another denomination. This gave rise to differences and indeed points of opposition, practices which before the Reformation were able peacefully to co-exist within the one Church but which now divided the churches from one another. As a result one can to a great extent be concerned for reunion and unity without this entailing each denomination having to give up what is especially important to it and what it is especially fond of. This of course will only happen if first of all there is a rapprochement on the fundamental differences of doctrine and if this is made the starting-point for the road towards unity. Otherwise any unity on sacramental doctrine would have feet of clay. But the Christian churches have already entered on this road.

In what follows we want to expound the differences in the Christian churches' sacramental doctrine. In this our aim is not to cover differences up but to describe them openly. Too hasty a tendency to bring things into agreement does not help progress. At the same time there are two points we must keep before our eyes. First, on many questions of sacramental doctrine theologians have of recent years already been able to reach a substantial measure of agreement, even if these areas of agreement have not yet been "officially" recognized – though on the other hand they have not been "officially" contradicted. Other differences that were strongly emphasized in earlier times are now at least on the way to being settled. Secondly, within the different Christian churches there has recently been an intensive effort to deepen sacramental doctrine and to rid it of one-sidedness. This arouses great hopes for all concerned for Christian unity. From this point of view it is not so easy briefly to describe the differences of doctrine concerning the sacraments, differences that in fact still give rise to opposition and as far as can be seen will still persist for some time. Only a general survey can thus be given.

There is a final point we must consider. As far as the Evangelical or Protestant churches are concerned there are no doctrinal definitions by a teaching authority such as exist in the Catholic church. But on the other hand as far as the Catholic church is concerned such definitions for the most part represent a drawing of boundaries rather than positive statements: what they say is rather what must *not* be thought and said than the view one must hold. This kind of demarcation of boundaries was necessary to bring about clarity in a quite distinct historical situation in a particular dispute. But to what extent can such definitions be "conclusive"? Their validity can only persist unchanged as long as the historical situation lasts that gave rise to them. Once it is past, then the question can be posed in a totally new and totally different way. These remarks do not mean that we should not take existing doctrinal differences seriously. But they should help to weigh up their social importance and aid us neither to undervalue nor to overvalue them.

The number of Christian sacraments

If one asks what the differences are between the denominations on sacramental doctrine, one prominent point of difference immediately leaps to the eye – the fact that the number of church rites that are termed "sacraments" is not the same in every denomination. The Catholic church lists seven sacraments. This finds its support in a long development that had already begun in the life of the primitive Church and to some extent was concluded by the end of the twelfth century. This development is related both to the administration and reception of the sacraments as well as to a deeper understanding of them. The Reformation in general recognized only baptism and the eucharist as sacraments, though Luther in addition to some extent recognized absolution in the sacrament of penance, while his colleague Melanchthon incidentally called ordination to the office of preacher a "sacrament".

The reason for the Reformers' limitation of the number of sacraments was that the term sacrament should in their view be restricted only to those rites of the Church imparting Christ's grace which were demonstrably instituted by Christ himself. Similar actions that were only first introduced by the Church, however venerable they might be, were to be strictly distinguished from the "sacraments".

Now, *all* the Churches are united in agreeing on the fundamental principle that the Reformers are applying here: all the sacraments must be instituted by Christ himself, otherwise they are not really means of grace. The doctrinal differences arise over where this principle is to be applied in individual cases. Even within the different denominations differences of opinion can arise on this question. The Protestant churches' requirement that the act of institution by Jesus must be capable of clear and unequivocal proof from Scripture has its basis in the Reformers' general principle that only Scripture has binding teaching authority in the Church. It is thus clear that different views on sacramental doctrine depend on much deeper and more general considerations.

Now, the concept of "sacrament" as we know it today does

not yet appear in Scripture itself, not even where baptism and the eucharist are mentioned. It took a long time for the word "sacrament" to become a fixed general theological technical term for certain actions or rites on the part of the Christian Church by means of which God's grace was imparted to the faithful. And even then the word "sacrament" was still used in a different sense. This has a decisive consequence. One must not only ask for what reasons this rite or that was termed a "sacrament" in the past, but one must also ask what view of this rite obtains in the Church today. Dependent on the answer to this question is the importance one attributes to the biblical proof that these "sacraments" were really instituted by Jesus. And the findings of exegesis and biblical theology in all fields today provide moreover a warning against being in too much of a hurry to take up positions on this question from which there is no retreat.

The question is thus not really whether one can prove from Scripture that Christ instituted the "sacraments". The question is rather whether in those actions on the part of the Church that for several centuries we have called "sacraments" the salvation achieved by Jesus Christ is effective with regard to those who "receive" them. Is it effective in the same way as for example it is in its own way in the preaching of the word? But even to ask these questions is not yet enough. In fact there can be no answer to these questions because they are far too general. This is shown by looking at the two major sacraments of baptism and the eucharist. There is so much difference even between these two that they cannot conveniently be forced into one and the same pattern. The effect would be only to begin by cramping and confining the fulness of what Christ has achieved for us and wants to communicate to us through the sacraments. It is thus clear how difficult it is to prove anything about the sacraments from Scripture. The difficulty grows greater when one admits how many and varied have been the forms adopted by the individual sacraments over the centuries and how many and varied have been the ways in which they have been understood. What precisely is it then that one wants to prove from Scripture?

If therefore we want to say something that is fruitful and helps us to proceed further, then it is better if we direct our attention not so much to the number of the sacraments but to the individual sacraments in themselves and try to grasp their essential nature. Biblical scholarship and history teach us that in fact there is obviously no question of deciding the number of sacraments by proof from Scripture.

The Catholic church is well aware of all these problems, even though it still holds to the sacraments disputed by the churches of the Reformation. According to Catholic teaching, these seven sacraments are, despite all their similarity, so different from each other that all seven do not merge or become included in the two or possible three sacraments of the Protestant churches. But in the Catholic view they are not in any way all equally essential and obligatory. And the opposite side of the coin is shown by the fact that many Protestant churches place a high value on the sacramental rites practised by the Catholic church – except that they do not call them "sacraments". This will become clear when we discuss each sacrament individually.

Baptism and the eucharist

With a few exceptions all the Christian churches adhere to baptism and the eucharist (the Lord's Supper) as sacraments in the strict sense of the word. We have seen what can jointly be said about them both in the Catholic and in the Protestant churches. But beyond this there are characteristic differences that once again arise from the fundamental differences between the churches.

In the case of baptism these are not a cause for division between the churches. The Catholic and Protestant churches mutually recognize each other's baptism if this is validly administered, that is by "washing" the person to be baptized with water while using the trinitarian formula: "In the name of the Father and of the Son and of the Holy Ghost." But since for both churches baptism means above all being received into the Church, their different views of the Church's essential nature affect their understanding of baptism. Catholic teaching understands the Church essentially as a community for which Jesus instituted a certain basic organizational structure. Hence according to the Catholic view baptism irrevocably makes the baptized person a member of this institutional community of the Church. One field where the Catholic encounters the consequences of this view is in the question of the canonical validity of marriages. As far as the Evangelical is concerned these are pseudo-problems because he has a different view of the Church. Further differences which are more than mere shades of emphasis arise from the fact that the Evangelical view of the essential nature of faith in its relation to God's word leads to a different view of the mode of operation of the sacraments from that more usual in the Catholic church. (This point will be considered in detail later.) Moreover not even in the bitterest disputes since the Reformation have the Protestant churches ever given up the conviction that baptism is the foundation on which they stand over against the world together with Catholics and all other validly baptized Christians.

A different situation obtains with regard to the eucharist, which is becoming the common ecumenical term for what the Catholics traditionally called the Mass, the Anglicans Holy Communion, and the Congregationalists, Presbyterians and other Protestants the Lord's Supper. Here mutual recognition that the eucharist is celebrated validly and according to Christ's institution is burdened with considerable reservations, to the extent that it has not yet really come about. Admittedly within Protestantism there is no longer any repetition of the old accusations that the Catholic eucharist is "idolatrous", while for its part the Catholic church no longer regards, say, the Evangelical eucharist as merely a subjective "pious exercise" (cf the Decree on Ecumenism § 22). The differences are not such as to exclude all hope of future unity. But at the moment they are still so large that numerous Christians in both churches regard any form of intercommunion or concelebration as dishonest, while the leadership of both churches continue up till the present to repudiate every experiment in this direction – admittedly no longer with complete success.

There are here three essential differences that still divide Catholics and Protestants. Two of them will be dealt with immediately, while the third will come up in connexion with the question of ordination.

The real presence of Christ in the eucharist

All the denominations are agreed that in all the sacraments Christ comes into contact with and is present to the faithful. At the second Vatican council the Catholic church explicitly laid down that it was not only with regard to the "eucharistic gifts" that one should speak of the "presence of Christ" (Liturgical Constitution § 7). Yet since the time of the early Church, Christianity has believed that in the eucharist Christ is present in a way that is exclusive to this sacrament. Hence Catholic theology talks of Christ's "eucharistic presence". The core of the matter is that in the eucharist the Lord is present not just as the giver of salvation but as the very gift of salvation proper to this sacrament.

The closer understanding of this idea is where the different denominations still go their separate ways. According to the Catholic view, and equally according to the Lutheran view, one must say that Jesus Christ, his body and his blood, is "really" present in the eucharistic gifts. The Lord's saying: "This is my body, this is my blood" is to be understood quite "realistically". The other Evangelical denominations prefer to talk of a mode of presence that is less "realistic" and is defined by the presence of Christ or rather is transmitted by the Holy Spirit. Alternatively one says that the Lord is present in the celebration of the commemoration that the eucharist itself is. Significant doctrinal differences do in fact still exist in this question of the real presence of Christ in the eucharist, and all those who are concerned about Christian unity are anxious to overcome them. Intensive "doctrinal dialogues" which include the eucharist in their subject-matter are taking place among different Protestant churches with the aim of establishing intercommunion where up to now it has not yet been possible.

But there is also a weighty difference between Lutheran and Catholic teaching, precisely at the point where one tries to explain more fully the jointly-held doctrine of the real presence of Christ and in particular how it comes about. For about a thousand years before the Reformation the conviction slowly took root in the Church that bread and wine were changed or transformed into the body and blood of Christ. Whatever fuller explanation was provided for this change, it was in every case held to be a direct and unavoidable conclusion if one wanted to take Jesus' words of institution seriously. If it is true that the words "This *is* my body" are validly applicable to the bread and "This *is* my blood" to the wine, then as a result the bread is no longer bread and the wine is no longer wine even if both still have the outward appearances of bread and wine. From the eleventh century onwards people preferred to express this by saying that when the priest spoke the words of consecration the "substance", the essential nature of the bread and wine, was changed, while the "accidents", the outward appearance, or what today we would call the physical and chemical structures, remained unchanged. By using these concepts, which had their origin in Aristotelian philosophy, a new technical term was coined for this unique transformation, the term "transubstantiation".

Luther (and the other Reformers) launched a bitter attack on this doctrine, One of the most important reasons for them was the fact that this doctrine could not claim the support of the one binding authority of Scripture, since Paul continues to call the bread given in the eucharist bread even after its consecration (cf 1 Cor 10: 16, 11: 26–8). The doctrine of transubstantiation could be held as a personal opinion but should not be declared as a binding part of the faith. Luther himself felt the evidence of Scripture constrained him to recognize the presence of Christ in the bread and wine *before* the consecration, and he sought to show that this kind of simultaneous co-existence of two "substances" is not impossible by quoting such examples as red-hot iron, which is both fire and iron at one and the same time, or, the highest possible comparison, the presence of both divinity and humanity in Christ.

At its thirteenth session in October 1551 the Council of Trent (1545–63) condemned the new eucharistic doctrine of *all* the Reformers and proclaimed the doctrine of transubstantiation as a dogma – though without going more deeply into its philososphical or theological explanations (cf especially canons 1 and 2 of the decree on the eucharist, DS 1651–2). Against this the Lutheran churches drew up the credal statement, in the 1577 Formula of Concord, that Christ's body was given to the faithful "in, with, and under" the eucharistic gifts (*Solida Declaratio* VII). This adopted formulations of Luther's. From this statement there developed in Lutheranism the view that it is only at the moment of reception that Christ is present in the eucharistic elements – a view that does not yet appear in this form in Luther himself.

This fixed an opposition that has not yet been overcome. The doctrine of Trent was explicitly reaffirmed for the Catholic church by Pope Paul VI in his encyclical *Mysterium fidei*, issued in 1965. Nevertheless the Catholic church too has been marked by an unexpected flow of discussion about the real presence of Christ in the eucharist, a discussion it is quite impossible to sum up adequately in a few sentences. If there is today hope of a rapprochement of views between the Catholic church and the churches of the Reformation, then, apart from the more or less unanimous interpretation that has been reached of the biblical passages concerned, it is above all because there is a deeper grasp of the insight that Christ's presence in the eucharist is a *personal* presence which should not be treated as equivalent to the way in which a thing is present. Hence such "material" terms as "substance" and "accidents" are today felt to be unsatisfactory and the attempt is made to replace them by more pertinent terms without betraying the traditional "realism". An essential impulse here is also that reform of the liturgy which in the Catholic church has brought with it new emphases in "eucharistic piety". These have led to a greater closeness to Evangelical sacramental piety than was recently regarded as possible.

QUESTIONS IN DISPUTE BETWEEN THE CHURCHES

The eucharist as sacrifice

The second major point of opposition concerns the Catholic doctrine of the Mass as "sacrifice". In comparison with the dispute over the real presence of Christ in the eucharistic elements, this dispute over the "sacrifice of the Mass" has to a considerable extent diminished in importance today. Luther originally saw in this doctrine the third and worst captivity of the Church (in his *De captivitate Babylonica Ecclesiae* of 1520, WA 6: 512 ff). The Council of Trent defended the doctrine – but without going into any detailed explanations of it (DS 1738–1759). Over succeeding centuries Catholic theology developed a number of theories, often indeed very misguided ones, to demonstrate the sacrificial character of the Mass and to avoid any impression of giving in to the Reformers.

Today all this is past history. The most recent relevant statement by the Catholic church – Pope Paul VI's encyclical *Mysterium Fidei*, mentioned above – does indeed defend the doctrine of the Council of Treat but explains it in so "prudent" a manner that a considerable part of Luther's complaints and those of Lutherans loses its substance. According to the Pope's explanations the sacrificial character of the Mass consists of the fact that in it Jesus' sacrifice on the cross is "actualized" (*repraesentatur*) and that his power is distributed in it. That is not to be understood in a "reified" or "material" sense, as though the Church sacrificed Christ like a "thing". Instead, by re-presenting the sacrifice of the cross on Christ's behalf, the Church is included in and enters into Christ's filial obedience to his Father. Nothing at all remains today, in official Catholic teaching at least, of what Luther came up against and attacked – ideas of the Mass as a *new* sacrifice in which Christ's death was repeated for our benefit, and that this gave rise to automatic and irresistible effects. The question is thus reduced to asking why the Catholic church insists on the *word* "sacrifice", including using it in its liturgical formulas, when what is meant, the Church's surrender of itself to God, could be expressed in quite different terms.

The answer is that it is to be understood as counterbalancing a tendency that is spreading in the Catholic church to place the exclusive emphasis on the eucharist as a meal. The traditional term "sacrifice" prevents the Church from celebrating and experiencing only itself and its own communion within itself in the eucharist seen as a community meal, and from no longer understanding that it stands before God with Christ and that it is devoted to God. The truth is that the meal, the community celebration, is the sign that Christ's cross and resurrection are effectively present, and that they open up to the celebrating community the way to God and to fresh obedience to him. Hence, as far as the Catholic view is concerned, meal and sacrifice in the eucharist are not contradictory, are not even in tension, but are the two aspects of the one eucharistic mystery.

Nevertheless it can hardly be disputed that once one leaves theological discussion it is still not uncommon to find quite crude ideas of the "sacrifice" of the Mass dominating popular Catholic piety. Hence it is understandable if Protestant theologians and other Christians press for this ambiguous term to be replaced by another in liturgical formulations too, and if they find it suspicious that the Catholic church has not yet done this, even though it could.

Confirmation

Confirmation as a second sacrament of initiation alongside baptism is rejected by, say, the German Evangelical churches – out of respect for baptism and because of insufficient biblical support. In the Catholic church it counts as an additional valid sacramental rite, but baptism remains *the* fundamental sacrament, since it is first and foremost baptism that imparts the life that Christ has gained for us. Confirmation presupposes baptism. It is therefore not on the same level as baptism but subordinate to it. Confirmation develops the life in Christ that at the fundamental level has been communicated by baptism and in a special way brings it to greater richness. The person who receives confirmation will lead his or her life as a Christian more deeply and more richly. In this way the Catholic church is able to see in all this no injustice to baptism, no misunderstanding of its fundamental significance and efficacy, and moreover no injustice with regard to Scripture, since Scripture too enables one to recognize a certain distinction between the event of baptism and the event of confirmation, between the salvific effect of the one and of the other. In the New Testament we read on the one hand that it is not only baptism that imparts the Spirit and on the other we read of a distinct rite in which those who have already been baptized receive the Spirit. This distinction provides the basis for the Catholic view acknowledging the sacramental character of confirmation. Equally the biblical evidence provides an understanding of the particular gift of confirmation: in confirmation the baptized person receives the Spirit as the power to bear public witness to his or her faith in word and deed.

Of course – and this applies to comparisons between all the sacraments – one must not press the distinctions too far. What is involved in all the sarcaments is Christ's unique saving grace, and this is not parcelled out piecemeal in the individual sacraments. Rather it is that, in the Catholic view, the Lord himself intends to be present with his salvation completely and yet in a manner that differs according to whether it is a question of baptism, confirmation, the eucharist, and so on.

In place of the rejected rite of confirmation the German Evangelical churches, after earlier foreshadowings during the Reformation itself, generally introduced from the seventeenth century onwards their own rite of confirmation which has continued in use up to the present. In this the Evangelical – usually at the age of fourteen – is introduced into the community as an active member in a solemn service involving the laying on of hands and prayer, and is also admitted to communion and endowed with all the rights and duties of a member of the congregation. There is no complete agreement over the way in which this Evangelical rite of confirmation is understood, together with the Church regulations connected with it, but the purport of the rite shows that it is very close to the Catholic rite of confirmation (which is even more true of the rite in the Book of Common Prayer). It is only that throughout it is not understood as a "sacrament" since this could lead to the misunderstanding that baptism was in need of being supplemented.

Ordination

In all the major churches those who hold office in the Church are installed in office by means of a special rite. In the Catholic church this is called ordination and is subdivided into ordination to the diaconate, to the priesthood or presbyterate, and to the episcopate. It is regarded as an individual sacrament in its own right, since Christ himself founded the ministry in the person of the apostles and endowed those called to it with the gift of special graces for their task. The sacrament and the gifts of grace it imparts are thus not primarily aimed at personal sanctification but at the service – the ministry – that the ordained person is to provide. This service or ministry consists of leading the community through the proclamation of the good news of the Gospel and the administration of the sacraments. Since the Church considers the ordained person to have been called by Christ himself, it regards it as beyond its powers to revoke the ordination it has imparted in the name of Christ. That is the meaning of the doctrine that ordination – like baptism – imparts an "indelible character" and is thus of life-long validity.

Since in the Catholic view the Church is hierarchically ordered, ordination raises the person ordained to a particular degree of the Church's officially organized ministry and thus distinguishes him from those who have not been ordained. Only someone who has been ordained – to be more precise, only someone who has been ordained to the priesthood – may preside over the celebration of the eucharist, since it is precisely this that belongs among the duties of his office. It follows from this that a celebration of the eucharist in the absence of a priest would not be a properly constituted celebration. This consequence prevents the Catholic church from regarding an Evangelical eucharist celebrated without a validly ordained minister as completely valid – and this is the third point of opposition, mentioned earlier, in the two denominations' understanding of the eucharist.

It is only the Anglican Communion among the non-Catholic churches that shares the Catholic understanding of the sacrament of order. Other Protestant churches have their own rite of ordination. Once again there are similarities in the outward form of the rite. As with the Catholic rite of ordination to the priesthood, the rite involves the laying on of hands, and – a fact of which many Catholics are not aware – it entails a lifelong commitment. But because the hierarchical constitution of the Church is disputed, ordination is neither regarded as a sacrament nor does it bestow a particular status in the Church. For it is the whole community of believers that is jointly responsible for the ministry (the "priesthood of all believers"). The reason for this is to be found in the Reformation doctrine of "Christ alone": it is Christ alone who is Lord of the Church, and there can be no other dominion, not even a holy dominion ("hierarchy"). And it is Christ alone who in the New Testament is called "priest": in him all earlier priesthood finds its conclusion. Hence the holder of office in the Church cannot possess the character of a "priest" in the proper sense of the word.

Once again the front lines on this question too have long since become fluid. Not only in the exercise of their ministry but also in their understanding of it Catholic theologians and clergy, in considering the church's hierarchical constitution, are trying, with the support of the documents of the recent council, to see office in the church less under the aspect of plenary powers but much more under the aspect of "service" or "ministry" and in connexion with the ministry of the laity. The other side of the picture is provided by the fact that the usual Protestant understanding of ordination does not in any way see it as a purely human, "democratic" appointment to office which the congregation has the sovereign authority to revoke at any time. If one considers that not only do different theological starting-points on matters of essential importance play a rôle here but that also there lie at any time behind the Church's understanding of its offices and the way they are structured the influences of views that are conditioned by the particular age and situation the Church finds itself in, then one must hope that the understanding and exercise of the ministry that are developing in response to new challenges will continually lead to new theological insights that will further the cause of unity.

Penance

Penance too, like confirmation and ordination, belongs to the category of rites that in certain forms are respected by almost all the churches but are only regarded as sacraments without any reservations in the Catholic church. There is no dispute between the denominations about the preconditions underlying penance: the fact that after baptism and "justification" the Christian can fall again into sin, and even into serious sin; that penance forms a life-long part of the Christian life; and that throughout his whole life the Christian is subject to God's judgment *and* under the promise of forgiveness. No Church therefore disputes penance as such. Moreover, most denominations are agreed that a definite form of confession is necessary and equally a corresponding pledge of forgiveness ("absolution") which the Church gives the individual sinner in the form of a liturgical rite. Where however the uncertainty comes in is whether one ought to talk plainly about a *sacrament* of penance. Many Protestant doctrinal statements use the same words as Catholic teaching. But others prefer to avoid such nomenclature, since confession lacks the "outward sign", that is to say material element like water in the case of baptism or bread and wine in the eucharist. But the major reason is that an individual sacrament of the forgiveness of sins does injustice to baptism as *the* sacrament of the forgiveness of sins. Penance in the context of the Church can only be always a return to baptism, but never an individual sacrament on its own which would then be necessary if baptism were "disrupted" by fresh sin. Objections of this kind make it clear once again how different the sacraments are in the symbols and words they use. And on the other hand we get the impression that the Protestant concept of "sacrament" which in every case includes a material element is narrower and stricter than the Catholic one. This is a point that should be considered when there is dispute over whether a rite is a "sacrament" or not.

The administration of the sacrament of penance, especially the imparting of absolution, is according to Catholic teaching fundamentally reserved to the ordained priest. In contrast, in the (German) Evangelical churches confession to a lay-person is basically possible. For them the promise of salvation in absolution is in itself God's word in such a way that it seems unnecessary for it to have to be mediated through a priest ordained specifically for this purpose. Of recent times the theological interpretation and the liturgical practice of confession in the different denominations have come closer to each other to an amazing degree.

At this point a reference to "indulgences" (originally meaning a remission of public penance imposed by the Church for a certain period) is not out of place. The major part played by indulgences in the Reformation squabbles is well known. Today that is no longer possible, not because the practice of indulgences has completely disappeared from the Catholic church, but because it is no longer subject to the appalling abuses recorded in the Middle Ages. Of course for many Catholics indulgences of any kind are unknown or a thing of the past. That is no matter for regret since indulgences do not enjoy a central position in the "hierarchy of truths". Nevertheless Catholic theologians today explain indulgences in a way that (as in the case of "purgatory") allows new possibilities of discussion with Protestant Christians: indulgences are seen now as the promise of spiritual support (through prayer) by the Church for sinful but penitent Christians who continue to struggle against the consequences of sin: ie, attitudes and behaviour by which even wrongdoing that is forgiven retains a hold in the human consciousness.

The anointing of the sick

In the Protestant churches there is no counterpart to the Catholic sacrament of the anointing of the sick (traditionally called "extreme unction"). On the basis of Jas 5: 14 and several other scriptural texts (cf Acts 3: 6–16; 4: 7–10; 9: 34; 19: 11–12) the Catholic church is of the conviction that the anointing of the sick is sufficiently attested as a particular promise of salvation in the Church and thus as a "sacrament" (cf the Council of Trent, session xiv, DS 1716–19). It is administered not just to the dying but as a matter of principle to anyone who is seriously ill. Its particular salvific gift is seen in its as it were dedicating the sick person to Christ: in other words, his illness is contained in Christ's victory over illness and death, and the sick person receives the power to endure sickness and if need be death as part of his road towards resurrection with Christ and thus to make them a concrete example of the living out of his faith.

The Protestant churches do not regard Jas 5: 14 as sufficient evidence for a sacramental anointing of the sick and regard the anointing to which witness is borne in that passage as a non-sacramental rite linked with prayer of intercession. But the Protestant churches do recognize the communion of the sick, or more precisely the celebration of the eucharist at the sickbed. The Catholic church by contrast distributes communion to the sick outside the celebration of the eucharist, a practice which finds its theological support in the Catholic view of Christ's presence in the eucharist, and if necessary this communion of the sick is linked with the anointing of the sick, and when there is danger of death is provided in the more solemn form of viaticum ("food for the journey"). Because it is in the dominion of sin that sickness and death find the profoundest reason for the sorrow and pain they bring, the grace imparted by the anointing of the sick includes the forgiveness of sins.

Matrimony

Together with the Orthodox churches the Catholic church counts matrimony as the seventh sacrament, while the Protestant churches usually dispute this view and in fact oppose it to a greater extent than in the case of other disputed sacraments. Since the opposition here is especially far-reaching and in addition since it affects the daily life of Christians belonging to the different churches to a greater extent than in the case of the other sacraments, it will be dealt with separately and in greater detail in a section on its own (chapter 27).

After considering the individual sacraments we must now ask where the real all-embracing point of opposition is to be found between Catholic and Protestant sacramental doctrine and whether there is any hope that it can be relaxed. We shall consider this question under two aspects which together comprise the disagreement since the Reformation.

Word and sacrament

Occasionally people have wanted to make a distinction between the Catholic and the Protestant versions of Christianity by describing the life of a Protestant as "existence based on the word" and that of a Catholic as "existence based on the sacraments". Behind this stands not only the idea of the greater number of "sacraments" in the Catholic church but also the reformation doctrine that God imparts salvation to mankind "by the word alone". This kind of dichotomy can be misunderstood. Nevertheless it contains something that aptly characterizes both the Reformation and the concrete forms that the different denominations still adopt today. At that time Luther was justified in setting up the oral word of preaching as the unique "vehicle of God's grace" in contrast to the exaggerated sacramental practice of the Catholic church of the time, a practice that was full of abuses. For him, as for the Protestant churches of today in general, a sacrament is a particular form in which the word appears, an actual and visible word (*verbum actuale, verbum visibile*). The sacramental event is made up of word and element (sign), but the decisive significance belongs to the word. The element or sign is thus linked with the word to make it clearer.

It would not be correct simply to describe the churches of the Reformation as the "church of the word" and the Catholic church as the "church of the sacraments" – even if this has a certain justification when one considers the life of the churches in the past. The formula "word and sacraments" can be understood and interpreted in a number of different ways. One thing is however certain, that no Christian denomination would agree to playing word and sacrament off against one another. But clearly on all sides there are differences of emphasis and a different order of precedence is established. Evangelical doctrine aims consciously and as emphatically as possible at giving the word precedence over the sacraments. It is the word alone that in the strictest sense is necessary for salvation. Luther indeed describes the word understood as the Gospel as "before bread and baptism the only, most certain and most eminent mark of the Church" (WA 7:721:9). The sacraments – and in this context, as we saw, one thinks most of baptism and the eucharist – are particular ways in which the word affects people. But first of all it is the word of the Gospel and the word that is preached that has power to promise and to effect salvation. One could say that the word is the first sacrament. The sacraments in the normal sense have the power of bringing salvation only inasmuch as this same word is proclaimed and promised in them too. Their salvific power thus belongs to them in a secondary sense. Clearly, this view does not in any way lead to a fundamental rejection of sacramental rites in Christ's Church. Rather are they decisively seen in relation to and subordinated to the word of the Gospel and of preaching. In addition this fundamental view was a factor in restricting the number of sacraments to baptism and the eucharist.

The formula "word and sacraments" thus seems to contain and summarize the entire difference in sacramental doctrine between the Catholic church and the churches of the Reformation. Nevertheless the actual opposition is narrower than might appear at first sight. The misunderstandings caused by historical factors and the overemphases due to the heat of the struggle must first be cleared out of the way before one can reach the problems at the heart of the matter. And these for their part can be tackled more easily and with greater hope than in the past. In part points of agreement are already apparent. Catholic teaching, like Protestant teaching, does not really place the word (the Gospel) and the sacraments side by side as if these were two or more means accepted in themselves whereby independently of each other God's grace was communicated to men. The word and the sacraments interpenetrate each other. They are not of course simply identical in every way. The word does not embrace and contain everything that is proper to the sacraments. Their relationship to each other is more complex. No sacrament is even conceivable as a "means of grace" effective for salvation without the word of personal assurance of salvation. And from the other point of view, as signs of salvation in the Church, the sacraments in their way as it were complete the effective power of the word that brings grace. For their particular nature consists in the fact that they affect those aspects of human life where the word alone is not able to penetrate. The word of God through whom the world has been created and redeemed, the Logos, has become flesh – and can thus be perceived by senses other than that of hearing. It wants to be apprehended not only in oral proclamation but also bodily. One cannot think about the word in this sense without quite automatically coming up against the question of the sacraments.

How the sacraments work

In the preceding discussion a further distinction in sacramental doctrine has already been hinted at several times. This is that different answers are given to the question how the sacraments work. Once again we must not overlook the fact that on this question most Protestant churches have only baptism and the eucharist in mind. The Evangelical churches' doctrine flows from their basic teaching that, just as all salvation and all grace is imparted to man by faith alone, so it is through faith alone that the sacramental rites of salvation are effective in Christ's Church. The aim of this view is to avoid the Christian seeing the reception of the sacraments as a "good work", a human contribution which God is bound to reward with grace. But this does not mean that according to the doctrine of the Reformation the effectiveness of the sacraments is *dependent* on faith. In order to exclude this misunderstanding emphasis was laid in Lutheran circles on the *manducatio impiorum*, the "eating of the impious". Because faith does not *create* but instead *receives* the sacrament, the unbeliever too eats the real body of the Lord if he receives communion – although not to his salvation. In opposition to this emphasis on faith, the Catholic church has taught since the Middle Ages, and still teaches today, that the sacraments are effective of themselves, through their accomplishment (*ex opere operato*). Does this not make the sacraments an independent human contribution before God which has its value in itself?

Now, all theologians of both denominations are agreed today that the Reformers did not understand the Catholic doctrine and the formula *ex opere operato* in the sense in which it was intended – that is, as an expression of the fact that the sacraments are instituted by God himself and that man cannot by his abuse bring to naught what God has instituted in this way. But this misunderstanding on the part of the Reformers was not something purely accidental. Late medieval theology had given the formula an interpretation which fed in popular piety the idea that the sacraments worked "automatically" like "magic". The Reformers were right to protest against this, except that what they were attacking was not the genuine Catholic doctrine. Nevertheless profound misunderstandings still continue to exist and urgently need to be got rid of. But no decisive progress will be made as long as no progress is made beyond the point where the Reformers' protest has its basis – in the question whether and in what sense salvation does in fact come about "by faith alone". Once there is unity on this point, then there would be unity on the question how the sacraments work.

Protestant doctrine thus sees the effectiveness of the sacraments as very closely linked with faith. The sacraments owe their power of salvation to God's saving word which is pledged to the faithful in them. But it is only faith that responds to the word. The sacraments strengthen and support this faith, but only faith receives the sacraments in such a way that they communicate salvation and grace. Catholic doctrine has indeed never asserted that the sacraments have nothing to do with faith because it is only in God's power that they are effective. All Catholic doctrine emphasizes is that it is only God who gives the sacraments their power. The subjective attitude of the person who administrates or receives the sacraments and their degree of piety, or even the attitude and piety of the whole congregation, are *not* decisive for the saving power of the sacraments. According to Catholic doctrine the Lord's will is that his grace should be distributed to the individual believer in the Church through the sacraments as well as and besides by means of the word of oral proclamation. It is for this and no other reasons that the sacraments administered in the Church are also the "guarantee" given by the Lord himself that he is there with his grace. In this way Catholic sacramental doctrine throughout contains the elements that were important to the Reformers. But at the time of the Reformation much had become confused in both doctrine and practice. Hence the Reformers placed more decided emphasis on the basic pattern of the connexion of word, faith and sacrament and renounced supplementary motives and traditions. In this way Catholic and Protestant sacramental doctrines in the first instance stand over against each other as two different and indeed opposed basic views of the sacraments. It is only slowly that both sides are learning from each other once again and moving towards an understanding of the sacraments that they can express jointly.

27   Marriage

Why another discussion of marriage when the subject has already been dealt with? A Protestant reader would indeed hardly notice the omission, since there has already been a suitable treatment of marriage within the chapter on ethics: according to the usual Protestant view of things marriage is concerned not with man's personal relationship towards God, and thus not with faith, but instead with his life among and with his fellow men, and thus with ethics, with the love that arises from faith.

Marriage and the Church

But, as has already been indicated, there is a particular question still in dispute between the Catholic and the Protestant doctrine of marriage. In general terms it could be formulated by asking what has the *Church* got to do with marriage. Here fundamental differences everywhere strike those who are acquainted with this field and above all those immediately affected. The Roman Catholic church links its doctrine of marriage with faith itself and with its own marriage law that is decreed in the name of the faith and is thus declared to be binding in conscience, while Evangelical churches are satisfied essentially with the regulations of the civil law.

Catholic doctrine sees marriage as a sacrament of the Church, just like baptism and the eucharist, while Evangelical doctrine rejects this and regards marriage, in a famous phrase of Luther's, as a "worldly thing", as something which the Church ought to be concerned about only in the preaching of God's word but otherwise only as little as it is about the Christian's secular occupation. According to Catholic teaching the canonical form of marriage is not only required for its canonical validity in the eyes of the Church but is also directly concerned with salvation just as the other sacraments are. As far as Evangelical doctrine is concerned on the other hand, marriage has no more to do with salvation than all the rest of the Christian's life in the world.

Hence for centuries the Catholic church has had strict laws against "mixed marriages". Anyone who contravened the canonical regulations without a dispensation, without in other words being dispensed from the requirements of canon law in his or her particular case, made himself or herself liable to ecclesiastical penalties. In many cases he or she was automatically "excommunicated", excluded from the Church. Some Protestant church constitutions also had regulations against mixed marriages and showed discrimination in their treatment of the partners of such marriages, though these regulations never went as far as Catholic canon law.

Many Christians of both denominations regard the age when such regulations concerning marriage, and particularly concerning mixed marriages, were in force as an evil time. But here too there is hope. The rigorous Catholic laws on mixed marriages are being interpreted and applied in such a way – especially since the new instructions issued by Rome in 1970 – that outsiders have the impression that these laws are gradually being dissolved, while in the Evangelical churches in Germany there are no longer any special rules with regard to mixed marriages.

In the Catholic church pastoral clergy and theologians who are concerned with the practical aspects of the mixed marriage question are meanwhile asking whether the rigid connexion between the Church's canon law on marriage and marriage as a sacrament is necessary because of the fundamental nature of the issue. From the Protestant side there is fresh talk about the "spiritual" character of Christian behaviour, the way in which it is orientated towards God, and as a result it is no longer seen to be necessary to begin by concentrating on opposing Catholic views. If we therefore ask what the Church has got to do with marriage, then our answer will certainly have to cover many points that are still disputed. At the same time, as with the other subjects of this section of the book, we are already able to put this question in a common form. The common denominator now becomes the question: What have faith and the Church got to do with marriage?

Marriage in history

On the basis of the good news of God's grace and the freedom of the Christian that this message proclaims the Church, in contrast to most religions, philosophies and ideologies, can as it were afford to see marriage as an historical dimension, that is to say not as a reality that develops and is bound to develop according to a pre-ordained programme but as something that has grown up together with the development of human society and has itself changed in the process. Supported by its faith, the Church can indeed propose using the means of historical criticism and scientific research into attitudes to investigate the reasons why marriage belongs to the stable and stabilizing institutions of this world and why this should have been so long before there was any ecclesiastical law of marriage, indeed "before any other structures of human society had been formed" (Bonhoeffer). Tied in with and supported by the family or kinship unit, marriage as an ordered sexual relationship guarantees from the start the stability and the further development of family, kin and nation. In all cultures the regulations pertaining to marriage were already always regarded as inviolable, with their roots in religion, and as a result they were not a subject for discussion. Marriage was understood as an institution, as a state of life with special obligations, which married people did not for their part have at their disposal but which rather had them at its disposal once they had given themselves to each other in it.

All this cannot of course prevent political, economic and social changes affecting and altering the pattern and legal framework of marriage. But, compared with developments in society as a whole, changes in marriage take place much more slowly and with less discontinuity. In this no part is played by whether monogamy or polygamy is normal, whether a patriarchal or matriarchal system obtains, whether people marry only within their own social group (endogamy) or are obliged to look for a marriage partner from another (exogamy). History moreover is not aware of these arrangements in any pure form. Recent research suggests that moderate monogamy was the rule at the beginnings of civilization, to the extent that these are open to investigation. Forms of polygamy denote a higher state of civilization or even the decadence of cultures in transition.

Monogamy therefore is not an "invention of Christianity". When the Christian faith entered history, the Western Roman Empire was in the process of doing away with survivals of polygamous customs. In the Eastern Empire this process was only partially successful. Later Islam revived polygamy and created mixed forms. The missionaries who evangelized the German tribes encountered among the upper classes of the "barbarians" a legal system that was founded on monogamy but in practice made polygamy possible. The Church admittedly forbade this kind of polygamy but it could never prevent it. It seems sensible of the Church too to have refused to impose an absolutely monogamous system: it allowed a second marriage not only after the death of the first partner but also in special cases, despite the fundamental ban on divorce, when he or she was still alive. The Church's view of the situation with regard to educating people in the faith was also such that it never seriously tried completely to do away with the rôle played by prostitutes, mistresses and concubines. In practice it contented itself with a monogamy that depended on the extent to which the situation allowed this to flourish, in other words with a "relative monogamy".

The legal systems of all known types of constitution recognize divorce as an exceptional possibility. It is only that the impediments on the way to divorce vary from state to state and are greater or smaller, more complicated or simpler. Modern sociology has indicated two interesting facts. First, a rise in the divorce rate due to social conditions does not threaten either the institution of marriage or that of the family. Secondly, in countries with no divorce (for example, Spain, Portugal and, until 1970, Italy) conditions are frequently much more confused than in countries where divorce is permitted. But even steps to make divorce easier, as in the Soviet Union in 1920, have been shown to be socially damaging in the long term and had to be reversed. Divorce therefore everywhere counts as an exception to the rule that marriage is understood as a legal association for life that includes the risk and uncertainty involved in a lifelong undertaking. With its character of permanence is linked a comprehensive socialization in three main directions: sexually, residentially and economically. Because of the first the legitimate children inherit the legal status of the father (or, in matriarchal societies, of the mother). The residential association is the basis for the development of the family as a legal and social union.

Marriage regulated by the Church

If the faith and the Church allow such a dispassionate consideration, then they cannot avoid the conclusion that marriage is in itself stable and has a stabilizing effect. Apparently it needs no outside help to this end, no higher valuation through religion to give it new strength, but rather needs social regulation corresponding to its nature.

Why then in the course of the eleventh century did the Church involve itself in the existing system for the regulation of marriage after having not only tolerated but even encouraged secular systems of marriage law up till then? To anticipate the answer, it was a great achievement – and also, in many people's opinion, a mistake that seriously needed to be put right.

From the ninth century onwards the tension between a West that was growing together spiritually and politically and local or regional legal systems had become so great that the demand for a unification of marriage law could not be ignored. The old forms for contracting marriage were no longer sufficient to offer a legal foundation for the development that was beginning towards a personal and individual experience of marriage. Until then the woman was transferred from the lordship of her father to that of her husband in various forms of legal transaction, such as solemn betrothal before the families concerned or a public wedding ceremony. Marriage was a change of lordship. But at this time customs and styles of life were increasingly taking on a bourgeois pattern, clans were splitting up into individual families, the individual was beginning to gain his freedom, the woman was winning greater independence. The Church did not hinder this development but in fact encouraged it. At the same time it helped a parallel form of marriage that had grown up among the "lower" classes but was looked down on by the "upper" classes to obtain something like an equal footing. This was the form of marriage based on love *without* any change of lordship. While in the case of one old form of marriage the family appointed someone to represent society at large, now a representative of society had to be found in order to ensure the legal validity of the new form of marriage. And this is where the priest came in as the representative of society as a whole.

He confirmed the correctness and validity in civil law of the promise of marriage. In modern terms his rôle outside the Church was that of a registrar, within the Church that of a pastor. And the practice soon began to be imitated in the case of the old form of marriage too. Since the formation of a unified system of law for the Empire meant that the introduction of a general marriage law now became inevitable, all that was needed was to link a custom that had grown up over two centuries with a system of "betrothal law" that was already valid in northern Italy and make it obligatory. Only the Church as the dominant spiritual and social force was able to impose as the only valid form of marriage this form that was related to the already socially accepted form. A couple were now reckoned to be legally married if they publicly promised themselves to each other in marriage for life.

The traditional two stages of the legal ceremony were retained but underwent a fundamental alteration, in that the ceremony of betrothal within the context of the family completely lost its legally binding character and its significance as part of the actual marriage ceremony. That survived only in the public legal wedding ceremony, to which the blessing of the Church was attached. The two evolved into a single ceremony in church. From the eleventh century on this rite was classified with baptism, the eucharist and the other sacraments and, as in the eastern church, equally regarded as a sacrament. Further background to this development was provided by early medieval tendencies of hostility towards the body and secular life which utterly rejected marriage along with the other sacraments and all Church institutions.

The conclusion of this development is reflected in the statement of Catholic canon law, itself based on the decisions of the council of Trent (1545–63, DS 1797–1812): "Christ the Lord raised marriage contracted between baptized persons to the dignity of a sacrament" (CIC 1012 § 1). What took place in the context of the Church now became the decisive and characteristic focus of all the ceremonies, even though traditional wedding customs today still recall former legal provisions.

The complexity and resulting uncertainty of the law was now controlled. But at the same time there was a sacrifice of tried and tested principles that had the effect of maintaining moral standards, such as the need for the parents' consent. Secret marriages increased as a result. The Council of Trent placed a rigorous ban on these "clandestine" marriages and declared them henceforth invalid (DS 1813–16).

This brief review leads to an important conclusion – that the Church's law on marriage is the product not only of theological convictions but also and to a far-reaching extent of secular conditions and needs. This leads to another conclusion – that the Church's marriage law can only retain its public legal significance as long as the Church represents society as a whole. And this is something one can no longer say today. The dialogue on marriage between the denominations has as its subject marriage as it must be lived under new pressures and needs. The more Christians of both denominations consider the historical character of their regulations and principles, the freer the dialogue is to take contemporary needs into account.

If we consider both tradition and the contemporary situation, the central question is whether the Church, as the community of believers, can use a legal code to safeguard and guarantee God's word concerning marriage, concerning its

ultimate meaning, concerning its nature that points beyond itself. In the opinion of many Protestants and incidentally of
many Catholics too, including Catholic theologians, it is here
that there is to be found the Church's mistake that seriously
needs to be put right, and this mistake consists of the fact that
the Church has not freely and at the right moment surrendered
the mandate of representing society as a whole that was once
necessary in those situations where in fact it can no longer
represent society in this way. This would of course mean
having to distinguish between, and separate from each other,
on the one hand the mutual promise of marriage as a valid
legal contract and on the other the sacrament of marriage.
The Catholic church believed it could not be disloyal to the
centuries-old contrary tradition. The Reformation, in contrast,
dared to take this step. The consequence was similar to that
in many other cases: the Counter-Reformation secured the
Church's secular deck-cargo even more firmly to the barque
of Peter. The two denominations' doctrines of marriage now
diverged far from each other and fortified their frontiers with
a ban on mixed marriages, a ban especially severe from
the Catholic side, the provisions of which were in any event
applied more or less flexibly according to the circumstances of
the time.

Marriage in the view of faith

The different systems of Church law and regulation have had
less effect on the basic Christian conception of marriage held
in common than might be supposed. We want to try to express
this basic idea in words that do not carry any denominational
overtones. This will also show the extent to which even in the
midst of their dispute the denominations can already bear
common witness to their belief concerning marriage. In doing
this we will be developing from the point of view of marriage
as a partnership what we have already touched on in another
context from the point of view of the individual and his or her
sexuality.

Just as Christians accept their lives from God's hands, just as they work at their jobs in a spirit of responsibility towards God, so they also see their marriage with the eye of faith. If faith is trust towards the God who has created us, has redeemed us in Jesus Christ, and has given us the spirit of freedom and of love, then the Christian cannot live his or her marriage apart from faith. It is also from God's hands that he accepts his partner for life. The fact that men and women are driven to each other by desire, that they mutually achieve complete sexual fulfilment, that they reproduce their life – these facts have nothing directly to do with faith but belong to the essential nature of men and women. But Christians ask what all this means beyond the biological and human sphere. We already know the profound answer of the Bible, an answer that is not conditioned by its age: "Then the Lord God said, 'It is not good that the man should be alone; I will make him a helper fit for him'" (Gen 2: 18), and the original Hebrew can well be translated "a female counterpart" rather than a "helper" or "helpmate". Man courts risks if he thinks he can live alone without the partner God intended and created for him. "Therefore a man leaves his father and his mother and cleaves to his wife, and they become one flesh (Gen 2: 24) – that is, a unity. The New Testament repeats this sentence without making any qualifications.

But unity does not mean being the same. The person who follows this biblical text accepts the other in his or her otherness, does not gauge him or her according to her or his ideal image of man or women, but loves him or her as he or she is, and as he or she is at any and every time: not just when erotic tension makes everything easy but also when loyalty and endurance are demanded. Everyone needs only to think of his or her own family to know what is meant. When the partner shows his or her "alien" side more strongly; when religious, political and social differences breed arguments and disputes; when the children's education throws up problems; when tensions arise over jobs; when love-making no longer automatically reaches the heights that irradiate everything and can express the way in which each is completely wrapped up in the other; when growing awareness of one's own weaknesses and those of one's partner not only helps but acts as a hindrance to mutual conversation; when the danger threatens of boredom and anger; when mistakes and lapses shake mutual confidence – it is then that loyalty becomes necessary to withstand the temptation to give it all up and break loose. To accept anew each day my partner in marriage as the person entrusted to me by God, to love him or her as myself – that is something that transcends man's ethical potentialities. It must continually be said to him "from outside" that despite guilt and sin he is accepted and loved by God and therefore is capable of loving despite everything. It is here that in every case the Church is concerned with marriage – however much or little it may be concerned in other respects. And it has no greater task with regard to marriage than continually to proclaim this to the community and to the individual.

To put it concretely, the Church must make the "frustrated" husband or wife aware of their rebellion against their own promises. It must help them no longer to persist in making accusations against their partner but to recognize themselves as sinners before God who need forgiveness to become capable of new love. Individually or together, mutually or through the "office that preaches reconciliation", it is in the forgiveness of guilt that Christians experience the ultimate worth of love that has been given and is to be given anew every day – and this precisely at the point where in purely human terms it is all too often felt only as a burden. And it is only at the point where this admission of guilt can be made and this reconciliation can be believed and trusted in that healing and salvation take place in marriage as in every other field of human relationship. This is what is meant when the couple promise before the altar, using almost exactly the same words whatever the denomination, to have and to hold each other "for better for worse, for richer for poorer, in sickness and in health, to love and to cherish, till death us do part". It is in this way that in the fulfilment of life together God's love can become visible in human love.

Neither is subject to the other in this love – or rather each is subject to the other, each is the other's helpmate. In Genesis

2: 24 matriarchal overtones survive in what otherwise is a text based on patriarchal suppositions, for the man leaves his father and mother to cleave to his wife. But this is already amended by the other account of Creation, more recent in date though standing first in the text, which provides a profound theological interpretation: "God created man in his own image, in the image of God he created him; male and female he created them" (Gen 1: 27). Whatever the social and legal system may have looked like in the context of which these words gained their authority two and a half thousand years ago, the text talks of man and woman together as the human being. Any fundamental subordination of woman to man is thus invalidated by "the word of God", even if Judaism and succeeding it the Church for a very long time confirmed in practice the existing superior status of the male and not infrequently proclaimed it as part of the divine order. It was only the Enlightenment of the eighteenth century that set the emancipation of woman in motion and started placing the sexes on an equal footing. If the churches had concentrated on their rôle of proclaiming the Gospel instead of maintaining positions that were already lost, then they would have been able to make their contribution to an emancipation of woman that would really do justice to the nature of woman earlier and better than actually has occurred.

Christian ethics means more of course than just equality of the sexes and partnership in marriage. This further depth of meaning is expressed in the Letter to the Ephesians, the author of which in the fifth chapter compares the love of man and wife with the love of Christ for his Church. No one with a little knowledge of the Bible can read this passage without being reminded of the Old Testament psalms and prophecies that proclaim God's loyalty to his faithless people. This loyalty of God becomes visible and concrete in Christ, in whom God himself has given himself for this people of his. To be subject to each other "in the fear of Christ" – Luther's literal translation of Eph 5: 21 (av "in the fear of the Lord"; rsv "out of reverence for Christ") – can make marriage the mirror of divine love, Christ's love for his Church the mirror of married love.

What is possible for the believer is a love whose power of forgiveness is so great that it willingly takes upon itself the cross that is laid upon it and can even cope with the partner's unfaithfulness.

This kind of faith and this kind of love cannot of course be gained by legal prescriptions nor can it be maintained by such prescriptions. It can only be demonstrated in trust in the word that grants this trust. But this is a personal matter: here everyone is alone before God and his neighbour. Faith has no collective power, even though faith is helped by the community of fellow believers. We can thus formulate a third conclusion: that to accept and love one's partner in marriage is to accept a gift of grace from God. And only faith can express this conclusion in the context of the world with regard to the many crosses involved in marriage.

But man and wife do not only accept each other as a gift of grace, they also assume the obligation laid on them jointly by God: "And God blessed them and God said to them, "Be fruitful and multiply, and fill the earth and subdue it" (Gen 1: 28). Even being alone together would not be good and would not correspond to God's plan. Marriage transcends pairing off and partnership. It urges people on towards children, towards the family. This desire too is built into the human being, above all into the woman and through her into marriage. Here there is no need for prescriptions even when the family has altered its image from the large extended family right down to the tiny nuclear family in keeping with the changes in society at large. This desire is not even changed to any lasting extent by the emancipation of sexuality that we have observed in our own days in response to a bourgeois morality that had become corrupt. All that is new is that today both churches emphasize the couple's personal responsibility for the number of their children.

What we have said does not mean any calumniation of the unmarried. In the Old Testament there were no celibates, no one who willingly remained unmarried. To be and to remain unmarried counted as misfortune and shame. But in the New Testament we find evidence of the expectation that this age in which marriages are entered into will come to an end. Hence some passages give remaining unmarried the sense of bearing witness to the conviction that the form of this world is passing away. Paul, having already reached this conviction, impressed upon his congregations the necessity for such celibacy to be based on a free personal decision (1 Cor 7: 25 ff).

Marriage as a sacrament?

If the foregoing can be said in common by all the denominations, where are the points of difference and opposition? The main point of difference between the Catholic and the Protestant doctrine of marriage lies unquestionably in the fact that the first links marriage between baptized persons to the Church and sees it as a sacrament. In the precise terms of dogmatic theology and canon law, the Catholic church understands as a sacrament the promise of marriage normally given before a priest and two witnesses. Hence the whole of married life can be understood as sacramental. "For as God of old made himself present to his people through a covenant of love and fidelity, so now the Saviour of men . . . comes into the lives of married Christians through the sacrament of matrimony. He abides with them thereafter so that, just as he loved the Church and handed himself over on her behalf, the spouses may love each other with perpetual fidelity through mutual self-bestowal. Authentic married love is caught up into divine love . . . Hallowed above all by Christ's sacrament, this love remains steadfastly true . . . It will never be profaned by adultery or divorce" (Pastoral Constitution on the Church in the World of Today, §§ 48 and 49).

The Catholic church protects this sacramental character of marriage with a comprehensive marriage law. It accepts the civil law of marriage for its members basically only with regard to its civil effects, such as the right of inheritance, and so on. From the Protestant point of view Catholics as it were can get married twice over: once in a civil and once in a religious ceremony. But in the Catholic view they only get married once, in the religious ceremony. The rite takes place in every case in the context of a service with scriptural readings, prayers, and in most cases also a sermon, but frequently too within the context of the eucharist, in what is called a nuptial Mass. Since 1970 Catholics have been able on application, particularly in the case of a mixed marriage, to contract a sacramental marriage not only before a Protestant minister but before a registrar.

In contrast to this, the Protestant churches recognize the couple's declaration of intent before the registrar as fundamentally a valid contracting of marriage in the eyes of God and the Church. They are of the view that they do not have to make any legal prescriptions with regard to marriage as long as the state guarantees the public nature of getting married and recognizes and protects the essential content of marriage: free choice of partners, marriage for life and monogamy. This does not mean proclaiming the state as all-powerful in place of the Church in marriage questions, as is continually feared on the Catholic side. It is rather that the state is bound to fulfil its obligation of protecting marriage, which as far as it is concerned is a pre-existing state of life and not one that it has established or ought to establish. A Protestant marriage ceremony can be a public service with a sermon on a biblical text, an avowal that the couple accept each other as given by God and want to conduct their marriage in responsibility towards God, prayer requesting God's blessing and the intercession of the congregation, and finally the assurance of God's approval of this marriage.

What is the meaning of this difference in the way in which marriage is understood, a difference that up till today has had the effect of dividing the churches? A few crude generalizations will make the position clear:

The Catholic church sees in any separation of civil law and Christian faith a secularization of marriage and a disintegration of its religious content. This can above all be recognized in the fact that a Protestant church tolerates divorce. But that means turning the "Church in miniature", marriage, permanently into its opposite.

The Protestant churches see in the Catholic fusion of faith

and law a dangerous ecclesiastification and therefore absolutizing of human law and in this a secularization of faith. This becomes especially evident through the fact that divorce is indeed forbidden but it is only after remarriage that divorced people are excluded from the sacraments while otherwise irregular sexual relationships are not as a rule subject to legal penalties. But this too means turning the sacrament permanently into its opposite.

It should be pointed out that both many Protestants and many Catholics are of the opinion that divorced people are excommunicated after remarriage. Strictly speaking, from the point of view of canon law, this is not so. They are excluded from the sacraments because the Church's canon law presupposes that such couples are committing bigamy and are therefore living in serious sin: their marriage cannot be terminated, as the verdict of a secular judge has no meaning for the Church. The reason for the incorrect view that is commonly to be found is that exclusion from the sacraments is as a rule the only effect of ecclesiastical penalties that someone who is excommunicated is likely to notice. Whether one agrees with the presupposition of canon law depends on the way in which one thinks of the Church's competence with regard to the contracting of marriage on the one hand and on the other of the absolute ban on divorce.

Mixed marriages – the exception or the rule?

It is neither possible nor suitable to bring out here all the mutual reservations each denomination has about the other's views on marriage and to go into the details of how each denomination justifies them. But one thing is clear. The differences are not really based on the view of marriage that the churches preach to their members but rather on their separate views of the Church. The extent to which the churches are able to understand each other's point of view, and to come to an understanding, on questions of marriage depends on the extent to which they are able mutually to recognize each other as Church. Our aim is to explain this with reference to the

dialogue on marriages between people of different denominations – usually referred to by the ugly term "mixed marriages".

This dialogue was often requested by the German Evangeli-
cals before the second Vatican council. Its way was then prepared by private initiatives. It later gained official tolerance
from the council and was finally encouraged by various official
decisions by both churches. It has followed a road similar to
that taken by the discussion of other questions in dispute
between the churches. The attempt is being made at last to
say jointly what is held in common and to prescind from what
for the time being must still be said and done in different and
indeed opposing ways for the sake of invariably different forms.
For the first time since the Reformation the two churches are
aiming at the joint pastoral care of mixed marriages.

Since the Catholic church has actively entered into dialogue
with the other churches in Germany, both sides have made a
similar discovery. Their own characteristic positions are being
called into question not only from outside but also from within
their own ranks. Within the Catholic church there is to be
heard not only criticism of the absolute ban on divorce and
the query whether this is really Christian but also new questions about the sacramental nature of marriage that as a result
call into question the linking of marriage as a sacrament and
the canon law on marriage. It is not only a question of a
fresh look at the nature of a sacrament in the light of linguistics and the history of ideas: it is also a question of a new
concept of the Church in which the sacraments occur. The
Church is no longer seen as a society closed in on itself, a
societas perfecta which has at its disposal all the means it
needs to achieve its goal, but as the community of Jesus'
followers which is able to cross frontiers and barriers. The
Church is and ought to be a sign of God's love in which alone
all oppositions are comprised and in which alone the lethal
nature of thinking in terms of categories and the barriers
between them is overcome (Gal 3: 27 ff; Eph 2: 11 ff). The
Church is not so much a principle of unity as rather a sign that
community is possible between men of different and indeed
opposing temperaments and styles of life.

The second assumption comes from the Protestant side. There the traditional understanding of the wedding ceremony has come under fire since it was always open to the misunderstanding that what was involved was a second marriage ceremony on a higher plane, that of the Church. More important, however, are the new questions about the character of the word. What power does the word of proclamation have with regard to marriage and what regulations must there be for its sake? Can one attribute to it something like a sacramental effect? Does it really achieve what it promises?

One of the most important questions encountered jointly by both churches is as follows. If in the various communities of the New Testament different theologies had already taken shape, then ought not the Church to take shape in different "denominational" forms that are in communion with one another despite different experiences of the faith and their correspondingly different theological expressions? If these denominational communities are living together in one nation in a limited area, must mixed marriages then only become a source of tension (as of course they only too often are) or can they not also become an image and example of a new relationship between these communities? If despite the weight of negative experience one is fundamentally obliged to answer this question positively, then not only from a statistical but also from a theological point of view one should see mixed marriages as no longer the exception but as the rule. At the same time even within one and the same denominational church the faith of that church today is showing more clearly widely different expressions. These differences, which extend as far as temperament and customs, are nowhere more profoundly evident than in marriage. It is of course the nature of marriage that two people who are alien to each other have discovered each other and are meant to go on discovering each other ever more profoundly. Many "good Catholic" and "good Protestant" marriages are in fact "mixed marriages" full of tensions, once we consider the range of the partners' human and religious perception.

What the partners to a marriage need to know about

marriage is something they have been told in the instruction and teaching of the Church and something they have seen their parents providing an example of in their own lives, sometimes positively, sometimes negatively. For the rest regular attendance at worship is everywhere the best training for marriage, because it keeps dialogue within the family going, and this dialogue includes dialogue about what one believes. It is only those marriages that are already shaky in themselves or have already broken down that need immediate pastoral care designed specifically for marriage – and then it is often already too late. Those with pastoral experience in both churches are aware that a standard of indissolubility that is only maintained under compulsion is not a crisis that has been stood up to and lived through – and thus not love that has endured suffering.

This growing realism with regard to both the ecclesiastical and secular aspects of the reality of marriage has made it possible for both churches mutually to recognize each other's marriage ceremonies. In the Catholic church a dispensation from the impediment of mixed religion, which the parish priest can grant on behalf of the bishop, is still needed, and in certain cases permission for the ceremony to take place before a Protestant pastor or priest, permission which the bishop grants on the application of the Catholic parish priest concerned. On the other hand the point has already been reached that at the special request of the couple concerned the clergy of both churches can take part in the ceremony. Probably such requests will automatically become simpler with time, the more there is a growth of real mutual recognition. Furthermore local synods, groups and individual Christians within the Catholic church are pressing Rome both to abolish the impediment of mixed religion and to remove the obligation of a Catholic ceremony.

A difficulty still remains with regard to the question of the education of the children. Both churches are rightly of the opinion that one can only be at home in *one* church. So it makes sense for the couple to settle before they get married which church allegiance it is that they want to bring their

children up in. Both churches have instructed their clergy not
to interfere in the freedom of this decision. However the
Catholic partner must still promise to do everything in his or
her power to ensure Catholic baptism and a Catholic education, but at the same time he may not be required to act not
just against his own conscience but also against that of his
Protestant partner. In cases of conflict the clergy of both
churches are instructed to make it clear to the couple that
ultimately all the churches can try to do is to help their members towards a good and fulfilled marriage that is lived in the
sight of God.

Marriage as a gift of grace

What then is a Christian marriage? Protestant theologians are
reserved with regard to this concept. Even its defenders are
aware that there is no one form of Christian marriage, in the
same way as there is no one form of a Christian nation or of
Christian politics. There is in reality hardly any difference
between marriages between Christians and marriages between
non-Christians. In the one case as in the other there are both
successful and unsuccessful marriages. Nevertheless it is still
possible even in the Evangelical understanding of faith to
talk of marriage as a gift of grace from God because his blessing rests on it. Any Christian who no longer takes God's gift
of grace seriously shares in the guilt for marriage becoming
the victim of the biologists and, what is much worse, the
victim of the moralists.

All the same, the Protestant way of understanding the faith
cannot take over the Catholic usage of "the sacrament of
marriage". To begin with it sees *all* marriages in the light of
the rôle God has given them and in the light of God's blessing
and cannot therefore "ecclesiastify" those involving Christians,
turn them into a special affair of the Church. Then Evangelical
thought understands the sacraments as gifts of grace only in
the context of faith, not as autonomous means of grace that
affect and alter reality. In marriage a couple can not only create
heaven – grace – for each other but can also make life hell.

These charges are taken seriously on the Catholic side. A self-critical Catholic doctrine of the sacraments is no longer prepared to commit itself to understanding the sacraments as autonomous means of grace that affect and alter reality, either on account of the long tradition behind this or because of its present standing. Nevertheless it can already be said on the Catholic side that marriage as a sacrament is a "sign of the fragmentation of all faith" and equally a "sign of God's inviolable and steadfast love for *this* unholy and sinful human being". Hence marriage is "the lifelong sacrament of earthly reality". Does this mean that it is not our love but God's alone that makes marriage a "holy state" – Luther's expression? A Catholic will hardly hold the opposite. But in that case Protestant and Catholic thought are once again closer to each other than it appeared in the question of marriage. Just as little as the Church as a whole does marriage contain its holiness and its grace in itself. It is God alone who makes both institutions holy – despite all unfaithfulness. Wherever Christians bear witness to this in what they do and what they say, then they are bearing witness to Christ who was crucified for them, and in their marriages too they are living out their faith in God's blessing in the midst of this world.

28   Mary

To a greater extent than in the case of the other subjects dealt with in this fifth part, we are concerned here with doctrines that are to be found only in one denomination – the Roman Catholic church, only partially in the Orthodox church too – while the other denominations for the most part remain silent about them except for protests against the Catholic teaching. To a lesser extent than in other fields are we able here to describe efforts at mutual understanding and the prospects of consensus. And, to a greater extent than in other fields, all this chapter can therefore do is present the Catholic church's position and its reason for adopting it, mention the objections

of the churches of the Reformation, and sketch the defence
Catholic theology offers against these.

The dogma

The Catholic church's dogmatic statements with regard to
Mary can be summarized as follows:

1. As the mother of Jesus Christ Mary is the mother of God
and as such remained ever virgin (the dogma of Mary's perpetual virginity).

2. Mary is holy thanks to an unmerited gift of God: from
the beginning she was preserved untouched by original sin, by
grace and through the merits of Christ (the dogma of the
immaculate conception, defined by Pius IX on 8 December
1854, DS 2803).

3. Mary, body and soul, is with the resurrected Christ (the
dogma of the assumption, defined by Pius XII on 1 November
1950, DS 3903).

Scripture

It is only the first of these statements that has an immediate
basis in Scripture. Admittedly Mary is never called the
"mother of God" in the New Testament but only the "mother
of Jesus" (Mk 3: 31 and parallel passages, Jn 2: 1–5; 19:
25–7; Acts 1: 14). But the title "mother of God" is logically
inevitable once the confession that Jesus is truly God, one in
substance with the Father, is put at the centre of the faith. The
title "mother of God" can then even become a criterion of
orthodoxy. This is what happened at the Council of Ephesus
(431) when, in order completely to exclude the idea that Christ
was only subsequently raised up or "adopted" to become the
Son of God, the Council decided on the formulation that
Mary was not only the mother of Christ (*christotokos*) but also
the mother of God (*theotokos*) (DS 252) – and the people
responded with enormous enthusiasm to having their doubts
cleared up.

Already two centuries earlier the formulation "the virgin

Mary" had entered what is known as the Apostles' Creed (in reality the baptismal creed of the western church dating from the end of the second or the third century). For this title Scripture provides more eloquent witness. The gospels of Luke and Matthew record Jesus' miraculous conception by the Spirit of God and his birth of the virgin Mary (Lk 1–2; Mt 1: 18 ff). But this twofold assertion is only to be found in these two passages. If one did not have them, then one would conclude without hesitation on the basis of a larger number of other passages that Jesus was conceived and came into the world in a different manner, like every other man, "born of woman, born under the law" (Gal 4: 4). Jesus' brothers and sisters are often mentioned (Mk 3: 31–5; 6: 3; Mt 13: 55 f; Jn 2: 12; 6: 42; 7: 2 ff; Acts 1: 14; 1 Cor 9: 5). One of them, James, was later to assume a leading place in the Christian community of Jerusalem (1 Cor 15: 7; Gal 1: 19; 2: 9 and 12; Acts 12: 17; 15: 13; 21: 18). The historian must conclude from this that the tradition of the virgin birth was still unknown to those who wrote or formulated these texts or their sources and that it arose comparatively late – both gospels were not written before AD 70. What is the purpose of this tradition?

The account in Luke (2: 1 ff), which has become the gospel reading for Christmas, is chiefly concerned with proclaiming not Jesus' miraculous conception and birth but the event of the birth of the Messiah for the salvation of all nations of the earth. The angel's announcement to the shepherds (Lk 2: 10–12) is the decisive focus of the story. If Luke did not at the start (2: 5 together with 1: 27) introduce Mary as Joseph's betrothed, every reader would naturally take Mary and Joseph for a wandering married couple. In contrast, in the preceding account of the annunciation of Jesus' birth by the angel Gabriel (Lk 1: 26 ff) Jesus' virgin conception and birth are presented as the special divine miracle with regard to Mary. In place of conception by a man we have conception by the Spirit of God: "Therefore the child to be born will be called holy, the Son of God" (1: 35). Is the virgin birth then the reason for Jesus being the Son of God? This kind of borrowing from Greek mythology, with its tales of demigods born of the union of a god with a mortal woman, is only apparently the natural interpretation. In the context of the passage as a whole the sentence quoted above expounds the preceding verses (Lk 1: 31–3). The Messiah who has been announced is to be called the Son of God because it is in him that the prophetic utterance of Is 7: 14 finds its fulfilment, and here as in the Christmas story of Lk 2 the prophecy represents the dominant centrepoint of the account.

Matthew too lays all possible emphasis on the fact that it is the *Messiah* who, according to the promise of Is 7: 14, is born of the virgin Mary as the promised redeemer of Israel (Ps 130: 8; Mt 1: 18–25). This prophecy, the historian must conclude, has thus probably provided the impulse for the tradition of Jesus' birth of the virgin. But the real core of the accounts of Jesus' birth and their aim is to underline that Jesus is the promised *Messiah* of the house of David and as *such* is God's *Son* (Lk 1: 32). The term "Son of God" is therefore not in any way used here in the sense of the later dogma but in the sense of the Jewish expectation of the Messiah.

It was only when the title Messiah in its Greek translation Christos was firmly linked with the name Jesus to become virtually inseparable from it, and when the statement that this Jesus Christ as the Son of God moved to the central point of Christian doctrine, that the virgin birth, explained by the statement of Jesus' divine conception, became the decisive symbol of the incarnation of the Son of God and thus gained significance in the creed, in theology and in piety. *Symbol*, be it noted, of Jesus being the Son of God, not its reason. Nevertheless here the biblical statement of the virgin birth is linked with the post-biblical title "mother of God": Mary is the mother of God *because* the Son of God took flesh from her. The *symbol* of this unique human being is the unique *birth*.

Catholic mariology has a very ancient addition to the title "virgin": "ever virgin". Of this there is nothing in Scripture – and certainly nothing of the later elaboration "virgin before, during and after the birth" that is of course meant to be connected with Mt 1: 18. As far as the statement "virgin *during* the birth" is concerned, it has meanwhile been demonstrated that it does not belong to Catholic teaching but has always been only a theological opinion, deriving from some rather dubious sources such as the apocryphal Protoevangelium of James. As far as the other two parts of the statement are concerned ("before" and "after"), both the meaning of the biblical account and the extent to which they are contained in the dogma are disputed within Catholic theology too.

The two other dogmatic assertions about Mary cannot claim any direct scriptural support. Nor has the attempt ever been made to prove them "scriptural" in *this* sense. All that is claimed is that they do not contradict the statements of scripture. To prove them as an article of faith one must work from a different basis. This basis is the principle of *traditio constitutiva* according to which something can be a binding doctrine if it has unanimously been held as a doctrine of the faith in the Church from time immemorial.

Interpretation of the mariological dogmas

Even though it is a frequent occurrence, it is still misleading and injurious for the dialogue to describe the dogmatic statements quoted above as "the mariological dogmas". In the strict sense there is no "mariological dogma" as such: what there are rather are individual dogmatic statements about Mary that are linked to christological dogma. There is, therefore, as is very clearly shown by the Council of Ephesus, only one dogma about *Christ* which includes Mary as mother of him who brought salvation. And it should in any case be remembered that, despite the quality they have in common of being ultimately concerned with Christ, the various statements about Mary are not all of the same weight. Since the second Vatican council mentioned a "hierarchy of truths" (Decree on Ecumenism § 11) one must to a greater extent bear in mind the question how close to or far from the central dogma about Christ these statements are. In this context the following needs to be said in the way of interpretation of the dogmatic statements about Mary:

1. The most important and central statement is that about

Mary as the mother of God, because it forms part of the dogma of the incarnation. To deny that Mary is the mother of God is equivalent to denying that God became man, or at the very least to a view of Christ totally different from that portrayed by the New Testament, tradition, and the Church's creeds. But that would involve calling into question the foundations of belief in our redemption.

Mary's virginity, too, since the time of the Fathers of the Church has been understood by the Catholic tradition in connexion with the mystery of the incarnation. It is a symbol for the fact that salvation transcends this world, for Jesus Christ's incomparable uniqueness as a human being, and evidence of that grace that chooses the weak things of this world to confound the strong. The virgin birth makes it clear that God does not use the usual means of this world to save mankind: he does not use wealth, power, sexuality, but poverty and weakness.

2. The definition of Mary's "immaculate conception" is, just like the dogma of Mary's "assumption", significantly further on the edge of acknowledgment of faith in Christ. In its existing form the first definition is the outcome of progressively leaving on one side particular scholastic problems which brought the freedom from original sin enjoyed by Mary's soul into connexion with the philosophical doctrine of the infusion of the soul into the body. Just before the dogma was proclaimed Pius IX removed a clause to this effect, with the result that the wording today is free of philosophical and anthropological ballast and only presents the pre-effective power of God's grace: "... by a unique grace and privilege of almighty God, with regard to the merits of Christ Jesus, Saviour of the human race, was preserved untouched by every stain of original sin ..." (DS 2803).

3. With regard to the definition of the assumption, Pius XII used a formulation which prescinds from questions of detail: "At the end of her earthly life, the immaculate mother of God, Mary ever-virgin, was taken up body and soul into the glory of heaven" (DS 3903). The usual translation of Mary's assumption to heaven already detracts from the precision of the dogma's

Latin text, which talks of her being taken up into "heavenly glory" (*ad caelestem gloriam*). The formulation thus avoids any spatial conception in the sense of "up there" and "down here" and "going up to heaven" and above all all the images that are available to us from apocryphal writings and from many works of art. There is also no mention of how much "time" has elapsed between the "end of her life" and her assumption, nor is Mary's death once mentioned. All that is portrayed is Mary's glorification: nothing is said about *how* this happened.

Joint problems

It must first be remembered that the dogmatic statements about Mary are automatically affected as soon as new perspectives appear in our understanding of the person and of the redeeming work of Christ. That in fact is the case today.

Even on the basis of a quite "traditional" view of Christ, the title "mother of God" already raises difficulties. In the unique situation of the disputes at the Council of Ephesus this title was certainly unavoidable and was also quite clear in its meaning. Outside and apart from this context into which it fitted so simply it can be misunderstood. *God* cannot be born. All that can be born is a human being in whom faith acknowledges the presence of God. But this does not mean that God is now present in this human being in such a way that I can talk about him as I can about other objects. The sentence "The man Jesus is God" has a structure quite different, for example, from the sentence "Jesus is a man". For theologians there arises here the problem that has fascinated them since antiquity, the problem of the "exchange of properties" (*communicatio idiomatum*) – the problem of the way in which what is divine can be predicated of the man Jesus and what is human of God, one test being whether one maintains the complete paradox of the Chalcedonian dogmatic formulation ("truly God and truly man") or provides oneself with a concept of God's incarnation that indulges in imprecise reification. People have again become more strongly aware of this in connexion with the renewed discussion concerning the meaning of the term "son of

God", and this is strengthened still further if in keeping with the findings of contemporary exegesis – and in complete agreement with the Church – we must entirely exclude in addition the gentlest hint of the subsidiary idea that Jesus' being the son of God is to be understood in the sense of his descent and parentage.

It is above all from the point of view of exegesis that the statement about Mary the "virgin" has become a problem. There is no need at all to owe allegiance to any policy of unrestrained "demythologization" to have serious questions on this point. There is agreement that in the context of the New Testament the *account* of the virgin birth is meant to underline Jesus' uniqueness as the Messiah and son of God. But what *kind* of account is it? Is it a *report* of a historical event? Or is it an example of *midrash*, a tale told to bring some point of teaching home, like for example the story of the Magi from the east (Mt 2: 1–18)? If it is the latter, did the evangelists themselves regard it as historical reality or did they consciously make it up or take it over to put forward the teaching they were presenting? Was the real miracle as far as they were concerned the biological aspect of the story or was it not rather the fulfilment of the prophecy of Isaiah 7: 14, which is not to be interpreted as pointing to the "virgin birth" in the sense of the Church's doctrine? Is one not obliged to raise the same questions with regard to the "miracle" of the virgin birth as one raises with regard to the other "miracles" of Jesus? To sum up, is it the evangelists' intention to tie the reader's faith down to a *biological* interpretation of Mary's virginity? Does this mean that one has to interpret the passages about "Jesus' brothers" in the light of Mt 1 and Lk 1–2 or the other way round? The Church's ancient creeds, which all mention Jesus being born "of the virgin Mary", do not take us any further, since once again the same questions arise as in the case of the biblical passages.

The dogmas of the immaculate conception of Mary and of her assumption into the glory of heaven are intrinsically difficult, to begin with because of contemporary problems concerning the concept of "original sin" and the extent to which it is a truth of faith, and in the other case both because of new questions about the validity of distinguishing between "body" and "soul" on the one hand and on the other because of new questions about the possibility of making statements about man's ultimate fulfilment.

Non-Catholic objections

The questions mentioned above preoccupy *all* the denominations jointly – even if within the Catholic church there is more hesitation and objections are raised. But beyond this there are specific objections against the Catholic teaching about Mary that come from the non-Catholic, and especially from the Evangelical, side.

There are hardly any objections raised against the title "mother of God' – particularly wherever people adhere to the traditional acknowledgment of Christ as found in the creeds. Not least among the reasons for this is that the title "mother of God" does not appear in the most important creeds, the Apostles' Creed and those of Nicaea and Constantinople.

The title "virgin" is equally for the most part left undisturbed, even though no one commits himself to a definite interpretation of this title in view of the findings of biblical exegesis. A balanced and representative Lutheran view is that Scripture does not indicate with any clarity whether the virgin birth is a *fact* or only a *symbol. If* it is a fact, then it is not for its own sake but for the sake of representing Christ. Nobody is bound in conscience to believe it as a *fact* but is however bound to believe what it *represents*: the uniqueness of Jesus Christ.

Very considerable objections are brought against the two most recent dogmas about Mary. From the Evangelical point of view they have no foundation in Scripture and indeed contradict Scripture, since Scripture does not admit any exception from the universality of the fate brought about by sin. Scriptural texts like Lk 1: 28 or Lk 11: 27 do not provide any sufficient support. The two dogmas therefore depend on a creative tradition (*traditio constitutiva*) that is extra- and post-biblical.

As a foundation for Marian piety this might still pass, because it would fall within the freedom of the individual. But once it is turned into a dogma the Church's teaching office has placed itself above Scripture and enslaved conscience. At the same time it has given an impetus to a kind of Marian piety that was already doubtful but could earlier at least be tolerated, an impetus which obscures consideration of Christ as the one and only mediator between God and man despite all the theoretical safeguards. The attempts that have failed over the past two centuries to push through the dogma of Mary as co-redemptrix were merely a consequence of this.

The Orthodox church adheres to Mary's assumption into heaven, indeed with greater emphasis than the Catholic church. But it rejects the dogma of the immaculate conception, for reasons diametrically opposed to those of the Evangelical church: it brings original sin too much into the centre of things and belittles Mary's merits because her free will would have had nothing to overcome.

The Catholic rejoinder

Contemporary Catholic teaching about Mary is no longer prepared to adhere to everything to be found on the subject in pre-conciliar textbooks of dogmatic theology. Everywhere there is evidence of a tendency towards sobriety and towards avoiding exaggerations.

There is just as little readiness to defend dogmatically everything that takes place in the liturgical cult of Mary – even though the Church also refuses, for example, to launch a drastic attack on the popular piety of southern Italy or of Latin America simply for the sake of Protestants. There is moreover no doctrinal decision on the part of the Catholic church that the Christian is *obliged* to honour Mary. The discussion of the question whether biblical passages like Mk 3: 31–5 (and parallel passages), Lk 1: 48 and 11: 27 f, and Jn 2: 1–11 and 19: 25–7 provide a basis for the liturgical veneration of Mary is a completely open one in the Catholic church too.

Nevertheless Catholic theology judges itself capable of

justifying the dogmatic statements about Mary. The question whether a dogma can be proclaimed that has no direct biblical basis is in this context not a specifically Mariological question but a question concerned with the Church's teaching office and thus with the structure of the Church. But intrinsic reasons for the Marian dogmas are seen.

According to the witness of the Bible, Jesus' mother served God by enabling him to enter into our history. In this God acted from pure grace (Lk 1: 34 f): he did not come through the will of flesh and blood (Jn 1: 13). Nevertheless in this Mary was not simply the "means" whereby God became man: Mary did not serve God only in a purely physical capacity. God became man through her *response of faith* (Lk 1: 38 and 45). This faith of Mary's, however, is not a human contribution but the acceptance of the grace and mercy of God, who achieves everything in everyone (Lk 1: 46–50). Her faith was also not confined to Jesus' conception and birth but proved itself in all the trials of her life (Lk 2: 35 and 49 f; 8: 19–21 with parallel passages 11: 27 ff; Jn 2: 4) right up to and including the cross (Jn 19: 25–7).

Mary is thus the primary image of the Christian, of the person who is affected by the approach of God's grace, accepts it, and builds on it through all the dark stretches of his life. If the Christian believes Mary is with Christ and honours her as such and expresses this through many exuberant titles such as "helper", "mediator", "queen", and so on, all that means is that in possessing this primary image she retains her significance as the first among all Christians.

Catholic mariology thus sees itself as a fortunate synthesis between the "Pauline tendency" of the Evangelical view and the "Johannine tendency" of the Orthodox church. Together with the Orthodox, the Catholic church places the emphasis on the entire seriousness and the complete reality of God's incarnation, in which Mary now has her unassailable place. But it does not share the Eastern church's view whereby basically the incarnation is already the whole of redemption – a view that to some extent has brought the liturgical veneration of Mary more into the centre of the Church's life than in the Catholic church. Here Catholic mariology is closer to the Evangelical, "Pauline" view, which emphasizes the continuing world of sin and stresses the cross and faith.

Finally, taking its cue from ideas of the Fathers of the Church, the Catholic church develops the biblical statements by seeing in Mary not only the primary image of the individual believer but also the primary image of the *Church*, which *receives* itself, the meaning of its existence, entirely from God and at the same time by *responding* is always completely with Christ. Just as salvation came into the world through Mary's response to God, so salvation comes to the individual man or woman through the Church's response.

Once again this view, which is typical of more recent Catholic mariology (cf the chapter on Mary at the conclusion of the second Vatican council's dogmatic constitution on the Church), meets with the most vigorous protest from Evangelical theologians. It is precisely at this point where Catholic doctrine wishes to make its most fully developed statement about Mary that Evangelical theology sees exemplified and summed up the Catholic church's original sin: that it places itself not *under* Christ but at his *side*, as a *receiving mediator*. Every time Mary is "revalued" – remember the question of Mary as a co-redemptrix – the Church is, in the judgment of Protestants, covertly trying to revalue itself and push its status that little bit higher. Because (eg) the Evangelical church passionately rejects the Church's interpretation of itself as mediator, it does not regard Catholic mariology as a harmless peripheral phenomenon. And it is for the same reason that one can detect practically no tendency at all to revive the Evangelical liturgical tradition of honouring Mary that was retained by Luther, that was supported by the magnificent music of Johann Sebastian Bach, and that only disappeared with the Enlightenment. The more general question of veneration of the saints does not seem to induce such rigidly opposed ideas. Of course the churches of the Reformation for the most part reject the veneration of the saints as they do mariology, whereas the Catholic church retains it (cf ch. 7 of the constitution on the Church of the second Vatican council).

Nevertheless the veneration and invocation of the saints are less to the centre of Catholic doctrine than mariology. In present-day Catholic piety they are nothing like as important as they were at the time of the Reformation or in the following centuries, when Catholics were accustomed to lay great stress on everything that Protestants rejected, without consideration of actual degrees of importance. Veneration of the saints in its modern Catholic acceptation is open to understanding by Protestants: the main intention of the veneration of the saints is to glorify God's grace in real men as they exist in historical time. Veneration of the saints is not adoration of the saints, but celebration of them as witnesses to the triumphant grace of God and as models for the Christian life – which can mean severe self-reproach by the church. When the saints are asked to intercede for men in this world they are not expected to do what they have not already done in this life, instead such an invocation is an expression of the belief that their earthly life in faith, hope and love has now acquired lasting validity before God and the world. In the Catholic viewpoint, anyone for whom the community of the faithful as the "people of God" in faith is a reality, and anyone who is filled with true hope in everlasting life, can hardly take offence at a form of veneration of the saints freed from all superstitious accretions.

29 The Church

We have been reminded a number of times already in this book that today, in contrast to the time of the sixteenth-century Reformation, the differences between the denominations are sharpest in their ideas about the nature of the Church. This fundamental difference keeps alive a whole range of further differences. If we are not to give up all hope of agreement, it is in this area that the most careful work must be done to clarify the points of dispute. Only thus can we really tackle the problem in mutual tact and honesty.

I. THE CHURCH AND ITS AUTHORITY

It is not a straightforward task to describe the different views of the Church and the structures to which they give rise because both have undergone a number of changes in the course of history.

For example, Luther's doctrine of the Church is not in complete agreement with the views of Melanchthon and later Lutheran theology (what is called "Lutheran orthodoxy"). In its turn, modern Protestant theology has brought new emphases. A process of this sort constantly uncovers new realities which make it necessary to look at everything from a different point of view.

Much the same is true of the development of the Catholic teaching about the Church ("ecclesiology"). A good example is the doctrine of apostolic succession. In the face of gnostic doctrines of redemption which promised men a way to salvation by means of secret traditions and flight from the world, Irenaeus (who died in about 202) stressed public, historically demonstrable succession in office as a means of ensuring the preaching of correct doctrine in the historical Church. The question is fundamental. Did God speak his redeeming word into *history*, that is, publicly, or does redemption take place apart from history, in an esoteric circle of initiates who have to strip off the evil material world and its activities in order to proceed by stages to a pure existence?

Because Irenaeus believed that the word of God had become flesh in history, he stressed the importance in the Church of public, visible authority and its transmission as a guarantee that the word of God will be constantly made present in history anew by public preaching. In other words, for Irenaeus and the early Church, apostolic succession (the authoritative transmission of office and authority) was inherently connected with correct preaching. But only a little later, with Augustine, ensuring correct preaching becomes quite unimportant as the aim of the public, historical transmission of authority. Instead, Augustine sees the apostolic succession as a guarantee of the valid administration of the sacraments and (*as such*) a means for distinguishing the true Church from the false. This emphasis has been retained down to the theology of the second Vatican council.

From this we can see two things. First, the doctrine of the Church held today in the various denominations does not as a matter of course retain all the insights developed in the course of history. We must be prepared in advance for certain narrowings, historical developments, and even forgotten truths. It can be valuable to rediscover such forgotten truths and abandoned attitudes. They show that the area of possible agreement could be larger than it is at present, and that objections on both sides often have less foundation than we think. Second, in spite of historical changes, the understanding of the Church in each of the two main confessions displays a number of main lines which, as it were, make up the features of the confessions. We must now describe the most important of these.

Luther on the Church

Following a tradition which goes back to Augustine, Luther distinguishes between an invisible, spiritual, hidden or inner Church and the externally visible Church. For him the first is the communion of saints, the body of Christ, the people of God, the *Catholic* Church.

"The first way according to the Scriptures is that Christendom is a gathering of all Christ's faithful on earth. So we pray in the creed, 'I believe in the holy Spirit, a communion of saints.' This community or gathering is to include all those who live in true faith, hope and love. That is, the essence, life and nature of Christendom is not a bodily assembly, but an assembly of hearts in one faith. As Paul says in Eph 4: 5: 'One baptism, one faith, one Lord.'" (*Weimarer Ausgabe* 6: 292, 35). The inner, spiritual Church is not a phenomenon outside history. It stands for the community of those who really believe, hope and love. This Church, however, cannot be located by external criteria, because faith, hope and love cannot be certainly detected from outside. It is true that faith, hope and love show themselves in words, judgments and forms of behaviour, but these may always include impure motives and deceit. To that extent faith, hope and love are "invisible" and yet affect history. For inter-denominational discussion the important thing about this way of describing the Church is that it excludes no believing Christian. For Luther there is not a number of churches, but *one* communion of saints. Our familiarity with the different denominational churches has largely obscured this truth. This Church is holy because the Lord makes it holy. It is *catholic* or "common to all".

Although the boundaries of this Church cannot be clearly defined from outside, there are features by which it can be recognized. According to Luther, "The signs by which we can see externally where the same Church is present in the world are baptism, the sacrament (ie, the eucharist), and the Gospel, but not those of Rome or this or that place. Wherever there is baptism or the Gospel, no one need doubt that there are also saints, though they be no more than children in cradles. But Rome and papal power cannot make saints like baptism and the Gospel" (*Weimarer Ausgabe* 6: 300, 37). At other places in his writings Luther gives a longer list of distinguishing features: in addition to the Gospel, baptism and the eucharist, *Of Councils and Churches* mentions the power of the keys, ecclesiastical offices, prayer and the cross (*Weimarer Ausgabe* 50: 628–41). The reason why the Church can be recognized from the marks listed lies in the power of God, who kindles faith, hope and love in men's hearts through his word, through baptism, the eucharist and the other distinguishing marks. "For God's word does not return empty, but must have at least a portion of the field" (*Weimarer Ausgabe* 50: 629). Because all these means belong to the Lord himself, even unworthy service cannot debase them. "We know and consider that the Pope and his crew are not the true Church, and yet when they baptise, ordain ministers of the Church, unite people in marriage, we do not consider this false, but admit that their baptism is true. . . . Office and person must be separated. A public sinner is not in the unity of the Church, and yet the office he holds in the Church is not for that reason to be despised. The reason? It is not his, but belongs to the Lord Jesus Christ (*Weimarer Ausgabe* 44: 310).

In other words, in Luther's view the one, holy catholic Church is provided by God with a range of gifts – which includes authority – by means of which God makes contact with men in history and leads them to salvation. Luther describes all these gifts which make the Church visibly present, and at the same time promote its invisible growth, predominantly in terms of the word. And just as the word is first among the marks of the Church, the nature and features of all the other marks are defined in terms of the word. This is clear in Luther's view of the eucharist and the ministry in the Church. Luther attacked the Catholic eucharistic practice of his time fiercely because the words of institution were said in Latin and also whispered. This meant that the people were being deprived of the very thing the Lord intended them to have: the promise of forgiveness of sins through the sacrifice made once for all by Christ. This word and faith in it are what the eucharist is all about. Similarly, Luther thinks of the ministry in the Church in terms of the word: ministers are necessary for the sake of the community, so that it can be constantly built up anew by the word.

The task of preaching has two aspects for Luther. By baptism every Christian is consecrated and anointed to a royal priesthood. All therefore have the right and duty to preach the word of God where no provision for the ministry of preaching so far exists. "First, when he is in a place where there are no other Christians, he requires no other call than the fact that he is a Christian, inwardly called and anointed by God. In this situation he has a duty to preach to the ignorant heathens or non-Christians and teach them the Gospel, from his obligation of brotherly love, even if no one appoints him to do so" (*Weimarer Ausgabe* 11: 412). But if a community exists, it is its duty to appoint a suitable Christian, whom the ecclesiastical authority will then confirm and "ordain". All the official duties of the ordained minister, including the administration of the sacraments, are included essentially in the task of preaching. The standard of all preaching is Scripture.

Ministries are part of the Church by God's will. Luther regards the purpose of ministries as essentially service to the community through the word. Ordination gives the recipient a function. Because this understanding of ministry is "functional", Luther rejects the Catholic doctrine that priestly ordination gives the ordained person an "indelible character" which continues to distinguish him from "ordinary" Christians even when he no longer performs the functions of his ministry.

Calvin on the Church

Calvin too distinguishes between a visible and an invisible Church, but his emphases are different from Luther's. The invisible Church is the one "into which those only are accepted who by the grace of acceptance into sonship are children of God and by the sanctification of the Spirit true members of Christ. This Church includes not only the saints who live on earth, but all the elect who have been since the beginning of the world" (*Institutio christianae religionis* IV, 1). This invisible, spiritual Church is *one*; it is *catholic* or "universal". It is the Church of the chosen, who have been made part of the body of Christ by God and "therefore nevermore fall from salvation" (III, 21).

From this invisible communion of saints Calvin distinguishes "the whole throng of men scattered through the world who confess that they worship the one God and Christ, who have been introduced by baptism into faith in him and show their unity in love and true doctrine by partaking of the eucharist, are unanimous in the word of the Lord and for the preaching of the word maintain the ministry instituted by Christ" (*ibid*).

The visible Church also includes among the believers hypocrites, who have no part with Christ, but anyone who lives in faith in the visible Church receives the innumerable gifts which God bestows and enters into fellowship with the exalted Lord.

This visible Church is necessary for men. "There is no other way by which we can enter life than by being conceived in her womb, born of her and fed at her breast and taken under her protection and guidance until we put off our mortal flesh and become like the angels (Mt 22: 30)" (IV, 1). According to Calvin, outside the visible Church there is no forgiveness of sins and therefore no hope of salvation. This is because it is in the Church that God's word is preached and his sacraments administered. In it are the ministers through whom Christ works – Calvin mentions apostles, pastors, evangelists and teachers. But it is the word and sacraments which produce their fruit, though perhaps not in all. This one Church unites in itself the many individual churches in towns and villages which are in themselves the Church complete, and rightly so called.

Like Luther, Calvin thinks of the ministry and the sacraments – baptism and the eucharist – essentially in terms of the word. He even describes the Church as a school and Christians as its lifelong pupils. Preaching or teaching is consequently the centre of life in the Church. However, Calvin distinguishes essential and less important points of doctrine. On the less important differences of opinion are possible, but the essential ones "are so necessary to know that they must be accepted by all firmly and without doubt, as being as it were the true principles of religion. These include the following statements: There is one God; Christ is God and the Son of God; Our salvation rests on God's mercy; and other statements of the same sort" (IV, 1).

If these central points of doctrine are not preserved and preached without distortion, and where the sacraments are not administered accordingly, Calvin says that the Church dies. It is as though the most important organ of the Church has been injured and the whole organism made incapable of survival. "This is the state of things under the papacy, and from it we can see what remains of the Church there. Instead of the service of the word, there is a perverted tyranny built out of lies" (IV, 2). In the Roman Catholic church Calvin recognizes only traces and remnants of the Church, of which the most important is baptism.

According to Calvin the dispute with the Church of Rome is

not about whether it is entitled to the name "Church" – for this is still justified in some sense by the remains of the Church which survive in it. The real point is the proper structure of the Church and life in the Church, and above all fellowship in doctrine.

The second Vatican council on the Church

The second Vatican council has rightly been described as the council of the Church. Almost all the council's documents discuss or touch on the Church. This is a good reason for using these as the basis for an outline of the contemporary Catholic understanding of the Church.

The council's general description of the nature of the Church agrees to a remarkable extent with the basic texts already quoted from Luther and Calvin: "He [the Father] planned to assemble in the holy Church all those who would believe in Christ. Already from the beginning of the world the foreshadowing of the Church took place. It was prepared for in a remarkable way throughout the history of the people of Israel and by means of the Old Covenant. Established in the present era of time, the Church was made manifest by the outpouring of the Spirit. At the end of time it will receive its glorious fulfilment. Then, as may be read in the holy Fathers, all just men from the time of Adam, "from Abel, the just one, to the last of the elect', will be gathered together with the Father in the universal Church" (*Constitution on the Church*, 2).

The Church is described as the gathering together by God of all who believe in Christ. It includes all believers, and is the one catholic Church sanctified by Christ. This Church, the people of God, the body of Christ, is made up of many members, all of whom have been given their particular gift for the service of all. It is visible in its "state of pilgrimage", but at the same time must grow invisibly in all its members in faith, hope and love. As God's holy ones, all members of the Church possess the status of prophets, priests and kings, and all share in Christ's mission to the world.

This community of believers is born "through the word of the living God" (9). The sacraments are the Church's means of life. Although on the whole the "word of God" is not given as much emphasis as in the writings of the Reformers, the word of God contained in Scripture and transmitted in preaching is called "the supreme rule of faith" and "the support and energy of the Church" (*Constitution on Divine Revelation*, 21). But – and here we see the difference from the Reformers' statements – the word of God in Scripture is never considered independently of tradition and the ceaseless process of interpretation in the Church. The authoritative position of Scripture in the process of transmission and its normative status in relation to tradition are indicated when the study of Scripture is called "as it were, the soul of sacred theology" (*Revelation*, 24). Some implications of this for the study of theology are mentioned in the *Decree on Priestly Formation:* "In the study of sacred Scripture, which ought to be the soul of all theology, students should be trained with special diligence . . . Dogmatic theology should be so arranged that the biblical themes are presented first. Students should be shown what the Fathers of the Eastern and Western Church contributed to the fruitful transmission and illumination of the individual truths of revelation, and also the later history of dogma and its relationship to the general history of the Church" (16). In other places, however, Scripture and tradition are simply mentioned side by side, without any more precise definition of the relation between them. This way of talking can give the impression that two fully equal entities are involved.

The documents of the second Vatican council place particular emphasis on authority in the Church, and in this they do no more than continue the tradition since the council of Trent. It is true that in the discussions on the *Constitution on the Church* the chapter on the people of God was placed before that on authority to make clear that authority means *service* to the people of God. Nevertheless the "hierarchical structure" of the Church, and in particular the episcopal office, retains great importance.

"For the nurturing and constant growth of the people of

God, Christ the Lord instituted in his Church a variety of ministries, which work for the good of the whole body. For those ministers who are endowed with sacred power are servants of their brethren, so that all who are of the people of God, and therefore enjoy a true Christian dignity, can work toward a common goal freely and in an orderly way, and arrive at salvation" (*Constitution on the Church*, 18).

These ministries go back to Jesus Christ himself, who called the twelve and gave them a share in his mission. "These apostles (cf Lk 6: 13) he formed after the manner of a college or fixed group, over which he placed Peter, chosen from among them (cf Jn 21: 15–17)" (19). Since the Gospel has to be handed down for all time, "the apostles took care to appoint successors in this hierarchically structured society".

In other words, according to this document, Jesus' group of disciples was from the beginning a hierarchically structured community. The purpose of the appointment of successors was to preserve this basic character of the Church. The document goes on to refer to the Petrine office, and repeats the teaching of the first Vatican council (1869–70) on the primacy of jurisdiction and the supreme teaching authority of the Church. The bishops are successors of the apostles "by divine institution". According to the documents of the second Vatican council, episcopal structure is one of the fundamental features of the ministry in the Church and so of the Church itself.

All this gives a somewhat different impression from what was said previously in this book. We do no one an injustice in noting that the council fathers paid insufficient attention to what modern historical and exegetical study has discovered about the gradual development of the ministries in the early Church. The group of the twelve which Jesus appointed is not simply identical with the post-Easter "apostles", a group which also includes Paul. The function and tasks of the "twelve" are clearly different from the function of the apostles. Only Luke retrospectively equates the twelve and the apostolic college. Moreover, in the period of the Church's foundation the ministry of the apostles was the most important, whereas in the post-apostolic period the office of presbyter and the college of presbyters and "overseers" predominates. Within this basic structure the Jewish Christian communities of Palestine had in turn a different structure of ministries from the communities in Greek areas. The "monarchical" episcopate, the government of the community by a single bishop to whom the presbyters are subordinate, did not develop until the turn of the first century, when it spread quite rapidly to all the communities.

It is of course quite reasonable and proper to see the whole development of the early communities as a process guided by the Holy Spirit, and one which, having given the Church its original shape, is a standard for later periods. It was also in this period that the normative writings of the Church, the New Testament, were produced. But this view also gives us great freedom to take seriously the historical influences on the development of the Church's ministerial structures. The Spirit does not guide the Church directly from above, but by allowing people in the Church to confront historical conditions and take appropriate action. This allows us to draw two conclusions. (1) The structures of the Church are the product of history and therefore not inherently unchangeable. But (2), they came into being under the guidance of the Holy Spirit and we cannot just take them or leave them.

One difference between the Protestant and Catholic views of the ministry is worth particular attention. Luther and Calvin both think of the ministry in relation to the word, while the Catholic tradition puts more emphasis on the power to administer the sacraments. The second Vatican council's *Constitution on the Church* says: "Among the principal duties of bishops, the preaching of the Gospel occupies an eminent place" (25), but on the whole the consideration of this ministry concentrates on the priestly and sacramental function. In this respect a sharp distinction is made between the office-holder and the layman: "The common priesthood of the faithful and the ministerial or hierarchical priesthood . . . differ from one another in essence and not only in degree" (*The Church*, 10). Only the ordained priest possesses the power to celebrate the eucharist. The practice still reported by Hippolytus of Rome

(who died around 235) of recognizing as priests, without impo-
sition of hands, Christians who had been imprisoned for their
faith in time of persecution soon fell into disuse. The deeper
reason for this increasing emphasis on the power of office
derives from the idea that the whole structured ministry in
and for the Church as a community of believers rests not on
human initiative, but on God's saving activity. As contrasted
with the Protestant view, this means that the connexion
between the office-holder and the source, the Christ-event, is
not primarily in the written word but more through the chain
of office-holders and communities through the centuries. With
some over-simplification we can say that for the Catholic
church the "word" always exists as word preserved in the
community. This gives ordination within the apostolic succession its meaning: it is an expression of the fact that this
community remains the same community through history.

Hopes

We have seen that there is agreement between Protestant and
Catholic Christians in the description of fundamental features
of the Church. The same is true of the Anglican and Orthodox
churches. All join in accepting the one, holy, catholic or universal Church as the assembly of all who believe in Christ. No
less important, all join in accepting Scripture, baptism, the
eucharist and a structural ministry as essential features of the
Church. If there is acceptance in principle of genuine diversity
in the Church, the different emphases on word and community
or sacrament should act as a stimulus rather than a divisive
force, always provided that no denomination denies the inherent validity of points of view stressed by others.

The real difficulty comes only with the different views of
authority in the Church. This requires the denominations to
begin a joint effort at learning and reflection. The experience of
the Reformed churches in the course of history with the territorial churches should have made them readier to see the need
for universal structures. On the Catholic side a theological
exploration of the full range of structural forms and views of

the ministry in the Church is still a long way off. There is far too little consideration of their possible legitimacy in the Roman Catholic community. The findings of biblical theology will have to be given a much larger place than previously in the official Catholic teaching on ministry. The development of early Catholicism, which has shaped both the Eastern and the Anglican churches, must be taken more seriously into account by Protestant theology. There must be a critical re-examination of the criticisms made of the late medieval Church and the Renaissance papacy by Luther and the other Reformers to see if they apply without alteration to the Catholic church today.

Church history shows that church reforms always start "from below" and make their way to "the top" only painfully. On the other hand, reforms only come into full force when the authorities in the Church take them up and support them. Without some pressure from the "grass roots" the churches will never move closer together – certainly not in the area of church structures. This makes co-operation and commitment on the part of church leadership particularly necessary in this field.

II.   THE POPE AND INFALLIBILITY

In spite of the great progress towards agreement on the nature of the Church made by the churches and their theologians, one great obstacle to agreement remains – the position of the pope. It is hard enough for Protestant Christians to accept the pope's so-called "primacy of jurisdiction", the supreme and universal authority over all members and office-holders of the Church attributed to him in the Catholic church. It is even harder, indeed impossible, for them to understand and accept the Catholic doctrine of the infallibility of the pope's teaching authority.

The very word "infallibility", especially in common usage, conjures up ideas of spotlessness, perfection in every way and even sinlessness. It has to do with a basic human limitation, the *possibility* of "making a mistake". In this sense to call a person "infallible" is to turn him into a superman. But who can really seriously deny that human talk about the truth involves finitude, fragility and weakness, even and especially where God's truth is concerned? "Infallibility" as a distinct term to describe the teaching authority of the pope first appears in the fourteenth century. Catholic theology is well aware of the liability of the word to cause misunderstanding and offence, and because of this it has for a long time been looking for alternative terms. Suggestions include "inerrancy", "inability to deceive", "freedom from error", and most recently "indefectibility and permanence in the truth" (Hans Küng). But we shall probably have to live with "infallibility" it would be hard to ban it now. This makes it all the more important to see clearly what the Catholic dogma of this name says – and almost more important still, what it does *not* say.

What the first Vatican council said

The authoritative definitions on this subject were made by the first Vatican council (1869–70). The Council was preparing a draft on the infallibility of the *Church,* but in the dogmatic constitution on the Church, *Pastor Aeternus,* it made a binding statement only on "the infallible teaching office of the Bishop of Rome" – this is the title of chapter 4 (Denzinger-Schönmetzer 3065–75). In context, the crucial text runs as follows: "When the Bishop of Rome speaks as supreme teaching authority (*ex cathedra*), that is, when, in the exercise of his office of pastor and teacher of all Christians, he definitively decides (*definit*), by the supreme, apostolic power of his office, that a teaching on faith or morals is to be held by the whole Church, he possesses, in virtue of the divine assistance promised to him in St Peter, that infallibility with which our divine redeemer willed to endow his Church in final decisions on teaching about faith or morals. These final decisions (*definitiones*) of the Bishop of Rome are therefore, of themselves and not in virtue of the agreement of the Church (*ex sese, non autem ex consensu Ecclesiae*) unalterable (*irreformabiles*)" (Denzinger-Schönmetzer 3074). How are we to understand these statements? The record of the council give us some help.

1. Infallibility is "personal" to all popes and each individually. It is not, however, a personal privilege of the successor of Peter which separates him from the Church and sets him above it. The pope is not infallible because he is the pope – or the Bishop of Rome or the Patriarch of the West. He is infallible when he speaks as supreme teacher of all the faithful, with the supreme authority of that office (*ex cathedra*). In other words, infallibility is not an attribute of an office-holder as such, but of particular acts which he performs. The pope must therefore himself make it clear when he is performing such an act: that is, when he intends to make such a decision on doctrine. Anyone who *claims* that the pope has made such a decision has to prove it. For the period before the first Vatican council that is not always easy.

A further limitation on papal infallibility comes from its subject-matter. The only doctrinal decisions which can be infallible are those dealing with faith and morals – not, for example, if the pope expresses an opinion on science or politics. The purpose of an infallible decision is to establish that a particular teaching is indeed revealed by God, since only in this case can a doctrinal decision command the unquestioned obedience of faith. Infallibility means that when the pope speaks under *these* conditions and restrictions, and in *this* way, he is preserved by the assistance of the Holy Spirit from leading the faithful into error. It is therefore incorrect, because incomplete, to say: "In Catholic teaching the pope is infallible". The correct statement, and the only one which agrees with the council documents, is "The *exercise by the Bishop of Rome of his teaching authority* is, under carefully defined conditions, infallible or without error".

2. Even under the strict conditions specified, the infallibility of the pope's doctrinal pronouncements is not "absolute", in the sense of separate from the Church. Indeed the faith of the whole Church is a criterion binding on the pope when he is preparing a doctrinal decision which he intends to proclaim with infallible status. There is only *one* infallibility in the

Church, that of the Church as a whole, but it is given effect in a variety of forms, one of which is particular doctrinal decisions of the pope. But the main point of the Catholic doctrine is that *ex cathedra* decisions of the pope do not possess infallibility as a result of a sort of delegation by the Church to the pope of its permanence in the truth. Rather, as guarantor of the unity of the faith and of the Church the pope *directly* possesses the spiritual gift (or charism) of infallibility, which for the benefit of the Church preserves him from error in such decisions.

Papal doctrinal decisions of this sort are also dependent on the faith of the Church, not only in the sense that the faith is the goal of the decision, but also in that it is its norm. The dogma itself obliges the pope to use all human means of discovering the truth, even though the council did not see fit to bind the pope in his choice of means. It is obvious that a search of the Scriptures and tradition is an essential part of the process. The assistance of the Spirit promised to the pope in the dogma has no more than a "negative" effect, as a guard against error. The pope is not promised a positive inspiration or any new revelation.

3. Most of the trouble was caused – both at the time and now – by the statement that the "decisions of the Bishop of Rome are, *of themselves and not in virtue of the agreement of the Church, unalterable*". However, what this statement means is not as objectionable as it sounds. The council was not claiming that there is no connexion between an infallible doctrinal decision of the pope's and the faith of the Church. On the contrary, the decision is a testimony to the faith of the Church. The pope can never separate himself from the faith of the Church; if he did he himself would be outside the community. The "of themselves" (*ex sese*) does not mean that the pope can dictate articles of faith to the Church at choice. All it excludes is the view that papal doctrinal definitions derive their irrevocability from a particular legal procedure like ratification by parliamentary vote. Such opinions did exist as the legacy of the theological movements known as "Gallicanism" (because it was particularly strong in France [*Gallia* in Latin] and pressed for a large measure of independence from Rome for the French

Church) and "conciliarism" (which wanted to give the authority of councils more or less precedence over that of the pope).
The intention of this provision was to avoid making the validity
of papal pronouncements dependent on either the agreement
of rulers and bishops as representatives of the people or the
direct agreement of believers as a whole. As a guard against
these tendencies, the controversial wording was introduced
into the text of the constitution at the last working session of
the council.

Whether it was really necessary to force through this text,
which became a source of many objections and misunderstandings, is disputed even today. Neither conciliarism nor
Gallicanism was as vigorous in 1870 as the defenders of this
wording at the council believed. Nevertheless today Protestant
theologians too take great pains to understand the unfortunate
(because ambiguous) term "agreement of the Church" (consensus Ecclesiae) in its proper technical and historical context
in order to avoid misplaced controversy in the famous case of
the "infallible magisterium".

History, limits and results

In many ways the formulations of the first Vatican council
were the result of a long drawn-out argument and gradual reconciliation between the extreme "infallibilists" and a respected
minority, which maintained a more moderate position. In the
period after the council both supporters and opponents of the
dogma each in their own way exaggerated the infallibility of
the papal teaching authority. The effects have lasted into the
middle of this century and have still not been completely overcome. There were theological theories according to which
almost every utterance of the pope's at least came close to
being infallible. Such theories receive no support from the texts
of the first Vatican council.

Nevertheless these theories did not arise by accident. The
first thousand years of Christianity were always familiar with
the idea that the Roman Church and its bishop enjoyed a
certain precedence in teaching – at least it was never denied in

principle. Later, however, during the second millennium of Christianity, the conviction of the "inerrancy" of the whole Church visibly concentrated on its culmination in the papacy. It was only after the Reformers had denied the binding doctrinal authority of the pope, and the Enlightenment had rejected the idea of any binding dogma, that the infallibility of the papal teaching authority was really emphasized. Before the first Vatican council this led to ideas of an unlimited infallibility of the pope and to a "pope worship" which even Catholics today would find hard to understand.

Though the first Vatican council did not confirm, but indeed rejected, such exaggerations, it did make possible a one-sided emphasis and an interpretation which extended the scope of papal infallibility. There was no discussion of the way in which the infallibility of the Church is related to that of the pope. There was a complete absence of detailed discussion of the rich variety of firmness, reliability and "infallibility" of faith, in a slightly different sense, shown by "ordinary" Catholics in their lives. Instead, the certainty of faith was transferred into a doctrinaire form of preaching and then applied to individual statements. The connexion between the infallible preaching authority and the individual statement which owes its certainty to this is finally strengthened by the particular legalistic form in which the statement is proclaimed as a dogma. This shows the effect of the primacy of jurisdiction on the primacy of teaching: the one decides infallibly, the other makes acceptance obligatory by forces of law.

What the second Vatican council added

The second Vatican council supplemented Vatican I. Naturally the dogma of 1870 was not revoked. In fact, paradoxically, more was said about the pope and his function than a hundred years previously. This time, however, the connexion between the pope's teaching authority and the Church was made a great deal clearer. Three points must be mentioned in this connexion.

1. The infallibility of the pope is placed within the

infallibility of the whole people of God. "The body of the faithful as a whole, anointed as they are by the Holy One (cf Jn 2: 20, 27), cannot err in matters of belief" (*Constitution on the Church*, 12).

2. The college of bishops is explicitly brought into the process of proclaiming infallible teaching. "Although individual bishops do not enjoy the prerogative of infallibility, they can nevertheless proclaim Christ's doctrine infallibly. This is so, even when they are dispersed around the world, provided that while maintaining the bond of unity among themselves and with Peter's successor, and while teaching authentically on a matter of faith or morals, they concur in a single viewpoint as one which must be held conclusively" (*The Church*, 25).

3. To say that in the pope "the charism of the infallibility of the Church herself is individually present" (*The Church*, 25) means that the distinctive character of the Church, that of being an indestructible community of faith in Jesus Christ, is given in the pope a functional and supreme personal incarnation, becomes as it were visible in his doctrinal definitions. Most theologians today, on the basis of the council's statement, believe that there is in the Church only *one* possessor of infallibility, the college of bishops under the leadership of the pope. But this college can perform its task of proclaiming doctrine in different ways. The pope can express the faith of the Church "alone" – and in the process he can and must secure the agreement of the Church in various ways. But the pope can also make the collaboration of all clearer by calling a council and proclaiming the faith of the Church jointly with it.

Why infallibility?

Up to this point we have attempted to understand the Church's doctrinal testimony. How can we understand the thing itself?

Any consideration of the infallibility of the Church in general and of the pope in particular must start from the belief of Christians that God's revelation in Jesus Christ has an "eschatological character": ie, that it is the final and insurpassable revelation. God will speak to the world no new word, fundamentally different from his promise to the world in the person and work of his Son, that he loves the world and has accepted it. The community of believers confesses this faithfulness of God in his love; what makes it a community of faith is its confession of this faithfulness of God. As a result, this word of God is, as it were, entrusted to the Church; it shares in the faithfulness of God and is for this reason promised indestructibility in the Scriptures (Mt 16: 18). The Lord will remain with the Church always (Mt 28: 20). The Spirit of truth will not leave it (Jn 14: 15 ff; 16: 13). As the Church of the living God, it is the pillar and bulwark of the truth (1 Tim 3: 15). All Christian denominations share the conviction that in this radical and fundamental sense the Church is invincible and, as long as it relies on Christ and the foundation of the apostles and prophets, also free from error. The statements of faith produced at the Reformation also bear witness to this indestructibility and inerrancy of the Church as a whole (cf the *Augsburg Confession* VII and the commentary on it in the *Apologia for the Augsburg Confession* VII.

The differences between the Catholic church and the other churches appear in connexion with the question whether this "indestructibility" can or must extend to specific acts of acceptance or rejection of particular statements, statements which are part of a legal system of obligations and obedience. Today more than ever, Catholic theology must take care that, whenever the infallibility of the Church and the pope is mentioned, it draws attention to the fundamental fact of "an underlying continuance of the Church in truth" (Hans Küng). Infallibility is not an end in itself. Nevertheless, for Catholics it follows from the definitive nature of God's revelation in the incarnation of his Word that, in the midst of all the defects and weaknesses of human language, the "indefectibility and permanence of the Church in truth" can take shape in binding statements of the Church's doctrine. The strict conditions and criteria have been mentioned. If they are met, such statements are, in their substance – not in their wording – *permanently binding,* and in that sense final.

The witness of Scripture

In claiming that under certain conditions the Petrine office is endowed with infallibility in this sense, the Catholic church invokes the support of the New Testament. Tradition here has bequeathed several different orders of ecclesiastical offices. Those testimonies which lay stronger emphasis on the Petrine office constitute only one strand among the many traditions. Hitherto this has created difficulties which are not easy to surmount in discussions as to which ecclesiastical offices or orders of offices can be recognized and agreed upon among the churches. On the other hand it is precisely the inquiries of modern exegesis into the Petrine office that enable us to achieve a deeper understanding of the objective reality itself.

1. In important New Testament passages and traditions deriving from different spheres, varying in antiquity, and in practice belonging to all epochs in which the New Testament writings emerged, we find Peter accorded a special pre-eminence.

2. Peter's special position amounts to something more than a mere exemplary pattern of discipleship. Rather, according to Mt 16: 18, it has the force of an "official" function. "Thus the teaching of Jesus entrusted to him and vouched for by him is declared valid and binding for the entire Church on earth; the decisions arrived at in heaven, ie, at the Last Judgment, will be in accordance with the decisions taken by Peter" (Bornkamm). Peter is granted teaching and disciplinary power as a unity. He is "the guarantor and the authorized interpreter of the teaching of Jesus" (Bornkamm).

3. Catholic theology must recognize the difficulty that in the New Testament there is no explicit reference to any *successors* to Peter's official function. At the same time it cannot be definitively proved that there were no such successors, or that what is in question here is an unique task assigned to Peter at one specific point in history such that his "official" function dies with him. For we can recognize, admittedly from the New Testament itself, that the traditions about Peter had an impor-

tance and a validity which (unlike, for instance, those concerning the office of apostle) extended beyond the age of the foundation of the Church. In fact we find fresh assertions of the principle that "Peter" had the force of an "official" position in the second and third generation after the age of the foundation also. This is illustrated by passages such as Jn 21 or the two epistles which circulated in the Church under the name of Peter but which derive from a later epoch. Thus even within the New Testament itself the question of the existence and continuity of the "Petrine office" is already to be discerned.

Many particular questions of exegesis remain which are far from having been solved by the recognition of this, yet it becomes apparent that precisely the more recent findings of research in *both* confessions contribute important points of departure for the discussion concerning the teaching authority of the Petrine office.

Borderlines and borderline cases

Yet the crucial problem is one which can hardly be solved by the approach of historico-critical research. Catholic doctrine upholds the conviction that the Church cannot remain in the truth in accordance with the promise of God unless it is also possible in cases of dispute to discover a concrete form for this truth and criteria capable of determining it. It must be possible to have reliable statements of faith. The charisma of infallibility attached to the teaching office exists to provide this reliability. It is not a mark of distinction attached to persons but an "assurance" attached to statements – and not even to statements as such, for these can in their turn be incomplete, limited, or inadequate, but to the objective realities expressed in them. Despite all appearances to the contrary the teaching office is not *above* Scripture so as to be able to manipulate it. "The teaching office is not above the word of God but serves it" (second Vatican council, *Constitution on Revelation,* 10). Again the teaching office, or those vested with it, must first *hearken* to the word before they (infallibly) proclaim it. The fact that they do not fall into error in this is a gift of the

Spirit, a "charisma of the truth", which never passes into their "possession".

If all this is to be credible, then he who is vested with the teaching office must make it clear in the form and expression of the teaching he proclaims that the office he holds carries responsibilities and has the character of service. Moreover it is understandable, but nevertheless inadequate as an interpretation, when we seek almost spontaneously to "fill in" the material content, as it were, of the concept of an "infallible teaching office" by identifying it with the particular mode and expression of the dogma in which it was formulated in 1870 or with the two Marian dogmas defined by the pope "alone", those namely of 1854 (the immaculate conception of Mary) and 1950 (the bodily assumption of Mary into heaven). In the normal case – we are speaking, therefore, of the "ordinary" teaching office – the infallibility and inerrancy of the teaching office are, as it were, embedded in the daily life and preaching of the Church, in her prayer, her liturgy, the administration of the sacraments and in practices of fraternal aid. In such cases the question never arises of any statements being specially singled out and having the claim of infallibility explicitly attached to them. The number and importance of the points that have, over a long period, come to be preached and lived by as true and "infallible" in this way is infinite, and in no case has someone specially laid down that the point concerned is infallible and devoid of error. When a truth already taught and believed in in the Church acquires the force of an explicit dogmatic definition this does not of itself mean that it is either more or less important than before. The classic example of this is the "apostles' creed". Never made the subject of formal dogmatic definition yet always believed in, it is nevertheless nowadays coming to have the force of a firm foundation for preaching on certain critical questions.

From this it is apparent, therefore, that doctrinal decisions of the pope "alone" are extreme cases, generally having been arrived at in crisis situations. In such situations the truth of the faith *had to be* expressed in an "extraordinary" manner. The Catholic doctrine of the infallible teaching office of the pope lays down that this truth *can* also be expressed in this manner at such times.

Perspectives for discussion

Not only on the Protestant but on the Catholic side the dogma of the infallibility of the Church and of the papal teaching office is often misunderstood and presented without any attempt at penetrating its deeper theological meaning. It is only in recent times, and as the outcome of a renewed and much discussed attack by Hans Küng, that the question of the dogma of 1870 has been made the subject of renewed discussion. At all events, this much can be said with certainty: the more the question under dispute is thought out right from its very roots, the more non-Catholics too will be able to arrive at a right understanding of the purpose and meaning of the dogma, even though they may still even then feel unable to agree to it. Over and above this it will be helpful for future discussion to draw attention to a few further aspects, briefly to be enumerated as follows:

1. Absolute infallibility is proper to God alone. In virtue of the promise of God it is given to the Church to *share* in this infallibility of divine truth. But this merely means: *God himself* keeps the Church indefectibly in the truth because it is *his* Church. The Catholic church should take warning from past misunderstandings and emphasize as strongly as possible, precisely in its discussion with the churches of the Reformation, that infallibility is wholly and solely a gift of the Spirit and never comes to be a "possession" of the Church itself. Relying upon this gift it is solicitous to ensure that the truth entrusted to it shall be rightly understood and interpreted. It is true that in exceptional cases this may lead to a certain *confrontation* between the community and the preaching office of the Church. In this sense this office can and must have a certain "autonomy". There are sound reasons for this, not the least of which is that no one can in fact guarantee that the desires and tendencies arising within the community of believers will not at some point actually turn *against* the truth.

2. Even when faced with irrevocable statements of faith, the conscience of the individual Christian is still not absolved from its responsibility. On the contrary it is and remains the closer and more immediate standard of decision.

3. Irrevocable definitions constitute the exception in the Church's doctrinal preaching. Hence they should not be arrived at unnecessarily, and any appearance of "arbitrariness" must be avoided in them – and the Christian affected by them can assess them in the light of this question.

4. Side by side with the infallibility promised and bestowed upon it, a further factor to be found in the Church is a history of errors, deceptions, prejudices, missed opportunities, points recognized too late. Catholic theology has no need to escape from this "experience of opposites" by taking refuge in the dogma of infallibility, nor is it even permissible to do so.

5. We must not lose sight of the basic aim behind infallible statements of doctrine: he who commits himself to the Church and its word must be certain that he is committing himself to the truth. The question of the infallibility of the papal teaching office is an intrinsic part of the basic question of the relationship between word, Spirit and Church.

6. In the history of Catholic theology there is a whole series of "forgotten" (sometimes actually suppressed) questions, the answers to which would influence and change to a notable extent the way the dogma of 1870 appears to us and our understanding of it.

Among these are to be numbered questions such as the following: Can a pope fall into errors of faith (heresy)? How is the acceptance ("receiving") of papal decisions arrived at by the Church, and how do we recognize that they have been accepted? Are there never any situations in which the council can stand above the pope (we are thinking of crisis situations such as the "Great Schism" of 1378 to 1417, when for whole decades at a time there was both a pope and an anti-pope)? Again is it possible for the pope to be able to enact positive laws restricting his own rights, or to produce new and different juridical measures governing his relations with the college of bishops and the council, and in fact the means to be used and the ways to be followed in discovering the truth? To this day, unresolved tensions still remain between the Christianity of the first and the second centuries respectively in their understanding of the Church, and no satisfactory way of resolving these tensions has so far been found. Questions that have been prompted – in a different historical situation – by moderate conciliarism still await an adequate answer. Nowadays it is wholly in the sphere of ecumenical discussion that this quest is pursued. Theological discussion, and especially dialogue with non-Catholic churches, can lead to positive proposals and so contribute in their own way to ensuring that the door remains open to a deeper understanding of the teaching function, teaching authority and teaching office in the Church.

30 The significance of the denominations today

The earlier questions of dispute between the confessions – this much has become apparent – are nowadays on the way towards agreement at numerous points. Yet it has become equally important not to overlook the fact that there are not a few points on which the confessions stick fast in a state of confrontation between old and new. Indeed in several areas reversals and fresh obstacles seem to arise on the road to unity. Firmness threatens to turn into an obstinate hardening of opposed attitudes. Thus on many questions the confessions seem on the way to achieving reconciliation, while on many others they seem more open than ever in recognizing the state of division between them.

Now that we have characterized the present situation as one of simultaneous advance and holding firm, can we go on from this to say something of that in which the importance and the function of the confessions consists or ought to consist nowadays? In this question we are summing up the fifth section, viewing the points contained in it in new perspectives, and attempting to bring this "common book of the faith" to a conclusion that is not an ending but rather an opening up.

Earlier questions of dispute from new standpoints

The manifold advances towards unity achieved between the confessions have their basis in the following fact: whereas in the sixteenth century certain differences and conflicts led to the Church being divided up into a number of mutually opposed confessions, nowadays those same conflicts can hardly be regarded any longer as capable of producing sectarian divisions within the Church. In this connexion we may remind ourselves especially of the basic Reformation doctrine of justification by faith alone, the "article by which the Church stands and falls" (Luther). We owe this new insight to a comprehensive programme of theological study and a process of intensive reflection on the historical and material issues involved within the confessions themselves which have been achieved within the last few decades. In this connexion we have come to recognize that the doctrine of justification as understood by the Reformers is not irreconcilably opposed to the basic assertions of the Catholic doctrine of justification. The matter has indeed been discussed on every side, and different terms and ideas have been used. As a result many of the relevant factors which were proper to a specific epoch in history have repeatedly and radically been misunderstood, so that it has been possible for things to appear irreconcilably opposed whereas in reality they were not necessarily so. This doctrine is so basic to the Reformation that for the sake of it Martin Luther once resolved to carry the pope in his hands and kiss his feet if only he would accept it (*Werke* – Weimarer Ausgabe, 40 I/181, 1–3). Yet a truer reading of the facts has enabled us to recognize that this basic doctrine no longer gives rise to any opposition capable of splitting the Church. It neither requires nor compels us – indeed it does not even allow us – to live in separated confessions on account of it.

Again the connected term "alone" as used by the Reformers, with its manifold shades of meaning, is on closer examination revealed to bear a sense which Catholic theology must recognize as justified: Scripture alone, grace alone, the word alone, Christ alone – this means: all this lies at the origins, without rival, unique, and setting the standard for all the rest. Conversely Protestant theology has come to recognize something similar about the Catholic use of the term "and": Scripture and tradition, grace and works. The "and" in all these phrases is not intended to combine two factors as of equal rank and value, but to express an interconnection and unity between them instituted by God himself, and one which, so far from being in contradiction to the term "alone", is actually rooted in it.

A similar point must be made about what the Reformers understood by "faith". The essence of faith is man's self-surrender to God, who comes close to him in Jesus Christ – a definition of the essence of faith which the second Vatican council has taken over in the Constitution on Revelation. The same can be said of two phrases currently used to characterize the Church, "Church of the word" and "Church of the sacrament". So far from being incompatible with one another, these likewise turn out, in so far as they have any meaning at all, to constitute two aspects of the *one* Church.

As a result of the Reformation which took place in the sixteenth century, with all it entailed and all its consequences, the term "reform" and the reality it stands for have for long enough constituted grounds for a sundering of spirits between the confessions. Yet for all this the fact remains that nowadays it is precisely this real essence of what reform means that has become a programme uniting all the confessions and laying a common duty upon them all. It is a programme which the Roman Catholic church explicitly made its own at the second Vatican council, and which determines its present course and the position in which it currently stands. Now a will to renewal implies a will to break out of established positions, to be on the move, to change. We must be ready to say farewell to that which constitutes a mere mode of expression conditioned by a particular epoch, and not the indispensable reality of the Church itself. No church can any longer suppose that the only way of ensuring its survival is to present that which is proper to it as the opposite of that which is to be found in other churches.

A new self-understanding

The new relationship between the confessions which enables them to arrive at a fresh recognition and appraisal of their functions today has its roots in a further fact: that the confessions view themselves in a different light than has been usual for a long time, a time during which it was believed that that which was usual had also to be that which was necessary. Terms such as anathema, heresy, apostasy, idolatry have been withdrawn from circulation. The quest for truth remains as serious as before. But despite this fact no one any longer believes that the ultimate wisdom, or even the essence of Christian and ecclesiastical living, are to be found in self-righteous polemics and controversies. On the other hand a mere neutralizing presentation, in which all the confessions are regarded as equal, is shown to be inadequate.

A new language has been developed, one in which the ideas of "brotherhood" – between those who are still separated – "dialogue", and "co-operation" are the determining factors, these being the appropriate modes of mutual encounter and intercourse between the confessions. And this does not merely show greater humanity. It is based on theological insights and practical experience with regard to the Christian and ecclesiastical reality of the confessions. In noteworthy contrast to almost all earlier councils, the second Vatican council has had a pastoral and ecumenical orientation. In answer to the question of whether and to what extent the other confessions are or are not the "Church" the distinction – hitherto normal – between the "body" of the Church and its "soul" is no longer invoked. It is based upon a psychological idea superimposed upon the biblical image of the Church as "Body of Christ". In general this image has been relegated to a secondary place (*Constitution on the Church*, ch 1, 7 compared with ch 2). Its place in the foreground has been taken by the description of the Church as "people of God". All Christian confessions are alive in virtue of the same essential constituents of the people of God. This makes it possible – indeed necessary – to apply to them the designation of "Church", taking this to signify the instrument of salvation.

Thus confessions are characterized not primarily by that which divides them but by that which unites them and is common to them all. What divides them is not suppressed, but it is assigned a different place and acquires a different and lesser importance. Measured by the basic statement of the *hierarchia veritatum*, the "hierarchy of truths" (*Decree on Ecumenism*, 11) which the council has provided as a general orientation the common factors outweigh the differences. To affirm that which is proper to oneself no longer means to reject that which is proper to another. The latter is something which we can and may openly recognize and value. We can and may even go so far as to utter criticisms against ourselves. We can and may put forward the thesis that in the other confession Christian realities are often presented more convincingly, and the demands of the Gospel are fulfilled in a way which carries greater conviction than in our own church. Thus the confessions can stimulate a healthy and desirable rivalry on the question of what it means to live by the Gospel, by the mind of Jesus Christ, in preaching his message and fulfilling his task and his promise.

The common faith in danger

A third factor characterizes the current relationship between the confessions: that which is proper to each confession is not merely viewed in a different light nowadays, it has actually ceased any longer to constitute the central point of theological interest for the confessions and for the individuals living in them. All too often we have the impression that inter-church and inter-confessional dialogue is marking time, seeing that – despite all the joy we may feel at the achievements of theological study at the ecumenical level – a theological debate arises ever afresh about the questions which are still openly disputed between the confessions.

The demands which the present age makes upon the Christian confessions bear not upon those areas in which the distinctive characteristics proper to each are to be found. On the contrary, the points which are nowadays called in question are precisely such as were not in dispute between the confessions at the time of the Reformation, and on which they are nowadays united. It is the Christian faith as such that is being called in question today, in respect of its content and its realization. The intellectual forces of the age are no longer the confessions and that which moves them, but rather these: science of a kind that has become atheistic first in its methodology and then in its content, social and political programmes and ideologies which reject faith and religion, philosophies of life which are hostile to Christianity. It is these that constitute a challenge to the tenets which are common ground uniting the confessions. It seems that in so far as anything needs to be justified it is not humanity that needs it in God's sight but rather God in humanity's.

This book has been written under the impression of a shifting of the frontiers of this kind. Other questions no less central might run as follows: How and in what sense can the universal and exclusive claim of Jesus Christ be justified in face of the comprehensive knowledge that has come to be achieved of the history of men and their religions? What chance and what right to existence has the Christian faith or have the churches in an age in which both are palpably losing ground day by day in terms of confidence, conviction, effectiveness or adherents? From many points of view the impression is given that we only need to let matters take their course and develop unimpeded for them to lead very shortly to the downfall of Christianity. One does not need any special gift of prophecy to predict that.

What contribution has Christian faith to make in throwing light on the meaning of human existence and human history? What contribution does faith make – for it is in fact something more than a mere upholding of doctrines; it is a fundamental way of life for man as well – in coping with the problems of the world? How can it contribute to justice, peace, brotherhood and solidarity, to the overcoming of racism or war, or to altering unjust conditions and social structures? What contribution can be offered by Christian faith and the hope based upon it towards the shaping of the world in such a way that it remains a world of man and becomes so more and more? What doors does Christian hope have to open leading to possibilities for the future?

These and other questions go to the very roots in which all Christian confessions are united. The answers to them cannot be given in terms of "specifically confessional" interests, but only in terms of the word of Christian faith as such, that is in terms of that in which all Christians are or ought to be unanimous and united. Admittedly this answer should include resonances deriving from that which has been and is a living force in theological reflection, in experience and ways of coping with human life, and in the zeal and piety within the various confessions. For that which is proper and distinctive to each particular confession has left its stamp, its special "style", so to say, upon all these factors. And the variety and multiplicity of these different characteristics are not such as to divide the Church, not the expression of a fragmentation within it, but rather a sign of the riches of Christian faith, the definitions it arrives at, and the possibilities of expression open to it. Precisely in this way the Christian faith can provide an answer that is varied and manifold in form in response to the challenge of the present.

This challenge, at once the summons and the opportunity of the hour, is designed as few others have been to point the confessions to what constitutes their heart and centre, that from which they sprang, and so to bring about to an ever increasing extent the unity of Christians. A primordial law is being brought to bear here: encounter, community and union are achieved not merely through dialogue between two parties, by efforts at mutual understanding. They are achieved by to-gether looking towards the future: a common goal, a common challenge, an all-engaging commitment. This seems to apply to the position in which the Christian confessions stand today. It does not imply any diminishment, but rather a heightening and enriching of the possibilities and chances open to them.

The motto hanging over the first half of the twentieth cen-tury is: "Century of the Church – century of the ecumenical movement." This characterization is no longer applicable to-day. Interconfessional questions have yielded pride of place to questions about God, about the meaning of existence, about the contribution which the Christian faith makes to humanity and to the peace of the world. These questions are usually accompanied by a pronounced aggressiveness against the Church and the denominations, and by a surging "away from the Church" movement which is clearly recognizable and growing in strength. While earlier lines of questioning are changing or fading out, this does not imply any loss to the reality and significance of the churches. Its effect is merely to make it clear that the Church is not the chief subject of faith, but is rather at the service of this faith and of the inquiry into God and Christ which move it. In other words its position is that not of the goal but of the mean of attaining it. This new appraisal of the function and position of the Church as "relatively speaking" one of service, together with the challenge it represents, is a path which the confessions open up for one another, and in their relationships one to another they can discover fresh ways of arriving at a deeper unity.

New questions of dispute

What we have said so far is still not sufficient to characterize the relationship between the confessions. Certainly this much is true: differences which were once accounted sufficient to divide the churches are so no longer today. On the fundamental affirmations of faith which are nowadays being inquired into and called in question there is unity between the confessions. These questions are concerned with God, Christ, salvation and its meaning. But in saying that the churches are at one upon them we must not suppress the fact that in the very manner in which these questions are formulated within the theologies of the various confessions both past and future considerable tensions are to be noted extending even to the so-called "death-of-God" theology, this in turn taking many forms. Yet on the other hand these theological differences are not simply representative of the confessions as such at any given time. Often such theological strivings are, on their own admission, merely attempts, experiments, hypotheses – designed to be submitted to theological criticism and discussion, to be corrected or modified. Thus again and again it becomes apparent that tensions, differences and even conflicts, precisely on those basic questions on which the confessions are united, are ironed out and put right by theological criticism and discussion, though admittedly this should be pursued more boldly and more forcefully. Hence, though we may sometimes find ourselves faced with risky, one-sided or even extreme theological theses, that is no reason for straightway speaking of the dissolution or selling out of the Christian factor.

There is however yet another fact which must be spoken of in the current scene, in place of the earlier conflicts which divided the churches among themselves, new ones have arisen which, as is often maintained, make it not merely justifiable but actually necessary to maintain and even to confirm the division between the churches. The conflict between the confessions has shifted from the doctrine of justification, and is now chiefly concerned with the question of the Church and the position of Mary. This is significant to the extent that it is in these areas that the more recent dogmatic decisions of the Catholic church have been put forward. In the field of Mariology we have the dogma of the immaculate conception of Mary (1854) and of her bodily assumption into heaven (1950), while in the field of ecclesiological inquiry we have the decision of the first Vatican council on the primacy of the pope and the infallibility of his *ex cathedra* decisions on matters of Christian faith and morals. These facts of more recent church history seem to be the most difficult obstacles in the path towards unity between the churches, the more so since these decisions have explicitly been confirmed by the second Vatican council. For many Protestant theologians the effect of these dogmatic decisions has been to make it possible to recognize even more clearly what the real point of the Reformation was, and of its insistence on the term "alone" with all its manifold shades of meaning. If from time to time it has seemed as though bridges had been built and doors opened between the confessions, then, after what has taken place in 1854, 1870, and 1950, the door has finally and definitively closed. More than in the doctrine of justification the true point of difference between the confessions has been laid bare in the doctrine of the Church. It is only today, therefore, that we can recognize how necessary it was to decide upon the Reformation.

Even judgments such as these are an intrinsic part of the current reality of the confessions. This remains true even though it can hardly be said that there is any unanimity on these questions within or between the confessions. But the fact that the abiding conflicts and the great obstacles in the path towards unity between the churches lie in the sphere of the doctrine of the Church and the doctrine of Mary the mother of the Lord, and that it is chiefly on these grounds that the division between the churches remains and is plain to all eyes – this is an incontestable fact. Otherwise indeed it would certainly have been possible to achieve unity. The special difficulty consists not so much in the fact that a new dogma has been put forward concerning the doctrine of the papacy and especially the primatial power and teaching office ascribed to it, but in the fact that here a principle finds expression under which all particular points of content are *a priori* subsumed: the function of the teaching office in its bearing upon the faith of the individual and the power to orientate, bind, and direct which this entails. At this point we find ourselves faced with a difference between the confessions which at first sight seems utterly hopeless, a difference primarily affecting the relationship between the Roman Catholic church and the churches of the Reformation, but also to a notable extent that between the Roman Catholic church and the Anglican and Orthodox churches. This difference is rendered still more acute when the individual vested with this teaching office exercises his office in a way which, from the point of view of theological content, exposes it to criticism and attack as much as, for instance, the encyclical *Humanae Vitae.* "Ecumenism mourns" – thus one commentator, a well-wisher, expressed himself upon the matter.

Appendix
Agreed Statements

ANGLICAN–CATHOLIC, METHODIST–CATHOLIC AND LUTHERAN–
CATHOLIC STATEMENTS ON THE EUCHARIST AND THE
MINISTRY

*AN AGREED STATEMENT ON EUCHARISTIC DOCTRINE OF THE
ANGLICAN–ROMAN CATHOLIC INTERNATIONAL COMMISSION*

Introduction

The following Agreed Statement evolved from the thinking and the discussion of the International Commission over the past two years. The result
has been a conviction among members of the Commission that we have
reached agreement on essential points of Eucharistic doctrine. We are equally
convinced ourselves that, though no attempt was made to present a fully
comprehensive treatment of the subject, nothing essential has been omitted.
The document has been presented to our official authorities, but obviously
it cannot be ratified by them until such time as our respective Churches can
evaluate its conclusion.

We would want to point out that the members of the Commission who
subscribed to this Statement have been officially appointed and come from
many countries, representing a wide variety of theological background. Our
intention was to reach a consensus at the level of faith, so that all of us might
be able to say, within the limits of the Statement: this is the Christian faith
of the Eucharist.

*Henry Ossory, Alan Elmham: Co-Chairmen of the
Anglican–Roman Catholic International Commission*

1 In the course of the Church's history several traditions have developed
in expressing Christian understanding of the eucharist. (For example, various
names have become customary as descriptions of the eucharist: Lord's supper,
liturgy, holy mysteries, synaxis, mass, holy communion. The eucharist has
become the most universally accepted term.) An important stage in progress
towards organic unity is a substantial consensus on the purpose and meaning
of the eucharist. Our intention has been to seek a deeper understanding of
the reality of the eucharist which is consonant with biblical teaching and with
the tradition of our common inheritance, and to express in this document the
consensus we have reached.

2   Through the life, death and resurrection of Jesus Christ God has reconciled men to himself, and in Christ he offers unity to all mankind. By his word God calls us into a new relationship with himself as our Father and with one another as his children – a relationship inaugurated by baptism into Christ through the Holy Spirit, nurtured and deepened through the eucharist, and expressed in a confession of one faith and a common life of loving service.

I   The Mystery of the Eucharist

3   When his people are gathered at the eucharist to commemorate his saving acts for our redemption, Christ makes effective among us the eternal benefits of his victory and elicits and renews our response of faith, thanksgiving and self-surrender. Christ through the Holy Spirit in the eucharist builds up the life of the Church, strengthens its fellowship and furthers its mission. The identity of the Church as the body of Christ is both expressed and effectively proclaimed by its being centred in, and partaking of, his body and blood. In the whole action of the eucharist, and in and by his sacramental presence given through bread and wine, the crucified and risen Lord, according to his promise, offers himself to his people.

4   In the eucharist we proclaim the Lord's death until he comes. Receiving a foretaste of the kingdom to come, we look back with thanksgiving to what Christ has done for us, we greet him present among us, we look forward to his final appearing in the fulness of his kingdom when "The Son also himself (shall) be subject unto him that put all things under him, that God may be all in all" (1 Cor 15:28). When we gather around the same table in this communal meal at the invitation of the same Lord and when we "partake of the one loaf", we are one in commitment not only to Christ and to one another, but also to the mission of the Church in the world.

II   The Eucharist and the Sacrifice of Christ

5   Christ's redeeming death and resurrection took place once and for all in history. Christ's death on the cross, the culmination of his whole life of obedience, was the one, perfect and sufficient sacrifice for the sins of the world. There can be no repetition of or addition to what was then accomplished once for all by Christ. Any attempt to express a nexus between the sacrifice of Christ and the eucharist must not obscure this fundamental fact of the Christian faith.[1] Yet God has given the eucharist to his Church as a means through which the atoning work of Christ on the cross is proclaimed and made effective in the life of the Church. The notion of *memorial* as understood in the passover celebration at the time of Christ – ie the making effective in the present of an event in the past – has opened the way to a clearer understanding of the relationship between Christ's sacrifice and the eucharist. The eucharistic memorial is no mere calling to mind of a past event or of its significance, but the Church's effectual proclamation of God's mighty acts. Christ instituted the eucharist as a memorial (*anamnesis*) of the totality of God's reconciling action in him. In the eucharistic prayer the Church continues to make a perpetual memorial of Christ's death, and his members, united with God and one another, give thanks for all his mercies, entreat the benefits of his passion on behalf of the whole Church, participate in these benefits and enter into the movement of his self-offering.

III   The Presence of Christ

6   Communion with Christ in the eucharist presupposes his true presence, effectually signified by the bread and wine which, in this mystery, become his body and blood.[2] The real presence of his body and blood can, however,

only be understood within the context of the redemptive activity whereby he gives himself, and in himself reconciliation, peace and life, to his own. On the one hand, the euchaistic gift springs out of the paschal mystery of Christ's death and resurrection, in which God's saving purpose has already been definitely realized. On the other hand, its purpose is to transmit the life of the crucified and risen Christ to his body, the Church, so that its members may be more fully united with Christ and with one another.

7 Christ is present and active, in various ways, in the entire eucharistic celebration. It is the same Lord who through the proclaimed word invites his people to his table, who through his minister presides at that table, and who gives himself sacramentally in the body and blood of his paschal sacrifice. It is the Lord present at the right hand of the Father, and therefore transcending the sacramental order, who thus offers to his Church, in the eucharistic signs, the special gift of himself.

8 The sacramental body and blood of the Saviour are present as an offering to the believer awaiting his welcome. When this offering is met by faith, a life-giving encounter results. Through faith Christ's presence – which does not depend on the individual's faith in order to be the Lord's real gift of himself to his Church – becomes no longer just a presence *for* the believer, but also a presence *with* him. Thus, in considering the mystery of the eucharistic presence, we must recognize both the sacramental sign of Christ's presence and the personal relationship between Christ and the faithful which arises from the presence.

9 The Lord's words at the last supper, "Take and eat; this is my body", do not allow us to dissociate the gift of the presence and the act of sacramental eating. The elements are not mere signs; Christ's body and blood become really present and are really given. But they are really present and given in order that, receiving them, believers may be united in communion with Christ the Lord.

10 According to the traditional order of the liturgy the consecratory prayer (*anaphora*) leads to the communion of the faithful. Through this prayer of thanksgiving, a word of faith addressed to the Father, the bread and wine become the body and blood of Christ by the action of the Holy Spirit, so that in communion we eat the flesh of Christ and drink his blood.

11 The Lord who thus comes to his people in the power of the Holy Spirit is the Lord of glory. In the eucharistic celebration we anticipate the joys of the age to come. By the transforming action of the Spirit of God, earthly bread and wine become the heavenly manna and the new wine, the eschatological banquet for the new man: elements of the first creation become pledges and first fruits of the new heaven and the new earth.

12 We believe that we have reached substantial agreement on the doctrine of the eucharist. Although we are all conditioned by the traditional ways in which we have expressed and practised our eucharistic faith, we are convinced that if there are any remaining points of disagreement they can be resolved on the principles here established. We acknowledge a variety of theological approaches within both our communions. But we have seen it as our task to find a way of advancing together beyond the doctrinal disagreements of the past. It is our hope that, in view of the agreement which we have reached on eucharistic faith, this doctrine will no longer constitute an obstacle to the unity we seek.

Windsor, 1971

Notes

1 The early Church in expressing the meaning of Christ's death and resurrection often used the language of sacrifice. For the Hebrew *sacrifice* was a traditional means of communication with God. The passover, for example, was a communal meal; the day of Atonement was essentially expiatory; and the covenant established communion between God and man.

2 The word *transubstantiation* is commonly used in the Roman Catholic Church to indicate that God acting in the eucharist effects a change in the inner reality of the elements. The term should be seen as affirming the *fact* of Christ's presence and of the mysterious and radical change which takes place. In contemporary Roman Catholic theology it is not understood as explaining *how* the change takes place.

ROMAN CATHOLIC–METHODIST STATEMENT ON THE EUCHARIST
[The Joint Commission summarizes the hopeful measure of agreement it has so far reached, and also some outstanding points of difference.]

Points of Agreement

I The Real Presence
1 Both Methodists and Catholics affirm as the primary fact the presence of Christ in the eucharist.
2 This is a reality that does not depend on the experience of the communicant.
3 It is only by faith that we become aware of the presence of Christ in the eucharist.
4 Within the worship of the Church, the eucharist is a distinctive mode or manifestation of the presence of Christ.
5 Christ in the fulness of his being, human and divine, crucified and risen, is present in the sacrament.
6 The presence of Christ is mediated through the sacred elements of bread and wine over which the words of institution have been pronounced.
7 Bread and wine do not mean the same outside the context of the eucharistic celebration as they do within that context. Within the eucharistic celebration they become the sign *par excellence* of Christ's redeeming presence to his people. To the eyes of faith they now signify the body and blood of Jesus, given and shed for the world; as we take, eat and drink, and share the bread and wine we are transformed into him. The eucharistic bread and wine are therefore efficacious signs of the body and blood of Christ.

II The Sacrifice
1 The eucharist is the celebration of Christ's full, perfect and sufficient sacrifice, offered once and for all, for the whole world.
2 It is a memorial which is more than a recollection of a past event. It is a re-enactment of Christ's triumphant sacrifice and makes available for us its benefits.

3   For this reason Catholics call the eucharist a sacrifice, though this terminology is not used by Methodists.

4   In this celebration we share in Christ's offering of himself in obedience to his Father's will.

III   Communion

1   The perfect participation in the celebration of the eucharist is the communion of all the faithful.

2   By partaking of the body and the blood we become one with Christ, our Saviour, and one with one another in a common dedication to the redemption of the world.

Points of Disagreement

I   The Presence

1   For Methodists the presence in the eucharist is not fundamentally different from the presence of Christ in other means of grace, ie preaching.

2   For some Methodists the preaching of the Word provides a more effective means of grace than the eucharist.

3   To the faith of the Catholic, the bread and wine within the context of the eucharistic celebration are transformed into another reality, ie the body and the blood of the glorified Jesus. The externals of the bread and wine remain unchanged. For the Catholic this transformation takes place through the words of the institution pronounced by a validly ordained priest.

4   Worship of the Blessed Sacrament is linked with the Roman Catholic doctrine of the transformation of the elements, and does not obtain in Methodism.

II   Intercommunion

Methodists welcome to the Lord's table any Christians who can conscientiously accept the invitation – Roman Catholics extend eucharistic communion only to those who share the same faith (except in cases of urgent necessity). We welcome the continuing study of this problem, and look forward to the day when we can partake of the eucharist together.

Denver, Colorado, 1971

THE EUCHARIST: A LUTHERAN–ROMAN CATHOLIC STATEMENT

As a result of our conversations on the eucharist, we Roman Catholic and Lutheran theologians wish to record, chiefly and first of all, our profound gratitude to God for the growing unity on this subject which we see in our day.

Our responsibility is to try to articulate and explain this increasing agreement to the people and leadership of our churches, so that they may test for themselves what we have discussed and draw whatever conclusions in thought and action they find appropriate.

What we have to report is not so much original with us as simply one manifestation of a growing consensus among many Christian traditions on the Lord's Supper.

Ours, however, is a specifically Roman Catholic–Lutheran contribution. It attempts to go beyond the more general ecumenical discussion of the eucharist to an examination of the particular agreements and disagreements of our two traditions. While we have considered the biblical and patristic sources of eucharistic doctrine and practice in our preparatory conversations, this statement deals with problems that have become particularly acute for Lutherans and Roman Catholics as a result of the sixteenth-century controversies. It does not try to treat the sacrament of the altar comprehensively.

Our attention has focussed on two issues: the eucharist as sacrifice, and the presence of Christ in the sacrament. These issues have been especially divisive in the past and are involved in most of our historical disagreements on eucharistic doctrine and practice. For this reason it seems to us important to enunciate our growing agreement on these two points, even though there are other aspects of the sacrament of the altar we have not yet discussed.

I   The Eucharist as Sacrifice

With reference to the eucharist as sacrifice, two affirmations have not been denied by either confession; four aspects of the problem have been major points of divergence.

1 (a) Lutherans and Roman Catholics alike acknowledge that in the Lord's Supper "Christ is present as the Crucified who died for our sins and who rose again for our justification, as the once-for-all sacrifice for the sins of the world who gives himself to the faithful". On this Lutherans insist as much as Catholics, although, for various reasons, Lutherans have been reticent about speaking of the eucharist as a sacrifice.

(b) The confessional documents of both traditions agree that the celebration of the eucharist is the Church's sacrifice of praise and self-offering or oblation. Each tradition can make the following statement its own: "By him, with him and in him who is our great High Priest and Intercessor we offer to the Father, in the power of the Holy Spirit, our praise, thanksgiving and intercession. With contrite hearts we offer ourselves as a living and holy sacrifice, a sacrifice which must be expressed in the whole of our daily lives".

2 Historically, our controversies have revolved around the question whether the worshipping assembly "offers Christ" in the sacrifice of the mass. In general, Lutherans have replied in the negative, because they believed that only thus could they preserve the once-for-all character and the full sufficiency of the sacrifice of the cross and keep the eucharist from becoming a human supplement to God's saving work, a matter of "works-righteousness".

(a) First of all, we must be clear that Catholics as well as Lutherans affirm the unrepeatable character of the sacrifice of the cross. The Council of Trent, to be sure, affirmed this, but Lutheran doubts about the Catholic position were not resolved. Today, however, we find no reason for such doubt, and we recognize our agreement in the assertion that "What God did in the incarnation, life, death, resurrection, and ascension of Christ, he does not do again. The events are unique; they cannot be repeated, or extended or continued. Yet in this memorial we do not only recall past events: God makes them present through the Holy Spirit, thus making us participants in Christ" (1 Cor 1:9).

(b) Further, the Catholic affirmation that the Church "offers Christ" in the mass has in the course of the last half century been increasingly explained in terms which answer Lutheran fears that this detracts from the full sufficiency of Christ's sacrifice. The members of the body of Christ are united through Christ with God and with one another in such a way that they become participants in his worship, his self-offering, his sacrifice to the Father. Through this union between Christ and Christians, the eucharistic assembly "offers Christ" by consenting in the power of the Holy Spirit to be offered by him to the Father. Apart from Christ we have no gifts, no worship, no sacrifice of our own to offer to God. All we can plead is Christ, the sacrificial lamb and victim whom the Father himself has given us.

(c) Another historically important point of controversy has been the Roman

Catholic position that the eucharistic sacrifice is "propitiatory". Within the context of the emphases which we have outlined above, Catholics today interpret this position as emphatically affirming that the presence of the unique propitiatory sacrifice of the cross in the eucharistic celebration of the Church is efficacious for the forgiveness of sins and the life of the world. Lutherans can join them up to this point. They reject, however, what they have understood Trent to say about the mass as a propitiatory sacrifice "offered for the living and the dead", even though the Apology of the Augsburg Confession concedes with respect to prayer for the dead that "we do not forbid it". We have not discussed this aspect of the problem; further exploration of it is required.

(d) In addition to the growing harmony in ways of thinking about the eucharistic sacrifice, there is a significant convergence in the actual practice of eucharistic worship. Doctrine is inevitably interpreted in the light of practice, as well as vice versa, and consequently oppositions on this level can negate apparent doctrinal agreement. For example, the Reformers and later Lutherans have believed that the multiplication of private masses and the associated systems of mass intentions and mass stipends are evidence that Roman Catholics do not take seriously the all-sufficiency of Christ's sacrifice, and this suspicion has been reinforced by such statements of Catholic theologians as "the sacrificial worth of two masses is just double the sacrificial worth of one mass". Now, however, the second Vatican council in its Constitution on the Sacred Liturgy has declared that the nature of the mass is such that the communal way of celebrating is to be preferred to individual and quasi-private celebrations. As the liturgical renewal progresses in this and other respects, each group in these discussions finds it increasingly easy to understand and approve what the other says about the eucharist in general and its sacrificial aspects in particular.

The question of eucharistic sacrifice is closely related to other issues. The problem of the "real presence" has been the first to claim our attention. Do we, in the eucharist, genuinely encounter Christ in the full reality of his person and sacrificial action? It is therefore to this subject that we now turn.

II The Presence of Christ in the Lord's Supper

Here, too, there are areas in which this group believes that Roman Catholics and Lutherans can make the same affirmations and others in which our agreement is not yet complete.

1 (a) We confess a manifold presence of Christ, the Word of God and Lord of the world. The crucified and risen Lord is present in his body, the people of God, for he is present where two or three are gathered in his name (Mt 18:20). He is present in baptism, for it is Christ himself who baptizes. He is present in the reading of the Scriptures and the proclamation of the Gospel. He is present in the Lord's Supper.

(b) We affirm that in the sacrament of the Lord's supper Jesus Christ, true God and true man, is present wholly and entirely in his body and blood, under the signs of bread and wine.

(c) Through the centuries Christians have attempted various formulations to describe this presence. Our confessional documents have in common affirmed that Jesus Christ is "really", "truly", and "substantially" present in this sacrament. This manner of presence "we can scarcely express in words", but we affirm his presence because we believe in the power of God and the promise of Jesus Christ: "This is my body ... This is my blood ..." Our traditions have spoken of this presence as "sacramental", "supernatural", and "spiritual". These terms have different connotations in the two traditions, but they have in common a rejection of a spatial or natural manner of presence, and a rejection of an understanding of the sacrament as only commemorative or figurative. The term "sign", once suspect, is again recognized as a positive term for speaking of Christ's presence in the sacrament. For, though symbols and symbolic actions are used, the Lord's supper is an effective sign: it communicates what it promises: "... the action of the Church becomes the effective means whereby God in Christ acts and Christ is present with his people".

(d) Although the sacrament is meant to be celebrated in the midst of the believing congregation, we are agreed that the presence of Christ does not come about through the faith of the believer, or through any human power, but by the power of the Holy Spirit through the word.

(e) The true body and blood of Christ are present not only at the moment of reception but throughout the eucharistic action.

2 In the following areas our historical divergences are being overcome, although we are unable at present to speak with one voice at every point.

(a) In reference to eucharistic worship:

i We agreed that Christ gave us this sacrament in order that we might receive him and participate in his worship of the Father.

ii We are also agreed that the Lord Jesus Christ is himself to be worshipped, praised and adored; every knee is to bow before him.

iii We are further agreed that as long as Christ remains sacramentally present, worship, reverence and adoration are appropriate.

iv Both Lutherans and Catholics link Christ's eucharistic presence closely to the eucharistic liturgy itself. Lutherans, however, have not stressed the prolongation of this presence beyond the communion service as Catholics have done.

v To be sure, the opposition on this point is not total. Following a practice attested in the early Church, Lutherans may distribute the elements from the congregational communion service to the sick in private communion, in some cases as an extension of this service, in some cases with the words of institution spoken either for their proclamatory value or as consecration.

vi Also in harmony with a eucharistic practice attested in the early Church, Roman Catholics have traditionally reserved the consecrated host for communicating the sick, which, according to the Instruction of 25 May 1967, is the "primary and original purpose" of reservation. The adoration of Christ present in the reserved sacrament is of later origin and is a secondary end. The same Instruction repeats the insistence of the Constitution on the Sacred Liturgy that any adoration of the reserved sacrament be harmonized with and in some ways derived from the liturgy, "since the liturgy by its very nature surpasses" any non-liturgical eucharistic devotion.

(b) In reference to the presence of Christ under both species, a divergence of practice concerning the cup for the laity has been one of the most obvious signs of disunity between Roman Catholics and other Christians. Catholics of the Eastern rites in union with the Roman See have always retained the practice of communion under both species. The Lutheran confessions emphasize the desirability of communion in both kinds of obedience to "a clear command and order of Christ", but do not deny the sacramental character of communion administered to a congregation in one kind only. At Vatican II the Roman Catholic church reintroduced, to a modest but significant extent, communion under both kinds for the western church. The Council thereby recognized that this practice better expresses the sign of the mystery of eucharistic presence. Recent liturgical directives have explicitly acknowledged this principle and have extended this usage.

(c) Lutherans traditionally have understood the Roman Catholic use of the term "transubstantiation" to involve:

a An emphatic affirmation of the presence of Christ's body and blood in the sacrament. With this they are in agreement.
b An affirmation that God acts in the eucharist, effecting a change in the elements. This also Lutherans teach, although they use a different terminology.
c A rationalistic attempt to explain the mystery of Christ's presence in the sacrament. This they have rejected as presumptuous.
d A definitive commitment to one and only one conceptual framework in which to express the change in the elements. This they have regarded as theologically untenable.

It can thus be seen that there is agreement on the "that", the full reality of Christ's presence. What has been disputed is a particular way of stating the "how", the manner in which he becomes present.

Today, however, when Lutheran theologians read contemporary Catholic expositions, it becomes clear to them that the dogma of transubstantiation intends to affirm the fact of Christ's presence and of the change which takes place, and is not an attempt to explain how Christ becomes present. When the dogma is understood in this way, Lutherans find that they also must acknowledge that it is a legitimate way of attempting to express the mystery, even though they continue to believe that the conceptuality associated with "transubstantiation" is misleading and therefore prefer to avoid the term.

Our conversations have persuaded us of both the legitimacy and the limits of theological efforts to explore the mystery of Christ's presence in the sacrament. We are also persuaded that no single vocabulary or conceptual framework can be adequate, exclusive, or final in this theological enterprise. We are convinced that current theological trends in both traditions give great promise for increasing convergence and deepened understanding of the eucharistic mystery.

Conclusion

There are still other questions that must be examined before we Catholic and Lutheran participants in these conversations would be prepared to assess our over-all agreements and disagreements on the doctrine of the sacrament of the altar. To mention two important omissions, we have not yet attempted to clarify our respective positions on the roles of the laity and the clergy, the "general" and "special" priesthood, in sacramental celebrations, nor have we discussed the pressing problem of the possibilities of intercommunication apart from full doctrinal and ecclesiastical fellowship.

On the two major issues which we have discussed at length, however, the progress has been immense. Despite all remaining differences in the ways we speak and think of the eucharistic sacrifice and our Lord's presence in his supper, we are no longer able to regard ourselves as divided in the one holy catholic and apostolic faith on these two points. We therefore prayerfully ask our fellow Lutherans and Catholics to examine their consciences and root out many ways of thinking, speaking and acting, both individually and as Churches, which have obscured their unity in Christ on these as on many other matters.

St Louis, Missouri, 1967

A STATEMENT ON THE DOCTRINE OF THE MINISTRY AGREED
BY THE ANGLICAN–ROMAN CATHOLIC INTERNATIONAL
COMMISSION

Preface

At Windsor, in 1971, the Anglican–Roman Catholic International Commission
was able to achieve an Agreed Statement on Eucharistic Doctrine. In accordance with the programme adopted at Venice in 1970, we have now, at our
meeting in Canterbury in 1973, turned our attention to the doctrine of
Ministry, specifically to our understanding of the Ordained Ministry and its
place in the life of the Church. The present document is the result of the
work of this officially appointed Commission and is offered to our authorities
for their consideration. At this stage it remains an agreed statement of the
Commission and no more.

We acknowledge with gratitude our debt to the many studies and discussions which have treated the same material. While respecting the different
forms that Ministry has taken in other traditions, we hope that the clarification of our understanding expressed in the statement will be of service to them
also.

We have submitted the statement, therefore, to our authorities and, with
their authorization, we publish it as a document of the Commission with a
view to its discussion. Even though there may be differences of emphasis
within our two traditions, yet we believe that in what we have said here both
Anglican and Roman Catholic will recognize their own faith.

H. R. McAdoo, Alan C. Clark, Co-Chairmen

I Introduction

1 Our intention has been to seek a deeper understanding of ministry which is
consonant with biblical inheritance, and to express in this document the
consensus we have reached. This statement is not designed to be an exhaustive
treatment of Ministry. It seeks to express our basic agreement in the doctrinal
areas that have been the course of controversy between us, in the wider
context of our common convictions about the ministry.
2 Within the Roman Catholic Church and the Anglican Communion there
exists a diversity of forms of ministerial service. Of more specific ways of
service, while some are undertaken without particular initiative from official
authority, others may receive a mandate from ecclesiastical authorities. The
ordained ministry can only be rightly understood within this broader context
of various ministries, all of which are the work of one and the same Spirit.

II Ministry in the Life of the Church

3 The life and self-offering of Christ perfectly express what it is to serve
God and man. All Christian ministry, whose purpose is always to build up the
community (*koinonia*), flows and takes its shape from this source and model.
The communion of men with God (and with each other) requires their reconciliation. This reconciliation, accomplished by the death and resurrection of
Jesus Christ, is being realized in the life of the Church through the response
of faith. While the Church is still in process of sanctification, its mission
is nevertheless to be the instrument by which this reconciliation in Christ is
proclaimed, his love manifested, and the means of salvation offered to men.
4 In the early Church the apostles exercised a ministry which remains of
fundamental significance for the Church of all ages. It is difficult to deduce,
from the New Testament use of "apostle" for the Twelve, Paul, and others, a

precise portrait of an apostle, but two primary features of the original apostolate are clearly discernible: a special relationship with the historical Christ, and a commission from him to the Church and the world (Mt 28:19; Mk 3:14). All Christian apostolate originates in the sending of the Son by the Father. The Church is apostolic not only because its faith and life must reflect the witness to Jesus Christ given in the early Church by the apostles, but also because it is charged to continue in the apostles' commission to communicate to the world what it has received. Within the whole history of mankind the Church is to be the community of reconciliation.

5 All ministries are used by the Holy Spirit for the building up of the Church to be this reconciling community for the glory of God and the salvation of men (Eph 4:11–13). Within the New Testament ministerial actions are varied and functions not precisely defined. Explicit emphasis is given to the proclamation of the Word and the preservation of apostolic doctrine, the case of the flock, and the example of Christian living. At least by the time of the Pastoral Epistles and 1 Peter, some ministerial functions are discernible in a more exact form. The evidence suggests that with the growth of the Church the importance of certain functions led to their being located in specific officers of the community. Since the Church is built up by the Holy Spirit primarily but not exclusively through these ministerial functions, some form of recognition and authorization is already required in the New Testament period for those who exercise them in the name of Christ. Here we can see elements which will remain at the heart of what today we call ordination.

6 The New Testament shows that ministerial office played an essential part in the life of the Church in the first century, and we believe that the provision of a ministry of this kind is part of God's design for his people. Normative principles governing the purpose and function of the ministry are already present in the New Testament documents (eg Mk 10:43–5; Acts 20:28; 1 Tim 4:12–16; 1 Pet 5:1–4). The early churches may well have had considerable diversity in the structure of pastoral ministry, though it is clear that some churches were headed by ministers who were called *episcopoi* and *presbyteroi*. While the first missionary churches were not a loose aggregation of autonomous communities, we have no evidence that "bishops" and "presbyters" were appointed everywhere in the primitive period. The terms "bishop" and "presbyter" could be applied to the same man or to men with identical or very similar functions. Just as the formation of the canon of the New Testament was a process incomplete until the second half of the second century, so also the full emergence of the threefold ministry of bishop, presbyter, and deacon required a longer period than the apostolic age. Thereafter this threefold structure became universal in the Church.

III The Ordained Ministry

7 The Christian community exists to give glory to God through the fulfilment of the Father's purpose. All Christians are called to serve this purpose by their life of prayer and surrender to divine grace, and by their careful attention to the needs of all human beings. They should witness to God's compassion for all mankind and his concern for justice in the affairs of men. They should offer themselves to God in praise and worship, and devote their energies to bringing men into the fellowship of Christ's people, and so under his rule of love. The goal of the ordained ministry is to serve this priesthood of all the faithful. Like any human community the Church requires a focus of leadership and unity, which the Holy Spirit provides in the ordained ministry. This ministry assumes various patterns to meet the varying needs of those whom the Church is seeking to serve, and it is the role of the minister to co-ordinate the activities of the Church's fellowship and to promote what is necessary

and useful for the Church's life and mission. He is to discern what is of the Spirit in the diversity of the Church's life and promote its unity.

8 In the New Testament a variety of images is used to describe the functions of this minister. He is servant, both of Christ and of the Church. As herald and ambassador he is an authoritative representative of Christ and proclaims his message of reconciliation. As teacher he explains and applies the word of God to the community. As shepherd he exercises pastoral care and guides the flock. He is steward who may only provide for the household of God what belongs to Christ. He is to be an example both in holiness and in compassion.

9 An essential element in the ordained ministry is its responsibility for "oversight" (episcope). This responsibility involves fidelity to the apostolic faith, its embodiment in the life of the Church today, and its transmission to the Church of tomorrow. Presbyters are joined with the bishop in his oversight of the church and in the ministry of the word and the sacraments; they are given authority to preside at the eucharist and to pronounce absolution. Deacons, although not so empowered, are associated with bishops and presbyters in the ministry of word and sacrament, and assist in oversight.

10 Since the ordained ministers are ministers of the Gospel, every facet of their oversight is linked with the word of God. In the original mission and witness recorded in Holy Scripture lies the source and ground of their preaching and authority. By the preaching of the word they seek to bring those who are not Christians into the fellowship of Christ. The Christian message needs also to be unfolded to the faithful, in order to deepen their knowledge of God and their response to grateful faith. But a true faith calls for beliefs that are correct and lives that endorse the Gospel. So the ministers have to guide the community and to advise individuals with regard to the implications of commitment to Christ. Because God's concern is not only for the welfare of the Church but also for the whole of creation, they must also lead their communities in the service of humanity. Church and people have continually to be brought under the guidance of the apostolic faith. In all these ways a ministerial vocation implies a responsibility for the word of God supported by constant prayer (cf Acts 6:4).

11 The part of the ministers in the celebration of the sacraments is one with their responsibility for ministry of the word. In both word and sacrament Christians meet the living word of God. The responsibility of the ministers in the Christian community involves them in being not only the persons who normally administer baptism, but also those who admit converts to the communion of the faithful and restore those who have fallen away. Authority to pronounce God's forgiveness of sin, given to bishops and presbyters at their ordination, is exercised by them to bring Christians to a closer communion with God and with their fellow men through Christ and to assure them of God's continuing love and mercy.

12 To proclaim reconciliation in Christ and to manifest his reconciling love belong to the continuing mission of the Church. The central act of worship, the eucharist, is the memorial of that reconciliation and nourishes the Church's life for the fulfilment of its mission. Hence it is right that he who has oversight in the church and is the focus of its unity should preside at the celebration of the eucharist. Evidence as early as Ignatius shows that at least in some churches, the man exercising this oversight presided at the eucharist and no other could do so without his consent (Letter to the Smyrnaeans 8:1).

13 The priestly sacrifice of Jesus was unique, as is also his continuing High Priesthood. Despite the fact that in the New Testament ministers are never called "priests" (hiereis), Christians came to see the priestly role of Christ reflected in these ministers and used priestly terms in describing them. Because the eucharist is the memorial of the sacrifice of Christ, the action

of the presiding minister in reciting again the words of Christ at the Last Supper and distributing to the assembly the holy gifts is seen to stand in a sacramental relation to what Christ himself did in offering his own sacrifice. So our two traditions commonly use priestly terms in speaking about the ordained ministry. Such language does not imply any negation of the once-for-all sacrifice of Christ by any addition or repetition. There is in the eucharist a memorial (*anamnesis*) of the totality of God's reconciling action in Christ, who through his master presides at the Lord's Supper and gives himself sacramentally. So it is because the eucharist is central in the Church's life that the essential nature of the Christian ministry, however this may be expressed, is most clearly seen in its celebration; for, in the eucharist, thanksgiving is offered to God, the gospel of salvation is proclaimed in word and sacrament, and the community is knit together as one body in Christ. Christian ministers are members of this redeemed community. Not only do they share through baptism in the priesthood of the people of God, but they are – particularly in presiding at the eucharist – representative of the whole Church in the fulfilment of its priestly vocation of self-offering to God as a living sacrifice (Rom 12:1). Nevertheless their ministry is not an extension of the common Christian priesthood but belongs to another realm of the gifts of the Spirit. It exists to help the Church to be "a royal priesthood, a holy nation, God's own people, to declare the wonderful deeds of him who called [them] out of darkness into his marvellous light" (1 Pet 2:9).

IV Vocation and Ordination

14 Ordination denotes entry into this apostolic and God-given ministry, which serves and signifies the unity of the local churches in themselves and with one another. Every individual act of ordination is therefore an expression of the continuing apostolicity and catholicity of the whole Church. Just as the original apostles did not choose themselves but were chosen and commissioned by Jesus, so those who are ordained are called by Christ in the Church and through the Church. Not only is their vocation from Christ but their qualification for exercising such a ministry is the gift of the spirit: "our sufficiency is from God, who has qualified us to be ministers of a new covenant, not in a written code but in the Spirit" (2 Cor 3:5–6). This is expressed in ordination, when the bishop prays God to grant the gift of the Holy Spirit and lays hands on the candidate as the outward sign of the gifts bestowed. Because ministry is in and for the community and because ordination is an act in which the whole Church of God is involved, this prayer and laying on of hands takes place within the context of the eucharist.

15 In this sacramental act, the gift of God is bestowed upon the ministers, with the promise of divine grace for their work and for their sanctification; the ministry of Christ is presented to them as a model for their own; and the Spirit seals those whom he has chosen and consecrated. Just as Christ has united the Church inseparably with himself, and as God calls all the faithful to lifelong discipleship, so the gifts and calling of God to the ministers are irrevocable. For this reason, ordination is unrepeatable in both our churches.

16 Both presbyters and deacons are ordained by the bishop. In the ordination of a presbyter the presbyters present join the bishop in the laying on of hands, thus signifying the shared nature of the commission entrusted to them. In the ordination of a new bishop, ·other bishops lay hands on him, as they request the gift of the Spirit for his ministry and receive him into their ministerial fellowship. Because they are entrusted with the oversight of other churches, this participation in his ordination signifies that this new bishop and his church are within the communion of churches. Moreover, because they are representative of their churches in fidelity to the teaching and mission of the

apostles and are members of the episcopal college, their participation also ensures the historical continuity of this church with the apostolic church and of its bishop with the original apostolic ministry. The communion of the churches in mission, faith, and holiness, through time and space, is thus symbolized and maintained in the bishop. Here are comprised the essential features of what is meant in our two traditions by ordination in the apostolic succession.

V Conclusion

17 We are fully aware of the issues raised by the judgment of the Roman Catholic church on Anglican orders. The development of the thinking in our two communions regarding the nature of the Church and of the ordained ministry, as represented in our statement, has, we consider, put these issues in a new context. Agreement on the nature of ministry is prior to the consideration of the mutual recognition of ministries. What we have to say represents the consensus of the Commission on essential matters where it considers the doctrine admits no divergence. It will be clear that we have not broached the wide-ranging problems of authority which may arise in any discussion of Ministry, nor the question of primacy. We are aware that present understanding of such matters remains an obstacle to the reconciliation of our churches in the one Communion we desire, and the Commission is now turning to the examination of the issues involved. Nevertheless we consider that our consensus, on questions where agreement is indispensable for unity, offers a·positive contribution to the reconciliation of our churches and of their ministries.

Notes

1 Cf *An Agreed Statement on Eucharistic Doctrine*, para. 1, which similarly speaks of a consensus reached with regard to the Eucharist.

2 In the English language the word "priest" is used to translate two distinct Greek words, *hiereus* which belongs to the cultic order and *presbyteros* which designates an elder in the community.

3 Cf *An Agreed Statement on Eucharistic Doctrine*, para. 5.

4 Anglican use of the word "sacrament" with reference to ordination is limited by the distinction drawn in the Thirty-nine Articles (Article 25) between the two "sacraments of the Gospel" and the "five commonly called sacraments". Article 25 does not deny these latter the name "sacrament", but differentiates between them and the "two sacraments ordained by Christ" described in the Catechism as "necessary to salvation" for all men.

© *H. R. McAdoo, Bishop of*
Ossory, Ferns and Leighlin;
Alan C. Clark, Bishop of
Elmhalm, 1973   *Canterbury, 1973*

ROMAN CATHOLIC–METHODIST STATEMENT ON THE MINISTRY

I Areas of agreement – (which await further discussion and action)

1 The primary authority and finality of Jesus Christ as the One through whom the ministry, whether sacramental or otherwise, is both identified and ultimately authorized. The minister participates in Christ's ministry, acts in Christ's name.

2 The importance of the work of the Holy Spirit in calling people to the ministry (however this call may come, gradually or suddenly . . .).

3 The understanding of the ministry primarily in terms of

(a) the *full-time* dedication to Christ *for life*, for studying and communicating the Gospel, and

(b) the functions of the minister (administering the sacraments, preaching the word, teaching Christian truth, defending the faith, nurturing souls in spirituality, and, by teaching and example, showing leadership through acts of reconciliation and of service to people in need).

4 The understanding of the ministry as, in some mysterious way, an extension of the incarnational and sacramental principle whereby human beings (as ministers), though their souls and bodies, become, by the power of the Holy Spirit, agents of Christ for bringing God into the lives and conditions of men. This means also that they are agents for enabling men to find their way towards God.

5 The recognition of prophetic and special ministries with their distinctive moral and charismatic qualities.

6 The "connectional" character of the ministry, whereby everyone who is authentically called by the Holy Spirit is both authorized by that same Spirit through duly recognized persons (for Catholics, bishops) in the community of faith and assigned a place of service in that community. Each is bound to the other through varied connectional systems to form a "ministry" in the corporate sense.

7 The need for high standards of education and spiritual training for the ministry and for its exercise today. The Catholic *Ecumenical Directory*, Part II, points the way towards joint study of common problems and towards collaboration in some areas of ministerial training.

8 Awareness of problems arising in an age of rapid change concerning the meaning and function of ministry.

Denver, Colorado, 1971

Index